Y0-BSE-887

ICONS OF HORROR AND THE SUPERNATURAL

ICONS OF HORROR AND THE SUPERNATURAL

An Encyclopedia of Our Worst Nightmares

VOLUME 2

Edited by S. T. Joshi

Greenwood Icons

GREENWOOD PRESS
Westport, Connecticut • London

Library of Congress Cataloging-in-Publication Data

Icons of horror and the supernatural : an encyclopedia of our worst nightmares / edited by S.T. Joshi.
    p. cm.—(Greenwood icons)
    Includes bibliographical references and index.
    ISBN 0-313-33780-2 (set : alk. paper)—ISBN 0-313-33781-0 (vol 1 : alk. paper)—
    ISBN 0-313-33782-9 (vol 2 : alk. paper)
    1. Horror tales—History and criticism. 2. Supernatural in literature. 3. Horror films—History and criticism. 4. Supernatural in motion pictures. I. Joshi, S. T., 1958-
    PN56.H6I26   2007
    809'.9164—dc22   2006031212

British Library Cataloguing in Publication Data is available.

Library of Congress Catalog Card Number: 2006031212
ISBN: 0-313-33780-2 (set)
       0-313-33781-0 (vol. 1)
       0-313-33782-9 (vol. 2)

First published in 2007

Greenwood Press, 88 Post Road West, Westport, CT 06881
An imprint of Greenwood Publishing Group, Inc.
www.greenwood.com

Printed in the United States of America

The paper used in this book complies with the Permanent Paper Standard issued by the National Information Standards Organization (Z39.48-1984).

10 9 8 7 6 5 4 3 2 1

Contents

List of Photos   vii

Preface   ix

Volume 1

The Alien, *Donald R. Burleson*   1

The Angel and the Demon, *Matt Cardin*   31

The Cosmic Horror, *Brian Stableford*   65

The Cthulhu Mythos, *S. T. Joshi*   97

The Curse, *Alan Warren*   129

The Devil, *Darrell Schweitzer*   161

The Doppelgänger, *Tony Fonseca*   187

The Ghost, *Melissa Mia Hall*   215

The Ghoul, *Scott Connors*   243

The Haunted House, *Steven J. Mariconda*   267

The Immortal, *Brian Stableford*   307

The Monster, *Richard Bleiler*   341

The Mummy, *Paula Guran*   375

Volume 2

The Psychic, *Tony Fonseca*   409

The Sea Creature, *Mike Ashley*   441

The Serial Killer, *Hank Wagner*   473

The Siren, *Melissa Mia Hall*   507

The Small-Town Horror, *John Langan*   537

The Sorcerer, *K. A. Laity*   565

The Urban Horror, *Rob Latham*   591

The Vampire, *Margaret L. Carter*   619

The Werewolf, *Stefan Dziemianowicz*   653

The Witch, *Bernadette Lynn Bosky*   689

The Zombie, *June Pulliam*   723

General Bibliography   755

Notes on Contributors   761

Index   767

List of Photos

The Alien (page 1) is present in this still from Ron Haskin's 1953 film *The War of the Worlds* © Paramount/The Kobol Collection. Courtesy of Picturedesk.

A still from William Freidkin's 1973 film *The Exorcist* turns us to The Angel and the Demon (page 31). Courtesy of Photofest.

The Cosmic Horror (page 65) is made vivid with this still from the 1993 film *Necronomicon*. © Hadida/Davis Film/Yuzna Prods/The Kobol Collection. Courtesy of Picturedesk.

For the Cthulhu Mythos (page 97), what better than a reproduction of this June 1936 cover of *Astounding Stories*, illustrating H. P. Lovecraft's "The Shadow out of Time" and Peaslee's encounter with the Great Race. © Mary Evans Picture Library/Alamy.

The Curse (page 129) is evoked by this poster for Jacques Tourneur's 1957 film *Curse of the Demon*. Courtesy of Photofest.

The Devil (page 161), is revealed with serial killer Gilles de Rais. Accused of evoking the Devil by sacrificing children, for this and other wickedness he was condemned to death. © Mary Evans Picture Library/Alamy.

Frederic March (as Dr. Henry Jekyll and Mr. Hyde) in Rouben Mamoulian's 1932 film *Dr. Jekyll and Mr. Hyde* portrays The Doppelgänger (page 187). © Paramount Pictures/Photofest.

A drawing of Florence Cook conjures The Ghost (page 215). © Mary Evans Picture Library/Alamy.

What would be more appropriate for The Ghoul (page 243) than this picture of Boris Karloff starring in Hunter T. Hays' 1933 film *The Ghoul*. © Gaumont-British/The Kobol Collection. Courtesy of Picturedesk.

The Haunted House (page 267) is classically depicted with this still from Robert Wise's 1963 film *The Haunting*. © MGM/The Kobol Collection. Courtesy of Picturedesk.

The Immortal (page 307) is imaged here as The Wandering Jew, condemned to journey the earth without rest until Judgment Day for refusing to allow Jesus to rest on his doorstep when bearing the cross. © Mary Evans Picture Library/Alamy.

The Creature in Jack Arnold's 1954 film *Creature from the Black Lagoon* seemed the perfect embodiment for The Monster (page 341). © Universal/Photofest.

To unearth The Mummy (page 375), we again turn to Boris Karloff, this time as Imhotep and Ardath Bey in Karl Freund's 1932 film *The Mummy*. © Universal Pictures/Photofest.

The Psychic (page 409), is called forth by Margaret Wycherly (as Madam Rosalie La Grande) in Tod Browning's 1929 film *The Thirteenth Chair*. © MGM/Photofest.

A Sea Serpent from *Historia de Gentibus Septentrionalibus* by Olaus Magnus, published in Rome in 1555, depicts The Sea Creature (page 441). © Visual Arts Library (London)/Alamy.

The Serial Killer (page 473) recalls Anthony Hopkins (as Hannibal Lecter) in Jonathan Demme's 1991 *The Silence of the Lambs*. Courtesy of Photofest.

The Siren (page 507) is appropriately graced by John Waterhouse's *The Siren*. © Visual Arts Library (London)/Alamy.

To illustrate The Small-Town Horror (page 537) we turned to Christopher Lee starring in Robin Hardy's 1973 film *The Wicker Man*. © British Lion/The Kobol Collection. Courtesy of Picturedesk.

For The Sorcerer (page 565) we use the frontispiece to *Dr. Faustus* by Christopher Marlowe. © Mary Evans Picture Library/Alamy.

A still from Albert and Allen Hughes' 2001 film *From Hell* captures The Urban Horror (page 591). Courtesy of Photofest.

The Vampire (page 619) pictures Max Schrek (as Count Orlaf) in F. W. Murnau's 1922 film *Nosferatu*. Courtesy of Photofest.

The Werewolf (page 653) could hardly be imaged by anything other than Lon Chaney Jr. starring in George Waggner's 1941 film, *The Wolf Man*. © Universal/The Kobol Collection. Courtesy of Picturedesk.

For The Witch (page 689) we have a splendid 1863 woodcut of the Witches from *Macbeth*. © Mary Evans Picture Library/Alamy.

The Zombie (page 723) is gruesomely depicted with a still from Lucio Fulci's 1979 film *Zombie Flesh Eaters*. © Variety/The Kobol Collection. Courtesy of Picturedesk.

Preface

Although the genre of supernatural horror can be thought to date to the earliest writings of human civilization, it has gained particular importance and popularity within the last century, and particularly within the last three decades. Such popular writers as Stephen King, Anne Rice, J. K. Rowling (whose works tread the borderline between the supernatural and pure fantasy), Peter Straub, Clive Barker, and Neil Gaiman have brought the genre unprecedented attention in the literary world; less popular but perhaps even more accomplished writers such as Ramsey Campbell, Thomas Ligotti, and Caitlin R. Kiernan have elevated the supernatural to the highest levels of literary craftsmanship. The inclusion of H. P. Lovecraft, in many ways the father of twentieth-century supernatural writing, in the prestigious Library of America shows that this field can attain canonical status. Paralleling the growth of supernatural literature is the burgeoning of the supernatural in film, television, comic books, role-playing games, and other media, so that it can truly be said that we live in a haunted age.

Icons of Horror and the Supernatural examines twenty-four of the leading icons of supernatural and nonsupernatural fiction, tracing their roots in folklore and legend and discussing their prevalence in literature, film, and other media as well as in popular culture and society as a whole. The articles, written by leading authorities in the field, are aimed at a general audience of students and interested readers and written without the use of the technical jargon of literary criticism; but, because of their comprehensiveness, they will be of interest to scholars as well. Because the articles are substantially longer than conventional encyclopedia entries, ranging between 12,000 and 15,000 words, they allow for an exhaustive coverage of their topic, but are nonetheless not as lengthy as full-length books on the subject, which would make them less convenient as introductions to their chosen subjects. The articles, arranged alphabetically, use an eclectic mix of critical approaches—historical, thematic, philosophical/religious—as dictated by the subject matter. Since the supernatural literature has drawn many of its central concepts from ancient religious and folkloristic beliefs, many of the articles discuss the anthropological roots of these icons in order to contextualize their continuing use in present-day media. But since horror can be manifested in a nonsupernatural manner—such as the icon of the Serial Killer—some articles examine the social and political implications of their subjects.

Each article concludes with a thorough primary and secondary bibliography, including full information on all works cited in the text and suggestions for further reading. These works include not only printed works but also Web sites and other electronic sources. In addition, the articles are augmented by sidebars featuring quotations from important literary works discussed, lists and chronologies that readers may find helpful for an understanding of the scope and parameters of the subject, and brief discussions of tangential issues related to the subject.

It is hoped that *Icons of Horror and the Supernatural* will be a useful guide to a genre that continues to evolve dynamically and innovatively, if current specimens in literature and other media are any guide, and that continues to elicit the enthusiasm of millions of readers, listeners, and viewers. As a genre that exposes our deepest fears—not only fears of injury or death, but fears engendered by our ignorance of the fundamental nature of the world and the universe—the supernatural will always have a place in human society, and will always stand in need of explication by authoritative hands.

—S. T. Joshi

The Psychic

by Tony Fonseca

DEFINITION AND ORIGINS

According to *The Skeptic's Dictionary* (http://www.skepdic.com/psychic
.html), the term psychic was first used by renowned chemist William Crookes.
In 1871, Crookes attended a séance and came away convinced of the presence
of spirits. Although parapsychologists have subsequently determined that
virtually every medium who has ever been tested under controlled conditions

has been proven not to possess any supernatural ability, they have also determined that more often than not people who believe they have psychic powers are not frauds; they genuinely believe in their untested powers. *The Skeptic's Dictionary* posits that the main reasons for belief in paranormal powers are the perceived accuracy of psychic predictions and readings; the seemingly uncanny premonitions that many people have, especially in dreams; and the seemingly fantastic odds against such premonitions or predictions being correct by coincidence or chance.

This may seem to fly in the face of reason, for the belief in psychic powers is universal, harkening back to the practice of early magic and witchcraft (in fact, certain types of psychics, namely diviners or clairvoyants, are in many ways related to witches and their predecessors, oracles). The other major division of psychic phenomena, those powers possessed by physical mediums, or those psychics who produce objects and noises, or those who master levitation, is usually incorrectly categorized as magic. Perhaps this miscategorization accounts for the fact that, typically, the profession that has most often taken on the job of exposing fraudulent physical mediums is that of prestidigitation. Both Harry Houdini (born Ehrich Weiss, 1874–1926) and The Amazing Randi (born James Randi, b. 1928) are numbered among those professional magicians who see the policing of psychics as a calling, a responsibility. Houdini wrote several books on the subject (his investigations, teamed with friend and fellow skeptic Sir Arthur Conan Doyle [1859–1930], have been fictionalized by H. R. Knight in the recent novel, *What Rough Beast* [2005; originally published under the byline Harry R. Squires in 2001]); The Amazing Randi routinely offers $1,000,000 to anyone who can demonstrate proven psychic powers.

In *A History of Witchcraft: Sorcerers, Heretics, and Pagans* (1980), Jeffrey B. Russell points to various primitive cultures that recognize the existence of humans who can, as Brian P. Copenhaver describes it in the introduction to *Hermetica*, "manipulate the divine and natural worlds for more or less concrete and immediate purposes" (xxxvi). Russell gives as example the Zande of the southern Sudan, who distinguished between good, benevolent, oracular magic, familial revenge-oriented magic, and evil magic, performed for personal gain or at the request of an individual who may gain personally. Likewise, the Bechuana of Botswana distinguish between beneficial "day-sorcerers" and terrifying "night-witches." In recent history, sorcery and witchcraft have been placed into the latter categories, seen as evil magic performed by night-witches. Historians agree that diviners and oracles were part of both Egyptian and Graeco-Roman cultures, and they were revered for their talents. Similar supernaturally inclined practitioners, such as astrologers, alchemists, and divinely inspired prophets, all promised the ability to bridge the gaps between the natural and divine worlds, and they were often welcomed in royal courts. Much medieval science was occupied with alchemy, and kings hired alchemists to develop some drugs and chemicals, that is until the Church condemned alchemy.

Russell theorizes that Eastern European cultures, because of the influence of Christianity, ultimately began to represent the precursors to physical psychics, in other words witches and sorcerers, as evil. At one time they were believed to be in league with Lucifer, to the point where various representations show them as having sexual intercourse with the devil (20). Although Agrippa of Nettesheim (1486–1535) called his major work on natural magic *De Occulta Philosophia* (*On the Occult Philosophy*), what we know as modern occultism (from the French word *occultisme*) did not become fashionable until the nineteenth century. When Austrian physician Franz Anton Mesmer (1734–1815) began practicing "mental healing," little did he know that his theory of a "laying on of hands" in order to produce a positive energy that would help cure would ultimately lead to the Spiritualist Movement. Mesmer, who was born in Switzerland and later studied medicine at the University of Vienna, was looking into the possibilities that a doctor's physical presence, that is, his ability to produce positive feelings in a patient, is fundamental in medical treatment. Ultimately, he posited the theory of the healing force or fluid called "animal magnetism." As James E. Beichler explains, Mesmer

> tried to unify the early physics of magnetism with life.... [He] made use of a common scientific method of explaining phenomena outside the realm of Newtonian mechanism in terms of a non-mechanical, unspecified and mass less fluid. He then considered the possibility that an imbalance of this hypothetical fluid in the human body caused illnesses.... Other psychic phenomena, such as telepathy, were also observed within the practice of Mesmerism. (30)

Dismissed in Vienna, Mesmer moved to Paris in 1778 and was favorably received by the public. However, medical authorities refused to countenance him, and in 1784 the government appointed a commission of members of the Faculty of Medicine, the Société Royale de Médecin, and the Academy of Sciences; the commission dismissed animal magnetism, claiming that Mesmer's patients simply had overactive imaginations. Mesmer's ideas were kept alive by a few of his students and reemerged during the next century. Later studies of Mesmer's work by James Braid and others in England introduced the term "hypnotism." Well-known writers who use occult motifs, for example Edgar Allan Poe (1809–1849) and E.T.A. Hoffmann (1776–1822), are in some way or other influenced by Mesmer's theories.

SPIRITUALISM

In a 2003 issue of *Aries*, Cathy Gutierrez points out the relationship between Mesmerism and Spiritualism: "Mediumship shared phenomenological characteristics with several similar movements of its day, foremost

Mesmerism.... Spiritualism was both dependent on and an elaboration of early experiments with hypnotism.... Mesmerism clearly included a mystical as well as medical component, and in certain cases mesmerized patients reported a facility for the paranormal and the ability to talk to the dead" (57–58). Although most scholars argue for 1848 as the official birth of the Spiritualist movement, there is some argument that it can be traced back to the lectures of J. S. Grimes (1807–1903) on the physiology of the nervous system and phrenology in Poughkeepsie, New York, in 1843. Some point out that there were indeed even earlier movements in Spiritualism and philosophy in Europe prior to the 1840s. British skeptic, well-known psychical investigator, and author Frank Podmore (1856–1910) theorizes that Spiritualism was the child of both Mesmerism and a belief in witchcraft and phenomena associated with it (Beichler 31). S. G. Soal writes of early spiritual mediums in his "Spiritualism" entry in Julian Franklyn's *A Survey of the Occult*, noting what could be the first instance of spiritualism, in the form of automatic writing, in the mid- to late 1840s, when shoemaker Andrew Jackson Davis published a bulky tome called *The Principles of Nature, Her Divine Revelations and a Voice to Mankind* (1847). Davis claimed that the entire book, which attempts to trace the genesis of cosmic evolution, was dictated while he was in a hypnotic trance over a period of fifteen months (Soal 215).

Most agree, however, that the Spiritualist movement proper got its start circa 1848 in upstate New York, at the home of a blacksmith named John Fox. Fox lived with his wife and two daughters, ages twelve and fourteen, in Hydesville (near Rochester). The girls began to communicate with the spirit of a murdered traveling sales representative, manifested by an outbreak of percussive activity; this lead to their local reputation as mediums. Eventually neighbors were called in to witness the Fox sisters, Kate (born Catherine Fox, 1839–1892) and Margaret (1833–1893), as they communicated with the ghost. Eventually, Quaker abolitionists Amy and Isaac Post of Rochester heard about the two girls, and soon the two had a captive audience. Eventually, the Fox Sisters lost control of their lives when their older sister became their manager and they became professional mediums. The sister, [Ann] Leah Fox (1814–1890), published a book in 1885, claiming that psychic power ran in the family. The girls' veracity was often attacked and questioned; they were proven a fraud during a few experiments; and they confessed (and later recanted) that they tricked people by creating the sounds physically, by cracking an ankle joint. At the time of their deaths, their lives were riddled with alcoholism, poverty, instability, and loneliness (Braude 18).

Mesmerism clearly included a mystical as well as medical component, and in certain cases mesmerized patients reported a facility for the paranormal and the ability to talk to the dead.

—*Cathy Gutierrez, Aries, 2003*

It would be a mistake to think that only the uneducated rural population was taken in by the Spiritualist movement in the United States. By the 1850s, New York State Supreme Court Judge John Edmonds became interested in séances and mediumship, and on at least one occasion an array of literati gathered at a New York clergyman's house to hear the Fox Sisters' rapping communications in 1850. These notables included James Fenimore Cooper, George Bancroft, William Cullen Bryant, Nathaniel Parker Willis, and *New York Tribune* editor Horace Greeley. Greeley was convinced of the value of mediumship, and in 1851 he published a transcript of a December 15 séance (Braude 16, 21, 27). A veritable who's who populated the audiences and believers of the movement. Other notables known for their belief were Charles Beecher, Isabella Beecher Hooker (Harriet Beecher Stowe investigated the phenomenon but never became entranced by it), William Lloyd Garrison, Sarah Grimke, Angelina Grimke, U.S. Senator N. P. Talmadge, Ohio Congressman Joshua Giddings, and First Lady Mary Todd Lincoln. Given the official and overwhelming acceptance of Spiritualism, mediums ultimately sprung up throughout the state of New York. Following in the vein of the Fox Sisters, most American mediums were female, perhaps because, as Elizabeth Cady Stanton, Susan B. Anthony, and Matilda Joslyn Gage wrote in the four-volume *History of Women's Suffrage* (1887), "the only religious sect in the world...that has recognized the equality of woman is the Spiritualists" (quoted in Braude 2).

In fact, as Ann Braude points out in *Radical Spirits: Spiritualism and Women's Rights in Nineteenth-Century America* (1989), mediums, at least in America, were seen as necessary passive conduits, as negative and passive, in other words, as feminine (23). Eventually word of Spiritualism reached Europe. By 1852 or so, mediums started becoming conduits for vocal communications from spirits, and by then England witnessed the emergence of what Soal calls "the first [professional] rapping medium," a Mrs. Hayden, who according to Soal, gave sittings for a small fee (220). By 1855, one of the most famous psychics of all time, a Scottish physical medium raised in America named Daniel Douglas Home (1833–1886), also visited England. In one of his better-known feats, Home is rumored to have floated out of the window of an adjoining room and in through the window of a séance room. Home had begun hearing "raps" at the age of seventeen, after his mother's death, and his signature feat was the appearance of "spirit hands" at his séances. His audiences included Elizabeth Barrett and Robert Browning, the latter sternly believing Home was a charlatan. Browning's poem, "Mr. Sludge the Medium," is a thinly veiled attack on Home. Other famous European psychics included Helene Smith (1861–1929) and Charles Bailey (1870–1947). Smith, born Catherine Elise Muller, operated in Geneva in the early 1890s, claiming that Victor Hugo was her spirit protector (he was later replaced by a mysterious spirit named Leopold, and then the deceased spirit of an Italian-born mystic, Cagliostro). Smith was also a physical medium, moving objects at a distance and producing items, and she ultimately claimed that she was the reincarnation of Marie Antoinette and that her astral

---

Séance attendees during the heyday of Spiritualism included New York State
Supreme Court Judge John Edmonds, James Fenimore Cooper, George
Bancroft, William Cullen Bryant, Nathaniel Parker Willis, *New York Tribune*
editor Horace Greeley, Charles Beecher, Isabella Beecher Hooker, William
Lloyd Garrison, Sarah Grimke, Angelina Grimke, U. S. Senator N. P. Talmadge,
Ohio Congressman Joshua Giddings, First Lady Mary Todd Lincoln, Elizabeth
Barrett, and Robert Browning.

---

projection visited Mars in 1894. Australian born Bailey began his professional
mediumship in 1889 and eventually gained the patronage of American-born
Melbourne millionaire T. W. Stanford, the brother of the founder of Stanford
University. His signature was the production of a large range of objects, which
he claimed were from past civilizations.

While Mesmerism sprang from Vienna and Spiritualism in the United
States, both were imported to Victorian England, adopted into the culture in
such a way that they were viewed as new sciences. Perhaps this is because The
Industrial Revolution and Darwinism created a sense of doubt, resulting in
the need for a search for meaning. This search was not limited to the working
classes. Nandor Fodor in *Between Two Worlds* (1964) argues that there is
evidence of Queen Victoria's attending séances and using a medium. Charles
Dickens practiced Mesmerism on his own wife (Kaplan 70). Dr. John El-
liotson (1791–1868), president of the Royal Medical and Chirurgical Society
of London and the first great exponent of animal magnetism in England and
founding member of the Phrenological Society (1838), represented these occult phenomena in such a way that they were viewed as acceptable by educated society. In 1838 approximately 170 of the 1,000 members of the
Phrenological Society were physicians and surgeons, giving even more cre-
dence to Spiritualism (Cooter 29). This is rather difficult to understand by
today's standards of scientific, and even pseudo-scientific theories. But as
Beichler points out, "the evolution of modern spiritualism, especially in its
scientific aspects, was not due to any failure of science to cope with the occult
and religion, but it was instead due to the success of science in its expansion
into previously questionable territories of human perception and thought. . . .
The modern spiritualism movement coincided with the first attempts of science to define itself relative to the human mind" (33). In 2005, Clare Wilson,
in *New Scientist*, attempted to account for the early (and sometimes current,
depending on the demographic) popularity of psychics. She reports that one
of the most remarkable features of an encounter with a professional medium,
astrologer, or fortune-teller is the uncanny insight that many psychics seem to
have about their customers. For believers, the clairvoyants' apparent omni-
science is no mystery: their source of information is their spirit guide, tarot
cards, or crystal ball. They assuage grieving and ostensibly provide heavenly
knowledge. And for women, as Gutierrez insightfully notes, "spiritualism

provided the possibility that anyone, and particularly women, might have the necessary talent to be invested with quasi-religious authority" (56).

Charles Dickens practiced Mesmerism on his wife.

HOUDINI AND THE SKEPTICS

Skeptics, on the other hand, continue to believe the psychic is deceiving the sitter in an elaborate con; they argue that charlatans are not above cheating by hot reading, or by planting a co-conspirator in the audience, a practice as old as Spiritualism itself. Yet repeated charges of fraud did little to stop the proliferation of fakes in the late nineteenth and early twentieth centuries. It was not until the 1920s that magicians such as Houdini (renamed after magician Jean Eugene Robert-Houdin) exposed the techniques and methods of deceit used. As a teen, he had read *Revelations of a Spirit Medium; or, Spiritualistic Mysteries Exposed* (1891), written and published anonymously by A. Medium. This book exposed the tricks of phony psychics, who after being tied up would secretly release themselves to make ghostly things happen in darkened rooms. Houdini, in *Miracle Mongers and Their Methods* (1920), attempts, as he writes in his introduction, to expose marvels "held to be supernatural . . . for the tricks they were" (x). The exposé informs readers of the tricks used in fire eating, razor and umbrella swallowing, snake eating, snake handling, feats of strength, and heat resistance. Houdini continued in the same vein in the better-known *A Magician among the Spirits* (1924). Here, he begins with the discrediting of the Fox Sisters (they had recanted their confession of fraud), then traces the history of particular psychics like Home, Eusapia Palladino (1854–1918), Ann O'Delia Diss Debar (a.k.a. Swami Laura Horos [b. 1849]), and the slate writer Dr. Henry Slade (1835–1905), as well as various other phenomena such as spirit photography and ectoplasm; Houdini then debunks each of the psychics and psychic phenomena. He also devotes one chapter of this important historical "skeptical" publication to his friend and fellow debunker Conan Doyle. Ironically, Houdini's "spirit" was the star of his final narrative, *The Houdini Messages: The Facts Concerning the Messages Received Through the Mediumship of Arthur Ford* (1929), a tract that chronicles a séance in which his wife Bess attempted to contact his spirit. Today this publication ranks as a rare piece of Houdini memorabilia.

PARAPSYCHOLOGY AND PSYCHICAL RESEARCH

Of course, every phenomenon produces an equal need for serious study, so by the late nineteenth century the science of parapsychology began to emerge. Sources agree that the term "parapsychology" was coined in 1889 by German psychologist and founder of the Gesellschaft für Experimental Psychologie

(The Society for Experimental Psychology) Max Dessoir (1867–1947), who was known for his experiments in muscle reading, thought-transference, and hypnotism. According to Marco Frenschkowski in *Supernatural Literature of the World: An Encyclopedia* (2005), Dessoir's goal was the scientific study of various aspects of occultism, including extrasensory perception, spiritualism, and other psychic phenomena (866). Similar institutions, The Society for Psychical Research and The Theosophical Society, were founded in 1882 London and 1884 New York City, respectively. These organizations brought about a focus on the religious as well as the scientific aspects of the occult. The Society for Psychical Research was founded principally on the initiative of various academics at Cambridge University, in response to the avid followings that Mesmerism and Spiritualism had engendered. Henry Sidgwick, Sir William Barrett, and Frederick W. H. Myers, as well as Balfour Stewart, R. H. Hutton, Hensleigh Wedgwood, and Edmund Gurney, were instrumental in its inception.

William James (1842–1910) became involved with The Society for Psychical Research and became one of the guiding forces behind the American chapter of the society, as he was (in the words of Gardner Murphy) "eagerly and actively concerned with the investigations by these societies into alleged hauntings, apparitions, and communications with the deceased" (James 14). James examined parapsychology with an empiricist's eye, pursuing throughout his life many types of psychological phenomena rejected by science. In 1884 he discovered Mrs. L. E. Piper, who, in the sittings given to his wife, himself, and his mother-in-law, had referred to information she could not have acquired other than through mediumship. In a much-quoted essay, "What Psychical Research Has Accomplished" (1897), he asserted that telepathy, as represented by Piper's experiences, constituted a true scientific breakthrough. James was not the only psychologist of note to spend considerable time researching psychic phenomena. Sigmund Freud (1856–1939) had, by 1921, reached what *The Encyclopedia of Occultism and Parapsychology* terms a "reluctant private conclusion that there might be something to telepathy" (after a few secretive experiments with the Hungarian psychoanalyst Sandor Ferenczi). Freud once wrote, "[I]f I had my life to live over again, I should devote myself to psychical research rather than to psychoanalysis," and his interest in the paranormal is evident in "The Uncanny" (1919). And although he always had a skeptic's predisposition, C. G. Jung did valuable work in psychoanalysis of occult phenomena by investigating a fifteen-year-old spirit medium, Miss S. W., who claimed to have had experience with astral projection through space (Soal 202).

Psychology and parapsychology have quite a bit in common, and often intersect in studies on phenomenon like near-death experiences and after-death communication. Even a hard science like statistics can get thrown into the mix, as studies (e.g., Houck 2005) that attempt to measure the frequency and uniqueness of after-death communication statistically, using frequency analysis, to determine the randomness of the phenomenon. Briefly defined, parapsychology is "the scientific study of experiences which, if they are as they seem to be, are in the principle outside the realm of human capabilities as presently conceived by conventional scientists" (Irwin 1). Implied in this definition is the possibility that this decade's parapsychological theories may be next decade's accepted psychology, for as H. J. Irwin writes in *An Introduction to Parapsychology* (1989), parapsychological events are those that are equated with the extrasensory; these experiences are differentiated from the paranormal (2). As any good scientist, parapsychologists began by categorizing various phenomena, based on commonalities. Many of these parapsychological events have been grouped together under the umbrella term "psi phenomena" by R. H. Thouless and B. P. Weisner for *The Proceedings of the Society for Psychical Research* (1948). Their categories include mediumship, both physical and spiritual; precognition; retrocognition; automatic writing; spirit photography; telepathy; clairvoyance; clairaudience; telekinesis; and psychokinesis.

Mental mediums are, strictly speaking, intermediaries between two worlds, or two dimensions, acting as an intervening body through which an entity from a spirit dimension can be transmitted. In this respect, they act as a means of communication. Mediumship is the category of psychic phenomena that is most commonly thought of as synonymous with the term psychic. A physical medium is also a conduit, and he or she is able to tap into an abundance of etheric energy, ectoplasm, and matter, physically transporting it, in various manifestations, from one realm into another. Usually, but not always, the physical medium must be in a deep trance, which helps clear the mind so that it can be used as a transporter. The implication is that the mind can literally affect or control matter. In physical mediumship, the spiritual realm can manifest itself in diverse ways. In what is called direct voice, the spirit guide creates an ectoplasm voice box, an instrument called a trumpet, which can be used to speak to a séance audience, often while being levitated around the room. Apportation occurs when the spirit realm causes objects to materialize in the sitting room, apparently from nowhere; the apported object can be permanent or temporary. These objects can include stones, gems, animals, ancient relics, and even people. What are called raps and taps are a common form of activity where sharp bangs are heard, often from within the area of the table the audience is gathered around. These sounds take the form of a code that can convey specific messages to the sitters. Spirit Lights take the form of flashes or balls appearing on or near the medium. In materialization,

---

Briefly defined, parapsychology is "the scientific study of experiences which, if they are as they seem to be, are in the principle outside the realm of human capabilities as presently conceived by conventional scientists."

—*H. J. Irwin,* An Introduction to Parapsychology

the spirit realm uses what is called ectoplasm to create an image or molding of the contacted human before death, with the degree and strength of the materialized form varying per medium. This ectoplasm is pure energy, similar to Mesmer's animal magnetism, and it can be used by mediums to move objects, as it can be manipulated into hardened rods. When it is used to raise objects, it is called levitation ectoplasm. Precognition—extrasensory knowledge or perception of the future—is the most frequently reported of all psychic experiences, occurring most often in dreams. It may also occur spontaneously in waking visions, as flashing thoughts entering the mind, accompanied by a sense of knowing. Precognitive knowledge may be induced through trance, mediumship, and oracular divination. It differs from premonition in that the former involves a sense or feeling that something is going to happen, while precognition involves specific knowledge. Retrocognition is a type of clairvoyance involving extrasensory knowledge of an event after its occurrence.

Automatic writing is sometimes regarded entirely as a function of channeling via mediumship. However, like many forms of divination, such as casting runes or turning Tarot cards, it relies ostensibly on unconscious muscular movements of the hand to convey, through writing, information that is not accessible to the conscious mind. Although the medium often claims that the words are being delivered by a spiritual presence, psychical researchers believe that most of the information conveyed through automatic writing comes from the writer's subconscious mind, perhaps based on something read as a child. Automatic writing does not have to occur solely during a séance; it can manifest spontaneously in the course of everyday correspondence, and it is characterized by the writing being in an unknown hand, and it tends to flow faster than conscious writing. In addition, words may be joined together and perhaps be spelled unusually. Automatic writing can also be in mirror script (written left to right, even starting at the bottom right of a page), can take the form of verse, or even Latin. Spirit photography, or the ability to capture the physical essence of deceased persons, is synonymous with the name William H. Mumler (1832–1884), who took the first spirit photograph. According to Crista Cloutier, once Mumler discovered the marketability of capturing spirits and ectoplasm on film, he "presented himself as a medium who was in the service of spirits. . . . [His] manner was often theatrical" (21).

The word telepathy, which describes types of mind-to-mind communication, comes from the Greek *tele*, meaning distant, and *patheia*, which translates as feeling. It is the innate talent to communicate information without the use of speech or body language, and it can be shared not only between humans, but between a human and an animal as well. Sometimes it is found in an individual who also possesses other paranormal abilities, such as precognition and clairvoyance. Like with mediumship, it would be a mistake to assume that only uneducated individuals buy into psi phenomena like telepathy. In 1930 Pulitzer winner Upton Sinclair (1878–1968) published *Mental Radio*, which describes the ability of his wife to reproduce sketches made by himself and others, even when separated by several miles. Telepathic phenomena have been tested fairly thoroughly by various institutes and researchers (including recently at universities such as Duke). Western scientific investigation of telepathy is generally recognized as having begun with the Society for Psychical Research, which produced an influential report entitled *Phantasms of the Living* (coauthored by Edmund Gurney, Frederic William Henry Myers, and Frank Podmore, 1886, reprinted 1970), a text that introduced the term telepathy (which had earlier been referred to as thought transference). In 1917, psychologist John E. Coover conducted a series of telepathic card tests (the precursors to Zener cards) at Stanford University, but he found no overwhelming evidence to support the phenomenon. The term clairvoyance originates from the French words *clair*, which means clear, and *voyance*, meaning seeing. It is defined as a form of extrasensory perception whereby a person perceives distant objects, persons, or events. This can include the ability to see through opaque objects and the talent of detecting types of energy not normally perceptible. Typically, such perception is reported in visual terms, but may also include auditory impressions (resulting in what is called clairaudience). Unfortunately, the term clairvoyance is often misused to refer to all forms of information reception that is wholly dependent on extrasensory, inexplicable means. Historically, clairvoyance occurs more often with young adults, and it is one of the phenomena observed in the behavior of mesmerized and entranced patients. The earliest recorded report of somnambulistic clairvoyance is credited to the Marquis de Puysegur, a follower of Mesmer, who in 1784 was treating a local peasant, who became fluent and articulate, forgetting everything when he came out of the trance state.

Telekinesis or psychokinesis refers to the ability to move objects without using physical contact, as well as reshaping them (as in key or spoon bending) using the mind's energies. The term psychokinesis (sometimes called PK) comes from the Greek words *psyche*, meaning life or soul, and *kineisis*, which translates as to move. This phenomenon harks back to Mesmer's theories of animal magnetism, in that an invisible physical energy is created by the electromagnetic impulses (what is sometimes referred to as psychic energy). An interesting psychological sidelight of telekinesis is that teenagers, at puberty, often express an interest in developing these powers, as well as other psychic talents, particularly telepathy, which accounts for the popularity of Ouija Boards, automatic writing, and Tarot among the age group. Parapsychologists in recent times have devised various tests for PK, such as determining if a subject can affect the outputs of random number generators. Notable researchers include Helmut Schmidt (b. 1928), Robert [George] Jahn (b. 1930), along with his associates at the Princeton Engineering Anomalies Research Lab center (PEAR). Schmidt designed experiments in which a subject was asked to influence the output of a random number generator after the output had already been recorded. Theoretical physicist Henry Stapp wrote an article for the *Physical Review* in 1994 in which he attempted to show how PK might be consistent with a generalization of quantum theory, and that such phenomena merited further study. Some religious scholars believe that PK is a spiritual gift, related to astral projection, yogic flying, and psychic healing.

To get an idea of how prevalent parapsychology as a serious pseudo-science has come, all one need do is investigate the number of journals devoted to the subject. At present, there are some 250 periodicals that cover various areas of extrasensory perception. A list of just those still being published and housed by fifty or more libraries (a mark that attests to their authority) would include, in order of popularity: *The Skeptical Inquirer* (Committee for the Scientific Investigation of Claims of the Paranormal), *The Journal of Parapsychology* (Duke University Press), *The Journal of the American Society for Psychical Research* (American Society for Psychical Research), *Bibliographic Guide to Psychology* (G. K. Hall), *Journal of the Society for Psychical Research* ([London] Society for Psychical Research), *Proceedings of the American Society for Psychical Research* (American Society for Psychical Research), *Proceedings of the Society for Psychical Research* ([London] Society for Psychical Research), *Biographical Dictionary of Parapsychology* (Garret Publications), *Eranos-Jahrbuch* (Rhein-Verlag), *International Journal of Parapsychology: Revue Internationale de Parapsychologie* (Parapsychology Foundation), *Journal of Near-Death Studies* (Human Sciences Press), and *The Journal of Religion and Psychical Research* (Academy of Religion and Psychical Research). This does not even take into account two of the more popular periodicals that are now defunct, *The Zetetic* (Committee for the Scientific Investigation of Claims of the Paranormal, 1976–1977) and *Parapsychology Review* (Parapsychology Foundation, 1970–1990). Web-based organizations that study parapsychology have also sprung up, such as the Committee for the Scientific Investigation of Claims of the Paranormal (http://www.csicop.org/).

PSI PHENOMENA IN POPULAR CULTURE

Modern-day Americans are more than familiar with psychics and psychic phenomena, as it has once again become a big business, and psychics have adapted themselves to new demands and new technologies. Spurred on by the fact that contemporary U.S. presidents such as Ronald Reagan routinely consult soothsayers, various psychic hotlines have cropped up, briefly thriving before meeting their demise, the best known of these being Dionne Warwick's Psychic Friends Network, which went bankrupt in 1998. Miss Cleo's (born Youree Dell Harris, b. 1962) psychic hotline was closed down by the Federal Trade Commission on the grounds that she was guilty of deception and misrepresentation, as it turned out that the alleged Jamaican mystic was actually an out-of-work actress from Los Angeles. And then there are the

Internet astrologers, such as Ferdie Pacheco, son of the famous boxing doctor to legend Muhammad Ali, who claims to help people discover the perfect relationship. Psychics being accepted at the highest levels of government are not inimical to the United States. In his book *For the Record: From Wall Street to Washington* (1988), former Reagan chief of staff Donald Regan noted that First Lady Nancy Reagan relied on her astrologer when creating the former president's schedule. Recently, British Prime Minister Tony Blair's wife Cherie was the subject of a national scandal, after she admitted seeking regular help from a spiritual adviser, and Princess Diana had admitted to taking counsel from clairvoyants (Brottman B16).

A quick study of popular culture reveals that the average person, generally speaking, is still quite curious about psi phenomena. This is true in comics, for example, especially in Ki and Ki-based ESP anime and manga. According to Eri Izawa's *Use of the Psychic in Manga and Anime* (http://www.mit.edu/ ~rei/manga-psychic.html), boys' comics that center around intrigue, fighting, or martial arts heavily exploit the notion of Ki, which informs the "The Force" of Star Wars fame. Ki comes from Eastern martial arts training, and has extended into popular Japanese and now American culture. Much like with ESP connections, characters sense each other's presences from far away, feel impending danger when asleep, and sometimes create a protective force around themselves, making them impenetrable. In addition, characters often possess auras "that glow like fire." A different form of psychic energy, psionics, is also present in some anime and manga. This allows not only for fantastical powers such as teleportation, but a more controlled, purer form of telepathy, as well as controlled telekinesis. Psionic characters can heal others as well. Television, arguably the best gauge of popular culture, has no shortage of psychic syndicated shows, episodes, and characters. One well-known medium who has recently been given his own shows is James Van Praagh ("Beyond with James Van Praagh"; "Possessed Possessions"), author of the best-selling spiritual advice books *Talking to Heaven* (1997), *Reaching to Heaven* (1999), and *Healing Grief: Reclaiming Life after Any Loss* (2000). In addition, he is the subject of a 2002 biographical CBS mini-series starring Ted Danson (*Living with the Dead*, directed by Stephen Gyllenhaal). The most popular of the television mediums is undoubtedly the John Edward, whose show "Crossing Over with John Edward" had been a major success with the SciFi network. Edward specializes in cold readings. Taking mediumship about as far as possible seems to be the idea behind pet psychics like Sonya Fitzpatrick, who has become so popular that the *Chronicle of Higher Education* has run a story on her (pet psychics have raised the ire of some veterinarians, as Michael A. Obenski's article in *DVM: The Newsmagazine of Veterinary Medicine* attests). Psychics who act as detectives or who help the police are also still in demand by the viewing public. "Medium" (NBC) stars Patricia Arquette as a Phoenix, Arizona, psychic who lends her services to crime investigations, especially when the people who come to her are trying to reach the souls of the dead (the real-life Dubois had earlier lent her services to Paramount on an unsuccessful reality pilot, "Oracles," starring a panel of five seers). Even in person psychics still draw large crowds. A December 2005 issue of *American Libraries* reports that a psychic whose lecture at a northern California library had been canceled then rescheduled drew a record-breaking crowd of 145 people to a November 2005 presentation. Irma Slage discussed her work in police investigations and her book *Phases of Life After Death* (2000) at a branch of the Stockton-San Joaquin County Public Library.

Horror films in which psychic phenomena play a large role include Wolf Rilla's *Village of the Damned* (1960; based on John Wyndham's *The Midwich Cuckoos*) and Anton Leader's sequel *Children of the Damned* (1963), which take place in the English village of Midwich and the big city environment of London, respectively. In Rilla's small town horror classic, the entire citizenry of Midwich falls into a deep, mysterious sleep for several hours in the middle of the day, and months later every woman capable of child-bearing is pregnant. The eerily similar Aryan children grow much too quickly and have the power to compel even adults to do their bidding simply by concentrating on them. The 1970s saw more than its share of alternate states films, including *The Eyes of Laura Mars* (1978), directed by Irvin Kershner. This haunting pseudo-psychic detective story tells of a woman who finds herself with the power to see through the eyes of a serial killer as he commits his crimes. She contacts the police and tries to stop the murderer; of course, the twist is that since she sees what he sees while killing, she cannot see his face. Two Stephen King telepathy and telekinesis texts made into movies in the 1980s: David Cronenberg's *The Dead Zone* (1983) and Mark L. Lester's *Firestarter* (1984), based on King's novels of 1977 and 1981, respectively. The first tells the story of a young schoolteacher who survives an accident, but spends five years in a coma. Coming out of it, he discovers he has an ability to see the future of any individual with whom he comes into physical contact with (this same talent is used briefly by M. Night Shyamalan in the film *Unbreakable*, 2000). *Firestarter* chronicles how a couple who met while serving as subjects for a psychic experiment in college is somehow affected reproductively. The couple's daughter possesses the ability to start fires by merely concentrating. Shyamalan's *The Sixth Sense* (1999) turns the parapsychological ability to commune with the dead on its head, as the main character, a child psychologist who does not realize that he is himself dead, attempts to help a child who acts as a medium for spirits of recently deceased individuals. Robert Zemeckis, in *What Lies Beneath* (2000), a more traditional psychic tale, has the spirit of a murdered woman attempt to contact a professor's wife, in an attempt to both solve her own murder and warn the wife of impending danger. The only film that gives psychic ability an ethnic face is the black magic piece *Eve's Bayou* (1997), directed by Kasi Lemmons, set in Louisiana. One character has what she calls psychic premonitions, and another character uses voodoo magic to control reality. Some well-received mainstream films treat psi phenomena (there are some 400 films that deal solely with psychics), including the brilliantly acted (starring Tyrone Power) *Nightmare Alley* (1947, directed by Edmund Goulding), which introduces an over the hill charlatan mentalist who is part of a traveling carnival, and Akira Kurosawa's *Rashômon* (1950), the twelfth-century Japan classic on subjectivity in which a samurai and his wife are attacked by a notorious bandit. The samurai ends up dead, but the trial of the bandit leads to so much confusion that a psychic is brought in to allow the murdered man to give his own testimony. In the realm of science fiction, characters with supernatural powers are featured in Josh Whedon's *Serenity* (2005), a science fiction adventure futuristic comedy about a merchant crew that specializes in smuggling and robbery and has unfortunately taken on an unstable, fugitive telepath, and in Andrei Tarkovsky's *Stalker* (1979), which tells a dystopian tale about an unnamed fascist city that contains The Room, a place where one's secret hopes come true, but only if one is, or is accompanied by, a stalker, a human who possesses special extrasensory powers that allow a psychic connection. Psychic phenomena also plays roles in some blockbusters, such as Gore Verbinski's *The Ring* (2002) and the Hughes brothers' *From Hell* (2001), two films based on graphic novels, although the graphic novel for the former is itself based on the first two books in Koji Suzuki's Ring novels (*Ring* [1991], *Spiral* [1996], *Birthday* [2004], and *Loop* [2005]).

PSYCHICS IN SCIENCE FICTION AND HORROR

The idea of having supernatural mental abilities is an appealing one for fantastical literature. Poe's "The Facts in the Case of M. Valdemar" opened the door for writers who wanted to delve into the darker and more supernatural recesses of human psychology. First published in the *American Whig Review* in December 1845, the story brought to the fore some of the more controversial practices of Mesmerism, especially the belief in hypnotism, practiced by some physicians in both the United States and Europe. This shocking tale places the hypnotic state on trial, with its questioning of whether human death could be postponed if a subject were placed under a mesmerist's spell at the moment of demise. In London the piece was published as a pamphlet and included a preface that indicated it was not fictional, but "a plain recital of facts." J. Sheridan Le Fanu's "Green Tea" (*All the Year Round*, October 23–November 13, 1869) is more explicit in its satire of Mesmer and his theories. It owes as much to the theories of mystic Emanuel Swedenborg (1688–1772) as it does to those of Mesmer. This story of a Reverend Mr. Jennings, which is part of the Dr. Hesselius series, is one in which the psychic realm is breeched by means of an unnatural concentration of the mental facilities of the main character, brought on by his decision to combine a study of religious metaphysics with the imbibing of green tea, an agent rumored to help focus the mind. Jennings then becomes haunted by an apparition of a somewhat deformed and deranged monkey (in addiction terminology, one might say he literally has a monkey on his back), which follows him around and encourages him to act out his impulses. Like Poe, Le Fanu toys with Mesmerism, more specifically the existence of the invisible fluids related to animal magnetism. In the conclusion to the frame tale, Hesselius takes over as narrator after Jennings's suicide; he explains the case as thus, speaking of the function of the human brain (which he examines in his text *The Cardinal Functions of the Brain*): "and the nature of that fluid [in the brain] is spiritual, though not immaterial, anymore than, as I have re-marked, light or electricity are so. By various abuses, among which the ha-bitual use of such agents as green tea is one, this fluid may be affected as to its quality.... This fluid being that which we have in common with spirits... communication is thus more or less effectually established" (206–7).

Other nineteenth-century fiction that deals with psychic phenomena in-cludes Guy de Maupassant's "The Horla" (short version in *Gil Blas*, October 26, 1886; long version in *Le Horla*, 1887). Here, an unnamed narrator with either an overactive imagination or an acute sense of the paranormal brought on by research on mysticism (Maupassant leaves this up to the reader) senses an invisible presence that at first threatens only him. However, as the story progresses, he realizes that what he is seeing is just the tip of the psychic ice-berg, for the Horla, as he learns the presence is called, will destroy all hu-manity. The narrator understands that the presence he has somehow invoked is "he whom disquieted priests exorcised, whom sorcerers evoked on dark nights.... Mesmer divined him, and ten years ago physicians accurately dis-covered the nature of his power, even before he discovered it himself" (39). Maupassant's reference here to animal magnetism as a type of electric power would not be lost on his contemporaries.

Mesmer's theories are still being examined in fictional universes today, by well-respected authors such as Richard Matheson. For example, *A Stir of Echoes* (1958) introduces problems unanticipated in the hypnotic trance, creating a situation where a doorway to other psychic dimensions is opened. An average blue collar worker goes under an experimental trance and is then turned into a medium of sorts, now an open (albeit unwillingly so) conduit to the spirit of an allegedly murdered neighbor. Perhaps the best-known modern psi text is the horror and mainstream classic, *The Haunting of Hill House* (1959), by Shirley Jackson. Ostensibly a haunted house story, this novel re-volves around an isolated house that is the architectural equivalent of a car-nival funhouse. With its Byzantine architecture, seemingly impossible angles, and general coldness, Hill House has either driven out all of its occupants, or has made them suicidal. Throw into this equation an academic interested in paranormal research and two women who possess psychic abilities and can therefore communicate with the house's spirits, and you have the makings

---

A Chronology of Important Films about Psychics

1933 *Supernatural* (Victor Halperin)

1947 *Nightmare Alley* (Edmund Goulding)

1950 *Rashômon* (Akira Kurosawa)

1951 *The Medium* (Gian Carlo Menotti)

1960 *Village of the Damned* (Wolf Rilla)

1963 *Children of the Damned* (Anton Leader)

1963 *The Haunting* (Robert Wise)

1973 *Hell House* (John Hough)

1975 *Carrie* (Brian de Palma)

1978 *The Eyes of Laura Mars* (Irvin Kershner)

1979 *Stalker* (Andrei Tarkovsky)

1980 *The Shining* (Stanley Kubrick)

1983 *The Dead Zone* (David Cronenberg)

1984 *Firestarter* (Mark L. Lester)

1988 *Paperhouse* (Bernard Rose)

1990 *Ghost* (Jerry Zucker)

1997 *Eve's Bayou* (Kasi Lemmons)

1999 *The Sixth Sense* (M. Night Shyamalan)

2000 *Unbreakable* (M. Night Shyamalan)

2000 *What Lies Beneath* (Robert Zemeckis)

2001 *From Hell* (The Hughes Brothers)

2002 *The Ring* (Gore Verbinski)

2005 *Serenity* (Josh Whedon)

---

of an unforgettable tale. *The Haunting* (1963), directed by Richard Wise, is a fairly faithful version of Jackson's novel. Similarly, Matheson's novel of some thirty years later, *Hell House* (1971), places a group of people with psychic abilities in a haunted abode to determine if their talents make it possible to engage the supernatural forces within; *Hell House* was made into a movie in 1973 by John Hough. This trope has been updated recently by Douglas Clegg in *The Infinite* (2001), part of the Harrow Trilogy. Three strangers with unusual psychic abilities, including a "ghost hunter," are hired to investigate a series of supernatural events at a haunted boarding school. Mediums hosting séances and average people dabbling with extrasensory perception have also been fictionalized by various novelists, most notably in the horror field.

Popular cross-genre writers such as Barbara Michaels and Thomas Tryon have tried their hands at producing psychic literature. In Michaels's *Ammie, Come Home* (1968), a playful séance leads to the possession of a young girl. Tryon's *The Other* (1971) is a modern classic in which twin preteen boys who experiment with ESP and astral projection destroy not only themselves, but family members who are unfortunate enough to interact with them (Tryon balances the story between a supernatural and a psychological explanation for the turn of events, hinting that nonetheless the twins have a psychic connection to each other). Similar connections between minds can be seen in Mary Stewart's crossover mystery romance *Touch Not the Cat* (1976) and Bernard Rose's first film, *Paperhouse* (1988), but in both cases the ESP abilities of the protagonist are positive forces. In Stewart's novel, the protagonist has the ability to communicate via ESP with an unknown cousin, even at great distances. In Rose's *Paperhouse*, a young teenaged girl discovers mental communication with a young boy she believes she created by drawing a world on paper. Meanwhile, across the city, a young, terminally ill boy finds he has a psychic connection with a fictional girl. Other mediumship turned possession narratives include Gary Holleman's *Ungrateful Dead* (1999). Here, a young woman is possessed by a very familiar spirit (perhaps giving a new meaning to Freud's uncanny) when she is controlled by the ghost of her mother, who happened to be a sociopath. Even the most respected of all contemporary British Gothic and horror authors, Ramsey Campbell fictionalizes the negative repercussions of mediumship in *The Parasite* (1980), where the skill leads to a horrifying experience: A young woman leaves herself open at a séance and becomes possessed by the spirit of an occultist. Campbell adds the twist of making his protagonist pregnant and raising the possibility that a human being can pass a possessing spirit on to an unborn child. Likewise in film, psychic activity can often lead to possession by a spirit, as in Victor Halperin's *Supernatural* (1933), wherein an evil spirit possesses and controls a virginal heiress, causing her to adopt behaviors not accepted for women at that time.

Clairvoyance, clairaudience, precognition, telepathy, telekinesis, hypnosis, and astral projection are all prominent in horror fiction. Some of the more notable examples of psychic fiction include the biggest names in the horror genre, such as Dean R. Koontz. *The Face of Fear* (1977; published under the pseudonym Brian Coffey), a well-received novel, is about a clairvoyant who foresees mutilations by a New York serial killer known as "the butcher." He eventually sees his own death at the hands of the killer, and must escape based on his extrasensory knowledge. Stephen King and Peter Straub have teamed up to produce recurring characters who dabble in the occult and black arts in their Talisman series, *The Talisman* (1984) and *Black House* (2001). In the first of these novels, a young man named Jack Sawyer discovers that he can project himself into a parallel universe which holds the key to saving his mother's life; later, as an adult in the sequel, Homicide Detective

Sawyer finds himself being once more drawn to the alternate occult universe of the talisman in order to stop a vicious serial murderer. Both King and Straub have solo works with psi themes. *If You Could See Me Now* (1977) and *Shadowland* (1980), both by Straub, explore the dark side of magic. Straub's story "Blue Rose," which was first published by Underwood-Miller in 1985 and later collected in *Cutting Edge*, a 1986 anthology edited by Dennis Etchison, portrays a tense domestic atmosphere in which the mesmerizing powers of hypnotism can take an evil turn. King has more than his share of humans who commune with spirits, as in his early story "The Reach" (*Yankee*, November 1981). King revisits this theme later in his career in *Bag of Bones* (1998). Here, the novelist as protagonist is an unwilling conduit for the spirit of his deceased wife, which visits him in the form of cryptic refrigerator magnet messages that indicate he is caught in a battle of good and evil spirits that will usher in the extermination of an entire town because of a past race crime. Early in his writing career, King portrayed the dark side of psychic powers in novels like *Carrie* (1974) and *The Shining* (1977). In the latter, telepathy plays a larger role, as Danny Torrance, a young boy, possesses "the shining," or the ability to communicate telepathically with other humans who likewise possess this power. Teen Carrie White, on the other hand, is cursed with the power of telekinesis, an ability that comes across as being much more difficult to harness in this and other texts. Both King novels were made into films by Brian de Palma in 1976 (*Carrie*) and Stanley Kubrick in 1980 (*The Shining*), and both are considered modern masterpieces of horror, thus guaranteeing that more horror fictions dealing with the two psi phenomena would continue to draw audiences.

Other notable authors in the horror genre who have produced tales of various types of psychics include Kurt Siodmak, Graham Masterton, Nancy A. Collins, Brian Lumley, Kim Newman, and, most recently, Poppy Z. Brite and Thomas Tessier. In *Donovan's Brain* (1942), the first of his Patrick Cory novels, Siodmak creates a dark science fiction universe where not only a human can develop telepathic powers, but a brain kept alive in a jar can as well. Masterton's classic *The Manitou* (1975) actually has as its protagonist a psychic charlatan, but one whose true psychic skills must be tapped in order to save the world from an evil Native American mythological figure, the spirit of a powerful medicine man. This novel was made into a film in 1978 by William Girdler, and the theme of the fake psychic accidentally discovering real powers has been the basis for at least two movies, the all-but-forgotten *The Medium* (1951), directed by Gian Carlo Menotti, and the romantic dark comedy classic *Ghost* (1990), directed by Jerry Zucker. Collins's first novel, and the beginning of her Sonja Blue series, *Sunglasses after Dark* (1989), stars a telepathic vampire huntress who is part human, part creature of the night. Collins further examines occult magic in *Tempter* (1990). Lumley's Necroscope series originates with *Necroscope* (1986), which pits various types of psychics against one another. The novel begins with the anthropomancer

Boris, who is juxtaposed against the "necroscope," Harry Keogh. Harry directly communicates with the dead by visiting cemeteries to hear their thoughts. Telepathy also plays a role in Lumley's Vampire World series: *Blood Brothers* (1992), *The Last Aerie* (1993), and *Bloodwars* (1994). Newman's early novel *Jago* (1991) tells of a small English village that falls under the spell of Reverend Anthony Jago, the telepathic leader of the Agapemone cult, who seems to have a knack for mass mesmerism. Tessier's *Fog Heart* (1998), which received many laudatory reviews, looks at the psychological aspects of paranormal activity, as it follows the effects that a psychic's readings have on members of two couples who seem receptive to ghosts. Brite's first two novels, *Lost Souls* (1992) and *Drawing Blood* (1994), may be informed by vampires, ghosts, and haunted houses, but psychics play a large role in furthering her story line. *Lost Souls* takes a new look at the vampire legend, introducing a gang of nihilistic vampire Gothic punks who roam the streets in search of drugs, sex, and blood, as well as a Southern rocker with psychic gifts. *Drawing Blood* features not a human being, but a haunted childhood home, itself the most fascinating character, for it breathes and pulses and retains images of horror reminiscent of King's *The Shining*. It also reintroduces Brite's psychic musician, nicknamed Ghost. Psychics have even made their way into the alternative fiction Dracula series, a fan favorite penned by Fred Saberhagen. In *Séance for a Vampire* (1994), Holmes and Watson find themselves confronted with the paranormal. Psychics have also proven fodder for espionage slapstick. Michael Shea's mainstream satire, *Lord Vishnu's Love Handles: A Spy Novel (Sort Of)* (2005) introduces successful entrepreneur Travis Anderson, who has psychic abilities (which account for his dot.com success) and owes a debt of millions to the government, which is determined to have him pay by using his abilities.

According to Brian Stableford in *The Historical Dictionary of Science Fiction Literature* (2004), the idea of psi powers was adopted into science fiction by John W. Campbell, "whose enthusiasm prompted a 'psi boom' in the early 1950s" in magazines such as *Astounding* (first named *Astounding Stories*, then *Astounding Science-Fiction*, then *Analog*) and *Galaxy* (277). Campbell, who became the editor of *Astounding*, was a firm believer in the experiments of Duke University's Dr. J. B. Rhine (1895–1980), one of the first scientists in America to conduct in-depth investigations into such phenomena as clairvoyance and mental telepathy, performing some 90,000 experiments over a four-year period at his Duke University laboratory and coining the term extrasensory perception, or ESP (see www.rhine.org). Rhine wrote or coauthored eight benchmark texts on the subject, *Extra-sensory Perception* (1934), *New Frontiers of the Mind: The Story of the Duke Experiments* (1937), *Extra-sensory Perception after Sixty Years* (1940), *The Reach of the Mind* (1947; rev. ed. 1961), *New World of the Mind* (1955; rev. ed. 1962), *Parapsychology: Frontier Science of the Mind* (1957), *Parapsychology from*

Duke to FRNM (1965), and *Parapsychology Today* (1968), and edited one collection, *Progress in Parapsychology* (1971).

One such science fiction author who delved in the soft science of parapsychology was A. E. van Vogt. He produced, in the words of Hazel Pierce, "a melange of intriguing situations spiced with telepathy, teleportation, shape control, inner and outer space, mass consciousness, time shifts, [and] technological wonders beyond count" (956). In characters such as Johnny Cross of *Slan* (1946), van Vogt's first and perhaps best novel, he introduces readers to a superhuman telepath who not only possesses psychic skills but also hones them through training. Extrasensory perception also plays a role in his "space opera" Null-A novels. Theodore Sturgeon, known for his eschewal of hard science in favor of human stories, published many of his stories in *Astounding*. One such tale is "Blabbermouth" (1947), in which a woman's study and use of psi powers are trivialized for profit. In the International Fantasy Award winner *More Than Human* (1953), derived from his short story "Baby Is Three," Sturgeon creates the quasi-science psi concept of "homo gestalt," his term for the development of group consciousness. Here, psionics may be the missing link in completing a Unified Field Theory. The prolific science fiction author Mack Reynolds brought ESP to the foreground in one of his utopian texts, *After Some Tomorrow*, about an elitist group called the Monad Foundation, which awards scholarships to people with special powers in order to study extrasensory perception's socioeconomic value.

PSYCHICS IN OTHER LITERARY GENRES

Action adventure paranormal texts that feature ESP include the sci-fi spy thriller *Brainfire* (1979), by Campbell Black, who produced two fine psi novels in *Letters from the Dead* (1985) and *The Wanting* (1986). *Letters from the Dead* is concerned with two single mothers who take their children to a long-abandoned country house for a quiet vacation and discover haunted presences who communicate via an Ouija Board; *The Wanting* presents us with a young boy who is under the power of two elderly neighbors. In the Cold War–influenced *Brainfire*, the sibling of a political advisor who had seemingly committed suicide figures out that there is a Soviet plot to defeat the United States by using mind control. CIA espionage novels are also not immune to parapsychology. *The Sensitives* (1987), *Strange Bedfellows* (1988), and *Brain Damage* (1992), by Herbert Burkholz—best known for his Bondesque UKDs (Unusual Killing Devices) in *The Death Freak* (1979)—envision a spy agency that uses teams of mind readers, or "sensitives" (so called because they can sense the thoughts of others), assembled to collect information on other individuals and foreign governments, in a blend of thriller, science fiction, espionage, and sometimes romance. Romance novels (often suspense crossovers) that feature characters with ESP include *Change* (1975), by Ann Maxwell (1944–); *Eyes of the Night* (1992), by Diana Bane; and *The Geneva Rendezvous* (1997), by Julie Ellis. Of these, Maxwell's is by far the most intriguing, containing elements of almost every genre. Although, since her first novel, she has sold over twenty million books and has been nominated for seven Nebula Awards, Maxwell began her career as a writer under A. E. Maxwell, a pseudonym for the writing team of her and her husband Evan. The science fiction romance *Change* features the psychic Selena Christian, who must be rescued from a futuristic earth where her talents are condemned, and taken to the planet Change, a psychic realm.

Clairvoyants and mediums seem to be a particularly big draw in young adult literature. Texts include an early novel by benchmark author Lois Duncan, best known for the award-winning *I Know What You Did Last Summer* (1973; made into a blockbuster film by Jim Gillespie in 1997), began the trend of juvenile ESP texts with *A Gift of Magic* (1971). As is the case with most psychic fiction, by notables such as Allan W. Eckert and Margaret Mahy, protagonists must learn to control their erstwhile destructive abilities. Eckert's uplifting *Song of the Wild* (1980) is a unique story where a young boy discovers the ability to project his being into animals. Mahy's *The Haunting* (1982) involves clairvoyant powers that are seen as a family curse. Mary Towne, in *Paul's Game* (1983), highlights the androgyny of YA psi fiction (historically and in film, psychics are more often depicted as female, emphasizing their receptivity). In it, an experiment in ESP mentally links a teenaged girl to a mysterious boy. In many cases, psychic abilities become a repressed youth's best defense, as in *Shadow* (1994), by Joyce Sweeney. In this sibling rivalry tale, the fighting between an older brother and his sister escalates to the point where she is in imminent danger; the sister then discovers that she has the power of mediumship. Sweeney adds a wrinkle to the typical psychic tale; however, for the spirit that helps to guide the protagonist is not a human one, but the ghost of her beloved pet cat. Tim Bowler gives readers another misfit with whom to identify in *Midget* (1994). Here, a smallish fifteen-year-old boy who is constantly abused by his brother discovers that he can influence events by using his mind, a skill that grants him control of his life and leads to an extremely violent confrontation. Children also use paranormal skills to escape oppressive adults, as in *Skullcrack* (2000), by Ben Bo (pseudonym for V[iv] A. Richardson), which tackles topics such as the psychic bond between twins, mysticism, Celtic lore, and magic, juxtaposed against the violence of alcoholism and domestic abuse. Award-winning and popular YA author Stephanie S. Tolan, who specializes in tales of misfits, adds ethnicity and currency to the paranormal tale in *Flight of the Raven* (2001). She writes of a nine-year-old African American boy with unusual mental powers and a special ability with animals. Taken as a hostage by a terrorist militia group, he must learn to control his powers to survive.

PSYCHIC DETECTIVES

Young adult authors have also produced their share of psychic detectives and detectives who deal with occult cases. In fact, parapsychological concerns have even made their way into the most seminal of juvenile detective series, the Hardy Boys Mysteries, with *The Case of the Psychic's Vision* (2003), by Franklin W. Dixon (the pseudonym used by a variety of authors who write the Hardy Boys novels for the Stratemeyer Syndicate). Lois Duncan, in *The Third Eye* (1984; published in the U.K. in 1985 as *The Eyes of Karen Connors*), introduces readers to a high school senior who sees her psychic powers as realistically as possible; they are a possible way for her to be ostracized. She, however, eventually agrees to become somewhat of a psychic detective, helping a young police officer locate missing children. ESP has seeped its way into the more modern (currently up to nine books) Invisible Detective series, by Justin Richards, with the recent publication of *Double Life* (2005). The series itself explores the possibilities of retrocognition, as it is based on the ability of a fourteen-year-old boy to envision the 1936 adventures of "the Invisible Detective," even though he is unsure of how he came to this knowledge. Female psychic detectives are also prevalent in YA literature, such as Jennifer Allison's creation, Gilda Joyce. In *Gilda Joyce, Psychic Investigator* (2005), the thirteen-year-old protagonist becomes involved in mediumship when her father dies (one of her methods of communication is through letters to the deceased, as she attempts to channel his spirit through his typewriter). She decides to visit distant relatives in San Francisco to solve her first paranormal mystery, involving one of the most common Gothic tropes, a mysterious presence being held in a boarded-up tower. Terrance Dicks, the extremely prolific writer of *Doctor Who* fame, is also known for his Cassie books: *Cassie and the Devil's Charm* (2000), *Cassie and the Conway Curse* (2001), *Cassie and the Cornish Ghost* (2001), and *Cassie and the Riviera Crime* (2002) feature a British female teenage psychic detective who goes after kidnappers, murderers, and ghosts.

Perhaps the first historical psychic detective was French dowser Jacques Aymar. In 1692 he reportedly used a divining rod (a practice that was not all that unusual) to track and then positively identify a trio of murderers who had killed a wine merchant and his wife. With time, new versions of divining criminals emerged, so that, as Joe Nickell points out in *Psychic Sleuths: ESP and Sensational Cases* (1994), by the "heyday of Spiritualism, some

---

Perhaps the first historical psychic detective was French dowser Jacques Aymar. In 1692 he reportedly used a divining rod (a practice which was not all that unusual) to track and then positively identify a trio of murderers who had killed a wine merchant and his wife.

---

séance mediums claimed to solve crimes through contact with the spirit world" (11–12). Such high profile cases continued into this century, as with the case of an English schoolgirl who disappeared in 1937. Medium Estelle Roberts claimed that she communicated with the allegedly murdered girl, and reportedly led police to her murderer (Nickell 12). Psychic defenders Arthur Lyons and Marcello Truzzi have written a book called *The Blue Sense: Psychic Detectives and Crimes* (1991), in which they challenge various studies that found psychic detectives to be nothing more than charlatans, or sometime fortunate guessers who were more often than not wrong (Truzzi 99–129). Various psychic detectives have made claims that they help police, including Peter Hurkos (born Pieter van der Hurk, 1911–1988), Gerard Croiset (1909–1980), Dorothy Allison (1925–1999), Noreen Renier (b. 1937), Bill Ward (b. 1942), Rosemarie Kerr, Phil Jordan, and Greta Alexander (b. 1932). However, according to Nickell's *Psychic Sleuths*, none of these claims hold up under scrutiny, as these psychics often fudged their "résumés." Nickell argues that despite the uncritical news reports and pseudo documentaries that continue to tout the alleged successes of "psychics," most police departments (72 percent according to researchers) have not used psychics and those who have often recognize the basic trick of psychics, called retrofitting, where several vague "clues" are interpreted to fit the true facts after they become known. Nickell argues that psychic detective claims and actually hurt investigations as they misdirect police efforts and waste funds.

Psychic Detectives in Fiction

Although Poe's C. Auguste Dupin and Doyle's Sherlock Holmes often solved cases that verged on the supernatural, Tony Fonseca in *Supernatural Literature of the World: An Encyclopedia* pinpoints the creation of the literary equivalent of the occult or psychic detective as occurring in 1898, in *Pearson's* magazine (864). E. and H. Heron (the pseudonym of Kate O'Brien Ryall Prichard Hesketh and Hesketh V. Prichard, a mother-son writing team) found a fan base for their psychic sleuth, Flaxman Low. His tales were eventually collected in *Ghosts: Being the Experiences of Flaxman Low* (1899). Soon, other fictional supernatural investigators were gracing the pages of literary magazines: Alice and Claude Askew's Aylmer Vance, Algernon Blackwood's John Silence, William Hope Hodgson's Carnacki the Ghost Finder, and the lesser-known Rose Champion de Crespigny's Norton Vyse (created c. 1919 for David Whitelaw's *Premier Magazine*). These supernatural sleuths would hire themselves out to solve crimes of a seemingly paranormal nature. Recently, many of the exploits of these characters have been published by Ash-Tree and Dover. Ash-Tree Press's Occult Detectives series, edited by Jack Adrian, at present includes a collection of Alice and Claude Askew's Aylmer Vance stories, in *Aylmer Vance: Ghost Seer* (1998; eight stories featuring Vance's companion, Dexter); collected tales of Crespigny's Norton Vyse, in *Norton*

Vyse, Psychic (1999); and various stories featuring Harold Begbie's Andrew Latter, in *The Amazing Dreams of Andrew Latter* (2002). Dover Publications has thus far released Blackwood's John Silence stories, collected by S. T. Joshi, in *The Complete John Silence Stories* (1997). Silence, a favorite among genre fans, was created around the turn of the century, partly inspired by Doyle's Holmes tales. In 1999, Stephen Jones collected tales of diverse supernatural sleuths in *Dark Detectives: Adventures of the Supernatural Sleuths* (1999). These eighteen stories are written by masters such as William Hope Hodgson, Manly Wade Wellman, and Basil Copper, as well as contemporary notables like Brian Mooney, J. S. Russell, Brian Lumley, Clive Barker, Neil Gaiman, and Kim Newman.

Oddly enough, the first contemporary psychic detective novel, by Paul Victor, was one written not to examine the soft science of parapsychology, but to serve as a reader for students of English as a second language. The brief and lexically controlled *The Psychic* (1982) told of the exploits of a gifted psychic who aided the police in criminal investigations. Some of the bigger names in science fiction and horror have dabbled with supernatural sleuths, including the aforementioned Harris and Hooper, are Marion Zimmer Bradley and the lesser-known David Bowker. Bradley's *Gravelight* (Tor, 1997) introduces a small town where researchers in parapsychological phenomenon open a gate to the underworld. Bowker's *The Death Prayer* (White Wolf, 1995) and *The Butcher of Glastonbury* (Gollancz, 1997) introduce Chief Superintendent Vernon Laverne, a police detective who must learn to use his abilities of astral projection in order to stop an evil magician who uses a mysterious incantation as a murder weapon and a mysterious serial murderer who mutilates its victims. Romance mystery readers also seem fond of supernatural sleuths, as evidenced by novels such as *Now You See Her* (2005), by Cecelia Tishy. The novel tells the story of a clairvoyant Boston divorcée who is pressed into service as both an exorcist and a psychic detective. Her talents are used on a cold case of some thirteen years.

Of the contemporary detective novels with extrasensory themes and characters, most were published in the horror genre. A handful of mainstream mysteries contain supernaturally empowered characters, on both ends of the

> *Dr. Silence was a free-lance . . . among doctors, having neither consulting-room, bookkeeper, nor professional manner. He took no fees, being at heart a genuine philanthropist, yet at the same time did no harm to his fellow-practitioners, because he only accepted unremunerative cases, and cases that interested him for some very special reason. . . . The cases that especially appealed to him were of no ordinary kind, but rather of that intangible, elusive, and difficult nature best described as psychical afflictions; and, though he would have been the last person himself to approve of the title, it was beyond question that he was known more or less generally as the "Psychic Doctor."*
>
> —Algernon Blackwood, "A Psychical Invasion," *John Silence—Physician Extraordinary*

Oddly enough, the first contemporary psychic detective novel, by Paul Victor was one written not to examine the soft science of parapsychology, but to serve as a reader for students of English as a second language. The brief and lexically controlled *The Psychic* (Longman, 1982) told of the exploits of a gifted psychic who aided the police in criminal investigations.

criminal investigation. Fiction by Ellen Hart, Lori Foster, and Jody Jaffe pit detectives against clairvoyants. In Hart's *Wicked Games* (1988), a Minneapolis restaurant owner and sleuth investigates her new tenant, a writer with psychic powers who claims to have witnessed murders (or may have actually been the culprit, another recurring motif in psychic fiction). Foster's recent *Jamie* (2005) is the fifth novel in the Visitation series. Here, a former parapsychological research institute employee, who also happens to be a mother with a psychic child, hunts a reclusive psychic who was once housed at the institute. Jaffe's clever *In Colt Blood* (1998) takes on the recent fad of the animal psychic, in this case a horse whisperer. Here, a North Carolina reporter investigates the murder of a horse breeder, with suspicion centering on a psychic who specializes in horses. Rochelle Jewel Shapiro and Dayna Dunbar present readers with an interesting side effect of having psychic powers, that is, being able to better one's life, as well as the lives of family members and friends. In *Miriam the Medium* (2004), Shapiro introduces a part-time third generation psychic who is considered somewhat of a charlatan, but who actually possesses extrasensory skills. Here, the psychic uses her abilities first to bring in money, as a phone psychic, to try to keep her husband's business from going under, and later to save her daughter from a ending up in a bad marriage. In *The Saints and Sinners of Okay County* (2003), Dunbar creates the oddball Aletta Honor, a thirty-something woman who is carrying her fourth child and is blessed—or cursed, depending on one's point of view—with clairvoyant abilities. Dunbar deals with the idea of being a psychic more realistically than most, delving into not only the effect on the psychic and his or her immediate family, but on an entire community, as it attempts to come to terms with Honor's being an empty vessel and passing on "truths" which may be painful and unsettling. Even best-selling novelist Andrew M. Greeley has a psychic detective series, featuring Nuala Anne McGrail: *Irish Whiskey* (1998), *Irish Eyes* (2000), *Irish Love* (2001), *Irish Stew!* (2002), and *Irish Cream* (2005). In these a young woman has a psychic vision when she visits the grave of her grandparents and becomes a psychic detective after finding the murderer of a 1920s Chicago gangster. Relatively newcomer Victoria Laurie also ties the psychic detective with the mob in *Better Read than Dead: A Psychic Eye Mystery* (2005). Her psychic character is hired not by the police but by a mob boss who makes her an offer she cannot refuse.

As with psi phenomena and powers, when it comes to psychic detectives, most of the texts come from writers who are normally categorized as publishing in the horror genre, perhaps because, in general, the motif of the psychic or occult detective goes hand in hand with the production of atmospheric, dark tales. The portrayal of the chase, the manhunt for what invariably turns out to be a deeply disturbed serial killer, often takes its toll psychologically on the protagonist, the psychically gifted detective who is in charge of the case. Thomas Harris's *Red Dragon* (1981) is the quintessential example. The novel emphasizes the almost psychic bond between the FBI profiler Will Graham and serial killers who he attempts to arrest, in this case the tattooed, sexually and psychically disturbed. More recently, Kay Hooper has emerged from being a romance novelist to one who has successfully made forays into the world of horror fiction, drawing readers into the mental and emotional worlds of clairvoyant Maggie Barnes. Hooper not only focuses on her catching mutilators of women, but also chronicles her fragile psychic state when she is allowing extrasensory information to filter into her consciousness.

CONCLUSION

Purveyors of parapsychology or psychical research continue to study the evidence for and against extrasensory ways of knowing, and mentally induced methods of influencing the world, without the use of our recognized senses and motor systems. The various manifestations of psi phenomena, including telepathy, clairvoyance, precognition, and psychokinesis, have been and should be continued to be ingenuously and methodically researched in both their spontaneous forms and in controlled situations. Psi research is relevant to both psychology and hard science, as is research on the afterlife and on spiritual communication, and this holds true no matter how controversial the evidence and conclusions pertaining to inquiries dealing with apparitions of the dead, hauntings, poltergeist occurrences, mediumistic communications, mediumistic physical phenomena, astral projections, some near-death experiences, and past lives. These phenomena continue to inspire popular culture and literature as well as the hard and soft sciences, perhaps because they examine that part of the human condition which Albert Einstein would have classed as one of those mysteries which make life worth examining.

BIBLIOGRAPHY

Primary

Allison, Jennifer. *Gilda Joyce, Psychic Investigator*. New York: Sleuth-Dutton, 2005.
Askew, Alice and Claude. *Aylmer Vance: Ghost Seer*. Ashcroft, BC: Ash-Tree Press, 1998.

Bane, Diana. *Eyes of the Night.* New York: Jove, 1992.

Begbie, Harold. *The Amazing Dreams of Andrew Latter.* Ashcroft, BC: Ash-Tree Press, 2002.

Black, Campbell. *Brainfire.* New York: Morrow, 1979.

———. *Letters from the Dead.* New York: Villard, 1985.

———. *The Wanting.* New York: McGraw-Hill, 1986.

Blackwood, Algernon. *The Complete John Silence Stories.* Ed. S. T. Joshi. New York: Dover, 1997.

Bo, Ben. *Skullcrack.* Minneapolis: Lerner Sports, 2000.

Bowker, David. *The Butcher of Glastonbury.* London: Gollancz, 1997.

———. *The Death Prayer.* Clarkson, GA: White Wolf, 1995.

Bowler, Tim. *Midget.* London: Aladdin, 1994.

Bradley, Marion Zimmer. *Gravelight.* New York: Tor, 1997.

Brite, Poppy Z. *Drawing Blood.* New York: Dell, 1994.

———. *Lost Souls.* New York: Dell, 1992.

Burkholz, Herbert. *Brain Damage.* New York: Atheneum, 1992.

———. *The Sensitives.* New York: Berkley, 1987.

———. *Strange Bedfellows.* New York: Atheneum, 1988.

Campbell, Ramsey. *The Parasite.* New York: Macmillan, 1980.

Clegg, Douglas. *The Infinite.* New York: Leisure, 2001.

Collins, Nancy A. *Sunglasses After Dark.* London: Onyx, 1989.

———. *Tempter.* London: Onyx, 1990.

Crespigny, Rose Champion de. *Norton Vyse, Psychic.* Ashcroft, BC: Ash-Tree Press, 1999.

Davis, Andrew Jackson. *The Principles of Nature, Her Divine Revelations and a Voice to Mankind.* New York: S. S. Lyon & W. Fishbough, 1847.

Dicks, Terrance. *Cassie and the Conway Curse.* London: Piccadilly, 2001.

———. *Cassie and the Cornish Ghost.* London: Piccadilly, 2001.

———. *Cassie and the Devil's Charm.* London: Piccadilly, 2000.

———. *Cassie and the Riviera Crime.* London: Piccadilly, 2002.

Dixon, Franklin W. *The Case of the Psychic's Vision.* London: Aladdin, 2003.

Dunbar, Dayna. *The Saints and Sinners of Okay County.* New York: Ballantine, 2003.

Duncan, Lois. *A Gift of Magic.* New York: Pocket, 1971.

———. *The Third Eye.* Boston: Little, Brown, 1984.

Eckert, Allan W. *Song of the Wild.* Boston: Little, Brown, 1980.

Ellis, Julie. *The Geneva Rendezvous.* London: Severn House, 1997.

Fodor, Nandor. *Between Two Worlds.* West Nyack, NY: Parker, 1964.

Foster, Lori. *Jamie.* New York: Zebra, 2005.

Greeley, Andrew M. *Irish Cream.* New York: Tor/Forge, 2005.

———. *Irish Eyes.* New York: Tor/Forge, 2000.

———. *Irish Love.* New York: Tor/Forge, 2001.

———. *Irish Stew!* New York: Tor/Forge, 2002.

———. *Irish Whiskey.* New York: Tor/Forge, 1998.

Harris, Thomas. *Red Dragon.* New York: Putnam, 1981.

Hart, Ellen. *Wicked Games.* New York: St. Martin's Press, 1988.

Heron, E. and H. *Ghosts: Being the Experiences of Flaxman Low.* London: Pearson, 1899.

Holleman, Gary. *Ungrateful Dead*. New York: Leisure, 1999.

Jackson, Shirley. *The Haunting of Hill House*. New York: Viking Press, 1959.

Jaffe, Jody. *In Colt Blood*. New York: Fawcett, 1998.

Jones, Stephen. *Dark Detectives: Adventures of the Supernatural Sleuths*. Minneapolis, MN: Fedogan & Bremer, 1999.

King, Stephen. *Bag of Bones*. New York: Scribner, 1998.

———. *Carrie*. Garden City, NY: Doubleday, 1974.

———. *The Shining*. Garden City, NY: Doubleday, 1977.

King, Stephen, and Peter Straub. *Black House*. New York: Random House, 2001.

———. *The Talisman*. New York: Viking Press, 1984.

Knight, H. R. *What Rough Beast*. New York: Warner, 2001 (as by "Harry R. Squires"); New York: Leisure, 2005.

Koontz, Dean R. *The Face of Fear*. Indianapolis: Bobbs-Merrill, 1977 (as by "Brian Coffey").

Laurie, Victoria. *Better Read Than Dead: A Psychic Eye Mystery*. New York: Bantam, 2005.

Le Fanu, J. Sheridan. "Green Tea." In *Best Ghost Stories*. New York: Dover, 1964, pp. 178–207.

Lumley, Brian. *Necroscope*. London: Grafton, 1986.

———. *Vampire World I: Blood Brothers*. New York: Tor, 1992.

———. *Vampire World II: The Last Aerie*. New York: Tor, 1993.

———. *Vampire World III: Bloodwars*. New York: Tor, 1994.

Lyons, Arthur, and Marcello Truzzi. *The Blue Sense: Psychic Detectives and Crimes*. New York: Mysterious Press, 1991.

Mahy, Margaret. *The Haunting*. New York: Atheneum, 1982.

Masterton, Graham. *The Manitou*. Jersey, UK: Neville Spearman, 1975.

Matheson, Richard. *Hell House*. New York: Viking Press, 1971.

———. *A Stir of Echoes*. Philadelphia: Lippincott, 1958.

Maupassant, Guy de. "The Horla." In *Selected Tales of Guy de Maupassant*. New York: Random House, 1950.

Maxwell, Ann. *Change*. New York: Popular Library, 1975.

Michaels, Barbara. *Ammie, Come Home*. New York: Meredith Press, 1968.

Newman, Kim. *Jago*. London: Simon & Schuster UK, 1991.

Poniewozik, James. "Spirits of the Age." *Time* 165 (February 14, 2005): 55–56.

Reynolds, Mack. *After Some Tomorrow*. New York: Belmont, 1967.

Richards, Justin. *Double Life*. New York: Putnam, 2005.

Saberhagen, Fred. *Séance for a Vampire*. New York: Tor, 1994.

Shapiro, Rochelle Jewel. *Miriam the Medium*. New York: Simon & Schuster, 2004.

Shea, Michael. *Lord Vishnu's Love Handles: A Spy Novel (Sort Of)*. New York: Simon & Schuster, 2005.

Siodmak, Kurt. *Donovan's Brain*. London: Barrie & Jenkins, 1942.

Slage, Irma. *Phases of Life After Death: Written in Automatic Writing*. N.p.: Xlibris, 2000.

Stewart, Mary. *Touch Not the Cat*. New York: Morrow, 1976.

Straub, Peter. *If You Could See Me Now*. New York: Coward, McCann & Geogheghan, 1977.

———. *Shadowland*. New York: Coward, McCann, 1980.

Sturgeon, Theodore. *More Than Human*. New York: Farrar, Straus, 1953.

Sweeney, Joyce. *Shadow*. New York: Dell, 1994.

Tessier, Thomas. *Fog Heart*. New York: St. Martin's Press, 1998.

Tishy, Cecelia. *Now You See Her*. New York: Mysterious Press, 2005.

Tolan, Stephanie S. *Flight of the Raven*. New York: HarperCollins, 2001.

Towne, Mary. *Paul's Game*. New York: Dell, 1983.

Tryon, Thomas. *The Other*. New York: Knopf, 1971.

Van Praagh, James. *Healing Grief: Reclaiming Life After Any Loss*. New York: Dutton, 2000.

———. *Reaching to Heaven*. New York: Dutton, 1999.

———. *Talking to Heaven*. New York: Dutton, 1997.

van Vogt, A. E. *Slan*. Sauk City, WI: Arkham House, 1946.

Victor, Paul. *The Psychic*. London: Longman, 1982.

Secondary

Beichler, James E. "From Spiritualism to Spirituality." *Proceedings (Academy of Spirituality and Paranormal Studies)* (2003): 27–50.

Braude, Ann. *Radical Spirits: Spiritualism and Women's Rights in Nineteenth-Century America*. Boston: Beacon Press, 1989.

Brottman, Mikita. "The Quick (to Make a Buck) and the Dead." *Chronicle of Higher Education* 49 (March 21, 2003): B16.

Chéroux, Clément, et al. *The Perfect Medium: Photography and the Occult*. New Haven: Yale University Press, 2004.

Cooter, Roger. *The Cultural Meaning of Popular Science: Phrenology and the Organization of Consent in Nineteenth Century Britain*. New York: Cambridge University Press, 1984.

Copenhaver, Brian P. *Hermetica: The Greek Corpus Hermeticum and the Latin Asclepius in a New English Translation, with Notes and Introduction*. Cambridge: Cambridge University Press, 1992.

Fonseca, Tony. "Occult Detectives." In *Supernatural Literature of the World: An Encyclopedia*, ed. S. T. Joshi and Stefan Dziemianowicz. Westport, CT: Greenwood Press, 2005, pp. 863–65.

Frenschkowski, Marco. "Occultism." In *Supernatural Literature of the World: An Encyclopedia*, ed. S. T. Joshi and Stefan Dziemianowicz. Westport, CT: Greenwood Press, 2005, pp. 865–70.

Gutierrez, Cathy. "From Electricity to Ectoplasm: Hysteria and American Spiritualism." *Aries* 3, no. 1 (2003): 55–81.

Houck, James A. "The Universal, Multiple, and Exclusive Experiences of After-Death Communication." *Journal of Near-Death Studies* 24 (2005): 117–27.

Houdini, Harry. *A Magician among the Spirits*. New York: Harper & Brothers, 1924.

———. *Miracle Mongers and Their Methods*. New York: Dutton, 1920. Reprint, Amherst, NY: Prometheus, 1993.

Irwin, H. J. *An Introduction to Parapsychology*. Jefferson, NC: McFarland, 1989.

James, William. *William James on Psychical Research*. Ed. Gardner Murphy and Robert O. Ballou. New York: Viking Press, 1960.

Kaplan, Fred. *Dickens and Mesmerism: The Hidden Springs of Fiction*. Princeton, NJ: Princeton University Press, 1975.

Nickell, Joe, ed. *Psychic Sleuths: ESP and Sensational Cases*. Buffalo, NY: Prometheus, 1994.

Obenski, Michael A. "Pet Psychics Bridge Gap in Medical Knowledge." *DVM: The Newsmagazine of Veterinary Medicine* 34, no. 12 (December 2003): 5.

Pierce, Hazel. "A(lfred) E(lton) van Vogt." *St. James Guide to Science Fiction Writers*. 4th ed. London: St. James Press, 1996, pp. 955–58.

Regan, Donald. *For the Record: From Wall Street to Washington*. New York: Harcourt, Brace, 1988.

Rhine, J. B. *Extra-sensory Perception*. Boston: Boston Society for Psychical Research, 1934.

———. *Extra-sensory Perception After Sixty Years*. New York: Henry Holt, 1940.

———. *New Frontiers of the Mind: The Story of the Duke Experiments*. New York: Farrar & Rinehart, 1937.

———. *New World of the Mind*. New York: Sloane, 1955. Rev. ed. New York: Apollo, 1962.

———. *Parapsychology from Duke to FRNM*. Durham, NC: Parapsychology Press, 1965.

———. *Parapsychology: Frontier Science of the Mind*. Springfield, IL: C. C. Thomas, 1957.

———. *Parapsychology Today*. New York: Citadel Press, 1968.

———, ed. *Progress in Parapsychology*. Durham, NC: Parapsychology Press, 1971.

———. *The Reach of the Mind*. New York: Sloane, 1947. Rev. ed. New York: Apollo, 1961.

Russell, Jeffrey B. *A History of Witchcraft: Sorcerers, Heretics, and Pagans*. London: Thames & Hudson, 1980.

Sinclair, Upton. *Mental Radio*. New York: A. & C. Boni, 1930.

Soal, S. G. "Spiritualism." In *A Survey of the Occult*, ed. Julian Franklyn. London: Arthur Barker, 1935.

Stableford, Brian. *The Historical Dictionary of Science Fiction Literature*. Lanham, MD: Scarecrow Press, 2004.

Stapp, Henry. "Theoretical Model of a Purported Empirical Violation of the Predictions of Quantum Theory." *Physical Review A* 50, no. 1 (July 1994): 18–22.

Truzzi, Marcello. "Reflections on *The Blue Sense* and Its Critics." *Journal of Parapsychology* 59 (1995): 99–129.

Wilson, Clare. "Spellbound." *New Scientist* 187 (July 30, 2005): 32.

The Sea Creature

by Mike Ashley

INTRODUCTION

That great writer of sea stories, W. W. Jacobs, began his story "Over the Side" (*Today*, May 29, 1897) by saying: "Of all classes of men, those who follow the sea are probably the most prone to superstition." Moreover, a tall or exaggerated tale is often equated with a fisherman's tale about "the one that got away," so it is not surprising to find many tales of monsters and strange creatures of the sea. Howard Waldrop creates a clever spoof on the fisherman's boast in "God's Hooks" (*Universe #12*, 1982) in which Izaak Walton catches but loses a massive serpent.

Mankind's relationship to the sea has always been close, not only as a source of food or as a means of travel, but also as that lure known as "the call of the sea," which, like the "call of the wild," haunts us, compelling us to return to the sea whenever opportunity allows. The sea remains the last great unexplored area of the earth's surface. As so much is still unknown about what hides in the ocean depths, it allows us to continue to believe in creatures of myth and legend such as the sea serpent or the selkie or the kraken. Add to this tales of ghost ships, Atlantis, the Sargasso Sea, and the Bermuda Triangle, and we find that the sea is probably home to more believable creatures and creations of myth and superstition than any other area of the supernatural.

This chapter will look at all forms of sea creatures and legends. While the emphasis is on supernatural creatures, it is difficult to determine a firm dividing line between the impossible and the possible when it comes to giant sea creatures, and so this essay will trespass into the domain of science fiction while seeking to define the borderland.

It will cover not only creatures of the sea, including mermaids, mermen, selkies, seal maidens, sea serpents, kraken, lorelei, sirens, and other such denizens of the deep, but also the power and lure of the sea itself, which is perhaps the ultimate sea "creature." It will also touch on worlds beneath and beyond the sea and other bodies of water such as lakes and rivers, where there are common areas of myth and folklore.

EARLY LEGENDS AND FOLKTALES

Our links to the sea—both physical and spiritual—are so strong and so ancient that virtually every race and culture has legends and folktales of the sea. In ancient Mesopotamia the sea was personified as the goddess Tiamat. No images of her are known to survive, but she was believed to take the form of a giant dragon, not unlike a sea serpent. The legend tells that Tiamat, who was once calm and kindly, is angered following the death of her consort, Apsu, the god of fresh water. She creates an army of beings to help in her battle, and among them are fish-men and serpents. Tiamat is eventually defeated by Marduk, the Sun god. Tiamat is representative of both the power of the sea and its ability to flood the land.

There are versions of Tiamat in most cultural legends, including the Polynesian Takaroa, the Japanese Owatatsumi, the Chinese Yu-qiang, the Nordic Aegir, and the ancient Greek Tethys. Almost all these take the form of a dragon or serpent, suggesting that the image of the sea serpent dates back to our earliest belief systems. Tethys was the wife of Oceanus (the original earth-girdling waters), who is also portrayed as a giant serpent wrapped around the earth with its tail in its mouth. He is thus the equivalent of the Scandinavian Midgard serpent called Jormangard.

Many ancient legends also talk of specific sea creatures, usually spawned by the gods, but which have an independent existence. Probably the best known in western cultures are those in the Greek legends. Although Poseidon (the Roman Neptune) was originally the god of earthquakes, later classical legends converted him into the god of the sea, with an underwater domain. He was the father of Triton, who calms the ocean by blowing through his sea-shell. Triton is always depicted as having a man's head and torso but the body and tail of a fish or dolphin, and thus is the original personification of the merman.

Triton's mother was Amphitrite, whose father was Nereus, known as the "Old Man of the Sea." Nereus is always portrayed as a very old man but according to Homer (*Iliad* 18.36) was capable of changing his shape, and thus is sometimes depicted as having a fish's tail. His wife, Doris, was the daughter of Oceanus, and they were the parents of the Nereids, the nymphs of the sea, who were always depicted as mermaids. Chief among the Nereids was Thetis, the primary goddess of the sea, whose name is derived from Tethys (and thus Tiamat). In one form or another she has appeared in Greek legends from the earliest days; indeed, she looked after the young Poseidon when he was cast into the sea as a child. Thetis later married a mortal, Peleus—the forerunner of many legends of humans marrying sea-nymphs—and was the mother of Achilles. A later similar story concerns the Syrian goddess Atargatis, equated with the Phoenician Derceto. Ctesias tells how she fell in love with a youth and bore the child Semiramis, later queen of Assyria. Ashamed, Atargatis-Derceto threw herself into a lake and was transformed into a fish with a human head. Atargatis was worshipped throughout the eastern Mediterranean and had sacred fishponds dedicated to her.

These and other sea deities feature in many of the Greek legends, not least the great sea voyages of Odysseus and of Jason and the Argonauts. Odysseus on his long voyage home after the Trojan War had to face many dangers, including the sea monster Scylla and the enchanting song of the Sirens. When the Argonauts had to pass the Sirens, Orpheus was able to outsing them and, as a result, they cast themselves into the sea.

The sea monster also appears in the story of the Trojan War when the priest Laocoön and his sons are killed by two sea serpents sent by Apollo, who is angered when Laocoön warns the Trojans about the danger of the Wooden Horse.

One legend that has given rise to many later stories is that of the sea monster that ravages the land until a sacrifice is made. The best known of the Greek stories concerns Andromeda, whose mother, Cassiopeia, boasted that her child was more beautiful than the Nereids. Angered, Poseidon sent a sea monster to destroy the land. Andromeda was tied to a rock as a sacrifice, but was rescued by Perseus. Robert Graves suggests (*The Greek Myths* 244) that this incident owes its origin to the Mesopotamian myth, discussed earlier, of Marduk killing Tiamat. A similar Greek myth concerns the Trojan king Laomedon, whose daughter is sacrificed to a sea monster sent by Poseidon after Laomedon had failed to pay his dues. All this is symbolic of tales created to celebrate man's growing control over the sea, especially controlling the flooding of cultivated land.

Greek legends are not alone in their depiction of sea creatures. In Vedic myth the omnipotent Varuna, who maintains order in all things, is frequently depicted as riding a sea monster, the *makara*, sometimes described as a fish, a shark, a dolphin, a crocodile, or any combination thereof. The first incarnation of Vishnu was as the fish Matsya, which grew rapidly in size and saved mankind during the Deluge. The Polynesian god of fishes is Ika-Tere, some of whose children were also mermaids and mermen, though curiously it was usually the right side that was fish and the left side human. Ea (Greek, Oannes), the Babylonian god of wisdom, was a merman, described thus by the Babylonian priest Berossus in his now lost *Babylonaika* (c. 280 B.C.E.). "The whole body of the animal was like a fish; and had under a fish's head another head, and also feet below, similar to those of a man, subjoined to the fish's tail."

Perhaps the best known of the fish gods, because of its later incorporation into supernatural literature, is the Phoenician Dagon, who was also half-man, half-fish, though according to Michael Jordan (*The Encyclopedia of Gods* 69), this association was an Israelite mistranslation, and Dagon or Dagan was originally a god of grain and fertility. The Hebrew word *dagh* means giant fish and was also used to describe the "great fish" that swallowed Jonah (Jonah 1:17). The Bible refers to other monsters, most notably the Leviathan, which both Psalm 74 and Isaiah 27:1 equate with a sea monster. It may be that the word is symbolic for a major nation such as Assyria or Egypt. However, its use elsewhere, such as in the Book of Job, clearly means a water creature, and the reference at Job 41 is taken to mean a crocodile by most Bible scholars, as a parallel to the previous reference to *behemoth* (Hebrew for "great beast") in Job 40, which is usually taken as describing a hippopotamus.

> The universal belief in sea deities and monsters by ancient cultures has remained hidden deep in our collective consciousness and continues to permeate folk tales and legends of more recent vintage. These are common among the great maritime nations of the world, but those that feature predominantly in Western folklore come from Celtic and Scandinavian myth.

There is a passing reference to a mermaid in the twelfth-century Icelandic foundation saga *Landnámábok*, while the Irish *Annals of the Four Masters*, which survives in documents of the seventeenth century but compiled from ancient chronicles, records that in the year 558 C.E. the fisherman Beoan of Comhgall caught the mermaid Liban in his nets. Her story is preserved in the *Lebor na h-Uidre* or *Book of the Dun Cow*, compiled in the twelfth century from early documents and tradition. It tells how Eochaid, son of the king of Munster, was drowned in a well with his children, but Liban survived and underwent a sea-birth. She was transformed into a mermaid, half-human, half-salmon, and lived in Lough Neagh along with her dog, which had become an otter.

Such tales provide the fundament from which many later traditional tales and stories spring, and these are best explored by individual category.

MERMAIDS, MERMEN, SELKIES, AND SIRENS

In *The Magic Zoo*, Peter Costello refers to many recorded sightings of mermaids and mermen and even the occasional capture or discovery of a body. The earliest surviving physical description was recorded by the second-century Greek geographer Pausanias in his *Description of Greece*.

Most "captured" mermaids are dismissed as fairground fakes, and most sightings attributed to the heightened imaginations of sailors mistaking seals, manatees, or dugongs for mermaids. Even so, the folk belief is so deeply rooted that it is easy for us to hope that such creatures might exist—or have existed once—and this adds an extra dimension to the various folktales that have been preserved.

Among several merfolk stories recorded by T. Crofton Croker in *Fairy Legends and Traditions in the South of Ireland* (1825) is "The Soul Cages." Here Jack Dogherty befriends a merman, known in western Ireland as a merrow, and is taken to the merrow's underworld home. The merrow shows Dogherty the cages in which he has benignly stored the souls of drowned sailors, and Dogherty schemes as how to release them. The merrow, which is of a great age, is described as having "green hair, long green teeth, a red nose, and pig's eyes. It had a fish's tail, legs with scales on them, and short arms like fins." It also talks Irish fluently, enjoys liquor, and wears a cocked hat.

Jonas Lie records a not dissimilar story in "Finn Blood" (*Trold*, 1891). Eilart's boat capsizes, and it is all the young man can do to stay afloat and awake. He finds himself taken down into the sea by a mermaid and introduced

---

But a greater marvel still is the Triton. The grander of the two versions of the Triton legend relates that the women of Tanagra before the orgies of Dionysus went down to the sea to be purified, were attacked by the Triton as they were swimming, and prayed that Dionysus would come to their aid. The god, it is said, heard their cry and overcame the Triton in the fight. The other version is less grand but more credible. It says that the Triton would waylay and lift all the cattle that were driven to the sea. He used even to attack small vessels, until the people of Tanagra set out for him a bowl of wine. They say that, attracted by the smell, he came at once, drank the wine, flung himself on the shore and slept, and that a man of Tanagra struck him on the neck with an axe and chopped off his head. For this reason, the image has no head. And because they caught him drunk, it is supposed that it was Dionysus who killed him.

I saw another Triton among the curiosities at Rome, less in size than the one at Tanagra. The Tritons have the following appearance. On their heads they grow hair like that of marsh frogs not only in color, but also in the impossibility of separating one hair from another. The rest of their body is rough with fine scales just as is the shark. Under their ears they have gills and a man's nose; but the mouth is broader and the teeth are those of a beast. Their eyes seem to me blue, and they have hands, fingers, and nails like the shells of the *murex*. Under the breast and belly is a tail like a dolphin's instead of feet.

Pausanias, Description of Greece, *Book 9, section 20–21*

to a draug, a sea-demon in merman shape. Like Croker's merrow, this draug is fond of his drink, and he and Eilart enjoy a meal, although Eilart remains suspicious of the draug's intentions. Nevertheless, he is made welcome and eventually taken back to his boat. Later he learns it was a dream. The draug is described as

> a broad-shouldered, strongly built fellow, with a glazed hat shoved back on to the top of his head, with dark-red tangled hair and beard, small tearful dog-fish eyes, and a broad mouth, round which there lay for the moment a good-natured seaman's grin. The shape of his head reminded one somewhat of the big sort of seal, which is called Klakkekal, his skin about the neck looked dark and shaggy, and the tops of his fingers grew together.

While Dogherty's merrow and to some extent Lie's draug are relatively friendly, most folk tales treat merfolk with caution. Indeed, in Lie's other stories, including "The Fisherman and the Draug," "Tug of War," and "Jack of Sjöholm," the draug has more demonic powers, striking vindictive bargains through which it seeks to claim its victims. This is more like the mermaid of Celtic tradition. The sea-woman Seshelma, who appears in Sara Coleridge's *Phantasmion* (1837), the first fairy novel written in English, is portrayed as a scheming sorceress and is hideous to behold: "her skin was thick and glistering; there was a glaze upon it which made Phantasmion shiver." In "The Laird of Lorntie," collected by Robert Chambers in *Popular Rhymes of Scotland* (1847), a servant stops his lord from rescuing a girl whom he believes is drowning in the loch. Only then does the maiden reveal her true colors as she tells the lord she was after his blood for supper. In "Lutey and the Mermaid," collected by William Bottrell in *Traditions and Hearthside Stories of West Cornwall* (1870), a fisherman rescues a stranded mermaid and is granted three wishes, but there are conditions and after nine years the mermaid claims the man and takes him into the deep waters. In "The Haunted Ships," included by Allan Cunningham in *Traditional Tales of the English and Scottish Peasantry* (1822), a local man is menaced by two mischievous water-elves who inhabit two rotting hulks.

Generally mermen are considered as having greater wisdom than their human equivalents. In "The Wise Merman," collected by Jón Árnason in *Icelandic Legends* (1862), a merman, caught in a fisherman's nets, reveals facts to the human of which he is ignorant, even though they are right under his nose. Their wisdom, though, may also be part of their cunning. In George A. Baker's "The Merman" (*Mrs Hephaestus*, 1887), which may be based on similar Nordic legends as used by Jonas Lie, a merman (or in this case a seal man) who is captured by a fisherman proves evil and destroys the fisherman's family.

The basic plot of finding or confronting a merman or mermaid, friendly or otherwise, is in itself limited. The more interesting development was in exploring the relationship between a human and one of the merfolk. This has become the enduring theme in almost all subsequent merfolk stories. Initially they were allegories between Christianity and paganism, because it was frequently a requirement of the relationship that to secure the love of a human, and thereby acquire an immortal soul, mermaids (or mermen) must abandon their elemental spirit and become mortal. This is the premise behind the best known (and most imitated) of all mermaid stories, "Den lille Havfrue" ("The Little Mermaid," *Fairy Tales Told for Children*, 1837) by Hans Christian Andersen. Andersen tells how a young mermaid, just fifteen, rescues and falls in love with a prince. She is intrigued by the human world and learns that though humans die younger (merfolk can live to be three hundred years old), they have an immortal soul. She consults the sea-witch who gives her a potion that will transform her into human shape, but she warns the mermaid that she can never revert to her former shape, and if she fails to win the love of the human she will fade away, "like the foam on the sea." In payment for the potion the sea-witch takes the mermaid's beautiful singing voice, so that she becomes mute. Unfortunately, the prince does not reciprocate her love and marries another. Although given the opportunity to kill the prince, she refuses and sacrifices herself. She dissolves into foam but rises into the air and is greeted by the air elementals who tell her that because of her good deeds she may still receive an immortal soul one day.

Oscar Wilde used Andersen's story as the basis for "The Fisherman and His Soul" (*The House of Pomegranates*, 1891), where a fisherman finds he must lose his own soul in order to wed a mermaid, and though most of the story concerns the problems caused by his disembodied soul, there are some beautiful passages of sea lore and imagery.

Andersen's story is seen by some as a metaphor for the repression of women in society (Golden 98–101), though it is also an allegory for transcendence, showing that despite one's place in society, actions can brings rewards. Andersen had long been fascinated by the duality of sea and earth and of the suggestion of transformation from one existence to another. This fascination manifested itself in several of his tales (most notably "The Ugly Duckling"), and had been used before he started his fairy tales when he adapted a traditional folktale for his poem "Agnete og Havmanden" ["Agnete and the Merman"] (*Kjøbenhavnsposten*, November 14, 1833). Here the roles are reversed. A merman falls in love with a young human girl and lures her into his watery domain, where he fathers seven children. One day the woman hears the church bells of her former village and becomes homesick. The merman allows her to return on condition she reveal nothing, but she confesses everything to her mother and never returns to the sea or her children, despite the merman's forlorn cries. This tale was retold by Matthew Arnold as "The Forsaken Merman" (*The Strayed Reveller*, 1849).

The idea of love between merfolk and humans date back to the legends of Thetis and of Atargatis mentioned above. Another early tale, "The King and the Merman," was captured by Walter Map in his twelfth-century compendium of court gossip, *De nugis curialium* (*Courtiers' Trifles*). It tells of a merman who rescues a sorcerer's child and is granted legs while on the land but a tail when in the sea. He must spend time in the sea every day or his skin will shrivel. Unfortunately, he is captured by the king and put on show until rescued by the woman who loves him. However, she cannot follow him back to his watery domain. In the Italian folktale "Maredata and Giulio" (1826), translated as *The Ocean Spirit* (Cowie, 1834), a man rescues a woman from the sea, marries her, and has a child. She remains mute but when eventually she speaks, she reveals that she is a mer-woman and must return to the sea.

Perhaps the most interesting of the legends of the transformed sea-maiden is that of Mélusine, which was recorded in *Le Roman de Mélusine* by Jean d'Arras in 1392. The basic story is that Raymond of Poitou became infatuated with Mélusine, the daughter of a fairy. She agreed to marry him but only on condition that he never spy upon her on a Saturday. When he did, and saw her in her natural form, part-woman part-serpent, she turned into a spirit, remaining to keep a watchful eye on her children, who became the de Lusignan dynasty. The Mélusine story has inspired several medieval and later works of literature, art, and music, including *Die schöne Melusine* by Thüring von Ringoltingen, the Mayor of Berne (1456); *Histoire de Mélusine* by Paul-François Nodot (1698); Ludwig's Tieck's nouvelle *Sehr wunderbare Historie von der Melusina* (1799); and Maurice Maeterlinck's play *Pelléas et Mélisande* (1892), which further inspired an opera by Claude Debussy (1902).

Its most lasting influence was through the nouvelle *Undine* (1811) by Friedrich de la Motte Fouqué. Undine is a water elemental who is found and raised by a human couple. When old enough she falls in love with and marries the knight, Huldebrandt, but he later rejects her for another. Undine returns to her watery home but, encouraged by her uncle, she visits her husband one last time to impart a fatal kiss. Fouqué's treatment of the legend is regarded by many as definitive—George MacDonald, for instance, called it the "most beautiful" of all fairy tales—and as a consequence it has rarely been reworked and at best simply copied. It was adapted as a play, *Ondine* (Paris, April 1939), by the French writer Jean Giraudoux.

The Celtic equivalent of the undine is the *gwragedd annwn*, and John Rhys recorded several traditional tales about them in *Celtic Folk-lore* (1901). In these legends, these female water-sprites seek out human husbands on condition that if he strikes them three times they will return to their watery home, though they continue to watch over their children.

The more significant, and often more sinister, Celtic variant of the undine and mermaid is the seal-maiden or selkie. The word "selkie" is Orcadian (from the Orkney Islands) for seal, but through folklore has come to mean those seals that can shed their sealskin and transform themselves into human form, though they must retain their sealskin to return to seal shape. This transformation has become a strong metaphor, not just for paganism versus

Christianity, but also for civilized man versus the beings of nature. For instance, in "The Unchristened Child," one of the stories inspired by Cornish legends in *Drolls from Shadowland* (1893) by Joseph H. Pearce, an unchristened child is transformed into a seal and later seeks revenge. The title of Eugene Field's "The Pagan Seal-Wife" (*The Holy Cross*, 1893), says it all in this tale of a man whose mother and wife were both seal-maidens who return to the sea at the point of death. More recently, Delia Sherman explores the Christian-pagan dilemma in "The Maid on the Shore" (*F&SF*, October 1987) where a woman, whose father is killed by suspicious fishermen and whose seal-woman mother returns to the sea, considers whether and how she will exact her revenge.

William Sharp, hiding under the persona of Fiona Macleod, shows these opposing elements powerfully in two separate stories drawn from Celtic folklore. In "The Dark Nameless One" from *The Washer of the Ford* (1896), Black Angus, who may have inherited the spirit of Judas, has transformed into a seal, but he works his wiles on Kirsteen, a young Christian woman, whom he lures into the sea and she becomes a sea-witch or *cailleach-uisge*. In "The Judgment o' God" from *The Sin-Eater* (1895), young Murdoch has always been a strange child obsessed with the sea. One wintry night he disappears but is later seen being caressed by a seal and in a state of transformation. Murdoch then vanishes into the sea with the seal, his laughter sometimes being heard on stormy nights.

The Scottish solicitor and occultist John Brodie-Innes wrote what ought to have been the definitive novel on selkies, *Morag the Seal* (1908), but this tale of deviltry and magic, with Morag's seal-state explained as a psychic projection, is spoiled by occult technicalities. Nevertheless, at its core it maintains the sinister nature of the selkie.

John Masefield's poem "The Seal Man" (*Manchester Guardian*, April 12, 1907) and Victor Rousseau's story "The Seal Maiden" (*Cavalier*, November 15, 1913), the latter inspired by Newfoundland legends, while both telling the simple story of love overcoming physical and spiritual barriers, also depict the selkie as a personification of the call of the sea, an image evident in Fiona Macleod's "The Judgment o' God" and even more powerfully in "The Ninth Wave" (*The Sin-Eater*). When the tide turns, the Great Tide sends out nine waves, each with its own purpose, and those who hear the ninth wave cannot ignore it, for it is death itself. In this guise the call of the sea corresponds to the siren who lures sailors to their deaths with their songs.

The most famous siren of legend is the lorelei (originally *lurlei*) of the Rhine, near St. Goarshausen, a rocky promontory where once lived a beautiful maiden whose song caused boatmen to crash on the surrounding rocks. This image was first captured in literature in the poem *Die Lore Lay* by Clemens Brentano (1802) and later in Heinrich Heine's poem *Die Loreley* (1823). In "The Nymph of the Waters" (1826), Irish author Francis Saint Leger tells how when a Count's son seeks to capture the lorelei, one of his boatmen tries to kill her with an arrow and the nymph vanishes, never to be seen again.

"The Siren" (*Graphic*, Summer 1882) is an unusually somber story for F. Anstey, and tells of a siren who sacrifices herself in order that the sailor she loves, lives. *The Story of the Siren* (1920), by E. M. Forster, tells of a swimmer who is disfigured by a siren. He marries another who has been similarly deformed but locals, fearing their child will be a monster, kill the mother. In "The Wine-Dark Sea" (*Powers of Darkness*, 1966), Robert Aickman underplays the siren legend yet still creates a magical atmosphere of detachment when a holidaymaker is entranced by an uninhabited island only to find solace among its spiritual inhabitants.

The siren has been adapted into literature as the *femme fatale*. Oliver Onions retained some of the original concept in "The Painted Face" (1929), where a young girl reveals that she is the reincarnated spirit of a siren cursed by Poseidon. On land the girl is shy and withdrawn but when by water she blossoms. The erotic element of the siren is displayed in "The Sea-Witch" by Nictzin Dyalhis (*Weird Tales*, December 1937), where a retired professor rescues a women from the stormy seas, and in showing her appreciation she recants for actions in past lives that serve only to torment her savior. An equally dangerous sea demon appears in "The Merrow" by Seabury Quinn (*Weird Tales*, March 1948), who seduces men and sucks away their breath.

Because of the romantic or faery connotations of mermaids and, to a lesser extent, selkies, most modern interpretations tend to be written either for children or older girls, or the stories are humorous and presented as light entertainment.

Among children's fiction, E. Nesbit inevitably contributed a fantasy with her last novel, *Wet Magic* (1913), a rather lackluster story of children who rescue a mermaid from a fairground and then experience various undersea adventures—the submarine world becoming an allegory for the human imagination. Lucy M. Boston produced her own Nesbitesque version with *The Sea Egg* (1967), in which children hatch a triton's egg in Cornwall and are taken on a tour of the sea. Although Susan Cooper has retold the basic selkie folktale in the picture book *The Selkie Girl* (1986), she has created a more complex story in *Seaward* (1983), where two teenagers, one unknowingly a selkie, struggle through a bizarre world after the loss of their parents, until they reach their own goal. Cally, the selkie girl, is richly explored as is her growing awareness of her real world. Other books for young readers involving merfolk or selkies include the haunting *The Secret of Ron Mor Skerry* by Rosalie K. Fry (1959), filmed as *The Secret of Roan Inish* (1994); *The Seal-Singing* by Rosemary Harris (1971); *A Strange Came Ashore* by Mollie Hunter (1975), which is a particularly appealing reworking of the selkie story; *The Mystery in the Bottle* by Val Willis (1991); *The Selchie's Seed* by Sulamith Oppenheim (1996), in which a young girl becomes aware of her selkie heritage; and *The Merman* (1997) by Dick King-Smith. The most powerful selkie novel of recent years is *Daughter of the Sea* by Berlie Doherty (1996), and though marketed for young readers is a violent book probably better appreciated by older readers. Years after a fisherman finds and rears a young child, the sea uses both its power and its creatures to retrieve it.

Jane Yolen has reworked most of the essential motifs into her own philosophy and in "The Lady and the Merman" (*F&SF*, September 1976), "The White Seal Maid" (*Parabola*, 1977), and "Undine" (*F&SF*, September 1982) has the female spirits assert their independence and return to their worlds. Other works by Yolen are listed in the Bibliography.

Among romantic fiction, Theodore Sturgeon's "A Touch of Strange" (*F&SF*, January 1958) stands out because no mermaids or mermen are featured in it and yet they are the catalyst that brings together a human couple. In "The Drowned Mermaid" by Christopher Barzak (*Realms of Fantasy*, June 2003) a rescued mermaid becomes a surrogate child for a mother who lost her own daughter; when at length the husband returns the creature to the sea, the mother is determined to follow. In "Sealskin Trousers" by Eric Linklater (1947), a romance blossoms between two university students, one of whom is a sealman who has studied the human world and does not trust it.

The selkie myth contains much for young readers, especially young girls, as it is a powerful metaphor for the girl who feels different and not part of this world and who seeks and eventually finds love with another outcast. As a consequence, the theme appears both literally and figuratively in several romance books aimed at all ages, including *Selkie* by Anne Cameron (1996); *Alice at Heart* (2002) and its rather renegade sequel *Diary of a Radical Mermaid* (2004) by Deborah Smith; *The Selkie* by Melanie Jackson (2003); *The Last Mermaid* by Shana Abe (2004); and, in more adult mode, *The Mermaids Singing* by Lisa Carey (1998), an emotive study of three generations of women, and *The Seal Wife* by Kathryn Harrison (2003), a powerful story set in Alaska in 1915 and a young man's affair with a strange woman.

The comic interpretation of the merfolk motif goes back at least as far as H. G. Wells's *The Sea Lady* (1901), though Wells uses the idea of a mermaid marrying a human only as a basis for a satirical study of society. Both better and shorter is "Fintale the Merman" by Bertram Atkey (*Red Magazine*, September 15, 1919), which portrays an entire city of merfolk called Mermanchester, with streets lit by lantern fish. Fintale is bored by the perfection of the place and is lured to the world of humans by an old newspaper found in a wreck. However, he soon discovers that the "new woman" of the dawning twenties is not what he is after. A couple of tall tales include the inevitable bragging of Lord Dunsany's Jorkens in "Mrs. Jorkens" (*Cosmopolitan*, October 1930), in which Jorkens marries a mermaid, and the similar "Bowleg Bill and the Mermaid" by Jeremiah Digges (1938). In "Something Rich and Strange" by Randall Garrett and Avram Davidson (*F&SF*, June 1961), a gourmet sets out to taste the meat of a mermaid but discovers more fruitful abilities of the merfolk. Esther Friesner wonderfully spoofs the genre in her comic novel *Yesterday We Saw Mermaids* (1992), set in an alternate world at the time of Columbus's discovery of America, where his sighting of mermaids was for real.

Of special interest is *Peabody's Mermaid* by Guy and Constance Jones (1946) in which a husband while on holiday encounters a mermaid and tries to keep her hidden, much to the consternation of everyone else who believe that he is either trying to hide a wartime infiltrator or is having delusions. This novel was filmed effectively as a humorous fantasy in *Mr. Peabody and the Mermaid* (1948), starring William Powell and Ann Blyth. Most mermaid films tend to be humorous, such as *Miranda* (1948), based on the play by Peter Blackmore, its sequel *Mad About Men* (1954), and the Tom Hanks/ Darryl Hannah hit *Splash* (1984). It is uncommon for films to depict an evil mermaid—the imagery of *The Little Mermaid* is deeply imbedded in our psyche—but both *Night Tide* (1961) and *She Creature* (2001) are distinctive efforts that should be congratulated for their originality.

Dead or dying merfolk do not usually appear in fiction other than at the end of a story. However, two stories in particular show the extremes of treatment meted out to such discoveries. In "The Thing on Outer Shoal" by P. Schuyler Miller (*Astounding SF*, September 1947), a giant merman is washed up dead on a reef after a storm. Townsfolk investigate but then encounter a giant merwoman who, Grendel-like, comes looking for her husband. A naval helicopter fires on her and she returns to the sea. In "The Shoreline at Sunset" by Ray Bradbury (*F&SF*, March 1959), two beachcombers stumble across a beautiful mermaid, dead or dying. They are torn between selling her to a university and returning her to the sea. Compassion wins and thereafter the boys share a bond of having witnessed something wonderful.

There are all too few stories that seek to undertake a serious study of merfolk, but one striking exception is "Miss Carstairs and the Merman" by Delia Sherman (*F&SF*, January 1989). Miss Carstairs, an amateur naturalist in nineteenth-century Massachusetts, discovers a stranded merman and spends many weeks studying it. The result is a telepathic rapport with the creature that nearly seduces her into venturing into the sea. Another recent story is "Singing Each to Each" by Paul di Filippo (*Interzone*, May 2000), in which a collector of postcards tracks down the model for a mermaid photograph taken thirty years before and discovers she was not alone.

Inevitably recent writers have turned their thoughts to the scientific creation of mermen. This may be by surgical means, as in "Driftglass" by Samuel Delany (*Worlds of If*, June 1967), genetically engineered as in "Selkies" (*Asimov's SF*, March 1994) and its sequels by Mary Rosenblum, or the products of natural evolution ("homo aquaticus"), as in "Sea Wrack" by Edward Jesby (*F&SF*, May 1964). The abilities of mermen also led to two short-lived series: the *Attar the Merman* books (1975) by Joe Haldeman (writing as Robert Graham), where two genetically enhanced mermen can communicate telepathically with dolphins, and the TV series *The Man from Atlantis* (1977–1978) where the "mer-man" is a separate line of evolution

Selected Mermaid TV Shows and Movies

Acri (Japan, 1996). Directed by Tatuya Ishii, based on story by Shunji Iwai. Scientist undertakes research into existence of mermaids.

Chechu y familia (Spain, 1992). Directed by Álvaro Sáenz de Heredio. Script, Rafael Azcona. In the mode of *The Addams Family* where a young boy's relatives include mermaids.

Diver Dan (US TV, 1961) 40 seven-minute episodes. Directed by Mort Heilig and Leon Rhodes. Children's series where Diver Dan fights various menaces with the help of Minerva the Mermaid.

Dyesebel (Philippines, 1950). Based on a comic-book character created by Mars Ravelo, there were four other spin-off films, in 1973, 1978, 1991, and 1996. Dyesebel is a mermaid of human parents.

The Little Mermaid (US, 1989). Directed by Ron Clements and John Musker. Story, Roger Allers. There have been several short animated adaptations of Andersen's story, and an hour-long Japanese version (1975), but this is the first full-length English-language version from the Disney studios. Sequel *The Little Mermaid II: Return to the Sea* (2000). A more faithful adaptation is *Malá morská vila* (Czech, 1975).

Local Hero (UK, 1983). Written and directed by Bill Forsyth. Attempts by a Texas oil company to develop a Scottish village. Jenny Seagrove plays Marina, a marine biologist with webbed hands and toes.

Magic Island (US, 1995). Directed by Sam Irvin. Screenplay, Neil Ruttenberg and Brent V. Friedman. A boy runs away from home and is transported to a magical pirate island where he falls in love with a mermaid.

Manhoru no naka no ningyo (Japan, 1988) a.k.a. *Mermaid in the Manhole*. Directed by Hideshi Hino. An artist finds a mermaid in a sewer and though he chooses to paint her, can find no way of preserving her and she rots away.

Marinara (Philippines, 2004). Directed by Eric Quizon. A young mermaid goes in search of her sisters.

Mermaid Forest (Japan, 1991). Directed by Takaya Mizutani, based on comic-book series by Rumiko Takahashi. Yuta ate mermaid flesh 500 years ago and is now immortal and is seeking for a way to die. Sequel is *Mermaid's Scar* (1993).

Mermaids (US TV, 2003). Directed by Ian Barry. Teleplay, Daniel Cerone from story by Brent V. Friedman and Rebecca Swanson. Three mermaid sisters avenge the death of their father.

Mermaids of Tiburon (US, 1962). Written and directed by John Lamb. A man seeking lost treasure finds a greater treasure amongst the mermaids.

Miranda (UK, 1948). Directed by Ken Annakin from a play by Peter Blackmore. Various amusing adventures of the mermaid Miranda after she is rescued by a human. Sequel is *Mad About Men* (UK, 1954).

Mr. Peabody and the Mermaid (US, 1948). Directed by Irving Pichel. Screenplay, Nunnally Johnson from the novel by Guy and Constance Jones. Peabody tries to keep a mermaid hidden.

Night Tide (US, 1963). Written and directed by Curtis Harrington. A former sailor believes that a sideshow mermaid is real and discovers the true story of her past.

Phra Apai Mani (Thai, 2002). Directed by Chalart Sriwanda, based on the Thai classic poem *Soondhornpoo* by Sunthon Phu. A series of adventures in which a prince is captured by a sea witch and his brother seeks to rescue him.

Sea Creature (US TV 2001). Written and directed by Sebastian Gutierrez. Part 1 of *The Mermaid Chronicles*. A mermaid captured for a carnival takes her revenge.

Sea People (Canada, 1999). Directed by Vic Sarin. Screenplay, Wendy Biller and Christopher Hawthorne. A young woman believes she has rescued a man from drowning but the more she gets to know his family the more she discovers their links with the sea.

The Secret of Roan Inish (US, 1994). Written and directed by John Sayles from book by Rosalie K. Fry. A young woman in rural Ireland learns of the selkie legend of her family and seeks her baby brother, long ago washed out to sea.

Splash (US, 1984). Directed by Ron Howard. Screenplay by Bruce Jay Friedman and others from his development. Romantic comedy about a man who falls in love with a mermaid, not knowing she is one or that she had once rescued him as a child. There was a TV sequel, *Splash, Too* (1988). A Chinese version is *Ren yu Chuan Shuo* (Hong Kong, 1994), directed by Jing Wong.

The Thirteenth Year (US TV, 1999). Directed by Duwayne Dunham from a story by Jenny Arata. When a boy starts his teens he begins to develop fins and discovers his mother is a mermaid.

---

and a survivor from Atlantis. In both these series the mermen's abilities are used in an eco-war against megalomaniacs.

Behind several stories is the suggestion that the merfolk and selkies are of a dying race and may soon be extinct. It was inherent in Thomas Burnett Swann's "The Dolphin and the Deep" (*Science Fantasy*, August 1963), set in the prehistory world of legend when most creatures of faery still survived. The definitive treatment, however, is *The Merman's Children* by Poul Anderson (Putnam, 1979). This takes its cue from the same story of Agnete and the merman that inspired Hans Christian Andersen. Anderson portrays a race of mer-creatures excommunicated by the church and forced to seek refuge in the dwindling lands of faery. Unfortunately the relentless march of Christianity sees the merfolk being baptized and thus losing their spiritual roots and gradually passing from the world.

Selected Classic Mermaid Paintings

Edward Burne-Jones, *The Depths of the Sea* (1887)

John Collier, *The Land Baby* (1909)

Evelyn De Morgan, *The Sea Maidens* (1886)

Herbert James Draper, *The Sea Maiden* (1894), *The Water Nymph* (1898), *Water Baby* (1900), *Sea Melodies* (1904), *Ulysses and the Sirens* (1909), *The Kelpie* (1913)

Isobel Lilian Gloag, *The Kiss of the Enchantress* (1890)

Frederick Leighton, *The Fisherman and the Siren* (1858), *Actaea, the Nymph of the Shore* (1868)

René Magritte, *The Forbidden Universe* (1943), *Le Chant d'Amour* (1948), *Les merveilles de la nature* (1953)

Edvard Munch, *Mermaid* (1896)

Arthur Rackham, *Undine* (1916)

Collier Smithers, *A Race with Mermaids and Tritons* (1895)

Franz von Stuck, *Mermaid* (1891)

John Waterhouse, *Ulysses and the Sirens* (1891), *Studies for a Mermaid* (1892), *Naiad* (1893), *Hylas and the Nymphs* (1896), *The Siren* (1900), *A Mermaid* (1901)

Rowland Wheelwright, *The Enchanted Shore* (circa 1910)

The number and variety of stories dealing with mermaids, mermen, and selkies show how important the motif is in exploring relationships between humans and another race, one that may be both rewarding and dangerous. Merfolk have come to represent a forbidden desire, a metaphor of church versus paganism. Though some merfolk are depicted as cunning or dangerous, it is often the human who reveals a darker side and for whom the supernatural being must make some form of sacrifice. The stories are thus also parables of prejudice and humility.

SEA SERPENTS AND OTHER MONSTERS

While mermaids and selkies may be legendary, one cannot so easily dismiss sea serpents and other monsters of the deep. So little is known about the ocean depths that there is a willingness to believe that almost anything might exist and new species are being found on a regular basis—some, such as the giant squid (the kraken of legend), having been photographed alive for the first time only in September 2005.

Tales of sea monsters appear in many of the early travel tales. In the sixth century *The Voyage of St. Brendan* the eponymous Irish monk spends time on the back of a whale, believing it to be an island. A similar episode occurs in the equally fabled *Seven Voyages of Sinbad* in the *Arabian Nights*, which was appearing in the oral tradition at about the same time. St. Columba also lived at that time and his biographer, Adomnan, records how Columba confronted and subdued the Loch Ness Monster.

Ancient mapmakers would adorn the unknown extremities of their maps with dragons and other monsters though only one known map, the Lenox Globe of circa 1507 which actually used the phrase "*Hic Sunt Dracones*" ("Here be dragons"). Nevertheless, the implications were always there. Mercator's map of 1587 placed sea serpents in uncharted areas of the ocean, and later cartographers followed his example.

The earliest known reports of sea monsters may have been in the writings of the Carthaginian traveler and merchant Himilco, who lived around the sixth century B.C.E. and plied the route from Carthage to Britain. His writings are now lost, but the poet Festus Avienus referred to them in his *Ora Maritima* in the fourth century C.E., commenting on Himilco's siting of monsters in the western seas, as well as waters clogged by seaweed—perhaps the earliest reference to the Sargasso Sea.

The great expansion of naval conquest by European nations in the fifteenth and sixteenth centuries made people aware not only of the vastness of the oceans but also their strangeness. There were various reports of unusual creatures from such explorers as Columbus, Humphrey Gilbert, Martin Frobisher, and Richard Hakluyt. In the text accompanying his *Carta Marina* (Venice, 1539), the Swede Olaus Magnus refers to a 200-foot sea serpent that menaced the western coast of Norway.

By the eighteenth century, sightings of sea monsters were sufficiently frequent that the Norwegian Bishop of Bergen, Erik Pontopiddan, listed many in his *Natural History of Norway* (1752). He was the first to name and describe the *kraaken*, which was popularized by Lord Alfred Tennyson in "The Kraken" (*Poems, Chiefly Lyrical*, 1830).

Sea serpents found their way into popular literature via the *Arabian Nights*–style *Pacha of Many Tales* (1835) by Frederick Marryat. In the "Fourth Voyage of Huckaback" the narrator is on board a ship stricken in a hurricane and floating out of control in the Gulf Stream. They are preyed upon by a sea serpent a hundred feet long, which takes men one at a time. The narrator succeeds in driving the serpent away with a broom coated in coal tar. This technique animal bears some similarity to an old Celtic legend recorded by Walter Traill Dennison in *The Orcadian Sketch Book* (1880) as "Asipattle and the Mester Stoor Worm." The Stoor Worm was a giant serpent that terrorized the sea around the Orkneys. On one appearance a farm worker, called Asipattle, rowed out and took battle with the creature, killing it by ramming burning peat into its wounds.

There is a rousing report of the chase, struggle, and killing of a 103-feet-long sea serpent near the Marquesas in the Pacific provided by Charles Seabury, Master of the whaling ship *Monongahela* in the London *Times* of March 10, 1852, taking the details from the *New York Tribune*. Though later dismissed as a hoax, the report, together with a compilation of 186 other sea-serpent sightings, was included by Dr. A. C. Oudemans, Director of the Zoological and Botanical Society at The Hague in the Netherlands, as *The Great Sea Serpent* in 1892, which long remained the primary study on the subject.

Perhaps the best-known genuine sea monster of Marryat's age was Mocha Dick, a huge white sperm whale in the seas around Cape Horn, which allegedly defied over 100 attempts to kill it. Jeremiah Reynolds wrote a vigorous account of the defeat of the whale in "Mocha Dick" (*Knickerbocker Magazine*, May 1839), the story that inspired Herman Melville to produce *Moby-Dick* (1851). Here the whale becomes a symbol in an iconic quest from life to death, an image that the endless sea readily evokes.

Victor Hugo vividly describes an encounter with a kraken, which he calls a *poulp* or devil-fish, in *Les Travailleurs de la mer* (*Toilers of the Sea*, 1866), set off the Channel Islands. But the book that probably did most to encourage interest in the monsters of the deep was *20,000 Leagues under the Sea* by Jules Verne (1869–1870). Verne employs the fear of sea monsters at the outset when Captain's Nemo's submarine, *Nautilus*, preys on ships like a creature of the deep and sets imaginations on fire. He writes: "The human mind delights in grand conceptions of supernatural beings. And the sea is precisely their best vehicle, the only medium through which these giants (against which terrestrial animals, such as elephants or rhinoceroses, are as nothing) can be produced or developed." Verne adds a few giants of his own. When the explorers approach what prove to be the ruins of Atlantis, the narrator remarks on the "giant crustacea crouched in their holes; giant lobsters setting themselves up like halberdiers, and moving their claws with the clicking sound of pincers; titanic crabs, pointed like a gun on its carriage; and

---

As I am preparing a minute description of the serpent, I will merely give you a few general points. It was a male; the length 103 feet 7 inches; 19 feet 1 inch around the neck; 24 feet 6 inches around the shoulders; and the largest part of the body, which appeared distended, 49 feet 4 inches. The head was long and flat, with ridges; the bones of the lower jaw, separate; the tongue had its end like the head of a heart. The tail ran nearly to a point, on the end of which was a flat firm cartilage. The back was black, turning brown on the sides; then yellow, and on the centre of the belly a narrow white streak two-thirds of its length; there were also scattered over the body dark spots.

Charles Seabury, Master, Whale-ship Monongahela *of New Bedford,*
February 6, 1852

---

frightful-looking poulps, interweaving their tentacles like a living nest of serpents."

But Verne's most memorable scene deals with the giant "poulps" or squids, seven of which, at one point, attack the *Nautilus*. Verne's description of it, for readers who had never seen a squid, is powerful indeed:

> It was an immense cuttlefish, being eight yards long. It swam crossways in the direction of the Nautilus with great speed, watching us with its enormous staring green eyes. Its eight arms, or rather feet, fixed to its head, that have given the name of cephalopod to these animals, were twice as long as its body, and were twisted like the furies' hair. One could see the 250 air holes on the inner side of the tentacles. The monster's mouth, a horned beak like a parrot's, opened and shut vertically. Its tongue, a horned substance, furnished with several rows of pointed teeth, came out quivering from this veritable pair of shears. What a freak of nature, a bird's beak on a mollusc! Its spindle-like body formed a fleshy mass that might weigh 4,000 to 5,000 lb.; the, varying colour changing with great rapidity, according to the irritation of the animal, passed successively from livid grey to reddish brown.

Verne's novel is full of the wonders of the oceans; though none of his creatures is supernatural, they are as fearful as any monsters of legend, and both the giant squid and the sea serpent (which Verne mentions but does not exploit) have become truly iconic.

It was all too easy for authors of nautical adventures to incorporate a battle with a sea serpent or kraken, but apart from frequent recurrences in boys' fiction, it soon ceased to be of interest in mainstream literature. Even the reportage of it grew stale, to the extent that the London *Times* referred to another batch of sightings in 1871 as the "sea-serpent season" (*Times*, October 4, 1871). Rudyard Kipling used this as the basis for "A Matter of Fact" (*Many Inventions*, 1893), in which a journalist is witness to two sea serpents driven to the surface following an underwater earthquake, but is unable to sell the story because editors think it is another hoax. Sea serpents soon became parodies of themselves in such humorous stories of the early twentieth century as "The Sea Serpent Syndicate" by Everard Jack Appleton (*Royal Magazine*, April 1905), "The Call of the Wild Water" by Bertram Atkey (*Red Magazine*, November 1918), and, best known of all, "Daniel Webster and the Sea Serpent" (*Saturday Evening Post*, May 22, 1937) by Stephen Vincent Benét.

Authors had to be creative to breathe life into the sea monster story. In "The Water-Devil" (*Scribner's*, October 1874), Frank R. Stockton reveals that the underwater monster that seems to trap metal ships at a certain location is in fact a giant lodestone. In "The Rival Beauties" (*Million*, March 30, 1895) W. W. Jacobs has a sea serpent frightened away from a ship by the sound of the foghorn. Ray Bradbury later turned that idea on its head in "The Fog Horn" (*Saturday Evening Post*, June 23, 1951), where a serpent is attracted to a lighthouse by the sound of the foghorn. This was filmed as *The Beast from 20,000 Fathoms* (1953). In "The Sea Raiders" (*Weekly Sun Literary Supplement*, December 6, 1896) H. G. Wells has bathers along the South Devon coast suddenly threatened by a brief but deadly shoal of giant octopi, *Haploteuthis ferox* as he calls them, which go as mysteriously as they came.

In "Port of Many Ships" (*Manchester Guardian*, April 2, 1904) John Masefield has the sea serpent symbolic of the end of the world, like the Midgard Serpent, rising like a demon in the final apocalypse. Masefield was wonderfully creative in "The Yarn of Lanky Job" (*Manchester Guardian*, July 16, 1904), where certain rats have evolved into semi-human form and operate at sea, rescuing normal rats from sinking ships. Owen Oliver has giant fish attack English cities in "Out of the Deep" (*London Magazine*, July 1904). Morgan Robertson suggested invisible giant octopi that can be seen only in ultraviolet light in "From the Darkness and the Depths" (*New Story Magazine*, January 1913), while Frank Belknap Long introduced giant vampiric leeches in "The Ocean Leech" (*Weird Tales*, January 1925).

Sea serpents and kraken would continue to pepper fiction for many years—John Wyndham was able to use the symbolism as suitable for his appearance of an alien from beneath the ocean in *The Kraken Wakes* (1953), though in fact his novel was symptomatic of a new wave of monsters that would emerge from the post-atomic waters, of which the most notorious was the dinosaur-like Gojira (or Godzilla) in the Japanese film of that name in 1954. Godzilla and its many B-movie imitations of the 1950s and 1960s were, for the most part, atomic mutations, and while they are continuing evidence of the acceptability of the ocean depths as the home of giant monsters, they are not the same as the natural or supernatural monsters of myth and imagination.

Two authors were responsible for reworking the sea monster theme in two distinctive ways in the early years of the twentieth century and, in so doing, refreshed the concept and revived it for future generations. These were William Hope Hodgson and H. P. Lovecraft.

Hodgson spent seven years in the merchant navy (1891–1898) and during that time traveled several times around the world. His experiences served as the basis for many short stories and two of his novels. Hodgson had a fertile imagination and his stories avoid the traditional horrors and superstitions of the sea. Doubtless long hours on the night watch or becalmed in open seas allowed him time to speculate on what form organic life might take. His first nautical horror story, "A Tropical Horror" (*Grand Magazine*, June 1905), though crude in its development, reads like one of these nocturnal musings. A ship is menaced by a giant sea serpent with "a vast slobbering mouth a fathom across," from which hang many tentacles. But this is no ordinary serpent. It also has a giant claw, like a lobster's, with which it crushes anything in its way. Thereafter Hodgson endeavored to create new and ever more bizarre abominations. In "The Voice in the Night" (*Blue Book*, November 1907), sailors on a fog-bound ship learn the terrible story of two travelers shipwrecked on a fungus-covered island who find that they have also become fungoid. In "The Derelict" (*Red Magazine*, December 1, 1912) a rotting ship's hulk is smothered in a mold that has taken on a basic sentience. In "The Stone Ship" (*Red Magazine*, July 1, 1914) an undersea eruption brings briefly to the surface an ancient ship that has been petrified but which is also the home for several denizens of the deep, including huge red sea caterpillars and giant eels. Another undersea eruption brings another ancient hulk to the surface in "Demons of the Sea" (*Sea Stories*, October 5, 1923), though here they are tentacled seal-like creatures, "parodies of human beings." "Out of the Storm" (*Putnam's Monthly*, February 1909) presents arguably the ultimate monster, the sea itself, as if it has a being and purpose in its restlessness.

Among Hodgson's body of work are several that took as their milieu the weed-clogged Sargasso Sea, in the North Atlantic. Strong currents encircle this area, creating a large body of water that effectively rotates upon itself. Within that area is an aggregation of large bodies of weed, which the Portuguese called "sargaco" after its grape-like pods. The legend grew that ships became becalmed and trapped by the weed. In fact, the weed is not strong enough to do this, but the sea and weather conditions here do becalm ships, leading to growing superstition. This is the area known as the "horse latitudes" or "doldrums" and equates with the more recent idea of the Bermuda Triangle.

Jules Verne takes the *Nautilus* through the Sargasso in *20,000 Leagues under the Sea*, describing it rather poetically as "a perfect meadow, a close carpet of seaweed, fucus, and tropical berries, so thick and so compact that the stem of a vessel could hardly tear its way through it." His adventurers encounter no monsters, though they see small creatures in the weed, and it is indeed the home of many crabs and small fishes. Before Hodgson, several writers used the Sargasso as a setting for societies of people trapped there for generations. Julius Chambers has a colony descended from Spanish slavers 300 years earlier in *"In Sargasso" Missing* (1896). Thomas Janvier's *In the Sargasso Sea* (1898) is a journey through the hulks and remnants trapped in the sea, while Frank Atkins (writing as Frank Aubrey) has it as the home of survivors of Atlantis in *A Queen of Atlantis* (1899). Although the last book includes some unusual creatures, none of these focus on the Sargasso as a haunt of monsters.

This became William Hope Hodgson's speciality. In six stories and one novel he created an astonishing Sargassan world in which its victims have to cope with a variety of bizarre creatures. This is most evident in *The Boats of the "Glen Carrig"* (1907), in which survivors of a shipwreck try to make their way through the weed-clogged sea beset by giant crabs, octopodes, and tentacled devil-fish, as well as giant fungi and trees that howl. Perhaps worst of all were the weed men, which Hodgson calls "human slugs." In the other, unconnected stories we encounter further giant crabs, giant shrimps, kraken, devil-fish, and a ship alive with an intelligent strain of rats. Hodgson's Sargasso stories have been collected in *The Boats of the "Glen Carrig" and Other Nautical Adventures* (2003), while the best of his other sea horror stories has been assembled in *Adrift on the Haunted Seas* (2005).

Hodgson's Sargasso milieu inspired others including Ward Muir, who in "Sargasso" (*Pearson's*, October 1908) has trapped sailors menaced by a giant sea serpent, and most notably Dennis Wheatley, whose *Uncharted Seas* (1938) is an homage to Hodgson. It was filmed as *The Lost Continent* (1968). Others who brought some originality to the Sargasso include Joel Martin Nichols who, in "The Lure of Atlantis" (*Weird Tales*, April 1925), depicts the weed itself as a sentient monster, and Murray Leinster who, in "The Silver Menace" (*Thrill Book*, September 1–15, 1919), has a jelly-like mass that reproduces rapidly, like amoeba, and clogs the eastern American seaboard. A natural extension of this appeared in "Slime" by Joseph Payne Brennan (*Weird Tales*, March 1953), in which a protoplasmic ooze is disturbed from the seabed and terrorizes a coastal town. Stephen King used a similar idea of "killer scum" in "The Raft" (*Gallery*, November 1982).

Although H. P. Lovecraft was a great admirer of Hodgson's work, he had already commenced his tales of marine monsters long before he discovered Hodgson. Although these later developed into what came to be called the Cthulhu Mythos, the early stories were simple one-off ideas that nevertheless showed an interest in what lurks beneath the seas. The first was "Dagon" (*Vagrant*, November 1919), where a shipwrecked sailor discovers evidence of worship of a sea monster that subsequently appears and turns out to be the ancient fish-god Dagon. In "The Temple" (*Weird Tales*, September 1925), crimes at sea are punished by strange sea creatures that may once have been human. "The Call of Cthulhu" (*Weird Tales*, February 1928) set out the premise of the Cthulhu concept, wherein ancient powerful entities that once dominated the earth have been imprisoned in various places under the sea or the earth. Among them is many-tentacled Cthulhu, who is freed from the sunken city of R'lyeh by an earthquake. As the Cthulhu ideas permeated his stories, Lovecraft became fascinated with the idea of intermarriage between humans and other creatures. One such story is "The Shadow over Innsmouth" (1931). Several generations earlier Obed Marsh had brought back strange half-human sea people from the South Seas and allowed them to live on the reefs out to sea. These creatures mated with Marsh and others from Innsmouth, spawning descendants who are more at home in water than on land. They have the Innsmouth look, "queer narrow heads with flat noses and bulgy, stary eyes that never seem to shut" (*Dunwich Horror* 308). Their skin is scabby and their necks shriveled.

The idea of humanoid races evolving in the seas or through miscegenation on land has been around probably as long as the selkie legend. In *The Tempest* (Act 3, Scene 2) Shakespeare has Trinculo call Caliban "half a fish and half a monster." In "Fishhead" (*Cavalier*, January 11, 1913), Irvin S. Cobb describes similar horrors at a lake in the southern States where somehow a woman gave birth to a monstrosity with the body of a man but the head of a fish. Cobb's description is vivid:

> His skull sloped back so abruptly that he could hardly be said to have a forehead at all; his chin slanted off right into nothing. His eyes were small and round with shallow, glazed, pale-yellow pupils, and they were set wide apart in his head, and they were unwinking and staring, like a fish's eyes.
>
> His nose was no more than a pair of tiny slits in the middle of the yellow mask. His mouth was the worst of all. It was the awful mouth of a catfish, lipless and almost inconceivably wide, stretching from side to side.
>
> Also when Fishhead became a man grown his likeness to a fish increased, for the hair upon his face grew out into two tightly kinked slender pendants that drooped down either side of the mouth like the beards of a fish!

In "In the Abyss" (*Pearson's Magazine*, August 1896), H. G. Wells's adventurer witnesses a bizarre reptilian humanoid deep in the ocean trench who captures his bathysphere and takes it to a cavernous underwater city. Wells speculates on the possibility of intelligent aqua-vertebrates evolving deep in the ocean and developing their own society. Victor Rousseau took it a step further in *The Sea Demons* (*All-Story Weekly*, January 1–22, 1916), with Britain threatened by an intelligent humanoid aquatic race that has evolved to breathe air. They are transparent and thus almost invisible in water, and operate with a form of hive mind controlled by their queen.

Humanoid sea monsters were ideal for the movie industry, as it did not require so many special effects and could be potentially more realistic. *The Creature from the Black Lagoon* (1954), developed for the screen by Harry Essex and Arthur Ross, was a surprising hit for Universal Pictures and led to two sequels, *Revenge of the Creature* (1955) and *The Creature Walks among Us* (1956). The creature, dubbed the Gill-Man, is an amphibious human survivor from prehistoric times that survives in the Amazon. The success of the film led to a spin-off novelization by Vargo Statten [John Russell Fearn] (1954), and its continued popularity has led to two more novelizations: by Carl Dreadstone (1977) and by Larry Mike Garmon as *Black Water Horror* (2002). Paul di Filippo has written a sequel, *Time's Black Lagoon* (2006).

There have been many stories about undersea societies and cultures. As far back as 1873, in *Colymbia* (1873) the noted British homeopathic doctor, Robert Ellis Dudgeon, created a world peopled by descendants of British explorers who have interbred with the remnants of an ancient oceanic race and now live underwater. However, they have not evolved to breathe underwater and still require oxygen. Frequently, these undersea communities are populated by survivors from Atlantis. This occurs in both *The Scarlet Empire* by David M. Parry (1906), which includes episodes where criminals are fed to kraken, and Sir Arthur Conan Doyle's *The Maracot Deep* (1928), both of which have survivors of Atlantis living in air-filled caverns deep beneath the ocean. Both pepper their stories with bizarre undersea creatures, Doyle adding a spiritualist dimension with a strange supernatural being who may be the last remnant of an earlier malign race.

Most recent sea monster stories are little more than variants on earlier material with few moments of originality. "The Rig" by Chris Boyce (*Impulse*, September 1966) depicts a giant sea plant that becomes attached to an oil rig. John Gardner's *Grendel* (1971) is a variant on the *Beowulf* story, with the events told from the viewpoint of Grendel, who is a troll-like monster inhabiting an undersea cavern.

In "The Shark God" (*Unknown*, January 1940), A. E. van Vogt depicts a shark god who takes human form to intervene in the local slaughter of sharks but finds his human shape has its limits. Sharks, in particular the great white shark, was the cause of the return to popularity of the sea monster with the success of Peter Benchley's *Jaws* (1974). There is nothing supernatural in the novel, but the action and suspense provide the same thrills as any sea monster or serpent. Filmmakers and publishers alike pounced on the theme looking for other underwater horrors, resulting in such films as *Tentacles* (1977), *Piranha* (1978), *Barracuda* (1978), *Up from the Depths* (1979), *Monster* (1979), featuring a sea serpent, *Humanoids from the Deep* (1980), *Island Claws* (1980), with giant crabs, and so on.

Benchley himself pulled back on the throttle in *The Deep* (1976), but came back with a vengeance in *Beast* (1991), where the menace is a 100-foot-long giant squid, and again in *White Shark* (1994), later reworked as *Creature* (1998). In the latter, scientific experiments in hybrids produce a monster, which is half-man/half-shark.

Other writers took advantage of the resurgent popularity for sea monsters. There was *Night of the Crabs* from Guy N. Smith (1976); *Sphere* by Michael Crichton (1987), in which scientists investigating a strange artifact at the bottom of the ocean have to combat not only bizarre technology and their own neuroses but also giant squid and monster jellyfish; and *Megalodon* from Robin Brown (1981), featuring the prehistoric ancestor of the great white shark. That monster also appears in *Meg* by Steve Alten (1997) and its sequels, and *Extinct* by Charles Wilson (1997). In *Wurm* (1991) by Matthew Costello, exploration into undersea volcanic vents unleashes a parasitic worm that first devastates New York and, in the sequel *Garden* (1993), the rest of the world. In *Sea Change* (1999), James Powlik returned to a concept similar to Leinster's "Silver Menace," when plankton mutates and grows out of control, threatening to engulf the American seaboard.

Steve Alten's *The Loch* (2005) forms a link between the Sargasso Sea, where the main protagonist has an altercation with a giant squid, and Loch Ness, where he faces an old enemy from his childhood. The Loch Ness Monster is one of the best known of all aquatic monsters, but has seldom been given a serious treatment in fiction, tending to appear mostly in children's books, such as *The Water Horse* by Dick King-Smith (1990) and *The Boggart and the Monster* by Susan Cooper (1997). Inevitably, Doctor Who became involved when the monster began attacking oil rigs in *Doctor Who and the Lochness Monster* by Terrance Dicks (1976), while time travel also features in *The Ultimate Dragon* by Daniel N. Jason (TimeDancer, 1999), set in Scotland's past. John Christopher provided a more serious view of the creature's outlook in "Monster" (*Science Fantasy* #1, 1950), while Leslie Charteris wrapped it in an enigma in "Fish Story" (*Blue Book*, November 1953). One of the few longer stories is *The Monster of Loch Ness* by Fred and Geoffrey Hoyle (1971), where a scientist tackles other mysteries related to the loch.

The monster has not fared well in films, either, though the first of them, *The Secret of the Loch* (1934), directed by Milton Rosmer, was a reasonable attempt at a serious story. Far worse films include *The Loch Ness Horror* (1981), written and directed by Larry Buchanan, and the gratuitously violent *Beneath Loch Ness* (2001), written and directed by Chuck Comisky. Only the family film *Loch Ness* (1996), directed by John Henderson from a script by John Fusco, makes any attempt at a proper ecological assessment of the creature. Other lake monsters fare little better, although the film *Lake Placid* (1999), directed by Steve Miney from a script by David E. Kelley, featuring a massive crocodile, is effective. Joseph Citro's novel *Dark Twilight* (1991) is a serious treatment of the alleged monster in Lake Champlain.

The ocean depths will long hold their secrets, and authors will continue to invent new monsters or recycle old ones to frighten us. There is one other area in which the sea continues to capture our imagination, and that is when it gives up its dead.

GHOST SHIPS AND OTHER HAUNTINGS

The most famous of all phantom ships is the *Flying Dutchman*, though tellings vary on how the legend came about. The most common version is that a ship with a valuable cargo was returning from the Dutch East Indies to Holland and the Captain, Van der Decken, was determined to make it round the Cape of Good Hope despite the hostile weather. He swore to God and invoked the Devil and, as a consequence, was cursed to sail forever around the Cape without ever making landfall. There have been many alleged sightings of the ship over the years, always in full sail even when other ships are becalmed, and it is believed to bring bad luck to those who see her.

The dating of this incident is usually the mid-seventeenth century, but no written account actually naming this legend seems to have survived until 1813. In his poem *Rokeby*, Sir Walter Scott refers to the "Demon Frigate," "harbinger of wreck and woe" (327), and in his notes to the poem specifically names the Flying Dutchman, stating that this a "well-known nautical superstition" (389). His note refers to a different and possibly earlier version of the legend stating that murder and piracy had occurred on the ship and the crew was afflicted by the plague. No port would admit them, and the ship was forced to sail on forever.

Samuel Taylor Coleridge had included a phantom ship in *The Rime of the Ancient Mariner* (*Lyrical Ballads*, 1798) but did not name it. John Leyden refers to the fated ship, though again not by name, in his poem "Scenes of Infancy" (1803) where he states that it was the first ship to start the slave trade, leaving Benin (West Africa), and was cursed with plague. He concludes his vivid portrayal of the ship's fate with:

> The Spectre Ship, in livid glimpsing light,
> Glares baleful on the shuddering watch at night,
> Unblest of God and man:—Till time shall end,
> Its view strange horror to the storm shall lend.

The first to name the captain appears to be John Howison, to whom is attributed the anonymous "Vanderdecken's Message Home" (*Blackwood's Edinburgh Magazine*, May 1821), which tells how the crew try to get mail back to their loved ones who are now long dead. Washington Irving took the legend to American shores in "The Storm-Ship" (*Bracebridge Hall*, 1822) by having the ship approach the port of New Amsterdam and then continue sailing around Manhattan. Irving adds an interesting feature that when sailors row out to the boat they can never reach it, rather like the end of the rainbow. Doubtless the legend was in Poe's mind when he wrote his story "MS. Found in a Bottle" (*Baltimore Saturday Visiter*, October 19, 1833), in which a stricken ship encounters a vast ghost vessel manned by ancient sailors driven on to some inexorable fate.

The name itself became popularized in Britain through Edward Fitzball's *burletta* or light comic opera, *The Flying Dutchman; or, The Phantom Ship* (*Cumberland's Minor Theatre*, vol. 2, 1829). This was performed nightly at the Adelphi Theatre from December 5, 1826 and then at other London venues for well over a year, and encouraged many imitations throughout the nineteenth century as well as an anonymous penny weekly *The Flying Dutchman; or, The Demon Ship* (Foster & Hextall, 1827?).

The author who produced what most regard as the definitive story was Frederick Marryat in *The Phantom Ship* (1839). He allowed that Vanderdecken might be redeemed by kissing a fragment of the True Cross. Vanderdecken's son, in whose family is just such a fragment, sets off in what becomes a lifetime's quest for his father.

German writers further developed the story, starting with Heinrich Smidt in his poem "Der ewige Segler" ["The Eternal Seafarer"] (*Hammonia*, 1822), where the ship is called *Von Evert*, and culminating with Heinrich Heine, who incorporated a chapter on the legend in his bogus autobiography "Aus den Memoiren des Herren von Schnabelewopski" ["From the Memoirs of

Lord Schnabelewopski"] (*Der Salon*, vol. 1, 1834). In Heine's version the captain can only be redeemed by the love of a devoted woman, and he is allowed ashore once every seven years to seek such a woman. Although he marries, he remains restless and returns to the ship, but to show her devotion his wife casts herself into the sea. It was this version that became the source for Richard Wagner's renowned opera *Der fliegende Holländer* (Dresden, January 2, 1843).

Stories about the *Flying Dutchman* appeared throughout the nineteenth and twentieth centuries, as the captain became symbolic of the accursed wanderer. *The Death Ship* by W. Clark Russell (1888) is an overly long story of a traveler washed overboard who is rescued by the crew of the *Flying Dutchman* and experiences life on board, eventually trying to escape with another rescuee, a young woman. A more positive variant on this was "By the Light of the Lanterns" by Pierre MacOrlan (1931), in which the Dutchman, here called Peter Maus, rescues a child and rears him on board, but returns him to land when they are able.

In a neat twist that united two legends, George Griffith has an old sailor recount how he encountered the *Flying Dutchman* in its final days trapped in the weeds of the Sargasso Sea in "The True Fate of the 'Flying Dutchman'" (*Pearson's Weekly*, July 21, 1894). In "The Crew of the 'Flying Dutchman'" by Henry A. Hering (*Temple Bar*, January 1896) we learn how Vanderdecken finds his crew; while in "A Primer of Imaginary Geography" by Brander Matthews (*Scribner's*, December 1894), Vanderdecken takes the narrator on a tour of various lands of legend. The captain remarks that the Wandering Jew is the only person with whom he can now talk over old times!

More recently *The Flying Dutchman* has been parodied in *Flying Dutch* by Tom Holt (Orbit, 1991), and it is featured in the series for young adults by Brian Jacques that started with *Castaways of the Flying Dutchman* (2001). Nicholas Monsarrat used the legend for his planned series *The Master Mariner*, where, following an act of cowardice, a sailor is cursed to travel the seas till the end of time. Alas, Monsarrat died with only the first book, *Running Proud* (1978), completed. Other cursed ships in fiction will be found in "The Brute" by Joseph Conrad (*Daily Chronicle*, December 5, 1906) and *The Jonah Watch* by Jack Cady (1981).

Other similar tales of ghost ships include "The Ship That Saw a Ghost" by Frank Norris (*Overland Monthly*, December 1902) and *The Ghost Pirates* by William Hope Hodgson (1909), one of the best of all phantom ship stories, in which Hodgson speculates that such ships exist on another plane of existence, like another dimension, which he calls a "mist-world." Other ghostly pirates, so memorably portrayed in the film *Pirates of the Caribbean* (2003), directed by Gore Verbinski, will be found in *On Stranger Tides* by Tim Powers (1987).

Other ships have developed legends about them even more memorable than the *Flying Dutchman*. This includes the *Mary Celeste*, which was found floating unmanned in the Atlantic in 1872 but with everything on board indicating that the boat had only recently and hurriedly been abandoned. The mystery has never been adequately resolved. Much of the legend we know was established by Sir Arthur Conan Doyle in "J. Habakuk Jephson's Statement" (*Cornhill*, January 1884), which many readers believed to be true. Alfred Noyes reworked the basic story in "The Log of the *Evening Star*" (*Walking Shadows*, 1918), in which he proposes a supernatural solution. Howard Pease switched the locale to the Pacific but used the same idea in *The Ship without a Crew* (1934), while more recently Brian Freemantle reassessed all the facts and came up with his own solution, in fictional form, in *The Mary Celeste* (1980) under the alias John Maxwell.

The sinking of the *Lusitania* by a German U-boat in 1915 caused an outcry at the time and prompted several authors to write tales of ghostly revenge. In "The Lusitania Waits" (*New York Tribune*, December 31, 1916), Alfred Noyes has the ghostly victims of the ship take their revenge on a U-boat. F. Britten Austin's "From the Depths" (*Strand*, February 1920) is on similar lines. In "The Murdered Ships" (*Premier Magazine*, June 1918), James Francis Dwyer has the ghost of the *Lusitania* forever reliving its final voyage.

The *Titanic* is far and above the most famous of all lost ships. Most fiction about her tends to be either romantic, mystery, or science fiction. Some supernatural stories focus on the premonitions some of the travelers had beforehand, which caused them to avoid the journey. There is are also the remarkable cases of the stories *Futility* by Morgan Robertson (1898) and "The White Ghost of Disaster" by Mayn Clew Garnett (*Popular Magazine*, May 1912), both of which relate incidents which parallel the *Titanic* disaster in many ways. The last story appeared in print just a few days before the *Titanic* set sail. One of the better supernatural novels is *Something's Alive on the Titanic* by Robert J. Serling (1990), in which something unnatural is protecting the wreck and killing any who venture near. Perhaps the most striking novel to date is *Latitudes of Melt* by Joan Clark (2002), which, in its tale of the discovery of a young child on an ice-flow by a Newfoundland fisherman who is raised as their own and turns out to be an infant survivor of the *Titanic*, has a mythic quality that links it to the legends of sea-people.

The motif of the *Flying Dutchman* is also an allegory of that eternal quest through life seeking salvation, and the sea is an ideal symbol for both life and death. It was this concept of the eternal sea that permeated Coleridge's *Rime of the Ancient Mariner*, and Conrad Aiken used the same imagery in "Mr. Arcularis" (*Harper's*, March 1931), in which the eponymous victim undergoes an operation and, while under the anesthetic, dreams of a strange sea voyage. Compulsive sea voyages between life and death occur in C. S. Lewis's Narnia book *The Voyage of the Dawn Treader* (1952) and E. H. Visiak's *Medusa* (1929) and its spiritual companion, "The Shadow" (*Crimes, Creeps and Thrills*, 1936).

That the sea gives up its dead is hauntingly depicted in several stories and novels. Most depict weed-covered skeletons, but a few stories show more originality. Often the stories are about the drowned seeking revenge, as in "On the Elevator" by Joseph Payne Brennan (*Weird Tales*, July 1953), and effectively depicted in John Carpenter's film *The Fog* (1980). In "Out of the Sea" (*Isles of Sunset*, 1904), A. C. Benson has a goat-like creature emerge from the sea as the spirit of a murdered sailor on a local wreck. E. F. Benson turns the idea on its head in "The Outcast" (*Hutchinson's Magazine*, April 1922) and has the sea reject the body of a woman who dies at sea, because her body contains the spirit of a former suicide. "Ringing the Changes" by Robert Aickman (*The Third Ghost Book*, ed. Cynthia Asquith, 1955) tells how every year a small seaside resort rings its bells sufficient to raise the dead. These come both from the land and from the sea, and the shoreline is depicted by Aickman as a division between life and death.

Lakes may also give up their dead. Lakes are frequently bewitched or cursed as in Arthur Machen's "The Children of the Pool" (1936), H. Russell Wakefield's "Woe Water" (*Weird Tales*, July 1950), Ian Watson's "Evil Water" (*F&SF*, March 1987), and Matthew Costello's novel *Beneath Still Waters* (1989). L.T.C. Rolt brought several threads together in "Bosworth Summit Pound" (*Sleep No More*, 1948), in which the ghost of a murdered gipsy woman acts as a siren to lure men to their deaths in an eerie stretch of an old canal.

The ancients envisaged heaven or the other world as being beyond the sea, at the Isles of the Blessed. For many the sea remains symbolic of the barrier between life and death and beneath the sea lies all that thwarts or tempts us through life. It has a lure and fascination that we cannot deny and will both tempt and threaten us for as long as the human race survives.

BIBLIOGRAPHY

Primary

Alten, Steve. *The Loch*. West Palm Beach, FL: Tsunami, 2005.
———. *Meg*. New York: Doubleday, 1997.
———. *Primal Waters*. New York: Tor/Forge, 2004.
———. *The Trench*. New York: Kensington, 1999.
Benchley, Peter. *Beast*. New York: Random House, 1991.
———. *Creature*. New York: St. Martin's Press, 1998.
———. *The Deep*. Garden City, NY: Doubleday, 1976.
———. *Jaws*. Garden City, NY: Doubleday, 1974.
———. *White Shark*. New York: Random House, 1994.
Boston, Lucy M. *The Sea Egg*. London: Faber & Faber, 1967.
Brodie-Innes, John. *Morag the Seal*. London: Rebman, 1908.
Brown, Robin. *Megalodon*. New York: Coward-McCann, 1981.
Cady, Jack. *The Jonah Watch*. New York: Arbor House, 1981.
Carey, Lisa. *The Mermaids Singing*. New York: Avon, 1998.
Citro, Joseph. *Dark Twilight*. New York: Warner, 1991.
Clark, Joan. *Latitudes of Melt*. New York: Soho Press, 2002.

Climo, Shirley. *A Treasury of Mermaids*. London: HarperCollins, 1997.

Coleridge, Sara. *Phantasmion*. London: W. Pickering, 1837. Latest edition Banbury, UK: Woodstock, 1994.

Cooper, Susan. *The Boggart and the Monster*. New York: McElderry, 1997.

———. *Seaward*. London: The Bodley Head, 1983.

———. *The Selkie Girl*. New York: McElderry, 1986.

Costello, Matthew J. *Beneath Still Waters*. New York: Berkley, 1989.

———. *Garden*. New York: Twilight, 1993.

———. *Wurm*. New York: Diamond, 1991.

Costello, Peter. *The Magic Zoo*. London: Sphere, 1979.

Crichton, Michael. *Sphere*. New York: Knopf, 1987.

Dann, Jack, and Gardner Dozois, eds. *Mermaids!* New York: Ace, 1989.

———. *Seaserpents!* New York: Ace, 1989.

di Filippo, Paul. *Time's Black Lagoon*. New York: Dark Horse, 2006.

Digges, Jeremiah. *Bowleg Bill, the Sea Going Cowboy*. New York: Viking Press, 1938.

Doherty, Berlie. *Daughter of the Sea*. London: Hamish Hamilton, 1996.

Doyle, Sir Arthur Conan. *The Maracot Deep*. *Strand Magazine* (October 1927–February 1928). London: John Murray, 1929.

Field, Eugene. *The Holy Cross and Other Tales*. Chicago: Stone & Kimball, 1893.

Fouqué, Friedrich de la Motte. *Undine*. Berlin, 1811. Most recent edition, translated by Ben Barkow, London: Dedalus, 1990.

Friesner, Esther. *Yesterday We Saw Mermaids*. New York: Tor, 1992.

Fry, Rosalie K. *The Secret of Ron Mor Skerry*. New York: Dutton, 1959.

Garmon, Larry Mike. *Black Water Horror*. New York: Scholastic, 2002.

Giraudoux, Jean. *Ondine*. Paris: Grassat, 1939.

Golden, Stephanie. *Slaying the Mermaid*. New York: Three Rivers Press, 1998.

Graham, Robert [Joe Haldeman]. *Attar's Revenge*. New York: Pocket, 1975.

———. *War of Nerves*. New York: Pocket, 1975.

Haining, Peter, ed. *The Ghost Ship*. London: William Kimber, 1985.

Harrison, Kathryn. *The Seal Wife*. New York: Random House, 2003.

Hodgson, William Hope. *Adrift on the Haunted Seas*. Cold Spring Harbor, NY: Cold Spring Press, 2005.

———. *The Boats of the "Glen Carrig."* London: Chapman & Hall, 1907. Included with other stories in *The Boats of the "Glen Carrig" and Other Nautical Adventures*. San Francisco: Night Shade, 2003.

———. *Deep Waters*. Sauk City, WI: Arkham House, 1967.

———. *The Ghost Pirates*. London: Stanley Paul, 1909.

———. *Men of the Deep Waters*. London: Eveleigh Nash, 1914.

Hugo, Victor. *The Toilers of the Sea*. London: Routledge, 1866. Currently available in many editions including New York: Modern Library, 2002.

Jacques, Brian. *The Angel's Command*. London: Viking, 2003.

———. *Castaways of the Flying Dutchman*. London: Viking, 2001.

Jones, Guy, and Constance Jones. *Peabody's Mermaid*. New York: Random House, 1946.

Linklater, Eric. *Sealskin Trousers and Other Stories*. London: Hart-Davis, 1947.

Lovecraft, H. P. *The Shadow over Innsmouth*. Everett, PA: Visionary Press, 1936. Annotated ed.: *The Shadow over Innsmouth*. Ed. S. T. Joshi and David E. Schultz. West Warwick, RI: Necronomicon Press, 1994.

Macleod, Fiona [William Sharp]. *The Sin-Eater*. Edinburgh: Geddes, 1895.

———. *The Washer of the Ford*. Edinburgh: Geddes, 1896.

Manning-Sanders, Ruth. *The Book of Mermaids*. New York: Dutton, 1968.

Marryat, Frederick. *Pacha of Many Tales*. London: Saunders & Otley, 1835.

———. *The Phantom Ship*. *New Monthly Magazine* (March 1837–August 1839). London: Colburn, 1839.

Maxwell, John [Brian Freemantle]. *The Mary Celeste*. London: Hamlyn, 1980.

Monsarrat, Nicholas. *Running Proud*. London: Weidenfeld & Nicolson, 1978.

Nesbit, E. *Wet Magic*. *Strand* (December 1912–August 1913). London: T. Werner Laurie, 1913.

O'Clery, Helen. *The Mermaid Reader*. New York: Franklin Watts, 1964.

Osborne, Mary Pope. *Mermaid Tales from around the World*. New York: Scholastic, 1993.

Parry, David M. *The Scarlet Empire*. Indianapolis: Bobbs-Merrill, 1906.

Pearce, J. H. *Drolls from Shadowland*. London: Lawrence & Bullen, 1893.

Pease, Howard. *The Ship without a Crew*. Garden City, NY: Doubleday, 1934.

Powlik, James. *Sea Change*. New York: Delacorte Press, 1999.

Robertson, Morgan. *Futility*. New York: Mansfield, 1898. Included in Martin Gardner, ed. *The Wreck of the Titanic Foretold?* Amherst, NY: Prometheus, 1998.

Russell, W. Clark. *The Death Ship*. London: Hurst & Blackett, 1888.

Scott, Sir Walter. *The Poetical Works of Sir Walter Scott*. Ed. J. Logie Robertson. London: Oxford University Press, 1916.

Serling, Robert J. *Something's Alive on the Titanic*. New York: St. Martin's Press, 1990.

Smith, Guy N. *Killer Crabs*. London: New English Library, 1978.

———. *Night of the Crabs*. London: New English Library, 1976.

Statten, Vargo [John Russell Fearn]. *Creature from the Black Lagoon*. London: Dragon, 1954.

Strating, J. J., ed. *Sea Tales of Terror*. London: Fontana, 1974.

Takahashi, Rumiko. *Mermaid Forest*. San Francisco: Viz, 1994.

Verne, Jules. *20,000 Leagues under the Sea*. *Magasin d'Éducation et de Récréation* (March 20, 1869–June 20, 1870); trans., London: Sampson Low, 1872.

Visiak, E. H. *Medusa*. London: Gollancz, 1929.

Wells, H. G. *The Sea Lady*. *Pearson's Magazine* (July–December 1901). London: Methuen, 1902.

Wheatley, Dennis. *Uncharted Seas*. London: Hutchinson, 1938.

Wilson, Charles. *Extinct*. New York: St. Martin's Press, 1997.

Woodley, Richard. *The Man from Atlantis* (four-book series). New York: Dell, 1977.

Wyndham, John. *The Kraken Wakes*. London: Michael Joseph, 1953.

Yolen, Jane. *The Mermaid's Three Wisdoms*. New York: Collins, 1978.

———. *Neptune Rising*. New York: Philomel, 1982.

———. *The Sea King*. New York: Crocodile, 2002.

———. *The Sea Man*. New York: Philomel, 1998.

Secondary

Alban, Gillian. *Melusine the Serpent Goddess in Myth and Literature.* Lanham, MD: Lexington, 2003.

Árnason, Jón. *Icelandic Legends.* Reykjavik, 1862. Trans. George E. J. Powell and Eiríkur Magnússon. Felinfach: Llanerch Press, 1995.

Benwell, Gwen, and Arthur Waugh. *Sea Enchantress: The Tale of the Mermaid and Her Kin.* London: Hutchinson, 1961.

Bottrell, William. *Traditions and Hearthside Stories of West Cornwall.* Penzance, UK: privately printed, 1870.

Carrington, Richard. *Mermaids and Mastodons.* London: Chatto & Windus, 1957.

Chambers, Robert. *Popular Rhymes of Scotland.* Edinburgh: Chambers, 1847.

Croker, T. Crofton. *Fairy Legends and Traditions in the South of Ireland.* London: John Murray, 1825.

Cunningham, Allan. *Traditional Tales of the English and Scottish Peasantry.* London: Taylor & Hessey, 1822.

Dalley, Stephanie. *Myths from Mesopotamia.* Oxford: Oxford University Press, 1989.

Fenkl, Heinz Insu. "Folkroots" on Mermaid lore. *Realms of Fantasy* 10, no. 1 (October 2003): 34–40.

Forster, E. M. *The Story of the Siren.* Richmond, UK: Hogarth Press, 1920.

Graves, Robert. *The Greek Myths.* Rev. ed. Harmondsworth, UK: Penguin, 1960.

Hoyle, Fred, and Geoffrey Hoyle. *The Monster of Loch Ness.* London: Heinemann, 1971.

Jordan, Michael. *The Encyclopedia of Gods.* London: Kyle Cathie, 1992.

Kirk, John. *In the Domain of the Lake Monsters.* Toronto: Key Porter, 1998.

Lie, Jonas. *Weird Tales from Northern Seas.* London: Kegan Paul, Trench, Trübner, 1893; trans. R. Nisbet Bain with selections from the original Danish collections *Den Fremsynte* (Copenhagen, 1871), *Fortaellinger og Skildringer* (Gyldendal, 1872), and *Trold* (Copenhagen, 1891–1892). Latest edition, Alan Rodgers Books, 2005.

Map, Walter. *De nugis curialium.* Ed. Thomas Wright. London: Camden Society, 1850. Current ed. by C.N.L. Brooke. London: Oxford University Press, 1983.

Oudemans, A. C. *The Great Sea Serpent: An Historical and Critical Treatise.* Leyden: E.J. Brill, 1892.

Pontopiddan, Erik. *The Natural History of Norway.* London: Linde, 1755.

Rhys, John. *Celtic Folklore, Welsh and Manx.* Oxford: Clarendon Press, 1901.

Simpson, Jacqueline. *Scandinavian Folktales.* Harmondsworth, UK: Penguin, 1988.

Stonehouse, Frederick. *Haunted Lakes: Great Lakes Ghost Stories, Superstitions and Sea Serpents.* Duluth, MN: Lake Superior Port Cities, 1997.

———. *Haunted Lakes II.* Duluth, MN: Lake Superior Port Cities, 2000.

Sweeney, James B. *A Pictorial History of Sea Monsters and Other Dangerous Marine Life.* New York: Nelson Crown, 1972.

Web sites

Mermaid.net at http://www.mermaid.net/, which covers legends, stories, folklore, pictures and a wide range of mermaid merchandise.

Mermaids on the web at http://www.isidore-of-seville.com/mermaids/, which covers all aspects of mermaid lore especially in art.

Sea serpents and lake monsters at http://theshadowlands.net/serpent.htm, which concentrates on specific creatures of cryptozoology with reported sightings and related folklore.

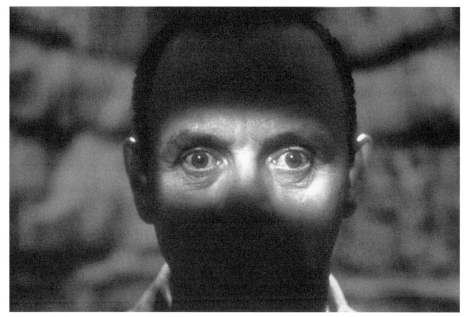

Courtesy of Photofest.

The Serial Killer

by Hank Wagner

INTRODUCTION

There is a clever little throwaway line in the Tim Burton film *The Addams Family* (1994) that is as chilling as it is humorous. Young Wednesday Addams, portrayed by Christina Ricci, is out trick or treating for Halloween. When questioned by an adult puzzled by her seeming lack of a costume, Wednesday coolly replies, "I'm dressed as a homicidal maniac, we look like everyone else."

Substitute "serial killer" for "homicidal maniac" and you capture the essence of the public's fascination with serial killers, contrasting the mundane aspects of these killers with their more outré characteristics: we fear them because they don't stand out, because they can be a lover, a friend, the guy with a cast on his arm asking for our help, someone we hire to entertain our children, a doctor, even someone prominent in our communities.

Mass murderers have always intrigued the public; they form the basis of numerous fairy tales and have provided fodder for the mass media since its infancy. Often saddled with catchy nicknames, they appeal to our basest, most prurient instincts, and our love for the sensational and the grim. In fact, serial killers are so much a part of modern pop culture that they even provide the inspiration for the lyrics of many modern songs, as attested by Kurt Weil's "Die Morität von Mackie Messer" (adapted by Louis Armstrong as "Mack the Knife," which later became a pop hit for Bobby Darin), the Doors's "Riders on the Storm" and "The End," The Rolling Stones's "Midnight Rambler," Warren Zevon's "Excitable Boy," Meat Loaf's "Bat out of Hell," and The Talking Heads's "Psycho Killer."

How much a part of our everyday consciousness have they become? Well, one indication is that a recent Google search of the words "serial killer" resulted in more than twenty million hits. Another is the presence of a serial killer storyline on the soap opera "Days of Our Lives" in 2003 and 2004. According to soapcentral.com, the reasons for adopting this story arc were simple and pragmatic: the daytime drama's head writer, James E. Reilly, was said to have pitched the idea of a serial killer storyline "as a way to accomplish two distinct goals—to devise an intriguing storyline to generate interest in the show and raise the ratings and to help trim the cast in an attempt to cut the show's operating budget."

Even though it did not have a formal label at the time, the general concept of a "serial killer" was first widely introduced in popular culture in 1960, with the premiere of Alfred Hitchcock's film adaptation of Robert Bloch's 1959 novel, *Psycho*. That film, with its infamous shower scene, told the story of a strange young man named Norman Bates, a troubled soul who dressed up as his mother to kill women to whom he was attracted sexually. The image of a sexual deviant who could only express his frustrations through violent acts became part of the cultural zeitgeist; over the ensuing decades, serial killers came to hold a special fascination for the general public, inspiring myriad works of nonfiction, novels, short stories, comic books, films, and even trading cards. The prominence of these killers in public consciousness reached a pinnacle in the latter part of the twentieth century with the rise of the fictional Dr. Hannibal Lecter (featured in Thomas Harris's novels, and portrayed by Sir Anthony Hopkins on the silver screen) to virtual superstardom. Like Frankenstein's Monster, Dracula, the Wolfman, and the Mummy, Hannibal the Cannibal has become a cultural icon, one that will be sending shivers down the spines of generations yet to come. Unlike the other monsters mentioned, however, the good doctor is a bit scarier for being all the more plausible a danger.

For all their recent notoriety, it's probable that serial killers have always been with us; as long as people have been living in groups, it's likely that serial killers have preyed on the fellow cave people, villagers, or city dwellers. Perhaps though, it's only the rise of the city, with an attendant rise in anonymity among citizens, that's allowed them to operate with greater ease. So maybe, just maybe, serial killers, who may have indeed inspired the fantastic legends of the werewolf or the vampire, are only finally being appreciated for what they truly are: damaged human beings who find release by killing and mutilating other human beings.

DEFINITIONS

The term "serial killer," first coined in the 1970s, entered the common parlance over the course of that decade, thanks to the prominence of the term in media coverage of such celebrated killers as Ted Bundy, David Berkowitz (a.k.a. "Son of Sam"), and others. The term allows criminologists to distinguish between three broad types of killers—the serial killer, the mass murderer, and the spree killer.

A *serial killer* is someone who commits three or more murders over an extended period of time.

A *mass murderer* is an individual who kills three or more people in a single event and in one location.

A *spree killer* commits multiple murders in different locations over a period of time that may last from a few hours to a few days.

A key factor in distinguishing these types of killers from one another is their actions in between their crimes. The serial killer blends into the woodwork, adopting what some have labeled a "a mask of sanity." Mass murderers often commit suicide after their outbursts; those who are captured often claim they

---

What Bloch had to say in *Psycho* influenced the whole art of horror writing. Back onto dusty shelves went most of the vampires, the werewolves, and other such beasties of the Victorian novelists. To front and centre came a probing of people's minds and an awareness of the frightening things to be found lurking there. Never mind the crumbling old castle, the mad scientist, the ancient, horrid gods we wrote about in *Weird Tales* and other grand old magazines. Those were good stories for their time and will always be fun to re-read or collect; of course they will! But take a good look now at your next-door neighbor who goes to an office every day or sells insurance or, in this case, runs a motel haunted by memories of an overpowering mother.

With this novel Robert Bloch took us from then to now in one big, scary leap, raising the hair of his readers while they eagerly turned the pages of what was scaring them, and showing writers how to handle a new kind of horror story.

Almost every present-day writer of horror has in one way or another been influenced by *Psycho*. Call it a milestone in horror fiction, written by one of the greats. That's what it is and what he is.

—*Hugh B. Cave on Robert Bloch's* Psycho

---

cannot remember their actions. Spree killers do not revert to normal behavior in between slayings; they tend to flare up, then burn out.

There is, of course, an almost desperate need to understand what creates a killer, arising from the desire both to treat and, more importantly, predict/prevent such deviant behavior. Are serial killers born that way, or are they a product of their environment? What compels them to kill? Although some maintain that serial killers will often manifest certain childhood behaviors—fire starting, cruelty to animals, and bedwetting—this idea has recently come under some fire (the TV psychologist Dr. Phil was recently lambasted for telling one of his TV patients that her son, who exhibited these behaviors, was on the path to becoming a serial killer). Still, the search for relevant characteristics and traits continues.

A 1984 study of thirty-six serial killers led the professionals conducting the research to publish a paper listing ten general traits associated with serial killers. Please note the deliberate use of the words like "most," "tend," and "generally" below—like any rules, there are always exceptions. Serial killers don't necessarily exhibit all of these traits, and people who exhibit these traits are not necessarily serial killers.

- Most are single white males.
- They tend to be smart.
- They tend to do poorly in school.
- Most have dysfunctional backgrounds.
- Many display a long history of psychiatric problems.
- Many are the victims of abuse—mental, physical, and sexual.
- They tend to have a great deal of trouble with male authority figures.
- They manifest psychiatric problems at an early age.
- They often feel suicidal as teenagers.
- They display a deep interest in deviant sexuality.

How prevalent is this behavior? How many serial killers are active at any given time? In the United States, estimates have ranged from 35 to 500. The lower figure was posited by the FBI in the 1980s and is probably the most realistic. This means that at any given moment in the United States, around thirty-five serial killers have committed at least one murder without being apprehended or stopped by other means, such as suicide or a natural death.

Statistics show that serial killers are more prevalent in developed Western nations, but this could be a function of more advanced detection techniques, a more sophisticated mass media, or the level of government censorship in any given region. Some have suggested that serial killings are distinctly American phenomena—true, they seem to be more prevalent in the United States, but they have surfaced in all parts of the world.

A SHORT HISTORY OF SERIAL KILLING

How far back does serial killing go? Probably to the dawn of mankind. But relatively few names register in our consciousness today. But oh, those that do! Below is a timeline of serial killing, beginning with ancient Rome and continuing through today.

First Century C.E.

Apparently a born psychopath, Nero displayed disturbing tendencies from a young age. Historians claim that he hunted human prey even as a boy, attacking pedestrians on the street and disposing of their bodies in the sewer system. He only grew worse as he matured, biting and ripping off the genitals of men and women tied to stakes. Among his more heinous acts: tearing out the womb of his mother Agrippina.

Fifteenth Century

One of the most famous serial killers of all time, Gilles de Rais, the original Bluebeard, was executed in 1440 for the torture and murder of 140 children.

Overshadowing de Rais, however, is Vlad III, Prince of Wallachia, more commonly known as Dracula (literally, son of Dracul, Romanian for Dragon). He was also known as Vlad the Impaler, due to reports of his habit of impaling his enemies on greased, pointed poles, relying on gravity to insure a slow painful death for those who opposed him.

Sixteenth Century

It is believed that Erzbet Bathory, also known as the "Blood Countess," was responsible for as many as 650 murders. Most of her victims were peasants whom she lured to her castle under false pretenses. Once inside, the girls were subjected to torture. It is reported that the Countess was fond of bathing in the blood of virgins, believing that it preserved her youth.

Seventeenth Century

Thomas Sherwood and Elizabeth Evans, also known as "Country Tom" and "Canterbury Bess," respectively, prowled the streets of London in search of their prey. Evans would lure men to a remote location where Tom would be waiting. These men were then murdered and stripped of all their possessions. They were believed to have been responsible for the deaths of at least five men. The dastardly duo was eventually apprehended, meeting their demise on the Newgate gallows.

Eighteenth Century

The murderess known as "La Tofina" was active in the late seventeenth and early eighteenth centuries. Operating in Naples, Italy, until well into her sixties, she would dispatch her victims with a specially brewed potion containing arsenic. After she was captured, she confessed to having committed 600 murders.

There is some dispute as to whether the legendary Sweeney Todd actually existed. One account claimed this mass killer was born in the slums of London in 1756. Todd acquired two skills as a youth. As a teenager, he was apprenticed to a cutler, during which time he became adept at handling and sharpening razors. Imprisoned after being accused of petty theft, he became a barber's assistant. At nineteen, he opened a barber shop on Fleet Street. Over the next quarter-century, Todd reportedly killed 160 patrons. Afterward, he butchered their bodies; his accomplice, Margery Lovett, used the body parts as a basic ingredient in the meat pies she sold in her bakeshop.

Nineteenth Century

Making a living as "resurrection men," or grave robbers, early in their careers, William Burke and William Hare hit on an easier method of obtaining corpses which they could sell to doctors and medical students looking for specimens to dissect and study—instead of digging them up, they'd make their own by poisoning Hare's lodgers.

A similar modus operandi was used by the Bender family of Labette County, Kansas. Around 1870, the Benders would murder visitors to their frontier inn, strip their corpses, and throw the bodies into their cellar. The Benders' criminal activity was halted in 1873, when a posse made up of local residents tracked them down and dealt them some lethal frontier justice. These events are mentioned in the memoirs of Laura Ingalls Wilder, who wrote that her father was one of the men who brought the Benders down.

Another American killer, the infamous Herman Mudgett, a.k.a. Dr. H. H. Holmes, was active in Chicago during the time of the 1893 World's Fair. He confessed to having committed more than two dozen murders, but many think he was responsible for several hundred deaths.

Of course, the most famous serial killer of the nineteenth century, and, perhaps, of all time has to be Jack the Ripper, a.k.a. Leather Apron, a.k.a. Saucy Jack. Active during August through November 1888, the Ripper slashed and killed five women (all prostitutes), his heinous acts causing a citywide panic. Not content to let the killings convey his message, the killer also wrote letters to a local news agency and to a local vigilance committee, ending one missive with the chilling send-off "From Hell." After taking his final victim, Mary Kelly, the Ripper was never heard from again.

The Ripper, however, was not to be forgotten. Since 1888, his activities and identity have provided fodder for hundreds of works of fiction and nonfiction. The most famous recent example of Ripper-mania is Patricia Cornwell's 2002 exposé, *Portrait of a Killer: Jack the Ripper, Case Closed.*

Twentieth Century

While other centuries have their notable serial killers, conditions in the twentieth century seem to have conspired to create a veritable explosion of aberrant behavior. Whether that is because modern conditions create more serial killers or because the media have made the public more aware of their presence in general is hard to say; the answer probably lies in a middle ground. Here is a brief list of some of the more infamous characters to surface:

Albert Fish (1870–1936). No one knows for sure how many victims fell prey to Fish, but experts feel sure he molested several hundred and killed at least sixteen. He was captured in 1934, when he wrote a letter to the mother of one of his victims. In custody, Fish opened up to Dr. Frederic Wertham (author of *Seduction of the Innocent*, the book that almost single-handedly destroyed the comic-book industry), revealing a personal history so horrifying that it shook even the good doctor, who had a wealth of experience dealing with such types.

Ed Gein (1906–1984). Warped by the fanaticism of his intensely religious mother, Ed found himself an "orphan" at the age of thirty-nine after she died. Living alone in an isolated Wisconsin farmhouse, Gein slipped into madness, carrying out abominable acts of depravity in the privacy of his home. When the local police arrived at his doorstep in November 1957 to question him in relation to a missing person's case, they found the corpse of the woman they sought, hanging from her heels in the summer kitchen behind his house. Exploring the property further, the authorities discovered a shocking museum of horrors: among other equally disturbing finds, they came upon chairs upholstered in human flesh, a boxful of noses, a shoe box containing preserved female genitalia, and the faces of nine women stuffed and mounted on a wall. Being more a ghoul/grave robber than a serial killer, Gein nevertheless admitted to killing two women. His exploits provided inspiration for Robert Bloch's seminal serial killer novel, *Psycho*, which was later adapted for a film by Alfred Hitchcock.

Charles Manson. Manson is unique among serial killers in that he was able to commit murder by proxy, sending his acolytes out into the night to kill to provoke the race war he felt sure was coming. The case was written up by prosecutor Vincent Bugliosi in his famous book *Helter Skelter* (1974).

Ted Bundy (1946–1989). Perhaps one of the most famous serial killers of modern times, Bundy began killing young women after dropping out of law school in 1973. Feigning an injury such as a broken arm, Bundy would lure his victims to his car under the pretense of needing their assistance. A sadist and necrophile who confessed to killing at least 30 women, he may actually have murdered 100 or more. Bundy was electrocuted on the morning of January 24, 1989.

Aileen Wuornos (1956–2002). Although many think she was the first female serial killer in America, Wuornos had predecessors. Wuornos was unique in that she aggressively attacked total strangers, as women nearly always kill someone with whom they already have a relationship. A prostitute, Wuornos would kill men seeking her favors; she eventually confessed to killing seven men, insisting all the murders were in self-defense. Wuornos was executed in 2002. Her story was made into a movie called *Monster*, starring Charlize Theron.

Jeffrey Dahmer (1960–1994). In 1991, the Milwaukee police answered a 911 call from a couple of black teenaged girls who were concerned about a young Asian boy they had seen running naked in the street. Arriving on the scene, the police could get no answers from the boy, who was incoherent; rather than relying on him to determine what was going on, they listened to an older white man who convinced them that the boy was nineteen and had fled his apartment during a lover's spat. The police accepted the man's story and left the boy with the man. That event has been recounted numerous times since, as people struggle to understand how Jeffrey Dahmer could have gotten away with subsequently strangling that boy and consuming parts of his body. Unbelievably, Dahmer had been killing boys in his Milwaukee home for years, keeping some body parts to eat and others as trophies. Dahmer was eventually charged with fifteen counts of murder and sentenced to fifteen life terms. Dahmer was murdered by an inmate two years into his prison term.

The list of twentieth-century American serial killers also includes Earle Leonard Nelson (1897–1928), Harvey Murray Glatman (1928–1959), John Wayne Gacy (1942–1994), Gary Heidnik (1943–1999), Henry Lee Lucas (and Ottis Toole), Edmund Emil Kemper III, Wayne Williams, and Joel Rifkin. Some were known initially by colorful nicknames, such as the Lipstick Killer (William Hierens), the Green River Killer (Gary Leon Ridgway), The Boston Strangler (Albert DeSalvo), the Night Stalker (Richard Ramirez), and the Son of Sam or .44-caliber killer (David Berkowitz). And those are the killers who were captured; others, like California's Zodiac Killer, are presumably still at large.

Twenty-first Century

The current century isn't even a decade old as of this writing, yet it has seen the capture of three of the more unusual killers in recent memory.

The first is the Beltway Sniper, John Muhammad who, traveling in a specially modified Chevrolet Caprice, terrorized the American capital and the surrounding area during the fall of 2002. Originally thought by profilers to be a white loner, Muhammad, the killer of at least fourteen people, turned out to be a black man who was accompanied by a young man named Lee Malvo.

On trial, both were found guilty of murder. In March 2004, Muhammad was sentenced to death, while Malvo received a sentence of life imprisonment. Muhammad reportedly plans to appeal his sentence.

The second was the German killer known as Armin M. who posted an ad on the Internet that read: "Wanted: Well-built man for slaughter." Astoundingly, someone answered the ad. Together, the two men dined on the respondent's privates. Later, M. stabbed him to death, carved him up, and stored parts of him in a freezer for later consumption. Said M. of the experience of dining with his victim, "It felt like communion." Only quick action by the German police prevented M. from claiming additional victims (he was caught after placing another ad), thus becoming a bona fide serial killer.

The third was Denis Rader, the self-dubbed BTK (for bind, torture, kill) killer, who terrorized Wichita, Kansas, for decades. Perversely proud of his deeds, Rader has readily confessed to ten killings. A careful planner who patiently stalked his victims before striking, Rader, whose bland façade makes him all the more frightening, blamed his demented behavior on an evil spirit he called Rex. Rader derived sick pleasure from killing people in front of their families and photographing victims' corpses in S&M poses.

It is evident from the cases described above that the shocking nature of this phenomenon is one key element in the elevation of serial killer from oddity to horror icon. Besides the mass media, another key element in keeping serial killers in the public eye is the development of an entire category of books on

---

Some Remarks by Real and Fictional Serial Killers

"Mary started to scream, and then the curtains parted further and a hand appeared, holding a butcher's knife. It was the knife that, a moment later, cut off her scream.
  And her head."

—Robert Bloch, Psycho

"For Heaven's sake catch me before I kill more. I cannot control myself."
—William Hierens, a.k.a. The Lipstick Killer

"Keep this letter back till I do a bit more work, then give it out straight. My knife's so nice and sharp I want to go to work right away if I get a chance. Good luck. Yours truly, Jack the Ripper."
—From a letter purportedly written by Jack the Ripper to police

"A census taker tried to quantify me once. I ate his liver with some fava beans and a big Amarone. Go back to school, little Starling."
—Hannibal Lecter, from The Silence of the Lambs

---

the subject, books written by journalists like Anne Rule about particular cases (among them *Green River, Running Red* [2004] and *The Stranger Beside Me* [2000]), or books written by professionals like former FBI agents like Robert K. Ressler, who wrote about his career spent trying to understand and track down killers (*Whoever Fights Monsters, I Have Lived in the Monster, Justice Is Served*). Indeed, there are even encyclopedias on the subject, among them *The Serial Killer Files* (2004) by Harold Schecter and *The Encyclopedia of Serial Killers* (2000) by Michael Newton. Intended to demystify the notion of serial killing, they also work against that notion, making these killers even more intriguing and fascinating to the general public.

FICTIONAL SERIAL KILLERS

Their exploits are the stuff of legend, their colorful nicknames a tabloid editor's dream come true. Thus, it is natural that serial killers would also inspire works of fiction, whether it be fairy tales, short stories, novels, films, or even television shows. Throughout history, and especially in modern times, serial killers have inspired numerous works of terror, suspense, and dread, building to the point where a member of their fictional ranks, Dr. Hannibal Lecter, has risen to icon status; his global recognition factor today certainly rivals that of other, more innocent pop icons such as Sherlock Holmes, Superman, and Mickey Mouse.

The tale of Bluebeard is perhaps one of the earliest recorded tales of a serial murderer. Originally included by Frenchman Charles Perrault in his famous collection *Contes du temps passé* (Tales of Past Times), known in English as *Mother Goose's Tales*, the story involves a wealthy gentleman who marries a young woman. He brings the woman to live with him at one of his country estates, allowing her access to all the rooms in the castle except one, which he specifically forbids her to enter. Curious, his young bride takes advantage of Bluebeard's absence to explore the room. Upon entering, she sees that the room contains the corpses of several women, all of whom Bluebeard had in turn married and murdered.

The Brothers Grimm also recorded tales of serial killers. In "The Robber Bridegroom," a young woman, hiding in her paramour's home, is shocked to witness the killing and consumption of a young woman by her boyfriend and his pals. In "Fitcher's Feathered Bird," a tale reminiscent of Bluebeard, a new bride enters a forbidden room and finds a vat filled with the dismembered remains of several human beings.

One need not look too deep to support the notion that the villains of fairy tales are actually serial killers. For example, consider the witch in "Hansel and Gretel," an old woman who is both a kidnapper and a cannibal. Even "Little Red Riding Hood" can be thought to be about a serial killer, albeit one suffering from lycanthropy, defined by the *American Heritage College*

Dictionary as "the magical ability to assume the form and characteristics of a wolf." Some experts believe that the degradations of some deranged individual may have given this tale its grisly subtext.

Serial killers began appearing more frequently in fiction as the nineteenth century drew to a close. A case could be made that, if looked at in a certain way, Bram Stoker's horror novel *Dracula* (1897) could also be about serial killing. If one ignores the vampirism angle, Dracula certainly fits the profile of a serial killer, and Van Helsing and his associates could be viewed as early profilers, professionals relying on a combination of modern science and their powers of observation and intuition to bring a killer to justice.

Richard Connell wrote about an exotic type of serial killer in his short story "The Most Dangerous Game" (1924). There, crazed Russian General Zaroff, a man who has hunted every kind of wild game there is to hunt, has resorted to hunting human prey, which he captures by luring ships to their doom on the rocks which surround his private island.

In his noir masterpiece *The Killer Inside Me* (1952), Jim Thompson takes readers inside the head of a serial killer. The story is narrated by small-town sheriff Lou Ford. Seemingly normal to outward appearances, Lou suffers from what he calls "the sickness," a penchant for killing people that first manifested itself in adolescence. Lou is drawn into a plot to rid the town of a prostitute with the potential to embarrass one of his town's leading families. After taking care of the problem at hand, Lou falls under suspicion, forcing him to eliminate an ever-growing number of human loose ends—including several people he claims to love. The genius of Thompson's classic noir novel is that he manages to describe the truly vicious murders and all the careful premeditation that goes into them—narrated in Lou's wonderfully deadpan voice—and yet still has you feeling for the man.

In 1954 William March published his disturbing novel *The Bad Seed*, the story of a doting mother who slowly comes to realize that her beautiful eight-year-old daughter Rhoda is a ruthless killer. The novel was adapted into a play and also into a memorable 1956 movie starring Patty McCormack as Rhoda. As an adult, McCormack starred in two features written and directed by mystery writer Max Allan Collins, which flipped the premise of *The Bad Seed*; instead of a mother realizing her child was evil, *Mommy* (1995) and *Mommy II: Mommy's Day* (1997) featured a child who discovers that her mother has been killing all those who she feels have wronged her baby.

Flannery O'Connor's short story "A Good Man Is Hard to Find" (1955) offers an interesting take on Southern manners and serial killers. The story begins with a combative Southern family embarking on a vacation trip to Florida against the wishes of an old woman in their midst, their grandmother. The woman is reluctant to travel to the Sunshine state because she has read about a crazed killer by the name of the Misfit; on the run from the law, the killer was last seen heading toward Florida. Decked out in her finest clothes for the sole purpose of being recognized as a lady in case someone sees her dead on the highway, the grandmother is forced to endure her family's antics while on the road. Stranded after the car is involved in an accident, the group is accosted by three men who arrive on the scene in their own vehicle. When the men exit their car, the grandmother suddenly realizes she is in the presence of the Misfit, who reveals himself to be quite amiable and polite despite the fact that he has just casually ordered his cronies to escort the rest of her family off into the woods to kill them. The grandmother and the Misfit engage in a strange, protracted conversation. Suddenly, the old woman has an epiphany; she reaches out to him and remarks, "Why you're one of my babies. You're one of my own children." The Misfit, who is obviously affected, shoots her three times.

One of the great crime novels of the twentieth century, Patricia Highsmith's *The Talented Mr. Ripley* (1955), is a warped but highly entertaining example of a bildungsroman. It tells the story of a young man, Tom Ripley, whose love of the good life leads to murder. The novel begins as Ripley, benefiting from a case of mistaken identity, is asked by the wealthy Herbert Greenleaf to find Greenleaf's son, Dickie, in Italy, and convince him to return home (Dickie is enjoying a sybaritic existence there with his girlfriend). Tom agrees and allows Greenleaf to sponsor his trip to Italy. There, Tom makes contact with Dickie, who takes him under his wing. He becomes comfortable living in this alternate reality, and soon finds that his passion for a lifestyle of wealth and sophistication transcends moral compunction. When Tom cannot win Dickie over, he kills him and assumes his identity. Highsmith brings this sympathetic sociopath to vivid life; Tom Ripley seduces readers into empathizing with him even as his actions defy all moral standards.

Robert Bloch explored the dark recesses of the psyche in three of his novels, *The Scarf*, *American Gothic*, and, most famously, *Psycho*. *The Scarf* (1947) was Bloch's first novel. The story is narrated by a young man turned into a serial strangler by a childhood trauma. It begins with the eerie lines: "Fetish? You name it. All I know is that I've always had to have it with me..." Published in 1959, *Psycho* was later made into a movie by Alfred Hitchcock. The serial killer was hardly new ground for Hitchcock, having directed *The Lodger* in 1927 and *Shadow of a Doubt* in 1943. Although he made some changes to adapt Bloch's book to the screen, he kept its basic plot intact: Marian Crane steals money from her boss and runs away to be with her boyfriend. She ends up in a small rundown motel run by the shy but noticeably odd Norman Bates. That evening, Marian is brutally slaughtered in her hotel shower by what appears to be an older woman wielding a knife. In one of the biggest, most stunning twists in literary and cinematic history, the "woman" is later revealed to be Norman, who, sexually aroused by Marian, dressed in his deceased mother's clothing and took on her warped personality.

American Gothic (1974) is Bloch's take on the activities of H. H. Holmes in Chicago circa 1890–1893. As is detailed in Erik Larson's excellent 2004 book *The Devil in the White City*, even as the Chicago World's Fair site was being built, Holmes was building "The World's Fair Hotel," a personal charnel house containing a dissection table, walk-in vault, greased wooden chute, gas chamber, and a 3,000-degree crematorium. No one can be sure, but some estimate that Holmes did away with upwards of 200 unfortunate souls. The main character of Bloch's novel, the handsome G. Gordon Gregg, is a doctor, pharmacist, hotel entrepreneur, ruthless thief, and killer. Like Holmes, Gregg dispatches dozens of victims in his house of horrors.

A murder mystery set in New York City, Lawrence Sanders's *The First Deadly Sin* (1973) focuses on killer Daniel Blank. Obsessive, orderly, and cold, Blank is driven to commit several horrendous murders on Manhattan's upper East side. Searching for Blank is retired police officer Edward X. Delaney (known as "Old Iron Balls" in his old precinct). As obsessive in his way as the man he is pursuing, Delaney is not above using questionable tactics to solve the crime. Delaney would go on to appear in Sanders's *The Second Deadly Sin* (1973), *The Third Deadly Sin* (1981), *and The Fourth Deadly Sin* (1985).

Written in 1978, Shane Stevens's groundbreaking *By Reason of Insanity* preceded *Red Dragon* by a few years, but many of the elements are similar, particularly the theory that serial killers are made, not born. Detailing a murderous rampage of a brilliant serial killer (the level of violence portrayed was uncommon at that time), the novel portrays him as more foxy, less a superman than someone like Hannibal Lecter. The killer's chief nemesis is a savvy journalist who gets inside his opponent's head as authorities race from one part of the country to another trying to apprehend the madman, always seemingly one step behind. Stevens ratchets up the tension with every scene, building toward a truly horrific climax, setting a tone in his prose that almost feels as if he is a journalist writing a book about the crimes a few years later, à la *The Executioner's Song* or *In Cold Blood*. Along the way, readers are exposed to the limitations of local law enforcement, wildly ambitious politicians, and national opinion makers out to add to their reputations; in addition to taking on the nature versus nurture argument, Stevens also presents all sides of the capital punishment issue.

One of the scariest serial killers in modern literature made his first appearance in Stephen King's 1979 thriller, *The Dead Zone*. The novel tells the tragic story of everyman Johnny Smith who, awakening from a lengthy coma, discovers that he has developed psychic powers that allow him to receive impressions through touch, and sometimes to glimpse the future. Asked by the Castle Rock, Maine, police to assist them in tracking down the serial killer who has been terrorizing their small town, Johnny continually receives the feeling that the killer thinks he is "slick." Johnny eventually realizes the killer is Frank Dodd, a Castle Rock policeman who commits suicide before he can be apprehended. Frank, it turns out, wore a slick yellow poncho each time he killed.

Ramsey Campbell has written many novels, both supernatural and nonsupernatural. They include *The Face That Must Die* (issued in a heavily edited version in 1979 and in a restored edition in 1983), the story of a homophobic serial killer, told largely from the killer's point of view. A more sympathetic serial murderer appears in the later novel *The Count of Eleven* (1991), which displays Campbell's gift for word play. Campbell has been quoted as saying that the novel is disturbing "because it doesn't stop being funny when you think it should."

A riveting exploration of lycanthropy and insanity, Thomas Tessier's *The Nightwalker* (1979) has several things going for it, among them the author's lucid prose, expert plotting, and a remarkable evocation of the city of London. The novel tells the story of American expatriate Bobby Ives, an aimless Vietnam veteran living in London with his girlfriend. The extremely volatile Ives is obsessed with two strange events in his past: the fact that he was declared dead in Vietnam via administrative error, and the time he experienced a vivid waking dream, in which he became a zombie.

Ives finds himself becoming more susceptible to uncontrolled rage; he also experiences quasi-fugue states where he lets that rage overwhelm him. In the midst of such a fugue state, he pushes his girlfriend into the path of an oncoming bus, killing her. Shortly after that "accident," he stalks and attacks a man in Hyde Park, tearing his victim's throat out. At first, he revels in the changes that occur. Then, realizing that he is swiftly losing control, he seeks help from a clairvoyant who seems to have insight into his condition. She initially refuses, and his rampages continue. Eventually, she relents, and tries to help him by imprisoning him. Her efforts prove unsuccessful, as he escapes confinement. Later, she is forced to kill him with a silver knife.

The Nightwalker is an effective and disturbing exploration of one man's descent into madness, exploring the chaos that results when a troubled individual gives in to his inner rage. Whether viewed as a terrifying novel of the supernatural or as a gripping psychological study, *The Nightwalker*, to paraphrase Stephen King's words in praise of the book (see *Danse Macabre*), is perhaps the finest werewolf novel of the past forty years.

Tessier would follow another man's descent into depravity with his 1986 novel *Finishing Touches*. It only takes a few pages for readers to realize they are in the hands of the master, as Tessier quickly and expertly establishes his characters and milieu. After completing his medical education, Dr. Tom Sutherland, an American in London, decides to spend some time in Europe before embarking on his career. At a major crossroads in his life, the twenty-eight-year-old Sutherland is unsure of himself as he embarks in a new direction. While in London, Sutherland meets the enigmatic Roger Nordhagen, a plastic surgeon who sees himself as the man who puts the "finishing touches" on his patients. Intrigued by the strange old man, Sutherland allows Nordhagen to show him a hidden London. His education is furthered by the lovely and dangerous Lina Ravachol, Nordhagen's assistant. Together, Nordhagen and Ravachol provide some unique and decidedly disturbing "finishing touches" to Sutherland's personality and psyche, ultimately transforming him into someone who can kill with impunity.

Jack Ketchum exploits a plot similar to the one that drives the classic horror films *The Hills Have Eyes* and *The Texas Chainsaw Massacre* in his groundbreaking work of horror, *Off Season* (1981). Accompanied by some friends, Carla, a book editor from Manhattan, travels to an isolated cabin in Maine for a few days of R&R. There, the group is attacked by a group of cannibals, plunging them into a battle for their very survival. Ketchum uses the devastation of a group of tourists by a band of cannibals not to titillate and shock, as so many horror writers might have done, but to explore the reactions of ordinary people placed in extraordinary situations.

In recent years, serial killers, like vampires, have come to occupy their own subgenre in horror and suspense. Many authors have attempted to tackle the subject, with varying degrees of success. No one, however, has been more successful with this subject matter than Thomas Harris, author of *Red Dragon* (1981), *The Silence of the Lambs* (1988), and *Hannibal* (1999). Taken together, these books constitute a bridge between such groundbreaking work as Robert Bloch's *Psycho* and the surfeit of serial killer novels published over the last three decades. These modern classics also introduced the public to the concept of serial killer as media star, featuring the most popular anti-hero of modern times, Dr. Hannibal Lecter.

Lecter is enigmatic, highly intelligent, and erudite. Before his capture, he killed and cannibalized at least nine people (the media later dubbed him "Hannibal the Cannibal"). As you might suspect, Lecter's activities created quite a stir, eventually bringing Will Graham, an FBI investigator, to Lecter's office (Lecter had actually been the treating physician for one of the victims). During a conversation with the doctor, Graham has an epiphany and realizes Lecter is the killer. Lecter, perceiving that Graham has found him out, attempts escape. Catching Graham off guard, he guts him with a linoleum knife and flees, only to be captured later by the authorities.

All this is background taken from *Red Dragon*. As the novel begins, Lecter resides in a high security mental facility, placed there by a court. Graham, recuperating from his wounds, is in semi-retirement. He is approached by Jack Crawford, his former boss at the FBI. Crawford seeks Graham's aid in the pursuit of a serial killer named Francis Dolarhyde, a.k.a. the Tooth Fairy (so named for his penchant for biting his victims), who has already slaughtered two innocent families.

Graham reluctantly agrees to help. Hoping to revive his investigative instincts, he visits Lecter in his lair. Lecter, unhelpful, nevertheless takes an interest in the case and manages to insert himself into the action, providing Dolarhyde with Will's home address. This information puts Will and his family in danger, as the hunted turns on the hunter. At the book's end, the Tooth Fairy is dead, and Will is disfigured for life. Despite being locked in a maximum security cell, Lecter has managed to achieve a measure of vengeance on Graham.

Lecter also plays a key role in the sequel to *Red Dragon*, *The Silence of the Lambs*. Clarice Starling, an FBI trainee, is asked by Jack Crawford to interview the doctor for a study on serial killers. Clarice visits Lecter, but is unable to convince him to participate in the study. Lecter, intrigued by young Clarice, offers her something better—his assistance on a current case involving a killer nicknamed "Buffalo Bill" (so named because he "skins his humps").

Clarice becomes an active participant in the hunt for Buffalo Bill, acting as intermediary between Lector and the FBI. Lector, with previous knowledge of the killer, cunningly manipulates all involved. His orchestrations eventually provide him with an opportunity to escape, one which he eagerly seizes. Clarice, acting on hints dropped by the doctor, eventually tracks Bill down, but her victory is tempered by the knowledge that Dr. Lecter is once again at large.

These two novels are acknowledged classics of suspense and the aforementioned serial killer genre. Well written, they do not rely on shock value alone to jolt readers. Harris masterfully creates and sustains tension, building to tremendous crescendos in both books. Other authors have written successfully in this genre, but they tend to rely on splatter to achieve their horrific effect, each subsequent novel trying to outdo its predecessors in terms of gore and perversion. Harris avoids this trap, relying on good old-fashioned story telling to make his point.

Harris resisted the obvious temptation to feature Lecter more prominently in these novels, showing admirable restraint in reining in this strong character, using him to enhance rather than dominate the action. It would have been very easy for Harris to allow the doctor to move to center stage—Lecter is mesmerizing. Like Sherlock Holmes, he transcends the boundaries of literature, leaving his many fans clamoring for more. Anthony Hopkins's riveting portrayal of Dr. Lecter on the screen only added to his luster, introducing him to an audience unfamiliar with Harris's novels.

Harris's *Hannibal* changed that forever. Featuring Lecter as its chief protagonist and Clarice Starling in a supporting role, this ambitious novel began to unravel the mystery behind the killer, providing tantalizing glimpses into his history and motivations. Many were upset by this, preferring Lecter's past to remain murky. A large portion of Harris's readership was also turned off by the book's ending, feeling that Starling's fate (brainwashed by Lecter, she becomes his companion) was inappropriate. However one views it, one has to admire the risks Harris takes, making Lecter into an almost "Bondian" hero, having him square off against the obsessive Mason Verger, a horribly scarred, megarich supervillain he helped create.

It is hard to say whether Michael Slade's *Headhunter* (1984) is a thriller, a mystery, or a work of horror. Extremely dark, this novel of psychological suspense functions splendidly as a mystery, yet also gleefully revels in the conventions of the horror genre, serving up shocking set pieces of brutal violence.

The story is set in Vancouver in October 1982. Robert DeClercq, a retired detective, has been summoned by the powers that be to spearhead an investigation into two murders which have been linked by the same weapon (the bodies have been savagely mutilated). DeClercq assumes command of the Headhunter Squad and immediately assembles a crack team of Special External (Special X) investigators to help ferret out the diabolical killer. As political pressure mounts and widespread hysteria begins to grip the city, DeClercq and his team race against time to snare their cunning adversary before another victim is butchered. Slade's debut has spawned numerous sequels featuring the members of Special X, the most recent being *Swastika* (2005).

Serial Killer Nicknames and Aliases

Serial killers are often tagged with memorable colorful names by the authorities and the media. Here are twenty especially evocative nom de plumes:

Richard Angelo	The Angel of Death
Joe Ball	The Alligator Man
Harvey Carnigan	The Want-Ad Killer
Nannie Doss	The Giggling Granny
Larry Eyler	The Interstate Killer
Carlton Gary	The Stocking Strangler
John Haigh	The Acid Bath Murderer
Colin Ireland	The Gay Slayer
Keith Hunter Jesperson	The Happy Face Killer
Ted Kaczynski	The Unabomber
Paul Knowles	The Casanova Killer
Posteal Laskey	The Cincinnati Strangler
George Metesky	The Mad Bomber
Earle Nelson	The Gorilla Murderer
Thierry Paulin	The Monster of Montmarte
Louis Pette	The Dutchess of Death
Melvin David Rees	The Sex Beast
John Scripps	The Tourist From Hell
Joseph Vacher	The French Ripper
Carol Eugene Watts	The Sunday Morning Slasher

Source: http://members.tripod.com/~SerialKillr/SerialKillersExposed/
index.html

Serial killers loom large in author Peter Straub's universe, so much so that his Web site has a special section on the topic ("The Serial Killers of Millhaven"). In *Koko* (1988), a group of Vietnam veterans tries to track down a serial killer who they fear was once a part of their unit. Led by one-time suspect Tim Underhill (a writer who dealt with serial murder in a novel called *The Divided Man*), the men learn that the killer's pathology is linked to a tortured childhood and the strangeness and savagery of their collective Vietnam experience. Tim Underhill figured in several of Straub's subsequent works, most notably *The Throat* (1993) and *lost boy lost girl* (2003), both of which are primarily set in Millhaven, Wisconsin, Straub's fictional version of Milwaukee.

The Throat, which deals with a series of killings collectively known as the Blue Rose Murders, focused on the serial killers Bob Bandolier, his son Fee Bandolier, John Ransom, and Walter Dragonette. Bob Bandolier was the original Blue Rose killer, named for the words found written on the walls above his victims. A victim of child abuse, Fee Bandolier, who took his first victim at the age of thirteen, found an outlet for his murderous impulses in Vietnam, where he traveled under the name Franklin Bachelor. John Ransom committed several murders using the second round of Blue Rose Killings as cover to conceal the murder of his wife, April. Dragonette, who untruthfully confessed to having committed the murder of April Ransom, murdered at least fifteen young men, had sex with their corpses, cooked and ate their body parts, and stored the remains, wrapped in Cling-Film, in his freezer. His actions were inspired, he claimed, at least in part by Tim Underhill's novel, *The Divided Man*.

lost boy lost girl details the deprivations of two more of Millhaven's finest, Joseph Kalendar and Ronnie Lloyd-Jones. The homophobic Kalendar was a master carpenter who added hidden rooms to the interior of his house. After killing his son and then his wife, Kalendar began abducting women and taking them to his house, where he terrorized and murdered them. He was eventually apprehended, tried, found insane, and sent to a state mental institution, where he was subsequently murdered by another inmate. The whereabouts of his daughter, who he tortured and sexually abused, are unknown.

Known as "The Sherman Park Killer" for the locale where he came upon his victims, Jones took numerous victims, nearly all of them boys between the ages of fourteen to nineteen. After his arrest, Jones tried to interest Tim Underhill in collaborating on the story of his life, which he saw at least in part as a tribute to the achievements of Joseph Kalendar. Tim declined. Two nights after his arrest, Lloyd-Jones killed himself in his cell. The Millhaven police department discovered sixteen bodies buried in his backyard.

Set in 1848, Cormac McCarthy's *Blood Meridian* (1985) initially focuses on a fourteen-year-old boy named the Kid, a vicious delinquent from Tennessee who travels down the Mississippi River, eventually reaching Texas.

There, he falls in with a rogue Army unit making raids into Mexico. After the unit is wiped out by Apaches in the Sonora desert, the Kid is imprisoned in a Mexican jail, where he meets and joins a group of bounty hunters retained by the government to collect Indian scalps as retaliation for a string of Apache massacres in remote border villages.

The gang, made up of misfits, outlaws, drifters, and psychopaths, is dominated by two of the nastiest characters ever to stride across a fictional landscape: the nominal leader of the group, Ike Glanton, a sadistic mercenary with a nasty temper, and Glanton's advisor, the fat, hairless, erudite, and volatile Judge Holden. The gang finds an Indian tribe—not Apache marauders but rather the denizens of a peaceful fishing village—and slaughters all its members. Unable to catch the elusive Apaches, the company elects to pursue easier prey, slaughtering the innocent denizens of villages and mining camps spread across the arid wastes of the Southwest. As their bounty hunt turns into a genocidal killing spree, the gang forgets its original motivations, becoming increasingly entranced by the overwhelming magnetism of the Judge, a madman who convinces them they are agents of a ruthless natural law.

The bestial Chaingang, the creation of the late Rex Miller, made his first appearance in Miller's debut novel, *Slob* (1987). A genius, the slobbering 500-pound giant, a.k.a. Daniel Edward Flowers Bunkowski, likes to snack on the hearts of his victims. Jack Eichord is the detective who must hunt this human monster. Bunkowski subsequently appeared in the novels *Slice*, *Chaingang*, *Savant*, and *Butcher*. Eichord went on to star in his own series, which included the titles *Frenzy*, *Stone Shadow*, and *Iceman*.

James Ellroy's *Silent Terror* (1990) is the startling fictional autobiography of captured serial killer Martin Michael Plunkett. In this incredibly graphic novel, the articulate Plunkett tells his sordid story, providing the repulsive details relating to his life and his kills, right up to his eventual capture by FBI Serial Killer Task Force agent Thomas Dusenberry. Interspersed with his narrative are newspaper clippings detailing his murderous and depraved odyssey across 1970s America.

According to *Publishers Weekly*, John Sanford's debut novel, *Rules of Prey* (1990), took "a stock suspense plot—a dedicated cop pursuing an ingenious serial killer—and dressed it up into the kind of pulse-quickening, irresistibly readable thriller that many of the genre's best-known authors would be proud to call their own." In that novel, Lieutenant Lucas Davenport (star of sixteen "Prey" books at this writing) is called in to aid a Minneapolis task force scrambling to stop a psychopathic serial woman-slayer. Viewing his activities as a game, the self-styled "mad dog" murderer takes pride in choosing his victims and in setting up obstacles for the police.

Although Bret Easton Ellis's *American Psycho* (1991) contains some truly repulsive scenes, these set pieces need to be viewed in the context of the book as a whole; the horror does not lie in the killer's actions, but in the society they reflect. In the first third of the book, Patrick Bateman, a twenty-six-year-old Wall Street professional, describes his designer lifestyle in excruciating detail—brand names abound. It becomes obvious that Bateman inhabits a very superficial world. Then, out of the blue, Bateman coldly blinds and stabs a homeless man. From here, the body count rapidly escalates, as he kills a male acquaintance and sadistically tortures and murders two prostitutes, an old girlfriend, and a child he passes in the zoo. The brutalization of Bateman's victims is made even more horrible by his cold, flat, impersonal first person narration.

The Corinthian, from Neil Gaiman's Sandman series, is the source of both humor and horror. Featured prominently in Gaiman's second major Sandman story (collected in a graphic novel called *The Sandman: Volume II: The Doll's House* [1991]), the Corinthian, a minion of Gaiman's main character Dream, is the ultimate serial killer. He first appears in Gaiman's story "Collectors," which concentrates almost exclusively on serial killers. While, on the surface, mass murder would not appear to be particularly amusing, Gaiman concocts a scenario wherein famous serial killers attend a "Cereal" convention at a hotel. The story is a hilarious send-up of genre conventions and America's fascination with serial killers.

Along Came a Spider (1993) by James Patterson introduced his continuing character Dr. Alex Cross, who has appeared in several subsequent novels with titles like *Cat and Mouse* (1997), *Roses Are Red* (2000), *Violets Are Blue* (2001), and *Four Blind Mice* (2002). In *Along Came a Spider*, Cross investigates crimes committed by a serial killer who finds his targets in the ghettos of Washington, D.C. Cross, a ghetto resident himself, is vexed when he is suddenly called away, along with his partner John Sampson, to investigate a kidnapping at an exclusive academy. Patterson weaves these and other threads together, providing glimpses into the mind of the kidnapper, as Cross eventually discerns a connection to the ghetto serial murders.

Caleb Carr's *The Alienist* (1994) is set in 1896 New York City. A serial killer who preys upon cross-dressing boy prostitutes is on the loose. The police are making no progress on the case; in fact, someone with power or influence seems to be bent on hindering the investigation. A team formed by police commissioner Theodore Roosevelt is charged with finding the killer. Leading the unconventional group is "alienist" Dr. Lazlo Kreizler (in the nineteenth century, when psychology was in its infancy, the mentally ill were considered "alienated" from themselves and society, and the experts who treated them were therefore known as "alienists"). Dr. Kreizler's team includes his former Harvard classmate, *New York Times* crime reporter John Moore; Moore's longtime friend, feisty heiress-turned-NYPD-secretary Sara Hamilton; and two former mental patients who now work as his servants.

The Alienist is filled with rich details about both the seamy underside and more privileged sections of late-nineteenth-century New York City and then-novel crime detection techniques such as fingerprinting. For instance, to help in apprehending the elusive killer, Kreizler's team develops a psychological profile for him.

Carr followed *The Alienist* with another adventure featuring Kreizler's team in 1997. Titled *The Angel of Darkness*, the story centers on the kidnapping of the infant daughter of a Spanish diplomat just as tensions between Spain and the United States have reached critical mass. The group soon discovers something even more horrific: their chief suspect seems to have been involved in the murders of several other young children, (including two of her own) and seems to be willing to take any measures necessary to cover her tracks. It becomes a race against time to save her latest victim.

In *Zombie* (1995), Joyce Carol Oates attempts to get inside the mind of a serial killer. This short novel, which purports to be the diary of one Quentin P——, includes strange capitalizations and crude drawings. As is typical of Oates, the language used adds to the overall feeling of disquiet she is trying to create; the simple prose creates an intimacy that becomes almost too much to take, as readers experience the killer's dark obsession and heinous acts (he's trying to create a zombie, attempting to achieve his goals by performing crude lobotomies on his victims) first hand. Oates never lets the tension ease as one victim after another falls prey to the killer.

In *Serial Killer Days* (1996), David Prill satirizes society's fascination with serial murder and its love affair with commerce, with a story about the small town of Standard Springs, Minnesota, where an annual visit and murder (twenty years in a row!) by a serial killer has become, in fine American tradition, a tourist attraction, replete with floats in a "Parade of Fear," and the crowning of a "Scream Queen." Although some regret the loss of life, nobody really wants the killer caught because his activities have proved a welcome boon to the local economy.

In *The Poet* (1996), a departure from his crime novels featuring Los Angeles Police Department's Harry Bosch, Michael Connelly tells the story of journalist Jack McEvoy. Apparently distraught over his inability to crack a murder case, Jack's twin brother, Sean, a Denver homicide detective, appears to have committed suicide. Jack's investigation uncovers a series of cop suicides across the country, all of which have in common both the cops' deep concerns over recent cases and their last messages, which Jack recognizes as having been taken from the works of Edgar Allan Poe. As his information reopens cases across the United States, Jack joins forces with a team from the FBI's Behavioral Science Section. In a shocking twist, the killer, known as The Poet, turns out to be a member of that task force.

Connelly delivered a sequel to *The Poet* in 2004 called *The Narrows*. In that book, retired Los Angeles homicide detective Harry Bosch investigates the death of his friend, ex-FBI profiler Terry McCalab. Bosch's inquiry leads him directly to a burial site that the FBI has been trying to conceal from the media, as it may be the work of the Poet, who, until now, was presumed dead. Teaming up with Rachel Walling, the FBI agent who discerned the

Poet's identity some eight years before, Bosch attempts to bring the killer to justice.

Stephen Dobyns's *The Church of Dead Girls* (1997) begins with a description of an attic containing the bodies of three girls, two aged thirteen, one aged fourteen. The bodies are seated in straight back chairs, bound loosely by rope. Their mummified corpses have been dressed in velvet, and their frocks contain a variety of symbols, together with fragments of words like "CK" and "NT" and "TCH" and "FIL." Each girl has had her left hand severed at the wrist. This macabre image sets the tone for the entire novel, creating a feeling of foreboding that author Dobyns sustains over the rest of his compelling narrative. Readers are offered clues as to how these girls came to be in the attic on nearly every page, as Dobyns describes the profound effects their disappearances have on the insular upstate New York town of Aurelius.

Jeffery Deaver has written seven novels about paraplegic Lincoln Rhyme and his partner/paramour policewoman Amelia Sachs, including the series debut, *The Bone Collector* (1997), and his latest, *Cold Moon* (2006). In each installment, Rhyme battles larger-than-life villains with colorful monikers like The Conjurer and the aforementioned Bone Collector by utilizing his keen mind and the principles and techniques of modern forensics. In *The Bone Collector*, Rhyme squares off against a killer who is recreating crimes which occurred at the turn of the century in New York City.

Eric Bowman (a pseudonym for Mark Frost) looks deep into the mind of a killer in his 1997 novel *Before I Wake*. Famous for bringing serial killer Wendell "the Slug" to justice, New York City homicide detective Jimmy Montone is accustomed to the spotlight, and so doesn't think twice before agreeing to allow British novelist Terence Peregrine Keyes to observe as he works a case "from start to finish." Soon after agreeing to this arrangement, Montone is confronted with the apparent suicide of TV news anchor Mackenzie Davis. Skeptical from the start, Montone quickly determines that the "suicide" was staged: someone forced Davis to tape a suicide video, then hurled him from the window of his thirty-fifth-floor apartment. Days later, when Montone's new girlfriend is found dead under similar circumstances, he realizes that the killings are meant as a personal attack. It takes him longer, however, to realize that the murderer, one Terry Keyes, has been under his nose the whole time.

In *Endless Honeymoon* (2001), Don Webb chronicles the exploits of a serial killer with a unique obsession: the aptly named "Shitkiller," on a personal mission to rid the world of those who delight in the misery of others, targets only the mean and cruel spirited. Although he has made dozens of kills across America over the course of several decades, the FBI has few clues as to his identity or motive. The job of tracking down this legendary killer has ended several careers, most recently that of Abel Salazar. Although severed from the Bureau, Salazar, funded by a mysterious benefactor, continues the pursuit, obsessively following up every lead regarding his nemesis, including several uncovered by his successor in the investigation, the hapless Special Agent William Mondragon. Recent events have led Mondragon to focus on Willis and Virginia Spencer, a couple who, stumbling upon an early version of the killer's victim selection software, have put it to an entirely different use: instead of killing the targets, they play elaborate pranks on them, hoping to scare them into changing their ways. Unfortunately for the well-meaning couple, their activities bring them into direct contact with their spiritual "mentor" when they one night find they have selected the same target. That fateful encounter is a catalyst for the rest of the novel, setting in motion a bizarre scenario where all parties are eventually thrown together. The results are by turns outrageous, tragic, and comic.

In *Black House* (2001), their sequel to their collaborative effort, *The Talisman* (1984), Stephen King and Peter Straub drop in again on the hero of that fantasy novel, Jack Sawyer. Now in his thirties, Jack has thoroughly repressed all memories of his fantastic past. Since that time, Jack has become, to use his own word, a "coppiceman," a Los Angeles Police Department detective whose exploits have garnered considerable attention in the national press. Apparently, his success is largely related to his time spent in the alternate reality known as the Territories and his experiences with the mystical Talisman. One of Jack's greatest professional triumphs occurred in the small town of French Landing, Wisconsin, where he apprehended a killer who had taken a life while visiting Los Angeles. Jack's visit to the Landing left a deep impression on him, so profound that he retired there shortly after closing the case. Jack had looked forward to a peaceful retirement, but that was not to be. French Landing is being terrorized by the Fisherman, a serial killer who dismembers and cannibalizes young children, a la Albert Fish. Baffled by the complete absence of leads, the local sheriff asks Jack for assistance. Although initially reluctant to become involved, Jack decides to help, in part due to the prodding of his friend, blind disk jockey Henry Leyden. Immersing himself in the case, Jack realizes that the killings are only the tip of the iceberg when it comes to the evil present in French Landing.

On her way home from school on a wintry December day in 1973, fourteen-year-old Susie Salmon, the narrator of Alice Sebold's bestseller *The Lovely Bones* (2002), is lured into a makeshift underground den in a cornfield and brutally raped and murdered, the latest victim of a serial killer, who is one of her neighbors, Mr. Harvey. The description of the crime is chilling, but never vulgar, and Sebold maintains this delicate balance between homey and horrid as she depicts the grieving process that Susie's family and friends go through. Sebold's debut novel unfolds from heaven, where "life is a perpetual yesterday"; Susie narrates and keeps watch over her loved ones and her killer. Though maudlin at times, *The Lovely Bones* is a moving exploration of loss and mourning.

In his 2002 novel *The Straw Men*, Michael Marshall (a.k.a. Michael Marshall Smith) delivers a tale of paranoia and despair, told, until late in the novel, on two parallel tracks, one dealing with the Los Angeles Police Department homicide detective John Zandt's hunt for The Upright Man, a serial killer who taunts the authorities with a unique calling card, the other with ex-CIA agent Ward Hopkins's search for the truth behind his parents' untimely death. Their independent investigations lead to discoveries that rock both their worlds. Marshall has written three sequels to this novel: *The Upright Man* (2004), *The Lonely Dead* (2005), and *Blood of Angels* (2005).

Gregory Frost gave "Bluebeard" and "Fitcher's Feathered Bird" a unique spin in his 2002 novel *Fitcher's Brides*. Frost's version takes place in 1830, in New York's Finger Lakes district. That district is the site of a community founded by Elias Fitcher, a community that prays and works while awaiting the end of the world prophesied for 1843. Inspired by Fitcher's preaching, the Charter family moves there with their three daughters to await the final days. Fitcher first marries Vernelia Charter, who disappears, then Amy Charter who also vanishes, finally moving on to Catherine, the youngest Charter daughter. In order to survive, Catherine must rely on her wits and the information passed on from her sisters before they disappeared. Frost riffs on the plots of the classic short stories even as he explores more mature themes of lust and desire.

Robert Frost's poem provides a title and an epigram to Blake Crouch's engrossing first novel, *Desert Places* (2004), the pulse-pounding tale of an outwardly civilized man forced into acting in an uncivilized (to say the least) manner. That man is Andrew Thomas, best-selling author of suspense novels with titles like *Blue Murder* and *The Scorcher*. Thomas lives the good life until the day he receives a letter in the mail, telling him that a woman's body has been buried on his property, a body soaked in the author's blood. Confirming this sad fact, Thomas is forced to play a serial killer's twisted game, one which requires him to make a journey to Wyoming, where he ultimately must confront his own mortality, and question his morality and sanity.

Crouch's sequel, *Locked Doors* (2005), picks up seven years after the conclusion of *Desert Places*. Having barely survived the events related in that harrowing thriller, famous writer Andrew Thomas, now one of America's most wanted criminals, has settled in the Yukon after many years on the run. Believing his ordeal over, Thomas is stunned to learn of the murder of a friend's wife and the kidnapping of a former flame. Apparently, someone is trying to send him a message that the trials that commenced seven years prior are not over, and that a reckoning must occur. Thomas travels to North Carolina and the Outerbanks island of Ocracoke to confront his adversary, setting the stage for an epic battle between the author and a man who can only be described as a relentless killing machine.

Dexter Morgan, the hero of Jeff Lindsay's subversive 2004 novel *Darkly Dreaming Dexter* (and its 2005 sequel *Dearly Devoted Dexter*), is a highly respected lab technician specializing in blood spatter for the Miami Dade Police Department. He is handsome and polite, and rarely calls attention to himself. He is also a sociopathic serial killer whose "Dark Passenger" drives him to commit the occasional killing and dismemberment. Adopted as a toddler, Dexter has learned, with help from his strangely accepting policeman father, to focus his talents, killing only those who deal with death themselves. Dexter has found his niche, but when a new serial killer working in Miami stages several grisly scenes that Dexter discerns are actually attempts at communication from one killer to another, he finds himself facing a dilemma. Should he help find the fiend? Or should he locate this new killer himself, so he can talk shop?

In Robert Randisi's *Arch Angels* (2004), the fifth Joe Keough mystery, the detective returns to his old stomping grounds when it becomes apparent that a serial killer is kidnapping and murdering young boys in St. Louis. It is a bittersweet experience for Keough for several reasons besides the killings. One is that he is now considered an outsider by local police, having spent the last year working for the Federal Serial Killer Task Force in Washington, D.C. Another complication occurs when he is brought face-to-face with his ex-partner Marc Jeter, with whom he has some very serious unfinished business. Finally, it appears as if the killer, or a copycat with a similar modus operandi, is snatching young girls off the street a few hundred miles away in Chicago, always within days of the St. Louis killings. Still, Keough endures, relying on razor sharp instincts to bring the killer down.

Florida writer Tim Dorsey has written a series of books featuring the antics of a serial killer named Serge Storms. Also somewhat of a political activist/terrorist, Serge takes on numerous pet projects to fill the time when he's not killing someone. Witness his to do list from *Cadillac Beach* (2005), the sixth novel to feature the homicidal lunatic:

> Develop and market my new line of South Beach energy drinks, complete rehabilitation and release of Loxahtachee marsh mouse, solve mystery of grandfather's death, recover fortune in missing diamonds from America's largest gem heist, cripple the mob in South Florida, embarrass Castro on the global stage, help Chamber of Commerce with image crisis, restore respect for the brave men and women of the US intelligence community, lure the Today Show to Miami for local pride/economic boost, participate in my times like Robert Kennedy (depending on the weather), and accomplish it all through the launch of my new-economy, clean-burning, earth friendly venture capital business that involves spiritual growth, historical appreciation, and the Internet. (27)

Of course, Serge notes, the list is "subject to change without notice."

A happy blend of police procedural and international thriller, *The Sacred Cut* (2005), David Hewson's third Nic Costa novel, finds the trinity of Costa, Peroni, and their chief, the irascible Leo Falcone, in fine form, fearlessly grappling with criminals, bureaucracies, significant others, and the American intelligence community in their pursuit of the truth. It is five days before

Serial Killer Profilers

Professional profilers, experts who use their knowledge of serial killers to construct detailed descriptions of these killers, have in the last decade also become popular players on television dramas. The trend began in the early 1990s with the characters of Mulder and Scully in "The X-Files," developed by Chris Carter. Although they specialized in investigating the paranormal, they cut their professional teeth as FBI profilers. Carter also created the show "Millennium," which featured a former FBI profiler named Frank Black, who unknowingly was a player in a larger battle between good and evil. The trend continued, resulting, inevitably, in a short-lived show predictably called "Profiler."

Christmas, and Rome is covered in snow. Braving the elements on this cold winter night are policemen Nic Costa and Gianni Peroni, accompanied by civilian Mauro Sandri. A photographer, Sandri is assembling a documentary on the policeman and their city. Summoned to the Pantheon by a shaken security guard, the policemen are ambushed by an intruder, who begins shooting before fleeing into the night. The policemen are unharmed, but the photographer is fatally wounded. Later, a woman's body, bearing knife marks in the elaborate pattern of the so-called Sacred Cut, is found on the premises. Seeking justice for the photographer, Costa and Peroni begin searching for the murderer; their investigation will bring them into conflict with one of the strangest killers they have ever faced, a man out to settle scores with origins in the days of Desert Storm.

PLAYS

An argument can be made that one of Shakespeare's most complex villains, the wicked Iago, was a serial killer. In *Othello* (1604), the completely amoral Iago will do anything to secure what he perceives as his rightful position. Iago begins scheming when Othello gives the "ignorant, ill-suited" Cassio the position the evil one desires. Infuriated, Iago plots to steal the position he feels he justly deserves. A consummate liar, Iago guiltlessly manipulates those around him to his benefit. Scarily pragmatic, Iago kills anyone who stands in his way, starting with his friend Roderigo and moving on to his spouse, Emilia. Many readers of *Othello* considered him evil personified; today, Iago would readily be labeled a psychopath.

Serial killers made their way to Broadway in 1939 with the premiere of Joseph Kesserling's *Arsenic and Old Lace*, later adapted to film in 1944 by Frank Capra. This play focuses on the travails of one Mortimer Brewster, a newspaperman who has come to Brooklyn, New York, to inform his eccentric aunts, Abby and Martha Brewster, of his impetuous engagement to the girl of his dreams. During his visit, he discovers his aunts have been quietly murdering old men without families to spare them the agony of growing old alone; the results of their efforts are buried in their basement. His efforts to cover up his aunts' crimes are complicated by the reappearance of his psychopathic brother Jonathan, whose body count rivals that of Abby and Martha. As Mortimer (essayed in the movie version by Cary Grant) tells his fiancée: "Look, I probably should have told you this before, but you see, well, insanity runs in my family. It practically gallops."

Serial mayhem would again hold sway over Broadway when Stephen Sondheim's grand guignol, *Sweeney Todd: The Demon Barber of Fleet Street*, opened in 1979. Based on the exploits of the legendary barber, the play won eight Tony Awards including the best musical. To quote the play's clever tag lines, "Sweeney Todd, hell-bent on revenge, takes up with his enterprising neighbor in a delicious plot to slice their way through London's upper crust. Justice will be served—along with lush melody, audacious humor and bloody good thrills."

FILMS/TELEVISION

A serial killer who preyed on children was featured in Fritz Lang's film, *M.* (1931). Starring Peter Lorre as the despicable killer, the film tells the story of a criminal element that feels threatened by the intense police scrutiny resulting from a string of child murders. Realizing it is in their best interests, the criminals launch an intense search for the killer.

As mentioned above, Alfred Hitchcock directed a handful of movies dealing with serial killers. Starting with *The Lodger* in 1927, he moved on to *Shadow of a Doubt* in 1943. This particularly suspenseful movie focuses on a young girl named Charlie (Teresa Wright) who slowly becomes convinced that her namesake, her beloved Uncle Charlie (Joseph Cotten), temporarily living under the same roof with her, is actually the murderer the media has dubbed The Merry Widow Killer. Following *Psycho*, Hitchcock directed the thriller *Frenzy* (1972), featuring a madman known as "The Neck-Tie Killer."

Brian DePalma would later pay homage to Alfred Hitchcock's *Psycho* in his 1980 film *Dressed to Kill*, at its heart a retelling of that movie set in modern Manhattan. Angie Dickinson plays the sexually frustrated, middle-aged wife who becomes the razor-wielding killer's first victim, confessing her sexual fantasies to her psychiatrist (Michael Caine). After she is cut down, the focus of the film switches to a murder witness (Nancy Allen) and Dickinson's grieving son (Keith Gordon), who team up in an attempt to track the killer down. The plot twist upon which the story turns is slyly hinted at in the film's title.

Fans of Wes Craven's more recent work (e.g., the *Scream* series) may not appreciate his second feature, *The Hills Have Eyes* (1977), but many consider it a classic example of 1970s horror. Originally titled *Blood Relations*, this unsettling fable of disparate cultures clashing strands a suburban family in the desert, then pits them against a clan of inbred cannibals. Working from a similar premise, *The Texas Chainsaw Massacre*, the over-the-top but extremely influential 1974 low-budget horror movie directed by Tobe Hooper, follows a group of teenagers who pick up a hitchhiker and wind up in a backwoods house of horror where they endure grievous tortures inflicted on them by a demented cannibalistic family, including a masked, aproned giant known as Leatherface. This chainsaw toting maniac, himself inspired in part by Ed Gein, no doubt provided inspiration for the next generation of cinematic serial killers, including the larger-than-life (or death) Michael Myers (of *Halloween* fame), Freddy Krueger (from The Nightmare on Elm Street series), Jason Vorhees (from the Friday the 13th franchise), and Charles Lee Ray (a.k.a. Chucky).

Nearly twenty years after its premiere, *The Stepfather* (1987) is still considered a classic by many. Directed by Joseph Ruben and sporting a screenplay from crime novelist Donald E. Westlake, the film is based on the true story of New Jersey family killer Joseph List. The movie's version of List is real estate agent, Jerry Blake (Terry O'Quinn). Jerry is outwardly calm and reasonable. Underneath that pleasant façade, however, lurks a psychopath, a man flies into murderous rages when his family fails to live up to his unrealistically high standards—presumably, that is why he kills his first family, an act that is revealed to the audience as the film's opening credits roll. The film picks up one year later, with Jerry living in a new home. He has got his new wife eating out of his hand, but her rebellious teenage daughter is less than thrilled by her stepfather. In fact, she knows something is wrong with Jerry from the moment they meet, despite Jerry's best attempts to win her over. The more she rebels, the closer Jerry comes to snapping once again.

The 1986 film *Henry: Portrait of a Serial Killer* was loosely based on the life of Henry Lee Lucas, reputedly one of the most prolific serial killers in American history (though Lucas has since recanted previous confessions). From the beginning, Henry plunges the audience into a world seen solely through the eyes of a sociopath. The power of Henry lies in its grounding in the mundane existence of everyday life. Michael Rooker plays Henry with great subtlety, not as a raving lunatic, but as the frumpy guy next door, a drifter who takes out his frustrations on random victims and escalates his body count after teaming up with the violent ex-con Otis (Tom Towles). Director John McNaughton's straightforward, matter of fact presentation creates a chilling sense of realism.

In *Serial Mom* (1994), director John Waters delivers a wickedly funny black comedy starring Kathleen Turner as Beverly, the ultimate suburbanite, a woman so obsessed with order and perfection that she kills a neighbor for not complying with her town's recycling mandates. Her spouse Sam Waterston and kids Matthew Lillard and Ricki Lake don't have a clue that it is in fact their June Cleaver clone of a mom who is offing the neighbors. The final courtroom scene is hilarious, as Beverly is turned into a celebrity defendant, long before O.J.

Peter Jackson's 1996 film *The Frighteners* manages to evoke both laughs and chills. Ever since the car accident that took the life of his wife, Frank Bannister has been able to see ghosts. Exploiting this talent, Frank sets up shop as a ghost buster. The only problem with his job is that he is the one who put the ghosts in his customer's homes in the first place. In other words, he is a con artist, enlisting his ghostly friends The Judge (John Astin), Stuart (Troy Evans), and Cyrus (Chi McBride) to create other worldly mayhem, such that folks will hire him to rid their homes of the spirits. When a series of mysterious murders take place in town, FBI Agent Milton Dammers, who believes Frank is responsible for the deaths of his wife and of the recent victims, appears on the scene to assist local law enforcement. The demented FBI agent will stop at nothing to catch Frank. Frank, who can see ghostly numbers on the foreheads of future victims, knows who the real killer is but can't prove it. In the early 1960s, a serial killer named Johnny Charles Bartlett (Jake Busey) murdered what was then a record number of victims ("That's one more than Starkweather!" he crows at one point), with the help of his teenage girlfriend Patricia Ann Bradley (Dee Wallace-Stone). The new killings all point to Bannister, but Bannister soon figures out that Bartlett, who was executed decades before, is once again active, having somehow found a way to bolster his kill count from beyond the grave.

One of the most visceral and frightening serial killer movies ever made, *Se7en* (1995), is based on an intriguing notion—a serial killer named John Doe who dispatches his victims by forcing them to act out one of the seven deadly sins, afterwards artfully arranging the murder scene into a tribute to a particular mortal vice. From its jerky opening credits to its horrifying twist ending, *Se7en*, directed by David Fancher, leads viewers further into a murky abyss, ratcheting up the tension to almost unbearable levels. Morgan Freeman and Brad Pitt play the detectives who dog the killer's footsteps, all the while unaware that the hunters can easily become the hunted.

JACK THE RIPPER

Jack the Ripper's activities in Whitechapel triggered myriad fictional interpretations. One early take was Marie Belloc Lowndes 1913 novel, *The Lodger*, later made into the 1927 film of the same name directed by Alfred Hitchcock.

One of the more famous short stories in the horror genre, "Yours Truly, Jack the Ripper," written by Robert Bloch, appeared in *Weird Tales*, July

1943. The tale is one of the most famous pieces about the most notorious of all serial killers, and it has been reprinted in countless anthologies. The narrator is one John Carmody, a psychiatrist living in Chicago. Carmody is approached by Sir Guy Hollis of the British Embassy who has an interesting theory: he hypothesizes that Jack the Ripper did not grow old, and asks Carmody's help to capture the killer, who he thinks is presently active in Carmody's home town. In an alley Hollis finds out that his hunch was right. "Never mind the 'John,'" Carmody whispers, revealing a knife. "Just call me...Jack" (20). The adaptation of this story for radio resulted in Bloch's own radio series, "Stay Tuned for Terror," in 1945.

Bloch would later use the Ripper in another short story, "A Toy for Juliette," which appeared in the Harlan Ellison's famous anthology *Dangerous Visions* (1967). Ellison himself used Bloch's story as a springboard for a Ripper story of his own called "The Prowler in the City at the Edge of the World" (1967), featuring the madman in a futuristic setting.

In 1967, Jack was the subject of a "Star Trek" episode, also written by Bloch, called "Wolf in the Fold." That second-season story found Captain Kirk and Dr. McCoy escorting Chief Engineer Scott, who is recovering from a head wound accidentally inflicted on him by a female crewmember, to a nightclub on the planet Aregelius II. There, Scotty becomes enamored of a lovely dancer and they leave together. Kirk and McCoy remain in the bar. A scream sends them to a mist-filled alley adjacent to the bar, where they find Scotty holding the dancer's corpse and a bloody knife. McCoy suggests that perhaps Scotty's subconscious distrust of women since his accident has manifested itself in murder. Hengist, the local constable, wants to arrest Scotty, but Kirk intervenes. Unfortunately, another local is killed, and, once again, Scotty appears to be the perpetrator. Before she dies, the woman says that something with an insatiable hunger and hatred of women is present in the room. Scotty still claims to have amnesia during the time when the women were killed. In the end, the entity turns out to be an ancient life form that calls itself Redjac, which Spock identifies as an alternate name for Earth's Jack the Ripper. The entity reveals itself as a non-corporeal vampire who thrives on others' fear. Apparently, it preys on women because they "are more easily frightened." Hengist is its current host; when discovered, it leaves his body and takes over Kirk's ship, the U.S.S. *Enterprise*. Seeking to thwart the creature, McCoy administers tranquilizers to all on board, dampening their fear. Enraged, the entity is forced to return to Hengist's body. Hoping this would happen, Kirk beams it into space at maximum dispersal, where it will presumably die for lack of nourishment.

Director/writer Nicholas Meyer put the killer to interesting use in his 1979 movie *Time After Time*, which had the Ripper escape to modern-day America using a time machine created by H. G. Wells. Wells (played by Malcolm McDowell) follows the killer (played by David Warner) to the future, hoping to bring him to justice.

In the late 1990s, the creative team of Alan Moore and Eddie Campbell created a lengthy graphic novel based on Moore's research into the Ripper's crimes titled *From Hell* (2004). This critically acclaimed work, which originally appeared (appropriately) serially in a standard comic book format, pinned the murders on the Queen's physician, William Gull. Moore and Campbell's graphic novel eventually became the basis for the 2001 film of the same name, featuring Johnny Depp, Heather Graham, Ian Holm, and Robbie Coltrane.

Horror writer Richard Laymon offered an interesting solution to the Whitechapel murders; like others, he guessed that the Ripper had escaped to America, where he resumed his killing ways on the frontier. Laymon's novel *Savage* (1993) tells the story of Trevor, a young man impacted by the killer's actions, who tracks him to America, hoping to put an end to the madman.

In Michael Slade's *Ripper* (1994), American feminist Brigid Marsh is found hanging dead in Vancouver, her face flayed. Local Mountie Nick Craven calls in Robert de Clerq, commander of Special X, an elite division of the Mounties specializing in outré crime. Marsh's murder has the hallmarks both of satanic ritual and serial murder and, as other grisly deaths ensue, they seem to be following a pattern established in *Jolly Roger*, a new paperback thriller due to be published soon. As de Clerq uses the novel to trace the motivations of the group of killers back to the same demons that drove the original Jack the Ripper, a coven of mystery writers and an ex-police chief find members of their group being killed off as they try to solve the mystery on an isolated island.

CONCLUSION

Serial killer mania seemed to reach its zenith in the early 1990s, an era marked by the premiere of the film version of *The Silence of the Lambs* and the issuance of a 54-card set of serial killer trading cards by Eclipse Enterprises. Despite a noticeable lessening of interest in them since then, serial killers have never totally been out of the spotlight since (witness the news coverage in the aftermath of the capture of the BTK killer in 2005). Because the media understandably focus on sensational news, real life serial killers will continue to be obsessively scrutinized whenever they emerge, thus insuring that they will remain a part of the public's collective consciousness. As a result, consumers in search of thrills will continue to eagerly seek out fictional treatments about these killers, whether it be through film or literature (for instance, Thomas Harris's next book featuring Hannibal Lector, listed on Amazon.com as *Behind the Mask*). Hopefully, through advances in medical science's understanding of the causes of this sad phenomenon, serial killers may one day become a part of folklore, rather than continuing to dominate current events.

BIBLIOGRAPHY

Primary

Fiction

Bloch, Robert. *American Gothic*, New York: Simon & Schuster, 1974.

———. *Psycho*. New York: Simon & Schuster, 1959.

———. *The Scarf*. New York: Dial Press, 1947.

———. "A Toy for Juliette." In *Dangerous Visions*, ed. Harlan Ellison. Garden City, NY: Doubleday, 1967.

———. "Yours Truly, Jack the Ripper." In *The Best of Robert Bloch*. New York: Ballantine, 1977.

Bowman, Eric. *Before I Wake*. New York: Putnam, 1997.

Campbell, Ramsey. *The Count of Eleven*. London: MacDonald, 1991.

———. *The Face That Must Die*. 1979. Santa Cruz, CA: Scream Press, 1983.

Carr, Caleb. *The Alienist*. New York: Random House, 1994.

———. *The Angel of Death*. New York: Random House, 1997.

Cave, Hugh B. "*Psycho* by Robert Bloch." In *Horror: 100 Best Books,* ed. Stephen Jones and Kim Newman. London: Xanadu, 1988.

Connell, Richard. "The Most Dangerous Game." 1924. In *The Most Dangerous Game*. Whitefish, MT: Kessinger, 2004.

Connelly, Michael. *The Narrows*. Boston, MA: Little, Brown, 2003.

———. *The Poet*. Boston: Little, Brown, 1996.

Crouch, Blake. *Desert Places*. New York: St. Martin's Press, 2004.

———. *Locked Doors*. New York: St. Martin's Press, 2005.

Deaver, Jeffrey. *The Bone Collector*. New York: Viking, 1997.

Dobyns, Stephen. *The Church of Dead Girls*. New York: Metropolitan, 1997.

Dorsey, Tim. *Cadillac Beach*. New York: Morrow, 2005.

Ellis, Bret Easton. *American Psycho*. New York: Vintage, 1991.

Ellison, Harlan. "The Prowler in the City on the Edge of the World." In *Dangerous Visions*, ed. Harlan Ellison. Garden City, NY: Doubleday, 1967.

Ellroy, James. *Silent Terror*. New York: Avon, 1990.

Frost, Gregory. *Fitcher's Brides*. New York: Tor, 2002.

Gaiman, Neil. *The Sandman, Volume II: The Doll's House*. New York: Vertigo, 1991.

Harris, Thomas. *Hannibal*. New York: Delacorte Press, 1999.

———. *Red Dragon*. New York: Putnam, 1981.

———. *The Silence of the Lambs*. New York: St. Martin's Press, 1988.

Hewson, David. *The Sacred Cut*. London: Macmillan, 2005.

Highsmith, Patricia. *The Talented Mr. Ripley*. New York: Coward-McCann, 1955.

Kesserling, Joseph. *Arsenic and Old Lace*. New York: Random House, 1941.

Ketchum, Jack. *Off Season*. New York: Ballantine, 1981.

King, Stephen. *The Dead Zone*. New York: Viking, 1979.

King, Stephen, and Peter Straub. *Black House*. New York: Random House, 2001.

Laymon, Richard. *Savage*. London: Headline, 1993.

Lindsay, Jeff. *Darkly Dreaming Dexter*. New York: Doubleday, 2004.

Lowndes, Marie Belloc. *The Lodger*. London: Readers Library, 1913.

March, William. *The Bad Seed*. New York: Rinehart & Co., 1954.

Marshall, Michael. *The Straw Men*. London: HarperCollins, 2002.

McCarthy, Cormac. *Blood Meridian*. New York: Random House, 1985.

Miller, Rex. *Slob*. New York: Signet, 1987.

Moore, Alan, and Eddie Campbell. *From Hell*. Marietta, GA: Top Shelf Productions, 1994.

Oates, Joyce Carol. *Zombie*. New York: Dutton, 1995.

O'Connor, Flannery. "A Good Man Is Hard to Find." In *A Good Man Is Hard to Find*. New York: Harcourt Brace, 1955.

Patterson, James. *Along Came a Spider*. Boston: Little, Brown, 1993.

Prill, David. *Serial Killer Days*. New York: St. Martin's Press, 1996.

Randisi, Robert. *Arch Angels*. New York: St. Martin's Press, 2004.

Sanders, Lawrence. *The First Deadly Sin*. New York: Putnam, 1973.

Sanford, John. *Rules of Prey*. New York: Putnam, 1990.

Sebold, Alice. *The Lovely Bones*. Boston: Little, Brown, 2002.

Slade, Michael. *Headhunter*. Toronto: Penguin, 1984.

———. *Ripper*. London: Hodder & Stoughton, 1994.

Stevens, Shane. *By Reason of Insanity*. New York: Simon & Schuster, 1978.

Stoker, Bram. *Dracula*. London: Constable, 1897.

Straub, Peter. *Koko*. New York: Dutton, 1988.

———. *lost boy lost girl*. New York: Random House, 2003.

———. *The Throat*. New York: Dutton, 1993.

Tessier, Thomas. *Finishing Touches*. New York: Atheneum, 1986.

———. *The Nightwalker*. London: Macmillan, 1979.

Thompson, Jim. *The Killer Inside Me*. New York: Lion, 1952.

Webb, Don. *Endless Honeymoon*. New York: St. Martin's Press, 2001.

Films

Dressed to Kill. Directed by Brian De Palma. Filmways, 1980.

Frenzy. Directed by Alfred Hitchcock. Universal, 1972.

The Frighteners. Directed by Peter Jackson. Universal, 1996.

Henry: Portrait of a Serial Killer. Directed by John McNaughton. Maljack, 1986.

The Hills Have Eyes. Directed by Wes Craven. Blood Relations Co., 1977.

The Lodger. Directed by Alfred Hitchcock. Gainsborough, 1927.

M. Directed by Fritz Lang. Nero-Film, 1931.

Psycho. Directed by Alfred Hitchcock. Paramount, 1960.

Serial Mom. Directed by John Waters. Polar Entertainment Corp., 1994.

Seven. Directed by David Fancher. New Line Cinema, 1995.

Shadow of a Doubt. Directed by Alfred Hitchcock. Universal, 1943.

The Stepfather. Directed by Joseph Ruben. ITC, 1987.

The Texas Chainsaw Massacre. Directed by Tobe Hooper. Vortex, 1974.

Time After Time. Directed by Nicholas Meyer. Warner Bros., 1979.

Secondary

Castledon, Rodney. *Serial Killers*. London: Time Warner, 2005.

Greig, Charlotte. *Evil Serial Killers*. New York: Barnes & Noble, 2005.

Newton, Michael. *The Encyclopedia of Serial Killers.* New York: Checkmark, 2000.
Ressler, Robert K., and Thomas Schachtman. *Whoever Fights Monsters.* New York: St. Martin's Press, 1992.
Schecter, Harold. *The Serial Killer Files.* New York: Ballantine, 2004.

Web sites

www.crimelibrary.com
www.mayhem.net
www.wikipedia.org

The Siren

by Melissa Mia Hall

At first she sang "Come to Love," and of the sweetness of Love she said many things. And next she sang, "Come to Life;" and life was sweet in her song. But long before I reached her, she knew that all her will was mine: and then her voice rose softer than ever, and her words were, "Come to Death;" and Death's name in her mouth was the very swoon of all sweetest things that can be...

Dante Gabriel Rossetti, "The Orchard Pit" (1868) (Weeks 30)

"All men are my slaves and—glad to be!"

Marlene Dietrich in *The Devil Is a Woman* (1935)

This seductive icon of horror and the supernatural is often associated with her equally alluring sister, the femme fatale. The roots of this enchanting but often deadly icon run deep into the ocean of Greek myth, but now no longer remain strictly in the water or in the air. Now she finds her admirers (or victims) on land as well.

Homer wrote about them in Book IV and Book XII of the *Odyssey*. In the beginning, Sirens were merely lovely, unlucky sea-nymphs cursed by Circe, a jealous and very dangerous sorceress who turned any man who approached her into a beast. The naiads are thought to be the daughters of Zeus, and they reigned over fresh-water sources such as fountains, wells, streams, and springs. As enchanted half-women, half-seahawks, sometimes they are confused with the monstrous winged harpies, who were sisters of Iris, daughter of Electra and Thaumas. Originally Hesiod (*Theogony*) described the harpies as two "lovely-haired creatures" (99), but as the myths were retold, the harpies increased in number and transformed into fierce ugly creatures who not only stole human food but ruined what they didn't eat. They also had an extreme fondness for torturing people. So the confusion over the beautiful Sirens and repulsive harpies creates both a dark agent of destruction as much as well as a gorgeous sexual temptress. Factor in extraordinary musical ability, the evolution of Greek Siren into today's glamorous Femme Fatale is not surprising, and her place in horror and the supernatural continues to expand with her claws digging with a vengeance. The Siren's path also cuts into other genres, including comedy, mystery (film noir especially), general fiction, fantasy, and paranormal romance. She can be found flourishing in all areas of entertainment literature and visual media. Beauty plus talent plus power equals an enduring and beloved dark icon. Whether an intelligent empowered vixen, a misunderstood woman in a thriller, refusing to be a victim or a shrill, brazen hussy in a sexploitation potboiler, she is a stunner who enlightens and entertains her captive audience.

Such a dangerous combination is not only valued in contemporary society; it appears to frighten those who do not have it. The gorgeous woman (or man?) of supernatural power, especially in the bedroom, appeals to everyone even as it creates tension. Someone totally self-absorbed, using such power for their own ends, is terrifying if their own ends means something awful will happen to you if you don't submit.

Plato saw the Sirens producing the harmony of the Speres in the *Republic*, and throughout time they have been used as metaphors for the lust for knowledge as well as lots and lots of sex and turbulent desire for power.

Sirens have also been transformed into harpies, screaming monsters, and the "winged things that hunt in the night" of Robert E. Howard ("Wings in

A Legend in Her Own Mind

One of the best examples of a femme fatale who doesn't know she has lost her power is Norma Desmond in Billy Wilder's *Sunset Boulevard* (1950). Gloria Swanson plays Norma Desmond, a forgotten silent screen Siren hoping for a comeback, praying for another close-up. William Holden plays Joe Gillis, a young writer who is being kept by her. Swanson was only fifty-three when she made the film, although Desmond seems much older (mentally she's unstable). Curiously, the character is supposed to be only fifty years old, a reflection of the era in which it was made, when women of a certain age suddenly became, well, ancient.

In *The Great Movies* (349) Roger Ebert notes:

> "*Sunset Blvd.* remains the best drama ever made about the movies because it sees through the illusions, even if Norma Desmond doesn't. When the silent star first greets the penniless writer inside her mansion, they have a classic exchange. 'You used to be big,' he says. Norma responds with the great line 'I *am* big. It's the pictures that got small.' Hardly anyone remembers Joe's next line: 'I knew there was something wrong with them.'"

the Night," *Weird Tales*, July 1932), who have more in common with vampire bats than mystical Sirens. And the bloodthirsty and sexy Queen in Howard's "The Moon of Skulls" (*Weird Tales*, June–July 1930), who may or may not be a vampire, certainly qualifies as a Siren who has turned into a femme fatale. The original Sirens were great beauties who could captivate lonely, love-starved sailors and lure them to their doom or captivity. The lonely Sirens did not necessarily enjoy watching a sailor die. And some mermaids in folklore take human shape in order to be loved by an earthbound man. She might then lure him deep into Poseidon's watery kingdom because she wants him to become a merman, not because she wants him to drown. Or maybe she just wants to have fun, like the Southern Sirens who tempt the three hapless escaped convicts in Ethan and Joel Cohen's *O Brother, Where Art Thou?* (2000), a wry Depression-era update of the *Odyssey*. Ulysses Everett McGill (George Clooney) and his pals encounter three gospel-singing naiads who seduce them into a river of temptation, then vanish after leading one of the trio straight into the hands of the law.

The harpy aspect is not to be confused with the mermaid or lovely sea nymph whose siren song—

> . . . To seek the unforgotten face
> Once seen, once kissed, once reft from me
> Anigh the murmuring of the sea.

—lures a certain golden haired Greek hero into a blissful sleep and summons her fellow sisters of the deep to capture the hopelessly enamored Theban Hylas (who was foolish enough to visit a mermaid haunted place) and drag him into the depths of the sea—wondering:

> At all his beauty they desired so much.
> And then with gentle hands began to touch
> His hair, his hands, his closed eyes; and at last
> Their eager naked arms about him cast,
> And bore him, sleeping still, as by some spell,
> Unto the depths where they were wont to dwell'
> And with small noise the gurgling river hid
> The flushed nymphs and the heedless sleeping man.
> But ere the water covered them, one ran
> Across the mead and caught up from the ground
> The brass-bound spear, and buckler bossed and round,
> The ivory-hilted sword, and coat of mail,
> Then took the stream; so what might tell the tale,
> Unless the wind should tell it, or the bird
> Who from the reed these things had seen and heard?
>   William Morris, *The Life and Death of Jason* (1867), Book 4

Contrast that depiction with Book V's description of the harpies (also referred to as "Snatchers") tormenting Phineus and later, poor Jason and the Argo crew:

> The dreadful Snatchers, who like women were
> Down to the breast, with scanty coarse black hair
> About their heads, and dim eyes ringed with red,
> And bestial mouths set round with lips of lead,
> But from their gnarled necks there began to spring
> Half hair, half feathers, and a sweeping wing
> Grew out instead of arm on either side,
> And thick plum underneath the breast did hide
> The place where joined the fearful natures twain.
> Grey feathered were they else, with many a stain
> Of blood thereon, and on birds' claws they went.

Not so attractive an image, not like the Germanic legend, Lorelei or Lore Lay as Clemens Brentano dubbed her in 1801, in his ballad about a Rhine maiden whose eyes no man could apparently resist. Only poor Lorelei killed herself because she couldn't handle being a Siren, but she still sings to warn sailors *away* from dangerous rocks.

LILITH AND OTHERS

In Judeo-Christian myth, Lilith, Adam's supposed first wife, is thrown over for Eve, kicked out of Eden because she was not a good wife or perhaps because she wanted to be equal to Adam. Was it the first divorce? Was it a bad one? Was Lilith just a bitch or a femme fatale? George MacDonald, a Scottish author who excelled in children's fantasy literature, wrote a feverish adult fantasy about her mystique, *Lilith* (1895). And Lilith has also inspired many other works, including Remy de Gourmont's play *Lilith* (1892). Jules Lemaître wrote a story about her in "Lilith" (1890), and Penelope Farmer wrote a feminist novel, *Eve: Her Story* (1985).

Brian Stableford described the deadly femme fatale as a "a woman whose powers of sexual attraction are so great that her pursuers become utterly careless of their own well-being, often perishing as a result" (Joshi and Dziemianowicz 411). Stableford edited *The Dedalus Book of Femme Fatales* (1992). He cited Salome, another archetypal femme fatale of Judeo-Christian myth. Salome, the daughter of Herodias, not only pleased Herod with her dancing and claimed the head of John the Baptist as her reward; she served as the muse in *Salome* (1893) by Oscar Wilde; *Salome the Wandering Jewess* (1930) by George Sylvester Viereck and Paul Eldridge; *Salome, Princess of Galilee* by Henry Denker (1952), *Veils of Salome* (1962) by John Jakes, revised by Jay Scotland (1976), and "Herodias" (1877) by Gustave Flaubert.

Enter Cleopatra, another ancient Siren whose legendary power over men has figured in film and in literature for years. French author Théophile Gautier wrote "Un Nuit de Cléopâtre" ("One of Cleopatra's Nights," 1838), serving as an early expert in discovering the erotic power of this femme fatale. He also wrote "La Morte Amoureuse," often translated as "Clarimonde."

Are all Sirens just angry women out for blood or a better bank account? And what about blood-drinking lamias or the sexy vampire brides in *Dracula* by Bram Stoker (1897), the lesbian vampire in "Carmilla" (*Dark Blue*, December 1871–March 1872) by J. Sheridan Le Fanu, or Akasha, the mother of all vampires in *The Queen of the Damned* by Anne Rice (1988)? The blood-sucking predator who has become a vampire via another's "curse" or "bite" kills for survival by seducing victims not only with her magnetic beauty but also the considerable lure of immortality. The vampire appears to be just another variation of the Siren theme.

Fritz Leiber honed in on the Siren as the "model" vampire, focusing on man's desire for a very primal, predatory "image" that devours as much as it satisfies in his timeless story, "The Girl with the Hungry Eyes" (1949). This story heralds the arrival of the contemporary fashion/pop icon as Siren and begs the question, whether a man or woman turns a victim into a vampire by seduction, which makes the vampire a blood relation (pun intended) to the Siren.

Witches are also related to Sirens dating back to the Arthurian era. Remember Morgan Le Fey? King Arthur's beloved Merlin could testify to the dangers of dealing with a Siren enchantress: his seductive nemesis certainly knew how to work her fatal powers. Being ensorcelled into a tree, Merlin, a wizard as well, still suffered from a Siren who knew how to ensnare men to do their bidding. Many fantasies have explored Celtic Sirens memorably. Arthurian classics include *The Once and Future King* (1958) and *The Book of Merlin* (1977), both by T. H. White, and Marion Zimmer Bradley's *The Mists of Avalon* (1982).

Fritz Leiber focused on the fear men have of being married to a Siren with weird powers in *Conjure Wife* (*Unknown*, April 1943). Anne Rice has explored the delights of the seductress Witch in *The Witching Hour* (1990) and *Merrick* (2000). And more mainstream authors like Alice Hoffman have examined the allure of contemporary sister Sirens who embrace being part of a family of witches in *Practical Magic* (1995). And who can forget the devilishly funny film *The Witches of Eastwick* (1987), based on the novel (1984) by John Updike, starring witchy Sirens, Susan Sarandon, Michele Pfieffer, and Cher taunting his Satanic majesty as played by Jack Nicholson?

The traditional witch canon is filled with sexy urban witches including the happy-go-lucky Tabitha, played by Elizabeth Montgomery in the popular 1960s sitcom "Bewitched" (Nicole Kidman in the flawed 2004 updated film tries and fails to capture the wit Montgomery brought to the role, although her nose-twitching skills were impressive). Other contemporary TV witches include the young vixens on "Charmed" (1998–): Prue (Shannon Doherty) is no longer on the show, but Phoebe (Alyssa Milano), Piper (Holly Marie Combs), and Paige (Rose McGowan) mix a little Siren mojo in with their wiccan skills on occasion to achieve their desires with flair but little, if any, evil intent.

Can a man be a Siren, an homme fatale who seduces his victim through his handsome charms? If he is sexy, elegant, and good with the drums, piano, or cars, well, why not? If "La Belle Dame sans Merci" (from the John Keats poem) meets the *man* without mercy, what do they beget? A glittering child of power who wants nothing more than to be fearless and in total control, a subject that lends itself to the creation of a monster or a saint. A monster or a saint can't be controlled if he or she is utterly fearless. Add in a sexually gorgeous body and abundant multi-talents (music, art, lust, gardening, or even extreme expertise in haute cuisine, Swedish massage, sports, financial wizardry, or acting) and a siren is a deadly diva, a master of erotic power, or merely a witch. By seduction we know the Siren. By fearlessness we know the femme or homme fatale.

In Germany and Scandinavia the shapeshifting Näcken or Nix are male water spirits who enchant listeners with their violin music. Pregnant women and children, especially unbaptised children, are thought to be especially vulnerable to the handsome Nix. Mysterious drowning deaths were sometimes attributed to hearing the spellbinding songs of these dangerous male Sirens, but some folk tales suggest they can also be harmless, unlike the female Siren of Greek myth. The Nixe is a river mermaid who can be male or female, who lures unsuspecting humans to a watery death, much like the Celtic Melusine, a female water spirit who appears to be a fish, serpent, or a dragon from the waist down. She can also mate with humans.

The Huldra is a Wild Woman mixture of Siren and femme fatale because she is not only female and gorgeous but can also use her considerable seduction skills to achieve her desires. She does not fly or live near water but in the forests of Scandinavia. She has a cow or fox tail and lures men to have sex with her. If she is pleased, he is rewarded; if not, he is cruelly punished.

The Wild Woman is a woman in touch with her primal self, like an animal or femme fatale, intent on survival at all costs. The Siren who has evolved into a deadly femme fatale and then grown up is the empowered woman who has thrown off Circe's curse. She can be good or evil. If she is vengeful, it is because she is protecting something or someone, but still has an almost magical power much like the Naiads before Circe took out her jealous wrath upon them. She is a Force of Nature who is free and in total control of her life, for good or ill.

CAN A MAN CREATE A FEMALE SIREN?

George du Maurier created Svengali, a fictional siren-maker in his self-illustrated novel, *Trilby* (1894). He is far more dangerous than Professor Higgins of *My Fair Lady* (inspired by George Bernard Shaw's *Pygmalion*), who merely transformed a grubby little flower seller into a glamorous high society Ascot-attending beauty. Fans of the classic musical might remember stuffy Rex Harrison falling for Audrey Hepburn's Eliza Doolittle. He was a charming, gently archaic, vaguely chauvinistic "Svengali" of sorts, but du Maurier's Svengali was evil and domineering, and his mesmerizing transformation of Trilby, the artist's model, into a singing "Siren" is one of the aspects of the Siren which should be remembered: A Siren is created by others, usually someone of power.

Svengali manipulated a young and beautiful artist model to his ends, hypnotizing her into singing a siren's song to achieve fame and fortune. Thus the false "siren" became a puppet for the true Siren, the manipulative Svengali whose power over her vanishes when she assumes her own self, throwing off her magic spell, much as a sailor might have survived the siren song heard off the island.

The Siren song of seduction that lures the sailor to the rocky shores of the lonely naiads changes over time. And the curse hurled at Sirens probably should be directed at the Circes or Svengalis who created them. It is significant that Sirens became winged harpies, devilish divas, vixens, vamps, femmes fatales, or wild women because they were *cursed or threatened* by jealous power-hungry entities. The sea nymphs were given the magic of flight; but due to the curse they did not know how to remove, they could not escape the area surrounding the Amazons' island. How could they control their own power in order to satisfy their needs?

The sailors who listened to the Siren's call are rumored in myth to have crashed their ships on the rocks near the fabled island populated only by warrior women, the Amazons. Thus the forbidden dark side of the Siren gave birth to the femme fatale and to the female vampire and the more feral aspects of the unfettered female, the wild woman.

Eventually, as the Siren left the sea and made landfall in the contemporary world, the manipulated siren controls her own destiny and revels in her power, whether it is to seduce or merely survive. A great modern cinematic symbol for this transformation is found in *La Femme Nikita* (1990). A young street punk is transformed into a gorgeous killing machine only to be manipulated by a covert French agency. Nikita, a Siren, thanks to the expert training and her own natural beauty and talent, chooses to take control of a bad situation and liberates herself from those who would manipulate her, doing what the original Sirens could not do—remove the curse. The original French film features a César award-winning performance by Anne Parrilaud and was written and directed by the formidable Luc Besson. This Siren is a wild woman who makes her own rules in order to survive. Nikita is a street junkie turned weapon for a secret government agency. This particular woman is beyond being empowered; she is triumphantly determined to survive at all costs, even if it means destroying or enchanting a man or a woman via questionable but glamorous means. But she uses her brains as much as her body. *Point of No Return* (1993) was an American remake of this French film, and a successful American TV series, "La Femme Nikita" (1997–2001), starring Peta Wilson, lasted five years.

DANGEROUS BEAUTY

The contemporary Siren handles the role well by celebrating it, but sometimes her sheer beauty and power may draw too much attention or tempt her to overestimate her strength when she makes a landfall. The sea-nymph Siren, the mermaid, and the harpy make earliest landfall most notably in the artistic and literary movement created by the Pre-Raphaelites. The art of the Pre-Raphaelites was notable for developing the earthly vision of sirens who did not have to be bound to the sea. Three young British artists John Everett Millais (1829–1896), Dante Gabriel Rossetti, and William Holman Hunt (1827–1910) originated the Pre-Raphaelite Brotherhood in 1848, and by the mid-1850s Millais and Hunt had fallen away from the group as others joined, including Algernon Charles Swinburne (1837–1909), William Morris (1834–1896), and Edward Burne-Jones (1835–1898).

Rossetti's romantic Pre-Raphaelite portraits come to mind. *Venus Verticordia* (1864–1868) is wonderful as Jane Burden Morris posing as a goddess who is either dead or alive. What we do know is that she is holding an arrow pointed at one of her exposed breasts. Rossetti idolized beautiful women, especially Lizzie Siddal, his doomed model/wife, and Fanny Conforth, another flame-haired stunner, but his absolute favorite model and object of somewhat unrequited lust was Jane Burden, the wife of William Morris. Janey became a lifelong obsession, but with Siren-like zeal her constant rejection of him appeared to hasten his death. One notable portrait, *Proserpine* (1873–1877) recalls another stunner so beautiful that the Greek god Hades stole her from earth to make her the Queen of his underworld.

Janey, though, was not as ethereal as his second great love. Elizabeth "Lizzie" Siddal was a flame-haired millinery clerk who first caught his eye. Her pale, delicate beauty also inspired John Everett Millais, another artist of the Pre-Raphaelite Brotherhood, to paint his iconic painting of Shakespeare's Ophelia (1852), a painting that has forever captured Lizzie's haunting Siren-like quality as she floats, in luminous death, hands outstretched.

Lizzie Siddal represents the tragic quality of the Siren. Rossetti fell in love with a fragile woman with her own artistic talent with an addiction to chloral (prescribed after a miscarriage) that caused her death in 1852. Lizzie was the archetype of what came to be known as the Pre-Raphaelite stunner who seduced artists such as Rossetti and Edward Burne-Jones and photographers like Julia Margaret Cameron, who was not immune to reproducing the PRB type in her Victorian photographs. Artists of later periods further glamorized or focused on the erotic image of the Siren archetype of devastatingly attractive icons, particularly the Symbolists and other early contemporary artists who were addicted to depicting sirens whose sexuality shouts off the canvas in an often feral way. Among them are Gustave Moreau; Fernand Hodler; Franz von Stuck, whose *Sin* (1897) depicts a pale bare-breasted diva shrouded in shadow; Emile Bernard; Paul Gauguin (*Ondine* [1889] evokes the Siren best); Gustave Klimt; Félix Vallotton; Toulouse Lautrec; Odilon Redon; Puvis de Chavanne; Henri Matisse; John William Waterhouse; Evelyn de Morgan; Edvard Munch; Jean Delville; Alphonse Mucha; and notably, two Surrealists, Salvador Dali (his wife Gala was very much a real-life femme fatale) and René Magritte. Picasso, of course, also heeded the Siren call, as did other contemporary artists such as Tamara de Lempicka, Vargas, Yves Klein, Joan Brown, and fashion photographers like Helmut Newton, Richard Avedon, Annie Leibovitz, and cheesecake photographers such as Bruno Bernard, David Hamilton, and others. Bernard's staged studio images of Marilyn Monroe echo the sad quality of how the original Sirens' eyes must have looked after Circe ensorcelled them, haunted and feral, the "hungry eyes" of women who have been cursed by fate or circumstances beyond their control.

Jan Marsh noted society's tendency to take PRB models and turn them into stars: "the romance of the Pre-Raphaelite women tends both to glorify them, raising them like Hollywood film stars above the level of ordinary mortals into a mythic realm of tragic heroine and fatal sirens, and paradoxically to diminish them, reducing their contradictory personalities and lives to flat figures in a fantasy landscape" (*Pre-Raphaelite Sisterhood* 3).

Siren worship thrives in pop media's fascination with fashion models ranging from vintage superstars Verushka, Twiggy, Lauren Hutton, and Iman, to younger mannequins like Naomi Campbell, Tyra Banks, and Kate Moss—whose every travail is covered with the same morbid delight as the sundry life stories of screen celebrities like Angelina Jolie, Julia Roberts, Pamela Sue Anderson, Demi Moore, Britney Spears, Madonna, Gwyneth Paltrow, Drew Barrymore, Jennifer Aniston, and other stunners. Will they gain the mystique of classic screen femmes fatales Greta Garbo, Marilyn Monroe, Jean Harlow, and Rita Hayworth? Only time will tell, but the key thing to remember is how they reflect a quality that all classic Sirens should have: beauty that tantalizes and lures men or women just as honey attracts bees.

THE SEDUCTIVE SHORT STORY

The Siren features in many short stories in all genres. It would be impossible to make a comprehensive "best of" list, but it is always fun to provide a menu of short stories that will remind readers why they are so enjoyable.

There are anthologies that feature Sirens, femmes fatales, wild women, or dangerous divas who use their seductive powers for revenge or just entertainment. A few titles: *The Dadelus Book of Femmes Fatales*, edited by Brian Stableford; *Wild Women*, edited by Sue Thomas (1994); *Wild Women*, edited by Melissa Mia Hall (1997); *Love Kills*, edited by Ed Gorman and Martin Greenberg (1997); *Sirens and Other Daemon Lovers*, edited by Ellen Datlow and Terri Windling (1998). Others target the Siren's (male and female) erotic powers as found in *I Shudder at Your Touch* (1991) and *Shudder Again* (2003), both edited by Michele Slung; *Alien Sex* (Dutton, 1990), *Little Deaths* (1994), and *Lethal Kisses* (1996), all edited by Ellen Datlow. *The Mammoth Book of Vampire Stories by Women*, edited by Stephen Jones (2002) provides many toothsome Vamp Sirens as well.

A chronological listing of pivotal sirens/femmes fatales stories:

I cannot, for my soul, remember how, when, or even precisely where, I first became acquainted with the Lady Ligeia. Long years have elapsed, and my memory is feeble through much suffering. Or, perhaps, I cannot now bring these points to mind, because, in truth, the character of my beloved, her rare learning, her singular yet placed cast of beauty, and the thrilling and enthralling eloquence of her low musical language, made their way into my heart by paces so steadily and stealthily progressive, that they have been unnoticed and unknown.

—*Edgar Allan Poe, "Ligeia"*

---

1. "Ligeia" (*Baltimore American Museum*, September 1838) by Edgar Allan Poe. Poe's early American grotesque tale of obsessive love might very well be his masterpiece. A perverse, nameless narrator falls in love with the Lady Ligeia, who sickens and dies but whose Femme Fatale persona leads him into opium addiction and encourages the torture of his beautiful young wife Rowena, whose dying body becomes the vessel for Ligeia's ill-fated return.

2. "Berenice" (*Southern Literary Messenger*, March 1835; revised and republished in *Broadway Journal*, April 5, 1845) by Edgar Allan Poe. Poe excelled in writing about Femmes Fatales, as they symbolized his mistrust of seductive women and romance in general. Egaeus, the narrator, lives with his beautiful cousin Berenice, who becomes ill. He obsesses about her changing appearance, especially her teeth, to the point where he goes to her grave, unearths her still living corpse, and pulls her haunting teeth.

3. "The Orchard Pit" (1886; in *The Dream Weavers*, ed. John Weeks) by Dante Gabriel Rossetti. This tale is of considerable significance but is often overlooked by readers of the Supernatural Siren. The Siren's evolution from a watery temptress into a more modern land-bound seductress is as important as much as Gautier's Cleopatra Femme Fatale in 1838 and the immortal lovers in John Keats's "Lamia" (1820) and Keats's Femme Fatale in "La Belle Dame sans Merci," whose beauty is the ultimate weapon. Rossetti's Siren story was written in 1869, not long before a failed suicide attempt, and was not published until seventeen years later in *The Collected Works of Dante Gabriel Rossetti* (1886). The lush poetic imagery in the short story becomes rapidly feverish as the protagonist falls deeper into the spell of the Siren of the glen, at first a childish memory, then a present-day beckoning He feels compelled to bite the Siren's apple, to heed her Siren call.

4. "The Great God Pan" (1894) by Arthur Machen. Much has been written about this often reprinted classic about Helen Vaughan, who becomes a

---

Men tell me that sleep has many dreams, but all my life I have dreamt one dream alone.

I see a glen whose sides slope upward from the deep bed of a dried-up stream, and either slope is covered with wild apple-trees. In the largest tree, within the fork whence the limbs divide, a fair golden-haired woman stands and sings, with one white arm stretched along a branch of the tree, and with the other holding forth a bright red apple as if to some one coming down the slope. Below her feet the trees grow more and more tangled and stretch from both sides across the deep pit below: and the pit is full of the bodies of men.

They lie in heaps beneath the screen of boughs, with her apples bitten in their hands' and some are no more than ancient bones now and some seem dead but yesterday. She stands over them in the glen, and sings for ever, and offers her apple still.

—Dante Gabriel Rossetti, "The Orchard Pit"

Siren by mysterious and hideous ways. Is she the progeny of a satyr and Mary, a servant girl who has been operated on by a mad doctor so she can see the Great God Pan? Helen is a Femme Fatale who grows up to have a deadly impact on many men.

5. "How Love Came to Professor Guildea" (1900) by Robert Hichens. A ghost as Siren, and a very unwelcome one at that—she haunts a cold-hearted genius to a tragic end. In this case, the Siren is not at all charming or seductive, she is the antithesis of what this professor believes to be desirable. The ghost is a Femme Fatale who is in love with him, love being something the professor can not understand, leading to heart failure. A tour de force of the imagination and the will of an extraordinary Siren.

5. "The Song of the Sirens" (*Sunset*, March 1909) by Edward Lucas White. White envisioned a more traditional Siren in this quiet jewel, written by the *Weird Tales* writer who also wrote "Sorcery Island" (1922), which featured a male Siren who holds an entire island in thrall.

6. "The Beckoning Fair One" (1911) by Oliver Onions. Onions produced a memorable ghost Siren/Femme Fatale haunting a writer first through a seemingly innocuous song suggested in the title, which also plays upon the musical bent of the original Greek Siren myth. Is he driven insane by the ghost or merely ensorcelled?

7. "The Seal Maiden" (*Cavalier*, November 15, 1913) by Victor Rousseau. Rousseau, a British-born American journalist who also wrote under the name H. M. Egbert, wrote about one of the Siren's well-known mythological relatives, a shapeshifting selky who just happens to be a seductive Femme Fatale in this early fantasy.

8. "Wings in the Night" (*Weird Tales*, July 1932) by Robert E. Howard. Howard tackles the harpies myth in this exciting Solomon Kane adventure, but these creatures are not very attractive. They may have wings but they represent the grotesque side of the Siren.

9. "The Rainy Moon" (1940) by Colette. An overlooked supernatural gem, Colette's exquisite tale is about a Siren's revenge. In Paris, a narrator, a writer much like Colette herself, hires Mademoiselle Rosita Barberet, a middle-aged typist, to temporarily fill in for her regular typist. Rosita lives with her lovely younger sister, Madame Délia Essendier, who is estranged from her husband Eugene—in a flat the narrator once lived in long ago. The flat has a window with an old wavy pane of glass that creates a mysterious colorful "rainy moon" when light shows through it, similar to a prism's rainbow shimmer, once charming and now sinister as the narrator learns what Délia is doing. The pretty neglected wife is one of the most convincing natural "witches" in European literature. She is a Femme Fatale who has decided to kill her husband by putting him to death through magical rituals. Why? Because he has fallen out of love with her. Colette's understated handling of dark magic and the narrator's growing unease with the rituals, cleverly conducted "offstage," enhance the chill factor of convoking and cast a relentless spell over the reader that lingers long after the story is done, much like the silence after a Siren's song has ended.

10. "The Daemon Lover" (*Woman's Home Companion*, February 1949) by Shirley Jackson. Jackson creates a memorable, if invisible, Siren for her lonely protagonist, Margaret, who goes in search of a James Harris, the Daemon Lover of the title. Is he real? Is her exhausting search fruitless? Horrific in its poignant portrait of a woman obsessed with finding a man to love, it also insists that readers make up their own ending.

11. "The Girl with the Hungry Eyes" (1949) by Fritz Leiber. Leiber dissects the glamor-girl complex and the ravenous aspect of the Siren as Goddess and how she is created to distract us from reality.

12. "Hot Eyes, Cold Eyes" (1980) by Lawrence Block. A wonderful story that complements Leiber's. It provides a timeless portrait of the Siren who scorns the adulation of men because of a savage mistrust, reflecting a more Circe-like trait than that of the Siren who does not willingly hurt the men she desires.

13. "Revenge" (1987) by Isabel Allende. Allende wrote several Sirenesque tales in this incredible collection "written" by the protagonist from Allende's novel, *Eva Luna* (1987). This one focuses on the plight of a Dulce Rosa Orellano, who at fifteen was crowned the Queen of Carnival during a civil war. A violent rebel, Tadeo Céspedes murders her father, Senator Orellano, and rapes the young virginal beauty but is forever tormented by his subsequent desire for her. When they meet again, she allows him to love her only to avenge his death and her sorrow in a brutal way on their wedding day.

14. "Tallulah" (1991) by Charles de Lint. De Lint's mysterious Siren in this bittersweet urban fantasy haunts a young Canadian writer. Tallulah or Tally, as she prefers to be called, seduces the writer with a poignant urgency, meeting him only at night in a crumbling section of a city much like Toronto. He falls in love with her and notes, "She mesmerized me—right from that very first night. I sensed a portent in her casual appearance into my life, though a portent of what, I couldn't say" (189). He believes she is a ghost, and her secretive aura about her past loves—"When they move away, they leave my life, because I can't follow them"—suggests that Tally might be cursed to haunt a place much like the island the Greek Sirens could never leave. De Lint's Siren song of lost love is also a shrewd depiction of the Siren motif reflecting the spirit of urban decay.

15. "Medusa's Child" (1991) by Kim Antieau. Antieau presents a Siren vampire/model who poses for artists in order to devour their creativity. It is a fresh take on the model/artist obsession, turning the tables on artists who take advantage of muses. It relates neatly to Leiber's "The Girl with the Hungry Eyes" and the whole bizarre Siren cult of beauty school.

16. "Predators" (1997) by Edward Bryant. This tale features a feral Femme Fatale who is pushed into a corner and retaliates. It is an uncanny exploration of how a Siren fights to survive, even if it means utilizing a physical attribute reminiscent of the traits Circe cursed the original Sirens with. Lisa Blackwell, a young African American, has attracted a violent stalker/serial killer's attentions, and shows how some Sirens must become

deadly Wild Women, not because they want to kill, but because they want to live.

17. "The Merry Widow" (*Mary Higgins Clark Mystery Magazine*, 1996) by Kate Wilhelm. Wilhelm's protagonist, Meg Summer, is a young single mom confronted with Effie Yates, a Femme Fatale favorite, the wealthy black widow. The deft portrait of She Who Could Not Care Less But Will Prevail at All Costs, even if it means leaving multiple murder, presents the symbol with an ironic twist.

18. "Psychofemmes" (1997) by Melissa Mia Hall. This contemporary take on fierce creatures who heed the Siren's call for revenge reflects the ongoing evolution of contemporary Sirens, some of whom become Wild Women and Avenging Angels while others remain unrepentant Femmes Fatales who happily lure men to their deaths. A suburban book club is actually a cover for a killing club for women (housewives, moms, and childless singles as well as career women) who dispatch men or women they perceive as deserving execution. Unfortunately, the leadership of the informal organization is unraveling because of some personal conflicts and dissension among the troubled members.

19. "Hunger" (*Alfred Hitchcock's Mystery Magazine*, 2001) by Joyce Carol Oates. Oates presents the seductive pull of a mysterious drifter ("Summoned by the long-haired young man. Like a dancer, summoned by music she can't resist" [122]) named Jean-Claude, a dangerous male Siren who wears briny-smelling cologne. He captures the heart of Kristine, a bored married mother of a five-year-old. Their first encounter is appropriately at Rocky Harbor, the seashore. An ex-dancer, she notices his graceful movements and his limp with a rush of love at first sight. As her obsession grows she sinks deeper into

---

It's at a distance she first sees him. Not knowing him then.

Yet seeming to recognize him. Shading her eyes as the chill Atlantic surf froths and foams over her bare feet. He's a silhouette crouched amid rocks and sand at the ragged edge of the surf; he seems to be washing his hands, his forearms, splashing water up onto his face. Then he stands, stretches, takes up a backpack, which he slings over his shoulder, and turns to move in her direction. Yet oblivious of her, she thinks. Striding along the beach like a pent-up, now released, young animal....

Kristine thinks, *He's a dancer. A wounded dancer like so many.*

It's one of those swift unexamined thoughts that sometimes fly into Kristine's head when she's in a heightened mood—not alone and not lonely yet alone in her mind—a childish wish (and in this case a lethal wish) that others for whom she feels a mysterious tug of kinship are persons like herself, sharing a secret unspoken bond.

A wounded dancer, an ex-dancer like me.

—Joyce Carol Oates, "Hunger"

---

a misguided, passionate connection leading to the creation of a nightmarish Couple Fatale with horrific consequences.

THE SIREN CALL OF NOVELS AND NOVELLAS

In literature the landscape populated by today's Sirens and femmes fatales is crammed with the deadly diva, most notably in the genres of suspense, mystery, and horror. She uses her beauty to attain whatever goal she has in sight, but she also has brains and considerable skill in many other departments aside from that of seduction.

But seduce she will, if that is what she must do to survive. What follows is the delectable...

Siren watchers are warned that such lists as the following are never conclusive, and the femme fatale in some aspect figures in many novels, whether in leading or supporting roles. Just watch for bad girls, naughty women, dangerous divas, and assorted wild, semi-wild, and very determined women (and men) who will do anything to insure their survival.

1. "Une Nuit de Cléopâtra" (*Presse*, November 29–December 6, 1838) by Théophile Gautier. This French pioneer of the dark fantastic joys found in exploring the Siren and her sibling spirits also wrote a Ghost Siren romance, *Sprite* (1877), about a love affair between a man and beautiful dancer's ghost. It has also been translated as *Spirit Love* and *Stronger Than Death*, which also aptly describes the allure of the Femme Fatale. Brian Stableford observed: "Gautier represents the zenith of Romantic Fantasy...Gautier created the modern Femme Fatale by arguing that death might be a small price to pay for the reward such magically attractive sexual partners might have to offer; his gloriously fantasized worldview is that which all neo-Romantics must attempt to transcend and to which they must default whenever their cynicism fails" (Joshi and Dziemianowicz 456).

2. "Carmilla" (*Dark Blue*, December 1871–March 1872) by J. Sheridan Le Fanu. In a class by itself, this novella about vampirism predates the better-known *Dracula* (1897) by Bram Stoker, who was influenced by its mystique. This vintage lesbian femme fatale is very scary in her elegant, relentless pursuit of a young woman. Dracula's Sirens are more toothsome and traditional but wonderfully unrepentant. But Samuel Taylor Coleridge left an unfinished piece, "Christobel" (1816), that features a female vampire as well.

3. *She* (1886) by H. Rider Haggard. Haggard wrote this to be read as juvenile literature, but it still seems more like an adult testament to the power of the Siren. It is a potboiler, but very memorable in its portrayal of a Goddess type who loses her femme fatale edge and immortality because of her love for a mere mortal, but not before a lot of teeth-gnashing and seductive Siren antics. Should Sirens turn into regular women because of men? Nah!

It was She herself!

She was clothed, as I had seen her when she unveiled, in the kirtle of clinging white, cut low upon her bosom, and bound in at the waist with the barbaric double-headed snake, and, as before, her rippling black hair fell in heavy masses down her back. But her face was what caught my eye, and held me as in a vise, not this time by the force of its beauty, but by the power of fascinated terror. The beauty was still there, indeed, but the agony, the blind passion, and the awful vindictiveness displayed upon those quivering features, and in the tortured look of the upturned eyes, were such as surpass my powers of description.

For a moment she stood still, her hands raised high above her head, and as she did so the white robe slipped from her down to her golden girdle, baring the blinding loveliness of her form. She stood there, her fingers clenched, and the awful look of malevolence gathered and deepened on her face."

—*H. Rider Haggard,* She

4. *Trilby* (1894) by George du Maurier. Du Maurier wrote and illustrated a Victorian masterpiece about how a Siren can be created not just by a Greek sorceress of myth, but by a modern man who uses mesmerism to give a lovely woman extraordinary singing ability.

5. *The Sea Demons* (*All-Story*, January 1–22, 1916) by H. M. Egbert. This hard-to-find early science fiction tale was actually written by a well-known American journalist who wrote under Victor Rousseau and often featured Femmes Fatales in his work. A gorgeous sea queen and her army of misty creatures decide to become Earth's dominant species. The tale shows what can happen when a Siren takes on a Circe-like thirst for domination.

6. *Gone with the Wind* (1936) by Margaret Mitchell. Scarlett O'Hara, Mitchell's unforgettable Southern belle, remains one of the most famous Sirens. Although she has no supernatural powers, Scarlett's vixen persona fits the requirements of the Femme Fatale. Watching Scarlett (Vivien Leigh) in the 1939 film begin to self-destruct after surviving the Civil War is tragic and horrific even as it also inspires viewers, confirming that at the core of the Siren is a delightful paradox—sometimes one must be bad to be good in order to get what one wants. That the reader must decide if Scarlett gets Rhett back is the cherry on the banana split in this sprawling and beguilingly romantic Civil War epic.

7. *Rebecca* (1938) by Daphne du Maurier. Du Maurier created an unforgettable femme fatale in this story about the power a dead first wife exerts over her husband's new wife. The ill Rebecca de Winter stages her own suicide to look like murder by her husband's hands. Made into an Alfred Hitchcock blockbuster in 1940, the novel also spawned two sequels: Susan Hill's *Mrs. De Winter* (1993) and Sally Beauman's *Rebecca's Tale* (2001).

8. *The G-String Murders* (1941) by Gypsy Rose Lee. Lee, a famous stripper, wrote two novels with the help of ghost collaborator, Craig Rice (Georgiana Randolph). Lee's burlesque background enlivened a potboiler that also served as the source material for the film *Lady of Burlesque* (1943), starring Barbara Stanwyck as the stripper crimesolver of multiple murders set against the vivid burlesque backstage world Lee knew so well. Who needs C.S.I. when you've got a stripper on the case? James Gunn wrote the film adaptation.

9. *Laura* (1944) by Vera Caspary. Caspary is not a familiar name to many romantic suspense readers but it should be. She wrote the source material for the more famous film of the same name about the murder of a beautiful woman who captivated many men, including the man investigating her murder. He is struck by a very Siren-like question: Can a man be seduced by a dead woman?

10. *Bedelia* (1945) by Vera Caspary. Caspary also wrote this chilling Black Widow novel. A "kitten with claws of steel," Bedelia uses her seductive Siren powers to produce a string of dead husbands dispatched with cool efficiency, without regrets.

11. *The Bloody Chamber and Other Stories* (1979) by Angela Carter. Carter's critically acclaimed short story collection is so cohesive that her retelling of fairy tales reflects an aspect of the Siren as enchantress, but on her own terms. The supernatural blends with magical realism and classic fantasy motifs that are turned upside down with particular flair. The darkly comic "The Lady of the House of Love" in particular should attract fans of the vampire Siren, as a young countess attracts a male virgin to her house only to find him singularly unappetizing. Carter influenced a new generation of adult fantasy enthusiasts that created an audience for anthologies filled with this new take on fairy tales typified by a series of anthologies beginning with *Snow White, Blood Red* (1993), edited by Terri Windling and Ellen Datlow.

12. *Earthbound* (1982; rev. ed. 1989) by Richard Matheson. This is a unique twist on the ghost femme fatale who seduces a man in order to siphon off his ectoplasm so she can achieve physical substance.

13. *Neptune Rising: Songs & Tales of the Undersea Folk* (1982) by Jane Yolen. Yolen is an award-winning author of both adult and children's literature. This collection of magical stories, beautifully illustrated by David Weisner, is suitable for readers of all ages.

14. *The Woman in Black* (1983) by Susan Hill. Hill's British tale of the supernatural not only has a great title reminiscent of Wilkie Collins's *The Woman in White* (1860), but includes a Ghost Siren out for revenge. It is narrated by a young lawyer who first sees the woman in black at a funeral. The novel is a good example of a Ghost Siren who doesn't have to look like Pamela Anderson, but she endures and usually gets what she wants, no matter what. Set in moody old England's nineteenth century, it was adapted by Stephen Mallatratt into a stage play in 1988.

15. *The Queen of the Damned* (1988) by Anne Rice. Rice's ability to portray vampires and witches as femmes fatales is well known. She has influenced many authors of erotic vampire fiction, including Laurell K. Hamilton of the popular Anita Blake series, Nancy Collins, Nancy Kilpatrick, Charlaine Harris, L. A. Banks, and many others. But the mother of all vampires in this particular book, who wishes to bend Lestat to do her bidding, is an exceptionally striking blend of femme fatale, Siren, and She Who Must Be Obeyed.

16. *Witch* (Little Brown, 1993) by Ian Rankin. The clever and very deadly protagonist in Rankin's thriller is dubbed "Witch," and her powers to elude capture verge on the supernatural. Witch is a wanted outlaw, an assassin who is beautiful, intelligent, a master of disguise and revenge. She is finally captured only after killing the only man she has ever hated, for good reason—her father. Is letting revenge rule her fatal flaw? Can a true Siren go beyond revenge as long as Circe's curse is upon her? Must she become a witch, a modern-day Morgan Le Fey, in order to survive?

17. *The Robber Bride* (1993) by Margaret Atwood. Atwood's satirical take on Zena, a sexy femme fatale, and her devastating impact on three friends. Learning how to deal with the destructive cyclone and the ruins left in the wake of Zena's wrath (or chicanery) in their lives, they also ponder on one of the most salient aspects of the femme fatale—she doesn't have to have a reason to destroy lives.

18. *On Blue's Water* (1999) by Gene Wolfe. Wolfe's first book of The Short Sun, a fantasy series—it takes place after Wolfe's four-volume Book of the Long Sun—features the beguiling Seawrack, a good Siren who becomes Horn's guide and beloved helpmate on an Odyssey-like seafaring search for Patera Silk, a wise leader who is much needed on Planet Blue. Seawrack is one Siren who has shaken off the bad curse karma but still has a bittersweet parting with the narrator who laments losing her.

19. *Femme Fatale* (2003) by Carole Nelson Douglas. Douglas has written a series of mystery novels expanding on Sir Arthur Conan Doyle's fringe

---

She didn't look out to sea, but she listened to it. The steady clash of waves, the whistling wind. Exhilarating. Her hair, pinned back, was still drying quickly, her scalp chilled by the wind. A sharp salt smell clung to her. Her eyes were closed slightly as she listened. Then in the distance, she heard a loudish pop, there and then not there. Like the meeting o f balloon and pin at a children's party. She knew she had measured the amount of the charge well, and had placed it well, too, down in the bowels of the boat. The hole blown in the hull would be a couple of yard in diameter. The vessel would sink in seconds, seconds of shock and horror for its crew. And if the explosion didn't kill the two men outright . . . well, what chance of their reaching land? No chance for the older man, minimal for the younger.

—Ian Rankin, Witch

---

character, Irene Adler, the only woman to outsmart Sherlock Holmes. In this installment Adler investigates her own mother's past to uncover the identity of one of the most notorious women of the nineteenth century.

20. *Holy Skirts* (2005) by René Steinke. Steinke delivered a fantastic fictional portrait of a real-life Siren, Baroness Elsa von Freytag-Loringhoven, who modeled for Man Ray and Marcel Duchamp. Set during the fabled years before and after World War I, it follows the lives and loves of a Wild Woman flamboyantly content with her Siren-like qualities. If longing is at the root of the original Greek Sirens who were punished for attracting the adulation of men that Circe wanted, Steinke expresses what can liberate the Siren from Circe's curse. Is it horrific or joyful? You decide.

21. *The Silver Bough* (2006) by Lisa Tuttle. This contemporary fairy tale is set in fey Scotland and provides an elusive Apple Queen as its heady Siren. One bite of a magical apple will also create a Siren who holds the key to a small town's renewal. Three hopeful American women heed the Siren's call, but this time it's about love's redemption and metaphorically lifts the dark veil of Circe's curse, making this an enchanting antidote to Rossetti's orchard Siren who lures her men to death. In this story the Apple Queen's gift of love seduces but rewards her captives who finally discover how to live.

THE FIERCE FILMS OF THE FEMMES FATALES

There are many films that feature Sirens, although they are not all supernaturally gifted and some are downright funny. All are significant because they chart the Siren's cinematic evolution.

1. *Cleopatra* (1917). Theda Bara was a silent screen Siren who starred in more than fifty movies from 1914 to 1926 with titles like *She Devil*, *Siren of Hell*, and *The Devil's Daughter*, the ultimate vamp of the silent screen era. Two other better-known Cleopatra remakes exist. In 1934, Claudette Colbert played the Egyptian diva in the Cecil B. de Mille classic, and Elizabeth Taylor had the honor in the plodding, unintentionally horrific 1963 version most notable for the love scenes with the man she would later marry, divorce, remarry, and act with again, Richard Burton.

2. *She* (1935). The RKO version of H. Rider Haggard's classic starring Randolph Scott is about an immortal woman and femme fatale who makes the mistake of falling in love. A later Hammerscope remake with Peter Cushing and Christopher Lee (1965) is primarily notable for Ursula Andress as Ayesha, She Who Must Be Obeyed.

3. *The Devil Is a Woman* (1935). This film stars Marlene Dietrich playing a Seville Femme Fatale who proudly proclaims "All men are my slaves—and glad to be." John Walker writes that it is "rather splendid in its highly decorative and uncommercial way, a treat for addicts" (233). This was the last Dietrich vehicle to be directed by Josef von Sternberg.

4. *Rebecca* (1940). File this spellbinder under "A dead Siren still has power." Alfred Hitchcock directed his American debut. It is a faithful adaptation of the classic Daphne du Maurier Gothic romance about a dead wife whose Siren call still controls her estate of Manderley, her obsessively devoted housekeeper, Mrs. Danvers, and Maxim de Winter's (Laurence Olivier) life. Her deadly influence corrupts the life of the second Mrs. de Winter, his innocent bride played by a luminous Joan Fontaine. In true femme fatale fashion, the demonically exotic Rebecca knew she was dying of cancer and staged a suicide to suggest that Maxim had murdered her. Donald Spoto noted the clever "Siren" reference: "The final solution to the mystery of the wicked and doomed Rebecca is connected with the sea where she was buried, that element of chaos in Hitchcock which finally yields terrible truth" (93).

5. *The Lady Eve* (1941). This Preston Sturges comedy depicts the power of the madcap Siren, a woman (Barbara Stanwyck) who always gets her man, in this case, Henry Fonda. Stanwyck plays a card sharp who preys on wealthy travelers; in short, a gold digger and a wild seductress (so bad, she's good). This represents the Siren as playful, possibly deadly, but never dull. Not horrific or supernatural, but it certainly represents the femme fatale's power of seduction.

6. *Double Indemnity* (1944). Barbara Stanwyck and Fred MacMurray star in this Billy Wilder classic that was film noir at its early sharp-edged best. "No, I never loved, you, Walter—not you, or anybody else. I'm rotten to the heart. I used you, just as you said. That's all you ever meant to me. Until a minute ago, when I couldn't fire that second shot"—from the screenplay by Billy Wilder adapted from a 1930s story by James M. Cain. Roger Ebert wrote: "*Double Indemnity* has one of the most familiar noir themes: The hero is not a criminal, but a weak man who is tempted and succumbs. In this 'double' story the woman and man tempt one another; neither would have acted alone. Both are attracted not so much by the crime as by the thrill of committing it with the other person" (*The Great Movies* 147). Ebert also noted, "The puzzle of Billy Wilder's *Double Indemnity*, the enigma that keeps it new, is what these two people really think of one another."

7. *Laura* (1944). Film noir doesn't get better than Otto Preminger's film of the Vera Caspary novel, adapted by Jay Dratler, Samuel Hoffenstein, and Betty Reinhardt. Solving Laura's murder is the mission of Waldo Lydecker (Clifton Webb), but the deeper the investigation goes, the more he discovers the Siren at the core of her persona. Gene Tierney played the Siren. Vincent Price, her fiancé.

8. *Leave Her to Heaven* (1945). Love drives a woman crazy, or at least this femme fatale who causes her own miscarriage, watches her brother drown, and poisons herself to implicate her sister. Does any self-respecting Siren kill herself for a man? Only if she is also insanely selfish and jealous. Gene Tierney chews the scenery with Cornell Wilde in a foot-stomping melodrama. Cycle forward a forty-six years to *Thelma and Louise* (1991), written by Callie Khouri and directed by Ridley Scott, where two feminist

femmes fatales played by Susan Sarandon and Geena Davis drive off a cliff to avoid capture.

9. *All About Eve* (1950). Bette Davis stars as the witty thespian and intelligent diva, Margo Channing, faced with a deceitful little actress named Eve Harrington who will stop at nothing to get what she wants (a suitable Siren trait) to usurp Margo's leading role in an upcoming play. Required for all serious drama students, this classic was written and directed by Joseph L. Mankiewicz. Davis is also notable for her role in *Jezebel* (1938), about a Civil War–era femme fatale who alas, becomes reformed.

10. *Carmen* (1954). Dorothy Dandridge plays the leading role in Oscar Hammerstein's updated, African American version of the famous opera. Carmen's sultry seduction of a man who is already spoken for has dangerous consequences for Harry Belafonte, who plays the jilted soldier she runs off with, only to discard for a prizefighter.

11. *Lolita* (1961). Vladimir Nabokov adapted his novel in this treasure directed by a young Stanley Kubrik. James Mason plays Humbert Humbert, a foolish European professor who moves to America and becomes obsessed with Lolita, his landlord's daughter, played by Sue Lyons. Lyons rocked the film world with her nubile femme fatale charm. Near the end, Humbert kills off a wildly unrepentant seducer Clare Quilty (played by Peter Sellers), despoiler of virgins, the playwright who seduced the willing Lolita. The now pregnant Lo' (by yet another man) breaks Humbert's heart after she discloses a past indiscretion and refuses to run off with him again. She then confesses glibly with true femme fatale self-absorption, "I'm sorry I cheated so much . . . I'll call you when we get to Alaska" while she gloats over the money he has just given her.

12. *Sisters* (1973). Brian de Palma's scary tale stars Margot Kidder and focuses on the plight of a woman having separation issues from a Siren, her dead and deeply disturbed Siamese twin. In the same year, *Coffy* stars Pam Grier as a femme fatale out to avenge the destruction of her eleven-year-old sister. See also *Cleopatra Jones* (1973) and *Foxy Brown* (1974), all often described as blaxploitation but enhanced by Grier's bravura acting skills.

13. *Splash!* (1974). This Tom Hanks comedy directed by Ron Howard is about the rewards of falling in love with a Siren who doesn't want to lose her man, a mermaid played by Darryl Hannah. An Americanized puff piece that is still a delight, much like the British film *Miranda* (1947) that predates it, set in Cornwall and written by Peter Blackmore, about a doctor in Cornwall on a holiday who also falls for a mermaid and takes her (played by Glynis Johns) to London. A cute modern film about a teen mermaid, *Aquamarine* (2006), based on an Alice Hoffman book for middle school readers, focuses, as *Splash!* did so well, on the joyful aspect of the good Siren sea creature, who means no harm but just wants to be loved and have friends.

14. *Annie Hall* (1977). Another comedic handling of a femme fatale who is not deadly nor evil, this Woody Allen gem won an Oscar in 1978 over *Star*

Check Out These B-Movies for Outrageous Femmes:

1. *Housewife* (1934). Bette Davis plays a babe (one of the original Desperate Housewives?) who knew it was her way or the highway.
2. *Cobra Woman* (1944). Maria Montez plays the dual role of sexy twin sisters from hell or, in this case, an island queendom.
3. *The Magic Carpet* (1951). Lucille Ball plays a had girl. That's right, LUCY as an evil femme fatale, the Princess Narah!
4. *Inferno* (1953). Rhonda Fleming plays an evil wife who plots to dump her rich hubby in the desert to die.
5. *Devil Girl from Mars* (1954). Patricia Laffan plays a Martian Siren who arrives on Earth to get men for breeding purposes.
6. *Queen of Outer Space* (1958). Zsa Zsa Gabor rules as the Queen Venusian Siren in this spaced-out epic. "Men caused the ruin of this world" is one of Gabor's best lines.
7. *Brides of Dracula* (1960). Marita Hunt and other alluring cuties lure a naughty disciple of Dracula to go on a blood-sucking rampage in an all girls' school.
8. *Faster Pussycat! Kill! Kill!* (1966). Tura Satana, Haji, and Lori Williams star as three exotic dancers on a wild girl-gang rampage proving that sweet femmes fatales are kittens with very sharp claws.
9. *Crazy Mama* (1975). Nobody gets in the way of Cloris Leachman, Linda Purl, and Ann Southern as they rip through the country on a crime spree.
10. *Species* (1995) and *Species II* (1998). Natasha Henstridge plays a hot half-human, half-alien who, of course, will do or eat anything to survive in an actually pretty entertaining modern sci-fi B movie, but this half-breed Siren gets a little too good by the time the sequel arrives—too bad!

Wars for the best picture. It features the Siren in a lighter vein, but its poignant message is ruefully horrific. Diane Keaton was Allen's muse before Mia Farrow and provided some of the best comedic work of her career as Annie, Alvy Singer's greatest love. Annie's elusive quality represents the Siren as the unattainable ideal, the one who got away because he couldn't accept her as she was.

15. *Fatal Attraction* (1987). Glenn Close turns in a stellar performance as the wronged Siren in a scary film that summed up the 1980s fear of the single career woman as much as it played on the fears of marital infidelity and the crumbling façade of the American family.
16. *La Femme Nikita* (1990). As mentioned earlier, this is a not so subtle reminder that this French seductress is a Siren and a femme fatale. The cable TV show spin-off is a pale imitation but entertaining and influenced other popular TV shows like "Alias 6."

17. *Basic Instinct* (1991). The original nightmarish thriller, with Michael Douglas and Sharon Stone in a lurid but intense game of cat and mouse, in a film written by Joe Eszterhaz, pulled no punches in its depiction of a deadly diva who could outsmart any man anytime. The long awaited sequel, *Basic Instinct 2* (2006), was a total disaster, making the Siren into a two-bit slut, horrific but not in a good way.

18. *Sirens* (1994). This Australian treasure starring Hugh Grant and Sam Neill is about a scandalous artist and his Siren models during the Victorian age. It echoes the Pre-Raphaelite preoccupation with the idea of extreme beauty that gives the women possessing it supernatural seductive powers. Sam Neill plays an artist making waves with his erotic nudes. His models include his wife and some sexy Sirens who help a young wife discover her sexual self and reignite her marriage to a minister, played by Hugh Grant. Elle MacPherson and Portia de Rossi play two of the enchanting Sirens.

19. *Practical Magic* (1998). Modern-day Sirens Sandra Bullock and Nicole Kidman star in this adaptation of the Alice Hoffman novel about bewitching sisters who must find a way to reverse a nasty curse, a dilemma those original Greek Sirens may have struggled with.

20. *American Beauty* (1999). Alan Ball wrote and directed this Academy Award–winning dark comedy starring Kevin Spacey, who also won a statuette for his portrayal of a suburban middle-aged married man tempted by a young Siren eerily unaware of her own power. It echoes the Lolita theme while exposing the tender flesh of the pale underbelly of modern suburban life.

21. *Chicago* (2002). In this multiple Academy Award–winning musical directed by Rob Marshal, based on a play by Bob Fosse and Fred Ebb, two showgirls battle it out on who is the best "celebrity" and femme fatale in the eyes of their true audience, the fickle public. Hilarious, poignant, and rambunctious, this "horrific" delight answers the question about what can happen when some good girls go bad but also shows how much fun can be had while doing it. It stars Catherine Zeta-Jones as Vilma Kelly and René Zellwegger as the rival bad girls and Richard Gere, who appeared as an homme fatale, a male prostitute framed for murder in *American Gigolo* (1980).

22. *O Brother Where Art Thou?* (2000). Inspired by the *Odyssey* of Homer and their own warped, hilarious vision, Joel and Ethan Coen wrote the script and Joel directed. Three chain-gang prisoners led by George Clooney (playing Everett Ulysses McGill) break free to search for treasure, encountering sexy Sirens, a one-eyed bad guy, the Klu Klux Klan, sweaty politicians, and all sorts of weird stuff.

23. *Frida* (2002). Frida Kahlo, directed by Julie Taymor, captures the Siren in all her glory as an art icon who was also a femme fatale. Frida was a brilliant, visionary Mexican artist and Diego Rivera's favorite muse; she seduced the world with her art and was a real-life Siren in many ways. This biopic starring the luminous Salma Hayek captures the seduction.

24. *He Loves Me ... He Loves Me Not (À la Folie ... pas du tout)* (2002). A French film written and directed by Laetitia Colombani about obsession, it features Audrey Tatou as Angelique, a young art student who becomes enamored of Loic, a married cardiologist played by Samuel Le Bihan, told from both viewpoints. Tatou's winsome performance heightens the shocking effect of the last reel. An underrated stylish thriller that examines the erotomania, an obsessive condition that might easily infect a modern Siren.

25. *Femme Fatale* (2002). Rebecca Romijn, in an erotic thriller directed by Brian de Palma, personifies the mixture of beauty and danger Nikita emanated. Through vivid cinematography in the later part of the film, it also suggests the femme fatale's origin in the Siren myth when he shows the character's death/rebirth through water. The dangerous trajectory of the empowered Siren suggests calamity in this film, and her salvation is through the watery rebirth that returns the Siren into making a choice to prevent a suicide, which then leads to her own miraculous redemption. The femme fatale then becomes the woman of life, of rebirth and hope.

26. *Kill Bill Vol. 1* (2003), *Kill Bill Vol. 2* (2004). Uma Thurman plays The Bride/Black Mamba in these Quentin Tarantino films that follow the cool assassin who wakes up after a four-year coma and decides it is time to get even. A too-long blood-drenched action epic, but with moments of sultry femme fatale glory, mainly due to Thurman's grace under pressure. *My Super Ex-Girlfriend* (2006) also features Thurman as a Siren in an Ivan Retiman-directed comedy. The mighty Uma plays G-Girl (a.k.a. Jenny Johnson) who decides to teach her ex, Matt Saunders (Luke Wilson), a serious lessonm about the perils of dumping a vixen with superpowers.

27. *Lady in the Water* (2006). In M. Night Shyamalan's uneven Gothic fantasy film, a sea "narf" (played by Bryce Dallas Howard) surfaces in the pool of a seedy apartment complex on a mission to find a writer who will inspire a future world leader. While the "narf" fits all the romantic physical criteria for a brilliant siren, she is not luring men to their deaths; instead, she is trying to save them.

THE SMALL SCREEN

In television the best-known examples of the femmes fatales can be found among the stellar cast of "Desperate Housewives" (2004–). They have all had their femme fatale moments, most notably Gabrielle Solis (Eva Longoria), the Latino spitfire and former model who has an affair with her yard boy, and the wickedly funny blonde realtor, Edie Britt, played by Nicollette Sheridan, who played a young Siren-in-the-making on "Knot's Landing."

"Alias" (2001–2006), created by J. J. Abrams, featured Jennifer Garner as Sydney Bristow, a strong empowered Wild Woman double agent for the CIA who has to deal with a femme fatale mother played by Lena Olin.

"Buffy the Vampire Slayer" (1997–2003). Sarah Michelle Gellar flirted with becoming a ferocious teen femme fatale in her popular role of Buffy. She certainly had some major Sirens surrounding her, including: Cordelia, played by Charisma Carpenter (who moved on to "Angel" [1999–2004], a spin-off series); Faith Lehane, a Vampire Slayer with issues; and a creepy vamp chick named Drusilla.

Classic nighttime soap operas like "Dynasty" (1981–1989) featured Joan Collins as a major femme fatale/Siren; just check out her character's name for a clue to this vixen's erotic charm: Alexis Morell Carrington Colby Dexter Rowan. Another soapy vehicle for a great Siren was "Knot's Landing" (1979–1993). The second longest running prime time soap featured Donna Mills as the evil temptress of the cul-de-sac, Abby Cunningham. The first longest running prime time soap was "Dallas," and if there was a true Siren on that show, it had to be the ornery homme fatale played by Larry Hagman: J. R. Ewing.

Daytime TV can report many divas among their casts, but Susan Lucci's Erica Kane of "All My Children"—which began in the 1960s and is still going strong—has no equal. Played by Emmy Award–winning (1999) Lucci, Erica is in a class by herself. Not only has she married and dumped more men than Alexis, Erica will stop at nothing to get what she wants, especially when it comes to protecting her husbands, jobs, or her children, even if it means committing a crime or two, including murder.

"Ally McBeal" (1997–2002), as played by the ever-insecure Calista Flockhart, does not qualify as a Siren, but Ling as played by Lucy Liu does. Cast as a supporting character, the fabulous Ling often stole the show as an insatiable Siren and femme fatale. Ling was difficult to please and an absolutely ruthless diva lawyer. Liu's bravura performance helped her land a role as a Charlie's Angel in the successful but wildly over-the-top film remakes, *Charlie's Angels* (2000) and *Charlie's Angels: Full Throttle* (2003), which also starred Drew Barrymore and Cameron Diaz. The classic TV version of "Charlie's Angels" (1976–1981) also had crime-fighting "angel" babes

---

Ten Films That Feature Notorious Femmes Fatales:

1. *Les Vampires* (1915) Musidora
2. *A Fool There Was* (1915) Theda Bara
3. *The Blue Angel* (1930) Marlene Dietrich
4. *The Devil Is a Woman* (1935) Barbara Stanwyck
5. *Leave Her to Heaven* (1945) Gene Tierney
6. *Gilda* (1946) Rita Hayworth
7. *The Lady from Shanghai* (1948) Rita Hayworth
8. *Body Heat* (1981) Kathleen Turner
9. *Basic Instinct* (1992) Sharon Stone
10. *Femme Fatale* (2002) Rebecca Romijn

(Farrah Fawcett, Jaclyn Smith, Kate Jackson, and Cheryl Ladd) kicking butt while looking luscious at the same time. But were they true femmes fatales? The jury is still out.

"Dark Angel" (2000–2002). Jessica Alba starred as a good femme fatale that showed kinship with *La Femme Nikita* as she was genetically enhanced to become a killing machine manipulated by a government agency in the future. Created by James Cameron.

Catwoman enlivened the "Batman" TV series (1966–1968) that starred Adam West and featured three actresses in the pivotal feline role: Julie Newmar, Lee Meriwether, and Eartha Kitt. All three had their glam pussycat moments, as did Michele Pfeiffer in the film *Batman Returns* (1991), with Michael Keaton as the masked superhero. Halle Berry took a turn at the role in *Catwoman* (2004) on the big screen, but the production featured a badly written script and no soul. Probably the best Catwoman can be found in comic book form. *Catwoman: Nine Lives of a Feline Fatale* (DC, 2004) showcases some vintage and newer scripts that capture the allure of this enduring pop icon.

A FINAL FEMME FATALE THOUGHT

The myth of Lilith, Adam's spurned "wife," is of course also at the root of the Siren mystique—or does that honor belong to Eve of biblical fame? The image of Eve offering the apple to Adam is at the very core of the deliciously dark side of temptation. Did Eve's beauty convince Adam to eat that apple, or was it his own hunger? Can a Siren succeed in her dark art of seduction if a man or a woman is not hungry? If her song is heard when no hunger exists, can the sweet notes induce hunger pains? Maybe, but a song can only be heard if someone is willing to be seduced. And if an apple is offered, there is always a choice to take it or to ignore it. One wonders if the account of Adam's first taste of Eve's apple is just as important as Homer's tales in the *Odyssey* in appreciating the evolution of the Siren femme fatale. And one wonders if this dangerous sea creature escaped Circe's curse to become the spurned Lilith who rejected Adam's rib in order to become the femme fatale...?

Did she then become the Siren in Rossetti's "The Orchard" or Marilyn Monroe, some hungry-eyed model staring down from a billboard or from a burlesque stage, a porno queen's video, a dancer on the street, an artist's model, a curse, a blessing, a wishing star...a pulp noir temptress, a mermaid, a girlfriend, a wife, a mother, or even a teen Lolita, a Siren's sigh?

Rossetti's lovesick, doomed narrator chooses to take the apple his lover offers, even though she warns him, " 'Do not eat, it is the fruit of the Siren's dell.' And I laughed and ate: And at the heart of the apple was the stain like a woman's mouth; and as I bit it I could feel a kiss on my lips" (Weeks 29).

What about Marilyn?

Norma Jean became a Hollywood Icon and Legendary Siren as Marilyn Monroe. She has inspired many authors, photographers, artists, and filmmakers to study her femme fatale qualities. But was she a true-life Siren? It doesn't appear that she was a Siren in her own mind, but only became one in the minds of those captivated by her beauty, humor, and childlike quality. At the core of the Siren who is cursed in the envied beauty. Remember Circe? One wonders if Marilyn was cursed by a jealous witch or just by her own fragility.

Check out:

Marilyn (Henry Holt, 1986) by Gloria Steinem

Marilyn: A Biography (Alskog, 1973) by Norman Mailer

Blonde (HarperCollins, 2000) Joyce Carol Oates (a novel)

Marilyn: Shades of Blonde (Tor/Forge, 1997), ed. Carole Nelson Douglas, an intriguing fiction anthology

And check out the film *Gentlemen Prefer Blondes* (1953), in which Marilyn plays Lorelei, a stunner of a showgirl who has this memorable line: "I always say a kiss on the hand might feel very good, but a diamond tiara lasts forever."

The femme fatale might have told him "A kiss is just a kiss, get over it!" but a Siren or Wild Woman who has shaken off the curse of Circe might have just kissed him again harder and then flew back to the orchard to pick some more apples.

BIBLIOGRAPHY

Primary

Allende, Isabel. "Revenge." In *Cuentos de Eva Luna*. Barcelona: Plaza & Janés, 1987. Trans. Margaret Sayers Peden as *The Stories of Eva Luna*. New York: Atheneum, 1991.

Antieau, Kim. "Medusa's Child." In *Final Shadows*, ed. Charles L. Grant. Garden City, NY: Doubleday, 1991.

Atwood, Margaret. *The Robber Bride*. Toronto: McClelland & Stewart, 1993.

Beauman, Sally. *Rebecca's Tale*. New York: Morrow, 2001.

Block, Lawrence. "Hot Eyes, Cold Eyes." In *Love Kills*, ed. Ed Gorman and Martin Greenberg. New York: Carroll & Graf, 1997.

Bradley, Marion Zimmer. *The Mists of Avalon*. New York: Knopf, 1982.

Bryant, Edward. "Predators." In *Love Kills*, ed. Ed Gorman and Martin Greenberg. New York: Carroll & Graf, 1997.

Carter, Angela. *The Bloody Chamber and Other Stories*. London: Gollancz, 1979.

Caspary, Vera. *Bedelia*. London: Eyre & Spottiswoode, 1945. Rpt. New York: Feminist Press, 2005.

———. *Laura*. London: Eyre & Spottiswoode, 1944. Rpt. New York: Feminist Press, 2005.

Colette. "The Rainy Moon." In *The Collected Stories of Colette*, ed. Robert Phelps. New York: Farrar, Straus & Giroux, 1983.

Datlow, Ellen, ed. *Alien Sex*. New York: Dutton, 1990.

———. *Lethal Kisses*. London: Millennium, 1996.

———. *Little Deaths: 24 Tales of Sex and Horror*. London: Millennium, 1994.

Datlow, Ellen, and Terri Windling, eds. *Sirens and Other Daemon Lovers*. New York: HarperPrism, 1998.

———. *Snow White Blood Red*. New York: Morrow/Avon, 1993.

de Lint, Charles. "Tallulah." In *Dead End: City Limits*, ed. Paul Olson and David Silva. New York: St. Martin's Press, 1991.

Denker, Henry. *Salome, Princess of Galilee*. New York: Thomas Y. Crowell Co., 1952.

Douglas, Carole Nelson. *Femme Fatale*. New York: Tor/Forge, 2003.

du Maurier, Daphne. *Rebecca*. London: Gollancz, 1938.

du Maurier, George. *Trilby*. New York: Harper & Brothers, 1894.

Egbert, H. M. [pseud. of Victor Rousseau]. *The Sea Demons*. N.p.: Long, 1924.

Farmer, Penelope. *Eve: Her Story*. London: Gollancz, 1985.

Flaubert, Gustave. "Herodias." 1877. In *Three Tales by Flaubert*. Trans. Arthur McDowall. New York: Knopf, 1924.

Gautier, Théophile. "One of Cleopatra's Nights" and "Clarimonde." In *One of Cleopatra's Nights and Other Fantastic Romances*, trans. Lafcadio Hearn. New York: Worthington, 1882.

———. *Sprite*. Eng. trans. as *Stronger Than Death*. Chicago: Rand, McNally, 1898.

Gorman, Ed, and Martin Greenberg, eds. *Love Kills*. New York: Carroll & Graf, 1997.

Gourmont, Remy de. *Lilith*. 1892. Trans. John Heard. Boston: John W. Luce, 1946.

Haggard, H. Rider. *She*. New York: Harper & Brothers, 1886.

Hall, Melissa Mia. "Psychofemmes." In *Wild Women*, ed. Melissa Mia Hall. New York: Carroll & Graf, 1997.

———, ed. *Wild Women*. New York: Carroll & Graf, 1997.

Hesiod et al. *Hesiod; The Homeric Hymns and Homerica*. Trans. Hugh G. Evelyn-White. Cambridge, MA: Harvard University Press, 1914.

Hichens, Robert. "How Love Came to Professor Guildea." In *Tongues of Conscience*. New York: Frederick A. Stokes, 1900.

Hill, Susan. *Mrs. de Winter*. New York: Morrow, 1993.

———. *The Woman in Black*. London: Hamish Hamilton, 1983.

Hoffman, Alice. *Practical Magic*. New York: Putnam, 1995.

Howard, Robert E. "The Moon of Skulls." In *Red Shadows*. West Kingston, RI: Donald M. Grant, 1968.

———. "Wings in the Night." In *Skull-Face and Others*. Sauk City, WI: Arkham House, 1946.

Jackson, Shirley. "The Demon Lover." In *The Lottery*. New York: Farrar, Straus, 1949.

Jakes, John. *Veils of Salome*. New York: Pinnacle, 1976.

Jones, Stephen, ed. *The Mammoth Book of Vampire Stories by Women*. New York: Carroll & Graf, 2002.

Lee, Gypsy Rose. *The G-String Murders*. New York: Simon & Schuster, 1941. Rpt. New York: Feminist Press, 2005.

Le Fanu, J. Sheridan. "Carmilla." In *Best Ghost Stories*, ed. E. F. Bleiler. New York: Dover, 1964.

Leiber, Fritz. *Conjure Wife*. 1943. New York: Twayne, 1953.

———. "The Girl with the Hungry Eyes." In *The Girl with the Hungry Eyes*, ed. Donald A. Wollheim. New York: Avon, 1949.

Lemaître, Jules. "Lilith." In *Dix Contes*. Paris, 1890.

MacDonald, George. *Lilith*. London: Chatto & Windus, 1895.

Machen, Arthur. "The Great God Pan." In *The Great God Pan and The Inmost Light*. London: John Lane, 1894.

Matheson, Richard. *Earthbound*. New York: Playboy Press, 1982. Rev. ed. London: Robinson, 1989.

Mitchell, Margaret. *Gone with the Wind*. New York: Macmillan, 1936.

Morris, William. *The Life and Death of Jason*. 1867. London: Longmans, Green, 1896.

Oates, Joyce Carol. "Hunger." In *The Female of the Species*. Orlando, FL: Harcourt, 2005.

Onions, Oliver. "The Beckoning Fair One." In *Widdershins*. London: Martin Secker, 1911.

Poe, Edgar Allan. *Tales of Edgar Allan Poe*. New York: Random House, 1944.

Rankin, Ian. *Witch*. Boston: Little, Brown, 1993.

Rice, Anne. *Merrick*. New York: Knopf, 2000.

———. *Queen of the Damned*. New York: Knopf, 1988.

———. *The Witching Hour*. New York: Knopf, 1990.

Rossetti, Dante Gabriel. *The Collected Works of Dante Gabriel Rossetti*. Ed. W. M. Rossetti. 2 vols. London: Ellis & Elvey, 1897.

Rousseau, Victor. "The Seal Maiden." *Cavalier* (November 15, 1913).

Slung, Michele, ed. *I Shudder at Your Touch*. New York: Penguin/Roc, 1991.

———. *Shudder Again*. New York: Penguin/Roc, 2003.

Stableford, Brian, ed. *The Dedalus Book of Femmes Fatales*. Sawtry, UK: Dedalus, 1992.

Steinke, René. *Holy Skirts*. New York: Morrow, 2005.

Stoker, Bram. *Dracula*. London: Constable, 1897.

Thomas, Sue, ed. *Wild Women: Contemporary Short Stories by Women Celebrating Women*. New York: Overlook Press, 1994.

Tuttle, Lisa. *The Silver Bough*. New York: Tor, 2006.

Updike, John. *The Witches of Eastwick*. New York: Knopf, 1984.

Viereck, George Sylvester, and Paul Eldridge. *Salome, the Wandering Jewess: My First Two Thousand Years of Love*. New York: Liveright, 1930.

Weeks, John, ed. *The Dream Weavers: Tales of Fantasy by the Pre-Raphaelites*. Santa Barbara, CA: Woodbridge Press, 1980.

White, Edward Lucas. "The Song of the Sirens." In *The Song of the Sirens and Other Stories*. New York: Dutton, 1919.

White, T. H. *The Book of Merlin.* London: Collins, 1977.
———. *The Once and Future King.* London: Collins, 1958.
Wilde, Oscar. *Salome.* 1893. Trans. R. A. Walker. London: Gollancz, 1957.
Wilhelm, Kate. "The Merry Widow." In *Wild Women,* ed. Melissa Mia Hall. New York: Carroll & Graf, 1997.
Wolfe, Gene. *On Blue's Water.* New York: Tor, 1999.
Yolen, Jane. *Neptune Rising: Songs and Tales of the Undersea Folk.* New York: Philomel, 1982.

Secondary

Atkins, Robert. *Art Speak: A Guide to Contemporary Ideas, Movement, and Buzzwords, 1945–Present.* New York: Abbeville Press, 1997.
Corey, Melinda, and George Ochoa, eds. *The American Film Institute Desk Reference.* New York: DK, 2002.
Doane, Mary Ann. *Femmes Fatales.* New York: Routledge, 1991.
Ebert, Roger. *The Great Movies.* New York: Broadway, 2002.
———. *The Great Movies II.* New York: Broadway, 2005.
Evslin, Bernard. *The Sirens.* New York: Chelsea House, 1988.
Gibson, Michael. *Symbolism.* Cologne: Taschen, 1995.
Hamilton, Edith. *Mythology.* 1942. New York: New American Library, 1969.
Joshi, S. T., and Stefan Dziemianowicz, eds. *Supernatural Literature of the World: An Encyclopedia.* Westport, CT: Greenwood Press, 2005.
Lao, Meri. *Sirens: Symbols of Seduction.* Trans. John Oliphant. Rochester, VT: Park Street Press, 1998.
Marsh, Jan. *The Pre-Raphaelite Sisterhood.* New York: St. Martin's Press, 1985.
———. *Pre-Raphaelite Women: Images of Femininity.* New York: Harmony, 1988.
O'Neill, Eileen, Tom Lisanti, and Louis Paul. *Film Fatales: Women in Espionage Films and Television 1963–1973.* Jefferson, NC: McFarland & Co., 2002.
Paver, Janine. *Femmes Fatales: Resistance, Power and Post-feminism.* N.p.: Wasteland Press, 2005.
Spencer-Longhurst, Paul. *The Blue Bower: Rossetti in the 1860s.* London: Scala, 2000.
Spoto, Donald. *The Art of Alfred Hitchcock.* New York: Hopkinson & Blake, 1976.
Turu, Tony. *Bad Girls: Film Fatales, Sirens, and Molls.* N.p.: Collector's Press, 2005.
Walker, John. *Halliwell's Film, Video & DVD Guide 2005.* New York: HarperCollins, 2005.
Yolen, Jane, ed. *Favorite Folktales from around the World.* New York: Pantheon, 1986.
Zalcock, Bev. *Renegade Sisters: Girl Gangs on Film.* London: Creation, 1998.

The Small-Town Horror

by John Langan

Since the mid- to late 1970s, the small town as a setting for horror narratives has become so common as to constitute one of the genre's hallmarks, an icon of the supernatural narrative. We find small towns in horror stories, horror novels, and horror films, and their prevalence makes them worth investigating. While there is a remarkable diversity in small-town horror narratives, they are also bound together by common concerns with authenticity, an anxiety about the difference between what we seem to be and what we in fact are.

In no small part, the ascendancy of small-town horror has been due to the tremendous success of Stephen King's stories and novels, a substantial number of which have been set in small towns—most of them in King's native

Maine—and which have employed their settings to considerable effect. More so than any horror writer before him, King has demonstrated the potential of the small town to serve as the stage for the writer's drama; in turn, his example has exerted considerable influence over other writers in the genre, both those of King's own generation (such as Peter Straub, Ramsey Campbell, and David Morrell) and those subsequent (such as Stewart O'Nan, Bentley Little, and Dale Bailey). A study of small-town horror fiction could do worse than focus on King's work, especially the novels *'Salem's Lot* (1975) and *Needful Things* (1991), whose settings are especially significant.

Profound as King's contribution to the development of this icon has been, however, it has not occurred in a vacuum. A number of important horror stories and novels to precede his have made use of the small town, and we will find it useful to give them our attention, since they establish many of the parameters for employing a small-town setting. In the process, we will have occasion to turn to several canonical works of American literature, which help in rounding off our understanding of the development of small-town horror. Neither works of horror or mainstream literature will prove much help in sorting out the place of small-town horror in the larger category of horror film, which has made infrequent and idiosyncratic use of the icon; although the written examples of small-town horror do contribute to our understanding of its cinematic appearances thus far. Though not a great deal of critical material has been written about small-town horror, Hank Wagner's recent essay on the subject in *Supernatural Literature of the World: An Encyclopedia* (2005) provides useful talking points.

While we can find strange towns as far back as Petronius's *Satyricon* (c. 61 C.E.), we might begin our discussion in the relatively recent past, with Nathaniel Hawthorne's story "Young Goodman Brown" (*New-England Magazine*,

---

Ten Leading Stories of Small-Town Horror

Nathaniel Hawthorne, "Young Goodman Brown" (1835)

Algernon Blackwood, "Ancient Sorceries" (1908)

William Faulkner, "A Rose for Emily" (1930)

H. P. Lovecraft, "The Shadow over Innsmouth" (1936)

Shirley Jackson, "The Lottery" (1948)

Jack Finney, *Invasion of the Body Snatchers* (1955)

Ray Bradbury, *Something Wicked This Way Comes* (1962)

Thomas Tryon, *Harvest Home* (1973)

Stephen King, *'Salem's Lot* (1975)

Peter Straub, "The Ghost Village" (1993)

April 1835). It is one of a half-dozen or so stories that help to stake out the boundaries of the small-town horror narrative; others include Algernon Blackwood's "Ancient Sorceries" (1908), H. P. Lovecraft's "The Shadow over Innsmouth" (1936), William Faulkner's "A Rose for Emily" (*Forum*, April 1930), Shirley Jackson's "The Lottery" (*New Yorker*, June 26, 1948), and Peter Straub's "The Ghost Village" (1993).

Hawthorne's story is a perennial favorite of high school and college English courses, in no small part because it is thick with symbols. The eponymous Goodman Brown, a Puritan colonial, leaves his wife, Faith, and the safety of their small town in order to walk the more dangerous woods with an old man who bears a striking resemblance to his grandfather. This man, who carries a walking stick in the shape of a snake, is a sinister, even satanic figure; what Goodman Brown thinks he is doing walking with him is something of a mystery. Brown has assured Faith that he intends to be away from her for only one night, but he has no idea of what lies in wait for him. As they journey together, Brown and the old man encounter a variety of the town's most respected figures, all of whom recognize and are familiar with Brown's sinister companion. It becomes clear that the old man is in fact the Devil, and that the pillars of the community are secretly his acolytes. The story reaches its climax in a forest clearing in which a Witches' Sabbath is being held; Brown finds the entire town in attendance, including his wife, and more people besides: political luminaries from far and wide, Native Americans. Brown calls out for his wife to resist the Devil, then swoons. When he awakes, he is alone in the forest, and Hawthorne asks if all he saw was a dream. Dream or not, Brown's experience leaves his disposition permanently altered, and for the worse: he becomes a gloomy figure whose dour demeanor keeps the rest of the community, even Faith, at arm's length. His dying hour, the story tells us, is gloom.

The tale effectively dramatizes the Puritan worldview, its Calvinist obsession with human depravity and damnation. Young Goodman Brown leaves the safety of the town and its structured community—and, most importantly,

---

Presently his eyes became glued to the windows of the opposite wall where the moonlight fell in a soft blaze. The roof overhead, and behind him, was reflected clearly in the glass, and he saw the outlines of dark bodies moving with long footsteps over the tiles and along the coping. They passed swiftly and silently, shaped like immense cats, in an endless procession across the pictured glass, and then appeared to leap down to a lower level where he lost sight of them. He just caught the soft thudding of their leaps. Sometimes their shadows fell on the white wall opposite, and the he could not make out whether they were the shadows of human beings or cats. They seemed to change swiftly from one to the other.

—*Algernon Blackwood, "Ancient Sorceries"*

---

his allegorically named wife—in order to flirt with his evil impulses, to lead himself, if not all the way into temptation, then close enough to its edge to have a good look. That the figure he meets in the forest assumes the shape of his grandfather indicates Brown's connection to a heritage of sin; when he realizes this relation, the knowledge destroys him. Encountering his individual link to evil provokes Brown to a vision of universal corruption. In a very real sense, in thinking he could walk with the Devil without consequences, Brown is lost before the story begins. His experience does not lead him to wisdom, to a greater tolerance for the imperfections of poor humanity; rather, it causes him to project his hyper-awareness of his fallen nature onto the world around him. If he is sinful, then so is everyone else, all of them hopelessly damned. The story's climactic scene is an index of how traumatic the recognition of his sinfulness is to Goodman Brown—and, by extension, to the Puritans in general.

So this first portrait of small-town horror uses the picture of an entire town given over to satanic practices to dramatize the protagonist's psychological processes. It is not too much of an exaggeration to say that most of the stories, novels, and films to follow Hawthorne have concerned themselves with taking his symbol and making it literal, with portraying actually sinister communities of one kind or another. One of the most interesting examples of these is Algernon Blackwood's "Ancient Sorceries." Although this story features John Silence, the "psychic doctor" who occasionally comes into direct conflict with the forces of darkness, Silence's role here is chiefly that of audience and interpreter. The story's true protagonist is Arthur Vezin, a nondescript Englishman who comes to Silence to relate a most extraordinary tale. While recently on vacation in France, Vezin was seized by the compulsion to abandon the train on which he was traveling for a small town not on his itinerary. Despite a cryptic warning from one of the other passengers about the sleep and the cats, Vezin plunged ahead. He took a room at an inn whose proprietress, he tells Silence, reminded him of a huge tabby cat, one that might leap across the room and pounce on him as if he were a mouse. In fact, all the town's population behaved in ways that reminded Vezin of cats. He had the sensation that he was under constant, if oblique, surveillance, but despite his growing unease about his decision to stop in the town, he found himself too lethargic to leave.

His desire to flee was moderated considerably by the appearance of the innkeeper's daughter, Ilsé, who was young, beautiful, and apparently drawn to the middle-aged Vezin. Their attraction progressed until Ilsé at last revealed the secret of Vezin's compulsion to visit the town and his inability to depart it: in a previous life, he had been one of its inhabitants; more importantly, he and Ilsé had been lovers. That past had returned him to the town, and the question before him now was whether he would stay and reclaim his former existence— a matter more complicated than renewing his affair with Ilsé. The entire town, it turned out, were witches, able to transform themselves into panthers through the application of a special salve. In his narrative's climax, Vezin was faced with the choice of joining Ilsé and the rest of the town in shedding his human form and taking part in the Witches' Sabbath, or fleeing. Though severely tempted, he chose flight. Vezin's conversation with John Silence concludes with another revelation: although, by his best estimates, Vezin was certain he had been in the town for more than a week, the calendar revealed that he had spent no more than a couple of days there. His last act is to show Silence marks on his shoulder and upper back, the places where Ilsé had embraced him.

"Ancient Sorceries" ends with a coda in which Silence discusses Vezin's story with an unnamed friend. Silence has verified Vezin's tale, both the specifics of his brief stay in the town and the more general facts of the town's historical connection to witchcraft. Vezin's experience, Silence proceeds, was essentially internal, not a dream or hallucination but a kind of psychic encounter with the manifestations of a persistent past. The story finishes with Silence brooding over the question of Vezin's returning to the town, which Silence doubts he will be able to resist doing.

It is tempting to read Blackwood's story as an expression of English Francophobia, but there is more to it than that. A comparison with "Young Goodman Brown" is helpful, in no small part for the direction in which it shows us the use of the small-town icon heading. The similarities between the stories are intriguing: both feature a protagonist who learns that the inhabitants of a town are not as they seem, and specifically, that they are all witches. Both narratives include vividly described Witches' Sabbaths, complete with infernal guests, which the protagonists attempt to resist and which they swoon away from. Brown and Vezin learn about their individual heritages, which make their discoveries about the towns, discoveries about themselves. Furthermore, the experiences of both men are largely internal. Viewed in this light, the stories appear varieties of psychodrama, using the figures of the small town given over to witchcraft to probe some aspect of their protagonists' psyche.

The divergences between the stories, however, are even more interesting. That Brown walks into the forest and Vezin into the French town is not so much a contrast as might first appear: in both cases, the men are entering foreign environments. What is more significant is the way in which Blackwood's story takes those points of convergence with "Young Goodman Brown" from the realm of the symbolic and pulls them towards the literal. Brown discovers his fellow townspeople to be witches, and we take it as a trope for his recognition of their sinfulness; Vezin discovers the inhabitants of the French town are witches, and we take his finding more literally. Hawthorne's Witches' Sabbath is the climax of Brown's vision of universal depravity; Blackwood's is an actual event that Vezin witnesses. Brown understands his own sinfulness, which he projects outwards onto the rest of the town; Vezin learns the nature of the French town's inhabitants, and that knowledge projects

At one extremity of an open space, hemmed in by the dark wall of the forest, arose a rock, bearing some rude, natural resemblance either to an altar or a pulpit, and surrounded by four blazing pines, their tops aflame, their stems untouched, like candles at an evening meeting. The mass of foliage that had overgrown the summit of the rock was all on fire, blazing high into the night and fitfully illuminating the whole field. Each pendent twig and leafy festoon was in a blaze. As the red light arose and fell, a numerous congregation alternately shone forth then disappeared into shadow, and again grew, as it were, out of the darkness, peopling the heart of the solitary woods at once.
—*Nathaniel Hawthorne, "Young Goodman Brown"*

itself into him. Brown's self-recognition is of his part in universal human fallenness; Vezin's connects him to a more restricted group. What Young Goodman Brown undergoes in the forest is a dream-journey; what Vezin undergoes in the French town, while largely intangible, is more externally real, a kind of interaction between his consciousness and an active past.

Perhaps the most striking difference is in the role the erotic plays in each story. In "Young Goodman Brown," the principle female character, Faith, is chastely married to the protagonist. In "Ancient Sorceries," the principle female character, Ilsé, is the protagonist's (former) highly sensual lover. There is little indication that the erotic is involved in Goodman Brown's experience—indeed, he largely abandons any such relationship in favor of his excursion into the forest—while sexual desire is very much part of Vezin's temptation.

The trend we find at work in "Ancient Sorceries," the move toward making the symbolic literal, is even more dramatic in H. P. Lovecraft's "The Shadow over Innsmouth," which takes Blackwood's psychic events and makes them material. Lovecraft's story presents us yet another out-of-the-way town visited by a wandering man, in this case, an unnamed, first-person narrator who recounts his adventure in the decayed seaport of Innsmouth, Massachusetts. Drawn to the town by the chance mention of it while on a tour to celebrate his coming of age, the narrator spends a good deal of the story wandering Innsmouth's streets and hearing the history of its decline from Zadok Allen, an old local. Allen's history begins with the loss of a good portion of the town's sailors and ships to a combination of causes, including the War of 1812 and several disasters at sea. One captain, Obed Marsh, attempted to maintain the town's connection with the East India/Pacific trade, in the course of which he came into contact with a group of South Sea islanders who had relations with a race of undersea creatures. Those relations included breeding with the creatures to produce hybrids manifesting varying degrees of their inhuman heritage—all of whom would, as they aged, grow steadily less human, until at last they took to the sea. Obed set up trade with the islanders and the creatures, as a result of which Innsmouth prospered, and also set about learning what he could about the creatures and how to summon them from their deep-sea homes. Eventually, he returned to the islands to find them wiped clean of inhabitants, presumably by neighboring people, but by that time he knew enough to bring the creatures up from the ocean near Innsmouth. Aided by his monstrous allies, Obed gradually took control of the town, instituting a new religious center, the Order of Dagon, and allowing and encouraging the interbreeding of the town's inhabitants with the creatures of the deep. As a result, the greater part of Innsmouth's remaining population is, to one degree or another, not fully human. What is more, Zadok Allen indicates that the creatures and townspeople have been working toward more sinister ends, using the houses at one end of the town to conceal things they have been raising form the ocean depths, some of which are more monstrous than the creatures themselves.

The town's less pleasant inhabitants spy Allen telling its secrets to the narrator, and after dark they strike, attempting to break into the narrator's hotel room. He escapes them, catching distant glimpses of his pursuers, and calls on the civil authorities, who raid the town, carry off a majority of its citizens to points unknown, and send a submarine to torpedo the creatures' undersea dwelling. Perhaps disaster has been averted.

Or perhaps not: the story does not end there, but continues to recount the narrator's horrified discovery that his grandmother was originally from Innsmouth, and that he has inherited her looks. As he feels his ancestry beginning to assert itself, he contemplates suicide, the choice of an uncle who had looked into the family's genealogy years before, but by the closing paragraphs the narrator has decided to embrace his transformation, swim out to the sea, and dwell in his new undersea world.

Just as it is tempting to read "Ancient Sorceries" as arising from English animosity toward the French, so does the temptation exist to read "The Shadow over Innsmouth" as springing out of American anti-immigrant xenophobia. As was the case with the previous story, though, there is more to the story than the simple expression of prejudice. A comparison between Lovecraft and Blackwood helps us see the path down which Lovecraft leads the small-town horror icon. Their stories resemble one another at several points. Each story comes to us from a man who, apparently by chance, stops in an old town with an ominous history to which he learns he is personally connected. The inhabitants of these towns transform themselves from human into some other shape and try to coerce the protagonist into joining them. Both men escape, but only temporarily; in the end, each will return to his ancestral home. The geographies of each town symbolize the protagonists' inner states: in "Ancient Sorceries," Vezin pictures the French town as an enormous cat, brooding over its inhabitants, the spires of its decayed cathedral forming the cat's ears—the scene a trope for Vezin's spiritual connection to the corrupt religious practices of the townspeople, especially their practice of abandoning their human identity in favor of a feline one—while Innsmouth's identity as a seaport, a place on the border between land and ocean, represents the narrator's interstitial identity.

Where the stories part ways is in the actuality of the events they relate. As Blackwood's story did vis-à-vis Hawthorne's, so does Lovecraft's story with Blackwood's, taking its concerns and bringing them even more fully into the realm of the physical. It is a change that is signaled by the difference in the stories' presentation of their narratives. Though Vezin tells his story to John Silence, we read that story largely in the third person, mediated to us by Silence's unnamed friend, who serves as Dr. Watson to Silence's Sherlock Holmes. In contrast, Lovecraft's protagonist speaks to us directly, and, aside from a brief, ominous opening that hints at Innsmouth's character, we learn about the town, and his connection to it, as the narrator does. As a consequence of that shift, Innsmouth's history is part of the protagonist's narration in a way that the French town's past isn't in Vezin's story. Vezin's link to his town's inhabitants is spiritual, determined by reincarnation, while Lovecraft's narrator's relation is physical, determined by genetics. Likewise, the witches of the French town consciously forsake their humanity for magical transformation into animal form, while the hybrid residents of Innsmouth are overtaken by a change analogous to the progression of a genetic disorder. The role of the erotic in each story is radically different: in Blackwood, the lure of his past is figured for Vezin by the promise of Ilsé; whereas in Lovecraft, the erotic is the very source of monstrousness, the origin of Innsmouth's, and the narrator's, troubles. He is drawn to Innsmouth by dreams of his grandmother transformed, by the appeal of family. Vezin's fate remains in just enough doubt for us to wonder at it, whereas the final lines of "The Shadow over Innsmouth" leave us certain of his future.

In all three of the stories we have been considering, knowledge serves as an integral—and horrifying—function. For each protagonist to learn the secret of his town is for him to learn the secret of himself. In their experiences of their respective towns, the protagonists discover what was already the case with themselves. Having acquired that information, there is no way for them to escape its implications. As is true in so much horror fiction, to know is to be damned; to become aware of your connection to the monstrous is to be drawn inexorably into its embrace. From this standpoint, this is what makes the ending of "The Shadow over Innsmouth" the most chilling of the three, its protagonist's acceptance, even embrace, of his fate. Obviously, all these stories incorporate a heavy dose of paranoia, but it is a paranoia that ultimately turns inward, to an anxiety over the protagonist's identity. In addition, atavism, another central concern of horror writ large, is a significant part of each narrative, the implication being that the primitive, whether savage rituals or genetic monstrousness, survives and even thrives within the boundaries of the small town.

Strictly speaking, neither William Faulkner's "A Rose for Emily" nor Shirley Jackson's "The Lottery" are stories of supernatural small-town horror, but both make contributions to the icon too important to be overlooked. Faulkner's story is significant for its use of the town's collective voice to relate the history of Miss Emily Grierson, in an apparent character study that winds up highlighting how little it is possible to know another person, as Miss Emily is revealed to have poisoned a lover who had jilted her and then slept beside his moldering corpse for decades. It is a story that is indebted to Sherwood Anderson's short story cycle *Winesburg, Ohio* (1919), which employs the grotesque as one of its central conceits. Anderson uses the term to refer to people who have become obsessed with a particular truth at the expense of a more complex and compound view of Truth; their monomanias warp their characters, causing them to twist and contort around their various truths. Of course, this provides the writer a wealth of material to explore. Anderson's and Faulkner's small towns are frequently unpleasant places. It is not just that their towns are remote from larger cities; the inhabitants of those towns are personally, even spiritually, remote from one another. It is as if the limited confines and circle of acquaintances of small-town life evoke a corresponding need for privacy, even secrecy; the smaller the town, the greater the need. We can trace links backwards from Anderson and Faulkner to Thomas Hardy and Honoré de Balzac, and forward to Gabriel García Márquez (whose short novel, *Chronicle of a Death Foretold* [1981], reads like an oblique response to "A Rose for Emily") and Stephen King. Faulkner's work bears mentioning in more general terms due to his setting the vast majority of his stories and novels in and around the invented town of Jefferson, Mississippi, the seat of the equally invented Yoknapatawpha County. Not the first to employ an imagined locale for his work, Faulkner is among the most successful, and his example, consciously or not, informs much of the small-town fiction, and small-town horror fiction, to follow him.

"The Lottery" reads like the culmination of a number of threads we have been discussing thus far. It moves back and forth among the perspectives of the members of a small town gathered to perform a spring ritual with an ease

---

There was a great deal of fussing to be done before Mr. Summers declared the lottery open. There were the lists to make up—of heads of families, heads of households in each family, members of each household in each family. There was the proper swearing-in of Mr. Summers by the post-master, as the official of the lottery; at one time, some people remembered, there had been a recital of some sort, performed by the official of the lottery, a perfunctory, tuneless chant that had been rattled off duly each year; some people believed that the official of the lottery used to stand just so when he said or sang it, others believed that he was supposed to walk among the people, but years and years ago this part of the ritual had been allowed to lapse.

—*Shirley Jackson, "The Lottery"*

that recalls Faulkner; while its conceit, that the town is engaged in a ceremony whose origins have been forgotten but which entails human sacrifice as
a means to insure a favorable harvest, takes the atavistic rites we find in
Hawthorne and Blackwood—and which are alluded to in Lovecraft—and
naturalizes them, treating them with an almost anthropological detachment.
Unlike Hawthorne, Blackwood, and Lovecraft, Jackson does not provide us
the perspective of a narrator whose encounter with the town is a vehicle for
his own voyage of horrified self-discovery. Instead, she opts to focus more on
the town as a whole. If there is a protagonist in the story—or, at least, a
character who receives slightly more attention—it is the woman whose fate it
will be to serve as the town's sacrifice. Her role brings her no enlightenment;
all it provokes from her is a protest at the unfairness of her fate, before the
town descends on her. Jackson pays meticulous attention to the details of the
eponymous lottery, which until its violent conclusion appears quaint, even
banal. Without a strong protagonist, the story directs our attention to the
small town as the source of horror through its blind perpetuation of terrible
practices. It is a savage, damning portrait.

Although small towns have featured in many other horror stories—enough
for their discussion alone to fill a book—the five stories we have considered
give us the icon distilled. In its concentrated form, the small-town horror story
represents the site of collective secrecy, of monstrousness metaphysical or
physical, and of atavism ritual and/or genetic. The small town functions as a
kind of composite monster, one whose monstrosity arises from its ability to
harbor the past, preserve tradition, resist change. The stories of small-town
horror we have looked at make paranoia an integral part of their narration,
often complementing it with xenophobia.

As a coda to our survey of small-town horror in short fiction, we might
consider Peter Straub's "The Ghost Village," which, although incorporated
into his 1993 novel, *The Throat,* was first published and can stand on its own.
It is a narrative that shows us some of the additional directions in which the
small-town horror icon can be taken. Set during the American war in Vietnam,
the story centers on an American patrol that comes across a deserted Vietnamese village. During their investigation of it, the soldiers discover a hut with
a trap door that leads to a subterranean chamber whose walls are covered in
paper filled with Vietnamese writing and spotted with dried blood. A pair of
upright supports, also bloodstained, anchor a pair of chains sets about four
feet high, their links rusted with blood. Though the lieutenant insists that the
soldiers have uncovered a secret Viet Cong interrogation room, the story's
narrator, Tim Underhill, understands that this is not the case; what the men
have found has nothing to do with the war that has brought them here. Underhill sees a young boy he realizes is a ghost, but it will not be until his patrol
has returned to its base that he will learn the village's story. A Green Beret, an
old acquaintance of Underhill's, tells it to him in a bar. The hut under which
the chamber was located, Ransom says, belonged to the village's chief, who

used the secret space to abuse and murder children, his own first, then several from the village. Eventually, the chief's crimes grew so grievous that ghosts started appearing in and around the village—not the specters of the dead children, but others of the town's previous inhabitants, summoned back to it by the horror and shame of the chief's actions. When the villagers pieced together what was happening, they bound the chief in his own torture chamber and turned him over to the Viet Cong, who first wrote the names of the children the chief had murdered on the room's walls, then tortured the chief to death. Following this, the villagers abandoned the village, unable to live any longer in the place that had become such a site of profound shame for them—shame because they had failed their children to the very man who was supposed to lead them; shame because perhaps they had known, after a certain point, that all was not right with the chief.

The story's title thus works on several levels. The Ghost Village is the deserted village; it is also the village filled with the ghosts drawn by the chief's crime. Most importantly, it is the village haunted by the catastrophic failure of its residents in one of their most fundamental responsibilities. We can draw a line between Straub's story and those of Jackson, Lovecraft, Blackwood, and Hawthorne in their concern with communities bound together in secret sin; we can also connect the story to Faulkner's in their representation of populations aware that something is wrong with one of their inhabitants, but failing to act on their knowledge until it is much, much too late. None of the previous stories we have considered give us communities especially conflicted about their particular secret; if anyone, it is the protagonists who rebel—for a time, anyway—against them. Straub's story gives us a town shattered by its collective shame, a shame so intense it continues to permeate the place they lived. It is the story in which the physical town, as opposed to its inhabitants, features most strikingly.

The small town comes into its own in horror novels in a trio of books published from 1955 to 1962: Jack Finney's *Invasion of the Body Snatchers* (1955), John Wyndham's *The Midwich Cuckoos* (1957), and Ray Bradbury's *Something Wicked This Way Comes* (1962). Both Finney and Wyndham present small towns as the starting points for alien invasions of the Earth. In Finney's novel, the inhabitants of Santa Mira, California—an idealized American small town—are being replaced by exact physical copies of themselves produced by alien pods, a kind of organic technology that arrives quietly and begins growing duplicates of the town's populace. While these "pod

---

I saw an empty room shaped like a giant grave. The walls were covered by some kid of thick paper held in place by wooden struts sunk into the earth. Both the thick brown paper and two of the struts showed old bloodstains.

—*Peter Straub, "The Ghost Village"*

people" dispose of their originals, they are not so much hyperbolically evil as they are frighteningly bland. They appear interested in little more than their plan of replacing the residents of Santa Mira, a plan they seem to be following as much because of their programming, as it were, as anything. Finney's novel brilliantly exploits those elements of paranoia we have seen in our survey of small-town horror short stories; indeed, the novel resembles a paranoid schizophrenic's delusion of a world of exact yet somehow different copies writ large. Enough ink has been spilled over the novel's possible implications as a dramatization of 1950s anti-communist hysteria for the subject to be considered addressed; what is of more interest is the way the book picks up the plot device we have encountered from Hawthorne to Jackson, that of a population whose normal appearance belies a collective otherness. Finney's novel helps us to see that otherness and the paranoia to which it gives rise as expressing a fundamental concern with authenticity, with what we are under the surface. Had we world enough and time, we could follow this concern's links to Protestant Christian theology based in an emphasis on a personal and genuine experience of salvation, which grows in turn from a more general Christian concern with hypocrisy and avoiding it; as well, we might examine the more historically recent conception of the small town as the site of genuine, untainted experience (a notion the British Marxist literary critic Raymond Williams analyses superbly in his study, *The Country and the City* [1973]); finally, we could address the anxiety over authenticity's relation to Freudian psychology (and its model of a psyche almost inherently inauthentic), Marxism (with its discussion of capitalism as a system of substitutions, of workers disconnected from their work), and Existentialism (especially Jean-Paul Sartre's interest in self-formation and -delusion). Given that our world and time are limited, we will have to settle for nodding in the direction of those many connections and noting that the anxiety over authenticity we find screaming beneath the surface of most small-town horror narratives is tied up with Modernity, broadly defined.

John Wyndham's *The Midwich Cuckoos* has much in common with *Invasion of the Body Snatchers*. Wyndham's novel also involves a small town, Midwich, which is threatened by aliens who look exactly like the inhabitants. Once again, we have a plot built around a quiet invasion. In Wyndham's novel, however, the invasion is being carried out through the agency of the town's children, the cuckoos of the title. They are the result of an event called the "Dayout," during which anyone within the bounds of Midwich is rendered unconscious; nine months later, a group of women give birth to children with golden eyes. These children grow at an accelerated rate, so that by the time their calendar age is eight, their physical development places them at approximately sixteen. They manifest paranormal abilities, including the capacity to communicate with one another telepathically and the power to control the actions of others. They use their advantages to remove anyone they consider a threat, a group that grows larger as the townspeople become more and more frightened by the children.

Like *Invasion of the Body Snatchers*, *The Midwich Cuckoos* has been discussed as a dramatization of anti-communist paranoia, which may be true so far as it goes, but which misses the book's more interesting aspects. It displays the same paranoia rooted in concerns over authenticity we have seen emerge as a common thread tying together small-town horror narratives, but it locates the source of that paranoia in the young. In this way, it is the opposite of much horror fiction, in which the horror has its source in the past, functioning as that past's embodiment; instead, the horror here is one of the future. It is difficult not to think of Wyndham's novel in conjunction with another novel published in 1955, a British one: William Golding's *The Inheritors*, which relates the story of a group of Neanderthals encountering *Homo sapiens* for the first time; both novels treat the horror of the new. We can relate this fear to a specific historical anxiety on the part of a Britain witnessing its imperial power fading and its position being taken over by other, younger countries, especially the United States, but we are not wrong in viewing the novel as expressing a more fundamental fear: that of the parent confronted with the child whose destiny it is to assume his or her place in the world.

Children are also at the center of *Something Wicked This Way Comes*, albeit as the novel's protagonists. Ray Bradbury's Green Town, Illinois, is his version of the idealized American small town we encounter in *Invasion of the Body Snatchers*, but where Jack Finney's Santa Mera—like John Wyndham's Midwich—is threatened by alien invasion, Bradbury's is menaced by something else: Cooger and Dark's Pandemonium Shadow Show, a sinister carnival. The Pandemonium Shadow Show arrives on the outskirts of town after carnival season has ended, its entertainments a mask for its true purpose. The carnival comes offering the adult population of Green Town a chance to escape the failures and frustrations of their lives, to transform those lives literally. It is the symbolic promise of any carnival made real, a kind of massive Faustian bargain. As is the case for Faust, the price the deal demands is frighteningly high, the carnival acting as a great vampire, draining the lives with which the town's inhabitants have become so dissatisfied. So changed by the fulfillment of their wishes, the townspeople become the same as the carnival's freaks, all of them the literalization of Sherwood Anderson's grotesques. The Pandemonium Shadow Show's ultimate goal is Jim Nightshade, one of the novel's pair of boy heroes, whose youthful rebelliousness the carnival desires to exploit and corrupt. Jim's only hope is his best friend, Will Holloway, and Will's father, Charles, the town librarian and the only one of the town's adults able to face the disappointments of his maturity and accept them. More spectacularly than Finney or Wyndham, Bradbury gives us the small town menaced by outside forces, yet those forces are drawn to Green Town and threaten it because of its most intimate secrets. As much as in any of the other narratives we have considered, the inhabitants of the town are joined in a common bond, one that is as universal as the sin that Goodman Brown encounters: it is the condition of maturity, of diminished expectations, and it draws the Pandemonium Shadow Show like a mosquito to blood. In a more basic way than in either Finney or Wyndham's works, the small town in Bradbury's novel is complicit in the threat to it.

This notion of the small town's complicity in the forces menacing it is at the core of Stephen King's novels; before we discuss them, however, we should mention a pair of other books, both of them set, interestingly, in small towns in Connecticut. Ira Levin's *The Stepford Wives* (1972) features a married couple, Joanne and Walter Eberhart, who leave Manhattan with their two children in favor of the idyllic town of Stepford. Once there, they discover that the women of the town fall into two groups: those, like Joanna, who embrace feminism to some degree or another, and the wives of the book's title, who are stereotypically, even comically traditional in their activities. When women from the first group start becoming women from the second group, Joanna grows suspicious, and her unease is well founded. The men of Stepford, alarmed at the implications feminism has for them and their comfort, have banded together to replace the women they married with much more compliant androids. Levin's novel adroitly dramatizes the anxieties generated by the women's movement of the 1960s, showing us the lengths to which half the inhabitants of the ideal small town will go to insure that the other half stay in their place. The novel is a thematic sequel to Fritz Leiber's *Conjure Wife* (1943/1953), which embodies gender conflict through the equally dramatic vehicle of witchcraft. Like *Invasion of the Body Snatchers*, Levin's novel presents a scenario in which the residents of a small town are being replaced by (almost) exact physical copies. The cause of this substitution, however, is much less grandiose than an extraterrestrial scheme; it is a jealous desire by the town's men to maintain the status quo. In this regard, the true secret of Stepford is not its women but its men, who act from motives more crass than any we have encountered thus far.

Thomas Tryon's *Harvest Home* (1973) also involves a small town whose quaint surface conceals a rotten core, but where Levin's terrors are high-tech, Tryon's are distinctly atavistic. Like *The Stepford Wives*, *Harvest Home* tells

---

Come, you slumberers, you lumps, arise from your legion of sleep and fly over the wild woods. Come, all you dreamers, all you zombies, all you monsters. What are you doing anyway, paying the bills, washing the dishes, waiting for the doorbell? Come on, take your keys, leave the bowl of candy on the porch, put on the suffocating mask of someone else and breathe. Be someone you don't love so much, for once. Listen: like the children, we only have one night.
—*Stewart O'Nan*, The Night Country

the story of a family who abandons Manhattan for the advantages of a small Connecticut town, in this case, Cornwall Coombe. Ned Constantine, his wife, and his daughter gradually learn that the town continues to practice violent fertility rites whose origins lie in the distant past; the residents of the town are the thematic cousins of the townspeople in Shirley Jackson's "The Lottery." Neither Ned nor his family escapes this knowledge; indeed, all three of them suffer terrible fates. It is possible to read Tryon and Levin's novels as responses to the flight from big cities in favor of suburban and rural homes that occurred in the United States during the decades following the Second World War. Levin employs his small-town setting as a microcosm in which he can play out gender tensions with greater focus, while Tryon's small town treats more general stereotypes of small towns as maintaining older customs with a vengeance.

Although *Carrie* (1974), Stephen King's first published novel, occurs in the small town of Chamberlain, Maine, it wasn't until his second book, *'Salem's Lot*, that the small town assumed the central place it would continue to occupy in his fiction. The novel's plot requires a single sentence to summarize: vampires overrun the small Maine community of Jerusalem's Lot. King has admitted the novel's debt to Bram Stoker's *Dracula* (1897), describing the manner in which he structured his novel as a self-conscious echo and response to Stoker's, and we can find numerous moments at which elements of the later book repeat those of the earlier. For the purposes of our discussion, though, what is more significant is the other influence on *'Salem's Lot* to which King has admitted: Thornton Wilder's *Our Town* (1938). Among the most famous of American dramas—taught, it seems, in every high school in the country; performed at small theaters across the nation; televised every few years—Wilder's experimental play follows the lives of two generations of the inhabitants of Grover's Corners, New Hampshire, crossing over at the very end into the world of the dead, juxtaposing the limited perspective of the living with the expanded view of the dead. The play moves from the picturesque to the nostalgic to the severe, and we can read *'Salem's Lot* as a kind of parody of it, as we also proceed from the perspective of the living to that of the (un)dead, which is nostalgic in the root sense of the word as the pain of return; reborn as thirsty vampires, the inhabitants of the Lot make a very painful return, indeed.

But the novel is about more than the simple corruption of the town. While the population of 'Salem's Lot either will be killed or transformed into monsters, this small town is not the idealized community we have encountered in *Invasion of the Body Snatchers*. In a series of scenes early in the narrative, King shifts viewpoints among the town's residents, peeling back the surfaces of their lives to reveal what lies squirming beneath—the lust, the greed, the anger, the resentment. King has always been a Naturalistic writer, admittedly indebted to Theodore Dreiser—which is to say, the majority of his characters are driven by their basest animal urges, their most primitive impulses. In this regard, he has inherited the concern with human depravity that runs back to the beginnings of American literature and that Hawthorne addresses in

"Young Goodman Brown." There is an interesting exchange later in *'Salem's Lot*, when Ben Mears, the protagonist, is talking to Susan Norton, his love interest. In response to Susan's complaint that the town is being overrun by the undead, Ben exclaims that the entire country is going to hell. Given the more immediate danger to life and limb posed by the vampires, Ben's response is, to say the least, curious; surely, we think, the state of the rest of the world can wait until the last vampire has been staked. The purpose of Ben's remarks, however, is to connect the particular monster with a global sense of a decayed culture, which King already has shown us, in miniature, in the town. There's an important sense in which 'Salem's Lot is doomed before the first vampire shows its bloodless face, in which the inhabitants' various failings make the vampires not so much a menace from outside as an embodiment of the corruption festering in the town's hearts. King picks from where Bradbury leaves off in *Something Wicked This Way Comes*, with an apparently external threat serving as an index of the community's shortcomings. The novel's title thus takes on an added meaning: it is not only the town's name, but a description of its lot, its fate, which is analogous to the earlier Salem, also torn apart from the inside out. To invoke the well-worn cliché, we have met the enemy, and he is us.

This pattern repeats itself in King's subsequent work, especially *The Tommyknockers* (1987) and *Needful Things*. In the former novel, the community of Haven, Maine, is transformed as a result of the unearthing of an enormous flying saucer, which gives the town's inhabitants wildly advanced technological abilities. The residents use their new-found knowledge not to cure cancer or end world hunger, but to seek revenge on one another for years of injuries and insults. The symbolism of uncovering the buried saucer is clear enough: what had been concealed is being brought to light, with dire consequences. When poet Jim Gardener, the novel's protagonist, who is immune to the saucer's depredations because of a metal plate in his head, enters the alien ship, he discovers the dried husks of its crew, long dead after a savage brawl in which most of them killed each other with their bare hands. He also learns the source of the ship's power: cables driven directly into the brains of the crew, who served as living batteries. Advanced technology does not guarantee advanced morality; in fact, the novel strongly suggests that the more sophisticated our tools, the greater our temptation to employ them in the service of our basest aims. It is too simple to refer to *The Tommyknockers* as *'Salem's Lot* with aliens, but the congruities between the two books are striking.

"It's just small-town life, though—call it Peyton Place or Grover's Corners or Castle Rock, it's just folks eatin pie and drinkin coffee and talkin about each other behind their hands."

—Stephen King, Needful Things

Needful Things takes the vision of the depravity lurking just under the skin of small-town life to its limit. It is set in Castle Rock, the fictitious Maine town that had served King as the stage for a number of stories and novels, including *The Dead Zone* (1978) and *Cujo* (1981). Though neither *The Dead Zone* or *Cujo* can be classified as a small-town horror novel in the sense in which we have been discussing the icon, both make effective use of the location. *Needful Things* announces the importance of the town to its story in its opening pages, in which a first-person voice meant to be a generic representative of the community—and perhaps a stand-in for Stephen King as narrator—gives us all the latest gossip about the town. The picture that emerges of Castle Rock from this introduction is of a community riddled with strife, from interpersonal tension to interfaith rivalry. It would not take much, we suspect, to push those conflicts over the line from verbal to physical, and the ensuing narrative confirms our suspicions. Castle Rock is visited by Leland Gaunt, an apparently charming and sympathetic dealer in antiquities who opens a store on Main Street called Needful Things. The store seems to hold each customer's heart's desire, which Gaunt is willing to sell at bargain-basement prices. Of course, there's a catch: in order to obtain the price, the customer must agree to perform a service for Gaunt, to which he gives the innocuous name of joke or prank. The actual tasks his customers undertake are far from innocent: they are designed to heighten the assorted tensions in the town to the point that they erupt into violence. Gaunt spends the first half of the novel setting up his dominoes; when he tips the first one over, they fall with ever-increasing speed, until we are riding breakneck through a town in flames, its inhabitants literally at one another's throats.

There is a scene fairly late in the novel where Ace Verrill—the villain from King's earlier novella, "The Body" (1982), whom King has brought back for one final hurrah and who has become Gaunt's henchman—takes his boss's car to a neighborhood in Boston that isn't on any map. In a garage there, Ace picks up lethal cargo, crates full of blasting caps, automatic handguns, and ammunition, all of it intended for Gaunt's grand finale. Scrawled on the wall of the garage, Ace reads the graffiti, "Yog-Sothoth Rules," an allusion to one of H. P. Lovecraft's invented monsters (409). The reference escapes Ace, who nonetheless is disturbed by the words, but it shouldn't escape us; in fact, it is shorthand for what is happening in the book. Yog-Sothoth is dealt with most directly in Lovecraft's 1929 novella, "The Dunwich Horror," which describes the entity as a gateway. Lovecraft leaves the precise meaning of such a statement open, but King picks up on it here. *Needful Things* is fundamentally concerned with passing through the gateway, that is, moving from internal anger toward another to external violence against others. The majority of its characters enact their roles under this sign.

Obviously, Leland Gaunt is a demonic, if not satanic, figure, and it is no surprise to learn that he has come for his customers' souls. Yet King rings a small but significant change to the deal-with-the-devil tradition. In this novel, it is not enough to barter away your soul verbally; in order to lose it, you must commit some act of depravity. The residents of Castle Rock are thus truly complicit in their own damnation. In all fairness, we should note that King does not present these people as being necessarily worse than the inhabitants of other small towns; rather, their doom arrives because of their common human fallibility. When, in the closing pages, their souls are saved from Gaunt by the intervention of the town's sheriff, whom Gaunt has succeeded in distracting for much of the novel, it is in no way because the townspeople deserve salvation; we might be watching the enactment of a Protestant Christian vision of salvation through Divine grace alone.

We find in King's novel an echo of Mark Twain's story, "The Man Who Corrupted Hadleyburg" (1900); certainly, in keeping with Twain's example, *Needful Things* is King's most satiric work (though *The Tommyknockers* is not too far behind). In terms of small-town horror, the work to which this novel and the others by him we have considered owe the most apparent debt is Bradbury's *Something Wicked This Way Comes*, especially for the way in which external evil is linked to the town's secret lives. In his study of the horror genre, *Danse Macabre* (1979), King distinguished between stories of exterior and interior evil, and without a doubt, at the level of narrated events, the distinction is valid and helpful. As we have found, however, in story after story, novel after novel, and as King's novels themselves have demonstrated, when we peer under the hoods of these narratives at the engines that drive them, we find that inner and outer evil are welded and wired together at a dozen places. Clearly, Leland Gaunt comes from outside Castle Rock, as the flying saucer does from Haven, as the vampires do from 'Salem's Lot; equally clearly, had the towns been less rent by secret angers, jealousies, resentments, lusts, they might have stood more of a chance against their invaders. We are back to the picture of humanity as hopelessly fallen that Goodman Brown embraces at the end of Hawthorne's story; the difference is that, whereas Hawthorne maintains sufficient distance from such a view to suggest it is being treated ironically, King appears to adhere more closely to a vision of what Mark Twain called "the damned human race." The title of *Needful Things* could stand for King's perspective on general humanity, we are all radically incomplete, insufficient creatures, driven and riven by desire.

As we noted at the beginning of this discussion, Stephen King's tremendous success has exerted a powerful influence on both his contemporaries and his successors in horror fiction. In some cases, this has meant stories and novels whose small-town settings (sometimes in Maine) have less to do with any necessity of plot or theme and more with blind adherence to a pre-established model. That said, the resultant upsurge in small-town horror narratives has yielded a number of impressive and innovative works of fiction and continues to do so, to the extent that it would require a second book—companion to our unwritten volume on the small town in horror short stories—to address them

The goods which had so attracted the residents of Castle Rock—the black pearls, the holy relics, the carnival glass, the pipes, the old comic books, the baseball cards, the antique kaleidoscopes—were all gone. Mr. Gaunt had gotten down to his *real* business, and at the end of things, the real business was always the same. The ultimate item had changed with the years, just like everything else, but such changes were surface things, frosting of different flavors on the same dark and bitter cake.

   At the end, Mr. Gaunt always sold them weapons... and they always bought.

—*Stephen King,* Needful Things

all adequately. A few, however, require our attention. Peter Straub's *Ghost Story* (1979) and *Floating Dragon* (1983) were among the first and best novels to follow King's lead. In the former book, the upstate New York town of Milburn is the site of a struggle between the four old men who comprise the Chowder Society, a conversation group, and a supernatural shapeshifter; in the latter book, the Connecticut town of Hempstead is under siege by either a deadly hallucinogenic gas, or an ancient evil linked to the town's history, or some combination of the two. *Ghost Story* is the more successful of the two novels; although *Floating Dragon*'s premise is bolder and more original, it fails to develop what may be its most interesting notion, the town's longstanding connection to the threat menacing it, in sufficient detail. Where both novels succeed is in their use and management of a large cast of characters, so that, by the conclusion of each story, we have gained a real sense of Milburn and Hempstead, to the extent that we feel we could walk their streets and stop into their diners for a plate of the daily special. Straub has acknowledged that King's work, especially *'Salem's Lot*, showed him the way forward with his fiction, and this is evident in these novels. While his view of humanity is, on the whole, more forgiving than King's, it mirrors real and figural feature prominently in both *Ghost Story* and *Floating Dragon*, pointing to a connection between the forces that menace his communities and those communities' residents.

   Ramsey Campbell's novel *The Hungry Moon* (1986) presents the small English town of Moonwell as menaced on several fronts: first, by the attentions of the American fundamentalist preacher, Godwin Mann, who comes to the town to decry its festival practices, vestiges of ancient pagan ritual; then by the entity he awakens and which possesses him; and finally by the town's inhabitants, who fall under the entity's sway. Generally speaking, Campbell has preferred to set his fiction either in cities or in even more remote and isolated locations; *The Hungry Moon* demonstrates his ability to exploit the narrative benefits of a small town. In its presentation of the small town as the site of a pre-existing menace—in this case, something far older than humanity—it is reminiscent of *Floating Dragon*. Like the inhabitants of some of the towns we have passed through, the inhabitants of Moonwell perform atavistic rituals, but where the other rites we have witnessed tend to express their town's corruption, these practices are intended to placate the ancient monster and maintain its prison in a well outside the town. Though Campbell's townspeople are no better able to handle the threat to them than are King's, the overwhelming sense we have from his novel is not so much of human depravity as of human fragility; there is simply no way for these men and women to resist what assaults them. Even Godwin Mann, responsible for releasing the evil from its cage, is more ignorant than malevolent—which does not make the consequence of his ignorance any less devastating.

Without in any way slighting their individual accomplishments, we can say that Straub and Campbell's novels together consolidate the gains Stephen King has made for the small-town horror novel, particularly the use of the panoramic, multi-viewpoint narrative. It is a model that continues to be used to great affect. Subsequent novels have suggested further possibilities for the small-town horror novel. In terms of presentation, Jack Cady's *The Off Season* (1995) and Stewart O'Nan's *A Prayer for the Dying* (1999) and *The Night Country* (2003) all merit mention. Cady's novel employs a collective narrative voice composed of five residents of the small town of Point Vestal, Washington, who are trying to make sense of recent strange and terrible events in their community. The tone is conversational, even sardonic, as Cady's narrators recount not only their story, but their continuing reactions to and interpretations of it. It is among the most sustained inventive responses to the example Faulkner sets in "A Rose for Emily." Point Vestal's location is a major contributing factor to the narrative; it has been built on cursed ground, which permits the spirits of its past inhabitants to remain visible, and which has done wonders for the town's tourist trade. When one of its most notorious inhabitants escapes his ectoplasmic cage, however, the town finds itself divided between those who welcome their predecessor's return for the further prosperity he promises them, an ever-increasing majority, and those who recoil

---

It was then that the most horrible impression of all was borne in upon me—the impression which destroyed my last vestige of self-control and set me running frantically southward past the yawning black doorways and fishily staring windows of that deserted nightmare street. For at a closer glance I saw that the moonlit waters between the reef and shore were far from empty. They were alive with a teeming horde of shapes swimming inward toward the town; and even at my vast distance and in my single moment of perception I could tell that the bobbing heads and flailing arms were alien and aberrant in a way scarcely to be expressed or consciously formulated.

—H. P. Lovecraft, "The Shadow over Innsmouth"

---

from his corruption, an ever-diminishing minority. The intervention of an itinerant, eccentric preacher saves Point Vestal from an apocalyptic fate, in return for which the residents stone the man to death. The novel closes on a dark note, as the townspeople bring a new curse down upon themselves: that of eternal life, so that they may dwell with their crime forever.

The voices of Stewart O'Nan's novels are equally diverse. In *A Prayer for the Dying*, a second-person narration gives us the combined sheriff, undertaker, and pastor of Friendship, Wisconsin, as his town succumbs with frightening speed to a diphtheria epidemic. *The Night Country* is told by the dead, one of a trio of teenagers killed in a car accident the previous Halloween; as the first anniversary of their deaths approaches, the ghosts of the teens are drawn back to the small town of Avon, Connecticut, by the memories of their families and friends. Although their insights into the psyches of those left behind are trenchant and penetrating, the ghosts are almost pathetically powerless, jolted from location to location by the anguish of those who knew them, unable to effect events in all but the most intangible of ways. These ghosts function more as Greek chorus than supernatural threat. Instead, the novel concerns itself with the town as a community bound together by grieving and guilt, the two forces that speed it toward a devastating conclusion.

Like *'Salem's Lot* and *Ghost Story* before it (and like "Ancient Sorceries" and "The Shadow over Innsmouth" before them), Dale Bailey's *The Fallen* (2002), the last novel for our consideration, features a protagonist who returns to a town with which he has a connection—in this case, Henry Sleep revisits his boyhood home of Sauls Run in the West Virginia mountains—in order to deal with the apparent suicide of his minister father. Once there, Henry begins to investigate the circumstances of his father's death, which in turn leads him in the direction of the town's great secret. Sauls Run is a kind of blue-collar cousin to those idealized towns we found in *Invasion of the Body Snatchers* and *Something Wicked This Way Comes*; it is not a perfect place, but it is an unusually peaceful one whose inhabitants enjoy better health than statistics would seem to allow. That peace and health are becoming increasingly disrupted, however, and we understand that what Bailey is writing is not the story of a small town jeopardized by supernatural evil, but a small town whose idyllic character owes itself to supernatural agency. In this way, Bailey neatly folds the security of the town and the supernatural together. As the underlying force that has provided the town's stability falters, various members of Sauls Run register it, none more dramatically than the town's sheriff, formerly a corrupt Los Angeles cop who fled his crimes and was able to reinvent himself

---

This December Milburn looked less like a village on a Christmas card than a village under siege.

—Peter Straub, Ghost Story

under the town's benevolent influence. Now, his control is slipping, the new life he has built crumbling as his darker impulses reassert themselves. The novel climaxes under the mountains on which the town is built, in a confrontation with the entity responsible for the town's prosperity, a benefit that appears to be so much dumb luck. Bailey's characters are as at the mercy of forces beyond their control—internal and external—as those of any of the narratives we have considered thus far, but they do not cease trying to understand their situation, seeking what comfort they can in their continuing effort at comprehension. It as a different attitude towards knowledge than we have seen expressed in most of the stories and novels we have looked at.

Given the number of stories and novels we have examined, and the even greater number to which we have alluded, it would seem a foregone conclusion that the small-town horror icon must have had its place in a plethora of films and TV shows. Strangely, this is not the case. In fact, only a handful of films have made effective use of small towns, two of them adaptations of books we have already discussed: *Invasion of the Body Snatchers*, filmed by Don Siegel in 1956, and *Village of the Damned*, Wolf Rilla's 1960 version of *The Midwich Cuckoos*. Both films are remarkably faithful to their source material, which leaves us little more to say about them. Alfred Hitchcock's *The Birds* (1963), though, is another story. This is literally true of the film: while nominally an adaptation of a short story by Daphne du Maurier, it jettisons all the story's elements except its central premise, that birds all over the world have become actively hostile to humanity. Hitchcock—and his screenwriter, Evan Hunter—relocate to the northern California town of Bodega Bay, and they provide a subtle rationale for the birds' attacks that bears out the observations we have made about small-town horror, particularly the way in which apparently external threats are the index of internal corruption. The film takes as its protagonists Mitch Bremmer and Melanie Daniels, played by Rod Taylor and Tippi Hedren, respectively. Mitch, the film implies, is a ladies' man who has left broken hearts scattered in his wake; Melanie is the glamorous new woman on whom he has set his sights. This provokes the animosity of Mitch's former lovers; Hitchcock takes care to show us the looks of resentment and hatred that cross their faces when they see Melanie. Those looks anticipate the initial bird attacks, and we realize that the birds are receiving the animosity of Mitch's old flames and acting on it. It is hard to say whether these women are conscious of what they are doing; the film doesn't dwell on the link between them and the birds, and more than one critic has described the movie as a study in random, inexplicable terror. Before long, the birds appear to have exceeded the women's intentions, visiting general destruction upon the town. It seems more likely that the initial behavior projected onto the birds alters their actions at a fundamental level. That said, the movie's ending, with Mitch, Melanie, and a few others leaving Bodega Bay while the gathered birds look on, suggests that the birds, if not acting under the direct control of Mitch's old flames, at least retain their basic motivation. Given the movie's more spectacular scenes—Melanie trapped in a phone booth as birds hurl themselves into it; Melanie struggling against a hurricane of birds in an attic—it is possible to miss the line Hitchcock draws between the birds' acts and the emotions of Mitch's former loves, but an attentive viewing of *The Birds* reveals it to be another case in which the threat to a small town has its roots in the community's secret life.

The Wicker Man (1973) is perhaps the greatest of small-town horror films; although, for much of its length, it plays more like a campy musical comedy than a tale of horror. It follows a Scottish police officer, Sergeant Howie, played by Edward Woodward, a rigid, humorless Christian, to the Hebridean island of Summerisle in order to investigate a possible missing persons case. Once on the island, Howie learns that the inhabitants, under the leadership of Lord Summerisle (Christopher Lee), have renounced Christianity in favor of a return to pagan practices. Mostly, this appears to involve a great deal of bawdy singing and female nudity, and the movie seems to be poking fun at some of the more hedonistic tendencies of the 1960s counter culture; although it is punctuated by moments of unease, even menace. Howie is certain that the islanders know more than they are letting on about the girl whose disappearance he is investigating, and we suspect he is right. Eventually, he dons a costume in order to go undercover at one of the island's festivals, and the islanders see right through his ploy. Howie is imprisoned in an enormous wicker figure shaped like a man, and Lord Summerisle reveals that Howie's mission to the island has been a fraud. There was no missing girl, only a ruse to draw Howie to the island so that its inhabitants might sacrifice him in order to restore fertility to their failing crops. This they do, setting the wicker man alight as the movie plunges us into outright horror. The film was released the same year Tryon's *Harvest Home* appeared, and it is hard not to be struck by the coincidence of their plots: outsiders coming to small communities practicing savage fertility rituals (with Shirley Jackson's "The Lottery" presiding over both). It is important to distinguish, however, that Summerisle has returned to its pagan ways only recently; unlike the residents of Cornwall Coombe, they lack the excuse of tradition for their actions. Their enthusiastic embrace of human sacrifice offers a view of human nature as dark as any we have seen. We might note, too, that here is a narrative of small-town horror in which the outsider remains an outsider until the bitter end; there is no moment when Howie discovers his connection to Summerisle's populace. He is different, and he dies for it; the film makes brilliant use of paranoia: everyone really is out to get Sergeant Howie.

In many ways, *The Fog* (1980), director John Carpenter's most successful foray into the small-town horror film (though his other efforts, *Halloween* [1978] and *In the Mouth of Madness* [1995], bear watching), is the most traditional of the films under discussion. The small town of Antonio Bay, California, which is celebrating the centenary of its founding, is blanketed by a

> And so, at twenty-nine years old, a narrow-framed man with the delicate features of a mother he barely remembered, Henry Sleep came home. He came on a frost-heaved ribbon of state road that twisted northwest through chinks in the barren January hills, and as the Appalachians drew up around him, as mute and hostile as a convocation of petrified giants, he felt the old midnight terror sweep over him, an icy tide shot through with currents of fresh anxiety, the bone-stark chill of his father's death—
>
> —*Dale Bailey,* The Fallen

heavy fog whose origin is mysterious and which conceals murderous spirits. After a certain amount of suspense and bloodshed, we learn that these are no accidental intruders; rather, their bloody antics are directly related to the town's origin. One hundred years before, a ship full of lepers had attempted to purchase coastal land on which to settle; lured by the promise of the lepers' gold, six locals agreed to sell them a stretch of coast, then provided them false directions to it, causing their ship to splinter on hidden rocks and all of the lepers to drown. The six men responsible used the money they had swindled to found their own town: Antonio Bay. Now the men the town fathers betrayed have returned to exact revenge on the current residents. As is the case with *The Birds*, confronted with the film's spectacle, it is easy to overlook that what is motivating the undead lepers is a wrong done to them; they are the embodiment of the town founders' crime, returned to bear awful witness to it. Granted, the vast majority of the town knows nothing of this history; their complicity in it is more diffuse than what we have seen in stories such as "Ancient Sorceries" and "The Shadow over Innsmouth." But it is clear that we are confronted, once again, by an invading menace whose roots are tangled with those of the community they threaten. Yet again, things are not what they seem, and even in so unlikely a place as a film about homicidal zombie lepers, we run into small-town horror's concern with authenticity.

Before we bring our discussion to a close, we might spare a mention for two television shows. The first, "Twin Peaks" (1990–1991), was the brainchild of the brilliant and eccentric director, David Lynch, and if the series occasionally stumbled in the course of its two seasons, it did a better job than perhaps any other movie or TV program at representing the varied lives of the inhabitants of the small town of Twin Peaks, Washington, showing us a community rife with secrets. The second, *Storm of the Century* (1999), was a four-part, made-for-TV movie based on a screenplay by Stephen King. It is another island story, set on Little Tall Island, off the coast of Maine, which is besieged by a sorcerer who may be demonic, and to appease whom the inhabitants agree to a terrible price. Both programs suggest the possibilities for small-town horror on the small screen; indeed, because of television's format, it may be better suited to exploring the ins and outs of small-town life than the big screen.

To conclude, then: in his essay on small-town horror in *Supernatural Literature of the World: An Encyclopedia*, critic Hank Wagner lists three categories we might use to classify small-town horror narratives. The first is that of the small town menaced by a stranger; the second that of the small town exposed to danger; the third that of the small town that is itself evil (Wagner 1037). These are helpful distinctions, particularly in trying to establish the principle plots in which small-town horror narratives tend to manifest themselves. We could arrange the works we have discussed according to it: *Needful Things* fits the first category, *'Salem's Lot* the second, *Harvest Home* the third. Underlying these three divisions, however, is, as we have seen time and time again, a common concern with authenticity that tends to compromise, if not collapse, the distinctions between the town's inhabitants and whatever is threatening them. Fundamentally, small-town horror narratives are interested in the tension between what we appear to be and what we really are, an interest that expresses a profound anxiety about our identity, about the subterranean forces that compel us. Small towns are microcosms, yes, but they are more than that: they are what Raymond Williams has called "knowable communities," and what we hope to learn from them is, when all is said and done, ourselves (Williams 165). The small-town horror story tells us that we won't like what that knowledge has to tell us, that any nostalgia we might feel for small-town life is a ruse designed to distract us from its less than pleasant realities. You can't go home again, not unless you're prepared for the monsters you'll find there, the vampires and the zombies and the demons who will look at you approvingly and say, "Welcome."

BIBLIOGRAPHY

Literary Works

Anderson, Sherwood. *Winesburg, Ohio*. 1919. New York: Penguin, 1987.
Bailey, Dale. "The Census Taker." In *The Resurrection Man's Legacy*. Urbana, IL: Golden Gryphon Press, 2003, pp. 156–80.
———. *The Fallen*. New York: Signet, 2002.
Blackwood, Algernon. "Ancient Sorceries." In *John Silence—Physician Extraordinary*. London: Eveleigh Nash, 1908. Rpt. in *Ancient Sorceries and Other Weird Stories*, ed. S. T. Joshi. New York: Penguin, 2002.
Bradbury, Ray. *Something Wicked This Way Comes*. 1962. New York: Avon, 1998.
Brite, Poppy Z. *Drawing Blood*. New York: Dell, 1994.
Cady, Jack. *The Off Season*. New York: St. Martin's Press, 1996.
Campbell, Ramsey. *Ancient Images*. New York: Tor, 1990.
———. *The Darkest Part of the Woods*. Harrogate, UK: PS Publishing, 2002.
———. *The Hungry Moon*. New York: Macmillan, 1986.
Clark, Simon. *Darkness Demands*. New York: Leisure, 2001.
Faulkner, William. "A Rose for Emily." In *Collected Stories*. New York: Vintage, 1995, pp. 119–30.

Finney, Jack. *Invasion of the Body Snatchers.* 1955. New York: Scribners, 1998.

García Márquez, Gabriel. *Chronicle of a Death Foretold.* 1981. Trans. Gregory Rabasa. New York: Ballantine, 1984.

Golding, William. *The Inheritors.* 1955. New York: Harvest, 1963.

Hand, Elizabeth. *Black Light.* New York: HarperCollins, 1999.

———. "Last Summer at Mars Hill." 1994. In *Last Summer at Mars Hill.* New York: Harper, 1998, pp. 1–49.

Hawthorne, Nathaniel. "Young Goodman Brown." In *Nathaniel Hawthorne's Tales,* ed. James McIntosh. New York: W. W. Norton & Co., 1987, pp. 65–75.

Jackson, Shirley. "The Lottery." In *The Lottery.* New York: Farrar, Straus, 1949, pp. 291–302.

Ketchum, Jack. *The Girl Next Door.* 1989. New York: Leisure, 2005.

King, Stephen. *Cujo.* 1981. New York: Signet, 1982.

———. *Cycle of the Werewolf.* 1983. New York: Signet, 1985.

———. *Danse Macabre.* 1979. New York: Berkley, 1982.

———. *The Dead Zone.* New York: Viking, 1979.

———. *Needful Things.* New York: Viking, 1991.

———. *'Salem's Lot.* Garden City, NY: Doubleday, 1975.

———. *The Tommyknockers.* New York: Putnam, 1987.

Lebbon, Tim. *Until She Sleeps.* Forest Hill: Cemetery Dance, 2002.

Levin, Ira. *The Stepford Wives.* 1972. New York: HarperTorch, 2004.

Little, Bentley. *The Town.* New York: Signet, 2000.

Lovecraft, H. P. "The Shadow over Innsmouth." 1936. In *The Call of Cthulhu and Other Weird Stories,* ed. S. T. Joshi. New York: Penguin, 1999, pp. 268–335.

McDowell, Michael. *Cold Moon Over Babylon.* New York: Avon, 1980.

O'Nan, Stewart. *The Night Country.* New York: Farrar, Straus & Giroux, 2003.

———. *A Prayer for the Dying.* New York: Picador, 1999.

Piccirilli, Tom. *A Choir of Ill Children.* San Francisco: Night Shade, 2003.

Ryan, Alan. *Dead White.* New York: Tor, 1983.

Shepard, Lucius. "How the Wind Spoke at Madaket." In *The Jaguar Hunter.* New York: Four Walls Eight Windows, 2001, pp. 91–157.

———. *Louisiana Breakdown.* Urbana, IL: Golden Gryphon Press, 2003.

———. *Trujillo.* 2004. San Francisco: Night Shade, 2005.

Simmons, Dan. *Summer of Night.* New York: Warner, 1992.

Straub, Peter. *Floating Dragon.* New York: Putnam, 1983.

———. *Ghost Story.* New York: Coward, McCann & Geoghegan, 1979.

———. "The Ghost Village." In *The Mists from Beyond,* ed. Robert Weinberg, Stefan Dziemianowicz, and Martin H. Greenberg. New York: Penguin/Roc, 1993. In Straub's *Magic Terror.* 2000. London: HarperCollins, 2002, pp. 78–115.

Tem, Melanie. *Revenant.* New York: Dell, 1994.

Tryon, Thomas. *Harvest Home.* 1973. New York: Dell, 1987.

Twain, Mark. "The Man That Corrupted Hadleyburg." 1900. In *The Complete Short Stories of Mark Twain.* New York: Bantam, 1984, pp. 351–92.

Wagner, Hank. "Small Town Horror." In *Supernatural Literature of the World: An Encyclopedia,* ed. S. T. Joshi and Stefan Dziemianowicz. Westport, CT: Greenwood Press, 2005, pp. 1037–40.

Wilder, Thornton. *Our Town*. 1938. New York: HarperPerennial, 1998.

Williams, Raymond. *The Country and the City*. New York: Oxford University Press, 1973.

Williamson, Chet. *Ash Wednesday*. New York: Tor, 1989.

Wyndham, John. *The Midwich Cuckoos*. 1957. New York: Penguin, 2005.

Films and Television

The Birds. Directed by Alfred Hitchcock. Universal, 1963.

The Fog. Directed by John Carpenter. Rank/Avco Embassy, 1979.

Storm of the Century. Directed by Craig R. Baxley. ABC, 1999.

"Twin Peaks." Produced by David Lynch and Mark Frost. ABC, 1990–1991.

The Wicker Man. Directed by Robin Hardy. British Lion, 1973.

The Tragicall Hiſtoy of
the Life and Death
of Doctor Fauſtus.

With new Additions.

Written by *Ch. Mar.*

LONDON,
Printed for *Iohn Wright*, and are to be ſold at his ſhop without
Newgate, at the ſigne of the Bible. 1610.

© Mary Evans Picture Library/Alamy.

The Sorcerer

by K. A. Laity

" 'Tis magic, magic hath ravished me—"
      Christopher Marlowe, *The Tragical History of Doctor Faustus*

Conjuring up the image of the sorcerer, inevitably we see many of the same things: a robe, a staff, an assortment of curious symbols drawn within a circle, and a mysterious attendant spirit. At the center of the scene stands a figure with wild eyes and a determined look. From antiquity to the present, this idea has changed little. The sorcerer treads a thin line between power and op-probrium, never quite inside nor outside of society. Unlike the closely related figure of the witch, it is usually "he" for the sorcerer must have access to education—a boon long denied too many women until very nearly the present. While early modern sorcerers like Faustus and Prospero may be most familiar to us, the roots of this icon lie in the distant past.

We can perhaps see the sorcerer as the offspring of the shaman. Like the shaman, the sorcerer traffics between worlds, however, he comes not directly from the natural world that births the shaman, but from the world of learning.

CLASSICAL

In the classical world, we find the double-edged perception of sorcerers. They were reputed to have wisdom, but also feared to be charlatans. The *magos*, as the Greek called him, could be a trusted philosopher who spoke to the gods or a con-artist who fleeced the gullible with the tricks of stage magic. From this time dates the art that comes to be most associated with the sorcerer over the centuries: *necromancy*, the use of the dead to offer prognostications. In part, the tradition of sorcery flowers in the ancient world because the Greek and Roman empires were melting pots of cultural collisions, assimilating the knowledge and practices of the civilizations they absorbed into their empires, from the Egyptians and Persians to the Sumerians, Hittites, and Jews. Curious philosophers who sought out the roots of knowledge delved into the same secrets purloined by swindlers in search of a quick coin or two. The borderline between philosophy and scientific inquiry was as blurred as that between magic and miracles. But even in this early period becoming a sorcerer required training, whether with the gods and their priests or with another master magician.

One of the earliest of the celebrated sorcerers was Apollonius of Tyana, who retained his fame even into Anglo-Saxon England centuries later. We know the details of his life from a defensive biography written by his admirer Philostratus. Apollonius traveled the world, visiting Brahmins in India and facing vampiric creatures like a Lamia and an Empusa in Corinth. He spoke with the dead, including the spirit of Achilles. While he made true predictions and healed mysterious maladies, Apollonius concentrated on the knowledge he gained from the experiences. He saw himself not as a magician, but as a philosopher like Pythagoras attempting to understand the natural world; it simply happened that the natural world was far more complex than the common people knew.

Apuleius of Madura presents a more complex case. His *Metamorphoses* (also known as *The Golden Ass*) provided an autobiographical account of a life of magical swindling that was eventually eclipsed by a religious awakening when he at last succumbs to the calls of Isis. Art imitated life, for

Apuleius also had to defend himself against charges that he had used magic to improve his life unfairly, particularly by his marriage to a wealthy widow. His neighbors found her infatuation inexplicable, and they were concerned about the magical accoutrements around his home. His novel suggested a rather more straightforward embracing of magic, for his hapless main character Lucius becomes transformed into an ass when he ignorantly steals a transformative ointment. While his conversion to Isis worship at the end of the novel suggests that he thought it wise to abandon magic, the charges levied against him and the detailed accounts of magical practices within the narrative suggest that he may not have been ready to part with this particular kind of learning.

One of the most notorious sorcerers of the ancient world was the pseudo-prophet Alexander. The second-century scholar Lucian offered a scathing account of this con artist that still serves as a monument both to sheer audacity and to public gullibility. Alexander was a student of a student of Apollonouis who had decided that chicanery paid better than genuine healing. His pupil decided to go further, and created his own god and oracle. He presented himself as a new prophet and trumpeted the powers of his oracle, Glycon the snake who contains the god Asclepius. With much smoke and mirrors—not to mention both a marionette dragon head and a well-trained pet snake—Alexander easily amazed the locals and persuaded them to make much of the insightful oracle, who offered healing remedies and insightful prognostications. To the cynical Lucian, only rubes could be taken in by such ploys and elaborate rituals, but taken in they were to the great benefit of Alexander and his staff of assistants.

With the spread of Christianity, the work of sorcerers and magicians whose work fell outside the church became suspect. While *theurgy*, the commanding of gods, had initially been part of the sorcerer's trade, the rise of Christian monotheism brought that practice into the realm of blasphemy, so the magician resorted instead to trafficking with lesser spirits (usually demons) and ghosts from the past. Since only priests of the church were allowed direct access to the divine, the sorcerer had to settle for lesser beings. Miracles were the province of the saints—sorcerers had to settle for magic.

MEDIEVAL

The sorcerers of the Middle Ages may be the most famous, but for much of the early part of the period they were the outlaws who needed to be eliminated. With the consolidation of the Western church, "magic" came under the province of the clerics, and the only acceptable form was miracles. Not that the difference was always clear, particularly to the audience. They were as willing to accept the sleight-of-hand of Simon the Magus as the authorized marvels of Jesus. The miracles of the early saints helped create the power of the orthodoxy; magicians were seen as a threat to that established order, to be outlawed and punished. Thus the laws of King Alfred the Great in the ninth century called for the death of those women who received enchanters, magicians, and witches. While there seemed to be an echo of Apollonius of Tyana in the early English proto-novel *Apollonius of Tyre* (MS, Corpus Christi College, Cambridge), the story of the itinerant sorcerer/philosopher has been turned into a romance of redemption and love. Apollonius uncovers the incestuous love of a king for his daughter and undergoes many trials and travels before miraculously (or magically) being reunited with his family.

Perhaps the first true sorcerer to emerge from the Middle Ages in Britain was the now world-famous Merlin. The irony is that this Welsh druid arose within the framework of the French-speaking Norman rule of Anglo-Saxon Britain in the twelfth century. In his *Historia Regum Britanniae* (History of the Kings of Britain), Geoffrey of Monmouth not only forged Britain's link to a glorious past in Troy with the glorious Brutus, but more famously built up the legendary King Arthur, defender of the Celtic Britons against the unruly Saxon invaders after the fall of Rome. This Welsh cleric at Oxford also created the sorcerer *par excellence*, Merlin. Primarily based on the Welsh figure known as Myrddin, Geoffrey reshaped the sorcerer into a much more grandiose figure. Although adapted by most later writers in the Arthurian realm as a protean magical individual, Geoffrey's Merlin was a no-nonsense man of learning who treated the kings who consult him with scorn for their appalling ignorance. In this way, Geoffrey connected his druid priest with the ancient past of learning and the emphasis on knowledge rather than simply magic. Nonetheless, many of his deeds were recognizably magic.

Perhaps one of the most notable of Merlin's accomplishments was the movement of the Giant's Ring from Ireland to England. Clearly this circle of colossal stones was none other than the monument we know today as Stonehenge, which Geoffrey sought to explain in terms of Merlin's powers. When King Aurelius wished to erect a monument to his soldiers fallen in the fight against the heathen Saxons, he summoned Merlin to him to foretell the future. The sorcerer refused, saying "Mysteries of that sort cannot be revealed except where there is the most urgent need for them. If I were to utter them as an entertainment, or where there was no need at all, then the spirit which controls me would forsake me in the moment of need" (196). However, he grudgingly suggested that a fitting monument could be made from the Giant's Ring. When Aurelius laughed, thinking the task impossible, Merlin coolly admonished him, "Try not to laugh in a foolish way, your majesty," then proceeded to tout the medicinal value of the stones, which were known by those who practice "certain secret religious rites." While Aurelius and his men made a game effort to budge the stones, they were quickly discouraged. Merlin laughed at their efforts, then got the necessary equipment together, dismantled the ring, and set them on board ships. Geoffrey emphasizes throughout the special knowledge to which Merlin had access, yet also maintains the connection to the secret rites of his order. As Geoffrey notes, "his artistry was worth more than any brute strength" (198).

Likewise, when called upon to facilitate Arthur's conception, Merlin seemed to show both prescience and a distaste for flashy magic. Utherpendragon developed an insatiable lust for Ygerna, the wife of Gorlois, the Duke of Cornwall. He consulted one of his closest friends, who declared that the only possibility of success would be to consult Merlin. When the sorcerer arrived, he declared the only solution was that "you must make use of methods which are quite new and until now unheard-of in your day. By my drugs I know how to give you the precise appearance of Gorlois . . . in this way you will be able to go safely to Ygerna in her castle and be admitted" (206–7). Geoffrey praised Merlin for his knowledge and skill, but also for his audacity. In the midst of the *Historia* he inserted the Prophecies of Merlin, originally intended to be part of a separate volume. These pronouncements, offered to King Vortigern, amazed listeners and predicted the coming ages (easy perhaps for Geoffrey to do, living as he was in the "future" world) and the success of Arthur.

As the character was adapted by later writers, Merlin became the instructor of Arthur himself and the heart of Britain. The twelfth-century French poem by Robert de Boron provided the matter for the fifteenth-century Prose Merlin, which also adapts material from France. It may seem ironic that the stories that form the chief mythological past of Britain became perhaps even more popular in France, but the frequent commerce between the two nations— particularly under Norman rule of England—led to a great deal of literary exchange. The last real flowering of the Merlin stories in the Middle Ages was Sir Thomas Malory's *Le Morte d'Arthur* (c. 1469). While Merlin plays a role in only the beginning of Arthur's story, his presence is key to all that happens to Arthur and his knights afterward. However, Malory also popularized a romantically tragic end for the sorcerer, who was undone by a woman of magic. Merlin meets Nimue, the Lady of the Lake, and is immediately smitten. While they pool their resources for a time, she eventually tires of him and tricks the old magician into his doom—sealed for all eternity in a cave beneath the earth.

The tragic love of the sorcerer propelled the Romantics visions of him in the nineteenth century, as in Sallie Bridges's poem that declared: "Mighty wizard was old Merlin, the wisest of his age; / But Love all living men subdues, and Love spared not the sage." The best-known of this vintage remains Alfred, Lord Tennyson's *The Idylls of the King* (1859). His poem "Merlin and Vivien" (Nimue) popularized the image of his lover as *la belle dame sans merci*, "born from death" as her mother died upon the corpse of her father on the battlefield. She sowed dissent in Camelot and finally, snakelike, charmed the deadly spell from the befuddled old magician until he lay as one dead, "lost to life and use and name and fame." This was the tragic ending that inspired so many of the contemporary painters, including Aubrey Beardsley, Arthur Rackham, and pre-Raphaelite Edward Burne-Jones's *The Beguiling of Merlin*.

Some Movies about Merlin

A Connecticut Yankee (1949)

The Sword in the Stone (1963)

7 Faces of Dr. Lao (1964)

Camelot (1967)

Excalibur (1981)

The Mists of Avalon (1991)

Merlin [mini-series] (1998)

But this romanticized view of the sorcerer moved him further away from the prototype. He became more wizardlike, his magic mystical and unknowable rather than learned. Gone was the practical know-how of Geoffrey's Merlin. Mark Twain seized upon the opportunity offered by this trivializing and made his Merlin in *A Connecticut Yankee in King Arthur's Court* (1889) the scheming villain, or in Hank Morgan's words, "That cheap old humbug, that maundering old ass" (977). Twain returned to Merlin as the sorcerer—in fact, he himself took up the role of Lucian, shaking a magical cloak to find science and logic beneath it. Morgan triumphs because of his New England resourcefulness and savvy can-do attitude and his recognition of Merlin's tricks. Twentieth-century narratives like T. H. White's *The Once and Future King* (1958) or Mary Stewart's *The Crystal Cave* (1970) often focused on the fantastic magic, making Merlin a wizard rather than a true sorcerer; White, in fact, imagined his Merlin almost as a kind of shaman, turning the young Arthur into different animals to learn the wisdom they could teach him, while Stewart returns him to his druid past. Marion Zimmer Bradley's epic feminist retelling of the Camelot legends, *The Mists of Avalon* (1982), necessarily reduced the impact of Merlin, making "the merlin" a position held by druid-poet bards rather than a sorcerer in his own right.

Eventually the work of the sorcerer crept back into the realm of the clerics. Not content to leave supernatural powers entirely to God or to the saints, medieval clerics began to become concerned with particular heresy that dealt with diabolical sorcery. While traffic with demons was seen as a normal danger of everyday life, to be guarded against in a variety of ways from the voicing of prayers to the carrying of blessed amulets, the sophisticated knowledge obtained by those scholars studying the problems of these particular heresies proved sometimes too tempting to resist. In particular, the rise of Hermeticism and its closely related art, alchemy, produced a new interest in the arts of sorcery within the Christian tradition in the West. Texts attributed to Hermes Trismegistus—himself a blending of Greek and Egyptian gods and traditions—became the core of new flowering of sorcery that continued in popularity through the Renaissance and, to a lesser form, right up to the present.

The return of learned magic grew first from Muslim Spain, then in part from the inadvertent commerce of the successive Crusades which began at the end of the eleventh century. While the primary aim of the incursions was to restore Western Christian control of the Holy Lands (an effort that overall created more misery than anything else), one influential effect of the cultural contact (both voluntary trading as well as looting and pillaging) was to restore Classical texts and knowledge to the West. While a combination of philosophical studies including alchemy, astrology, and theurgy motivated these scholars, many soon stepped beyond the bounds allowed by the church and sought forbidden knowledge.

Perhaps the most famous of these is alchemy. While the broad umbrella of Hermeticism in the Middle Ages and beyond moved away from its roots in the ancient Mystery religions, it contained a number of practices objectionable to the orthodoxy of the church. Alchemy itself, often seen as a precursor to the scientific method (Sir Isaac Newton was at first an alchemist), was chief among these practices. The principles guiding alchemy came from the Hermetic tradition: that all things derive from the one divine source; that the material reflects in all important ways the ethereal; that the small (microcosm) affected the whole (macrocosm); that all materials was made from varying combinations of the four elements: earth, air, fire, and water; and that the unity of opposing forces (male/female, light/dark, etc.) could prove enlightening.

While early alchemists were regarded as philosophers in pursuit of better understanding of the divine order, by the thirteenth century their work had become suspect. Clergy like Roger Bacon followed the trail of the divine in the natural world, but also attempted to aspire closer to divinity itself by searching for the legendary Philosopher's Stone and the Elixir of Life it created, the *aqua vitae* that could heal any illness and prolong one's life. As the backlash against reason and practical pursuits grew, the experimentation of the alchemists began to take on a more objectionable air. By the early fourteenth century, Pope John XXII expressly forbade clergy to practice alchemy. It is unlikely that all church personnel gave up this particular art of sorcery. However, this ban did have the unintended effect of opening the field to non-clerical alchemists, many of whom more nakedly pursued the devising of the Philosopher's Stone and the attendant power it might bring. Among these more business-oriented alchemists was Nicolas Flamel, made popular by the first *Harry Potter* book as the creator of the titular Philosopher's Stone. Although there was no evidence to suggest that Flamel succeeded in producing the stone, he did find monetary success sufficient to assure his fame, perhaps in part because he shared the wealth with his community, funding both hospitals and churches.

Perhaps one of the best-known of the alchemists of the late Middle Ages was Cornelius Agrippa, who combined alchemy with other magical practices (including theurgy, astrology, and divination) in a return to more recognizable sorcery. While Agrippa often fled persecution during his time, his works have proved to maintain a lasting fascination for students of the occult, particularly his *Libri tres de occulta philosophia* (Three Books of Occult Philosophy), still in print today. Agrippa was ahead of his time in many ways, writing a book on the essential equality of women with men and devising elaborate handbooks for those who would follow in his footsteps. While he often suffered persecution from those who either feared his magic or condemned his heretical views, Agrippa also maintained for a time influential positions within the German nobility, entertaining people with his prognostications and knowledge.

EARLY MODERN

The most influential sorcerer of the early modern period actually has his roots in the late Middle Ages. Faustus remains the model of the black magic sorcerer even in the modern era. The convention of selling one's soul to the devil emerged from the concerns of heresy and witchcraft that grew out of clerical musings upon the power and nature of devils. While devils in the early Middle Ages were tempters whispering in the ears of otherwise innocent folk, the clerical development of demonology created a body of knowledge that, ironically, led to theugistic attempts to use and control those supernatural figures. The experiments of alchemy and the influence of Hermetic thought—seeing Christianity in terms of symbolism rather than dogmatic literalism—influenced scholars who desired to go beyond the approved systems of study. This zeal became embodied in Faustus.

The historical Faustus turned up in sixteenth-century chapbooks that popularized the story of the scholar turned diabolist. Johann Georg Faust is said to have lived about 1480–1540, to have received a degree in theology from Heidelberg University, and to have practiced everything from alchemy to necromancy. Fiction and folklore have removed any chance of truly understanding the historical figure, in large part because he became attached to ideas already in circulation. The motif of selling one's soul to the devil had already been part of folkloric traditions. This arose out of medieval legends of demons and saints. The usual practice of devils was to work unseen in the material world, whispering in human ears to goad them into sinful behavior or frustrating their attempts to live a virtuous life. These teachings came from both the lives of saints and from moralistic writings varying from explications of biblical lessons to the lively morality plays of the late Middle Ages. The play *Mankind*, for instance, shows the titular character able to withstand the direct assaults of evil with the regurgitation of pious teachings offered by the character Mercy; however, when the unseen devil Titivillus continually frustrates his efforts to plow a field, Mankind at last gives into despair and is very nearly hung by the evil demons. Saints' lives, however, demonstrated that with the right powers it was possible to control these demons and force them to do as one commanded. Even demure virgin saints like Margaret and Juliana were able to subdue recalcitrant demons like the ever-popular Belial and force them to both reveal their secrets and become humble servants.

The Faust story grows out of this popular history as well as the learned disciplines of theology, alchemy, and necromancy. Necromancy, the art of raising spirits of the dead for divinatory purposes, had continued since ancient times despite prohibitions of the church and secular law. Just as numerous church reforms attempted to put a stop to various folk traditions of prognostication (often tied to seasonal festivals like midsummer), within the scholarly community of the church and then the universities, various efforts to outlaw or curtail the practice failed to have any lasting success. While the witchcraft prosecutions growing in the wake of the Reformation began to fasten on the misunderstood folk practices of common people, the learned traditions of magic that required knowledge of Greek and Latin (and, with the growing commerce in Near Eastern texts, Hebrew and Arabic) presented a quandary for the church hierarchy. While earlier efforts to weed out heresy provided a clear means for prosecution, the long acceptance of arts like alchemy provided a grey area of confusion. Where to draw the line between scholarly scientific inquiry and magic? The line was contested and often unclear. If saints could safely traffic with demons, could necromancy be wrong?

As the Faustus legend developed, it clearly became a question of agency. Who was really in control, the magician or the demon? If the demon was in control, then the soul was in peril of sin. One of the earliest Faustian narratives demonstrates that point unambiguously. The late fourteenth- or early fifteenth-century Dutch play *Mary of Nijmeghen*, attributed to Anna Bijns, presents a young woman whom others misuse until she finds a sympathetic ear in One-Eyed Moenen. He is, of course, a devil, and claims that he is a Master of Arts who never fails at what he undertakes. Eager to have access to knowledge of the seven liberal arts, Mary accepts his offer of teaching, even though he balks at teaching her necromancy, the art her uncle has such proficiency in that "he can make the devil crawl through a needle's eye, whether he likes it or not" (359). The devil hastily warns her of the dangers of that art: "If you were beginning to recite a spell with your pretty red lips, and you were to forget a word or a letter, so that you could not at once say the right thing to the spirit whom you had conjured, he would break your neck straight away." Mary shrinks from learning an art that could kill her, but does not immediately worry about the peril of her soul. Unlike her later reflection, Mary does eventually see the errors of her ways (fittingly enough, her revelation comes as she watched a morality play), and after true contrition and a very long penance her sins are forgiven and she ascends to heaven. While the play emphasizes the need for contrition and repentance (whatever the scope of one's sins), it also highlights the utility of necromancy. Moenen fears not only that Mary will be able to control him, but if she were to become proficient in the art she might indeed imperil all hell's inhabitants. It was not without dangers, but necromancy could definitely be a power for good.

This was less clear by the time of Elizabeth. In the context of religious divisiveness in England in particular (after Henry VIII's split from the Roman church and with the growing emphasis on Protestant reform across Western Europe), necromancy's dangers were far more apparent than any good it might have been able to achieve. This was particularly so when it came to the dramatic version written by Christopher Marlowe (1564–1593). It certainly did not help that Marlowe himself proved to be a figure of controversy for much of his life, especially given his sudden and violent death at the hands of a possible assassin. He was repeatedly charged with atheism—at this time, a very serious crime, tantamount to treason, for the English monarch was still newly become the head of the church—and associated with people like Sir Walter Raleigh who were associated with explorations of atheism, philosophy, and religion in a loose discussion group known as the School of Night. Marlowe's plays feature larger-than-life figures who dare far beyond the safe compass of Christian morality in philosophical, religious, and even sexual matters (many scholars have suggested that Marlowe's liaisons were primarily homosexual, although it is difficult to divide accusations from truth given the paucity of factual evidence). Marlowe's Faustus, like his Tamburlaine and his Barabas, is a character who refuses to be reigned in by convention or morality. While their hubris in the end leads to their downfall, the audience could vicariously enjoy their audacity throughout the bulk of the performance. This ambiguity created both his controversy and his popularity—and continues to do so today. His was the fame to which Shakespeare aspired, which Ben Jonson trumpeted.

While he undoubtedly had been inspired by the widely disseminated chapbook of Faust's life and downfall, Marlowe's Faustus is a scholar who tires of the traditional disciplines. One by one he examines the fields of his education: logic, medicine, law, and theology. Each only affords "external trash," and after his dismissal of the accepted arts, he turns to necromancy:

Notable Faust Films

Faustus (F. W. Murnau, 1926)

The Band Wagon (1953)

Bedazzled (1967)

Mephisto (1981)

Hellraiser (1986)

Faust (Jan Svankmajer, 1994)

The Devil's Advocate (1997)

"These necromantic books are heavenly / lines, circles, schemes, letters, and characters" (1.52–53). Marlowe brings the necromancer to the popular imagination in a vivid way that has since become the icon. Faustus's magic explicitly refers back to Bacon and Agrippa. He is conscious of the tradition he is joining, confident of the powers ("a sound magician is a mighty god": 1.64) he will be able to employ. Marlowe made indelible the image of the conjuring sorcerer, hidden away in a "solitary grove" and surrounded by books that, on their own, would offer a seemingly innocent library, but combined would show the way to magic and peril: Bacon, Albanus, the Hebrew Psalter, and the New Testament. While his friends Valdes and Cornelius claim to have the knowledge to attain the great powers that Faustus dreams of, it is he alone who appears in the grove with his books open and the circle drawn, ready to conjure a pliant spirit to his commands. His working requires writing Jehovah's name forward and backward, specifying the appropriate astrological symbols to find the appropriate conjuncts, then summoning forth the appropriate spirit with a poetic Latin directive.

Knowledge was the key to access. The necromantic sorcerer needed to know Latin, astrology, mathematics, and chemistry. As Cornelius noted, "he that is grounded in astrology, / Enriched with tongues, well seen in minerals, / Hath all the principles magic doth require" (1.140–42). Marlowe made much of the academic setting of Faustus's life, beginning and ending within the university's sphere, surrounding the scholar with other students who worried about his extracurricular activities, yet enjoyed the spectacle of Helen of Troy parading before them. Marlowe, the Cambridge graduate (just barely—the Privy Council had to intercede on behalf of the somewhat negligent student), sprinkled his play not only with Latin phrases and nuggets of elevated discourse on everything from astrology to cosmology, but also with serious questions about the nature of sin and damnation. Mephistopheles's existential despair ("this is hell, nor am I out of it": 4.78) reveals a sophisticated concept of hell quite different from the medieval focus on physical punishment. The world was opening up. When Faustus imagines how the pliant spirits will serve him, he takes into consideration all the lands in the new world trade: "I'll have them fly to India for gold, / Ransack the ocean for orient pearl, / and search all the corners of the new-found world / for pleasant fruits and princely delicates" (1.84–87). Necromancy will give him power of commerce not just between the material world and the spiritual, but across the vast riches of both.

That was also the primary objection against necromancy: not simply that it perverted the altruistic aim of learning (the universities, grown from medieval monasteries, were still chiefly designed to produce new generations of clergy), but that it did so for mere filthy lucre. While theurgy may have begun with the aim of commerce with the gods, within the monotheism of Christianity, magicians had access only to lesser spirits who were generally understood to be of infernal origins. Faustus is conscious of this. Within his circle of anagrams and astrological calculations, he calls directly to Hell, "Sint mihi dei Acherontis propitii!" (May the gods of Acheron be propitious to me, 3.16), using not the English name of hell, but the Greek river that leads to Hades, and referring to the devils as "gods." In keeping with alchemical traditions, he also beckons the spirits of air, fire, and water (leaving out earth seems a significant omission that spells already the future failure of the magician). But even his summons to *inferni* is spiced with the props of the church (the name of Jehovah, holy water, and the sign of the cross), keeping his work within the learned Christian context too.

What Marlowe made key to the legend of Faustus's overreaching was not the inevitable punishment required by Christian morality, but the questioning of that morality's veracity. It may have been less of a surprise from an author himself accused of atheism, but Faustus repeatedly suggested that he had little trust in the tenets of the faith he had been taught to follow. "Come, I think hell's a fable," he tells Mephistopheles. "This word 'damnation' terrifies not him, / For he confounds Hell in Elysium" (5.129, 3.60–61). Even when admonished by the Good Angel or the pious Old Man, Faustus wavers only momentarily before returning to his thoughts of pleasure and riches. Like the alchemists who succumbed to the desire for the Philosopher's Stone and its promise of unlimited wealth—and a long life in which to enjoy that bounty—Faustus thinks only of his own appetites.

The comic scenes inserted between the more tense dramatic scenes highlight this folly (although their authorship remains less certain). The parodic repetition of Faustus's contract-signing scene, played by his servant Wagner and the ever-present stock character the Clown, contrasts sharply with Faustus's knowing acceptance of the contract his very skin and blood object to signing. When the wily servant scornfully assumes that the fool would sell his soul for a bit of raw mutton, the clown surprises him with a clear understanding of the cost, declaring "By'r Lady, I had need have it well roasted, and good sauce to it, if I pay so dear" (4.11–13). While Marlowe assumed his audience would enjoy the vicarious thrills of Faustus's dissipation, taunting the pope, performing for royalty, and conjuring illustrious figures from history, he also gave them the required damnation with the increasingly frenzied fear of his ultimately unrepentant sorcerer, who counts down the final hours, then minutes of his life, grasping for scapegoats. The magician blames the demons who tempted him, the parents who engendered him, the books from which he learned both useful and infernal knowledge, but only briefly himself. With a few notable exceptions, later versions of the story focus on the horrors of the demonic tempter and the inevitable damnation of the deal rather than the sorcery of the protagonist. Necessarily, the devil became the central figure.

The Faust legend has had a lasting impact upon the Western imagination. He has not only appeared in the works of writers as diverse as Johann Wolfgang von Goethe, Thomas Mann, Gertrude Stein, and Clive Barker, but also inspired works in other media including operas by Charles Gounod and Konrad Boehmer as well as popular music by artists like Frank Zappa, Randy

Newman, and a litany of death metal bands. While this success might seem to reflect the triumph of Christian morality, it also point the way toward the success of the growing influence of scientific inquiry. Much that had been the realm of the sorcerer would soon become the part of the province of the scientist dispelling magic with careful observation and experimental repetition. For a while it appeared that the sorcerer would have to be resigned to the distant past.

Marlowe's contemporary, Shakespeare, decided to do just that with his sorcerer, Prospero. While equally influenced by the historical magicians infusing Elizabethan culture, Shakespeare's *The Tempest* takes place in a less definite time period, one that allows traffic in sorcery without immediate peril to one's soul. Nonetheless, the parallels between Prospero and Faustus are numerous. Each has his familiar spirit, though sprightly Ariel lacks the menace of Mephistopheles's infernal realm. Each requires the background of learning, purchased with hard toil. Each makes his elaborate preparations with circle and staff, Prospero with his cloak, Faustus with his girdle of invisibility. Each, too, realizes that his magical workings come with a cost. Faustus simply denies the reality of his, while initially Prospero seethes for revenge on behalf of his losses. But Shakespeare's play lacks the tragedy of Marlowe's vision. While the audience's introduction to Prospero offers a bitter man lusting for revenge, by degrees he grows more pliant, empathetic, and eventually forgiving. Many scholars have considered this play to have been Shakespeare's last, a meditation on the magical art of writing and its illusions and realities as much as on his magician character. Not that the writer ever shrank from comparing life to a stage (or vice versa), but this play in particular tests the effects of the writer as creator and his people as helpless puppets on their strings. But more recent scholarship has also pointed out the debt owed to the rapidly expanding colonial role of the British Empire, reflected in Prospero's immediate assumption of control over the inhabitants of his tiny island nation.

While the overarching memory of Prospero remains the kindly master of beautiful spirits, at the beginning of the play he is less charming. The action starts *in media res*, without the typical scene-setting of most plays of the period. The titular tempest rages while sailors shout orders and curses and the nobles on board interfere. A calm Prospero watches all this from shore while his more empathic daughter, Miranda, anxiously "suffered / with those I saw suffer" and begs "if by your art, my dearest father, you have / Put the wild waters in this roar, allay them" (1.2.5–6, 1–2). As the seas rage and the ships pitch, Prospero relates to his daughter the truth about his brother's betrayal and usurpation, as well as the unexpected kindness of old Gonzalo, who made sure that the pair had both food and more esoteric sustenance: "Knowing I lov'd my books, he furnish'd me / From mine own library with volumes that / I prize above my dukedom" (1.2.166–68). Fortune and "a most auspicious star" have combined to bring his enemies within reach of his magic, and the former Duke intends to make the most of the opportunity.

It is not only the lust for revenge that renders Prospero forbidding at the outset. Faustus is more friendly to his sometime tormentor Mephistopheles than Prospero is to Ariel, when the spirit dares mention the promised freedom. The magician at once reminds Ariel of the debt owed for releasing him from his prison within "a cloven pine" after a dozen fruitless years (ignoring his equal length of servitude for the sorcerer), repeating to him, "It was mine art . . . that made gape / The pine and let thee out" and threatening him, "If thou murmur'st, I will rend an oak / And peg thee in his knotty entrails till / Thou hast howl'd away twelve winters" (1.2.291–93, 294–96). Similarly, Prospero uses his powers to torment the creature Caliban with cramps and aches, although the source of his malice is revealed to date from Caliban's attempt to rape Miranda and people the island with little Calibans. Shakespeare went to great pains to make the monstrous Caliban both humorous and ultimately impotently dangerous. He pairs him with the drunkards Stephano and Trinculo, who accentuate the droll side of the hideous creature, of whom even Trinculo declares, "I shall laugh myself to death at this puppy / headed monster!" (2.2.154–55). Clearly, the audience was meant to share the universal revulsion for the strange creature (much as it may alarm audiences viewing the play from a post-colonial perspective), although they might still have some sympathy for Caliban at the end of the play, presumably alone once more on his island and king.

Despite these attempts to render his magic charming and even humorous, through much of the play the sorcerer chafes to enact his revenge upon his enemies, eager to see them suffer. In the third act, Prospero charges Ariel to appear to the conspirators as a harpy and accuse them as "three men of sin" who are "unfit to live" and set for a "ling'ring perdition worse than any death." Prospero looks upon his work with grim satisfaction, declaring "my high charms work, / and these, mine enemies, are all knit up / in their distractions. They are now in my pow'r" (3.3.53, 58, 77, 88–90). Yet at this moment of tragic fulfillment, the humor and generosity of spirit catch up with Prospero. In this way, the underlying Christian morality triumphs over the apparent setting in the past. Trained by Miranda's compassion and touched by old Ganzalo's tears, Ariel dares to speak his mind to his fractious master:

From the twelfth century on, the alchemists declared that for their transmutations an agent was necessary. This agent they called by many names—the philosopher's stone, the philosopher's powder, the great elixir, the quintessence, etc. When touching the liquid metals, the philosopher's stone was thought to change them into gold. . .Besides its power to transmute metals, the philosopher's stone had other marvelous virtues: it could cure all diseases and prolong life beyond its natural limits.

Kurt Seligman, The History of Magic and the Occult

Ariel: Your charm so strongly works 'em
That if you now beheld them, your affections
Would become tender.
Prospero: Dost thou think so, spirit?
Ariel: Mine would, sir, were I human.
Prospero: And mine shall. (5.1.17–20)

The sorcerer finds that like the scientist (or the penitent) his "nobler reason" strives against his desire for revenge. Virtue, while rarer than vengeance, wins the day. Thus by the end, Prospero denounces his magical arts, breaks his staff, and "deeper than did ever plummet sound" drowns his book of magic (5.1.56).

While Christian charity may have led to the final shape of Shakespeare's fantasy, the deliberate location in a vaguely ancient time sidestepped the need to address the deliberate heresy of Faustus's magical workings. While the sorcerer of the Early Modern period might have risked charges of both atheism and heresy, the past was out of the compass of the ongoing debates and hard-fought religious battles of the time. Prospero does not conjure in Latin and Greek, but calls upon "ye elves of hills, brooks, standing lakes and groves" (5.1.33). He does not summon devils and demons forth, but the goddesses Ceres and Juno—and then only to bless the wedding of Ferdinand and Miranda. Further, he relates to the dazzled young couple, they are in fact "all spirits" rather than the true gods, and once the show is over "these, our actors / are melted into air, into thin air," and "this insubstantial pageant faded" (4.1.148–55). Even as he stands within the magic circle, casting his final spell, Prospero declares: "this rough magic / I here abjure" (5.1.50–51), as if salvation for him also requires relinquishing "that damned art" as the Good Angel declared it to Faustus. Even removed from the concerns of the present, Shakespeare could not allow his magician to imperil his soul for long.

Prospero became the model for the more fantastical sorcerer in the centuries to follow. Not the tragic overreacher of Marlowe's Faustus, but the creator of delights and illusions, Shakespeare's magician provided a more benign figure who dwelt in the safety of the past, "such stuff / as dreams are made on" (5.1.156–57). Like the figure of the witch, he was closer to the natural world, though he yet required the special training and conduit spirits that were always part of the sorcerer's world.

However, there continued to be real figures who took up the mantle of sorcerer despite the often perilous nature of that pursuit. One of the most famous of these was the magician and astrologer to Queen Elizabeth, John Dee (1527–1609). Dee stood on the growing fault line between scientific inquiry and the magics of the past like alchemy. His close ties to both royalty and theater provided much of the allure that continues to cling to him. He was a founding fellow of Trinity College, Cambridge, but also invited to take a position at Oxford (which he declined). His penchant for astrology got him into trouble when he cast horoscopes for Queen Mary and (then) Princess Elizabeth. He had to appear at the dreaded Star Chamber and defend himself, but through these contacts made his way into the upper echelons of society. By the time Elizabeth took the throne in 1558, Dee was so securely established that he chose the most auspicious day for her coronation and became her close confidant and advisor. He wrote extensively on the Hermetic arts, navigation, and mathematics, but as time went on he focused his efforts on more esoteric arts. Using a scryer, he would attempt to contact angels to gain access to important information. These exercises in theurgy went better once he teamed up with the medium Edward Kelly (1555–1597), and together they developed a body of writings in the Enochian language of the angels. Kelly, however, had a much more slippery reputation than the Queen's astrologer. He was reputed to be an alchemist more interested in turning lower metals into gold (or, as some later writers have suggested, turning his credulous partner and other wealthy folk into paupers) than in the words of angels. For a time Dee and Kelly lived as itinerants in Central Europe, seeking the patronage of nobles. Apparently, when Kelly tired of the partnership—preferring the more materials gains of his alchemy to the esoteric correspondence Dee craved—he declared that the angels had indicated that the two should share all their possessions equally. Among the "possessions" to be shared were their wives. Many have assumed this was simply Kelly's way of dispensing with the partnership, although Dee did initially comply with the angelic order. However, he was unable to continue for long and departed with his wife for England once more. Kelly eventually died after being imprisoned repeatedly for his failure to produce the expected gold. Dee, protected during Elizabeth's reign, was abandoned during her successor's. James, who feared that supernatural powers surrounded him (he had claimed that witches were angling to assassinate him), had no interest in the man by then popularly believed to be an evil magician. Dee died disconsolate and alone. Many of his records of angelic conversations were published in the seventeenth century with a preface by the scholar Méric Casaubon, who argued that Dee was an unwitting tool of infernal spirits rather than the angels he believed. Only in the twentieth century did his accomplishments in fields like mathematics and navigation begin to receive acclaim. However, the damage was already done; in fictional works, Dee has become a figure of wild fantasy and often outright horror.

MODERN

In the seventeenth and eighteenth centuries, the growing appreciation of the scientific method separated magic from philosophy and alchemy from chemistry and natural science. Even in the late Middle Ages these beliefs had their roots. The alchemist Paracelsus, with his emphasis on practicality and medical efficacy, pointed the way toward the future even if he still relied on astrology and prognostication to fund his work. The work of the sorcerer became increasingly displaced by the inquiry of the scientist, while the philosophical questions central to alchemy and Hermeticism continued. As the tools to measure various phenomena improved, the immeasurable and incalculable lost its allure. There was so much to discover in the natural world that scholars became disenchanted with the immaterial, which began to take second place. Many kinds of magical practice, however, continued to be considered suspect. As the witch hunts continued into the nineteenth century, the practitioners of any kind of magical art faced possible punishments.

Of course, the focus on Cartesian rationality did not dispel the desire for magic and sorcery for long—if at all. As scholar Anthony Aveni writes, "So maybe the characterization of the dimming of the lights of magic in phase with the illumination of the rational view of the world is a little too simple, too elitist, too progressive a model" (146). It is human nature to desire shortcuts—and often the sorcerer seemed to offer them. And despite the Protestant revolution, many people still found themselves stymied in their attempts to touch the divine. A skilled intermediary would be called for, one who could guarantee answers beyond the reach of science. In the nineteenth and twentieth centuries, the figure of the sorcerer seemed to flower in different ways. The fictional sorcerer usually resided in the past, where matters of magic would be assumed to be both active and believed. In the real world, the sorcerer appealed to those who either rejected the exclusive focus on the material or hoped to reach beyond its claim.

The sorcerer appeared in Gothic stories, usually as the voice of doom sealing the fate of the hero or heroine based on a strange prognostication. Most of the magical work, however, was carried out by monks or nuns—as in Matthew Gregory Lewis's classic novel *The Monk* (1796)—in keeping with the anti-Catholicism of the genre. These were the type of stories that a young Mary Shelley had read (in addition to her copious studies in Latin, Greek, and German), although it was a collection of ghost stories that precipitated her writing of the timeless classic *Frankenstein; or, The Modern Prometheus* (1818). While Shelley's novel has often been counted as the first example of what was to be known as science fiction, its roots come much closer to sorcery—as her accusers no doubt believed. As a teen, Victor Frankenstein read the works of Albertus Magnus and Paracelsus. Arriving at the university in Ingolstadt shortly after the death of his mother, he greets his new studies in natural science with some disenchantment, particularly after being ridiculed by his natural philosophy instructor M. Krempe, who echoes the "sad trash" comment of his father regarding the work of the alchemists. But his eventual project of galvanizing life into a collection of bones and charnel house offal could be easily categorized as sorcery rather than science, particularly when readers consider his reluctance to divulge the details to his patient audience, Robert Walton. His methods remain in the realm of magic—or madness.

The roughly contemporary German writer Johann Wolfgang von Goethe not only provided a key text in Shelley's creature's education (*The Sorrows of Young Werther*) but continued the Faustian tradition with his own development of the character. Ironically, Goethe devoted much of his life to the pursuits of science, including what he considered his magnum opus, *Theory of Colors*. His interests in philosophy and culture colored his approach to the tale of *Faust* (part 1 published first in 1808, part 2 posthumously in 1832). Goethe's Faust is a scholar but no longer a necromancer (although his father was an alchemist who saved many lives with his cures). There is a section in part two where a homunculus is created by an alchemical process, but the magic has been transferred completely to Mephistopheles, taking on the cast of supernatural rather than the province of the sorcerer. This was in keeping with the other changes Goethe made to the tale—adding a tragic love story, examining the process of nation building and political maneuvering—but moves it outside the subject of the sorcerer. However, Goethe did produce another work on sorcery that, slight as it may be, has had surprising influence. This was of course the ballad "The Sorcerer's Apprentice" ("Der Zauberlehrling," 1797). This comic tale of magic run amok was based on a story from Lucian and itself inspired both the symphonic poem *L'Apprenti sorcier* by Paul Dukas and, perhaps more popularly, the Mickey Mouse section of the Disney film *Fantasia* (1940), which used Dukas's piece as the soundtrack.

A similarly humorous turn on the subject of sorcery drove the plot of Gilbert and Sullivan's *The Sorcerer* (1877). Gilbert's book of the operetta centered upon the workings of the sorcerer John Wellington Wells of J. W. Wells & Co., Family Sorcerers. As Wells assures the young man who summons him, "we practice Necromancy in all its branches." However, the efficacy of his "amulets, charms, and counter-charms" seems somewhat questionable after his opening song, which celebrates his mercantile success more than his magical.

> My name is John Wellington Wells,
> I'm a dealer in magic and spells,
> In blessings and curses
> And ever-filled purses,
> In prophecies, witches, and knells.

The young lover Alexis had summoned Wells because he needed to purchase a quantity of the "Patent Oxy-Hydrogen Love-at-first-sight Philtre" in order to stir up the libidos of the nobility who had shied from professions of love. His plan, predictably, goes awry, however, when the love potion kicks in and completely unsuitable couples fall into spontaneous love. When even the young lovers find themselves inextricably parted, all call for a solution, which Wells informs them can only come from the sacrifice of either Alexis or himself to "Ahrimanes." Urged on by the crowd (and unwelcome attentions from Lady Sangazure), Wells consigns himself to the fire, and the restored couples depart for a feast at Sir Marmaduke's mansion, singing of eggs, ham, and strawberry jam.

Much of the nineteenth-century interest in sorcery, however, proved far more serious. In keeping with the rise in spiritualism promoted by people like Madame Blavatsky and Eliphas Lévi, the return of interest in Hermetic traditions led to the formation of groups like the Golden Dawn. The Hermetic Order of the Golden Dawn grew out of the Rosicrucian and Masonic traditions in England, which required members to affirm their Christianity, even as they "gathered for the purpose of studying the cabbala [*sic*], the hermetic texts, and other arcane wisdom of the ancient and medieval world" (Hutton 72–73). The Golden Dawn, unlike many of its precursors, actively promoted the role of women (perhaps influenced by Blavatsky's indefatigable work) and included a female image as the Key of the Universe incorporating Isis, the Bride of the Apocalypse, the Cabbalistic Queen of Canticles and the "Great Feminine Kerubic Angel" (Hutton 79). The group maintained a Christian identity while pursuing increasingly complex rituals of magic. Among the more famous members of the Golden Dawn were Maude Gonne, William Butler Yeats, Arthur Machen, and Aleister Crowley. Crowley, however, is probably the only one who really pursued the ideal of the sorcerer, developing his own systems of magic and ritual.

Influenced by a wide study of magic since ancient times and visionary artists like William Blake, Crowley much of the time sought ecstatic experiences from his rituals, often incorporating drugs or sex to achieve them. His flamboyant personality and uncompromising opinions often shocked contemporaries, a reaction Crowley openly cultivated. Many wish to see in Crowley the Faustian prototype, citing his squandered wealth and increasingly caustic relations with companions. Crowley sought to define his *Magick* as a science, famously referring to it as "the art or science of causing change in conformity with will"

He was not wholly hostile to man; but sitting there leaning forward upon a table whereon one taper flared, he was brooding on problems so far from our work-a-day cares, so far beyond even that starry paling which bounds our imaginations, that men and women were not to him that matter of first importance they are to us, but only something to be noted and studied as we might study whatever rumours may come of life upon planets of suns that are other than ours. . . . Only in the rarest moments, perhaps as an organist sleeps, and his hand falls on to the keys playing one bar straight from dreams . . . or eastwards from here, where a player upon a reed in barbarous mountains hits ancestrally on a note that his tribe have known from the days of Pan . . . only at rarest moments comes any guess to us of those songs and splendours that the lonely man drew from the spaces that lie bleak and bare about the turn of the comet.

Lord Dunsany, The Charwoman's Shadow

---

or the "Science of understanding oneself and one's condition" (131, 133). Despite his serious—if often ironic—attempts to forge a magical tradition of lasting import, it was the persistent image of him as the scandalous libertine that has continued to hold sway over the public imagination, showing up in modern fictional portrayals of magicians and sorcerers, not too surprising for a man who actively courted the appellation "wickedest man in the world." He lampooned former associates in his own novels and, in return, found himself savaged by novelist W. Somerset Maugham in *The Magician* (1908). Yet his system of ceremonial magic has proved to have continual interest, as has his organization, the Ordo Templi Orientis, which continues to draw wide membership across the world. As his ideas and excesses have become less shocking, it has become possible to read his works without the sensationalist veneer. Crowley's influence can be found in modern witchcraft movements, some of which descend from the OTO: Gerald Gardner, founder of the Wiccan movement, had been an associate of Crowley for a time. Rock groups like Led Zeppelin claimed to be influenced by his works (Jimmy Page even bought Crowley's one-time home), and even the Beatles included him among the portraits adorning the cover of *Sgt. Pepper's Lonely Hearts Club Band*. Crowley remains a charismatic figure that will no doubt continue to influence the modern depiction of the sorcerer.

In the twentieth century, however, the figure of the sorcerer primarily lived in fictional works. A model for the age can be found in Lord Dunsany's lonely magician in *The Charwoman's Shadow* (1926). Set in the distant past, Dunsany's sorcerer owes much to the alchemists and necromancers of the past, including his regular intake of the *elixir vitae* to prolong his life. The young hero, Don Ramon Alonzo, has been sent to learn his arts in the hope that he will be able to contribute gold for his sister's dowry. Ramon Alonzo fears to imperil his soul, but his noble family's impoverishment seems an insurmountable barrier to happiness. Finding at last the hidden house of the magician, the young man stammers out his desire to learn the arts the magician might teach. The sorcerer patiently corrects him: "all those exercises that men call arts, and all wisdom and all knowledge, are but humble branches of that worthy study that is justly named the Art" (12). Dunsany's magician embodies the somewhat distant, distracted, and infinitely knowledgeable icon, with only one foot in this world. Once Ramon Alonzo decides to dedicate himself to rescuing the old woman's shadow (yielded in a Faustian bargain with the magician), he only slowly comes to realize the complexity of the Art that the master has had centuries to apprehend. Dunsany established a figure who was not deliberately evil, but one whose studies so far removed him from human sphere that he found it difficult to reduce his vision to their small world. This melancholy spirit, whose actions may have been inscrutable to mere man, nonetheless formed a sentimental attachment to the related species who might make the leap. The melancholy came, however, from the knowledge that this was a Golden Age that has passed. By the end of the novel, the magician has departed, taking with him all the magical creatures who were "beyond damnation" to the Country Beyond Moon's Rising. This was the exodus Chaucer's Wife of Bath laments in the fourteenth century, so even their departure fell in the distant past. This sense of nostalgia influenced much fantasy writing until the rise of urban fantasy in the late twentieth century.

One of Dunsany's key descendents was the influential medievalist J.R.R. Tolkien. Tolkien's wizard Gandalf was more witch than sorcerer, but the same cannot be said of his opponent in *The Lord of the Rings* (1954–1955), the evil Sauron. He was referred to even in *The Hobbit* (1937) as a necromancer, and his activities more clearly fall in the area of alchemy (forging of the One Ring) and necromancy (controlling the Nazgul). However, Tolkien was less interested in forging the role of the sorcerer than in portraying his world as an epic landscape of Christian allegory, where the seemingly powerless creatures triumph as much by their righteousness as by the help of Gandalf's natural (as opposed to Sauron's technological) magic. Tolkien's influence has assured that his many imitators often reflect that interest, although some have pursued the character of the sorcerer with more interest.

One of the liveliest arenas for the sorcerer has been in the medium of comics. The arcane knowledge, ethereal events, and otherworldly creatures provide excellent fodder for graphic realization. Among the most influential comics series has been *Doctor Strange*, part of the Marvel Comics Group. "The Sorcerer Supreme of the Earth" was created by artist Steve Ditko and scripter Stan Lee in 1963. Originally a surgeon, Strange was injured in a car crash and lost his lucrative abilities. Devolving into a shambling wreck, he lost his position and wealth, becoming homeless and bitter. However,

> In the Himalayas he sought out a fabled healer called The Ancient One, who ended up repairing Strange's soul instead of his hands. Redeemed from worldliness, the reborn hero also tacitly acknowledged the value of a race and culture other than his own, studying with the old master until he was ready to become a guardian protecting humanity from the intrusion of evil. He encountered wicked wizards, and also abstract entities like Nightmare and Eternity; in each battle his weapon was knowledge rather than force. (Daniels 116)

Strange hearkened back to the heyday of the alchemist and necromancer, while continuing the battle against evil more associated with the sentimentalized version of the sorcerer. Ditko's art blazed across the pages, bringing to life these etheric battles, arcane knowledge systems, and bizarre creatures. His influence extended far beyond the medium. "Dr. Strange was embraced by and influenced the American counter-culture in the mid-late 1960s," where "the Master of the Mystical Arts nevertheless quickly became a sort of touchstone for an American youth eager explore new realms of consciousness" (Kannenberg). His image appeared on concert posters album covers as well as in the pages of underground comics.

Strange's direct descendants illuminated the pages of comics during the British invasion of DC Comics beginning in the late 1980s. Perhaps the most direct inheritor of the mantle is John Constantine of *Hellblazer*, recently rendered as the film *Constantine* (2005). This series was first written by Jamie Delano and drawn by John Ridgway and Alfredo Alcala, with numerous other writers and artists picking up the story since then. However, Constantine originally appeared in the DC series *Swamp Thing*, first because artists Stephen R. Bissette and John Totleben wanted to draw a character who looked like Police lead singer Sting. Later, writer Alan Moore (himself deciding to become a magician on his fortieth birthday and to pursue both arcane knowledge and disseminate it in his comics series *Promethea*, drawn by J. H. Williams III and Mick Gray) breathed life into the image and created Constantine as a magician and investigator. The Liverpudlian sorcerer combined the con-artist image of the magician as charlatan with the genuine study of arcane knowledge. Constantine traffics with demons and elementals. He has something of the loneliness of Dunsany's magician, but rather than producing a sense of nostalgia, Constantine has effected a sense of existential isolation that he only rarely breaks through to engage the world and its inhabitants on a personal level.

Constantine was one of the figures in the "Trenchcoat Brigade" who introduced young Timothy Hunter to the magical life in *The Books of Magic*, the comic series written by Neil Gaiman and illustrated by John Bolton, Scott Hampton, Charles Vess, and Paul Johnson. Gaiman's previous series, *The Sandman*, had also begun with a setting in sorcery, with the title character (the personification of dreaming) captured by the arcane plotting of twentieth-century sorcerers who hearken back to the arts of alchemy and necromancy.

Writer Alan Moore, who decided to become a magician on his fortieth birthday, took up worship of the god Glycon, knowing "he was exposed as a glove-puppet in the second century." Moore turned to the fake snake god when his life was "hijacked" by the word balloon of one of his characters in the graphic novel *From Hell.* "A character says something like, 'The one place gods inarguably exist is in the human mind.' After I wrote that, I realised I'd accidentally made a true statement, and now I'd have to rearrange my entire life around it. The only thing that seemed to really be appropriate was to become a magician." Moore tells his erstwhile partner Eddie Campbell, "Lucian's scornful account of Glycon's true origins as a glove puppet struck me as a marvelous way to both, as you say, pre-empt the inevitable ridicule by worshipping a deity that was already established as historically ridiculous and also to illustrate something of my ideas as to the actual nature of gods. It is my belief that all gods are stories...but stories that have become in some way almost alive and aware" (5).

In the apocalyptic issue "24 Hours" a character who calls himself John Dee holds hostage a diner full of people and drives them insane by means of one of the Dream King's possessions. Dee tells another character in the previous issue, "I'm not a black magician . . . I'm an hermetic philosopher and a scientist, too. Truly" (16). While Gaiman clearly demonstrated an interest in the sorcerer, throughout the series he focused far more on the mythic level and witchcraft. Even in *The Books of Magic*, which had a more explicit connection to the magician's history, much of the emphasis was on the cosmic and mythic strands of the history. The spectacled trainee in magic with an owl perched on his shoulder (an image made world-famous years later in the *Harry Potter* series) was also a kind of magical key, capable of opening worlds and doors—and of being used by others. Like Diana Wynne-Jones's *Chrestomanci* series or J. K. Rowling's wizards school offerings, the connection to the sorcerer figure was usually fairly tenuous.

Perhaps the greatest flowering of the sorcerer figure in recent times has been the writings of Clive Barker. While his earliest work focused more on horror and the Faustian bargain (in his first novel *The Damnation Game*, 1985), he moved on to nostalgic fantasy (albeit in an urban setting) with *Weaveworld* (1987). The figure of the sorcerer took over his imagination for a few years, appearing in some of his best work, including the sprawling epic *Imajica* (1991) and the first and second books of The Art, *The Great and Secret Show* (1989) and *Everville* (1994), with a third book much promised (and delayed so far). *Imajica* presents the story of the swindling painter John Furie Zacharias, a.k.a. Johnny Gentle, who eventually discovers that he has been a great magician involved in a gigantic magical working meant to heal the rift between the Earth and its sister dominions. Recovering his memory is part of the task, but with his assistant, the shapeshifting mystif Pie'oh'Pah, Gentle must once more attempt the reconciliation at the propitious time. Barker used the motif of magic, of course, to comment upon the work of the creator of art, itself an Art for many. He pursued that line of argument even more directly in the Books of The Art, realizing in his seeker characters the desire to shape the world that motivates all artists, whether of the material or the immaterial. The first book began with the sad sack character Randolph Jaffe, who barely maintains the signs of life, merely existing in his dead-end post office job, until he uncovers a secret network of correspondence that seeks to understand the mystical workings of the world. After murdering his boss and covering his crime with a fire, Jaffe begins wandering in search of a suitable teacher. Along the way, he forms a connection with the scientist/alchemist Richard Wesley Fletcher. While the two initially bond over their similar paths to knowledge, their methods and morals ultimately divide them. Once enemies, they fuel the wars of successive generations as they fight for control of the dream sea Quiddity. At the center of all Barker's work has been a growing certainty of the artist's role as shaman and alchemist, reaching into the shared unconscious to work magic of healing and transformation.

While he has come a long way from his roots, the sorcerer rooted in ancient practice and arcane knowledge continues to hold sway even in a world dominated by devotion to logic and reason. Perhaps as Isaac Asimov famously remarked, all technology that cannot be understood will be assumed to be magical, so continuing developments will ironically always lead to magical interpretations.

BIBLIOGRAPHY

Apps, Lara, and Andrew Gow. *Male Witches in Early Modern Europe*. Manchester: Manchester University Press, 2003.

Apuleius. *The Golden Ass*. Trans. Jack Lindsay. Bloomington: Indiana University Press, 1960.

Aromatico, Andrea. *Alchemy: The Great Secret*. New York: Harry N. Abrams, 2000.

Aveni, Anthony. *Behind the Crystal Ball: Magic, Science, and the Occult from Antiquity through the New Age*. New York: Times Books, 1996.

Barker, Clive. *The Damnation Game*. London: Weidenfeld & Nicolson, 1985.

———. *Everville*. New York: HarperCollins, 1994.

———. *The Great and Secret Show*. New York: HarperCollins, 1989.

———. *Imajica*. New York: HarperCollins, 1991.

Bijns, Anna (attrib.). *Mary of Nijmeghen*. Trans. Eric Colledge. In *Medieval Women's Visionary Literature*, ed. Elizabeth Alvilda Petroff. New York: Oxford University Press, 1986, pp. 355–72.

Bradley, Marion Zimmer. *The Mists of Avalon*. New York: Knopf, 1982.

The Camelot Project at the University of Rochester. Ed. Alan Lupack and Barbara Tepa Lupack. March 9, 2006. http://www.lib.rochester.edu/camelot/cphome.stm.

Campbell, Eddie. "Alan Moore Interviewed." *Egomania* 2 (December 2002): 1–32.

Crowley, Aleister. *Magick in Theory and Practice*. 1929. New York: Dover, 1976.

Daniels, Les. *Marvel: Five Fabulous Decades of the World's Greatest Comics*. Introduction by Stan Lee. New York: Harry N. Abrams, 1991.

Delano, Jamie, John Ridgway, and Alfredo Alcala. *Hellblazer: Original Sins*. New York: DC Vertigo, 1997.

Dunsany, Lord. *The Charwoman's Shadow*. 1926. London: Unwin Paperbacks, 1983.

Gaiman, Neil, John Bolton, Scott Hampton, Charles Vess, and Paul Johnson. *The Books of Magic*. New York: DC Comics, 1993.

Gaiman, Neil, Sam Kieth, Mike Dringenberg, and Malcom Jones III. *The Sandman: Preludes & Nocturnes*. New York: DC Comics, 1991.

Geoffrey of Monmouth. *The History of the Kings of Britain*. Trans. Lewis Thorpe. London: Penguin, 1966.

Gilbert, W. S., and Arthur Sullivan. *The Sorcerer*. The D'Oyly Carte Opera Company. Avid Records, 2004.

Goethe, Johann Wolfgang von . "Der Zauberlehrling." 1797. In *Poems of Goethe*, ed. Ronald Gray. Cambridge: Cambridge University Press, 1966.

———. *Faust: A Tragedy*. 1808–32. Trans. Walter W. Arndt. New York: W. W. Norton & Co., 2000.

Goolden, Peter, ed. *The Old English Apollonius of Tyre*. London: Oxford University Press, 1958.

Hutton, Ronald. *The Triumph of the Moon: A History of Modern Pagan Witchcraft*. Oxford: Oxford University Press, 1999.

Kannenberg, Gene, Jr. "Strange Magic: Marvel's *Doctor Strange* from Comics to Culture." International Conference on the Fantastic in the Arts. Wyndham Ft. Lauderdale Airport Hotel, Ft. Lauderdale. March 16, 2006.

Lewis, Matthew Gregory. *The Monk*. London: J. Bell, 1796.

Lucian. *Selected Satires of Lucian*. Trans. and ed. Lionel Casson. New York: W. W. Norton & Co., 1968.

Luck, Georg. "Witches and Sorcerers in Classical Literature." In *Witchcraft and Magic in Europe: Ancient Greece and Rome*, ed. Bengt Ankarloo and Stuart Clark. Philadelphia: University of Pennsylvania Press, 1999, pp. 91–158.

Malory, Sir Thomas. *Le Morte d'Arthur*. Ed. R. M. Lumiansky. New York: Scribner, 1982.

Marlowe, Christopher. *The Complete Plays*. New York: Penguin, 2003.

Maugham, W. Somerset. *The Magician*. 1908. New York: Penguin, 1992.

Rose, Steve. "Moore's Murderer." *Guardian* (February 2, 2002). http://www.guardian.co.uk.

Seligman, Kurt. *The History of Magic and the Occult*. New York: Pantheon, 1948.

Shakespeare, William. *The Riverside Shakespeare*. Boston: Houghton Mifflin, 1974.

Shelley, Mary. *Frankenstein; or, The Modern Prometheus*. London: Lackington, Hughes, Harding, Mavor & Jones, 1818.

Stewart, Mary. *The Crystal Cave*. New York: Morrow, 1970.

Sutin, Lawrence. *Do What Thou Wilt: A Life of Aleister Crowley*. New York: St. Martin's Griffin, 2002.

Thorpe. Benjamin. *Ancient Laws and Institutes of England*. London: Eyre & Spottiswoode, 1840.

Tolkien, J.R.R. *The Hobbit*. London: Allen & Unwin, 1937.

———. *The Lord of the Rings*. 1954–1955. New York: Houghton Mifflin, 2005.

Twain, Mark. *A Connecticut Yankee in King Arthur's Court*. 1889. In *The Unabridged Mark Twain*, ed. Lawrence Teacher. Philadelphia: Running Press, 1976.

White, T. H. *The Once and Future King*. London: Collins, 1958.

Wooley, Benjamin. *The Queen's Conjurer: The Science and Magic of Dr. John Dee*. New York: Henry Holt & Co., 2001.

Courtesy of Photofest.

The Urban Horror

by Rob Latham

INTRODUCTION

The phrase "big city life" conjures a number of positive images—cultural diversity, stimulating entertainment, an exciting array of cosmopolitan experiences—but it also summons more negative associations: the lurking threat of crime, the squalor of crowded slums, the incessant sensory blitz of nameless faces and alien sounds. A deep-rooted fear of the city, with its menacing shadows and sheer looming mass (what Lewis Mumford, in his classic study *The Culture of Cities*, called its "shapeless giantism" [233]), has always gone hand in hand with its many allures, and world literature is filled with tales of small-town travelers whose hopeful sojourns to the metropolis result in tragedy and dissolution.

The tension between urban and rural life may be the most basic social division, marking a rupture between distinct economies, forms of experience, and systems of value. In the modern period, this rupture has only accelerated with the advent of industrialization, with its ceaseless, revolutionary dynamism. As Marx and Engels put it in *The Communist Manifesto*: "everlasting uncertainty and agitation distinguish the bourgeois epoch from all earlier ones. All fixed, fast-frozen relations, with their train of ancient and venerable prejudices and opinions, are swept away, all new-formed ones become antiquated before they can ossify. All that is solid melts into air" (476). Building on this analysis of modernity's pulverizing flux, sociologist Georg Simmel has argued that urban existence threatens the very stability of the self: "because it stimulates the nerves to their utmost reactivity until they can finally no longer produce any reaction at all," the city gives rise in its denizens to an affectlessness and anomie that Simmel calls the "blasé attitude" (329). The modern metropolis, according to Simmel, represents an unprecedented "hypertrophy of objective culture" (338), a measureless nexus of commerce and power that dwarfs the individual subject: "He becomes a single cog as over against the vast overwhelming organization of things and forces which gradually take out of his hands everything connected with progress, spirituality and value" (337).

The resulting isolation and disorientation produce a characteristic social type that Walter Benjamin, drawing on the essays of French poet Charles Baudelaire, calls the "flaneûr." An aimless browser of random cityscapes, drawn to yet repelled by the clamor of faceless crowds, from whose seething rhythms he derives a strange, lonely pleasure, the flaneûr is at once a member of the restless throng and obscurely detached from it, driven from scene to scene by "the wave motions of dreaming, the shocks of consciousness" (165). According to Benjamin, the flaneûr has a particular fascination for "the uncanny elements" of big-city life, those sites redolent with "[f]ear, revulsion, and horror" (174); indeed, aside from Baudelaire's writings, the touchstone text cited by Benjamin as defining this ambivalent creature is a work of supernatural literature by Edgar Allan Poe. It is thus in nineteenth-century European cities that urban horror in its modern form arises, and the flaneûr—the itinerant connoisseur of milling crowds and creepy milieux—is its first iconic hero.

MEN OF THE CROWD: NINETEENTH-CENTURY URBAN NIGHTMARES

The narrator of Poe's story "The Man of the Crowd" (*Casket*, December 1840) is a nameless urbanite who, recovering from a debilitating fever, sits idly scanning the passing scene from a London coffeehouse. The anonymous "tides of population"—clerks and pickpockets, gamblers and military men—wash past his window, some moving with "a satisfied business-like demeanor," others jostling and muttering, "as if feeling in solitude the very denseness of the company around" (180). As night draws on, seedier characters begin to emerge, the guttering gas-lamps casting "a fitful and garish lustre" over their stealthy scuttlings (183). Suddenly, amidst this dubious throng, a shabby old man appears whose striking countenance enthralls the narrator, suggesting as it does "ideas of vast mental power, of caution, of penuriousness, of avarice, of coolness, of malice, of blood-thirstiness, of triumph, of merriment, of excessive terror, of intense—of extreme despair" (183–84). Impelled by this startling vision, the narrator sets out to follow the man as he skulks among the eddying masses with a furtive intensity.

As the surrounding crowd begins to thin, the man grows agitated, darting abruptly down narrow side-streets until he comes to a busy shopping district, where he browses aimlessly, "with a wild and vacant stare" (185). When the shops start to close, the man, once again distressed, sprints "with incredible swiftness through many crooked and people-less lanes" (186), the narrator barely keeping up with him, until he arrives among some posh late-night revelers. This gathering too soon disperses, and the old man, frantic, leads the narrator to the very outskirts of the city, where he blends once more with a milling swarm of humanity, this time a horde of impoverished, drunken louts. This continues until dawn, whereupon he retraces his steps, "with a mad energy" (187), to the center of London, at which point the narrator, exhausted, abandons the chase. As the decrepit wanderer disappears into the morning crowd, the narrator speculates that he has witnessed the very "type and genius of deep crime," a parasitical monster spawned by and drawing sustenance from the endlessly cycling urban mob. *"He is the man of the crowd"* (188; emphasis in original).

While not among Poe's greatest stories, "The Man of the Crowd" is historically significant because it establishes a genre of urban horror that has proven remarkably resilient. The idea of the city's amorphous vices coalescing into an emblematic figure, a living symbol of urban terror and ugliness, would come to exert a powerful influence. While the narrator glimpses a dagger inside the wanderer's grubby coat, the man never overtly threatens anyone or commits any obvious crime; yet his loitering presence suggests a latent threat, a coiled possibility for violence subsequent writers would potently exploit. Moreover, the basic elements of the story would recur throughout nineteenth-century horror fiction: the lurking demon, the startled witness, the enveloping crowd, the dawning revelation, the breathless imminence of supernatural agency in an otherwise starkly secular milieu. From the short fiction of Guy de Maupassant (strongly influenced by Baudelaire's translations of Poe), to late Victorian classics such as Robert Louis Stevenson's *The Strange Case of Dr. Jekyll and Mr. Hyde* (1886) and Bram Stoker's *Dracula* (1897), to the various permutations of the Jack the Ripper legend, early urban horror follows the pattern set down by Poe, obsessively recounting "the hideousness of mysteries which will not *suffer themselves* to be revealed" (179; emphasis in original).

Maupassant's tales show how forcefully Poe's imaginative visions of London and Paris, in stories like "The Man of the Crowd" and "Murders in the Rue Morgue" (*Manuscript*, March 1841), resonated with the actual denizens of those cities. Both authors feature haunted or fanatical narrators, harried by the debilitating complexity of the modern metropolis, surrendering with a bleak ecstasy their consciences and finally their minds to obscure or half-glimpsed agencies. Rootless flaneûrs with delusions of grandeur and an air of seedy absurdity, they wander the city's labyrinth, miserably alone yet cherishing some secret complicity with the vectors of force surrounding them. Quasi-occult energies, mesmeric hallucinations, shimmer vaguely in the gaslight, and pestering phantoms reveal themselves as cryptic doubles, which may be merely the projections of disintegrating minds (as in Maupassant's most famous story, "The Horla" [1886]). It is as if the city itself were a vast subjective space, an externalized mental landscape, peopled with the half-formed apparitions of nightmare.

Maupassant's "La Nuit" (1887; translated as "A Night in Paris"), in fact subtitled "A Nightmare," is the morbid reverie of a decadent flaneûr whose haughty promenade descends abruptly into apocalyptic dissolution. Yet another unnamed Poe-esque narrator regales the reader with his feverish obsessions—this time, for the city at night, with its glittering boulevards and blazing cafés spread out beneath the sky's "black, exhilarating immensity" (192). Lying about in languid boredom during the day, the narrator is galvanized at twilight: seized by "an unexpected and overpowering thrill, a kind of exaltation which seemed like the fringe of madness" (193), he gloats on a fantasy of himself as a nocturnal animal, senses preternaturally alert, silently stalking the city's mazes. Yet this particular evening, something seems strangely awry: the air feels clammy and dense, the streets are deserted, and the gas-lamps have all been turned off. "I felt that I was about to witness something strange, something new" (194). Yet this *frisson* of anticipation soon gives way to panic: distant figures ignore his worried calls; time seems to halt in the absolute stillness. Wandering down to the Seine, he trails his fingers in the water, but it is frigid, unmoving—the world itself has stopped. A terrifying vision of total social abandonment, "La Nuit" is the man of the crowd's cry of anguish at his harrowing solitude, his isolation amidst the city's impersonal, clockwork complexity (the ticking of his watch is the only companion to the narrator's hectic thoughts). The tale is also, perhaps, an allegory for the onset of madness, a fate that would eventually claim Maupassant himself and that seems to lurk on the anxious margins of every flaneûr's experience.

Stevenson's and Stoker's classic novels are discussed in greater detail elsewhere in this volume (under the entries for Doppelgangers and Vampires, respectively), but they deserve to be analyzed briefly here in terms of how they contributed to the iconic representation of urban horror at the end of the nineteenth century. *Dr. Jekyll and Mr. Hyde* is the quintessential tale of an urban double life: well-respected bourgeois surgeon by day, drug-taking feral sensualist by night. As his alter-ego Edward Hyde, Henry Jekyll is free to enjoy a "vicarious depravity" (81): adopting the dress and manners of a low-life swell, he gives himself over to "leaping impulses and secret pleasures" (84), haunting bohemian Soho like a hedonistic demon. "He walked fast, hunted by his fears, chattering to himself, skulking through the less frequented thoroughfares. . . . Once a woman spoke to him, offering . . . a light. He smote her in the face, and she fled" (88). Hyde is Baudelaire's flaneûr with a pronounced sadistic streak, beating a man to death in "a transport of glee . . ., glorying and trembling, [his] lust of evil gratified" (85). Jekyll is impotent to contain these savage outbursts, the "insurgent horror" of Hyde's lusts and rages (89). Perhaps if Poe's narrator had tracked the man of the crowd to his lair at last, he would have come up short at the door to Dr. Jekyll's laboratory.

Stoker's *Dracula* might seem far removed from the tradition of the lonely urban stroller nostalgically evoked by Benjamin; yet recall the eponymous character's words to Jonathan Harker, as he envisions his new life in the British capital: "I long to go through the crowded streets of your mighty London, to be in the midst of the whirl and rush of humanity, to share its life, its change, its death, and all that makes it what it is" (26). As the novel's band of vampire-hunters soon discovers, Dracula's fiendish plans are actually augmented by urban anonymity: he can come and go as he pleases from pseudonymously rented houses, his personal business shielded from prying eyes by discreet solicitors, like any slumming aristocrat. Indeed, once returned to England after his harrowing experience in Transylvania, Harker spots the Count amidst a London crowd, leering hungrily at a young woman yet apparently arousing no particular attention. Like Poe's shabby prowler, like Maupassant's narrator, like Stevenson's Hyde, Dracula becomes a nocturnal predator of the cloaking cityscape, a drifting incarnation of urban crime and violence—an image film versions of the novel have definitively cemented, from Bela Lugosi molesting a flower girl outside an opera house (in Tod Browning's 1931 version) to Gary Oldman vamping Harker's fiancée in a cinematograph theater (in Francis Ford Coppola's 1992 treatment). Driven by a compulsive bloodlust from victim to victim, Dracula is Baudelaire's flaneûr as serial killer.

In fact, the figure that serves to link Hyde and Dracula is the world's first—and still most famous—serial murderer, Jack the Ripper. The unknown slayer of at least five London prostitutes during the summer and fall of 1888, Jack got his name from a series of taunting letters boasting of his crimes mailed to the press and various authorities (one containing half a kidney allegedly removed from one of his victims). Like Edward Hyde, Jack was conversant with low-life haunts, a furtive man of the crowd scheming in the solitude of his disordered mind. (Interestingly, a stage version of Stevenson's novel, which was running during the murders, featured an actor whose performance as Hyde was so authentically bestial that rumors swirled he might be the killer.) Like Stoker's vampire, the Ripper was an invisible peril, striking at night and leaving mutilated bodies in his wake. Yet he was a real-life horror and would thus merit no mention in this entry were it not for the endless train of literary and filmic adaptations his bloody exploits have spawned.

Of course, in legendary cases such as this one, the membrane separating fact from fancy is at best thin, at worst semi-permeable—as the numerous extravagant theories that have cropped up over the past century to explain the string of murders attest. The Whitechapel killings have generated more speculation, in more or less explicitly fictional form, than any other killing spree in history, and the Ripper has had a cultural career to rival that of another Victorian mainstay, Sherlock Holmes (who has often crossed paths with Saucy Jacky, as in the 1965 Hammer film *A Study in Terror*). The Ripper has been featured in an opera, Alban Berg's *Lulu* (1937), based on Fritz Wedekind's play *Pandora's Box* (1904), which also provided a memorable film vehicle for the great screen actress Louise Brooks (1912); a parodic philosophical dialogue by 1920s French surrealist Maurice Heine, in which Jack banters with the Marquis de Sade (1936); and countless novels and films, from Marie Belloc Lowndes's *The Lodger* (1913) and the eerie 1927 Hitchcock thriller based upon it, on down. The chapter "Gaslight Ghouls" in Donald Rumbelow's *Jack the Ripper: The Complete Casebook* (1988) provides a succinct historical overview of the Ripper's cultural legacy; as another chapter, "Beyond the Grave," amply demonstrates, the Ripper's influence extends past the realm of the literary to the literal, and epigones of gore from "Düsseldorf Ripper" Peter Kürten in the 1920s to "Yorkshire Ripper" Peter Sutcliffe in the 1970s have tipped their bloody caps to Springheel Jack.

Grisly as the conclusion might seem, *oeuvres* such as Kürten's and Sutcliffe's were actually more imaginative recollections of the Ripper's career than nearly all the literary treatments, which are generally dreadful. The Lowndes novel, for example, is a creaky bit of Edwardian fustian, and most of the Holmesiana is laughably bad, especially Michael Dibdin's (alas, inaccurately titled) *The Last Sherlock Holmes Story* (1978), in which the Ripper turns out to be Holmes himself. Robert Bloch's *The Night of the Ripper* (1986) is a tedious exercise in gratuitous nastiness that makes one wish the author had stood pat with his inventive gem of a story, "Yours Truly, Jack the Ripper" (*Weird Tales*, July 1943), in which the eponymous bogey turns out to be an immortal magician extending his bloody reign into the twentieth century. That memorable tale and Colin Wilson's 1960 novel *Ritual in the Dark*, a stark portrait of disaffected British youth that peripherally relates a contemporary reenactment of the Ripper slayings, were the only literary treatments worth serious attention before Paul West released his brilliant *The Women of Whitechapel and Jack the Ripper* in 1992.

Chronology of Major Jack the Ripper Stories

Fritz Wedekind, *Pandora's Box* (1904)

Marie Belloc Lowndes, *The Lodger* (1913)

Robert Bloch, "Your Truly, Jack the Ripper" (1943)

Colin Wilson, *Ritual in the Dark* (1960)

A Study in Terror (1965, dir. James Hill)

Time After Time (1971, dir. Nicholas Meyer)

Iain Sinclair, *White Chappell, Scarlet Tracings* (1987)

Alan Moore and Eddie Campbell, *From Hell* (1991–1993)

Paul West, *The Women of Whitechapel and Jack the Ripper* (1992)

Richard Calder, *Babylon* (2006)

Like Alan Moore and Eddie Campbell's superb graphic novel *From Hell* (1991–1993), West's book draws on the most notorious theory of the Ripper slayings: that they were the work of the royal physician, Sir Edward Gull (along with a small band of conspirators, including Impressionist painter Walter Sickert), that they were designed to cover up a sexual dalliance between Queen Victoria's grandson and a Catholic prostitute, and that they featured an array of distracting smokescreens, from press-baiting letters to Masonic rituals and popular anti-Semitism. Yet this gonzo theory is, for West, merely the vehicle for a darkly ruminative reverie, a bleak meditation on power, sex, violence, and corruption. Structured as a series of overlapping internal monologues, *The Women of Whitechapel and Jack the Ripper* evokes a textured vision of Victorian London that has a gripping, hallucinatory power.

It is also a slyly feminist story, as remarked by its very title, which inverts the usual pattern of emphasis in the case. As Judith Walkowitz has shown in her superb study *City of Dreadful Delight: Narratives of Sexual Danger in Late-Victorian London*, the "Whitechapel murders have continued to provide a common vocabulary of male violence against women" for over a century (228), and West interrogates this vocabulary by exposing its psychological roots. What Sickert shares with Gull, as West depicts it, is a detached, clinical attitude towards women, viewing their bodies as mere clay to be worked upon, surgically reshaped. Both men are obsessed with procreation, each jealously begrudging this female power and aching to usurp it, through art or science—or, failing that, through new frontiers of violence, "as if he had discovered a new life form that would love him for having coaxed it, fiendish and fragile, out of Creation's night" (112). The city itself seems a co-conspirator, a sordid labyrinth whose minotaur is unfettered male lust, a fact one of the doomed women subconsciously realizes: "It was like walking on a blade, and that was the city" (4). As Mary Kelly, the Ripper's most brutalized victim, observes of her dismal neighborhood: "there was always somebody screaming, in diabolical pain, and the sound went on in Mary's head for hours" (22–23). Her own cry of "Murder!" would go unheeded because such shouts were a nightly occurrence in the wretched slum where she met her grisly end. *The Women of Whitechapel and Jack the Ripper* distills out of an infamous hell of sexual violence an angry and challenging critical vision, arraigning Poe's man of the crowd for his egotism and festering misogyny. As such, it is worth more than all the leering tales of urban stalkers and slashers that have glutted the horror field for the past century put together.

INTO THE TWENTIETH CENTURY: SMOKE GHOSTS IN THE TWILIGHT ZONE

One would naturally expect that, as cities grew exponentially in size and population, tales of urban horror would also proliferate, generating new iconic images to match the novel sights and sounds of the burgeoning metropolis. In fact, however, during the first few decades of the twentieth century, as towering skyscrapers blossomed in downtown districts and waves of immigrants packed ethnic ghettos, horror literature turned its sights elsewhere, focusing less on fresh sources of dread than on ancient atavisms. The atmospheric ghost stories of M. R. James and Algernon Blackwood drew their terrors from medieval lore or the natural world rather than from the bristling skylines and teeming tenements of big-city life. When horror fiction did engage the city, it was largely in the form of distanced allegory: William Hope Hodgson's *The Night Land* (1912), a tale of far-future survivors besieged by demons in a massive megalopolis, may in part symbolize the pathologies of urban conglomeration, with its rampant paranoia and sense of perpetual beleaguerment. The *Weird Tales* circle of the 1920s and 1930s often located the supernatural in pre- or post-historic landscapes, such as Robert E. Howard's Cimmeria or Clark Ashton Smith's Zothique; and H. P. Lovecraft, while he did portray terror stalking the streets of modern Providence, generally evoked it in the form of archaic survivals, from looming Old Ones to reincarnated sorcerers like Joseph Curwen (in *The Case of Charles Dexter Ward* [written 1927, published 1941]).

This depiction was to prove influential, however: the evocation of primordial monstrosities erupting within an otherwise advanced and secular milieu would become one of the most recognizable horror set-ups of the twentieth century. Stoker's novel had pioneered this idea, of course; as senior vampire-hunter Abraham Van Helsing at one point observes, the potency of Dracula's threat derives in large part from the modern Londoner's skepticism about such lurking superstitions. But Lovecraft brought the scenario to a peak of achievement, such that hoary presences accosting startled denizens of the modern world is largely how the genre of supernatural horror is now understood by the casual reader. Some of Lovecraft's most memorable images trade on the affective charge of this shocking reversal, from misshapen ghouls feeding on trapped subway travelers (in "Pickman's Model" [*Weird Tales*, October 1927]) to the collage of newspaper clippings foreshadowing the imminent return of the Old Ones (in "The Call of Cthulhu" [*Weird Tales*, February 1928]). In *At the Mountains of Madness* (written 1931, published *Astounding Stories*, February–April 1936), he even reverses the reversal, bringing modern men into the heart of a primeval alien city hidden deep in the Antarctic wastes.

Lovecraft's most striking tale of specifically urban terrors is also one of his most controversial. "The Horror at Red Hook" (*Weird Tales*, January 1927) is set in the eponymous ethnic section of Brooklyn, "a maze of hybrid squalor" populated by a host of immigrants, legal and illegal, "swarthy, evil-looking strangers" (250) collectively emitting "a babel of sound and filth" (247). As the language here suggests, a palpably racist fear of otherness underlies the author's vision of "the polyglot abyss of New York's underworld" (246): unassimilated aliens observing their time-honored religious rituals are grimly slandered as devil-worshipping cultists who cannibalize white children, re-enacting "the darkest instinctive patterns of primitive half-ape savagery" (248). The protagonist, an Irish beat cop repulsed by the decline of his neighborhood into "a horror of houses and blocks...leprous and cancerous with evil dragged from elder worlds" (246), barely retains his sanity when confronted with the subterranean abominations lurking behind the tenement's brick facades. The tale's infamous translation of mundane fears of racial hybridization into the clutching phobias of supernatural terror has been satirized in T.E.D. Klein's 1980 story "Children of the Kingdom," where Lovecraft's unapologetic ethnocentrism is softened by liberal guilt: the real threat to the Caucasian narrator and his wife derives not from the loitering young blacks and Latinos he reflexively dreads, but from a race of blind albinos infesting the sewers, super-white grubs eager to mate with human women. Yet for all its satire, Klein's tale echoes Lovecraft's in its evocation of the essential *alienness* of big-city life, the inscrutability of every "menacing stretch of unfamiliar sidewalk down which, at any moment, anything might walk on any errand" (48).

Lovecraft's influence on the tradition of urban horror lay also in his generous mentorship of younger writers, especially Robert Bloch. Bloch, along with Henry Kuttner and Ray Bradbury, emerged during the 1930s and 1940s as creators of a new breed of horror rooted in the institutions and practices of everyday life. All three developed bodies of work that cross-pollinated pulp horror with science fiction and the hard-boiled detective story to produce a unique hybrid, at once eldritch and high-tech, feral-atavistic and *noir*-cosmopolitan. Bloch in particular pioneered not only a set of up-to-date themes (e.g., adapting Jack the Ripper myths into the modern serial killer story), but also a pervasive tone—wise-cracking, morbidly world-weary—that perfectly captured the psychic attitude of mid-century urban dwellers: suspicious, buffeted by change, clinging to quotidian rituals to fend off a sense of looming entropy. Aside from his path-breaking tales of sex-crazed murderers, culminating in *Psycho* (1959), Bloch's most characteristic stories feature modern Hollywood as a literal or figurative presence, its cinematic spawn infiltrating and shaping consciousness to sinister effect. In "Return to the Sabbath" (*Weird Tales*, July 1938), for example, two slumming studio drones stumble into a downtown burlesque show where they witness a sleazy low-budget horror film that leads them into contact with an underground cult of devil-worshippers. Other titles, such as "The Phantom from the Film" (*Amazing Stories*, November 1943) and "The Dream-Makers" (*Beyond Fantasy Fiction*, September 1953), continue Bloch's exploration of Hollywood's seamier haunts and grislier horrors, paving the way for later writers who would explore similar terrain, such as David J. Schow and Richard Christian Matheson.

The satirical, urban-hip attitude of Bloch's best stories, and their sense that transformative terror lurked behind every movie marquee and shabby storefront, helped forge a fresh post-Lovecraftian identity for urban horror. In March 1939, a new magazine debuted that gave this brand of fiction a brief but memorable home: *Unknown* (later *Unknown Worlds*), helmed by John W. Campbell, Jr., who also edited the premier science fiction pulp, *Astounding Stories*. The third issue, in fact, contained one of Bloch's most innovative early efforts, "The Cloak" (May 1939), in which a threadbare Halloween costume purchased at a corner shop fills its owner with vampiric bloodlust. Through its mere four years of existence, *Unknown* made an indelible mark on the genre, sweeping away a century of Gothic cobwebs and ushering in a skeptical, streamlined depiction of uncanny presences hovering on the margins of contemporary life. As Stefan Dziemianowicz observes in his fine study of the magazine, "Campbell preferred the psychological horror story [to the traditional Gothic] because its focus was on characters and their reactions, and because psychological horror was consistent with the spirit of the unknown—it could happen to anyone, anywhere, at any time" (32). (The first line of Fredric Brown's tale of Satanic incursion, "Armageddon" [August 1941], captures the attitude perfectly: "It happened—of all places—in Cincinnati" [187].) Lovecraft disciples like Bloch, Kuttner, and Frank Belknap Long found their voices in *Unknown*'s pages, as did unclassifiable talents such as Manly Wade Wellman and Jane Rice; but the most significant originator, the one who invoked novel icons that resonated for decades, was Fritz Leiber.

Like Bloch, Leiber had already begun to work this emerging vein in other pulp venues, but *Unknown* gave him the platform to convert these inchoate dabblings into a sharp-edged effort that reads, in retrospect, like a manifesto of modern urban horror. "Smoke Ghost" (October 1941) is, as its title implies, the tale of a ghastly haunting, but the eponymous specter is no conventional revenant; rather, it is the veritable incarnation of big-city squalor and malaise.

A grimy, shambling creature "with the soot of the factories on its face and the pounding of machinery in its soul" (129), it stalks the protagonist relentlessly, first as a series of sooty silhouettes glimpsed from his subway seat and high-rise office building, then as a demonic amalgam of all the psychological trials of urban life ("the hungry anxiety of the unemployed . . ., the jerky tension of the high-pressure metropolitan worker . . ., the aggressive whine of the panhandler . . ., and a thousand other twisted emotional patterns" [130]), and finally as a demonic idol demanding total subservience and devotion. "You rule this city and all the others," the protagonist grovels. "The world is yours to do with as you will, save or tear to pieces" (147). Leiber's smoke ghost is, in short, the embodiment of all of urban modernity's compelling contradictions: its boundless creativity and entropic decay, its brutal dynamism and boring stasis, its exhilaration and despair. The tone of the story—paranoid, borderline hysterical, nervously alert to subtle hints and lurking portents—would exert an enormous influence on future chroniclers of urban anxiety and dread, such as M. John Harrison and Ramsey Campbell.

On the heels of "Smoke Ghost," Leiber published a series of similar efforts, in *Unknown*, *Weird Tales*, and elsewhere, that explored specifically modern forms of horror, usually in an urban milieu; each of them has spawned a small tradition within the field. In "The Hound" (*Weird Tales*, November 1942), the title creature's animal sounds emerge from and merge with "the howls and growls of traffic and industry" (187). Replacing the werewolves of medieval folklore, it is a monster spawned by the "psychological environment" of the city itself (191), feeding on city-dwellers' fears and insecurities; it is also the prototype for Whitley Strieber's *The Wolfen* (1978), with its pack of supernatural predators thinning the human herd in contemporary Manhattan. Leiber's "The Girl with the Hungry Eyes" (1949) updates the conventions of the vampiric femme fatale for a world of modern consumerism: its lean, young advertising model, star of urban billboards and high-fashion magazines, is nothing short of the undead embodiment of consumer desire itself, of half-formed cravings that can never be fully satisfied. She is also the forerunner of an entire subgenre of contemporary vampire stories, including S. P. Somtow's *Vampire Junction* (1984) and Anne Billson's *Suckers* (1992), which link feral appetite with communications media and high-tech consumption. Leiber would continue to produce such tales of urban dread intermittently throughout his career, with his brilliant 1977 novel *Our Lady of Darkness* (discussed below) serving as a fitting capstone.

The potent blend of horror, science fiction, and urban *noir* that crystallized in the pages of *Unknown* in the early 1940s also percolated out into other media during the decade. While German émigrés Fritz Lang and Robert Siodmak brought Expressionist techniques and tones to genre crime pictures like *Scarlet Street* (1945) and *Cry of the City* (1948), evoking a brooding landscape of moral ambiguity and random violence, two other European expats, producer Val Lewton and director Jacques Tourneur, were forging a

Werewolves? He had read up on such things at the library, fingering dusty books in uneasy fascination, but what he had read made them seem innocuous and without significance—dead superstitions—in comparison with this thing that was part and parcel of the great sprawling cities and chaotic peoples of the Twentieth Century, so much a part that he...winced at the endlessly varying howls and growls of traffic and industry—sounds at once animal and mechanical; shrank back with a start from the sight of headlights at night—those dazzling unwinking eyes; trembled uncontrollably if he heard the scuffling of rats in an alley or mongrel dogs looking for food in vacant lots.

—*Fritz Leiber, "The Hound" (1942)*

corpus of dark, creepy horror stories laced with subtle shades of paranoia. The first of these, *Cat People* (1942), is a tale that could have come straight from the pages of *Unknown*: a New York architect marries a mysterious Serbian girl who refuses to consummate their love, convinced that, if aroused by passion, she will morph into a savage panther and kill him. Fearful for her sanity, he sends her to a psychiatrist, who unscrupulously attempts to seduce her, only to be mauled by her emergent animal nature. The most powerful moments in the film are obliquely menacing scenes of urban stalking, with characters listening fearfully for the softly treading predator they know haunts their footsteps. As in Bloch and Leiber, the big city seethes with shadowy alien presences, in this case a secret cult of cat-worshipping fanatics, which extends its influence in the 1944 sequel (directed by Robert Wise) *Curse of the Cat People*.

As the pulp magazines began to disappear during the early 1950s, the mélange of genres they had pioneered moved out to seed new arenas of cultural production, such as the pocketbook paperback and, eventually, television. Cheap and readily available, paperback editions of works by Bloch, Leiber, Bradbury, and others served to define the genre of urban horror for postwar readers, moving beyond specialty markets to reach a broad mainstream audience. This audience, attuned to large-scale social transformations such as the explosion of new technologies and the rise of suburban enclaves, found in urban horror a compelling series of metaphors that captured the uneasy essence of contemporary experience. New writers, such as Richard Matheson and Charles Beaumont, were readily assimilated to this tradition, updating its concerns for an era of Cold War threat, middle-class malaise, and technological proliferation.

Matheson's and Beaumont's urban dwellers are young and hip, moving to the rhythms of jazz and the new singles lifestyle. Sometimes brutally overworked, like the accountant in Beaumont's "The Vanishing American" (*F&SF*, August 1955) who is so ground down by a routinized job that he literally disappears, they nonetheless know how to enjoy themselves, stomping in a divey club to a wailing (and possibly supernatural) trumpet that "screams and snarls, like little razors shooting at you, millions of them, cutting, cutting deep" (Beaumont, "Black Country" [*Playboy*, September 1954], 182). Yet they are prone to a lingering paranoia, like the protagonist of Matheson's "Legion of Plotters" (*Detective Story Magazine*, July 1953) who becomes convinced the daily irritations he suffers—a man sniffing loudly on a bus, the vague mutterings and thumpings of his neighbors—are part of a systematic conspiracy to drive him insane. The frustrating oddness of the purely *ordinary* is a major theme of both writers; their fiction vibrates with a sense that quotidian life is merely a screen for invisible and irrational impulses. At the same time, they are alert to the growing influence of mass-produced fantasies, with Matheson's "The Creeping Terror" (1959) giving this theme a comic-apocalyptic twist, as Hollywood literally begins to metastasize, becoming a "meandering metropolis" (144) that colonizes the entire country.

The characteristic world evoked in their fiction would find a perfect name in the television program both wrote for in the early 1960s, "The Twilight Zone." During the five years the show ran on CBS (1959–1964), Beaumont contributed eighteen scripts and Matheson fourteen, an output exceeded only by series creator Rod Serling. What "The Twilight Zone" basically accomplished was to disseminate the ethos of urban horror pioneered in *Unknown* to a broad mainstream audience. A world of hapless losers and scheming conmen, paranoid white-collar workers and lonely suburbanites, the "twilight zone" is the landscape of postwar change and uncertainty writ large, its everyday confusions transformed into cosmic metaphors. As Scott Zicree puts it, "the characters inhabiting *The Twilight Zone* were average, ordinary people: bank clerks, teachers, petty hoods, salesmen, executives on the rise or decline. It took no great leap for us to . . . imagine that perhaps in some flight of fancy, some slight tangent from the reality of the ordinary routine, what happened to these characters might very well happen to us" (1). Several episodes suggest the lurking horror of quotidian technologies, a theme that would strongly influence later horror writers, such as Stephen King: Serling's episode "A Thing About Machines," for example, is a neat little tale of a sophisticated man beset by mundane objects that have grown overtly hostile to him, while "The Fever" (also by Serling) features a Las Vegas gambler who is pursued and killed by a slot machine. Another major theme of the series is the jolting paranoia of discovering your very identity to be a construct or delusion, as in Beaumont's "In His Image," where a harried New Yorker realizes he is actually a robot—a perfect allegory for the growing mechanization and alienation of big-city life. "The Twilight Zone" brings to a potent culmination the strain of urban horror devised by Leiber and Bloch, paving the way not only for later mass-media efforts such as *The Night Stalker* (1972, based on a script by Matheson) and "The X-Files" (1993–2002), but also ambitious literary treatments.

SORCERY AND SPLATTER: URBAN HORROR SINCE THE 1960s

Between the "Twilight Zone" crew and the splatterpunk movement of the 1980s, urban horror did not have a coherent defining center but instead proliferated in a number of provocative directions. Iconic sites of big-city life, such as apartment buildings and subways, became powerful loci of supernatural menace, as will be discussed in the next section. Also, new writers emerged, often associated with specific cities—for example, Anne Rice with New Orleans, Dennis Etchison with Los Angeles, M. John Harrison with London, and Ramsey Campbell with Liverpool. These diverse talents made urban horror uniquely their own, giving it the particular flavor of their favorite—or most dreaded—metropolitan haunts. Rice's *Interview with the Vampire* (1976), for example, peoples a richly imagined antebellum Big Easy with dreamily dissolute bloodsuckers, languid, androgynous creatures emblematic of that city's legendary exoticism, decadence, and soulful sensuality. This novel, and its many sequels, have cemented New Orleans as the preferred stalking-ground for the coolest and kinkiest of the undead, as witness Poppy Z. Brite's Goth-girl update of *Interview*, *Lost Souls* (1992).

Etchison, who began publishing short fiction in the early 1960s, has generated a brilliant corpus of work that manages to be at once aesthetically and sociologically distinctive, exploring the ambiguous landscapes of Southern California with a corrosive precision that recalls Raymond Chandler and Nathanael West. The characteristic scenes of his stories—half-empty multiplex cinemas, all-night laundromats and convenience stores, bleak highway rest-stops, neon-lit beachside motels—evoke the aimlessness and ennui of contemporary (sub)urban experience, a spiritual wasteland in which dark and sinister forces incubate. Stylistically, his tales are models of concision, stark montages of hallucinatory details pregnant with psychological nuance. "It Only Comes Out at Night" (1976), for example, captures the accumulating dread of a driver who realizes he is being tracked by a killer, while "The Nighthawk" (1978) offers a more subtle study of a young girl who suspects that her brother may be a shape-shifting monster. Only a few of the tales—such as "The Late Shift" (1980), in which dead-end service jobs are staffed by reanimated corpses—are overtly supernatural, most conveying mere glimpses of the numinous that remain inscrutable, hauntingly elusive. The co-ed murders in "White Moon Rising" (1977), the vanished pets in "The Dog Park" (1993) could be evidence of supernatural agency, or they could simply be the inexorable results of a hollow, decadent modernity. Filled with grim hints and nervous portents, Etchison's stories amount to a collection of cryptic snapshots of the contemporary cityscape and the lost souls that inhabit it.

Harrison's vision of London is similarly bleak, wedding a downbeat portrait of dissipated lives with a tone of stark, moody lyricism. Compelling tales such as "The Incalling" (1978) and "Egnaro" (*Winter's Tales* No. 27, 1981) invoke a blighted city obscurely seething with secret ceremonies, a shabby magic perceptible only to disintegrating psyches. Harrison's skill at depicting the hallucinatory labyrinth of the contemporary city achieved potent expression in his Viriconium Sequence—a sword-and-sorcery series, set in the eponymous urban dreamland, that skirts the metafictional terrain of Borges and Calvino in its exploration of delirious mindscapes, the shifting maze of a deliquescent far-future. His 1992 novel *The Course of the Heart* combines Harrison's characteristic strength at the delineation of physical and emotional wastelands with a fascination for Crowleyesque "sex magick": a scruffy little warlock named Yaxley oversees a cryptic ritual whose fallout damages the lives of a pair of bookish neurotics, as well as that of the nameless narrator, whose aching mid-life crisis points up the spiritual emptiness and deadened perception of secular modernity. Lured by a vague promise of transcendence, this graying cohort of ex-hippies struggles to realize a mystical vision of "the Coeur," a lost homeland that Yaxley seeks through squalid sorcery and the others through fugitive states of grace—thus suggesting that sordid (urban) horror may ultimately be purged by redemptive (rural) fantasy, with ruined landscapes of stone and steel giving way to an irrepressible natural fecundity. It is a rare moment of hope in an *oeuvre* otherwise chillingly disheartening.

Perhaps the finest of this generation of talents who came of age during the 1960s and 1970s is Ramsey Campbell. Liverpool, the major shipping center of Industrial-Age Britain, was brutally impacted by waves of capital flight and deindustrialization during the 1970s, and Campbell's fiction, which had begun as a pastiche of Lovecraft, evolved to limn the resulting social horrors with a cold intensity. A number of his short stories of the period convey a clutching terror of urban decay, finding in bits of street refuse or other detritus not only a lurking physical threat but also an emblem of cultural and spiritual putrefaction—for example, "Litter" (1974) and "In the Bag" (1977). The city's human castoffs—drifters, vagabonds, skinheads—also appear as icons of horror in Campbell's short fiction: in "The Man in the Underpass" (1975), children imagine a loitering masturbator to be a feral god demanding sacrifice, while in "Midnight Hobo" (1979) a vagrant haunting a railway bridge becomes a figure of shape-shifting loathsomeness. "Mackintosh Willy" (1979), perhaps Campbell's finest effort in this vein, conveys not merely the coarse vileness of the eponymous character—a drunken bum huddling in the darkness of a park shelter, perceptible only as "shapeless movement . . ., and a snarling" (208)—but also the casual cruelty of the middle-class children for whom he is little more than a subhuman bogey. Campbell's novels of the period—such as *The Face That Must Die* (1979), a masterful study of social isolation and murderous paranoia—also feature Liverpool as a brooding presence, a grim landscape of alienation and nightmare.

This generation of urban horror writers has inspired a fresh cohort. Following in the downbeat footsteps of Etchison and Campbell, younger talents such as Joel Lane and Nicholas Royle have taken their elliptical, hallucinatory, and paranoiac visions to further limits of extremity. Lane's harsh,

We never saw him until it was growing dark: that was what made him into a monster. Perhaps during the day he joined his cronies elsewhere—on the steps of ruined churches in the center of Liverpool, or lying on the grass in St. John's Gardens, or crowding the benches opposite Edge Hill Public Library, whose clock no doubt helped their draining of time. But if anything of this occurred to us, we dismissed it as irrelevant. He was a creature of the dark.

—*Ramsey Campbell, "Mackintosh Willy" (1979)*

fragmentary short stories, gathered in *The Earth Wire* (1994) and *The Lost District* (2006), surreally collapse psychic and physical topographies, evoking a crumbling, dreamlike, post-Thatcher Britain peopled with deracinated losers, drug-addled visionaries, and other noir-esque hard cases. Royle's sharply etched novels, while depicting a more upscale scene, have a similar febrile intensity: *The Director's Cut* (2000) and *Antwerp* (2004) link London's urban-chic film (sub)culture with various manifestations of erotic and criminal mania. More conventional in tone yet ingenious nonetheless, the work of Christopher Fowler—especially his London Quartet of novels: *Roofworld* (1988), *Rune* (1990), *Red Bride* (1992), and *Darkest Day* (1993)—portray a city scene rife with clandestine ritual and cryptic menace, while the short stories gathered in *City Jitters* (1986) and *The Bureau of Lost Souls* (1989) delineate an array of contemporary urban nightmares: malign buildings, shady civil servants, sinister bureaucracies.

For his part, M. John Harrison has also inspired followers; indeed, he is often seen as the godfather of the so-called "New Weird" aesthetic, with his shape-shifting Viriconium series inspiring more recent science-fictional urban Gothics by the likes of China Miéville (*Perdido Street Station* [2000]) and Alistair Reynolds (*Chasm City* [2001]). The work of Peter Ackroyd and Iain Sinclair also belongs within this general orbit, though their influences are more diverse, less based in a genre corpus. Still, like Harrison, they are both obsessed with a ceremonial world of violence and delirium lurking behind the bland façades of modern London: Ackroyd's *Hawksmoor* (1985) connects a secret history of satanic architecture with a series of grisly child murders, while Sinclair's first novel, *White Chappell: Scarlet Tracings* (1987), fuses a mordant portrait of contemporary book collecting with a grim retelling of the Jack the Ripper slayings. An even younger writer, Conrad Williams, has recently produced a novel, *London Revenant* (2004), that seems almost a synthesis of all these overlapping trends, a macabre meditation on a dark, fundamentally unknowable city alive with festering presences.

While these new generations of writers were busily adapting the tradition of urban horror staked out several decades before by *Unknown* magazine, several of the older authors who had pioneered that tradition were still actively publishing. While Robert Bloch seemed content to spin out endless variations on the *Psycho* theme, such as his 1974 novel *American Gothic*, which treated the career of Chicago serial killer H. H. Holmes, the ever-unpredictable Fritz Leiber produced one of the classics of urban horror of the postwar period: *Our Lady of Darkness* (1977). Set in modern San Francisco, Leiber's adopted home, and featuring as protagonist an aging horror writer and bibliophile who seems clearly an autobiographical projection, the novel is, like Alfred Hitchcock's film *Vertigo* (1958), a subtle evocation of the City by the Bay's buried history of supernatural legend. Deeply connected to a local tradition of the fantastic that goes back to Ambrose Bierce and Jack London, the story centers on a secret book, Thibaut de Castries's *Megapolisomancy: A New Science of Cities*, that elaborates a theory of "paramental entities," hostile emanations of "all that stuff accumulating in big cities, its sheer liquid and solid mass" (13). In an eerie echo of the narrative of "Smoke Ghost," our hero hurries anxiously through a growingly estranged city, "searching the dark sea of roofs" for "a swift pale brown thing stalking him," confident in its mastery of the landscape and "taking advantage of every bit of cover: a chimney and its cap, a cupola, a water tank, a penthouse large or tiny, a thick standpipe, a wind scoop, a ventilator hood, hood of a garbage chute, a skylight, a roof's low walls, the low walls of an airshaft" (85). Every feature of the skyline is a latent menace, every familiar scene transformed into an incipient wasteland of "electro-mephitic city-stuff," the entropic sediment of human conglomeration rife with ghostly predators. It is a brilliant and compelling novel.

But the most influential novel of the 1970s, in terms not only of seeding a new wave of urban dread but also inaugurating a boom in horror publishing that would last for the next two decades, was William Peter Blatty's *The Exorcist* (1971). This gripping tale gave mainstream readers a taste of the quotidian horrors genre writers such as Leiber and Bloch had been spinning out since the 1940s: in a tasteful suburb of Washington, D.C., in an environment entirely secular and mundane, a pleasant young girl is possessed by a demon. The atmosphere in the household as the possession deepens is chillingly conveyed, and the exorcism itself—with the transformed child raging and the furniture quaking—has a stark, archetypal power. In part through its own best-selling success, in part due to the blockbuster 1973 film based upon it, *The Exorcist* opened a wide new market for horror writers, and soon enough Stephen King and Peter Straub, among many others, would move in to exploit it. While best known as authors of small-town horror and thus falling outside the ambit of this entry, King and Straub had an immediate, skyrocketing success that paved the way for a host of fledgling talents who would explore urban terrors appropriate for an age of high crime, racial tension, and post-industrial decay. In the late 1980s and early 1990s, this fresh upsurge of city horror went by the general name of "splatterpunk."

The term, coined by the movement's shrewdest operator David J. Schow, was geared to evoke the in-your-face aesthetic of low-budget splatter films, with their hyperkinetic rhythms and unapologetic explosions of gore, as well as the streetwise attitudes of contemporary punk subculture. Controversial and confrontational, splatterpunk authors—especially John Skipp and Craig Spector, who collaborated on a series of novels that delineated the faction's grisly perimeter—stoked fights with proponents of quieter brands of horror, such as Charles L. Grant and William F. Nolan, who castigated the splatter-punks in the fan press as vulgar guttersnipes in thrall to cinematic sleaze. At the same time, the movement drew avid defenders, such as R. S. Hadji, who championed Skipp and Spector's rhetorical overkill against the older gen-eration's complaints, and Philip Nutman, who praised splatterpunk as a "survivalist" literature that "reflects the moral chaos of our times" (24). The polemical noise surrounding the movement has made it difficult for critics to assess its strengths and weaknesses. On the one hand, its exploitation of the temper and tactics of grindhouse cinema and music videos introduced a wider range of cultural reference and stylistic possibility to the genre, at least partially legitimating the jaundiced world-view of heavy-metal headbangers and hardcore gorehounds. On the other hand, of the various writers associated at one time or another with the movement, only Schow and Clive Barker are truly major figures, while Skipp and Spector, Richard Christian Matheson (son of Richard Matheson), and Joe R. Lansdale are occasionally arresting second-raters, and Ray Garton and Richard Laymon are fellow travelers of borderline competence.

Not every splatterpunk has engaged with the tradition of urban horror: Lansdale, for instance, tends to work the rural scene, and the pyrotechnic Barker is notoriously difficult to pigeonhole. But Matheson and Schow have followed Bloch in limning the noirish terrors of modern Hollywood, while Garton and Skipp and Spector have inflated Leiber's subtle vision of quintes-sentially city-based forms of monstrosity to truly hysterical proportions. Matheson's short stories, gathered in *Scars and Other Distinguishing Marks* (1987), invite comparison with Etchison in their bleak concision, but they lack

---

Significant Tales of Hollywood Horror

Henry Kuttner, "The Shadow on the Screen" (1938)

Richard Matheson, "The Creeping Terror" (1959)

Robert Bloch, "The Movie People" (1969)

Clive Barker, "Son of Celluloid" (1984)

Harlan Ellison, "Laugh Track" (1984)

Joe R. Lansdale, *The Drive-In* (1988)

David J. Schow, "Monster Movies" (1990)

Theodore Roszak, *Flicker* (1991)

Richard Christian Matheson, *Created By* (1993)

Dennis Etchison, *Fine Cuts* (2006)

---

that author's lyrical bite, tending to dissolve into easy ironies. Schow's tales, by contrast, are genuinely affecting: *Lost Angels* (1990) is perhaps the finest monument to the splatterpunk aesthetic, with its canny array of L.A. low-lifes, its fluent mimicry of trash-film conventions, and its tone of hip ennui. (Schow has also edited a solid collection of celluloid-based nightmares, *Silver Scream* [1988].) Garton's *Live Girls* (1987), though it has a clever premise (female vampires infesting Times Square sex clubs), spends its energy in tepid porn scenarios, while Skipp and Spector's ambitious trilogy of urban nightmares— *The Light at the End* (1986), *The Cleanup* (1987), and *Deadlines* (1989)—is deformed by adolescent posturing and tin-eared prose. Sprawling horrorshows (in more ways than one), these novels proffer incessant, tediously didactic broodings about urban decay rather than the stark, inferential images that make the work of Etchison and Campbell so effective. While Skipp and Spector deserve credit for tackling difficult themes—the simmering frustration of urban outcasts, the raw tensions of class and race, the dubious allure of vigilantism— their rampant stylistic excesses and their inability to maintain command of their plots finally (and fatally) compromise their achievement.

While never officially included in the splatterpunk canon, the films of Abel Ferrara and the fiction of Kathe Koja show peripheral connections with the movement's key themes and are, moreover, considerably more accomplished than the core group's general output. Ferrara's early low-budget films *The Driller Killer* (1979), *Ms. 45* (1981), and *Fear City* (1984) explore splatterpunk terrain in their unflinching vision of a corrupt, soul-destroying New York populated by deranged street people, hard-bitten strippers, and penny-ante mafiosi. His more accomplished later films include *The Bad Lieutenant* (1992) and *The Addiction* (1995), the latter a ferociously downbeat vampire story with a real feel for urban grunge. Koja's short stories and novels traverse a similarly scruffy world of hardened bohemians and social outsiders whose hunt for physical and psychological fulfillment leads them to the shadowy boundaries of big-city life. Written with a slangy energy, and attuned—as titles like *Skin* (1993) and *Kink* (1996) suggest—to depths of sexual darkness the male splatterpunks can only hint at, Koja's fiction moves with a feral grace among a subculture of artistic loners and decadent toughs. Yet for all her hard-boiled cynicism, Koja's main theme is the wounding misery of love, the baffled quest for connection in a chaotic and unfeeling world. With Ferrara and Koja, one potently senses, as one does not with Skipp and Spector, a vibrant heart beneath the world-weary pose and all the surface cruelties. If their work is true splatterpunk, it is the best of the breed.

ICONIC SITES OF URBAN HORROR

Koja's first novel, *The Cipher* (1991), was a tale of bizarre transformation set in an urban apartment building with a secret channel into unguessable dimensions. While brilliantly original in many ways, it nonetheless built on a recognizable subgenre of urban horror: the haunted apartment house story. Ira Levin's *Rosemary's Baby* (1967) is often credited with pioneering this form, but in fact, Levin's novel is merely a mainstream version of Roland Topor's deliriously offbeat *Le Locataire chimerique* (1964), which was published in English translation, as *The Tenant*, in 1966. Aside from the fact that both books were memorably filmed by Roman Polanski, the stories have much in common, centering on isolated, growingly paranoid apartment dwellers who fall prey to shadowy plots hatched by their nosy, conspiring neighbors. Both books powerfully exploit the sense of ersatz community pervading such anonymous dwellings, the prying curiosity regarding others' peccadilloes, the lurking ambiguity in every chance encounter in the hall or on the stairs. But whereas Levin ultimately resolves his mysteries, unveiling the conspirators as a coven of witches devoted to unleashing Satan's spawn, Topor trades in harrowing uncertainty, never unraveling the motives behind the scheme that drives his frazzled protagonist, Trelkovsky, to a grisly death.

This thirtyish schlemiel at first is hounded by fellow residents enraged by his slightest noise, their "furious thumpings on the ceiling" (43) causing him to cower in meek silence under the bedclothes; but soon a more sinister pattern of manipulation and coercion emerges. Secretive figures hold silent vigil in the common bath; Trelkovsky's room is ransacked and his belongings stolen, unmooring him from his already tenuous sense of identity; then, in the midst of an hallucinatory fever, he finds himself dressed in the clothes of the apartment's former tenant, a lonely young woman who had committed suicide by throwing herself from the window. Suddenly it dawns on him that his neighbors, by "a thousand shabby little tricks . . . were altering his whole personality" (85) in an effort to drive him also to a despairing self-annihilation. "They were no longer peaceful tenants, but killers in search of a victim" (54–55). Besieged in his room, Trelkovsky gazes in numb terror at an orgiastic pageant in the courtyard below, knowing he will soon succumb to this "vision of unutterable horror" (82) in which he finds himself engulfed. The gradual escalation of bizarre incidents is handled masterfully, creating a clutching mood of claustrophobic menace. The fact that Topor provides no settled conclusion only adds to the uneasy surrealism of the story, effectively conveying a sense of the inscrutability and drifting transience of urban life.

Rosemary's Baby is an altogether more conventional affair, narratively speaking. Guy and Rosemary Woodhouse, a seemingly content young couple, move into an uptown New York apartment building with something of an unsavory reputation. Soon, a young girl whom Rosemary had befriended in the laundry room leaps to her death from an upper floor, and shortly thereafter, the elderly couple with whom she had resided, Roman and Minnie Castavet, commence an aggressive friendship with the Woodhouses. Suddenly, Guy's sputtering career as an actor begins to take off, and he and Rosemary decide they can now afford to have a child. As we ultimately discover, however, Guy has fallen under the sway of the Castavets, the amiable center of a coven in the building, and in return for their sorcerous aid in advancing his professional ambitions, he has volunteered Rosemary to serve as a vessel for the devil's seed (the other girl's suicide having claimed their initial victim). In a scene narrated with a kitschy surrealism that provides a second-rate echo of Topor's technique, conception is effected by means of a drugged rape by Satan himself: imagining herself dreaming, Rosemary "opened her eyes and looked into yellow furnace-eyes, smelled sulphur and tannis root, felt wet breath on her mouth, heard lust-grunts and the breathing of onlookers" (81). As the alien baby burgeons within her, she finds herself being subtly separated from her former friends, drawn into the cozy world of the elderly witches, who ply her with potions and charms and protective advice. Eventually cottoning to their plot, she attempts escape only to be foiled, and the story ends with the young mother coming to accept the demonic child as her legitimate offspring, claws, tail, and all.

While *Rosemary's Baby* has long provided an efficient model for horror writers eager to exploit urban settings for their reserves of the eldritch and uncanny, Topor's work has also exerted its sly influence. Indeed, this contrast between clear-cut narratives of the occult and mutable dreamscapes of dread and desire can be traced through subsequent decades of haunted apartment house stories. On the one hand, novels such as Jeffrey Konvitz's *The Sentinel* (1975), Ken Eulo's *The Brownstone* (1980), and David J. Schow's *The Shaft* (1990) mine the vein Levin tapped in their depiction of city dwellings infested with more or less straightforward supernatural presences (with Stephen Laws's *Darkfall* [1992] adapting the model to evoke an eldritch downtown office complex); on the other hand, works such as J. G. Ballard's *High-Rise* (1975), David Cronenberg's 1975 film *Shivers*, and Hideo Nakata's film *Honogurai mizu no soko kara* (2002; remade as *Dark Water*, 2005) explore more ambiguous psychological terrain, with the urban residence becoming a potent symbol of modern-day disconnection and alienation.

Schow's novel is probably the best of the more conventional treatments of this general theme. *The Shaft* is the story of a decaying apartment house in a downscale suburb of Chicago, of its motley assortment of tenants leading lives of quiet desperation, and of the bizarre transformation that, one brutally cold winter night, brings the two—building and occupants—eerily, intimately closer together. The core plot involves a plan to rescue a bag of cocaine that, during a police raid, was tossed down the central air-shaft, a slimy, murky, foul-smelling cavity that leads into the labyrinthine bowels of the tenement, where Something dwells. The characters, an entertaining crew of scuzzy stereotypes (the evil drug dealer, the hooker with a heart of gold, the well-meaning dweeb), are little more than plot-fodder, easy prey for the creatures that infest the eponymous passage. The major strength of the novel lies in its absolute commitment to grossing the reader out: true to his splatterpunk roots, Schow proffers a cornucopia of sleaze, evoking an atmosphere so fetid and

> . . . the open tribal conflicts of the previous week had now clearly ceased. With the breakdown of the clan structure, the formal boundary and armistice lines had dissolved, giving way to a series of small enclaves, a cluster of three or four isolated apartments. . . . The residents of the high-rise were like creatures in a darkened zoo lying together in surly quiet, now and then tearing at each other in brief acts of ferocious violence.
>
> —*J. G. Ballard,* High-Rise *(1975)*

revolting you can almost smell it. The descriptions of the shape-shifting building and its inhuman cellar dwellers are effectively grotesque, and the many scenes of violence are handled with a bracing gusto. Unfortunately, the plot is a structural mess, with too many threads going nowhere, and as a result the supernatural elements pop up cartoonishly, often seeming more risible than terrifying. Schow's renowned style—brutally frank, telegraphically slangy, with an edge of instability that borders of hysteria—comes across as the genuine voice of big-city low-life, but it ultimately cannot carry a narrative so immersed in generic cliché.

Ballard's *High-Rise* could hardly be more different. While it too centers on an apartment building swiftly descending into chaos and ruin, the reason for this transformation is not a siege of neo-Gothic monsters, as in *The Shaft*, but the low-grade tensions and deep-seated rivalries that mark urban existence itself. The setting is a forty-story glass-and-steel skyscraper on the margins of London, inhabited by a range of white-collar functionaries (on the lower floors), bourgeois professionals (in the middle), and elite technocrats (on the upper levels). This blatant recapitulation of prevailing class divisions, coupled with the hedonistic isolation of high-rise living, allows the "thinly veiled antagonisms" (13) between these groups to be expressed without the usual filters of social deference and personal self-control. Soon, the edifice has literally balkanized into clannish factions, enforced by vigilante violence that only escalates as the building's various services—water, electricity, sewer—begin to break down. Regressing to primal savagery, the groups are driven to survivalist extremes, fighting for control of the stairs and elevators, ambushing stragglers who stray beyond their designated spaces, feasting on captured pets and, eventually, one another. An "architecture designed for war, on the unconscious level if no other" (9), the high-rise unleashes psychic tendencies modern culture has long struggled to sublimate, internecine hatreds and territorial aggressions that might otherwise find no outlet. "By its very efficiency, the high-rise took over the task of maintaining the social structure that supported them all. For the first time it removed the need to repress every kind of antisocial behavior, and left them free to explore any deviant or wayward impulses" (48). While not a work of supernatural horror, Ballard's novel, like Cronenberg's *Shivers*, is a disturbingly surreal examination of the tenuousness of civilization, evoking an eruption of the wanton irrationalism barely screened by the surface pleasantries of everyday life. Along with the author's other novels of the period—*Crash* (1973) and *Concrete Island* (1973)—it sets an unusually high standard for critically pointed interrogations of contemporary urban experience.

It is a standard few works in the subgenre of the haunted apartment house have equaled, though Nakata's film comes close. Indeed, one can glimpse, in the Hollywood remake of this brilliantly unsettling Japanese movie, an example of the containment and mainstreaming of subversive fantasy that is similar to Levin's quasi-revision of Topor's novel. Produced by the writer-director team that released the hugely successful *Ringu* (1998)—also remade in the United States as *The Ring* (2002)—*Honogurai mizu no soko kara* (which roughly translates as "From the Bottom of the Murky Waters") tells the story of Yoshimi Matsubara and her six-year-old daughter Ikuko, who are compelled to take up residence in a cheap apartment building on the outskirts of Tokyo while Yoshimi pursues a painful divorce. Though it is ultimately possible to resolve the mysterious incidents that plague the pair (a growing wet patch on the ceiling, a child's purse that keeps appearing on the roof, a shadowy girl in a yellow raincoat who haunts the corridors) into a straightforward tale of ghostly visitation, the overall effect of the film is profoundly disorienting, a moody and dreamlike meditation on the psychic fallout of abandonment and a longing for succor that can never be assuaged. The experience is quintessentially that of the modern urban dweller: deracinated, harassed by money worries, unable to sustain enduring bonds. The powerful set design of the film underlines this message, with its counterpoint between the sterile interiors of professional offices and the dingy, dismal apartment where Yoshimi and Ikuko take refuge. The endlessly falling rain, both outside and inside the building, suggests the absolute impermanence of these flimsy shells that populate the global urban landscape, offering their fragile illusions of domesticity.

While the downtown apartment offers the horror novelist a ready-made self-contained world, its physical borders—dismal roofs, towering walls, and shadowy basements—have also provided fodder for fictional exploration. Christopher Fowler's *Roofworld* (mentioned above) is a case in point, with its strange portrait of warring gangs traversing the bristling skyline, and Larry Cohen's film *Q: The Winged Serpent* (1982) is an entertaining gorefest featuring the eponymous mythic demon preying on unwary sunbathers and hapless window washers. John Shirley's *Cellars* (1982), a schlocky tale of murderous demons lurking beneath Manhattan, is viscerally compelling but lacks the humor of a film like *C.H.U.D.* (1984), whose eponymous Cannibalistic Humanoid Underground Dwellers turn out to be not occult beasties but mutated bums taking revenge on complacent yuppies. Stories of subterranean urban terrors also include monsters-in-the-subway scenarios like Thomas F. Monteleone's *Night Train* (1984) and Clive Barker's "The Midnight Meat Train" (1984), the latter a shrewd fusion of serial killer routines with Lovecraftian cosmic dread. In these various works, contemporary writers and filmmakers have mapped out the city's manifold possibilities for geographically focused menace, in the process bringing to fruition an iconic exploration of big-city horror that extends from Victorian vampires through Modernist smoke ghosts up to the postmodern atrocities of the splatterpunks.

BIBLIOGRAPHY

Primary

Ackroyd, Peter. *Hawksmoor*. 1985. New York: HarperPerennial, 1987.

Ballard, J. G. *Concrete Island*. London: Jonathan Cape, 1973.

———. *Crash*. London: Jonathan Cape, 1973.

———. *High-Rise*. 1975. New York: Popular Library, 1978.

Barker, Clive. "The Midnight Meat Train." In *Books of Blood, Volume 1*. London: Sphere, 1984; New York: Berkley, 1986, pp. 17–52.

Beaumont, Charles. "Black Country." In *The Hunger and Other Stories*. New York: Bantam, 1957, pp. 164–83.

———. *The Twilight Zone Scripts of Charles Beaumont*. Ed. Roger Anker. Springfield, PA: Gauntlet, 2004.

———. "The Vanishing American." In *The Hunger and Other Stories*. New York: Bantam, 1957, pp. 18–27.

Billson, Anne. *Suckers*. 1992. New York: Atheneum, 1993.

Blatty, William Peter. *The Exorcist*. New York: Harper & Row, 1971.

Bloch, Robert. *American Gothic*. New York: Simon & Schuster, 1974.

———. "The Cloak." In *Magic for Sale*, ed. Avram Davidson. New York: Ace, 1983, pp. 43–60.

———. "The Dream-Makers." In *Pleasant Dreams*. New York: Jove, 1979, pp. 17–48.

———. *The Night of the Ripper*. New York: Tor, 1986.

———. "The Phantom from the Film." In *The Fear Planet and Other Unusual Destinations*. Burton, MI: Subterranean, 2005, pp. 71–88.

———. "Return to the Sabbath." In *Pleasant Dreams*. New York: Jove, 1979, pp. 223–40.

———. "Yours Truly, Jack the Ripper." In *The Best of Robert Bloch*. New York: Ballantine, 1977, pp. 1–20.

Brite, Poppy Z. *Lost Souls*. New York: Delacorte Press, 1992.

Brown, Fredric. "Armageddon." In *The Unknown*, ed. D. R. Benson. New York: Jove, 1978, pp. 187–92.

Campbell, Ramsey. *The Face That Must Die*. 1979. New York: Tor, 1985.

———. "In the Bag." In *Cold Fear*, ed. Hugh Lamb. London: W. H. Allen, 1977. In Campbell's *Dark Feastsl*. London: Robinson, 1987, pp. 126–35.

———. "Litter." In *Vampires, Werewolves, and Other Monsters*, ed. Roger Elwood. New York: Curtis, 1974, pp. 95–110.

———. "Mackintosh Willy." In *Shadows 2*, ed. Charles L. Grant. Garden City, NY: Doubleday, 1979. In Campbell's *Dark Feasts*. London: Robinson, 1987, pp. 208–21.

———. "The Man in the Underpass." In *The Year's Best Horror Stories III*, ed. Richard Davis. New York: DAW, 1975. In Campbell's *Dark Feasts*. London: Robinson, 1987, pp. 86–96.

———. "Midnight Hobo." In *Nightmares*, ed. Charles L. Grant. Chicago: Playboy Press, 1979. In Campbell's *Dark Feasts*. London: Robinson, 1987, pp. 234–45.

Dibdin, Michael. *The Last Sherlock Holmes Story*. New York: Pantheon, 1978.

Etchison, Dennis. "The Dog Park." In *Dark Voices 5: The Pan Book of Horror*, ed. David Sutton and Stephen Jones. London: Pan, 1993, pp. 131–46.

———. "It Only Comes Out at Night." In *Frights*, ed. Kirby McCauley. New York: St. Martin's Press, 1976. In Etchison's *The Dark Country*. Los Angeles: Scream/Press, 1982, pp. 1–12.

———. "The Late Shift." In *Dark Forces*, ed. Kirby McCauley. New York: Viking Press, 1980. In Etchison's *The Dark Country*. Los Angeles: Scream/Press, 1982, pp. 111–26.

———. "The Nighthawk." In *Shadows 1*, ed. Charles L. Grant. Garden City, NY: Doubleday, 1978. In Etchison's *The Dark Country*. Los Angeles: Scream/Press, 1982, pp. 127–44.

———. "White Moon Rising." In *Whispers*, ed. Stuart David Schiff. Garden City, NY: Doubleday, 1977. In Etchison's *Red Dreams*. Los Angeles: Scream/Press, 1984, pp. 89–106.

Eulo, Ken. *The Brownstone*. New York: Pocket, 1980.

Fowler, Christopher. *Bureau of Lost Souls*. 1989. New York: Ballantine, 1991.

———. *City Jitters*. London: Sphere, 1986.

———. *Darkest Day*. London: Little, Brown, 1993.

———. *Red Bride*. London: Little, Brown, 1992.

———. *Roofworld*. New York: Ballantine, 1988.

———. *Rune*. 1990. New York: Ballantine, 1992.

Garton, Ray. *Live Girls*. New York: Pocket, 1987.

Harrison, M. John. *The Course of the Heart*. London: Orion, 1992.

———. "Egnaro." In Harrison's *Things That Never Happen*. London: Orion, 2004, pp. 93–116.

———. "The Incalling." In *The Savoy Book*, ed. David Britton and Michael Butterworth. London: Savoy, 1978. In Harrison's *Things That Never Happen*. London: Orion, 2004, pp. 55–80.

———. *Viriconium*. 1971–1984. New York: Bantam Spectra, 2005.

Hodgson, William Hope. *The Night Land*. 1912. Rockville, MD: Wildside Press, 2001.

Klein, T.E.D. "Children of the Kingdom." In *Dark Forces*, ed. Kirby McCauley. New York: Viking Press, 1980. In Klein's *Dark Gods*. 1985. New York: Bantam, 1986, pp. 3–72.

Koja, Kathe. *The Cipher*. New York: Dell, 1991.

———. *Kink*. New York: Holt, 1996.

———. *Skin*. New York: Dell, 1993.

Konvitz, Jeffrey. *The Sentinel*. New York: Ballantine, 1975.

Lane, Joel. *The Earth Wire and Other Stories*. London: Egerton, 1994.

———. *The Lost District*. Norwalk, CT: Nightshade, 2006.

Laws, Stephen. *Darkfall*. New York: Leisure, 1992.

Leiber, Fritz. "The Girl with the Hungry Eyes." In *The Girl with the Hungry Eyes*, ed. Donald A. Wollheim. New York: Ace, 1949. In *The Penguin Book of Vampire Stories*, ed. Alan Ryan. New York: Penguin, 1987, pp. 334–48.

———. "The Hound." 1942. In *Night's Black Agents*. New York: Berkley, 1978, pp. 185–200.

———. *Our Lady of Darkness*. 1977. New York: Berkley, 1978.

———. "Smoke Ghost." 1941. In *Unknown*, ed. Stanley Schmidt. New York: Baen, 1988, pp. 129–48.

Levin, Ira. *Rosemary's Baby*. 1967. New York: Dell, 1968.

Lovecraft, H. P. *At the Mountains of Madness*. In *At the Mountains of Madness and Other Novels*. Sauk City, WI: Arkham House, 1985, pp. 3–106.

———. "The Call of Cthulhu." In *The Dunwich Horror and Others*. Sauk City, WI: Arkham House, 1984, pp. 125–54.

———. *The Case of Charles Dexter Ward*. In *At the Mountains of Madness and Other Novels*. Sauk City, WI: Arkham House, 1985, pp. 107–235.

———. "The Horror at Red Hook." In *Dagon and Other Macabre Tales*. Sauk City, WI: Arkham House, 1986, pp. 244–65.

———. "Pickman's Model." In *The Dunwich Horror and Others*. Sauk City, WI: Arkham House, 1984, pp. 12–25.

Lowndes, Marie Belloc. *The Lodger*. 1913. New York: Dell, 1964.

Matheson, Richard. "The Creeping Terror." *Star Science Fiction Stories #5*, ed. Frederik Pohl. New York: Ballantine, 1959. In *Shock!* New York: Dell, 1961, pp. 139–53.

———. "Legion of Plotters." In *Shock!* New York: Dell, 1961, pp. 120–30.

———. *The Twilight Zone Scripts, Volume 1*. Ed. Stanley Wiater. Springfield, PA: Edge, 2001.

———. *The Twilight Zone Scripts, Volume 2*. Ed. Stanley Wiater. Springfield, PA: Edge, 2002.

Matheson, Richard Christian. *Scars and Other Distinguishing Marks*. Los Angeles: Scream/Press, 1987.

Maupassant, Guy de. "The Horla." 1886. In *The Dark Side: Tales of Terror and the Supernatural*. New York: Carroll & Graf, 1989, pp. 1–24.

———. "A Night in Paris. (A Nightmare)." 1887. In *The Dark Side: Tales of Terror and the Supernatural*. New York: Carroll & Graf, 1989, pp. 192–96.

Miéville, China. *Perdido Street Station*. New York: Tor, 2000.

Monteleone, Thomas F. *Night Train*. New York: Pocket, 1984.

Moore, Alan, and Eddie Campbell. *From Hell*. 1991–1993. Marietta, GA: Top Shelf, 2004.

Poe, Edgar Allan. "The Man of the Crowd." In *Selected Writings of Edgar Allan Poe: Poems, Tales, Essays and Reviews*, ed. David Galloway. New York: Penguin, 1967, pp. 179–88.

———. "The Murders in the Rue Morgue." In *Selected Writings of Edgar Allan Poe: Poems, Tales, Essays and Reviews*, ed. David Galloway. New York: Penguin, 1967, pp. 189–224.

Reynolds, Alistair. *Chasm City*. London: Gollancz, 2001.

Rice, Anne. *Interview with the Vampire*. New York: Knopf, 1976.

Royle, Nicholas. *Antwerp*. London: Serpent's Tale, 2004.

———. *The Director's Cut*. London: Abacus, 2000.

Schow, David J. *Lost Angels*. New York: New American Library, 1990.

———. *The Shaft*. London: Macdonald, 1990.

———, ed. *Silver Scream*. New York: Tor, 1988.

Shirley, John. *Cellars*. New York: Avon, 1982.

Sinclair, Iain. *White Chappell: Scarlet Tracings*. London: Goldmark, 1987.

Skipp, John, and Craig Spector. *The Cleanup*. New York: Bantam, 1987.

———. *Deadlines*. New York: Bantam, 1989.

———. *The Light at the End*. New York: Bantam, 1986.

Somtow, S. P. *Vampire Junction*. 1984. New York: Tor, 1995.

Stevenson, Robert Louis. *The Strange Case of Dr. Jekyll and Mr. Hyde*. 1886. Ed. Martin A. Danahay. Peterborough, ON: Broadview Press, 1999.

Stoker, Bram. *Dracula*. 1897. Ed. Nina Auerbach and David J. Skal. New York: W. W. Norton & Co., 1997.

Strieber, Whitley. *The Wolfen*. New York: Morrow, 1978.

Topor, Roland. *The Tenant*. 1964. Trans. Francis K. Price. 1964. New York: Bantam, 1967. Originally published as *Le Locataire chimerique*.

Wedekind, Fritz. *Pandora's Box: A Tragedy in Three Acts*. 1904. London: Boni & Liveright, 1918.

West, Paul. *The Women of Whitechapel and Jack the Ripper*. 1991. New York: Overlook Press, 1992.

Williams, Conrad. *London Revenant*. 2004. San Francisco: Night Shade, 2005.

Wilson, Colin. *Ritual in the Dark*. 1960. New York: Popular Library, 1961.

Secondary

Benjamin, Walter. "On Some Motifs in Baudelaire." 1939. In *Illuminations: Essays and Reflections*, ed. Hannah Arendt. New York: Schocken, 1968, pp. 155–200.

Dziemianowicz, Stefan. *The Annotated Guide to "Unknown" and "Unknown Worlds."* Mercer Island, WA: Starmont House, 1991.

Hadji, R. S. "Extreme Measures: The Fiction of John Skipp and Craig Spector." *Horror Show* 6 (Fall 1988): 10–16, 20, 33.

Heine, Maurice. "Regard sur l'enfer anthropoclasique." *Minotaure* 8 (1936).

Marx, Karl, and Freidrich Engels. *Manifesto of the Community Party*. 1848. In *The Marx-Engels Reader*, ed. Robert C. Tucker. 2nd ed. New York: W. W. Norton & Co., 1978, pp. 469–500.

Mumford, Lewis. *The Culture of Cities*. 1938. New York: Harcourt Brace Jovanovich, 1970.

Nutman, Philip. "Inside the New Horror." *Twilight Zone* 8, no. 4 (October 1988): 24–29, 85.

Rumbelow, Donald. *Jack the Ripper: The Complete Casebook*. Chicago: Contemporary, 1988.

Simmel, Georg. "The Metropolis and Mental Life." 1903. In *On Individuality and Social Forms: Selected Writings*, ed. Donald E. Levine. Chicago: University of Chicago Press, 1971, pp. 324–39.

Walkowitz, Judith. *City of Dreadful Delight: Narratives of Sexual Danger in Late-Victorian London*. Chicago: University of Chicago Press, 1992.

Zicree, Marc Scott. *The Twilight Zone Companion.* 1982. Los Angeles: Silman-
    James, 1992.

Filmography

The Addiction. Directed by Abel Ferrara. Fast, 1995.
The Bad Lieutenant. Directed by Abel Ferrara. Aries, 1992.
Bram Stoker's Dracula. Directed by Francis Ford Coppola. Columbia, 1992.
Cat People. Directed by Jacques Tourneur. RKO, 1942.
C.H.U.D. Directed by Douglas Cheek. New World, 1984.
Curse of the Cat People. Directed by Robert Wise. RKO, 1944.
Dark Water. Directed by Walter Salles. Touchstone, 2005.
Dracula. Directed by Tod Browning. Universal, 1931.
The Driller Killer. Directed by Abel Ferrara. Navaron, 1979.
The Exorcist. Directed by William Friedkin. Warner Bros., 1973.
Fear City. Directed by Abel Ferrara. Twentieth Century Fox, 1984.
Honogurai mizu no soko kara (*Dark Water*). Directed by Hideo Nakata. ADV, 2002.
Le Locataire (*The Tenant*). Directed by Roman Polanski. Paramount, 1976.
The Lodger. Directed by Alfred Hitchcock. Wardour, 1927.
Ms. 45. Directed by Abel Ferrara. Navaron, 1981.
The Night Stalker. Directed by Dan Curtis. ABC TV, 1972.
Pandora's Box. Directed by Laurence Trimble. General Film Co., 1912.
Phantom Lady. Directed by Robert Siodmak. Universal, 1944.
Q: The Winged Serpent. Directed by Larry Cohen. Arkoff International, 1982.
Rosemary's Baby. Directed by Roman Polanski. Paramount, 1968.
Scarlet Street. Directed by Fritz Lang. Universal, 1945.
Shivers (a.k.a. *They Came from Within*; a.k.a. *Orgy of the Blood Parasites*). Directed
    by David Cronenberg. Cinépix, 1975.
A Study in Terror. Directed by James Hill. Compton, 1965.
Vertigo. Directed by Alfred Hitchcock. Paramount, 1958.

Courtesy of Photofest.

The Vampire

by Margaret L. Carter

INTRODUCTION

Ernest Jones in *On the Nightmare* maintains that no superstitious belief is "richer or more over-determined than that in the vampire" and its "psychological meaning is correspondingly complicated" (98). Therefore, it is not surprising that vampirism in some form is found in folklore throughout the world. In his survey of vampire fiction, Brian Frost calls this creature the "monster with a thousand faces," the ultimate shapeshifter. Supernatural entities falling under the general classification of "vampire" include many varieties of blood-drinking demons as well as the animated dead that prey on the living, often feeding on blood but sometimes on other body fluids or simply spreading disease, draining life-force, or frightening victims to death. Some of them must return to their graves at dawn and can be trapped aboveground by scattering seeds they feel compelled to count, while at least one variety is active from midnight to noon. Some undead survive only forty days, while others maintain their quasi-life indefinitely, and still others (in one European tradition), if they survive the initial, most hazardous period of postmortem existence, eventually develop the ability to pass for human and reenter society in a community distant from their original home. Internationally, vampires range from men who return from the grave to live with and impregnate their widows to grotesque revenants who could not possibly be mistaken for ordinary people, such as the Maylasian penanggalan, a disembodied head trailing its stomach and intestines, and the chiang-shih of China, which may grow a coat of long, white hair. The wider European culture became aware of vampires as we know them in the early eighteenth century, in the aftermath of extended warfare between the Habsburg dynasty and the Ottoman Empire. Dom Augustin Calmet's 1751 "Dissertations on Those Persons Who Return to Earth Bodily" is the best-known and most frequently cited work of this period to explore vampire legends at length and attempt to explain them rationally. In the twentieth century, Dudley Wright's *Vampires and Vampirism* (1914) and two books by Gothic scholar Montague Summers, *The Vampire: His Kith and Kin* (1928) and *The Vampire in Europe* (1929), provide exhaustive surveys of the varieties of vampirism throughout the world's cultures.

Even within the familiar Central and Eastern European context, folk traditions vary widely. Among causes of vampirism, although victims often become transformed into the undead after death, many other events can cause an individual to become a vampire, such as being born on Christmas, with teeth, or illegitimately of illegitimate parents, or committing suicide, practicing sorcery, being cursed by one's parents or excommunicated, or having a cat jump over one's corpse. Prescriptions for destroying vampires also encompass many methods in addition to the best-known remedy of a stake through the heart, for example, beheading, cremation, immersion in running water, firing a blessed bullet into the coffin, and removing the heart and boiling it in oil, wine, or vinegar. To prevent a potential vampire from rising as one of the undead, the corpse might be buried face down so that it could not find its way out of the grave. Means of protection against vampire attacks include the familiar garlic and holy objects, but also thorny plants such as holly or wild roses. Modern theories of the sources of vampire beliefs range from the psychoanalytic, as advanced by Ernest Jones and other Freudian authorities, to the more pragmatic, such as the risks of premature burial in the centuries before modern medicine. Paul Barber's *Vampires, Burial, and Death* (1988) makes a convincing argument that, once belief in the undead became established, observation of phenomena associated with the decomposition of corpses reinforced this belief system. When bodies suspected of vampirism were disinterred, witnesses mistook normal variations in the process of decay for confirmatory symptoms of supernatural preservation and postmortem blood-drinking. Folk belief often associated vampirism with epidemic diseases, such as the bubonic plague. Deaths were blamed on victimization by the first person in the area to fall ill and die, a possible reason why most vampires were thought to prey first on their own families. Michael E. Bell researches an epidemic of supposed vampirism arising from an outbreak of tuberculosis in colonial Rhode Island in *Food for the Dead* (2001).

EARLY VAMPIRE STORIES

Vampire motifs frequently appeared in poetry from the late eighteenth century through the Romantic period. German poet Heinrich Ossenfelder's "The Vampire" (1748) illustrates that as soon as writers of this period began to make artistic use of vampirism, they associated it with erotic seduction. Ossenfelder's vampire attempts to lure an innocent maiden away from her mother's Christian faith. He vows, "And as softly thou art sleeping To thee I shall come creeping And thy life's blood drain away" (Moore 12), rather than pursuing a violent, gory attack. Quasi-vampiric creatures appear in Gottfried August Bürger's "Lenore" (1773), a ballad of an undead lover returning from the grave to claim the heroine (from which Bram Stoker quotes in an early scene in *Dracula*), and "The Bride of Corinth" (1797) by Johann Wolfgang von Goethe, in which a young man is seduced by his fiancée after her untimely death. In prose of the German Romantic period, "Wake Not the Dead" (1800), by Johann Ludwig Tieck, similarly mates the living with the dead, but Tieck's Brunhilda, resurrected by a sorcerer at the unwise request of her bereaved husband, appears ravenous and malevolent, in contrast to Goethe's melancholy revenant. The vampire motif appears in English poetry of the early nineteenth century before entering prose fiction. The hero of Robert Southey's *Thalaba the Destroyer* (1800) combats a vampire in the shape of his dead beloved. The first known poem in English concerned entirely with vampirism is John Stagg's "The Vampyre" (1810), featuring an undead monster in a medieval German setting. The poet prefaces the work with an "Argument" that attributes vampire legends to Germany and Hungary. This ballad of a ghastly, bloodstained walking corpse who rises to prey on his best friend adheres closely to the folklore image of the vampire as disgusting and terrifying. The mysterious Geraldine in Coleridge's unfinished "Christabel" (1816) prefigures later female vampires. Lord Byron alludes to vampire folklore in *The Giaour* (1813). Keats depicts supernatural female predators in "La Belle Dame Sans Merci" (1819) and *Lamia* (1820). The latter, based on Greek myth, presents a sympathetic perspective on the title character, a serpentine shapeshifter who, after taking human form to marry the young hero, is destroyed by a stern philosopher.

The first known prose vampire story in English, *The Vampyre* (1819), by Byron's physician, John Polidori, was inspired by an unfinished tale by Byron and, upon first publication, was mistakenly attributed to the latter. *The Vampyre* is prefaced by an introduction discussing the folklore background. Polidori supposes the superstition to have originated in Arabia and spread

"Lord Ruthven had dis-appeared, and Aubrey's sister had glutted the thirst of a VAMPYRE!" (Polidori, "The Vampyre," 24)

from there into Greece and Eastern Europe. He recounts the notorious Hungarian case of Arnold Paul, as reported in the *London Journal* of March, 1732. Polidori also alludes to *Thalaba* and Byron's *Giaour*. Although aware of the superstition that a victim killed by a vampire becomes one of the undead, as mentioned in a footnote to the essay, Polidori gives no indication in his story that either of the women destroyed by his vampire, Lord Ruthven, rise after death. Ruthven is based on Byron, even bearing the name Lady Caroline Lamb assigned to her villain in *Glenarvon* (1816), a *roman à clef* targeted at the poet, and Ruthven displays the predatory, seductive traits of Byron's dark heroes. Besides feeding on the blood of maidens, Ruthven preys on the innocent (both men and women) by luring them into corruption. The story ends with his attack upon the sister of the ineffectual young hero, Aubrey. The popularity of *The Vampyre* inspired a number of vampire melodramas on the early nineteenth-century stage, such as *Le Vampire*, by Charles Nodier, and *The Vampire, or, the Bride of the Isles*, by James Robinson Planche, both first performed in 1820.

The "penny dreadful" *Varney the Vampyre* (1847), sometimes attributed to Thomas Preskett Prest but now considered likely to have been written by James Malcolm Rymer, reflects Polidori's influence with such elements as a "dead" vampire's revival by moonlight and his compulsion to marry innocent maidens. A sensational, incoherent narrative of over 800 pages, which concludes with the repentant vampire's suicide, *Varney* even contains a minor character named Polidori. Among other inconsistencies, the story offers several contradictory accounts of how the title character became a vampire. Displaying the stereotypical traits of the Byronic villain-hero, Varney serves as a transitional figure between Ruthven and Dracula. The opening chapter, often reprinted, depicts Varney's violent assault upon the heroine Flora in her bedchamber. Another memorable scene, the staking of a female vampire in a graveyard, anticipates the destruction of Lucy in *Dracula*. Later in the novel, Varney displays softer character traits, begging Flora for aid and eventually showing remorse for his bloodthirsty deeds. Thus he foreshadows the sympathetic vampires of late-twentieth-century fiction.

Whereas the male vampire of the nineteenth century has roots in the Gothic novel and Byron's villain-heroes, the prevailing image of the female vampire can be traced back to the seductive females in the poetry of Coleridge and Keats. In American literature, Edgar Allan Poe creates vampirelike women in "Morella" (1835), "Ligeia" (1838), and "The Fall of the House of Usher" (1839). Both Morella and Ligeia use occult powers and sheer force of will to return from death by inhabiting the bodies of others, Morella possessing her own daughter and Ligeia the narrator's second wife. Madeline Usher returns from the grave, whether buried alive or literally undead, to precipitate the downfall of the House of Usher and the death of her twin brother. Théophile

Gautier introduces an early example of the sympathetic vampire in Clarimonde, the lover of a young priest in "La Morte Amoureuse" (1836). Clarimonde feeds on only token drops of blood from her beloved, and after the destruction of her remains by an older cleric, the protagonist's life becomes bleak and colorless. Gautier's narrative frames the young priest's affair with Clarimonde, whose deathbed he attends early in the story, as a nocturnal, dreamlike existence completely separate from his mundane life.

"With a plunge he seizes her neck in his fang-like teeth—a gush of blood, and a hideous sucking noise follows. The girl has swooned, and the vampyre is at his hideous repast!" (Rymer, Varney the Vampyre, *4)*

Before *Dracula* (1897), the most distinguished work in this field is J. Sheridan Le Fanu's novella "Carmilla" (1871). The story is framed as a case from the notes of Le Fanu's occult healer, Dr. Hesselius, a probable inspiration for Stoker's Professor Van Helsing, but Dr. Hesselius is not mentioned outside the prologue. Like Geraldine in Coleridge's "Christabel," Carmilla mysteriously threatens a motherless young woman, though Le Fanu's vampire has more success at winning the heroine's trust than Geraldine does with Christabel. Laura, the heroine, an English girl living with her father in the Gothic setting of Styria, narrates the story from a retrospective viewpoint years afterward. The cryptic childhood dream in which a young woman, later identified as Carmilla, appears in Laura's bedroom suggests a mystical connection between the two characters. This scene is never explained, nor is the identity of the old lady who poses as Carmilla's mother to introduce her into Laura's father's household. The heroine finds herself both attracted and repelled by her enigmatic guest, who displays extravagant affection for Laura and enthralls her with a thinly veiled story of her own victimization by the vampire who initiated her into the realm of the undead. Notable for its often-cited subtext of lesbian eroticism, "Carmilla" conveys an ambiguous, partially sympathetic image of its titular vampire, despite her conventional destruction by stake-wielding representatives of the political and scientific establishment.

Among other distinguished pre-*Dracula* stories in the traditional vein, "The Mysterious Stranger" (1860), a German story translated anonymously into English, foreshadows Stoker's novel with its Carpathian setting, a male vampire of noble aspect, the gradual draining of a young woman's blood, and the destruction of the vampire in his coffin. "The Family of the Vourdalak" (1847), by Alexis Tolstoy, is notable in its portrayal of an old peasant returning from death as the repulsive, voracious revenant of folklore rather than the Byronic figure created by English authors such as Polidori and Rymer. Julian Hawthorne presents a seductive female vampire in "Ken's Mystery" (1883). Ken, an artist traveling in a remote part of Ireland, spends a night with a mysterious woman whose embrace drains him; when he wakes, the luxurious house where he slept has transformed into a ruin. More exotic variations on the theme include the invisible monster of Guy de Maupassant's "The Horla" (1886), the blood-draining plant of H. G. Wells's "The Flowering of the

"I live in your warm life, and you shall die—die, sweetly die—into mine." (Le Fanu, "Carmilla," 89)

Strange Orchid" (1894), and the batlike, vaguely humanoid bloodsucking animal in Phil Robinson's "The Last of the Vampires" (1893). A nonsupernatural treatment of life-draining through the theft of blood in "Good Lady Ducayne," by Mary Elizabeth Braddon (1896), presents a medical mystery that anticipates elements of *Dracula*. A young doctor discovers that the elderly woman of the title has been preying on her young female hired companions by secretly having their blood transfused into her in order to maintain her vitality. Sir Arthur Conan Doyle explores the theme of psychic vampirism in *The Parasite* (1891).

STOKER AND HIS INFLUENCE

However, it was *Dracula* (1897) that established the stereotypical traits of the vampire for eighty years following its publication, until Anne Rice's *Interview with the Vampire* (1976) presented Stoker's Count with a rival for the position of iconic literary vampire. Bram Stoker acknowledges his debt to "Carmilla" in a deleted chapter (later published as "Dracula's Guest") in which Jonathan Harker, on his way to Castle Dracula, visits the grave of a vampire countess from Styria, the setting of Le Fanu's novella. The opening chapters of the novel as published, set in Transylvania, are composed entirely of passages from Jonathan's diary. Leaving the young English solicitor at the almost literally cliff-hanging moment of his attempt to escape from the castle where he believes himself abandoned to the mercies of the Count's vampire brides, the novel then shifts to Mina, Jonathan's fiancée in England. The epistolary structure of the rest of the book, with its multiple viewpoints, professes to offer documentary evidence of the fantastic events narrated therein, yet paradoxically the absence of any authoritative single narrator may also have the effect of casting doubt on the truth of the story. The modern reader who approaches the book without having seen a Dracula film (if such a reader exists) recognizes Mina as Jonathan's fiancée from the mention of her in his diary but otherwise must grope his or her way through a maze of bewildering "facts" along with the characters. Transylvania and England come together in the narrative when Dracula, shipwrecked in the harbor at Whitby, chooses Mina's sleepwalking friend Lucy as his prey, thus setting in motion the sequence of events that lead to his destruction. Count Dracula combines the Byronic villain-hero of Polidori and Rymer with the vampire of Eastern European folklore.

Nina Auerbach in *Our Vampires, Ourselves* (1995) convincingly argues that Dracula departs from his literary predecessors in his characterization as an alien invader, in contrast to the intimacy she perceives in the relationships of Ruthven, Varney, and Carmilla with their victims. Dracula also displays prominent animal traits, embodying the late Victorian fear of atavism and degeneration. The vampire's archaic, instinctual behavior contrasts with the values of late-nineteenth-century enlightenment and science, highlighted by Stoker's frequent allusions to modern technology. Van Helsing, leader of the civilized band that repels and destroys the barbarian invader, harnesses this technology in the service of what the novel frames as a religious crusade against evil. The sexual subtext of *Dracula* has, of course, been exhaustively analyzed, with the novel's erotic energy attributed to such diverse themes as infantile oral sadism, the unleashing of repressed female desire, latent homoeroticism, and the sexual threat of the Other. The epistolary narrative structure, with its multiple voices, invites a reading that foregrounds doubt and subjectivity; references to madness pervade the text. As for its plot elements, *Dracula* establishes the traits of the literary vampire for decades to come and contains a number of motifs that have become standard in vampire fiction, for example, garlic, crucifixes, bats, blood transfusions, hypnotism, the habit of sleeping in a coffin, the need for native soil, the gradual seduction and transformation of the victim, and the unearthing and staking of the vampire. Stoker's vampires, however, do not display one weakness that has become synonymous with vampirism in the popular imagination, the inability to survive in sunlight; that trait was adopted from film, beginning with the silent movie *Nosferatu* (1922). Stoker revisits the vampire theme in a later novel, *The Lady of the Shroud* (1909), in which the princess of a tiny Eastern European country disguises herself as one of the undead to hide from her enemies. The fragment posthumously published as "Dracula's Guest" (1914) has been frequently reprinted as a deleted first chapter of *Dracula*, although some commentators point out its inconsistencies with the novel as published and maintain that it was never intended as the opening chapter of *Dracula* in the book's present form.

The anxiety of influence generated by Stoker seems to have cast an inhibiting shadow over horror writers in subsequent decades, since few memorable vampire novels were produced between *Dracula* and the 1970s. The short story form proved more varied and fruitful in this period. Throughout the first half of the twentieth century, numerous authors of horror and science fiction wrote vampire stories that display the influence of Le Fanu and Stoker. "'For the Blood Is the Life'" (1905), by F. Marion Crawford, concerns a murdered girl who arises from her unmarked grave to seduce and drain the young man she hopelessly loved in her lifetime. "An Episode of Cathedral History" (1914), by M. R. James, features a spectral vampire released from her grave in the course of excavations in an ancient cathedral. "Count Magnus" (1904), also by James, portrays a man who happens upon the grave of the title character and foolishly expresses a wish to meet him. Thereafter, a shadowy figure hounds the protagonist to his death. The undead woman in "Mrs. Amworth" (1923) by E. F. Benson differs from the typical seductive female vampire in her

> *"Individual vampires may die . . . but as a species vampires have been our companions for so long that it is hard to imagine living without them."* (Auerbach, Our Vampires, Ourselves, 9)

"I felt in my heart a wicked, burning desire that they would kiss me with those red lips." (Dracula, *42*)

appearance of relentless normality; before her accidental death and subsequent return, she loves gardening. Benson's "The Room in the Tower" (1912) mediates vampirism through a haunted portrait. Another tale by Benson, *"Negotium Perambulans..."* (1923), deals with a repulsive nonhuman entity rather than the classic undead of the *Dracula*-derived tradition. This author creates a patch of land that drains energy in "And No Bird Sings" (1928), somewhat as Algernon Blackwood had done on a smaller scale in "The Transfer" (1912), which features a human energy-vampire as well. Earlier, Mary E. Wilkins Freeman presents a character study of a psychic vampire in "Luella Miller" (1902), about a small-town woman who sucks out the life of everyone who cares for her but may or may not be aware of her own debilitating influence. The conventional symptoms of vampirism became so well known that Sir Arthur Conan Doyle could have Sherlock Holmes solve a vampire hoax in "The Adventure of the Sussex Vampire" (1927). Sydney Horler's *The Vampire* (1935) imitates *Dracula* almost to the point of pastiche, though with the variation that Horler's Baron Ziska leads a cult of Satanists.

The pulp magazine fiction of mid-century produced a number of memorable vampire stories. C. L. Moore's "Shambleau" (1933) features an alien predator, a seductive female shapeshifter that transplants the myths of Medusa and the succubus into a science-fictional setting. H. P. Lovecraft's "The Shunned House" (1924) presents a vampire that at first appears to be a traditional revivified corpse but actually results from an unnatural transmutation of a dead body by an alien entity. August Derleth in "Bat's Belfry" (1926) follows the model of *Dracula* in associating an undead lord with a harem of female vampires. Derleth's less traditional story "The Drifting Snow" (1939) features an undead servant girl who returns on snowy nights to drain and transform, one by one, members of the family that caused her death. Southern fantasy writer Manly Wade Wellman treats vampirism from a traditional viewpoint in many stories, including "School for the Unspeakable" (1937), about a vampire coven infesting a boys' boarding school; "When It Was Moonlight" (1940), pitting Edgar Allan Poe against a devious female vampire; and "The Devil Is Not Mocked" (1943), in which Count Dracula exterminates Nazi troops who occupy his castle. In Wellman's "The Last Grave of Lill Warran" (1951), his occult detective John Thunstone uses a silver rapier to slay a traditionally seductive but evil female revenant, who rises from the grave to prey on the man she loved in life. With a blend of humor and sensuality, Robert Bloch portrays a hapless man transformed into a vampire by a magic cape in "The Cloak" (1939). Ray Bradbury's "The Homecoming" (1946), about a "normal" boy who feels like a misfit in a family of vampires, witches, and werewolves, offers an early example of sympathetic treatment of "monsters," an approach that later becomes prominent in the fiction of the 1970s. In "The Girl with the Hungry Eyes" (1949) Fritz Leiber explores the figure of the energy-draining vampire as incarnate in the images of modern mass media. C. M. Kornbluth's "The Mindworm" (1950), a story of a psychic vampire conceived under the shadow of an atomic bomb test but defeated by Eastern European immigrants who remember the old superstitions, reflects mid-century fears of nuclear weapons, as Richard Matheson's novel *I Am Legend* (1954) does. Matheson introduces a boy who yearns to be a vampire in "Drink My Red Blood" (a.k.a. "Blood Son" and "Drink My Blood," 1951) and a little girl vampire in "Dress of White Silk" (1951). The latter, a first-person narrative in the voice of a naïve child who has no inkling of the monstrous heritage she bears, has been acknowledged as an influence by Anne Rice.

It is noteworthy that in the nineteenth century, individual vampires might be portrayed with some sympathy, as in *Varney* and "Carmilla," but the assumption prevailed that vampirism in itself was evil. A vampire partook of "goodness" only in so far as he or she resisted the cursed condition. In the twentieth century, on the other hand, it became possible to regard vampirism as a neutral condition and vampires as capable of being, like other people, either good or evil depending on their individual choices. The vampire in "Share Alike" by Jerome Bixby and Joe E. Dean (1953) belongs to another humanoid species living secretly among us, creatures who wish only to survive and be left alone. Shipwrecked and stranded in a lifeboat with a single human companion, this vampire initiates a symbiotic relationship with his fellow castaway. William Tenn's "She Only Goes Out at Night" (1956) presents a sympathetic view of vampirism by interpreting the condition as a hereditary disease rather than a supernatural curse. Tenn's heroine proves to be a gentle young woman who yearns to lead a normal life, a goal she achieves through medical control of her syndrome, enabling her to live as a typical middle-class housewife. Evelyn E. Smith's story of a wistful, romantic vampire seducing a young career woman away from the cold practicalities of her modern urban milieu, "Softly While You're Sleeping" (1961), adopts its title from Ossenfelder's eighteenth-century poem, quoted above (although the characters attribute the line to an Albanian folk song). Smith's story anticipates the vampire romances popular from the 1980s onward, except that her heroine finally rejects the dreamlike seduction of the vampire to embrace ordinary life.

THE MODERN VAMPIRE

Although memorable book-length fiction in this genre is rare before the 1970s, a few distinguished pre-1970 novels deserve mention. Richard Matheson created the best-known and most meticulously detailed treatment of vampirism as infectious disease in *I Am Legend* (1954), with the apocalyptic story of the last "normal" man on earth facing a horde of vampires engendered by a bacterial plague. The protagonist, Neville, meticulously researches the characteristics of the disease, whose origin is attributed to bomb testing, to

"It is again and again the experience of that loss of my own life, which I experienced when I sucked the blood from Lestat's wrist and felt his heart pound with my heart. . . . for vampires that is the ultimate experience." (Rice, Interview with the Vampire, *32)*

sift fact from superstition. The ultimate victory of a group of survivors who have evolved to live in symbiosis with their infection problematizes the stark good-versus-evil contrast with which the novel begins. Simon Raven's *Doctors Wear Scarlet* (1960), a suspenseful tale of both physical and psychic vampirism, leaves the reader in doubt, almost until the end, whether the vampire's predation is supernatural or psychological. A nonsupernatural novel of blood-drinking, Theodore Sturgeon's *Some of Your Blood* (1961), uses an epistolary narrative structure and the viewpoint of an Army psychologist to reveal the truth about its sociopathic protagonist. Sturgeon evokes echoes of the supernatural vampire by making his troubled young blood-drinker the child of Hungarian immigrants and giving him the name "Bela." Leslie Whitten's absorbingly realistic murder mystery, *Progeny of the Adder* (1965), brings the traditional vampire of folklore, depicted as a repulsive, soulless predator, into a modern urban setting. Colin Wilson creates horrific alien, energy-draining vampires in *The Mind Parasites* (1967) and later, in *The Space Vampires* (1976), develops a complex treatment of the psychic vampire motif, juxtaposing the predation of alien invaders against naturally evolved psychic vampirism by both animal and human energy-drainers within the terrestrial ecosystem.

In the following two decades, vampire novels proliferated in unprecedented numbers. *The Dracula Archives*, by Raymond Rudorff (1972), set in the years just preceding Stoker's tale, shows Dracula telepathically reaching out from his entombed sleep to take possession of several people in turn, culminating in his release to new life on the book's final page. Stephen King, in *'Salem's Lot* (1975), transplants Count Dracula into a contemporary setting in the person of the aristocratic Barlow. King plays upon the isolation of a small town in Maine, exploring the possibility of its takeover by nonhuman forces, unknown to the rest of the world. While employing the standard components of vampire fiction made familiar by Stoker, including a band of heroes complete with an aging scholar as a Van Helsing figure, King downplays the erotic dimension of vampirism, prominent in "Carmilla" and *Dracula*, in favor of metaphors of power and corruption. *The Dracula Tape* (1975), by Fred Saberhagen, in sharp contrast to King's traditional portrayal of the vampire as demonically evil, provides one of the earliest novelistic treatments of the sympathetic vampire. In one of the first novels to present a vampire's story from his or her own point of view, Count Dracula retells the events of Stoker's book on the tape recorder of a car belonging to a descendant of Jonathan and Mina Harker. While generally adhering to the "facts" as recorded by Stoker, Saberhagen reinterprets them to show Count Dracula as the hero of the tale.

Interview with the Vampire, by Anne Rice (1976), although far from the first piece of fiction to present a story from a vampire's point of view, was the first in that mode to bring vampires to the notice of the general public. Unlike King, who in *'Salem's Lot* follows Stoker in presenting the vampire as the essence of evil, to be overcome by a dynamic faith in God, Rice places her vampires in a secularized universe. To the boy interviewer's questions about crucifixes, magical transformations, and the efficacy of a stake through the heart, the vampire Louis replies, "That is, how you would say today—bullshit?" (25). Rice's vampires display abnormal strength, speed, and sensory acuity, along with a drastically altered appearance that makes it difficult for them to pass for human, but they have none of the traditional fictional vampire's powers of transformation. Aside from sunlight and fire, they seem to have no vulnerabilities. In *The Vampire Lestat* (1985), the reader who accepted Louis as a reliable narrator must undergo a wrenching reversal of perspective, for Lestat, portrayed as a villain in the earlier book, contradicts Louis' interpretation of events and presents himself as an admirable character—at least, within the limits of the inhuman, amoral nature of Rice's vampires. *Queen of the Damned* (1988) abandons first-person narration for multiple points of view, both human and vampire. Lestat's quest for the source of his own existence leads him to the mythic Adam and Eve of the Undead, culminating in a battle between ancient vampires of unimaginable power. It would not be accurate to characterize this epic as a conflict between "good" and "evil" vampires; these creatures have their own values and goals, to which human standards of morality remain peripheral. Her work, including numerous books in the "Vampire Chronicles" series following the first three, not only stimulated a renewed interest in the vampire archetype but shaped much subsequent fiction, supplementing and, to some extent, displacing Stoker as the most influential author in this subgenre.

Hôtel Transylvania (1978), by Chelsea Quinn Yarbro, introduces Count Saint-Germain, based on the enigmatic historical figure of that name. Though less familiar to general readers than Rice, Yarbro has exerted a strong influence on many authors of vampire fiction. Against her meticulously researched historical backgrounds, intimate exploration of human (whether living or undead) emotions and relationships claims central importance. Saint-Germain may be described as Dracula with a difference. Another Transylvanian Count who lives on blood, sometimes transforms his victims into his own kind, casts no reflection, and rests on a bed of his native earth, Saint-Germain embodies the opposite of the unholy evil Stoker ascribes to Dracula. Rather than recoiling from Christian symbols, in Hôtel Transylvania Saint-Germain wields a consecrated Host to repel a coven of Satanists. To Saint-Germain, the taking of blood is an erotic experience, making this character the quintessential demon lover. Drinking blood offers him no satisfaction unless his partner attains sexual fulfillment. Hence he becomes the immediate ancestor of numerous sympathetic vampire protagonists who exhibit a ravishing sensuality that particularly appeals to female readers. The Saint-Germain series, set all over the world in centuries from ancient times to the present, exhibits an epic scope as well as meticulous historical research. Yarbro has also written novels

*"You are blood of my blood,
Madelaine. It would be as
impossible for me to leave you
as it would for me to cross the
Seine barefoot. Even if blood
did not bind us, I swear to you
that love would." (Yarbro,*
Hôtel Transylvania, *173)*

focusing on two of Saint-Germain's former lovers, Olivia and Madelaine, now transformed into vampires. Through these women's perspectives, Yarbro explores the social and political status of women in several different historical periods.

While it would be impossible to list all the vampire novels of interest in the past three decades, some of the most noteworthy can be mentioned: More or less traditional supernatural vampires appear in numerous works published in the 1970s and 1980s. In *The Black Castle* (1978), by Les Daniels, the Grand Inquisitor of Spain ironically employs his brother, the vampire Sebastian, as an instrument of terror in the service of the Church. *They Thirst* (1981), by Robert R. McCammon, resembles *'Salem's Lot* on an epic scale, featuring a satanic vampire lord, Prince Vulkan, bent on ruling Los Angeles. *The Delicate Dependency* (1982), by Michael Talbot, leads its human characters through a multilayered plot that culminates in an encounter with an esoteric society of vampires, who guide the history and nurture the genius of the inferior but indispensable human race. *Vampire Junction* (1984), by S. P. Somtow, a violent story of a boy vampire who becomes a rock star, draws upon Jungian theory to explain vampirism as a spontaneous birth from the collective unconscious.

Blood Hunt (1987), by Lee Killough, is the first memorable novel in the thriving subgenre of vampire detective fiction. Garreth Mikaelian, a San Francisco police officer, investigates murders committed by Lane Barber, a vampire who attacks and accidentally transforms him. The core of the novel concerns Garreth's gradual realization of and adjustment to the fact of his vampirism. His personality remains intact through his transformation. Instead of becoming a bloodthirsty demon, he stands in the far more interesting position of an ordinary, decent man required to adjust to a new set of limits and temptations. Moral ambiguity occupies the foreground in the highly successful "Vampire Files" detective series begun with *Bloodlist* (1990), by P. N. Elrod. The books are narrated by Jack Fleming, who (like Killough's Garreth) after becoming a vampire investigates his own murder. Elrod's series, however, set in Depression-era Chicago, has affinities with the hard-boiled private eye subgenre rather than the police procedural. In *Children of the Night* (1990), by Mercedes Lackey, psychic investigator Diana Tregarde defeats a gang of life-force predators with the aid of Andre DuPres, a sensual and witty vampire reminiscent of Yarbro's Saint-Germain. Tanya Huff combines mystery with romance in her series about vampire Henry Fitzroy, illegitimate son of Henry VIII, and Toronto private detective Vicki Nelson, who investigate occult crimes together, beginning in *Blood Price* (1991). Barbara Hambly's *Those Who Hunt the Night* (1988) features a husband-wife investigative team, Professor James Asher and his wife Lydia, in Victorian England. They reluctantly accept a commission from vampire nobleman Simon Ysidro to find out who has been murdering London's vampires. Hambly's undead resemble Rice's in their amorality, violence, and detachment from humanity. The novel's title has an ironic triple application—to the vampires, to the fanatical vampire-slaying antagonist, and to James in his role as detective. Hambly's novel illustrates the post-1970s shift in characterization of even less than "good" vampires from ravening demons to beings with individuality, free will, and the capacity for moral choice.

A number of late-twentieth-century novelists explore alternatives to the classic supernatural undead, frequently from a science fiction perspective. *The Vampire Tapestry* (1980), by Suzy McKee Charnas, presents its vampire, Dr. Edward Weyland, the sole survivor of his species, as a single-minded beast of prey with superior intelligence. The novel moves from an external view of this character as simply a ruthless predator to a more intimate and sympathetic perspective through the eyes of a teenage boy who befriends him and a middle-aged female psychologist who, faced with the task of "curing" Weyland of his vampiric "delusion," makes the imaginative leap of realizing that he actually is the nonhuman creature he claims to be. Finally, Charnas places the reader entirely within Weyland's viewpoint, demonstrating how he has grown and changed, unwillingly forced into relationships with the human beings he prefers to consider his "livestock." Animal metaphors dominate this story; Weyland is characterized as a lynx, tiger, or raptor in deceptively human shape, with his human appearance merely an evolutionary adaptation to enable him to mingle unnoticed with his prey. Miriam Blaylock in *The Hunger* (1981), by Whitley Strieber, another naturally evolved vampire, differs sharply from Weyland in her orientation toward the human race. Unlike Charnas's protagonist, who values his isolation and would not want to create his own rivals, Strieber's Miriam craves human company. She futilely attempts to use her own blood to transform her victims into immortal companions, who eventually degenerate into a grotesque living death. Thus Strieber uses the vampire-as-alien to achieve a fresh perspective on the familiar motif of the vampire's tragic isolation. *Fevre Dream* (1982), by George R. R. Martin, features a vampire subculture rather than a solitary predator. Set in the heyday of the Mississippi steamboats, this novel centers on Joshua, a vampire who, orphaned in childhood, grows up believing himself an aberrant human being. Eventually he realizes that he is neither human nor supernatural, but a representative of a species that combines features of the legendary werewolf and vampire. He invents a potion that substitutes for blood, freeing himself and his followers from the "red thirst" or "fever." Joshua's human partner, steamboat captain Abner Marsh, provides the viewpoint through which we learn about the vampire race and come to understand that vampires, like human beings, are individuals with both good and evil traits.

In *Sabella or The Blood Stone* (1980), by Tanith Lee, an alien entity takes over the body and memories of a child living on a colonized planet in Earth's near future and transmutes her into a vampire, a process of which she has no

"But we must understand that we are not speaking—in the case of the vampire, for example—of a blood-sipping phantom who cringes from a clove of garlic. Now, how would nature design a vampire?" (Charnas, The Vampire Tapestry, *25)*

clear memory, believing herself to be the girl Sabella. The novel follows the protagonist's pilgrimage of self-discovery in Lee's inimitably poetic style. Another alien vampire species, the luren, in *Those of My Blood* (1988), by Jacqueline Lichtenberg, also originate on a different planet rather than on Earth as a human mutation. Stranded on our world for generations, they have developed into two factions, the Residents, who believe in responsible coexistence with humanity, and the Tourists, who exploit human beings as prey and devote their energies to the goal of returning to their home world. As in many novels of this period, the conflict between vampire antagonists highlights issues of the ethics of predation and the possibility of harmonious relationships between human and nonhuman beings. *Shattered Glass* (1989), by Elaine Bergstrom, begins the saga of the Austra family, a clan of alien vampires who, despite their extraterrestrial origins, have been a part of human history for millennia. Bergstrom gives her vampires powerful psychic abilities, animal strength, speed, and feral grace, and a dislike for but not an exaggerated vulnerability to daylight. They also possess the ability to immerse their donors in their own memories so vividly that the donor feels he or she has lived the past event.

Sunglasses After Dark (1989), by Nancy Collins, is a violent, erotic novel that initially appears to be a tale of homicidal psychosis and multiple personality. The Other, Sonja Blue, inhabits the body of supposedly dead heiress Denise Thorne. In fact, Denise has died, and Sonja, the vampire, a new personality with Denise's memories, has come to birth in her body. Collins postulates a demonic race known as the Pretenders, who comprise a variety of subspecies that all prey on human beings. Like many contemporary vampire novels, *Sunglasses* enlists our sympathy with a creature traditionally regarded as a bloodthirsty monster by demonstrating that human beings can be guilty of far worse than a peculiar diet and occasional killing in self-defense. Many such novels extend contemporary respect for the integrity and civil rights of minority groups to that misunderstood and feared minority, the race of vampire. Twentieth- and twenty-first-century readers of fantasy and science fiction are not content to destroy the alien on sight. Authors of this period frequently respond to their audience's desire to understand the mind of the not-quite-human by creating fictional vampires—Saberhagen's Dracula dictating his apologia on tape, Louis and Lestat in Rice's trilogy, Joshua telling his life story to Abner in *Fevre Dream*, Charnas's Dr. Weyland revealing his secrets to his therapist—who seem eager to be understood. Jewelle Gomez, for instance, makes connections between vampirism and humanity by using her undead characters to explore the plight of marginalized members of human society in *The Gilda Stories* (1991), a series of episodes in the history of a black, lesbian vampire who begins life as a slave in the antebellum South.

"My revenge is just begun! I spread it over centuries, and time is on my side. Your girls that you all love are mine already." (Dracula, *267*)

Less gentle vampires, however, continue to thrive among the many different approaches to the theme explored from the 1980s on. Brian Lumley's *Necroscope* (1986) is the first volume in a series about a parasitic species of vampires from another dimension and the secret espionage bureau that battles against them. In *The Stress of Her Regard* (1989) by Tim Powers, three major Romantic poets—Byron, Shelley, and Keats— feature as victims of silicon-based, shapeshifting drinkers of blood and life- force. Powers combines a dazzling variety of mythical motifs in this sweeping novel. *Dracula Unbound* (1991), a time-travel tale by Brian Aldiss in which Bram Stoker features as a character, portrays the vampire species as reptilian predators completely alien to human emotions and ethics. Aldiss also meta- phorically associates vampirism with infectious disease, specifically syphilis. Yvonne Navarro in *AfterAge* (1993) portrays a postapocalyptic world in which a vampire plague has reduced those who remain human to cowering in hiding from the vampire hordes, a scenario reminiscent of Matheson's *I Am Legend*. *Carrion Comfort*, by Dan Simmons (1989), a novel of psychic vampirism, involves Nina and Melanie, a pair of antebellum Charleston belles, and Willi, a German aristocrat, who meet to perpetuate their long-term rivalry in what they variously call the Game, the Hunt, or simply Feeding. Ordinary human beings except for their mutant ability to drive others to violence by sheer mental force, they have learned to extend life and vitality indefinitely by feed- ing on the deaths they cause. Simmons explores the motif of vampirism as infectious disease in *Children of the Night* (1992), drawing connections with the AIDS epidemic and reflecting the political situation of the late twentieth century against the backdrop of the disruption caused by the downfall of Communism in Eastern Europe, as *I Am Legend* reflects an earlier decade's anxieties over potential nuclear war. Dracula appears in Simmons's novel as an aged despot directing the action behind the scenes.

Among many other revisionist treatments of Dracula as a character, Jeanne Kalogridis produced a trilogy, "Diaries of the Family Dracul," beginning with *Covenant with the Vampire* (1994). Kalogridis traces the malign influ- ence of Vlad Dracula over his kin through several generations, ending with events that overlap Stoker's novel. Chelsea Quinn Yarbro also wrote prequels to *Dracula*, dealing with the origins of the Count's three vampire brides. Each of these books is set in a different historical era, with the last having been designed to culminate just before Jonathan Harker's arrival at Castle Dra- cula. Two of the three planned "Sisters of the Night" novels were published, *The Angry Angel* (1998) and *The Soul of an Angel* (1999); the third appears to have been canceled. A recent bestselling novel by Elizabeth Kostova, *The Historian* (2005), adopts the traditional vampirc-hunting plotline, narrated in an epistolary format in homage to Stoker's *Dracula*. Kostova's hunters, however, are scholars, and the pursuit of Dracula, here identified with Vlad the Impaler, takes place mainly in libraries through the uncovering and analysis of hidden texts. The theme of a secret history underlying the public history known to the uniniated pervades the novel, echoed in the heroine's quest for the secrets of her own father's past.

Some authors of the 1990s revisit the traditional antagonism between vampire and mortal with a difference. As in older fiction of vampires as demonic predators, the two races can find no depth of common ground, but in these decentered works, the vampire point of view is privileged over the human. In Poppy Z. Brite's *Lost Souls* (1992), a postmodernist novel of literal and metaphorical alienation, a teenage boy named Nothing runs away from his adoptive parents in search of his true self. He discovers that he is the child of a vampire and a human woman, who died at his birth, as the mothers of vampire infants usually do. The common adolescent feeling of not belonging to one's family becomes literally true for Nothing. Batlike humanoids live secretly alongside modern human culture in Melanie Tem's *Desmodus* (1995). Essentially giant, blood-drinking bats in vaguely human form, they share the physiology and social structures of their lesser, unintelligent kin. In this innovative novel, humanity remains peripheral, bizarre and alien as viewed through the eyes of the Desmodus protagonist.

The emergent subgenre of vampire romance moves in precisely the opposite direction, toward intimacy rather than disconnection between human and nonhuman. Although vampires have occasionally featured as protagonists of love stories since the middle of the twentieth century, Lori Herter's *Obsession* (1991) was the first vampire novel to be sold expressly as a romance rather than shelved with horror or fantasy. The four-book series initiated by this novel signaled the advent of a new marketing category, which has since become extremely popular. Authors who followed soon afterward with multiple novels in this subgenre include Linda Lael Miller, Nancy Gideon, Nancy Kilpatrick, Maggie Shayne, and Amanda Ashley. Under the pen name "Rebecca Brand," Suzy McKee Charnas explores the traditional supernatural vampire in *The Ruby Tear* (1997), a revisionist take on vampire romance with suspense and touches of humor in a theatrical setting. The heroine, a stage actress who becomes entangled in an ancient vampire's quest to retrieve the eponymous jewel from her former fiancé, a playwright, must choose between human and vampire lovers, with an unexpected denouement. An unusual science fiction treatment of vampirism, Jean Lorrah's *Blood Will Tell* (2001), narrated from the viewpoint of a female police officer in a small town, dating a man with a mysterious past, at first appears to be a variation on the "vampire as alien" motif, then veers in a surprising direction. This novel postulates that vampires do not occupy the pinnacle of the terrestrial food chain but, rather, are bred and manipulated as prey for a still higher species. Christine Feehan creates nonhuman, naturally evolved vampires called "Carpathians" in a series that pits ethical members of the race against those who have succumbed to violent bloodlust. Feehan's system postulates that the most fortunate Carpathian males attain intimacy with human female "soulmates," a relationship seldom without tension.

The popularity of this kind of romance demonstrates female readers' attraction to vampire heroes that are both sympathetic and erotic. These novels strip vampire eroticism of the guilt that originally infused the sexual subtext in classic fiction, without quite abandoning the spice of the forbidden. Lynsay Sands and Kate McAlister, among other contemporary authors, combine vampire romance with humor. Vampirism blends with the subgenre of "chick lit"—novels focusing on young career women finding their way in the world of work and relationships—in the work of such authors as humorous paranormal novelist MaryJanice [*sic*] Davidson, beginning with *Undead and Unwed* (2002), told in the first person by a heroine who unexpectedly arises from the grave to discover that, not only has she become a vampire, the supernatural community believes her to be the prophesied queen of the undead. For vampire fiction suffused with a higher degree of explicit sexuality than found in mainstream romance, readers can seek out erotic romance and women's erotica novels from electronic publishers such as Ellora's Cave (www.ellorascave.com), Loose Id (www.loose-id.com), and Liquid Silver (www.liquidsilver books.com), books from major publisher Kensington's Brava imprint, and novellas in the "Secrets" anthology series from small press Red Sage.

One popular variant on the theme presents vampires, often along with other nonhuman characters such as werewolves, as acknowledged members of society in an alternate present-day society where supernatural creatures are known to be real. Kim Newman's alternate history series, beginning with *Anno-Dracula* (1992), postulates that Van Helsing's band of hunters did not succeed in slaying Dracula as in Stoker's novel. Instead, Dracula transformed the widowed Queen Victoria into a vampire, married her in order to become Prince Consort, and now rules England. Vampires and mortals exist in uneasy fellow citizenship. Newman's incorporation of dozens of characters from history and literature enriches the series with the reader's pleasure in recognizing the author's allusions, as well as the drama of the gradually unfolding variations on real-world history as we know it. Laurell K. Hamilton's series of novels narrated by Anita Blake, a professional necromancer with a license to kill vampires who transgress legal boundaries, is set in an alternate contemporary America in which supernatural creatures are publicly known to exist. Law and custom have been restructured to deal with vampires, werewolves, zombies, and other nonhuman beings. Anita's triangular relationship with a master vampire and a werewolf pack leader draws her deeper into increasingly violent and explicitly erotic situations as the series progresses. Similar worlds are constructed by Charlaine Harris, with her stories of reluctant psychic Sookie Stackhouse, who becomes entangled with vampires and other creatures of the night, and Kim Harrison, whose series focuses on a witch professionally partnered with a female vampire. Also creating their own unique mythologies are L. A. Banks in the "Vampire Huntress" series and Sherrilyn Kenyon in her "Dark-Hunters" books.

The mainline thread of supernatural vampirism flourishes alongside continued innovation, although with significant differences from older fiction. *Midnight Mass* (2004), by F. Paul Wilson, illustrates the tendency toward more nuanced treatment of character and ethics even in fiction harking back to the original concept of vampirism as a diabolical evil. In this novel, vampires have overrun the United States and forced the human remnant into hiding in most areas. A priest and a nun rally a group of survivors to take the offensive against the undead. When the priest falls victim to a deadly attack, he manages to restrain his encroaching vampiric nature and cling to his humanity long enough to continue supporting the heroes in their crusade. Science fiction author Octavia Butler, on the other hand places vampires at the center and human characters on the periphery in her recent novel *Fledgling* (2005). The first-person narrative is told by a preadolescent female member of a naturally evolved vampire species who suffers from amnesia following a murderous attack upon her family's home and rediscovers her true nature simultaneously with the revelation of her background to the reader. Unlike the humanoid bats of Tem's *Desmodus*, however, Butler's vampires depend on human blood donors for emotional connection as well as physical nourishment, and each individual forms a network of symbiotic relationships for that purpose.

YOUNG ADULT VAMPIRE LITERATURE

Fiction for children and teenagers in the past three decades has followed the precedent set by adult fiction in often portraying vampires as sympathetic characters, capable of ethical behavior. If presented as evil, they are usually more than one-dimensional villains, often morally ambiguous. Entertainment for younger children tends to portray them as amusing and harmless. The Count on the television program "Sesame Street" (1969–present), wearing a black cape and speaking in a Bela Lugosi accent, has an obsession with counting rather than bloodsucking. *Bunnicula* (1979), by James and Deborah Howe, narrated by a dog living in a middle-class American household, details the family cat's growing suspicions of Bunnicula, a pet rabbit with mysterious origins, who preys on vegetables by draining their juices, leaving them anemically white. In Mel Gilden's "Fifth Grade Monsters" series, analogies are drawn between the monsters and both the disabled and members of minority ethnic groups, deserving fair treatment and as capable of kindness and friendship as any other children. In the opening volume, *M Is for Monster* (1987), human protagonist Danny discovers that the four monster children who join his fifth-grade class, including C. D. Bitesky, a Transylvanian immigrant who wears evening clothes with a cape to school and carries a thermos of red liquid called Fluid of Life, make far better friends than the human class bully.

Angela Sommer-Bodenburg's "Little Vampire" series (translated from German), beginning with *My Friend the Vampire* (1982) has a sharper edge. The young vampire who befriends Tony represents a rebellion against adult norms, and his relatives, except for his little sister who is still too young to drink blood and lives on milk, appear overtly dangerous. The title character of Ann Jungman's *Vlad the Drac* (1982) and its sequels, by contrast, is a thoroughly domesticated vampire, even to the point of

> *"Before we began I told you that you are a vampire or you are not. . . . It is like having red hair and freckles." (Gilden,* How to Be a Vampire in One Easy Lesson, *90)*

trivialization. The humorous tone of the narrative underscores the harmlessness of this vegetarian vampire. Probably unique to Jungman is the literal reduction of the monster in both size and status; Vlad the Drac (a name he adopts in an attempt to sound frightening) is treated like a pet. Two English children on a Romanian vacation rescue the diminutive vampire from under a stone where he has been trapped for over a century and take him home with them. Serious issues, however, are hinted at by his fear of being the last of his kind and his resentment of popular culture stereotypes of vampirism, the latter a theme Jungman's series has in common with Gilden's. All these works illustrate the trend among children's authors of using vampire motifs to promote tolerance toward people of different backgrounds.

Jayne Harvey reverses this pattern in *Great-Uncle Dracula* (1992), in which a human child plays the role of outsider. When Emily Normal's father brings her and her brother Elliot to Transylvania, United States, to live with Great-Uncle Dracula, she becomes a misfit in a community of witches, werewolves, vampires, and ghosts. Transylvania is a parody of a generic American small town with the conventionally monstrous and normal reversed. By the story's end, Emily learns to appreciate her own unique qualities and recognize that her real friends can accept her for what she is. Another unusual variation on the theme, *Ma and Pa Dracula* (1989), by Ann M. Martin, focuses on a human boy's struggle with the discovery that his beloved adoptive parents are different from other children's families and are, in fact, vampires. His unsuccessful attempt to become just like all the other children ends in a renewed bond with his parents and appreciation for their unusual lifestyle.

For slightly older readers, *My Sister the Vampire* (1992), by Nancy Garden, depicts vampires for the most part in the traditional horror mode, as an evil fit only to be destroyed. The plot centers on young Tim's struggle to prevent his teenage sister from being transformed into one of the undead. At the climax, however, the vampires renounce their unnatural existence and thank the children for freeing them from their curse by leaving them bound to face the sun, another illustration of nuanced treatment of vampires even when framed as villains. L. J. Smith created one of the first vampire romance series for teenage readers in her "Vampire Diaries," beginning with *The Awakening* (1991). A stand-alone novel, *The Silver Kiss* (1990), by Annette Curtis Klause, involves a love story between Zoe, a teenage girl whose mother is dying, and

Simon, a 300-year-old vampire who appears about her age. His reluctant attraction to Zoe puts her in danger from his brother, Christopher, who became undead as a small boy. Zoe's experience with Simon helps her come to terms with her mother's imminent death, while he, in turn, gains the courage to end his unlife. Vivian Vande Velde presents a dangerous alliance between a human girl and a young male vampire in *Companions of the Night* (1995). When sixteen-year-old Kerry accidentally stumbles into a confrontation between vampire Ethan and a gang of would-be vampire hunters, she rescues him under the assumption that he is a human victim of deluded fanatics. Vande Velde maintains a dynamic balance between the allure and the lethal power of Kerry's bloodthirsty, secretive, charismatic ally. With a more positive view of vampires, although not discounting their predatory nature, L. J. Smith's "Night World" series explores relationships between human characters and members of a naturally evolved race of vampires. The first book, *Secret Vampire* (1996), is a romance in which the heroine's boyfriend saves her from a terminal illness by initiating her into the realm of vampirism. Young author Amelia Atwater-Rhodes published her first novel, *In the Forests of the Night* (1999), at age fourteen. The protagonist, lonely vampire Risika, is hunted by an unknown enemy while facing the memories of her past and trying to cling to the remnants of her humanity. Kate McAlister, under the name "Katie Maxwell," writes humorous novels for teenagers, beginning with *Got Fangs?* (2005), which gently satirizes the "soulmate" motif through the voice of the girl protagonist.

VAMPIRE CRITICISM

Literary criticism dealing with vampire fiction at first typically analyzed its psychological roots, applying Ernest Jones's Freudian model to fiction. Maurice Richardson, in "The Psychoanalysis of Ghost Stories" (1959), famously summarizes *Dracula* as "a kind of incestuous, necrophilious, oral-anal-sadistic all-in wrestling match" set in "a sort of homicidal lunatic's brothel in a crypt" (427). James Twitchell later takes a similar approach in *Dreadful Pleasures: An Anatomy of Modern Horror* (1985), analyzing vampire stories as an adolescent male fantasy. Psychological critiques of *Dracula*, in particular, encompass a wide range of supposed subtexts, including latent homosexuality, incestuous desires, and fear of female sexuality. Leonard Wolf's impressionistic meditation on the place of *Dracula* in modern culture, *A Dream of Dracula* (1972), also relies heavily upon a psychosexual approach to the vampire theme. Wolf followed this book with the first annotated edition of *Dracula* (1975), later revised and reissued as *The Essential Dracula* (1993). *In Search of Dracula* (1972), by Raymond McNally and Radu Florescu, popularized the theory of a connection between Stoker's Count and the historical Wallachian warlord Vlad the Impaler. McNally and Florescu wrote two later books focusing on Vlad's life and times, *Dracula: A Biography of Vlad the*

A Chronology of Major Vampire Films

Nosferatu (Prana, 1922)

Dracula (Universal, 1931)

Vampyr (Tobis-Klangfilm, 1932)

Dracula's Daughter (Universal, 1936)

Son of Dracula (Universal, 1943)

Horror of Dracula (Hammer, 1958)

Brides of Dracula (Hammer, 1960)

Dance of the Vampires (Ransohoff-Polanski Productions, 1967)

The Vampire Lovers (Hammer, 1970)

House of Dark Shadows (MGM, 1970)

Countess Dracula (Hammer, 1971)

Blacula (American International, 1972)

Dracula (Mirisch/United Artists, 1979)

Love at First Bite (Simon Productions/AIP, 1979)

The Hunger (MGM, 1983)

Fright Night (Columbia, 1985)

The Lost Boys (Warner Brothers, 1987)

Near Dark (De Laurentiis/Feldman-Meeker, 1987)

Bram Stoker's Dracula (Columbia, 1992)

Buffy, the Vampire Slayer (Twentieth Century Fox, 1992)

Interview with the Vampire (Warner Brothers, 1994)

Vampire in Brooklyn (Paramount, 1995)

Dracula: Dead and Loving It (Columbia, 1995)

From Dusk Till Dawn (Dimension, 1996)

Blade the Vampire Slayer (New Line Cinema/Amen Ra Films, 1997)

Underworld (Sony Pictures, 2003)

Van Helsing (Universal, 2004)

Impaler (1973) and *Dracula: Prince of Many Faces* (1989). They also edited an annotated *Dracula*, called, like Wolf's second edition, *The Essential Dracula* (1979). Other critics analyze Stoker's novel's narrative structure and its relationship to the social and political issues of its day. Many pioneering articles on *Dracula* from a wide range of critical viewpoints are collected in the anthology *Dracula: The Vampire and the Critics* (1988), edited by Margaret

L. Carter. Clive Leatherdale examines Stoker's work from a variety of historical, cultural, and literary perspectives in *Dracula: The Novel and the Legend* (1985).

Critical interest in *Dracula* permitted other works in the field to be considered worthy of scholarly attention. Basil Copper surveys the vampire theme in fiction, drama, and popular culture in general, including real-life bloodsuckers, in *The Vampire in Legend, Fact, and Art* (1973). Christopher Frayling's anthology *Vampyres: From Lord Byron to Count Dracula* (1978), including nonfiction as well as fiction and excerpts from Stoker's working notes as well as from sources used in writing *Dracula*, begins with an extensive essay on the history of vampire fiction and a chart summarizing the features of numerous major works. Several bibliographies of vampires in fiction and other media have been published, beginning with *Vampires Unearthed* (1983), a multimedia listing by Martin V. Riccardo. Margaret L. Carter covers fiction, nonfiction, and stage plays, with introductory essays on the history and evolution of vampire fiction, in *The Vampire in Literature: A Critical Bibliography* (1989). Greg Cox's more selective *The Transylvanian Library* (1993), confined to fiction, lists notable novels and stories with brief summaries and ratings graded by numbers of bats from one through four. Patricia Altner's *Vampire Readings* (1998) also contains useful summaries of the listed works to guide the potential reader. Brian Frost's *The Monster with a Thousand Faces* (1989) comprehensively surveys vampire fiction from its folklore roots and its literary inception in the eighteenth century to the 1980s. Carol A. Senf concentrates on selected periods and works in *The Vampire in Nineteenth-Century English Literature* (1988), which, despite its title, includes reflections on some twentieth-century authors. Senf later wrote a reader's guide to Stoker's novel, *Dracula: Between Tradition and Modernism* (1998). Gregory A. Waller's wide-ranging *The Living and the Undead: From Stoker's Dracula to Romero's Dawn of the Dead* (1986), as its subtitle suggests, deals with movies as well as print fiction and encompasses non-vampiric undead creatures such as zombies in addition to vampires. Ken Gelder's *Reading the Vampire* (1994) places fiction and movies in this genre in their historic and cultural context, drawing upon literary and psychological theory to analyze works from the nineteenth century through the late twentieth. Nina Auerbach, in *Our Vampires, Ourselves* (1995), also begins with the Romantic period and analyzes the vampire stories (and later, films) she views as characteristic of each period, with their social and political significance. David J. Skal explores the career of Bela Lugosi and the making of the classic Dracula films in *Hollywood Gothic* (1990). Skal's witty *V Is for Vampire* (1996) contains alphabetically arranged brief discussions of significant authors, characters, works, and themes related to vampires in popular media. *Vampire Legends in Contemporary American Culture* (2002), by Gothic scholar William Patrick Day, begins with the roots of vampire fiction but concentrates mainly on the cultural implications of late-twentieth-century novels, movies, and television.

The 1997 centenary of the publication of *Dracula* inspired several critical anthologies on Stoker's novel and vampires in literature, notably *Bram Stoker's Dracula: Sucking Through the Century, 1897–1997* (1997), edited by Carol Margaret Davison; *Blood Read* (1997), edited by Joan Gordon and Veronica Hollinger; and *The Blood Is the Life: Vampires in Literature* (1999), edited by Leonard G. Heldreth and Mary Pharr. James Holte, author of *Dracula in the Dark* (1997), a study of the film adaptations of *Dracula*, edited *The Fantastic Vampire* (2002), papers from the Dracula centennial year of the International Conference on the Fantastic in the Arts. Two new annotated editions of *Dracula* appeared around this time, *Dracula Unearthed* (1998), edited by Clive Leatherdale, and a Norton Critical Edition (1997), edited by Nina Auerbach and David J. Skal; the latter includes reviews and critical essays. Glennis Byron edited an edition of *Dracula* (1998) featuring an introduction directed to students and several appendices elaborating on elements of the novel's nineteenth-century background. A version edited by John Paul Riquelme (2002) contains similar contextual documents as well as several essays from various critical perspectives written especially for that volume. Elizabeth Miller writes in depth about Bram Stoker, his work, and Vlad the Impaler in *Reflections on Dracula* (1997) and *Dracula: Sense and Nonsense* (2000), exhaustively debunking popular misconceptions about Stoker, the writing of *Dracula*, and the confusion between Vlad and the fictional Count.

> *"Listen to them—the children of the night. What music they make!" (Stoker,* Dracula, *Norton Critical Edition, 24)*

VAMPIRES IN THE MEDIA

Cinematic treatments of vampirism began in the silent film era with *Nosferatu* (1922), a thinly disguised adaptation of *Dracula*. Stoker's widow successfully sued for plagiarism, and most copies of the movie were destroyed, with, however, a few surviving, fortunately for later vampire aficionados. This film originates the popular motif of the vampire's destruction by sunlight. Graf Orlock, the villain in *Nosferatu*, is associated with images of contagion and has a ghastly appearance combining batlike and ratlike traits. Bela Lugosi in the Universal *Dracula* (1931), the movie that established the stereotypical image of the vampire for all time, has, in contrast, a suave, seductive manner. The script was based on the stage drama (1927) by Hamilton Deane and John L. Balderston, in which Lugosi had played the leading role before being chosen to portray the Count on film. The action of the play takes place entirely in London. Although the movie includes opening scenes set in Dracula's Transylvanian castle, the remainder of it follows the play so closely that the tension and horror of the early scenes are not consistently maintained. Important actions occur offstage, including the climactic staking of Dracula. Universal Studios

"I never drink—wine."
(Dracula, *1931 movie)*

produced several sequels, notably *Dracula's Daughter* (1936), with a lesbian subtext and a partially sympathetic treatment of the title character's plight. A German expressionist film, *Vampyr* (1932), purports to be based on "Carmilla" but has little or no similarity to Le Fanu's tale. The first of several films produced by the British studio Hammer, *Horror of Dracula* (simply *Dracula* in England, 1958), introduced Christopher Lee as the Count. Bloodshed in full color and blatant (for the time) eroticism distinguished the Hammer Dracula movies sharply from the earlier Universal films. Lee portrays a tall, dark, menacing Dracula who speaks little dialogue and engages in physical combat with Peter Cushing's Van Helsing. Van Helsing but not Dracula reappears in the next Hammer vampire movie, *Brides of Dracula* (1960), which characterizes vampirism as an obscene cult that ensnares the young man who preys on his own mother early in the film and goes on to seduce several young women at a girls' school. Lee went on to play Dracula in other Hammer films and also in a non-Hammer production, *Count Dracula* (*El Conde Dracula*, 1971). Hammer produced a cycle of movies loosely based on "Carmilla," the first, *The Vampire Lovers* (1970), adhering closest to Le Fanu's novella. Hammer's *Countess Dracula* (1971), contrary to the title, is based on the life of Elizabeth Bathory, the "Blood Countess." Roman Polanski's *Fearless Vampire Killers* (also known as *Dance of the Vampires*, 1967) parodies the established conventions of the vampire film, sending an elderly vampire-hunter and his naïve young assistant into a vampire-haunted castle.

Variations on the traditional motifs appear in movies of the 1970s and beyond. In *Blacula* (1972) an African prince whom Count Dracula has transformed into a vampire awakens in contemporary America. The humorous *Love at First Bite* (1979), with George Hamilton as a romantic Dracula, satirizes familiar elements from the Lugosi film, including an insect-eating Renfield. In the same year, Frank Langella, who had also performed the part onstage, plays the Count as a seductive lover in a serious adaptation of *Dracula* (1979). Like the original Universal movie, this version is based more on the Balderston-Deane play than on Stoker's novel; in fact, unlike the Lugosi film, the 1979 version includes no Transylvanian scenes. Moreover, it reverses the roles of Lucy and Mina, making the latter Van Helsing's daughter and having her transformed into a vampire early in the story. *The Hunger* (1983), adapted from Whitley Strieber's novel, stars Catherine Deneuve in a sexually charged performance as the solitary vampire Miriam. *Lost Boys* (1987), with its theme of never growing up, connects vampirism with contemporary youth culture. Francis Ford Coppola's *Bram Stoker's Dracula* (1992) claimed to follow Stoker's novel more faithfully than any previous adaptation. While this movie does include every significant element from the book, including details missing from previous films such as all three of Lucy's suitors and a faithful rendering of Van Helsing's sometimes dictatorial and sometimes manic behavior, *Bram Stoker's Dracula* also inserts a reincarnation romance subplot completely alien to Stoker's original. *Dracula: Dead and Loving It* (1995) parodies every major Dracula film that preceded it, including Coppola's, and even includes a homage to the mirror scene in *Fearless Vampire Killers*. *Blade the Vampire Slayer* (1997), bringing to life a hero from Marvel Comics, reflects the more ambiguous treatment of vampires recently prevalent in both fiction and film, with Blade, although an implacable nemesis of the undead, displaying the effects of his prenatal exposure to vampirism through an attack on his mother. *Underworld* (2003) focuses on an ancient feud between vampires and werewolves, with a "Romeo and Juliet" plot involving a forbidden liaison between lovers from the two warring groups. The recent film *Van Helsing* (2004) pits the titular hero, entirely different in personality and background from Stoker's professor, against a menagerie of monsters in addition to vampires.

> *"Children of the night—shut up!"* (Love at First Bite, *1979 movie)*

Television pioneered mass audiences' acceptance of the sympathetic vampire with the introduction of Barnabas Collins (played by Canadian actor Jonathan Frid) to the soap opera "Dark Shadows" (1966–1971). Originally introduced as a supernatural villain to improve the program's weak ratings, Barnabas searches for the reincarnation of his lost beloved, Josette, and kidnaps a young woman he identifies with that role. Gradually, Barnabas's character softens, with increased emphasis on his remorse for his bloodthirsty past and his quest for a cure for his condition. *House of Dark Shadows* (1970) adapts Barnabas's attempt to regain his humanity and find love as a theatrical film. The TV series enjoyed a brief revival in 1991, with the role of Barnabas taken by Ben Cross, who had previously played a vampire in the 1989 made-for-TV movie *Nightlife*. The comic series "The Munsters" (1964–1966) includes two vampiric characters, Grandpa, a parody of a Lugosi-like Dracula figure, and his daughter Lily, although no overt blood-drinking occurs on the program. A made-for-television mystery, *The Night Stalker* (1972), about a cynical reporter who exposes a vampire, spawned a series, "Kolchak: The Night Stalker" (1974–1975), in which Kolchak investigates a new monster every week. Dracula himself made several appearances on television over the years. Jack Palance played Dracula in a network television adaptation (1974) produced by Dan Curtis of "Dark Shadows" fame. The first film to identify Stoker's Count with Vlad the Impaler, this production depicts Lucy as the reincarnation of Dracula's late wife, anticipating the same device in Coppola's movie adaptation. Louis Jourdan starred in a BBC production of *Dracula* (1978), arguably the most faithful to Stoker's novel ever produced. The anthology series *Cliffhangers* (1979) featured one storyline, "The Curse of Dracula," about the Count as a history professor teaching night classes in San Francisco. Michael Nouri portrays Dracula as an attractive, romantic figure. The vampire as television protagonist achieved cult status for a late-twentieth-century audience in the Canadian series about a vampire police detective, "Forever Knight" (1992–95), which was preceded by a made-for-television movie, *Nick Knight* (1989). The series differs from the feature film in that the medical examiner trying to help Nick find a cure for vampirism becomes a woman rather than a man, and Nick's vampire master, LaCroix, becomes a more nuanced, less unambiguously evil character. Also, Nick's backstory is changed, making him considerably older. The show's theme, Nick's search for redemption and his resolve to atone for his past sins by helping mortals, is reinforced by flashbacks linking present-day plots to past events in his eight centuries of existence. A failed series pilot, "Blood Ties" (1991), depicts vampires as a separate subspecies of humanity. Calling themselves Carpathian-Americans, most of them seek only to be allowed to live in peace, free of prejudice-induced violence, although an anti-assimilationist faction advocates treating human beings as prey. A short-lived British series, "Ultraviolet" (1998), takes a quasi-scientific approach to vampires, known as "leeches," which were hunted by a secret government organization. Another briefly flourishing cult favorite, *Kindred: The Embraced* (1996), derived from the "Vampire: The Masquerade" roleplaying game produced by the White Wolf gaming company, involves an elaborate subculture of vampire clans. As translated to television, the undead factions appeared more like rival crime syndicates than supernatural beings. The satirical light suspense movie *Buffy, the Vampire Slayer* (1992) became the basis for a wildly popular television series by the same name, when the film's creator, Joss Whedon, had the opportunity to return to his original intentions for the character and her world. Reversing the familiar horror cliché of a beautiful girl victimized by a monster, "Buffy the Vampire Slayer" (1997–2003) empowers its blonde, teenage heroine to become a hunter of monsters, the latest in a long line of Slayers who appear once (theoretically) in every generation. Guided by her Watcher, a middle-aged librarian who provides research, training, and occasional combat backup, Buffy confronts creatures and situations that often mirror and symbolize the horrors of adolescence as experienced in mundane life. Early in the series, demons in general and vampires in particular are framed as unequivocally evil, with no potential for moral choice. The exception, Angel, Buffy's romantic interest, achieves that status through a curse that restores his soul. Later, however, characters such as Spike demonstrate moral ambiguity and potential for personal growth even in soulless vampires. A spinoff program, "Angel" (1999–2004), transports the vampire with a soul to Los Angeles, where he solves mysteries as the hero of noir-style detective adventures. Dozens of novels based on these two series have been published.

Vampire anime (Japanese animation) has developed a large fan base among English-speaking audiences in recent years. The feature film *Vampire Hunter D* (1985), set in a post-apocalyptic world 12,000 years in the future, displays the influence of Western horror films such as Hammer's Dracula cycle. The vampire lord, Count Lee, inhabits a Gothic castle but has cybernetic as well as demonic servants. The hero, known only as D, is a dhampir, a human-vampire hybrid who possesses superhuman powers as a result of his mixed heritage.

Anime television series popular in the United States include the following: "Vampire Princess Miyu" (1988) stars Miyu, a gentle teenage girl vampire, who uses her supernatural powers to send wandering Shinma (demons) back to the darkness and sometimes takes blood as a reward from those she rescues, gifting them with peace and oblivion in the process. A Shinma she formerly defeated, Larva, accompanies her as ally and protector. In "Master of Mosquiton" (1996), set in the 1920s with a humorous tone, a Transylvanian schoolgirl resurrects the vampire Mosquiton and enlists him to help her search for the secret of immortality. "Night Walker: Midnight Detective" (1998) features half-vampire detective Shido hunting the demonic Nightbreed in Tokyo, in cooperation with his young female assistant Riho and Yayoi, a beautiful investigator from a secret government organization. "Descendants of Darkness" (2000) is a supernatural detective series with a homosexual subtext, about an elite class of vampires tracking down the lost souls of the undead. "Hellsing" (2002) centers on a secret organization of that name, directed by hereditary leader Integra Hellsing. The reformed vampire Alucard assists the Hellsing Organization in its crusade against vampires and other creatures of the night, and in the first episode of the series, Alucard transforms a young female operative, Seras Victoria, into a vampire to save her life. This series features violent, epic battles that often involve clashes between Hellsing and a covert Vatican-based society also dedicated to exterminating vampires.

Several popular vampire characters appeared in comic books from the 1960s onward. Gold Key released comics based on television programs "The Munsters" (beginning in 1964) and "Dark Shadows" (from 1969). Warren Publishing Company inaugurated *Vampirella* in 1969. The title character, a female vampire in a sleek, black costume, was an alien from the planet Drakulon, where blood replaced water. A sympathetic heroine, she avoided taking human life whenever possible. Marvel Comics launched its long-running *The Tomb of Dracula* in 1972. The team of hunters pursuing Dracula is led by an elderly Quincey Harker (son of Jonathan and Mina from Stoker's novel). After the demise of this publication in 1979, Marvel published six issues of a large-format, black-and-white *Dracula* magazine. The same company produced an anthology comic series called *Vampire Tales* beginning in 1973. Marvel also created the Morbius, a scientist who became a vampire by contracting a rare blood disease. He appeared as a villain in various different Marvel publications over the years, beginning in 1971. Blade the Vampire Slayer, an African American hero, first appeared in the July 1973 issue of *Tomb of Dracula*. His mother's murder by a vampire motivated his crusade against the undead. More recently, Chaos! Comics revived Vampirella from 1994 to 1996, Brainstorm Comics introduced the ancient vampire Luxura in *Vamperotica* (beginning in 1994), and the DC Vertigo series *Preacher* (begun in 1995) included an Irish vampire, Cassidy.

White Wolf's roleplaying game "Vampire: The Masquerade" offers players the opportunity to assume the identities of vampire characters in a world, like the setting of Anne Rice's novels, where vampires are central and ordinary mortals peripheral. Rather than the solitary predators like most classic vampires, the undead in the parallel universe of "Vampire: The Masquerade" belong to an elaborate subculture, divided into clans with distinguishing characteristics and complex histories, existing secretly in the underworld of human society. Sourcebooks have been published detailing the Kindred (vampire) culture and politics of various major cities. The game's terminology has crept into fiction with the now commonplace use of "sire" for the vampire who transforms another person into one of the undead, "embrace" for the process of transformation, and "ghoul" for a servant under a vampire's supernatural influence or control, just as admirers of Anne Rice have popularized the term "fledgling" for a newly spawned vampire. Vampires have also infiltrated computer and video games, two of the most popular series being *Castlevania* and *Legacy of Kain*. The *Castlevania* cycle begins with vampire hunter Simon Belmont's quest to slay Dracula, battling many other monsters along the way. In later games, other characters with more complex motives also set out to destroy the undead Count. In *Legacy of Kain*, the player assumes the role of a vampire rather than a slayer. Morally ambiguous and extremely powerful, the player, as Kain, consumes the blood and souls of others and sometimes possesses the bodies of victims.

Several researchers have published studies of the vampire motif's pervasiveness in popular culture, including the phenomenon of people who believe themselves to be, in some sense, "real" vampires. *American Vampires* (1989), by Norine Dresser, surveys television, movies, advertising, music, and fan clubs as well as the subculture of real-life blood-drinkers and self-styled psychic vampires. Carol Page's *Bloodlust* (1991) devotes an entire book to people who consider themselves vampires. Rosemary Guiley's *The Complete Vampire Companion* (1994), which includes contributions on its various topics from a number of different writers, covers folklore, movies, fiction, television, comic books, fan clubs, and the world of "real vampires." This book features numerous quotes from and brief interviews with writers and directors of vampire fiction and films. Katherine Ramsland, author of the Anne Rice biography *Prism of the Night* (1991), conducts in-depth research on real-life vampire phenomena in *Piercing the Darkness: Undercover with Vampires in America Today* (1998). She reports on vampire-oriented nightclubs, Internet groups, and Goth communities, with numerous firsthand conversations and anecdotes. Unlike most writers on this topic, she has immersed herself in the subculture that forms the object of her study. Ramsland, a psychologist, also has written the more speculative *The Science of Vampires* (2002), which contains a chapter on vampire sex with exploration of real-life practices among people who consider themselves vampires.

The vampire in his or her many guises continually transforms in response to contemporary culture and shows no signs of fading away. As Nina Auerbach suggests in *Our Vampires, Ourselves*, each decade gets the vampire it needs.

BIBLIOGRAPHY

Primary

Aldiss, Brian. *Dracula Unbound*. New York: HarperCollins, 1991.

Atwater-Rhodes, Amelia. *In the Forests of the Night*. New York: Delacorte Press, 1999.

Benson, E. F. "And No Bird Sings." In *Spook Stories*. London: Hutchinson, 1928.

———. "Mrs. Amworth." In *Visible and Invisible*. London: Hutchinson, 1923.

———. "Negotium Perambulans." In *Visible and Invisible*. London: Hutchinson, 1923.

Bergstrom, Elaine. *Shattered Glass*. New York: Berkley, 1989.

Bixby, Jerome, and Joe E. Dean. "Share Alike." *Beyond* (1953).

Blackwood, Algernon. "The Transfer." In *Pan's Garden*. London: Macmillan, 1912.

Bloch, Robert. "The Cloak." *Unknown* (May 1939).

Bradbury, Ray. "The Homecoming." *Mademoiselle* (October 1946).

Braddon, Mary Elizabeth. "Good Lady Ducayne." *Strand Magazine* (February 1896).

Brand, Rebecca. *The Ruby Tear*. New York: Tor, 1997.

Brite, Poppy Z. *Lost Souls*. New York: Delacorte Press, 1992.

Butler, Octavia. *Fledgling*. New York: Seven Stories Press, 2005.

Charnas, Suzy McKee. *The Vampire Tapestry*. New York: Simon & Schuster, 1980. Rpt. New York: Pocket, 1981.

Collins, Nancy A. *Sunglasses After Dark*. New York: New American Library, 1989.

Crawford, F. Marion. "'For the Blood Is the Life.'" *Collier's* (December 16, 1905).

Daniels, Les. *The Black Castle*. New York: Scribner's, 1978.

Davidson, MaryJanice. *Undead and Unwed*. Ellora's Cave, 2002. Revised rpt. New York: Berkley, 2004.

Deane, Hamilton, and John L. Balderston. *Dracula*. 1927. Rpt. ed. David J. Skal. New York: St. Martin's Press, 1993.

Derleth, August. "Bat's Belfry." *Weird Tales* (May 1926).

———. "The Drifting Snow." *Weird Tales* (February 1939).

Doyle, Arthur Conan. "The Adventure of the Sussex Vampire." In *The Case-Book of Sherlock Holmes*. London: John Murray, 1927.

———. *The Parasite*. London: Constable, 1891.

Elrod, P. N. *Bloodlist*. New York: Ace, 1990.

Freeman, Mary E. Wilkins. "Luella Miller." *Everybody's Magazine* (December 1902). In *The Wind in the Rose-Bush and Other Stories of the Supernatural*. New York: Doubleday, Page, 1903.

Garden, Nancy. *My Sister the Vampire*. New York: Knopf, 1992.

Gautier, Théophile. "La Morte Amoureuse." *Chronique de Paris* (June 1836).

Gilden, Mel. *How to Be a Vampire in One Easy Lesson*. New York: Avon, 1990.

———. *M Is for Monster*. New York: Avon, 1987.

Gomez, Jewelle. *The Gilda Stories*. Ann Arbor, MI: Firebrand, 1991.

Hambly, Barbara. *Those Who Hunt the Night*. New York: Ballantine, 1988.

Harvey, Jayne. *Great-Uncle Dracula*. New York: Random House, 1992.

Hawthorne, Julian. "Ken's Mystery." *Harper's New Monthly Magazine* (November 1883).

Horler, Sydney. *The Vampire*. London: Hutchinson, 1935.

Howe, James, and Deborah Howe. *Bunnicula: A Rabbit-Tale of Mystery*. New York: Macmillan, 1979.

Huff, Tanya. *Blood Price*. New York: DAW, 1991.

James, M. R. "Count Magnus." In *Ghost-Stories of an Antiquary*. London: Edward Arnold, 1904.

———. "An Episode of Cathedral History." *Cambridge Review* (June 10, 1914). In *A Thin Ghost and Others*. London: Edward Arnold, 1919.

Jungman, Ann. *Vlad the Drac: The Adventures of a Vegetarian Vampire*. London: Granada, 1982.

Kalogridis, Jeanne. *Covenant with the Vampire*. New York: Delacorte Press, 1994.

Killough, Lee. *Blood Hunt*. New York: Tor, 1987.

King, Stephen. *'Salem's Lot*. Garden City, NY: Doubleday, 1975.

Klause, Annette Curtis. *The Silver Kiss*. New York: Delacorte Press, 1990.

Kornbluth, C. M. "The Mindworm." *Worlds Beyond* (December 1950).

Kostova, Elizabeth. *The Historian*. Boston: Little, Brown, 2005.

Lackey, Mercedes. *Children of the Night*. New York: Tor, 1990.

Lee, Tanith. *Sabella or the Blood Stone*. New York: DAW, 1980.

Le Fanu, J. Sheridan. "Carmilla." *The Dark Blue* (December 1871–March 1972). In LeFanu's *Best Ghost Stories*. New York: Dover, 1964.

Leiber, Fritz. "The Girl with the Hungry Eyes." In *The Girl with the Hungry Eyes and Other Stories*. New York: Avon, 1949.

Lichtenberg, Jacqueline. *Those of My Blood*. New York: St. Martin's Press, 1988.

Lorrah, Jean. *Blood Will Tell*. Dubuque, IA: Awe-Struck, 2001.

Lovecraft, H. P. "The Shunned House." 1928. In *At the Mountains of Madness and Other Novels*. Sauk City, WI: Arkham House, 1985.

Martin, Ann M. *Ma and Pa Dracula*. New York: Holiday House, 1989.

Martin, George R. R. *Fevre Dream*. New York: Simon & Schuster, 1982.

Matheson, Richard. "Dress of White Silk." *Magazine of Fantasy and Science Fiction* (October 1951).

———. "Drink My Red Blood." *Imagination* (April 1951).

———. *I Am Legend*. Greenwich, CT: Fawcett, 1954.

Maupassant, Guy de. "Le Horla." *Gil Blas* (October 26, 1886).

Maxwell, Katie. *Got Fangs?* New York: Dorchester, 2005.

McCammon, Robert R. *They Thirst*. New York: Avon, 1981.

"The Mysterious Stranger." *Odds and Ends* (1860).

Moore, C. L. "Shambleau." *Weird Tales* (November 1933).

Moore, Steven. *The Vampire in Verse: An Anthology*. New York: Dracula Press, 1985.

Navarro, Yvonne. *AfterAge*. New York: Bantam, 1993.

Newman, Kim. *Anno-Dracula*. New York: Carroll & Graf, 1992.

Poe, Edgar Allan. "The Fall of the House of Usher." *Burton's Gentlemen's Magazine* (September 1839).

———. "Ligeia." *American Museum* (September 1838).

———. "Morella." *Southern Literary Messenger* (April 1835).

Polidori, John. "The Vampyre." *New Monthly Magazine* (April 1819). Rpt. in *Vampires*, ed. Alan Ryan. Garden City, NY: Doubleday, 1987.

Powers, Tim. *The Stress of Her Regard*. Lynbrook, NY: Charnel House, 1989.

Raven, Simon. *Doctors Wear Scarlet*. New York: Simon & Schuster, 1960.

Rice, Anne. *Interview with the Vampire*. New York: Knopf, 1976.

———. *Queen of the Damned*. New York: Knopf, 1988.

———. *The Vampire Lestat*. New York: Knopf, 1985.

Robinson, Phil. "The Last of the Vampires." *Contemporary Review* (March 1893).

Rudorff, Raymond. *The Dracula Archives*. New York: Arbor House, 1972.

Rymer, James Malcolm. *Varney, the Vampyre; or, The Feast of Blood*. London: E. Lloyd, 1847. Rpt. New York: Dover, 1972.

Saberhagen, Fred. *The Dracula Tape*. New York: Warner, 1975.

Simmons, Dan. *Carrion Comfort*. Arlington Heights, IL: Dark Harvest, 1989.

———. *Children of the Night*. New York: G. P. Putnam's Sons, 1992.

Smith, Evelyn E. "Softly While You're Sleeping." *Magazine of Fantasy and Science Fiction* (April 1961).

Smith, L. J. *The Awakening*. New York: HarperCollins, 1991.

———. *Secret Vampire*. New York: Pocket, 1996.

Sommer-Bodenburg, Angela. *My Friend the Vampire*. Trans. Sarah Gibson. New York: E. P. Dutton, 1982.

Somtow, S. P. *Vampire Junction*. Norfolk, VA: Donning, 1984.

Stoker, Bram. *Dracula*. London: Constable, 1897.

———. "Dracula's Guest." In *Dracula's Guest and Other Weird Stories*. London: George Routledge & Sons, 1914.

———. *The Lady of the Shroud*. London: William Heinemann, 1909.

Strieber, Whitley. *The Hunger*. New York: William Morrow, 1981.

Sturgeon, Theodore. *Some of Your Blood*. New York: Ballantine, 1961.

Talbot, Michael. *The Delicate Dependency*. New York: Avon, 1982.

Tem, Melanie. *Desmodus*. New York: Dell, 1995.

Tenn, William. "She Only Goes Out at Night." *Fantastic Universe* (October 1956).

Tieck, Ludwig. "Wake Not the Dead." 1800. Rpt. in *Popular Tales and Romances of the Northern Nations, Volume 1*. London: Simpkin, Marshall, 1823.

Tolstoy, Alexis. "The Family of the Vourdalak." 1847. Rpt. in Tolstoy's *Vampires: Stories of the Supernatural*. Trans. Fedor Nikanov. New York: Hawthorn, 1969.

Vande Velde, Vivian. *Companions of the Night*. New York: Harcourt Brace, 1995.

Wellman, Manly Wade. "The Devil Is Not Mocked." *Unknown Worlds* (June 1943).

———. "The Last Grave of Lill Warran." *Weird Tales* (May 1951).

———. "School for the Unspeakable." *Weird Tales* (September 1937).

———. "When It Was Moonlight." *Unknown* (February 1940).

Wells, H. G. "The Flowering of the Strange Orchid." *Pall Mall Budget* (August 1894).

Whitten, Leslie H. *Progeny of the Adder*. Garden City, NY: Doubleday, 1965.

Wilson, Colin. *The Mind Parasites*. London: Arthur Barker, 1967.

———. *The Space Vampires*. New York: Random House, 1976.

Wilson, F. Paul. *Midnight Mass*. New York: Tor, 2004.

Yarbro, Chelsea Quinn. *The Angry Angel*. New York: Avon, 1998.

———. *Hôtel Transylvania*. New York: St. Martin's Press, 1978.

———. *The Soul of an Angel*. New York: Avon, 1999.

Significant Editions of Dracula

Auerbach, Nina, and David J. Skal, eds. *Dracula*. New York: W. W. Norton, 1997.

Byron, Glennis, ed. *Dracula*. Peterborough, ON: Broadview Press, 1998.

Leatherdale, Clive. *Dracula Unearthed*. Westcliff-on-Sea, UK: Desert Island, 1998.

McNally, Raymond, and Radu Florescu, eds. *The Essential Dracula*. New York: Mayflower, 1979.

Riquelme, John Paul, ed. *Dracula*. New York: St. Martin's Press, 2002.

Wolf, Leonard, ed. *The Annotated Dracula*. New York: Clarkson N. Potter, 1975.

———. *The Essential Dracula*. New York: Penguin, 1993.

Secondary

Altner, Patricia. *Vampire Readings*. Lanham, MD: Scarecrow Press, 1998.

Auerbach, Nina. *Our Vampires, Ourselves*. Chicago: University of Chicago Press, 1995.

Barber, Paul. *Vampires, Burial, and Death*. New Haven: Yale University Press, 1988.

Bell, Michael E. *Food for the Dead: On the Trail of New England's Vampires*. New York: Carroll & Graf, 2001.

Bloom, Harold, ed. *Bram Stoker's Dracula*. Broomall, PA: Chelsea House, 2003.

Calmet, Augustin. "Dissertations on Those Persons Who Return to Earth Bodily, the Excommunicated, the Oupires or Vampires, Vroucolacas, etc." 1751. Rpt. as *Treatise on Vampires and Revenants: The Phantom World*. Westcliff-on-Sea, UK: Desert Island, 1993.

Carter, Margaret L., ed. *Dracula: The Vampire and the Critics*. Ann Arbor: UMI Research Press, 1988.

———. *The Vampire in Literature: A Critical Bibliography*. Ann Arbor: UMI Research Press, 1989.

Copper, Basil. *The Vampire in Legend, Fact, and Art*. London: Hale, 1973.

Cox, Greg. *The Transylvanian Library*. San Bernardino, CA: Borgo Press, 1993.

Davison, Carol Margaret. *Bram Stoker's Dracula: Sucking Through the Century, 1897–1997*. Toronto: Dundurn Press, 1997.

Day, William Patrick. *Vampire Legends in Contemporary American Culture*. Lexington: University Press of Kentucky, 2002.

Dresser, Norine. *American Vampires: Fans, Victims, Practitioners*. New York: W. W. Norton, 1989.

Frayling, Christopher. *Vampyres: From Lord Byron to Count Dracula*. 1978. Rev. rpt. London: Faber & Faber, 1991.

Frost, Brian. *The Monster with a Thousand Faces*. Bowling Green, OH: Popular Press, 1989.

Gelder, Ken. *Reading the Vampire*. New York: Routledge, 1994.

Glut, Donald F. *The Dracula Book*. New York: Scarecrow Press, 1975.

Gordon, Joan, and Veronica Hollinger, eds. *Blood Read: The Vampire as Metaphor in Contemporary Culture*. Philadelphia: University of Pennsylvania Press, 1997.

Guiley, Rosemary Ellen. *The Complete Vampire Companion*. New York: Macmillan, 1994.

Heldreth, Leonard G., and Mary Pharr, eds. *The Blood Is the Life: Vampires in Literature*. Bowling Green, OH: Popular Press, 1999.

Holte, James Craig. *Dracula in the Dark: The Dracula Film Adaptations*. Westport, CT: Greenwood Press, 1997.

―――, ed. *The Fantastic Vampire: Studies in the Children of the Night*. Westport, CT: Greenwood Press, 2002.

Jones, Ernest. *On the Nightmare*. New York: Liveright, 1951.

Leatherdale, Clive. *Dracula: The Novel and the Legend*. Wellingborough, UK: Aquarian Press, 1985.

McNally, Raymond, and Radu Florescu. *Dracula: A Biography of Vlad the Impaler*. New York: Hawthorn, 1973.

―――. *Dracula: Prince of Many Faces*. Boston: Little, Brown, 1989.

―――. *In Search of Dracula*. Greenwich, CT: New York Graphic Society, 1972.

Melton, J. Gordon. *The Vampire Book*. 2nd ed. Detroit: Visible Ink Press, 1999.

Miller, Elizabeth. *Dracula: Sense and Nonsense*. Westcliff-on-Sea, UK: Desert Island, 2000.

―――, ed. *Dracula: The Shade and the Shadow*. Westcliff-on-Sea, UK: Desert Island, 1998.

―――. *Reflections on Dracula*. White Rock, BC: Transylvania Press, 1997.

Page, Carol. *Bloodlust: Conversations with Real Vampires*. New York: HarperCollins, 1991.

Ramsland, Katherine. *Piercing the Darkness: Undercover with Vampires in America Today*. New York: Harper Prism, 1998.

―――. *Prism of the Night*. New York: Dutton, 1991.

―――. *The Science of Vampires*. New York: Berkley, 2002.

Riccardo, Martin V. *Vampires Unearthed: The Complete Multi-Media Vampire and Dracula Bibliography*. New York: Garland, 1983.

Richardson, Maurice. "The Psychoanalysis of Ghost Stories." *Twentieth Century* 166 (1959): 419–31.

Senf, Carol A. *Dracula: Between Tradition and Modernism*. New York: Twayne, 1998.

―――. *The Vampire in Nineteenth-Century English Literature*. Bowling Green, OH: Popular Press, 1988.

Silver, Alain, and James Ursini. *The Vampire Film: From Nosferatu to Interview with the Vampire*. New York: Limelight, 1997.

Skal, David J. *Hollywood Gothic*. New York: W. W. Norton, 1990.

―――, ed. *Vampires: Encounters with the Dead*. New York: Black Dog & Leventhal, 2001.

―――. *V Is for Vampire*. New York: Penguin, 1996.

Summers, Montague. *The Living Dead: The Vampire in Romantic Literature*. Durham, NC: Duke University Press, 1981. *The Vampire: His Kith and Kin*. London: Routledge & Kegan Paul, 1928.

―――. *The Vampire in Europe*. London: Kegan Paul, Trench & Trübner, 1929.

Twitchell, James B. *Dreadful Pleasures: An Anatomy of Modern Horror*. New York: Oxford University Press, 1985.

Waller, Gregory A. *The Living and the Undead: From Stoker's Dracula to Romero's Dawn of the Dead*. Urbana: University of Illinois Press, 1986.

Wolf, Leonard. *A Dream of Dracula: In Search of the Living Dead*. Boston: Little, Brown, 1972.

Wright, Dudley. *Vampires and Vampirism*. London: William Rider & Son, 1914.

Useful Web sites

Alt-Vampyres Newsgroup: www.altvampyres.net
Dracula: For the Dead Travel Fast: www.geocities.com/nansee_2000/dracula.html
The Dracula Library: www.cesnur.org/dracula_library.htm
Dracula's Home Page: www.ucs.mun.ca/~emiller/
Michelle Hauf's Ultimate Vampire List: www.vampire-books.com
Realm of the Vampires: www.simegen.com/reviews/vampires/vamprelm.htm
The Vampire Library: www.vampirelibrary.com
Vampire Readings: www.biblioinfo.com/vamp/vamp.html

© Universal/The Kobol Collection.

The Werewolf

by Stefan Dziemianowicz

INTRODUCTION

No one can say with complete certainty when the first tale of the werewolf was told. What seems indisputable, however, from a reading of Elliott O'Donnell's *Werewolves* (1912), Montague Summers's *The Werewolf* (1933), Basil Copper's *The Werewolf in Legend, Fact and Art* (1977), Charlotte F. Otten's *A Lycanthropy Reader: Werewolves in Western Culture* (1986), and other clinical and anecdotal histories, is that virtually every culture has a variant on the werewolf legend as part of its mythology and folklore. Indeed, accounts of human transformation into feral form (and, in some cases, vice versa) are just part of a larger body of myths concerned with shapeshifting into a variety of animal guises. In general, these stories range from marvelous accounts of unusual powers humans acquire by changing form and nature to cautionary tales in which the wicked backslide into a bestial state.

Although the werewolf legend is thousands of years old, its most popular version dates only to the middle of the twentieth century. Robert Siodmak's screenplay for the 1941 film *The Wolf Man* reduced the legend to bare essentials: The werewolf is a hapless victim who, once bitten in human form by another werewolf, changes into wolf form during the days of each month when the moon is full, between the hours of moonrise and sunrise. The human who is a werewolf usually is unaware of the supernatural side of his life, or at very least of his behavior after his transformation. As a werewolf, his sole purpose is to slaughter other creatures (especially humans), sometimes (but not always) for sustenance. Any injury he sustains as a wolf persists after his reversion to human form. The werewolf can be repelled only by wolfbane, and can be killed only by a silver bullet. Once killed, the werewolf immediately reverts back to his human form.

Most of the werewolf lore Siodmak put into his screenplay was taken from folktales or werewolf fiction that itself was derived from folk legend. However, the movie's impact cannot be underestimated. Reaching a larger audience than perhaps any werewolf narrative of the preceding century, it codified werewolf lore in the same way that Bram Stoker's novel *Dracula* created the template for all vampire fiction written in its wake. However, the cinematic werewolf deviated markedly from the literary werewolf, which had by that point enjoyed a rich and varied life for nearly 2000 years. Universal, the studio that produced *The Wolf Man*, had ten years earlier produced the film adaptation of *Dracula*, and Siodmak's werewolf is easily identifiable as a vampire in wolf's clothing. In literature, the werewolf has a distinctly different pedigree and speaks to different concerns and ideas than the vampire does. The canonical werewolf sprung from the film *The Wolf Man* was largely cut loose from the rich literary tradition that has made the werewolf one of the more fascinating and complex icons of horror literature.

THE PRE-GOTHIC WEREWOLF

The word "werewolf" (which translates roughly as "man wolf") is of Anglo-Saxon origin, and has been traced at least as far back as the eleventh century. Most other descriptive terms for the werewolf—*loup garou*, shapeshifter, lycanthrope—are of later derivation. The *concept* of the werewolf, however, appears in literature that predates this considerably. In his eighth Eclogue, which dates to 39 B.C.E., the Roman poet Virgil mentions in passing of "baneful herbs" from Pontus with which "full oft have I seen Moeris change / To a wolf's form, and hide him from the woods." Thus, in one of the earliest literary references, transformation of human into wolf is voluntary, and achieved by a means other than contact with another werewolf.

As with Virgil's account, most other evocations of the werewolf in classical literature are part of a larger catalog of supernatural marvels being described. Ovid, in the *Metamorphoses*, relates the transformation of Lycaon, the King of Arcadia, who is punished with bestial transformation by the god Jove on a visit to Earth. Unlike other mortals who grovel and pray in Jove's presence, Lycaon decides to test whether Jove is actually a god by serving him a meal of cooked human flesh. Lycaon's fate is possibly the first instance in literature of lycanthropy depicted as a curse brought on by an evil nature—and, as befits that nature, his transformation is permanent. Of significant interest is his physical transformation, which Virgil describes in nearly cinematic terms:

> Howling he fled, and fane he wou'd have spoke;
> But humane voice his brutal tongue forsook.
> About his lips the gather'd foam he churns,
> And, breathing slaughters, still with rage he burns,
> But on the bleating flock his fury turns.
> His mantle, now his hide, with rugged hairs
> Cleaves to his back; a famish'd face he bears;
> His arms descend, his shoulders sink away
> To multiply his legs for chase of prey.
> He grows a wolf, his hoariness remains,
> And the same rage in other members reigns.
> His eyes still sparkle in a narr'wer space;
> His jaws retain the grin, and violence of his face.

Petronius, in the *Satyricon* (c. 55 C.E.), treats an instance of lycanthropic change differently from either Virgil or Ovid. His narrator, Niceros, recounts how, when a servant, he one night took a walk with the host of an eating house to a graveyard, where the man shed his clothing, urinated in a circle around them, and transformed into a wolf which immediately bounded off to savage sheep in the countryside. Niceros can scarcely believe his own eyes, until he is informed by the owners of one sheep fold that a servant ran the marauding wolf through the neck with a pitch-fork: the next day he sees that his host bears a wound on his neck at the exact spot the pitch-fork would have injured. Many writers after Petronius contrived ingenious examples of humans bearing the stigma of injuries sustained in werewolf form as proof of their inescapable moral responsibility for their crimes.

For the most part the werewolf of classical literature is not an innately evil being. Even for Lycaon, bestial transformation is a punishment for sins he commits as a human. In the literature of the Middle Ages, werewolves are less sinister than they are sympathetic. Two of the better werewolf narratives from this period, the late-fourteenth-century tale "Arthur and Gorlagon," and "The Lay of the Were Wolf," attributed to Marie de France and dated circa 1150, tell basically the same story of werewolves who are victims of circumstance. In the first, a king whose garden contains a sapling that can turn the person struck with it into a wolf, is tricked by his unfaithful wife into demonstrating its power on himself, after which she turns him out into the wild. In the other, a husband who confesses to his wife that his regular nighttime disappearances are due to feral transformations, finds one day that she has stolen his clothes, preventing him from changing back and forcing him, too, into the forests. In both stories, the wives have schemed all along to replace their husbands with new lovers. The unfortunate men are forced to live the lives of wolves, even though they retain their human consciousness and are wolves only in outward form.

Ultimately, this curse proves their salvation, for in each case they ingratiate themselves with the king, who domesticates them as guardians. Through their benevolent and intelligent actions, the wolves reveal that they are more than animals, and ultimately are able to direct their keepers to the methods that allow them to be restored to human form—whereupon their deceitful wives are either executed or exiled with their lovers. The clear moral of these stories is that the truly virtuous can overcome the bestial, be it their own lupine form or the inhumane schemes of their fellow humans. A similar story can be found in *Guillame de Palerne*, a Middle English poem that dates to 1350, and which tells of Alphonse, heir to the throne of Spain, who is bewitched by his evil stepmother and turned into a wolf. In wolf form, Alphonse performs many good and heroic deeds, including protecting the lovers William and Melior. William ultimately attains the throne of Rome, and Alphonse's good deeds allow him to return to human form.

GOTHIC AND VICTORIAN PERIOD

The idea that humans are potentially a more potent source of evil than the werewolf persists into the early Gothic era in such stories as Sutherland Menzies's "Hugues, the Wer-Wolf: A Kentish Legend of the Middle Ages" (1838). Hugues Wulfric, the descendant of a family falsely assumed to be werewolves, finds himself so ostracized by townspeople that he watches his family die of neglect and is barely able to provide for himself. Desperate, Hugues pretends to actually be a werewolf by donning a costume found in a family chest: "the complete disguise of the wer-wolf:—a dyed sheepskin with gloves in the form of paws, a tail, a mask with an elongated muzzle, and furnished with formidable rows of yellow horse teeth" (62). In this outfit, Hugues is able to extort meat from the local butcher. When the man discovers the ruse, he cuts off the "werewolf's" paw. Only then does the supernatural enter the picture for, in a twist on the idea of the werewolf's severed limb turning back to human form, Hugues's lost limb becomes animated with un-holy life and eventually causes so much mayhem that the butcher is driven to suicide. Prejudice and superstition, not lycanthropy, are true crimes that this story warns of.

Nevertheless, it is in the Gothic period that the werewolf, like the vampire, becomes almost exclusively a figure of supernatural evil. George W. M. Rey-nolds's *Wagner, the Wehr-Wolf* (1846) is a werewolf story presented as an indirect sequel to the tale of Faust. Its protagonist, Fernand Wagner, is Faust's former servant and associate, now in his nineties. One day the Devil offers Wagner eternal youth and uncanny powers if he will agree to let himself transform into a werewolf one night a month during the full moon (one of the earliest stories to tie the werewolf's transformation to the lunar cycle). Wagner accepts, and many bloody adventures follow, including his capture by the Inquisition and close escape from the headsman through sheer brute force exercised in his werewolf form. In time, Wagner comes to realize, like Faust, that his supernatural powers are more curse than benefit, especially when he is shipwrecked on an island with his lover, Nisida, and finds he must exile himself from her each night of the month that he changes to a wolf. At various points the Devil intervenes and offers to relieve Wagner of his werewolf affliction in exchange for his soul. Wagner, who knows it will mean his damnation, steadfastly refuses, and ultimately meets up with a Rosicrucian who helps him find redemption and freedom from the werewolf curse. Reynolds's novel is memorable for scenes of Wagner's transformation to and from wolf form, which are colored by a sensuality that makes it easy to understand why Wagner so easily accepts being a werewolf:

> But, lo! What awful change is taking place in the form of the doomed being? His handsome countenance elongates into one of savage and brute-like shape;— the rich garment he wears becomes a rough, shaggy, and wiry skin; —his body loses its human contours—his arms and limbs take another form; and, with a frantic howl of misery, to which the woods give horribly faithful reverberations, and with a rush like a hurling wind, the wretch starts wildly away—no longer a man, but a monstrous wolf!
>
> ... in the midst of appalling, spasmodic convulsions,—with direful writhings on the soil, and with cries of bitter anguish,—the Wehr-Wolf gradually threw off his monster shape; and at the very moment when the first sunbeam penetrated the wood and glinted on his face, he rose a handsome—young—and perfect man once more! (23)

Black magic and the Devil also play a role in *The Wolf Leader* (1857) by Alexandre Dumas *fils*, where, once again, lycanthropic transformation is a consequence, rather than a benefit, of a satanic bargain.

The hero, Thibault, is initially a benevolent man with noble ambitions who one day finds himself unable to trap game by praying, and so instead calls upon the Devil to help him. A talking wolf appears and agrees to grant Thibault's every wish if Thibault will help hide him from an approaching hunting party. Thereafter, Thibault begins trying to advance ambitiously and becomes increasingly corrupted as the wolf's magic disposes of his enemies and removes obstacles that would prevent his rising in society. Every time he resorts to his unusual powers, though, one of his hairs turns the color of the wolf's pelt; until eventually his hair looks more like the wolf's mane than his own. At a point midway in the story, Thibault becomes the titular wolf-leader when outrage against him necessitates that a pack of wolves accompany him at all time.

Only at the story's end does the nature of lycanthropic transformation articulated. Despairing of the misery he has brought upon himself Thibault once again invokes the devil's name and the wolf appears offering his own position to the man. Each day, Thibault will be a wolf by night and a man by day, with the same supernatural powers. "This skin that covers me is impenetrable by iron, lead or steel" (423), the wolf tells him, and thus he will be immortal except for one day, when he must retain his wolf form for a full twenty-four hours, during which time he is vulnerable to any injury. Thibault accepts and, while fleeing a pack of wolf hunting dogs, he comes upon the funeral procession of a woman he once loved and whose death he caused directly. Smitten by his guilty conscience, Thibault asks to give up his life in exchange for returning hers. Heaven grants his wish, and by the time the dogs reach him, all that is left is an empty wolfskin.

A more subtle treatment of the werewolf theme can be found in Rudyard Kipling's "The Mark of the Beast" (*Pioneer*, July 12 and 14, 1890), which tells of Fleete, a British colonial in India who, while drunk one night, profanes a temple to Hanumann and is cursed by a leper serving as a temple priest. Fleete's bestial reduction under the curse is gradual: he develops a ravenous appetite for meat, horses begin shying away from him, he starts wallowing in dirt, and his eyes become lit behind from a greenish light. The less superstitious assume he has developed hydrophobia when he begins foaming at the mouth and howling like a wolf, but his friends ultimately locate the leper and torture him into removing the curse. In a story concerned with a sophisticated culture's clash with primitive magic, Kipling makes it clear that Fleete's own ignorant actions while drunk are themselves savage, as are the actions of his friends who, in torturing the leper, are aware they "had disgraced themselves as Englishmen forever" (62).

It is also in the Victorian era that female werewolves begin to gain currency. In "The Werewolf," a story excerpted from Frederick Marryat's novel *The Phantom Ship* (1839), a female lycanthrope is portrayed as the ultimate betrayal of domesticity, home and hearth. Krantz, a steward to a noble family, murders his wife and her lover, and flees with his three children to the Hartz Mountains where he encounters Wilfred and his daughter Christina, two travelers to whom he offers shelter while pursuing a white wolf. Christina is beautiful but there is something about her that the children instinctively fear:

She was dressed in a traveling dress, deeply bordered with white fur, and wore a cap of white ermine on her head. Her features were very beautiful, at least I thought so, and so my father has since declared. Her hair was flaxen, glossy and shining, and bright as a mirror; and her mouth, although somewhat large when it was opened, showed the most brilliant teeth I have ever beheld. But there was something about her eyes, bright as they were, which made us children afraid; they were so restless, so furtive; I could not at that time tell why, but I felt as if there was cruelty in her eyes; and when she beckoned us to come to her, we approached her with fear and trembling. (115)

Krantz is beguiled into marrying Christina, and not until two of the children are savaged by a marauding white wolf does Krantz realize that his bride and the wolf are one and the same. When he kills her he brings down a curse that ultimately claims the lives of all in the family.

The reversal of the traditional treatment of the werewolf in Marryat's tale—Christina is actually a wolf who transforms into a human shape—says a great deal about gender politics of the time and the perceived predatory nature of females in non-traditional roles. It is recapitulated in Clemence Housman's allegorical short novel *The Were-Wolf* (1896). Sweyn and Christian are twin brothers living as part of a community in northern lands when they are visited one night at the farm hall by a beautiful woman dressed in white furs. Her name is White Fell, and she quickly beguiles Sweyn with her beauty. Christian is wary of her, however, and comes to the realization that the victims of a spate of recent wolf-killings all were last kissed by White Fell and that Christian is next. The hardheaded Sweyn refuses to listen to his brother's warnings but Christian, whose very name suggests his appreciation of the mysterious side of life, subscribes to a bit of werewolf lore passed down by an elder in their community: "[Y]ou should watch the suspected person until midnight, when the beast's form must be resumed, and retained ever after if a human eye sees the change; or, better still, sprinkle the hands and feet with holy water, which is certain death" (298). On the next night that White Fell leaves the farm to avoid becoming trapped in human form, Christian follows her, maintaining her arduous pace in order to witness her transformation and thereby force her permanently into her wolf form. At the moment when it seems Christian will triumph, White Fell overwhelms him and, stabs him with knives. Christian, however, proves the victor, when the blood he sheds for his brother's sake kills White Fell even as he dies: "[H]e did not presume that no holy water could be more holy, more potent to destroy an evil-thing than the life-blood of a pure heart poured out for another in willing devotion" (316).

THE EARLY MODERN WEREWOLF

Until the 1900s the overwhelming majority of werewolf tales were written by British or continental writers. The first four decades of the twentieth century saw an explosion of werewolf fiction, much of it with American settings and by American writers, and these stories are notable for their treatment of lycanthropy as a taint associated with foreigners and emigrants to countries where old European superstitions have less of a foothold and outsiders are more likely to thrive unnoticed, or at the very least undisturbed.

Margery Williams was a British writer, but her novel *The Thing in the Woods* (1913; revised and reprinted as by "Harper Williams" in 1924) is set in a small Pennsylvania Dutch town recently beset by a series of inexplicable deaths and killings. Suspicion falls on Aaron Menning, whose brother Jake died of an apparent seizure a short time before. Aaron rouses immediate feelings of aversion in visiting doctor Austin Haverill, the narrator of the story: "His face, with unpleasantly close-set eyes, was scarred by smallpox, and apart from the repugnance which this disfigurement always inspires, more or less, I think I have seldom seen a countenance which impressed me more disagreeably" (180). Haverill's instinctive dislike of the man is well placed, for it transpires that the man is actually Jake, the more degenerate of the two brothers, who killed Aaron and is actually impersonating him. Jake and Aaron are the offspring of different fathers born to a Westphalian woman who is "a curious survival of the original peasant stock": "She had preserved a great deal of her native superstition and traditions, and was reputed to have a great knowledge of herbs and some skill in home doctoring and decoctions, when she could be induced to use it, by reason of which the neighbours, ready enough in such gossip, believed her to have actual powers of witchcraft" (243).

It turns out that Jake, who was born overseas, is a throwback of sorts. His mother toured with a traveling circus and when Jake reached the age of seventeen, he began to play the sideshow wild man—a role that perfectly fit his "apish and uncouth" character. Jake seems to have played his role a little too well, according to another doctor who knows the family: "There is a form of mania which takes just that expression, and it is possible that in Jakey's case it began out of sheer maliciousness, and developed later into something a great deal worse—a fixed mania which, with the rousing of the homicidal instinct, turned him actually, at moments, into the wild beast he pretended to be" (292). Only in the novel's finale, when Jake is dispatched in wolf-like form, is it established that Jake is not just a deluded victim of his homicidal psychosis, but an actual werewolf who inherited the condition from his father:

> Menning's mother came from Westphalia, one of the parts of Europe where the belief in lycanthropy is most widely spread and where its existence is still credited among the peasants of to-day. Lycanthropy was believed to be a hereditary taint, as transmissible as insanity, which may lie dormant through one or more generations, so much so that at one time the relatives of an accused man or woman were all held suspect. (291)

Greye La Spina's novel *Invaders of the Dark* (1960) first appeared in serial form in the American pulp magazine *Weird Tales* in 1925. It is the account of a trio of Russian werewolves who move into a part of Brooklyn, New York. Princess Irma Andreyevna Tchernova, her two retainers, and a pack of wolf-hounds move in and almost immediately set about preying on the locals. Even in human form, the Princess shows features drawn straight from folklore that suggest her bestial nature: "the beryl-green eyes that in dusk gleamed like garnets; the sharp white teeth; the small, low-set ears, pointed above ... the over-red lips; the narrowed lids under eyebrows that curved down to meet the base of the nose ... slender fingers on which the third finger was abnormally long," and a "slinking, sinuous walk ... that by its resemblance to the tireless gait of the wolf, would have betrayed her real personality to an expert" (89).

To these traditional folkloric elements La Spina adds several new and modern wrinkles. Werewolves are the disciples of evil entities inhabiting the ether who are endowed with the power to grant supplicants the power of transformation. "These infatuated people who believe in the Evil are actually metamorphosed—either at their own desire for some personal reason, or by someone evilly disposed toward them—into the form of a wolf, so that at night time they are impelled to go about mauling, killing and eating small animals, such as rabbits and sheep, until they come to the point where they prey upon human beings" (90). This transformation occurs at the atomic level for, as La Spina writes, in an unusual fusion of clinical scientific and conventional Christian belief, "everything in is composed of infinitesimal intelligences which I believe they call electrons" (92), which have free will, and can exercise it in a choice for evil much the same way the individual consciousness can. The Princess herself, seeking a mate, effects this transformation in an ordinary male character in the story with occult rituals, exposure to orchids associated with lycanthropic transformation, and imbibement of water "from some lycan-thropus stream" (109).

Ultimately, the narrator of this novel presents the threat the Princess poses in terms of an alien invasion of America:

> The world ought to know that these forces of the dark are organizing for the advancement of their own individual and collective purposes, just as the forces of light are cooperating for the advancement of humanity; that invasions from the dark will periodically be made, slyly, subtly, whenever opportunity offers; that embodied and disembodied evil is marching upon the New World, intent on conquest.
>
> And most terrible of all, the New World is ignorant of these potent influences on mind and body, attributing the ancient wisdom of the Old World along occult lines to the superstitious beliefs of ignorant peasants. (10)

Invaders of the Dark is similar to Gerald Biss's *The Door of the Unreal* (1919) not only in plot, but in its racially conscious treatment of the werewolf as a foreign invader from an alien culture. Its villain, Lycurgus Wolff, is a botanist who hails from Berlin and Vienna, and who has set up residence on a British estate with a mostly sinister entourage of fellow countryman. Biss gives Wolff many of the typical stigmata of the werewolf, and makes it clear that the foreignness of his appearance clashes with what one might expect to find in the otherwise ordinary surroundings:

> He was a very striking man of sixty with shaggy grey hair and beard, a pair of remarkably piercing black eyes under long, straight, slanting brows, which met in a point over his nose, and distinctly pointed ears set low and far back on his head, half-hidden by his long hair. His mouth under his straggling, unkempt moustache was full and red-lipped, and he had a very fine set of even, white teeth, especially considering his age. His hands were long and pointed, projecting curiously far at the third finger, and noticeably hairy with red, almond-shaped, curving nails. He was tall and rather lean, with a sight stoop, and walked with a peculiar long, swinging stride—altogether a strange and rather bizarre personality in the surroundings of sleepy Sussex, especially as in winter he always wore a Russian cap of grey fur and a heavy grey fur coat. (37)

Biss further emphasizes Wolff's foreignness by contrasting his appearance to that of his daughter Dorothy, a beautiful innocent who "was unlike the Professor as anyone could well be, and without the least trace of the Teutonic type" (38). Dorothy, as it turns out, is not Wolff's true daughter, but a ward who is the object of his experiments to bring about lycanthropic transformation through the occult properties of certain strange plants, which themselves represent an unnatural infiltration or infection of the setting. Wolff says of them that that they "are rare and unobtainable in this highly civilized country" (81), and the narrator, Lincoln Osgood, characterizes a particularly noxious bloom that Wolff makes Dorothy wear as "a flower the like of which I would dare have bet had never been seen in England before" (124).

Biss's and La Spina's novels were followed into print shortly after by Alfred H. Bill's *The Wolf in the Garden* (1931). Set in New York State in the years immediately following the American and French Revolutions, the novel is a crude and largely conventional werewolf thriller, notable for its use of racial identity and sexual menace. Its werewolf is an expatriate French nobleman who sums up the worst of his type, and the threat he poses is infection of the novel's heroine with his werewolf taint.

Robert Farrier is a clerk serving his uncle in the town of New Dortrecht when Monsieur de Saint Loup (an obvious reference to "wolf" that is just one of the novel's blatant signals) arrives seeking a home. He is an aristocrat who fled the terror in France, and who plans to take up residence in the States until it is safe for him to return to his home country. Arrogant, aloof, and somewhat dissipated, Saint Loup is off-putting to many of those whom he meets. He has a growling chuckle, and children and animals instinctively recoil from him. Shortly after his arrival a wolf begins causing mayhem around the town, including the slaughter of the miser whose house Saint Loup covets and then moves into once the obstacle of ownership has been removed.

There follows a mildly complicated plot in which Robert is informed that the miser had made him the sole beneficiary of his estate and money but that the will cannot be found. Robert is desperate to find the will, as the family business is in arrears and his uncle is compelled to let Saint Loup marry Felicity, a cousin whom Robert himself is in love with, in order to link himself to Saint Loup's fortune. Robert, the jealous suitor, aptly fears that Saint Loup, who has a reputation as a lecher and ladies man, will "devour" Felicity. Saint Loup is out of town for portions of the novel, but his wolfhound De Retz (named, as Saint Loup takes great pains to clarify, for Cardinal de Retz, not Gilles De Retz, the infamous child murderer) is always there when he is not, and it is only a matter of time before the townsfolk realize that the depredations of the marauding wolf, all of which seem to benefit Saint Loup directly or indirectly, began after the Frenchman's arrival, and that Saint Loup and De Retz never appear together.

The origins of Saint Loup's lycanthropy are never explained, but Saint Loup has a degenerate streak that makes it understandable. At one point in the story, he shows Robert a preserved strip of skin that hangs in his room as a decorative ornament. The skin is that of a Circassian slave who was flayed alive by a pasha friend of the Count's as he watched. Saint Loup takes delight in the handling of the skin, and later, in the only scene suggesting his werewolf transformation, Robert sees Saint Loup naked, having emerged from his lupine form, wearing the strip of flesh around him.

In the only part of the novel where lycanthropy is discussed, the rector Sackville, who has a more than healthy suspicion of Saint Loup's true nature, avers that "lycanthropy in our modern sense means only a form of insanity" in which "the unfortunate imagines that he is a wolf and acts accordingly" (49), but notes that in the past, when witchcraft and superstition were rampant, it was believed that selling one's soul to the devil, or the bite of another werewolf, could confer the curse. Echoing Charles Robert Maturin's Gothic novel *The Albigenses*, the rector then recalls how in olden times, it was assumed that the werewolf in human form simply wears his hairy coat on the inside of his skin. Robert is in fact bitten by De Retz but saved from transformation owing to the intervention of Felicity's Haitian nursemaid. Saint Loup is eventually dispatched with a silver bullet.

Even as the authors of these werewolf tales were deploying mostly traditional folkloric elements, other writers were attempting interesting variation of the theme in novels combining science, psychology, and mythology. Jessie Douglas Kerruish's *The Undying Monster* (1922) is one of the more elaborate werewolf tales of the early twentieth century and shows the inventive extremes to which writers were resorting in their effort to revitalize a classic horror theme.

Ten Essential Werewolf Novels

Wagner, the Wehr-Wolf by George W. M. Reynolds (1846–1847)

The Undying Monster by J. D. Kerruish (1922)

The Werewolf of Paris by Guy Endore (1933)

Grey Shapes by Jack Mann (1938)

Darker Than You Think by Jack Williamson (1940; 1948)

The White Wolf by Franklin Gregory (1941)

The Wolfen by Whitley Streiber (1978)

The Nightwalker by Thomas Tessier (1979)

Thor by Wayne Smith (1992)

Walking Wolf by Nancy Collins (1995)

The monster in question is a curse of the Hammand family, who for centuries have been visited by a monster no one lives to describe: the victims are the eldest born, who either die as a result of the confrontation or kill themselves shortly afterward. There are many theories as to the monster's origin, not the least that the first in the family line made a pact with the devil to keep the Hammands at Dannow forever. This elder is rumored to live still in a secret room in the estate house, emerging every so often to drink blood of a family member. Another theory has it that the creature is half-human half-animal. The legend of the Undying Monster has given rise to a cryptic couplet: "While the monster is alive, Hammand's race shall live and thrive." It has also inspired an effigy of a strange-looking animal with rounded paws under the feet of one Hammand ancestor: "The beast's head was vaguely doglike, with long nose and prick ears, the body slim in the waist, and the tail snaky and ending in what might have been either a tuft of hair or the conventional barb that ends the conventional devil's tail" (60). The monster appears only on frosty nights, on Thunderbarrow Shaw, a rise surrounded by pines and fir trees.

The recent resurgence of the monster's activity, after it lay dormant for centuries, is blamed on a family ancestor, known as the Warlock who, in the sixteenth century, excavated portions of the Shaw and removed artifacts found there, including parts of a Viking longboat and a sword, which he believed to be imbued with occult powers that he might harness. The sword is traceable back to the eighth century, and it is presumed that its removal from the Shaw removed a protective seal that had kept the monster in place for centuries.

Such is the belief that the modern-day heroes and heroines of the story act in, trying to apprehend the monster's meaning through historical and archeological investigation, and even hypnosis of Oliver Hammand, the current family scion, in order to stir up racial memories of the monster that family members have carried silently in their brain for centuries. In fact, something altogether different is stirred up by psychic Luna Bartendale, the occult investigator consulted for the case. It is discovered that the Hammands are descendants of Sigmund of the Volsung line, an eighth-century Viking whose family was persecuted until only he and his sister sere left, and she died while Sigmund was forced to survive by fighting a wolf in hand-to-hand combat. Maddened by grief and the apparent abandonment by his gods, Volsung took on a curse. "He made a solemn vow that in the Final Warring, the Norse Day of Judgment, when all heroes shall come to life and ride behind the Asa Gods to the Final War with the Powers of Evil, instead of having him—Sigmund the human hero—to help them, they should find him opposing them; *as a wolf* on the side of the Evil Powers" (224).

Sigmund made this vow "in a wood of firs and pines, on a frosty starlit night," and was so smitten by his alliance with the wolf that he was subject to a bout of wolf mania in which he believed he actually had become a wolf. So firmly did he believe this that it became impressed upon his brain as a type of racial memory blending nature and nurture: "the impression on Sigmund's brain was so acute that it passed on to his descendants, and to this time at uncertain intervals a man has been born in his line liable to turn, mentally, into a wolf in this combination of circumstances:—a wood with pines and firs in it, a cold starlit night, and only one human companion" (225). Even when the curse was long forgotten, the memory of it lurked in the subconscious recesses of the Hammand brain. Each generation of the Hammands has so expected the curse of the wolf that befell Sigmund that any prompt of the night Sigmund made his blasphemy stimulates the racial memory of the family and revives the strain of wolf-mania that is the Undying Monster. Hence, the monster is not a product of the fourth dimension, which is the dimension inhabited by the supernatural. As Luna Bartendale explains, "The Monster did not enter into you Mr. Hammand, simply because the monster has never had any existence. It is purely a creation of the Fifth Dimension, and the Fifth Dimension is—the human mind" (208–9). In a unique exorcism, Luna succeeds in hypnotizing Oliver, and taking him back along the path of racial memory to become one with Sigmund, whereupon she convinces Sigmund that Ragnarok has come and it is time for him to become wolf for the final time and ride with the powers.

Two other novels echo Kerruish's tale and further develop ideas she introduces. Jack Mann's *Grey Shapes* (1933) is the second in his series of novels featuring detective Gregory George Gordon Green (known as "Gees"). Gees is summoned by Tyrrell, a squire in Cumberland, to investigate the regular marauding of Tyrrell's sheep by a pack of dogs or wolves when none are known to live any closer than twenty miles away. The killing of the sheep has coincided with the letting of Locksborough Castle by Diarmid McCoul and his daughter Gida. It does not take long for Gees to realize from poking around in local history and folklore that Locksborough's pedigree can be traced back to Norse times, and that it was populated 2000 to 3000 years before by an older race: "Flint men, one may call them.... A people who believed in fierce gods, made human sacrifices to them, and were fierce themselves. Evil, from our point of view. They are the race that our people here call 'the old dead' " (103). The history of this race dovetails with Daione Shih, or Shee—the faery folk, and the legends Etain, a fairy princess who dallied briefly in the mortal world, leaving a daughter, half human, half fairy. She is the origin of a race that survives into the present day, of whom Diarmid and Gida are descendants, as well survivors of a family from centuries before who disappeared mysteriously. The two have returned to the modern age as werewolves (shapeshifting being one of the powers of the Shee) and it is they who periodically savage Tyrell's flock. Their home serves as a locus that amplifies the evil necessary for them to transform lycanthropically. As one character observes:

> "Don't you see that—there you have a place stained and soaked in evil.... A place, humanly speaking, abhorrent, haunted by evil, if not by visible ghosts, and a place from which all the people of the district shy away. What more probable than that the more evil of the Shee, the dregs of the sub-human race, say, should use it, haunt it, come there to consort with their familiars." (278)

In Franklin Gregory's *The White Wolf* (1941), as in Kerruish's novel, lycanthropy is a family curse. Eight hundred years before an ancestor of Pierre de Camp D'Avenes committed blasphemy. After his death, "he was not seen as a man. He was seen as a wolf, a huge white wolf, burdened with chains. And on still, dark nights, they said you could hear his bay from the forest as if he were in pain." An occultist awakens the impulse to lycanthropy in Pierre's daughter Sara, who secretly indulges her wolfish appetites in and around suburban Philadelphia. Her lycanthropy is described in terms of a contagion, which also infects a lover through her. Ultimately, the werewolf transformations are attributed to an expression of the fourth dimension, or dimension of the supernatural.

The werewolf tale hit its height of creativity just on the eve of the release of the film *The Wolf Man* in Jack Williamson's novel, *Darker Than You Think* (1948), the original, shorter version of which appeared in 1940 in the pulp magazine *Unknown. Unknown* specialized in fiction that surveyed the everyday events in the modern world and saw behind them machinations of the fantastic and supernatural. The result was stories that were patently fantastic yet that grew from the sort of logic one associates with science fiction. In this novel, Williamson proposed a lycanthropic race that coexists with mortal humanity and that has been manipulating the course of human events since prehistoric times.

Events in the novel build around the return to the United States of an expedition to the Gobi Desert led by anthropologist Professor Mondrick. Mondrick went to the desert hoping to find the remains of the Garden of Eden and the origins of the human race. What he found, instead, were the remains of an advanced race, *Homo lycanthropus*, who evolved independent but parallel to *Homo sapiens*. More sophisticated, they developed powers of telepathy, clairvoyance, and prophecy that allowed them to dominate and subjugate the weaker race of *Homo sapiens*:

> "For hundreds or thousands of years, all through the main intergalacial period...those witch people were the hunters and the enemies and the cruel masters of mankind. They were cunning priests and evil gods. They were the merciless originals of every ogre and demon and mean-eating dragon of every folk tale." (260)

As mental giants who could literally exert mind over matter, they also possessed the power to shift shape. The horror of what they represented impressed itself upon humanity's racial consciousness in the form of superstitions regarding witches, werewolves, and supernatural being that have come down through history in the form of superstitions and legends:

> "Almost every primitive people is still obsessed with the fear of the loup-garou, in one guise or another—of a human-seeming being who can take the shape of the most ferocious animal of the locality to prey upon men. Those witch people, in Dr. Mondrick's opinion, learned to leave their bodies hibernating in their caves while they went out across ice-fields—as wolves or bears or tigers—to hunt human game." (259)

Ultimately, humanity rose up and overthrew *Homo lycanthropus* although they failed to eliminate them entirely. For more than 100,000 years, *Homo lycanthropus* has lived unobtrusively among human beings. Those whose powers were uncovered were stigmatized as witches, sorcerers, werewolves, and other supernatural beings persecuted down through the ages. The beings have bred with the human race, refining their skills and increasing their numbers, until they have reached the point in evolution where their reemergence is inevitable. That time is now.

The novel's hero, Will Barbee, is a journalist who was once a student of Mondrick's until he was exiled from Mondrick's group for reasons he has never completely understood. Shortly after Mondrick's team returns, members of the expedition are killed savagely, one by one, through a series of animal attacks, before Barbee can interview them about their findings in the desert. Barbee is afflicted with dreams in which, under the instruction of April Bell, an alluring woman he met at the airport where Mondrick's plane landed, he transforms into a variety of animals—wolf, tiger, snake, even prehistoric creatures—and strikes at the expedition members. He consults a psychoanalyst, who dismisses the dreams as delusions brought on by guilt and other subconscious emotions. In fact, psychoanalysis itself is revealed to be a tool of *Homo lycanthropus*, created to deflect humanity from an understanding of the true meaning of psychological impulses rooted in *Homo sapiens'* instinctive fear of *Homo lycanthropus*. It is just one of many scientific rationales Williamson offers to explain *Homo lycanthropus* and their powers, including the properties that silver and sunlight have to neutralize the werewolf because they interfere with mind-matter vibrations crucial to shapeshifting.

The meaning behind all of this eventually become manifest to Barbee, who also realizes that his dream transformations are accompanied by an exhilarating sense of liberation he has never known before: "Those painful bonds, that he had worn a whole lifetime, were abruptly snapped" (101), he acknowledges while changing into a wolf. And when he transforms into a snake, "In this glorious awakening from the long nightmare of life, all his values were changed" (208). He is, he discovers, the prophesied Dark Child, who will lead *Homo lycanthropus* to ascendancy once more.

THE MANY VARIETIES OF MODERN WEREWOLF FICTION

Hundreds of werewolf stories have been written since the 1940s and as might be expected for a genre staple the majority feature the canonical werewolf immortalized in *The Wolf Man* and the legends and fiction that inspired the film. Even so, writers have worked numerous variations into their plots, if not into the actual thematic foundations of their stories, such that the werewolf tale now assumes a multitude of shapes, forms, and guises. The werewolf has taken the role of hero in Anthony Boucher's "The Compleat Werewolf" (1942), Seabury Quinn's "Bon Voyage, Michele" (1947), and Richard Jaccoma's *The Werewolf's Tale* (1988) and *The Werewolf's Revenge* (1991). The werewolf story has been crossbred with the tale of crime and detection in Les Whitten's *Moon of the Wolf* (1968), George R. R. Martin's "The Skin Trade" (1988), Geoffrey Caine's *Wake of the Werewolf* (1991), and Crosland Brown's *Tombley's Walk* (1991). Werewolves are sympathetic and misunderstood beings in Bruce Elliott's "Wolves Don't Cry" (1954) and objects of romance in Manly Banister's "Eena" (1947), Jane Toombs's *Under the Shadows* (1992), and Cheri Scotch's *The Werewolf's Touch* (1992) and *The Werewolf's Kiss* (1993). There is even a subcategory of werewolf lifestyle fiction, which includes Scott Bradfield's "Dream of the Wolf" (1984), Whitley Strieber's *The Wild* (1991), Michael Cadnum's *St. Peter's Wolf* (1993), and other tales that juxtapose the natural and full-blooded life characters live in wolf form to the stunted and stressful lives they lead during their human hours.

While these approaches and treatments have broadened and expanded the body of werewolf fiction, some perspectives on the theme have yielded particularly significant work that has accelerated the evolution of the werewolf as an iconic figure of horror.

Wolfe Wolf was no longer primarily a scholar. He was a werewolf now, a white-magic werewolf, a werewolf-for-fun; and fun he was going to have. He lit his pipe, stared at the blank paper on his desk, and tried desperately to draft a letter to Gloria. It should hint at just enough to fascinate her and hold her interest until he could go south when the term ended and reveal to her the whole wonderful new truth.... He could see Gloria now and claim her in all his wolfish vigor.

—Anthony Boucher, "The Compleat Werewolf"

THE PSYCHOLOGICAL WEREWOLF

Psychological interpretations of the werewolf theme in fiction have complemented supernatural treatments for over two centuries. It is easy to understand why. The werewolf is unique among monsters insofar as it is both human and inhuman at the same time. Consequently, some writers choose to view the werewolf's predatory activities as extensions or exaggerations of ordinary human behavior. Just as the separation between the human and wolf aspects of the werewolf is often ambiguous, so in many werewolf tales are the distinctions between supernatural and psychological motivations for lycanthropic behavior. The werewolf's divided nature has been used in horror fiction as a symbol for a variety of psychological conditions, ranging from the sociopathic serial killer to the victim of psychotic delusion, split personality, or multiple-personality disorder.

Some authors have presented lycanthropy as largely a phenomena of mind over matter. Charles Robert Maturin, in his novel *The Albigenses* (1824), presents a character who acts in a wolf-like manner, although there is no outward physical transformation: he claims that his fangs and fur grow on the inside. In "A Pastoral Horror" (1890), Sir Arthur Conan Doyle presents a troubled clergyman prone to fits of madness in which he kills with the savagery of a wild animal.

The best-known psychological werewolf story features no traditional werewolf at all. Robert Louis Stevenson's *Strange Case of Dr. Jekyll and Mr. Hyde* (1886) is the classic tale of a personality split into human and bestial halves. Its protagonist, Henry Jekyll, is a scientist who recognizes the dual nature of the ordinary human being and concocts a formula for separating them out:

I not only recognized my natural body for the mere aura and effulgence of certain of the powers that made up my spirit, but, managed to compound a drug by which these powers should be dethroned from their supremacy, and a second form and countenance substituted, none the less natural to me because they were the expression, and bore the stamp, of lower elements in my soul. (77)

At the time he undertakes the experiment Jekyll fails to appreciate that the "lower elements" of his soul, incarnated in the form of his dark alter ego, Edward Hyde, will express themselves so powerfully that Hyde will completely overwhelm the benevolent side of Jekyll's personality, and begin manifesting spontaneously, without the need for the drug infusions that first bring him out. The crimes the liberated Hyde commits are memorable for their brutality. And though Hyde appears in a semblance of human form, his coarseness has a bestial quality that can be understood in terms of lycanthropic transformation:

> The hand of Henry Jekyll (as you have often remarked) was professional in shape and size: it was large, firm, white, and comely. But the hand which I now saw, clearly enough in the yellow light of a London mid-morning, lying half shut on the bed clothes, was lean, corded, knuckly, of a dusky pallor and thickly shaded with a swart growth of hair. It was the hand of Edward Hyde.

There is no traditional werewolf to speak of either in Fritz Leiber's "The Hound" (1942). Rather, Leiber conjures a predatory entity that is an expression of humanity's collective subconscious. The protagonist of the story is a young man living in a modern city who periodically sees a scavenging dog or wolf-like being in his peripheral vision and sometimes hears distant baying. Increasingly anxious, he begins to sense that he is being stalked or driven by something he cannot explain. A casual conversation with a friend about the translation of basic human superstition from the medieval age to the modern urban frontier finally brings it all into focus for him:

> "[W]hat's happening inside each one of us? I'll tell you. All sorts of inhibited emotions are accumulating. Fear is accumulating. Horror is accumulating. A new kind of awe of the mysteries of the universe is accumulating. A psychological environment is forming, along with the physical one.... Our culture becomes ripe for infection. From somewhere. It's just like a bacteriologist's culture...when it gets to the right temperature and consistency for supporting a colony of germs. Similarly, our culture suddenly spawns a horde of demons. And, like germs, they have a peculiar affinity for our culture."...
>
> "How would you know the infection had taken place...Why, they'd haunt us, terrorize us, try to rule us. Our fears would be their fodder. A parasite-host relationship. Supernatural symbiosis. Some of us—the sensitive ones—would notice us sooner than others. Some of us might see them without knowing what they were. Others might know about them without seeing them." (160)

In effect, Leiber suggests that the modern werewolf would be a psychological manifestation with all the force of an occult monster, a creature spawned and nourished by the neuroses and anxieties of modern life:

> "I think there'd be werewolves among our demons, but they wouldn't be much like the old ones. No nice clean fur, white teeth and shining eyes. Oh no. Instead

you'd get some nasty hound that wouldn't surprise you if you saw it nosing at a garbage pail or crawling out from under a truck. Frighten and terrorize you, yes. But surprise, no. It would fit into the environment. Look as if it belonged in a city and smell the same. Because of the twisted emotions that would be its food, your emotions and mine. A matter of diet." (160)

Joseph Payne Brennan takes Leiber's idea that the werewolf is largely a projection of our own psyches down another avenue in "Diary of a Werewolf" (1960). The protagonist of this story is a former city resident who moves to rural Hemlock House to recover from a variety of dissipations, including heroin addiction. Over the months of April to July in 1958, he records in brief diary excerpts his developing desire to drop to all fours and hunt like a wolf. He reports killing small game at first before moving on to humans: an old woman, a derelict, and finally a young girl. Making the most of his first-person narrative, Brennan presents the story almost exclusively from the narrator's point of view, making it virtually impossible to establish whether he actually transforms into a werewolf, or is merely projecting his psychoses. There is no doubt, however, in the mind of the narrator, who goes so far as to suggest that historical legends of the supernatural werewolf are merely embellished accounts of killers like him who have existed throughout the ages:

> I am convinced that werewolves like myself have existed for centuries. Harassed peasants may have invented some of the trappings in the first place, but I can clearly see now that there is a solid basis of fact for the many legends that have come down through the ages. There must have been many like me! External trappings invented for effect are as nothing compared to the hidden horrors which exist unseen in the convolutions of our brains—brains subjected to who knows what monstrous pressures, derangements, diseases, hereditary taints. (10)

In the last forty years the werewolf tale has become the template for many horror stories featuring serial killers. A number have followed Brennan's lead, narrating the story from the viewpoint of a killer whose judgment is not to be trusted during (or even outside) his rampages. David Case's "The Cell" (1969) is related in the form of a diary written by a man who monthly turns into a werewolf—or so he tells the reader. At the approach of the full moon, he allows his wife to lock him into a specially constructed cell in their basement. He blames his condition on a peculiar hereditary taint, and repeatedly reassures his readers of his sanity. Even though he himself is aware of that, he has no physical proof to offer:

> I am completely sane.
>   It occurs to me that I have not stated that, and it is necessary. If anyone ever reads this they must understand that I am not crazy. It is not a disease of the mind, it is a disease of the body. It is purely physical. It must be, to cause the physical change that it does. I haven't yet written about the change. That will be

hard, although I can see it objectively. I can see my hands and body, and feel my face. I cannot see my face, of course, because there is no mirror. I don't know if I could bear it if I had a memory of what my face must become. And I don't know if I can describe it honestly, or honestly describe it. (14)

The narrator never refers to himself as a werewolf, and as his narrative unfolds it seems increasingly clear that he is deluded about his condition. Since childhood he has been unable to control or explain violent outbursts. He is romantically remote toward his wife (which he justifies on the basis of not wanting to produce offspring who would inherit his condition), and expresses aversions that suggest he is sexually inhibited. Stridently self-righteous, and lacking the self-consciousness to connect himself to vicious unsolved murders that he reads took place at sites he visited, he is a textbook psychopath who looks to blame society for his crimes:

The middle classes have such a ridiculous idea that man-made laws have some higher right than the man who is behind them. I cannot understand how people can be so dense, so easily led. How can they regard the rules of society as the rules of God? They make no distinction between descriptive laws and laws that are relative to the situation; between eternal laws of nature and God and morality and the fluctuating and often wrong laws that men create to hinder themselves and others. It truly bothers me that this is so, that prejudice has made it so. Just think how it applies to myself...I would be scorned and hated and punished if anyone knew of my affliction. The authorities would most likely pass a law to make it illegal to have this disease. But what good would that do? Diseases are not governed by the laws of governments, and I would be thought a criminal although powerless to help myself. That is why no one must ever know about it. The old, almost forgotten prejudices and fears and superstitions would join forces with the new powers of the authorities and destroy me. It is a terrible thing. One sees it everywhere, and can do nothing to combat it. I feel very bitter about it. If I had lived three hundred years ago I would have at least been feared and acknowledged by anyone who knew. Now I would simply be legislated against. It is a good thing that I am a well-balanced man, as there is no telling what such stupidity would drive me to. (45)

In his novel *The Nightwalker* (1979), Thomas Tessier seeks a middle ground between the psychological and supernatural. The protagonist, Bobbby Ives, is an American expatriate who finds himself suddenly afflicted with inexplicable headaches, strange body sensations, and violent tendencies. He tells his girl-friend that he has also had dreams of a life in the historical past where he lived as British colonialist on the island of Guadalupe and witnessed a voodoo ceremony, after which he was bitten on the way home by a feral man. He died of his injuries, but quickly came back to life as a werewolf and was eventually killed by the islanders. Ives also served as a soldier in Vietnam, and had an experience there where he was clinically dead, but successfully resuscitated.

His symptoms of illness have been manifesting ever since, and getting increasingly stronger.

By the time he consults a psychic Ives has murdered his girlfriend and taken the lives of several other people. The psychic informs him that she sees the mark of the wolf on him (including a ring finger as long as his middle finger). But her explanation for his condition is far from the traditional explanation for a werewolf:

> "You see, you aren't possessed, in the strict sense, by an outside spirit or demons. Only by yourself. Some of the powers that are part of lycanthropy, the physical transformations for instance, are supernatural. But think of the word 'supernatural'. It doesn't necessarily mean an omnipotent, external force of either good or evil." (140)

According to the psychic Ives may have an innate proclivity for his behavior that comes out only under the proper set of circumstances. His, and all forms of lycanthropy, may or may not have an occult basis:

> "[L]ycanthropy may need something to trigger it off within a person. We know so little. In the old stories lycanthropy came about through a pact between an individual and the devil, and I'm sure that's what many people believed, absolutely. Because it is such a terrible thing, to become a wolf-man-creature. But if you take the devil away, why couldn't the seed still be there in some people, perhaps everyone? Manifesting itself, growing, taking control *only after* something or some set of conditions triggers it? (145)

Although enough happens to suggest that Ives is the victim of a supernatural curse that replicates itself through serial incarnations, there is never enough objective proof to establish that he is a true werewolf. The few scenes of physical transformation are presented through his eyes and it is never resolved whether Ives's dreams of past lives have a basis in reality or are simply the delusions of a psychotic mind.

The psychological and the supernatural also work in tandem in Stephen King's *Cycle of the Werewolf* (1985), which relates a series of werewolf-like killings that terrorize the town of Tarker's Falls, Maine for twelve months of one year. The murders are eventually revealed to be the handiwork the Reverend Lester Lowe, a Baptist minister whose bestial side is just an expression of what he refers to in his sermons as "The Beast," or the natural human capacity for evil. Although Lowe assumes the classic werewolf form, there is no explanation for how or why he transforms. In a final twist, King suggests, if only through thoughts that may be a madman's self-delusion, that Lowe's lycanthropy may serve some divine purpose:

> "I do good here, and if I sometimes do evil, why, men have done evil before me; evil also serves the will of God, or so the book of Job teaches us; if I have been

cursed from Outside, then God will bring me down in his time. All things serve the will of God..." (111)

THE SCIENCE-FICTIONAL WEREWOLF

Science fiction treatments of the werewolf theme are at the opposite extreme of psychological interpretations. Where the one attempts (for the more part) to rationalize lycanthropy in terms of aberrant psychology and dismiss it as a supernatural phenomena, the other attempts to explain how the seemingly supernatural elements of lycanthropy can be explained within the realm of known science.

One of science fiction's earliest explorations of the werewolf, Jack Williamson's *Darker Than You Think*, proposes that werewolves are members of the species *Homo lycanthropus*, a race superior to *Homo sapiens* owing to their ability to psychically manipulate probability in order to shift shape. "The stability of atoms was a matter of probability," concludes the main character, who understands the significance of being able to manipulate matter at the atomic level through powers of the mind. "The direct mental control of probability would surely open terrifying avenues of power." Indeed, it explains extraordinary powers of shapeshifting, invisibility, and even telepathy that hitherto would have been attributed to the supernatural:

> "No common matter is any real barrier to us, in this free state...Doors and walls still seem real enough, I know—but wood is mostly oxygen and carbon, and our mind-webs can grasp the vibrating atoms and slip through them, nearly as easily as through the air. Many other substances we can possess for our vehicles, with a little more effort and difficult." (113)

In James Blish's "There Shall Be No Darkness" (1950), virtually everything about the traditional werewolf is demystified when explained in terms of standard biology. The ability of the werewolf to shift shape, for example, is attributed to hormonal rather than occult factors. Hyperpinealism, "the little-known aberration of a little-known ductless gland," contributes to "a plastic, malleable body, within limits. A wolf is the easiest form because the skeletons are so similar. Not much pinearin can do to bone, you see. An ape would be easier still, but lycanthropes don't assume shapes outside their own ecology...As the pinearin blood level increases the cellular surface tension is lowered so much that the cells literally begin to boil away" (110–11).

The werewolf's reaction to wolfsbane and garlic can be explained in terms of anaphylaxis: "The herbs, for example, are antispasmodics—they act, rather, as ephedrine does in hay fever, to reduce the violence of the seizure" (110). Aversion to religious symbols, on the other hand, is due purely to ingrained superstition. "As for the religious trappings, their effects are perhaps solely psychological"—meaning that its quite that an artifact like the crucifix would have no effect against a religiously skeptical werewolf. The werewolf's bite infecting another with lycanthropy can be explained in terms of disease vectors: "The pinearin in the wolf's saliva evidently gets into the bloodstream, stimulates the victims pineal gland" (125).

The werewolf in Poul Anderson's "Operation Afreet" (1956) is also a hyperpineal who is able to control his transformations with a simple tool built to aid transformation in a wartime situation: "How hard to believe that transforming had depended on a bright full moon until only ten years ago! Then Wiener showed that the process was a simple one of polarized light of the right wavelengths triggering the pineal gland, and the Polaroid Corporation made another million dollars from its WereWish lens." He explains that the laws of conservation of energy apply when shapeshifting, with the result that human weight translates directly into wolf weight, no matter how big a wolf it produces. Anderson's scientifically inclined werewolf is also able to describe clinically the experience of being a werewolf, which is usually lost in the oblivion suffered by most supernatural werewolves:

> A lot of writers have tried to describe how it feels to be were, and every one of them has failed, because human language doesn't have the words. My vision was no longer acute, the stars were blurred above me and the world took on a colorless flatness. But I heard with a clarity that made the night almost roar, way into the supersonic; and a universe of smells roiled in my nostrils, wet grass and teeming dirt, the hot sweet odor of a scampering field mouse, the clean tang of oil and guns, a faint harshness of smoke—Poor stupefied humanity, half-dead to such earth glories!
>
> The psychological part is hardest to convey. I was a wolf, with a wolf's nerves and glands and instincts, a wolf's sharp but limited intelligence. I had a man's memories and a man's purposes, but they were unreal, dreamlike. I must make an effort of trained will to hold them off and not go hallooing off after the nearest jackrabbit. No wonder weres had a bad name in the old days, before they themselves understood the mental changes involved and got the right habits drilled into them from babyhood. (51)

Several writers have looked beyond scientific explanation for the werewolf to regard it in the same terms as extraterrestrials and aliens. In Jack Williamson's "Wolves of Darkness" (1932), invaders from another dimension assume the form of frightening wolf-like creatures. Clark Ashton Smith, in "A Prophecy of Monsters" (1954), imagines the darkly amusing consequences of a future where a ravenous werewolf does not realize until too late that its quarry is a humanoid robot. Larry Niven's "There's a Wolf in My Time Machine" (1971) sends its luckless time traveler to an alternate future where all human are lycanthropes, descended from wolves rather than apes, while Michael Swanwick, in "A Midwinter's Tale" (1988), imagines a wolf-like race of extraterrestrials who periodically feed on humans to absorb their thoughts and thereby strengthen a mutually beneficial symbiotic relationship. In Al Sarrantonio's *Moonbane* (1991), earth is invaded by extraterrestrial werewolves who come, not surprisingly, from our moon.

There have also been numerous science fiction takes on the werewolf's ability to transform physically. In A. Bertram Chandler in "Frontier of the Dark" (1952), characters acquire the power to shift shape lycanthropically following a mishap with a spaceship atomic drive during interstellar travel. The werewolves in Clifford D. Simak's *The Werewolf Principle* (1967) are actually androids constructed to genetically mimic the life on any planet where they live (including one that is home to a wolf-like species) and transform back upon leaving it. In Michael Flynn's "Werehouse" (1990), lycanthropic shapeshifting is a new form of illicit thrill-seeking entertainment made possible through nanotechnology.

THE WEREWOLF AS SYMBOL OF RACIAL AND POLITICAL IDENTITY

In early horror fiction the werewolf was frequently presented as an alien to the culture it preyed upon as much as a supernatural anomaly. The ethnicity of title character of Clemence Housman's *The Were-Wolf* is not clear, except that she is an outsider to the close-knit northern society she insinuates her way into. Likewise, the werewolves in Gerald Biss's *Door of the Unreal*, Greye La Spina's *Invaders from the Dark*, and Alfred H. Bill's *The Wolf in the Garden* all are foreigners who, even in human form, provoke unease through suspicious behaviors associated with their nationalities. The depiction of the werewolf as a foreign invader intent on undermining its adopted culture is a dominant strain in horror fiction that persists in contemporary horror novels including Jerry and Sharon Ahern's *Werewolvess* (1990), which features a werewolf contingent of the Nazi army, and Jeffrey Sackett's *Mark of the Werewolf* (1990), in which neo-Nazi white supremacists attempt to use a werewolf to breed a fascist army for the Aryan nation.

Modern werewolf fiction features an abundance of stories in which the werewolf serves as a symbol not only for the social outsider, but for a wide variety of political and racial issues. In his novel *The Werewolf of Paris* (1933), Guy Endore deliberately juxtaposes the activities of his nineteenth-century werewolf, Bertrand Caillet, to the natural cruelty of humans down through history. Caillet's history begins with two rival households in medieval France, the Pitavals and the Pitamonts. When one of the Pitamonts is captured after having murdered two of the Pitavals, he is subject to a brutal imprisonment that reduces him to a howling beast. Centuries later, a priest descended from the Pitamonts molests a young woman, Josephine, and their union yields Bertrand. Bertrand bears some of the typical stigmata of the werewolf, including eyebrows that meet and hair on the palms of his hands. His earliest kills

---

Thirteen Groundbreaking Werewolf Short Stories

"The Were-Wolf" by Clemence Housman (1890)

"The Mark of the Beast" by Rudyard Kipling (1890)

"The Camp of the Dog" by Algernon Blackwood (1908)

"The Werewolf of Ponkert" by H. Warner Munn (1925)

"The Compleat Werewolf" by Anthony Boucher (1942)

"The Hound" by Fritz Leiber (1942)

"The Refugee" by Jane Rice (1943)

"There Shall Be No Darkness" by James Blish (1950)

"The Cell" by David Case (1969)

"The Company of Wolves" by Angela Carter (1979)

"The Dream of the Wolf" by Scott Bradfield (1984)

"Twilight at the Towers" by Clive Barker (1985)

"Boobs" by Suzy McKee Charnas (1989)

---

are livestock, but eventually he progresses to human prey. Owing to his community's disbelief in superstitions, and to Bertrand's own ignorance of his condition, his atrocities are often blamed on others, who tend to be the poor and those on the margins of society incapable of defending themselves or articulating their innocence.

Once he realizes his true nature, Bertrand flees to Paris that is in a state of chaos at the height the Paris Commune uprisings. In a city facing starvation where domestic animals and vermin are being killed for food, and where executions under martial law are common, Bertrand's activities go all but unnoticed. In fact, he joins the National Guard and applies himself all the more zealously to his duties under the protection of his rank. Bertrand is "cured" temporarily by the selfless love of a woman who regularly yields her blood to him, but eventually he is apprehended and put into prison, where he commits suicide. There is no question that Bernard is a genuine werewolf—his skeleton, exhumed years later, is that of a wolf. But Endore sees the evil that Bertrand represents as just a facet of a greater evil infecting humanity. The narrator of the novel writes, "I have often wondered if several such monsters might not, by geometrical progression, infect whole nations in a few days," but the behavior Endore describes is clearly endemic to humanity, regardless of Bernard's presence:

[C]ertainly Paris seemed to be infected, though the cause is more easily traced to the horrors of war than to werewolves. The bitter winter, with multitudes starving, with babies dying like flies, with shells bursting in all directions, was an experience likely to weaken many characters. The city was full of hate and suspicion. A man of a too Germanic name or a too Germanic cast of countenance was likely to suffer for what was scarcely his fault. Every strange house was people with spies. Poor people who took to sewers for warmth and refuge from a wintry night might wake rudely to find themselves vehemently suspected of planting bombs to blow up the city. (145)

A superior officer later puts the evil that Bernard represents in its proper context:

> "Evil exists. And evil breeds evil. The horrors and cruelties of history link hands down the ages. One deed engenders another, nay multiplies itself. One perpetrator of crime infects another. Their kind increases like flies. If nothing resists this plague, it will terminate with the world a seething mass of corruption.
>   "[T]he bars have been let down, the doors are opening wide and monsters of old, in new disguises, will soon throng the world. The new terror will not lurk in the forest, but go abroad in the market place; it will not attack lonely wayfarers but will seize the throats of nations. There will be such wars as the world has never seen, and inhumanities such as no one has dreamed of." (183)

In his novel *The Wolfen* (1979), Whitley Strieber takes the werewolf out of the realm of good and evil by imagining a predatory wolf-like race that has coexisted with humanity for 10,000 years or more. This race is the foundation of werewolf tales told by primitive man. As human civilization progressed, the tales came to be regarded as myths. Not only did the skepticism and disbelief of modern times afford this race the cover of superstition to move about among mankind, as a scientist in the novel realizes, but the inevitable shortcomings of the social contract in any expanding human civilization allowed them to flourish. The wolfen have a particularly strong foothold in the cities, where they prey upon societies outcasts. As a scientist in the book realizes:

> [T]he werewolves, tormented for generations by humanity's vigilance and fear, had found a way to hide from man. Their cover was now perfect. They lived among us, fed off our living flesh, but were unknown to all except those who didn't live to tell the tale. They were a race of living ghosts, unseen but very much a part of the world. They understood human society well enough to take only the abandoned, the weak, the isolated. And toward the end of the nineteenth century the human population all over the world had started to explode, poverty and filth had spread. Huge masses of people were ignored and abandoned by the societies in which they lived. And they were fodder for these werewolves, who range through the shadows devouring the beggars, the wanderers, those without name or home. (141)

The marginalization of non-Caucasian cultures in America has given rise to a number of variations on the werewolf theme. In *Moon Dance* (1989), S. P. Somtow weaves the werewolf myth into the myth of the American frontier.

Set in 1880s in America's Dakota territory, it tells of a turf war between the Shungmanitu, who are members of the Lakota Sioux, and the retinue of Count von Bächl-Wölfing, a German immigrant who hopes to appropriate Native American land in the name of Manifest Destiny and to fulfill his own perverted take on the American Dream. Both represent werewolf races, and their struggle reprises the American immigrant experience insofar as immigrants oppressed in their own countries fled to America only to displace Native Americans from their own lands.

Nancy Collins builds on Somtow's theme in her novels *Walking Wolf* (1995) and *Wild Blood* (1994). *Walking Wolf*, a period western, features young Billy Skillet, who is the offspring of a human mother and a werewolf father. Raised by the Comanches, Billy seeks entry into the society of white men with whom he has much more in common. In *Wild Blood*, Skinner Cade has long presumed he was of Native American descent, insofar as he is persecuted for his looks by the white men in the contemporary American southwest. Both endure the prejudice the dominant culture directs towards outsiders, even though they neither are Native American. Rather Billy and Skinner are both *vargr*, the name shapeshifters call themselves (werewolf being considered a pejorative name invented by humans). Billy learns the true background for his kind:

> I learned that what I was, in truth, was a species of being known as a metamorph, a creature who could take the shape of man or beast at will. I also learned that there are many different kinds of metamorph scattered all over the globe. There were the *kitsune* of Asia, the *naga* of India, the *birskir* of the Arctic Circle, the *anube* of the Nile, the *bast* of Africa, the *silkie* and *undine* of the north and south seas...and the *vargr* of Europe.
>
> The *vargr*, my particular clan, are wolves...they were the most successful (meaning the most aggressive) breed of metamorph on Earth. Europe had proven a fertile home for their packs, and many had come into power in the world of man as popes and kings and warlords, albeit in human guies.
>
> In fact the *vargr* had proven so successful in getting what they wanted that they had grown bored with their original territory and begun traveling with their unwitting human cattle to the New World, often coming into conflict with the breeds of metamorphs and other Pretender races already established there. The *vargr*, like the Europeans they had tied themselves to, were champion exploiters and imperialists. (211)

Indeed, in *Wild Blood*, the *vargr* openly persecute the *ulfr* and the *coyotero*, other species of metamorphs whom the *vargr* deem inferior and persecute as they themselves are persecuted by humans.

Kim Newman extends the idea of the werewolf as a symbol for the fringe members of a dominant culture in "Out of the Night, When the Full Moon Is Bright..." (1994), a variation on the legend of Zorro. In this story the Mexican peasant Diego Vega becomes an avenger of the oppressed after he is transformed into a werewolf. The popular legend of Zorro as a masked outlaw who etches his signature letter "Z" in the clothing or skin of his victims with his rapier is actually just a bastardization of the story of the true Zorro (who makes the mark with his claws). Newman's tale is set in a modern racially divided Los Angeles in which Zorro still lives and in which his services are needed more than ever. As Zorro tells the hero of the story, a black man: "At first, I understood that I killed for *my* people. I was wrong, I killed for my *kind*. Chicano, black, white, whatever. My kind is all colours. I am of the pobres, the poor, the oppressed, the neglected, the inconvenient. I am the cry of the sad, the true grito de Dolores" (492).

One of the more ingenious stories deploying the werewolf as a political metaphor is Clive Barker's "Twilight at the Towers" (1985), which explores personal identities in the context of Cold War politics. Barker populates a Berlin still divided by the Iron Curtain with werewolves whose own divided natures make them the perfect double agents in the game of espionage played between East and West. Ultimately, their loyalties and allegiances become so confusing and unpredictable that all they can embrace with any certainty is the dividedness of their own natures.

THE FEMINIST WEREWOLF

In early werewolf fiction, women were usually limited to playing the thankless roles of villain or victim. Women cast as werewolves in Frederick Marryat's "The Werewolf" or Clemence Housman's *The Were-Wolf* were portrayed as predatory monsters who used female vulnerability and sexual allure to seduce and deceive their unwitting prey. By contrast, the women in Gerald Biss's *The Door of the Unreal* and Alfred H. Bill's *The Wolf in the Garden* are traditional imperiled innocents whose purpose is to be rescued by masculine heroes. In a small but significant number of stories from the same period, notably J. D. Kerruish's *The Undying Monster* and Greye La Spina's *Invaders from the Dark*, plucky heroines use superior intelligence and guile to fight werewolves. The culmination of this trend is Jane Rice's "The Refugee" (1943), in which a woman facing starvation in wartime France dallies with a young man whom she knows is a werewolf long enough to catch him off guard and kill him so that she can feed off his carcass.

Positive treatments of female werewolves began appearing regularly in the early twentieth century, in romances by Seabury Quinn, Arlton Eadie, and other pulp writers. However, it was not until the 1960s that writers began looking to the werewolf as a symbol of feminine identity. The title character of Peter S. Beagle's "Lila the Werewolf" (1974) is a young woman whose ly-canthropy is depicted as an expression of her liberal, exuberant personality which resists the conformity and repression that her steady lover and her family would impose upon her. In Angela Carter's "The Company of Wolves" (1979), a retelling of the fairy tale of Little Red Riding Hood, the wolf who disposes of the young girl's grandmother is not a villain, but rather a symbol of her own sexuality whom she embraces at the story's end. In Carter's "The Werewolf" (1979), grandmother turns out to be the wolf, and once the girl has disposed of this figure of parental authority, she becomes the mistress of the family house.

The idea that lycanthropy represents a liberation rather than a curse is predominant in Suzy McKee Charnas's "Boobs" (1989), which parallels a young girl's transformation into a werewolf with the onset of puberty. On the day she begins menstruating, Kelsey Bornstein experiences her first change into a werewolf. Whereas Kelsey as a human feels embarrassed and disgusted about the transformations of womanhood, as a wolf, she comes to appreciate her appearance: "I was a werewolf, like in the movies they showed over Halloween weekend. But it wasn't anything like your ugly movie werewolf that's just some guy loaded up with pounds and pounds of makeup. I was *gorgeous*" (32). Not only does Kelsey's feral side give her a sense of comfort, it provides her with a feeling of empowerment that she has never known. Speaking of her domineering stepmother, she says: "I realized, all of a sudden, with this big blossom of surprise, that I didn't have to be scared of Hilda, or anybody. I was strong, my wolf-body was strong, and anyhow one clear look at me and she would drop dead" (31). This new-found confidence, which expresses itself vividly in wolf form when she attacks a pack of dogs, extends to her human life where she unapologetically kills in cold-blood the most merciless of the boys in her class who tease her for her developing body.

In the wake of the researches of Clarissa Pinkola Estes, whose sociological text *Women Who Run with the Wolves* (1991) used the wolf as a symbol of the instinctive side of femininity, several novelists have used lycanthropy to explore aspects of modern female experience. The heroine of Dennis Danvers's *Wilderness* (1991) is a young woman who has treated her werewolf identity as a guilty secret most of her life. Revealing it to her lover and her psychiatrist proves the first step in her journey to self-fulfillment and psychic wholeness. By contrast, in Pat Murphy's *Nadya* (1996), Nadya Rybak, a werewolf of European descent who emigrates to America in the nineteenth century, and Elizabeth Metcalf, the woman with whom she has an intimate romance, both accept the uniqueness of a relationship that places them beyond the norms of the proper society of their times. In *Wilding* (1992), Melanie Tem describes a matriarchal clan of werewolves who cherish the integrity and strength of their wolf pack, even though the impulse to lycanthropy in their teenage children manifests as restlessness, emotional liability, anger, and promiscuity. In *Bitten* (2002), Kelley Armstrong, takes the opposite tack, presenting her heroine, Elena Michaels, as the only female werewolf in what is essentially a werewolf fraternity:

> "The werewolf gene is passed only through the male line, father to son, so the only way for a woman to become a werewolf is to be bitten to survive, which, as I've said, is rare. Given the odds, it's not surprising I'm the only female. Bitten

on purpose, turned into a werewolf on purpose. Amazing, really, that I survived. After all, when you've got a species with three dozen males and one female, that one female is something of a prize. And werewolves do not settle their battles over a nice game of chess. Nor do they have a history of respect for women. Women serve two functions in the werewolf world: sex and dinner, or if they're feeling lazy, sex followed by dinner." (18–19)

Not only the sole female werewolf, but someone who understands her outsider status within the pack, Elena comes to understand her importance when she is enjoined to help hunt down renegade independent werewolves not that much unlike herself.

THE CINEMATIC WEREWOLF

Although no werewolf film produced since *The Wolf Man* has had a similar impact on the popular consciousness, the cinematic werewolf is an important figure whose influence is intimately bound up with that of the werewolf in horror fiction. There are hundreds of werewolf films, a significant number of which have been adapted from stories and novels, and in them one can frequently find the same ideas and concerns that have distinguished the werewolf as potent monster of horror fiction.

The film generally acknowledged as the first with a werewolf theme is *The Werewolf* (1913), a short silent film about the daughter of a Navajo witch woman who assumes the form of a wolf to attack the white men she has been raised to hate. One hundred years after her death, she even returns from the dead to seek out the reincarnation of the man who killed her lover. This relatively unconventional story, steeped in Native American lore, might suggest that the cinematic werewolf has a wilder and more unconventional history than the literary werewolf. In fact, the majority of werewolf films made in the

---

Eight Essential Werewolf Films

Werewolf of London (1935)

The Wolf Man (1941)

I Was a Teenage Werewolf (1957)

Curse of the Werewolf (1961)

The Howling (1980)

The Company of Wolves (1985)

Teen Wolf (1985)

Wolf (1994)

---

near-century since has been largely conventional in their telling, although several stand out for their ingenious twists and their unique telling.

The first feature-length werewolf film, Stuart Walker's *Werewolf of London* (1935), is a product of Universal Studios, who would also produce *The Wolf Man* and its numerous sequels. The film's basic story concerns scientist Wilfred Glendon who, while on an expedition to Tibet to find the rare mariphasa plant, is attacked by a wolf-like creature. Back in London, while training a moon lamp on the plant in order to stimulate its growth, Glendon is shocked to discover that his hand, when accidentally exposed to the light, grows hairy and wolf-like. He is reminded of a conversation he had with a colleague, Dr. Yogami, who showed up after his return from Tibet claiming to have met him there. According to Yogami, a man bitten by a werewolf will himself become a werewolf, a condition for which the mariphasa provides only temporary relief. Once Glendon realizes he is becoming a werewolf, he seeks the healing power of his mariphasa plant, only to discover on two successive occasions he has been pre-empted by Yogami, who is not only a werewolf himself but the very one who bit Wilfred in Tibet. Although somewhat original in its use of botany, the film introduces several ideas that would become staples of werewolf lore, including the werewolf's transformation by moonlight, and its reversion to human form at death. Notwithstanding the similarity of their titles, the special effects extravaganza *An American Werewolf in London* (1981), which tells of an American traveling in England who is transformed into a werewolf, and its sequel, *An American Werewolf in Paris* (1997), about a werewolf subculture perfecting a drug that will allow them to shape at any time, have little to do with the original.

Also introduced by *Werewolf of London* is the notion of lycanthropy as a foreign menace with a primitive or uncivilized origin. This idea was developed further in George Waggner's *The Wolf Man* (1941), which became the bible for most werewolf films that followed it. In this story, American Lawrence Talbot is visiting his family's ancestral home in Wales when he is mauled by a wolf that he manages to kill with his silver-headed cane. The wolf is actually a werewolf, from a visiting gypsy camp but Talbot, now tainted by the bite, is prone to lycanthropic transformation at the full moon, during which he loses human awareness and transforms into a ravenous wolf. This movie was the first to tie the werewolf to the pentagram, which the werewolf supposedly sees the image of in the hand of his next victim. More important, the film captured the essence of the werewolf's turmoil as a reluctant victim. Talbot experiences no joy in his transformation, which has the look of physical torture. In a scene where his family is attending mass and he finds himself curiously unable to enter the church, there is a sense of deeply conflicted emotions, and inexplicable impulses boiling inside of him. The true horror he feels is the slow and ineluctable revelation that he is the killer in the many unsolved crimes he becomes aware of. Silver is used to kill the wolf in this story, but not a silver bullet: in a deeply symbolic final scene Talbot is bludgeoned to death with the same cane he killed the first werewolf with, only this time it is wielded by his own father.

The Wolf Man yielded four sequels from Universal: *Frankenstein Meets the Wolf Man* (1943), *House of Frankenstein* (1944), *House of Dracula* (1945), and *Abbott and Costello Meet Frankenstein* (1948). As the titles suggests, these films were uninspired commercial products. The most interesting werewolf film from this period, *She Wolf of London* (1946), is only nominally concerned with werewolves. In essence, it is a murder mystery in which a family curse is invoked to deceive an heiress into believing she bears a hereditary taint of lycanthropy.

The most notorious of all werewolf films after *The Wolf Man* is Gene Fowler Jr.'s *I Was a Teenage Werewolf* (1957), one of the slough of horror and science fiction B-movies aimed at the youth culture of immediate post–World War II America. Its main character, Tony Rivers, consults Dr. Alfred Brandon, who subjects him to treatment combining hypnotherapy with scopolamine (or truth serum) for his troubled behavior. But the treatment backfires in Jekyll and Hyde fashion, liberating Tony's savage side in werewolf form. As Stephen King wrote in *Danse Macabre* (1979), the werewolf of the film, played by Michael Landon, transcends its cinematic vehicle to provide a commentary on the politics of adolescence: "Landon becomes the fascinating embodiment of everything you're *not* supposed to do if you want to be good . . . if you want to get along in school, join the National Honor Society, get your letter, and be accepted by a good college" (74).

I Was a Teenage Werewolf was not the last film to use the werewolf as a symbol of adolescent experience. *Teen Wolf* (1985) is the story of a young man who discovers he has werewolf tendencies and parlays them for social acceptance. When average, anxiety-ridden teen Scott Howard discovers he has inherited lycanthropy through his family, he exploits his powers to become a top basketball player and social celebrity. Rather than being repulsed or horrified by his transformation, Scott's peers accept his special character. As Scott discovers, though, they begin to prefer his flamboyant and more rambunctious wolf self to his human side. Ultimately, the film explores the pressures of teenage conformity and its price. *Ginger Snaps* (2000), on the other hand, is more faithfully struck from the mold of *I Was a Teenage Werewolf*, in its story of two teenage sisters, members of the Goth subculture, who share an unhealthy fascination with death. On the night of her first period, Ginger is bitten by a werewolf and thereafter begins acting more and more wild and promiscuous as the full moon approaches.

The werewolf has been featured in all manner of movies ranging from the serious to the silly, and in a manner of guises that can be gleaned from the titles alone: *Werewolf on Wheels* (1971), *Werewolf of Washington* (1973), *Werewolf of Woodstock* (1975), *Curse of the Queerwolf* (1989), and so on. The most original werewolf film at the end of the twentieth century was *Wolf* (1994), set in the world of modern business. Will Randall (played by Jack

Nicholson) is senior editor at a publishing house that is being bought out by a corporate conglomerate who hopes to squeeze him out. Bitten by a wolf that he accidentally hits while driving one night on a foggy road, the hitherto acquiescent Will begins to develop aggressive tendencies that soon make him a formidable opponent against the new owners and an ambitious underling eager to climb the corporate ladder. The film is memorable for its use of the werewolf as a symbol for the dog-eat-dog business world, which it depicts as a sort of Darwinian proving ground where humans have free reign to indulge in aggressive and brutish behavior that might otherwise be criticized outside its boundaries.

BIBLIOGRAPHY

Ahern, Jerry, and Sharon Ahern. *Werewolves.* New York: Pinnacle, 1990.

Anderson, Poul. "Operation Afreet." In *Tomorrow Bites*, ed. Greg Cox and T.K.F. Weiskopf. New York: Baen, 1995.

Anonymous. "Arthur and Gorlagon." In *A Lycanthropy Reader: Werewolves in Western Culture*, ed. Charlotte F. Otten. New York: Syracuse University Press, 1986.

Anonymous. "Guillame de Palerne." In *A Lycanthropy Reader: Werewolves in Western Culture*, ed. Charlotte F. Otten. New York: Syracuse University Press, 1986.

Armstrong, Kelley. *Bitten.* New York: Plume, 2003.

Banister, Manly. "Eena." In *Book of the Werewolf*, ed. Brian J. Frost. London: Sphere, 1973.

Barker, Clive. "Twilight at the Towers." In *The Mammoth Book of Werewolves*, ed. by Stephen Jones. New York: Carroll & Graf, 1994.

Beagle, Peter S. "Lila the Werewolf." In *Werewolf! A Chrestomathy of Lycanthropy*, ed. Bill Pronzini. New York: Arbor House, 1979.

Bill, Alfred H. *The Wolf in the Garden.* New York: Longmans, Green, 1931.

Biss, Gerald. *The Door of the Unreal.* London: Eveleigh Nash, 1919.

Blish, James. "There Shall Be No Darkness." In *Tomorrow Bites*, ed. Greg Cox and T.K.F. Weiskopf. New York: Baen, 1995.

Boucher, Anthony. "The Compleat Werewolf." In *The Compleat Werewolf and Other Tales of Fantasy and Science Fiction.* New York: Simon & Schuster, 1969.

Bradfield, Scott. "Dream of the Wolf." In *Dream of the Wolf.* New York: Knopf, 1990.

Brennan, Joseph Payne. "The Diary of a Werewolf." In *Shapes of Midnight.* New York: Berkley, 1980.

Brown, Crosland. *Tombley's Walk.* New York: Avon, 1991.

Cadnum, Michael. *St. Peter's Wolf.* New York: Carroll & Graf, 1993.

Caine, Geoffrey. *Wake of the Werewolf.* New York: Diamond, 1991.

Carter, Angela. "The Company of Wolves." In *The Bloody Chamber and Other Adult Tales.* New York: Harper & Row, 1979.

———. "The Werewolf." In *The Bloody Chamber and Other Adult Tales.* New York: Harper & Row, 1979.

Case, David. "The Cell." In *The Cell: Three Tales of Horror*. New York: Hill & Wang, 1969.

Chandler, A. Bertram. "Frontier of the Dark." In *Tomorrow Bites*, ed. Greg Cox and T.K.F. Weiskopf. New York: Baen, 1995.

Charnas, Suzy McKee. "Boobs." In *Woman Who Run with Werewolves*, ed. Pam Keesey. Pittsburgh, PA: Cleis Press, 1996.

Collins, Nancy. "Walking Wolf." In *Dead Man's Hand: Five Tales of the Weird West*. Stone Mountain, GA: White Wolf, 2004.

———. *Wild Blood*. New York: Roc, 1994.

Copper, Basil. *The Werewolf in Legend, Fact and Art*. New York: St. Martin's Press, 1977.

Danvers, Dennis. *Wilderness*. New York: Poseidon, 1991.

De France, Marie. "The Lay of the Were Wolf." In *A Lycanthropy Reader: Werewolves in Western Culture*, ed. Charlotte F. Otten. New York: Syracuse University Press, 1986.

Doyle, Arthur Conan. "A Pastoral Horror." In *The Captain of the 'Pole Star': Weird and Imaginative Fiction*. Ashcroft, BC: Ash-Tree Press, 2004.

Dozois, Gardner, and Sheila Williams, eds. *Isaac Asimov's Werewolves*. New York: Ace, 1999.

Dumas, Alexandre. "The Wolf Leader." *Weird Tales* (August 1931–March 1932).

Endore, Guy. *The Werewolf of Paris*. 1933. New York: Ace, 1962.

Flynn, Michael. "Werehouse." In *Tomorrow Bites,* ed. Greg Cox and T.K.F. Weiskopf. New York: Baen, 1995.

Frost, Brian J. *The Essential Guide to Werewolf Literature*. Madison, WI: Popular Press, 2003.

Greenberg, Martin H., ed. *Werewolves*. New York: DAW, 1995.

Gregory, Franklin. *The White Wolf*. New York: Random House, 1941.

Housman, Clemence. *The Were-Wolf*. 1896. In *A Lycanthropy Reader: Werewolves in Western Culture*, ed. Charlotte F. Otten. New York: Syracuse University Press, 1986.

Jaccoma, Richard. *The Werewolf's Revenge*. New York: Fawcett, 1991.

———. *The Werewolf's Tale*. New York: Fawcett, 1988.

Jones, Stephen, ed. *The Mammoth Book of Werewolves*. New York: Carroll & Graf, 1994.

Keesey, Pam, ed. *Women Who Run with the Werewolves*. Pittsburgh, PA: Cleis Press, 1996.

Kerruish, Jessie Douglas. *The Undying Monster*. London: Heath, Cranton, 1922.

King, Stephen. *The Cycle of the Werewolf*. New York: NAL/Signeet, 1985.

———. *Danse Macabre*. 1979. New York: Everest House, 1981.

Kipling, Rudyard. "The Mark of the Beast." In *Werewolf! A Chrestomathy of Lycanthropy*, ed. Bill Pronzini. New York: Arbor House, 1979.

La Spina, Greye. *Invaders of the Dark*. Sauk City, WI: Arkham House, 1960.

Leiber, Fritz. "The Hound." In *Werewolf! A Chrestomathy of Lycanthropy*, ed. Bill Pronzini. New York: Arbor House, 1979.

Mann, Jack. *Grey Shapes*. London: Wright & Brown, 1933.

Marryat, Frederick. "The Werewolf." In *The Dark Dominion: Eight Terrifying Tales of Vampires and Werewolves*, ed. Anonymous. New York: Paperback Library, 1970.

Martin, George R. R. "The Skin Trade." In *Night Visions 5*, ed. Douglas E. Winter. Arlington Heights, IL: Dark Harvest, 1988.

Maturin, Charles Robert. *The Albigenses: A Romance*. New York: Arno Press, 1974.

Menzies, Sutherland. "Hugues, the Wer-Wolf: A Kentish Legend of the Middle Ages." In *Book of the Werewolf*, ed. Brian J. Frost. London: Sphere, 1973.

Murphy, Pat. *Nadya*. New York: Tor, 1996.

Newman, Kim. "Out of the Night, When the Full Moon Is Bright..." In *The Mammoth Book of Werewolves*, ed. Stephen Jones. New York: Carroll & Graf, 1994.

Niven, Larry. "There's a Werewolf in My Time Machine." In *Werewolf! A Chrestomathy of Lycanthropy*, ed. Bill Pronzini. New York: Arbor House, 1979.

O'Donnell, Elliott. *Werewolves*. London: Methuen, 1912.

Otten, Charlotte F., ed. *A Lycanthropy Reader: Werewolves in Western Culture*. New York: Syracuse University Press, 1986.

Ovid. *Metamorphoses*. In *A Lycanthropy Reader: Werewolves in Western Culture*, ed. Charlotte F. Otten. New York: Syracuse University Press, 1986.

Petronius. *Satyricon*. In *A Lycanthropy Reader: Werewolves in Western Culture*, ed. Charlotte F. Otten. New York: Syracuse University Press, 1986.

Preiss, Byron, ed. *The Ultimate Werewolf*. New York: Dell, 1991.

Pronzini, Bill, ed. *Werewolf! A Chrestomathy of Lycanthropy*. New York: Arbor House, 1979.

Quinn, Seabury. "Bon Voyage, Michele." In *Is the Devil a Gentleman?* Baltimore: Mirage Press, 1970.

Reynolds, George W. M. *Wagner, the Wehr-Wolf*. New York: Dover, 1975.

Sackett, Jeffrey. *The Mark of the Werewolf*. New York: Bantam, 1990.

Sarrantonio, Al. *Moonbane*. New York: Bantam, 1991.

Scotch, Cheri. *The Werewolf's Kiss*. New York: Diamond, 1992.

———. *The Werewolf's Touch*. New York: Diamond, 1993.

Simak, Clifford D. *The Werewolf Principle*. New York: Putnam, 1967.

Smith, Clark Ashton. "A Prophecy of Monsters." In *Werewolf! A Chrestomathy of Lycanthropy*, ed. Bill Pronzini. New York: Arbor House, 1979.

Somtow, S. P. *Moon Dance*. New York: Tor, 1989.

Stevenson, Robert Louis. *The Strange Case of Dr. Jekyll and Mr. Hyde*. In *The Strange Case of Dr. Jekyll and Mr. Hyde and Other Stories*. New York: Barnes & Noble, 2004.

Strieber, Whitley. *The Wild*. New York: Tor, 1991.

———. *The Wolfen*. New York: Morrow, 1978.

Summers, Montague. *The Werewolf*. London: Kegan Paul, Trench, Trübner, 1933.

Swanwick, Michael. "A Midwinter's Tale." In *Tomorrow Bites*, ed. Greg Cox and T.K.F. Weiskopf. New York: Baen, 1995.

Tem, Melanie. *Wilding*. New York: Dell, 1992.

Tessier, Thomas. *The Nightwalker*. London: Millington, 1979.

Toombs, Jane. *Under the Shadows*. New York: Roc, 1992.

Whitten, Leslie H. *The Moon of the Wolf*. Garden City, NY: Doubleday, 1967.

Williams, Margery. *The Thing in the Woods*. London: Duckworth, 1913.

Williamson, Jack. *Darker Than You Think*. Reading, PA: Fantasy Press, 1948.

———. "Wolves of Darkness." In *Wolves of Darkness*. Royal Oak, MI: Haffner Press, 1999.

The Witch

by Bernadette Lynn Bosky

INTRODUCTION

The classic witch is easy to depict, but the icon in all its variety is difficult to
define. We imagine a woman, old and baleful, perhaps with a long, warty nose
and one clouded eye. She is accompanied by a familiar, a supernatural helper in
the shape of an animal, especially a black cat. She meets others in a coven,
usually a group of thirteen, to call upon the devil to work magic. This magic is
always harmful, usually involving herbs, recited spells, or a doll that symbol-
izes her victim. She often ends up getting burned at the stake.

   Even in the witch trials of medieval and early modern Europe, male as well as
female witches were condemned, and in England and its colonies, they were
not burned, but hanged or pressed to death. Both fiction and fact include
witches who are young and attractive, good as well as bad witches. Their
power can come from the devil or demons, from a benevolent goddess, from

their ancestors, from study of books to gain knowledge of the right words and herbs, from items with supernatural power, or from being qualitatively different, supernatural creatures themselves. From a modern perspective, the witch may be an innocent victim of superstition, a master of the powers of suggestion, or perhaps someone with abilities that should be studied by a parapsychologist. Moreover, those who fight witches—the "witch doctors"— often become confused and identified with what they fight, in part because their powers seem similar.

The approach of this chapter is like that of the DSM, the diagnostic manual used by psychiatrists, in which anyone with a number of the key symptoms qualifies, and no patient is expected to demonstrate them all. The main criterion, in fact or fiction, is of course that the person is called a witch. However, an old, unattractive woman with supernatural powers would still qualify, even without the label; so would a young child who works destructive magic. Satanic worship is so closely associated with the term "witch" that it alone could lead to accusations of witchcraft, as is having a familiar.

The themes witches represent—their psychological resonance, their social implications—vary as widely as the witches do. A witch, in one short story, may evoke disgust as the abject, reviled "other," while in another, she or he is the inciter of uncontrollable desire. One story of a witch may evoke our sympathy for an innocent victim of persecution, while another may chill us about how easy it is to be corrupted by power. Even the lessons of historical cases of witchcraft have changed as various eras reinterpreted them in the light of different values and beliefs. At the core, though, there still lies a figure who is like us because she or he is human (or seems to be), and also not like us because he or she is said to really have powers that most of us have fantasized about. As Stefan Dziemianowicz writes in his editorial introduction to *100 Wicked Little Witch Stories*, "It is this dual nature that makes witches so fascinating—and so frightening" (xiii).

ASPECTS OF THE WITCH

For most of history, in most of the world, the prevailing view of witches is that they represent some kind of threat. From Australian aboriginals "pointing the bone" at the person they want dead through the mysterious menace of the move *The Blair Witch Project* (1999), one of the defining characteristics of the witch is the capability of and inclination to do supernatural harm. For the study of the icon of the witch, it is irrelevant whether this harm—or any other actions of the witch—were real results (of supernatural power, of psychic ability, or of the powers of suggestion) or not. Hexing or cursing is often a charge directed by one person against another, but it also may be a power claimed by individuals themselves. In either case, it defines a major aspect of the figure of the witch.

Culturally and historically, although people may also believe in other kinds of witches, the belief in witches who cause harm to others is nearly universal. In many cultures, witches are said to have "the evil eye"—the power to harm by looking at someone, not necessarily deliberately. Roman mosaics, including one from the second century C.E., depict weapons or threatening animals drawing towards the eye, presumably a protective image. Other protections against the evil eye include inscribed amulets, cowrie shells, or a stone with a natural hole in it. Cuneiform tablets from ancient Assyria include instructions for curses; a curse "to dispose of someone who stands in the path of you and your desires" was collected by a folklorist in Essex, England, in 1971. Ancient Greek spells include one to stop the speech of a rival orator—the same effect that a male African American witch achieves for the lawyer protagonist of the movie *The Devil's Advocate* (1997), directed by Taylor Hackford and written by Jonathan Lemkin, based on the 1990 novel of the same name by Andrew Neiderman. Throughout the world, spells might be directed against individuals, their children, their domestic animals, and even their property. In medieval and early modern Europe and the English colonies in America, witches were said to curdle milk or cause cheese not to set.

Melanesia, Africa, and Asia have strong traditions of harmful magic. In Africa today, AIDS is often thought to be caused by witchcraft, and anthropologists are working with health-care professionals to help them explain prevention and treatment within that paradigm. In fact, evil witches are a vital part of African life. Curses are accepted as a factor in all aspects of life, from family relationships to politics. Individuals accused of witchcraft were burned to death by lynch mobs in South Africa as recently as 1995, and the Congolese Human Rights Observatory reported that forty people in that country were burned or buried alive as witches in 1996.

Fictional third-world malign witches have a strong and embarrassing place in colonial and post-colonial literature. The stories inspire genuine horror, but say more about European fears than about actual African magic. Edward Lucas White's "Lukundoo" (1927) concerns a curse by an African sorcerer with peculiar effects upon the British victim's body; "The Mark of the Beast" (*Pioneer*, July 12 and 14, 1890) by Rudyard Kipling, and "Pollock and the Porroh Man" (*New Budget*, May 23, 1895) by H. G. Wells, involve curses on Europeans by an Asian and an African black magician, respectively. In each case, the European has done something to deserve the curse—quite serious mockery of the statue of a god in the former story—and yet the reader's sympathy for the European victim is assumed. In "The Snake" by Dennis Wheatley, a relative latecomer (in *A Century of Horror Stories*, 1935), an African "witch doctor" kills a European to whom he owes money, by turning his staff into a living snake. More recent and authentically based fiction about African magic tends to concern protective magic, but Charles Saunders provides an interesting and well-written exception: "Ishigbi," a 1982 short story concerning twins, one evil and one good.

The ancient Celtic Druids were said to cast deadly spells, but they are primarily known for sacrificing people to give themselves magical power. A person was placed in a huge humanoid figure made of straw and wicker, and this was set alight, burning the sacrifice alive. Because of stories about this, the Druids represent wasteful evil in the later poems of William Blake (1757–1827). *The Wicker Man*, a 1973 movie for which Anthony Shaffer wrote the screenplay and then did a novelization, concerns a modern revival or continuation of this tradition in contemporary England. A police officer stumbles on the situation when he comes to an isolated island community to investigate a teenaged girl's disappearance. The movie creates sympathy for the locals, yet horror at what they do.

Of course, the height of European belief in evil witches, or at least official opposition to it, occurred in the sixteenth and seventeenth centuries. During that time, many people were put to death as witches—although more likely 60,000 to 100,000 instead of the 7 or even 11 million, some sources say. Another section of this chapter will examine the causes and effects of this persecution; here the subject is the image of the threatening witch that developed in those trials. Besides harming individuals, their families, and their property, these witches were seen as threats to the social order and an offense to God, because they had made a pact with the Devil to achieve their powers. Descriptions of the gatherings of such witches became more specific and more specifically anti-Christian as time went on, especially in Catholic countries, from general revels to a specific Black Mass complete with desecrated or parodic hosts (the latter made of a slice of black turnip, or a concoction of unsavory ingredients including menstrual blood). One could well say that the witch trials created Satanism, which later people actually began to practice.

Among the many weapons of the witch, two that stand out in folklore and in fiction are the book of evil spells and the doll, poppet, or manikin used to project curses on an individual. The book, sometimes called a grimoire, contained words of incantations, instructions for rituals and herbal spells, and the names of devils, demons, and spirits to summon. These books were frequently thought to have power in themselves, as well as powerful information. Perhaps the most well-known evil book is the *Necronomicon*, featured in the stories of H. P. Lovecraft (1890–1937) and others. Stories about evil books include "The Book," a terrifying and often reprinted piece by Margaret Irwin (1889–1967); "The Minister's Books" (*Atlantic Monthly*, August 1942), by Stephen Vincent Benét, is less frightening but equally well crafted. Fiction also uses references to historical books of magic, such as *The Key of Solomon*, probably written in the thirteenth century. Some of the fantasy stories by Manly Wade Wellman (1903–1986) feature *Pow-wows; or, Long Lost Friend*, a book in the Pennsylvania Dutch tradition of magic written by George Hohman and published in 1820.

Most systems of magic have had some form of curse made by identifying an image with a person and then damaging it. Ovid (43 B.C.E.–17 C.E.) mentions sticking needles into wax marked with the victim's name as a way to do harm; a plastic doll with pins stuck into it was found on a doorstep in Manchester, England, in the 1960s. Historically, the image need not be a doll, as the example from Ovid shows: a calf's or sheep's heart pierced with thorns was also common in England. However, it is the doll that predominates in fiction. "The Witch's Vengeance" (*International*, 1930), by William Seabrook (1886–1945), a world traveler who also wrote nonfiction about witchcraft, is just one example. Theodore Sturgeon's "A Way of Thinking" (*Amazing Stories*, October–November 1953) provides an interesting twist on the poppet, as do Robert Bloch's "Sweets to the Sweet" (*Weird Tales*, March 1947) and Fredric Brown's "The Geezenstacks" (1943).

One particularly horrible offense, held against witches in many cultures and some fiction, is the killing and even eating of children. Of course, this is the fear behind the fairy tale "Hansel and Gretel." A little-known work by Ulrich Molitor, from 1489, alleges that witches eat newborn children and presents a woodcut of their doing so at a table under a tree. The protagonist of "Hunger Gulag" (1995), by Martin Mundt, is a horrific witch who fights an angel in order to eat a newborn baby.

Moreover, in the United States today, many people believe in satanists who sexually abuse children, kill them, use their bodies in rituals, and sometimes even eat some of the flesh. Real satanists do exist—especially in members of groups such as the Temple of Set or the Church of Satan who do no physical harm but may cast harmful spells; rare but real murderous magical groups such as the one behind the murders in Matamoros, Mexico, in April 1989; and troubled individuals, often teens such as Sean Sellers, who combine interests in satanism and murder for personal reasons. In addition, due to uncritical publicity and the same process by which urban folklore stories spread, many people believe stories of a vast satanic conspiracy which have never actually been proven to exist. Some books, even by credible psychologists, support this view, but the lack of evidence, such as the bodies of those sacrificed, is telling.

Movies concerning malign witches are too common to more than suggest here. Sometimes, the witch has good reasons for vengeance, but terror at her destructive powers is still the driving force of the work, as in *Black Sunday* and *Witchcraft* (1964), directed by Don Sharp and written by Harry Spalding. Other works primarily concern ritual sacrifice, including *The Witches* (1966) and *The Seventh Victim* (1943), directed by Mark Robinson and written by DeWitt Bodeen and Charles O'Neal.

Fiction about the harmful witch also abounds, from fairy tales such as "Rapunzel" to novels such as *Darkfall* by Dean Koontz (1984) and *Furnace* by Muriel Gray (1997). Besides African and Asian witches, Sabbath-attending witches and Black Mass–attending Satanists, purely supernatural creatures, and spiteful women with poppets, stories may concern the American Halloween hag, such as "Yesterday's Witch" (*Witchcraft & Sorcery*, 1973) by Gahan Wilson. "The Cookie Lady" (*Fantasy Fiction*, June 1953), by Philip K. Dick, never uses the word "witch," but no one could mistake the old lady who offers sweets but delivers menace. In fact, there is a small subgenre of stories concerning people who do not practice magic per se but have the effects of witches, including the title character of "The Warlock" by Fritz Leiber (*Saint*, February 1960), who through some unknown psychic power brings insanity to those around him. Stephen King's novel *Thinner* (1984) features a curse by an aged, ugly gypsy witch, in this case a man.

At least since the 1920s, as will be shown, the image of the good witch has gained prominence, until in some ways it may be the dominant image of the witch in the early twenty-first century. However, the harmful witch persists, not only in fiction, but also in reality—at least culturally defined reality.

One particular kind of horror the baleful witch can present is that of a hidden organization, a secret conspiracy. For instance, the classic story "Young Goodman Brown," by Nathaniel Hawthorne (*New-England Magazine*, April 1835) presents the title character's horror and disillusionment when he discovers that the most respected people in his town and his innocent-seeming wife all meet regularly at the witches' sabbat. This fear is also well conveyed in *Conjure Wife* by Fritz Leiber, and in Algernon Blackwood's 1908 story "Ancient Sorceries." Elizabeth Hand's novels concerning the Benandanti and worshippers of an ancient goddess, discussed in the next section, have much of the same impact. People love to think of secret conspiracies, an idea that is frightening and yet at least implies some order in the world, some group-shaping events instead of everything happening chaotically. In addition, these stories, like those of Hermetic magic and other traditions, imply a hidden dimension of supernatural experience, available to us for good or ill, if we only knew.

WITCHES AS HEALERS AND PROTECTORS

Though it has gained strength since the 1940s, the idea of the good witch is far from recent. As long as people have feared harm from supernatural creatures and human practitioners of magic, they have turned to supernatural or human witches for protection from magic and help in other ways. For instance, protective amulets against sorcery were made in ancient Egypt. Moreover, when medical practice declined after the fall of the Roman empire, many people relied on spells and charms to stop bleeding, cure illness, and help women conceive. However, the terms "white witch" or "good witch" are more the product of writers than of the benign practitioners and those they aid.

In England, those who provide services have generally been called "cunning men" or "cunning women"; they also have been called "conjurers" and "pellars" (apparently from "spell"). This tradition survived into the nineteenth century, when it was studied by folklorists who first used the term "white witch." Most of the people in the English countryside and even city had some knowledge of charms or herbs, but the cunning folk were specialists who knew more, were considered to have more power, and even possessed magical books. People came to them, and paid them, to cure their own illnesses or those of their domestic animals, to recover lost or stolen property, to find treasure, to tell their fortunes, and to provide love charms. Also, if someone had been cursed by a witch, the cunning man or woman could identify the witch and remove the spell; they also offered preemptive protection against witchcraft. Lesser practitioners, sometimes called charmers, specialized in one skill, such as curing warts. James Murrell was a well-known cunning man.

Historian Carlo Ginzburg's studies *The Night Battles: Witchcraft and Agrarian Cults in the Sixteenth and Seventeenth Centuries* (originally published in 1966, English translation 1983) and *Ecstasies: Deciphering the Witches' Sabbath* (first appearance in English 1991) take evidence from rural European witch trials and other sources to show that some medieval and early modern beliefs about witches may have come from an age-old tradition of counter-witches called the Benandanti. They reported going out to battle witches; if the witches won, the crops would be bad, and if the Benandanti won, the crops would be good. Because they were so closely associated with witches, and because they themselves gathered either in person or in shamanistic trances, they came to be tried as witches, and stories of their gathering contributed to the idea of the witches' sabbat. Ginzburg's argument is interesting, and much better documented than Margaret Murray's similar attempts to find a real lineage for many of the characteristics of medieval and early modern witchcraft, but as with her work, time and future scholarship are needed before his work can be accepted as truth. Taken as the basis for fiction, the concepts are fascinating. Elizabeth Hand has written three novels in which the Benandanti is indeed a secret organization with stupendous magical powers, and the witches they oppose are also powerful worshippers of an ancient mother goddess: *Waking the Moon* (1995), *Black Light* (1999), and *Mortal Love* (2004). In these novels, both groups think they are in the right and both are ruthless and uncompromising.

The African "witch doctor" fills a similar role to the cunning folk and Ginzburg's Benandanti, although the term is often misrepresented, especially in fiction. Sometimes the "witch doctor" is used for a harmful witch, as in the 1966 movie *The Witches* and Dennis Wheatley's "The Snake," both discussed above. Other times, including as a common image in cartoons from the 1930s through the 1970s, the term is used for a witch who is a doctor, that is, a medical practitioner who works through ritual and magic (and wears an exotic mask but little else). Actually, like cunning folk and charmers, witch doctors do cure disease, but that is because culturally many diseases are seen as the creations of sorcery. The main business of the witch doctor is to thwart evil magic. In Zaire and Sudan, they detect and stop negative magic with herbs and amulets. There are two Zulu words for such practitioners: *inyanga* is one who specializes in herbs, while *sangoma* refers to someone who uses divination. In modern Kenya, one can buy magical help in getting pregnant or getting and keeping a lover.

This helpful figure does appear in some fiction, although it is still much less common than the evil, and stereotypical, African witch. Janet Berliner Gluckman and George Guthridge refer to the tradition in their 1995 story "Inyanga." Richard Matheson's story "From Shadowed Places" (*F&SF*, October 1960) uses "witch doctor" to refer to a Zulu native who delivered a curse, but primarily concerns a real witch doctor, a Black anthropologist who studied counter-magic among the Zulus. She emerges as a heroic figure, and the story is as much about many kinds of prejudice as it is about magic.

As universal as practitioners of counter-magic and healing-magic are, the image of the good witch received its biggest boost with the development of a view of witches now known to be false, crystallized and popularized by Dr. Margaret Murray (1863–1963), and the development of a real religion and magical system, variously known as witchcraft, paganism, neo-paganism, and Wicca. In her book *Witch-Cult in Western Europe* (1921) and others, Murray argued that the witches persecuted in the sixteenth and seventeenth centuries were actually adherents of a goddess-worshipping nature religion that extended back to prehistoric times. By now her work is completely refuted, but the idea had such undeniable appeal that Gerald Gardner and others actually created the religion, often claiming they worked from secretly transmitted traditions.

Wiccans use the term "witch" for both men and women; "warlock," which is usually understood to derive from the Old English *wærlog*, meaning deceiver or oath breaker, is considered an insult. Modern Wiccans and neo-pagans come in all ages, may be anywhere on the socio-economic ladder from professionals to manual laborers, and definitely inhabit the cities as well as the countryside. They tend to be pantheistic, worshipping one or more deities, usually a god and goddess, who represent nature. Some are materialists who view the energies raised during a magical ritual as psychic, or due to some other natural force we do not yet understand. Above all, Wiccans and neo-pagans are never the same as Satanists; some say that the Christian Satan is too modern an invention for them to care about. These modern witches avoid any curses or harmful magic; many believe in "the law of three," according to which any harm they do will come back to them threefold.

With the founding of Wicca, the witch gained a new—and more benevolent—presence in fiction as well. Many of the fiction writers are themselves Wiccans or neo-pagans. The novels of Diana Paxson, a priestess from San Francisco, include *Paradise Tree* (1987), the story of a witch who uses a Cabalistic brand of neo-paganism to defeat evil magic. Rosemary Edghill has written a series of novels featuring an occult detective, Karen Hightower, who goes by the name of Bast: *Speak Daggers to Her* (1994), *The Book of Moons* (1995), and *The Bowl of Night* (1996). The heroine is a Wiccan who lives in New York City, and the background of the books reflects real events and people in modern witchcraft, with added supernatural menaces. Neo-pagan and Wiccan protagonists appear in Benjamin Adams's "Alexa, Skyclad," Lillian Csernica's "On the Wings of the Wind," and other stories in the 1995 collection *100 Wicked Little Witch Stories*. On television, Willow, the witch in "Buffy, the Vampire Slayer" (1997–2003), shows Wiccan influence, as do the witches in "Charmed" (1998–2006), the opening episode of which is titled "Something Wicca This Way Comes."

Not all good witches in fiction are Wiccans or neo-pagans, of course. Besides Old Nathan, African witch doctors, and others who work against evil magic, many witches in children's literature are helpful. Before benevolent witches were very popular, *The Good American Witch* (1957), by Peggy Bacon, featured a witch who granted children's wishes; there was always a price, which the witch tried to alleviate as much as she could. *Strega Nona*, written and illustrated by Tomie De Paola (1975), concerns a generally nice witch, although the plot of the story concerns a "sorcerer's apprentice" in which someone she has hired to do chores uses her magic pasta-producing pot but cannot make it stop. Good witches also appear in the movies, including *Kiki's Delivery Service* and *Bedknobs and Broomsticks*.

WITCHES AS FIGURES OF POWER

Both the hexing, sacrificing witch and the healing, protective witch come from one root: the witch is essentially a being defined by supernatural power. Some modern practitioners of witchcraft view magic as a neutral force, often compared to electricity that can power a lifesaving respirator or an electric chair. An example of this from comic books is The Scarlet Witch: her ability to change reality is actually a mutant power, and it has been used for both good and evil during her career in Marvel Comics such as *The Uncanny X-Men*.

In literature, history, and modern practice, many witches have tended to take one side or the other: the witch who curses and the cunning man or woman who removes the curse, the modern Satanist and the modern Wiccan. Often, fictional works ensure conflict by having both a good witch and a bad witch, most famously Glinda the Good Witch and the Wicked Witch of the West in L. Frank Baum's Oz books (1900–1920) and the movie *The Wizard of Oz* (1939). Among all the good witches in the Harry Potter books, from Albus Dumbledore and Harry Potter himself on down, we find the evil witch, Lord Voldemort. The conflict between good and bad witches also shows up in *Bedknobs and Broomsticks*.

However, historically, the two uses of power probably coincided in the same witch's practice more than most people imagine. Apart from the idea of one magical source of energy behind all magic, which is relatively recent in human history, the same kinds of power often unavoidably can be used for good or ill. For instance, witches often have control over weather: the Druids

He looked at her, trying to comprehend it. It was almost impossible to take at one gulp the realization that in the mind of this trim modern creature he had known in completest intimacy, there was a whole great area he had never dreamed of, an area that was part and parcel of the dead practices he analyzed in books, an area that belonged to the Stone Age and never to him, an area plunged in darkness, acrouch with fear, blown by giant winds. He tried to picture Tansy muttering charms, stitching up flannel hands by candlelight, visiting graveyards and God knows what other places in search of ingredients. His imagination almost failed. and yet it had all been happening right under his nose.

—*Fritz Leiber,* Conjure Wife

were said to command thunder and lightning, and in many cultures witches can control the winds and weathers of the sea. Even those European witches who sold good winds to sailors—often bound in the knots tied in a cord—must have been tempted to produce bad weather on some occasions. Still more ambiguous is the knowledge of herbs and potions that witches from ancient Israel and ancient Greece to the present are reputed to have. Often, witches who worked as healers and midwives almost certainly also supplied abortions, and it may not be too large a step from there to eliminating a patron's unwanted husband.

The last example also shows that good versus bad may be a matter of perspective. Legend has it that the defeat of the Spanish Armada by storms in May 1588 was caused by patriotic English witches. Who is to say whether that was, or would have been, good magic or bad? Similarly, in the films *Burn, Witch, Burn* and *Conjure Wife*, each witch advances her husband's career at the expense of everyone else's husband, whether they do it by curses or by protective spells. The story "The Chestnut Beads" by Jane Roberts (*F&SF*, October 1957), also presents the moral ambiguity of power, in this case involving women made witches without their knowledge, in preparation for a later good. Showing that benevolence and malevolence can be a matter of perspective, some revisionist novels have improved the respectability of famous harmful witches by providing background regarding their motives. In Gregory Maguire's novel *Wicked: The Life and Times of the Wicked Witch of the West* (1995), the Wizard is an arrogant oppressor, especially of the sentient animals of Oz, and the witch is called wicked because she opposes him. *The Third Witch*, by Rebecca Reisert (2001), presents a background to Shakespeare's *Macbeth* (1605–1606) in which Macbeth killed the family of one of the witches, so their action is vengeance rather than pure spite.

African American traditions such as voodoo and mojo tend to be less polarized than European or even African traditions of the witch and counter-witch. In voodoo, despite its evil reputation in most fiction and movies, the gods, called Loa, curse and bless with equal willingness. "Mojo," a term with origins in Africa, originally meant a charm; in the United States, from slavery times through the early twentieth centuries, it meant a small bag, filled with herbs, written prayers or spells, magical ingredients such as cemetery dust, and hair or fingernail clippings to tie the magic to an individual. Also called the mojo hand, conjure bag, and nation sack, such bags were usually protective, but could be used in casting a harmful spell. References to these charms are common in blues songs, including those by Blind Willie McTell, the Memphis Jug Band, Lightnin' Hopkins, Blind Lemon Jefferson, and Robert Johnson (who, incidentally, was rumored to have sold his soul to the devil for his musical gifts). As the term became known through popular culture, it became more widely applied to magic, on the one hand, and sexual urges, especially male sexual urges, on the other. Nalo Hopkinson, who often uses African-Caribbean folklore in her own fiction, has edited an excellent anthology called *Mojo: Conjure Stories* (2003). Its major flaw may be that it does not include any fiction by the editor; for instance, the story "Greedy Choke Puppy" in her collection *Skin Folk* (2001) is a frightening story of malign magic.

Finally, the witch often represents female freedom and power, which is itself often the cause of ambivalent responses. This is, for instance, clearly the theme of *The Witches of Eastwick*. There, the empowerment is genuine, but not without cost—and in the novel, John Updike is quite clear about the petty and self-serving use of power as well as its positive social, psychological, and artistic potential. In moralizing stories of witchcraft, the sense of freedom and power is illusory, as in "The Nocturnal Meeting" (a chapter from *The Lancashire Witches*, 1849) by W. Harrison Ainsworth (1805–1882). However, it is difficult to look at many drawings of witches on the way to the Sabbath—on a pitchfork, a shovel, a hurdle, a goat, or, yes, a broomstick—and not imagine the joy of flight. The delirious delight is even conveyed within the generally negative and Satanic depiction of witches in the "Night on Bald Mountain" segment of the Disney movie *Fantasia* (1940). Nancy Holder's 1995 story "The Only Way to Fly" explicitly uses the flight of the witch as a metaphor for freedom from imposed limitations and joy in an active life.

LEGENDARY OR MYTHIC WITCHES

Given that belief in witches and witchcraft dates to the earliest periods of human history, it is not surprising that folklore and early literature have depicted a number of legendary or mythic witches whose powers range from the benevolent to the spectacularly evil. We present capsule biographies of thirteen such witches:

1. The traditional witch from folklore, known in Russian as Baba Yaga—in Polish, Czech, and Slovak as Baba Jaga, and in Serbian as Baba Roga—flies through the forest in a mortar, using the pestle to steer. Her house has giant

chicken legs and can turn away or come when told to; her fence is made of human bones with skulls on top. She is ugly, thin, and old: according to some versions, she ages a year for every question she is asked, and people always come to her to ask questions. She is a profoundly ambivalent figure. She undeniably is a fearsome hag who eats children. In other stories, she aids those who are pure of heart. In between are stories of a girl, Vasilisa, who outwits her and escapes.

Baba Yaga and her hut are popular subjects for pictorial art and music. Jane Yolen has written a children's book about her, *The Flying Witch*, with illustrations by Vladimir Vagin (2003). The Bone Witch, in R. Garcia y Robertson's *Firebird* (2006)—a fixup novel made from previously published novellas and novelettes—is based on Baba Yaga. Baba Yaga has also gotten interesting treatments in comic books, including Neil Gaiman's *Sandman* and Bill Willingham's *Fables*. A useful recent study is *Baba Yaga: The Ambiguous Mother and Witch of the Russian Folktale*, by Andreas Johns (2004).

2. The Witch of Endor appears in the Hebrew Bible as a necromancer who calls up the dead prophet Samuel. King Saul of Israel, in disguise, goes to the witch for this service; the prophet's ghost does not give Saul the advice he wants but predicts Saul's downfall. The story appears in 1 Samuel, 28:4–25. Medieval theologians decided that the spirit was not the ghost of Samuel but a demon or imp taking Samuel's form. In Theodore Sturgeon's short story "The Hag Seleen" (*Unknown*, December 1942), a clever modern-day tale of evil magic, the ending turns upon a reference to the Witch of Endor. In the television series "Bewitched," Samantha's mother is named Endora.

3. The Thessalian witches are so named because they lived in Thessaly, a part of Northern Greece bordering Macedonia, that was known in classical times as a hotbed of sorcery and black magic. The devoted and enthusiastic servants of the goddess Hecate, the witches used herbs both to kill and to cast love spells and were able to shape-shift into birds or other animals. They were also the first witches said to "draw down the moon"—that is, use lunar forces magically.

In Neil Gaiman's *Sandman* comics, the story arc "A Game of You" (1991–1992) introduces Thessaly, the last of the Thessalian witches, who appears to be an innocuous, bespectacled young woman. In that story, Thessaly shows that for her, "drawing down the moon" is no metaphor or psychic experience: doing so, even though she puts it back, creates a storm and tsunami that ravages New York City. Thessaly became a popular character and has starred in two spin-off miniseries; hers is always a harsh, gritty magic, atavistic and dangerous.

4. Circe, in Homer's *Odyssey* (c. eighth century B.C.E.), is the child of the Titan Helios and an Oceanid (a type of nymph) named Perse; she is a sorceress, highly skilled in the use of drugs and potions. Her home, a stone mansion in the clearing of a dense wood, is surrounded by people she turned into lions and wolves. When she serves a feast to Odysseus's crew, the potion in the food turns the men into pigs. Odysseus, advised by Hermes, comes to her

protected by the herb moly and makes her turn the men back. He and his crew spend a year with her, and she falls in love with Odysseus.

Circe has appeared in works from Nathaniel Hawthorne's *Tanglewood Tales* (1853) to *Wonder Woman* comic books; she has inspired characters from Acrasia in Edmund Spenser's *The Faerie Queene* (1593) to the Marvel Comics character Sersi. Circe appears in the short story "Justice," by Elizabeth Hand (first published 1993). Of course, she also appears in any retelling of the *Odyssey*, from James Joyce's *Ulysses* (1922) to David Drake's science fiction novel *Cross the Stars* (1984).

5. Medea, the daughter of the king of Colchis, is the niece of Circe and is often described as a priestess of Hecate, a many-faceted goddess who governs sorcery. In the story of Jason and the Argonauts, Medea magically helps Jason with the tasks her father gives him: for instance, the dragon that guards the golden fleece is put to sleep with narcotic herbs. She is also an expert with poisons and can foretell the future. Medea falls in love with Jason and sails away with him. However, in Corinth, Jason leaves Medea for the king's daughter, Glauce; Medea gives Glauce a cursed dress that burns her to death. In the play *Medea* by Euripides (431 B.C.E.), Medea kills her own children by Jason for vengeance on their father.

   Euripides's play has inspired many newer versions, including Robinson Jeffers's *Medea* (1946) and *By the Bog of Cats* (1998), by Marina Carr, which adapts the action to an Irish setting. Austrian poet-playwright Franz Grillparzer tells the entire story in his three plays, *The Host* (1818), *The Argonauts* (1819), and *Medea* (1820). The Medea of Pier Paolo Passolini's disturbing film by that name (1970) is definitely a witch.

6. Erichtho is a famous Thessalian witch who appears in *Pharsalia*, a Roman epic poem by Lucan (c. 61 C.E.). There, Erichtho is said to have raised a spirit for Pompey the Great's son, Sextus Pompeius. Her incantation calls upon Hermes, Charon, Hecate, Proserpina, and Chaos. She is also mentioned as a necromancer in Dante's *Inferno* (1308–1321).

7. Morgan Le Fay, also called Morgaine or Morgana, is a powerful sorceress in the legends of King Arthur. She is half-sister to Arthur and often his nemesis. She is also a healer as well as a shape-shifter, but grows more troublesome as the story developed within the Christian tradition. In *The Mists of Avalon* (1982), by Marion Zimmer Bradley, Morgaine is the protagonist, with second sight and other magical abilities. A goddess worshipper, she at first fights against the coming of Christianity and then comes to terms with it. She is also a central character in Gene Wolfe's novel *Castleview* (1990). In some modern versions of the story, such as John Boorman's film *Excalibur* (1981), she seduces Arthur and gives birth to his adversary Mordred.

8. Aradia began as fiction but has influenced Wiccan practice. In the novel *Aradia; or, The Gospel of the Witches* (1899), by Charles Leland, she is the daughter of the goddess Diana and the fallen angel Lucifer, and she comes to Earth to teach witchcraft. Leland claimed that his work was based on a hidden historical tradition from Tuscany; this is probably not true, although one modern witch, Raven Grimassi, claims evidence that Aradia was the

name of a goddess and a fourteenth-century Italian witch (*strega*). Certainly, a speech by Aradia in the first chapter of the book is sometimes used as an important piece of Wiccan ritual called The Charge of the Goddess.

9. Gilles de Rais (1404–1440), after a distinguished military career and time as a national hero, retired to his estate; there he tortured, raped, and killed as many as 200 young boys (higher estimates, up to 600, are inaccurate). He was tried and executed by hanging. The charges included heresy; he was accused of performing the Black Mass; he has a significant reputation in folklore as a practitioner of black magic, with the murders also serving as sacrifices. In *The Witch-Cult in Western Europe* (1921), Margaret Murray argues that he was the practitioner of a surviving pre-Christian cult that worshipped Diana. While this is almost certainly not true, it does indicate and did shape his image as a witch. In *Là-Bas* (1891), a decadent novel of sorcery and sanctity by J.-K. Huysmans, the protagonist is researching a biography of Gilles de Rais. In one videogame he appears as a vampire, but there is a niche for fantasy fiction that treats him as a witch.

10. Elizabeth Bathory (1560–1614), in modern folklore now thought of as a vampire because she killed young women for their blood, was at the time thought to be, and may have thought of herself as, a witch. A Hungarian countess, she certainly was, like Gilles de Rais, a serial killer of staggering proportions—such that even royalty could not get away with. She was caught in torture and murder; she was never tried, but kept isolated in her own rooms until she died. She was rumored to be influenced by a local Satanic witch, Anna Darvula, who died before Bathory was stopped; under torture, others confessed to practicing witchcraft alongside Bathory. One letter to her husband mentions her learning a fatal spell. She has inspired many works, predominately factual studies or works in which she is a vampire. The fantasy novel *This Rough Magic* (2003), by Mercedes Lackey, Eric Flint, and Dave Freer, does depict Bathory's bloodletting as a kind of magic.

11. Catherine Deshayes, known as La Voisin, was burned alive as a poisoner and witch in 1680. The French court of Louis XIV was tolerant of witchcraft, and there was even a fad for love potions, séances, fortune-telling, and other magic—up to a point. A scandal began over three Black Masses arranged by La Voisin and conducted by an infamous priest named Guiborg; the altar was the naked body of the Marquise de Montespan, the king's mistress, who sought magical help in keeping his attention. The mass invoked Satan and his demons and reputedly included the sacrifice of children. La Voisin also worked as a midwife and probably engineered abortions, so one child, said to be "obviously premature," may well have been already dead. No charges were brought against Madame de Montespan.

12. James Murrell practiced as a cunning man in Hadleigh, England, from 1810 until his death in 1860. He made a living curing warts, finding lost or stolen property, treating both human and animal illnesses, and breaking spells by evil witches. He used books, herbs, prayers, and amulets in his work. Most educated people disliked him but left him alone, while the common people admired him and became his customers. One fictional counterpart of

Murrell is Old Nathan, the eponymous protagonist in a collection of stories by David Drake (1991). Like Cunning Murrell, Old Nathan bills himself as "the devil's master." Old Nathan can also talk to animals, and he generally prefers their company to that of human beings.

13. Marie Laveau, "the Witch Queen of New Orleans," was born in the 1790s, a "free person of color." She married and is also known as the Widow Paris. She learned her craft from a "voodoo doctor"; by 1830 she was known as a voodoo queen, but she soon became *the* voodoo queen. She performed rituals on the banks of Bayou St. John on June 23, St. John's Eve, and sold charms or hexes to the wealthy. Her position was also built on a strong network of informants, whose information made her respected and feared. She was also a devout Catholic and saw no conflict between that and voodoo. People still visit her tomb in New Orleans and leave flowers and other tokens. Marie Laveau appears in the novel *Voodoo Dreams*, by Jewell P. Rhodes (1993) and in Francine Prose's well-regarded *Marie Laveau* (1977). She is the subject of the 1971 song by the group Redbone, "The Witch Queen of New Orleans." She also appears in Neil Gaiman's novel *American Gods* (2001).

WITCH HUNTS AND THE PERSECUTED WITCH

Long before the founding of Wicca and the rise of the image of the good witch in fiction and popular culture—separate though sometimes related trends—fiction presented witches, or those accused as witches, in a positive light compared to their persecutors.

The witch hunts are definitely shameful moments in history; earlier historians of the early modern European witch hunts tended to emphasize the condemnable superstition, while more recent historians have explored the psychological and social scapegoating. Generally, historians now agree that the European witch hunt began in the Alps and other mountain regions, and that they had less to do with any indigenous pagan or magical tradition than with the then-recent extermination of heretics such as the Cathars. In various places, lepers, heretics, Jews, and witches would be killed during or immediately after times of misfortune such as famine and pestilence. Since suspects were tortured, and punishment might be lessened if the accused confessed and named other witches, the number of witches naturally increased like a snowball rolling downhill.

Even at that time, many people objected to the witch trials and found the methods of the witch finders unsound. In 1584, Reginald Scot's *The Discoverie of Witchcraft* argued that witchcraft was not supernatural, but trickery and perhaps hysteria. Many officials protested against the Salem witch trials at that time, and less than twenty years later the colony officially restored the rights of the accused, declared them not guilty, and gave 600 pounds to their heirs in restitution.

Salem, a Year of Witch Fever

Salem, Massachusetts, was founded in 1629; in 1641, witchcraft became a crime punishable by death under English law. Other witch trials had been held in the new world, including that of Anne Glover in Boston, executed in 1688. However, the events in Salem and surrounding towns, resulting in twenty executions, took place within one year, 1692. Approximately 150 people were imprisoned, of whom seventeen died in custody; the last accused were pardoned and released from prison in May 1693.

The following is a chronology of the major events of the Salem witch panic:

Late January: Abigail Williams, age eleven, and Elizabeth Parris, age nine, begin acting strangely, including seizures, trances, and screaming out blasphemies. Soon other Salem children show similar symptoms.

Mid-February: The girls' doctor states that witchcraft may be causing their behavior.

Late February: Elizabeth identifies Tituba, the Parrises' Carib slave, as a witch; the girls also name Sarah Good and Sarah Osborne.

March 1: Tituba confesses to witchcraft.

March 11: Anne Putnam and other girls also say they are victims of witchcraft.

March 12–28: Martha Cory, Rebecca Nurse, and Elizabeth Proctor are accused of witchcraft. Magistrates Hathorne and Corwin begin examination of accused witches.

April 3: After defending Rebecca Nurse, her sister Sarah Cloyce is accused of witchcraft.

Early April: Mary Warren, the Proctors' servant, admits to lying when accusing Elizabeth Proctor.

April 11: Elizabeth Proctor's husband, John, who protested his wife's situation, is the first man accused of witchcraft.

April 13: Giles Cory is accused.

April 19: Mary Warren is examined by the magistrates; she recants her statement and rejoins the "afflicted." Deliverance Hobbs confesses to practicing witchcraft.

April 22: Hathorne and Corwin examine Mary Easty, also a sister and defender of Rebecca Nurse, and eight others, three men and five women.

April 30: Former Salem minister George Burroughs is accused of witchcraft.

May 4–7: Burroughs is arrested in Maine, imprisoned back in Salem.

May 10: Sarah Osborne dies in prison.

May 18: Mary Easty is released from prison, then re-arrested. Roger Toothaker is arrested for witchcraft.

May 27: Sir William Phipps, new governor of the colony, orders a Court of Oyer and Terminer (hearing and deciding), appointing seven men, including John Hathorne, as judges.

June 2: Bridget Bishop is tried and convicted of witchcraft.

June 10: Bishop is hanged at Gallows Hill.

June 16: Roger Toothaker dies in prison.

July 19: Rebecca Nurse, Susanna Martin, Elizabeth Howe, Sarah Good, and Sarah Wildes are hanged at Gallows Hill.

August 6: Elizabeth Proctor is tried and condemned; her hanging is delayed because she is pregnant.

August 19: George Jacobs Sr., Martha Carrier, George Burroughs, John Proctor, and John Willard are hanged at Gallows Hill.

September 9: Dorcas Hoar is tried and found guilty. She escapes execution by confessing to witchcraft.

September 19: Giles Cory is pressed to death for refusing to enter a plea and undergo a trial for witchcraft. He takes two days to die.

September 22: Martha Cory, Margaret Scott, Mary Easty, Alice Parker, Ann Pudeator, Wilmott Redd, Samuel Wardell, and Mary Parker are hanged.

October 29: Sir William Phipps dissolves the Court of Oyer and Terminer; he stops arrests and releases many accused witches from prison.

November 25: The General Court of the Colony creates the Superior Court to try the remaining witchcraft cases. None will be convicted.

From http://www.salemweb.com/memorial/ and http://www.law.umkc.edu/ faculty/projects/trials/salem/ASAL_CH.HTM

Thus, it is not surprising that a significant body of fiction treats the witch finders as the real villains. Many of these works are not supernatural, but historical novels. *The Amber Witch* by Wilhelm Meinhold, which first appeared in an English translation in 1844, concerns an innocent girl tried as a witch and saved just in time; a detailed historical novel, it has sometimes been taken as fact. Elizabeth George's *The Witch of Blackbird Pond*, a popular and Newbery Award winning book from 1958, for young adult readers, presents a fictional protagonist, teenage Kit Taylor, who is accused of being a witch in the Connecticut Colony in 1867. "The Witch-Baiter," a story by R. Anthony (pen name for Richard A. Muttkowski) first published in *Weird Tales* (December 1927), has no supernatural component but is a horror story, concerning vengeance enacted upon a witch-finder named Mynheer van Ragevoort. Of course, the most famous work that presents a sympathetic picture of those who were tried and condemned as witches is Arthur Miller's play *The Crucible* (1953). Miller presents the hysteria of the Salem witch hunts as a tragedy in its own right and a metaphor for the persecution of suspected communists in his own time.

One of the most famous witch hunters was Englishman Matthew Hopkins, who declared himself, or was declared by the Puritan Parliament, "Witch-finder Generall." He worked from 1644 to 1646, primarily in Suffolk, Essex, and East Anglia; he is also known for writing *The Discovery of Witches*. Torture was technically illegal, but he extracted confessions by psychological intimidation, sleep deprivation, and "swimming"—testing to see if the water would reject the witch, which often amounted to partial if not complete drowning. Ronald Bassett's 1966 novel *Witch-Finder General*, a historical novel about Hopkins, was made into the 1968 movie, *Witchfinder General*, directed by Michael Reeves, with a script by Tom Baker. Neither has any supernatural element. The film, starring Vincent Price, is also called *The Conqueror Worm*, although it has little connection to Poe's poem by that name, artificially referenced to link the film to a popular series of movies based on Poe's stories and starring Price. Julie Hearn's 2005 novel *The Merrybegot*, which blends history and fantasy, includes a negative portrait of Matthew Hopkins and a positive one of a young witch, conceived on the morning of May 1, which is Beltane, a traditional Gaelic holiday also celebrated by Wiccans.

The most well-known witch trial in England, referred to as that of the Pendle Witches or Lancashire Witches, has also inspired historical fiction, though it is not as consistently sympathetic to the accused. In 1612, ten men and women were hanged for alleged murder by witchcraft; one woman, found guilty of witchcraft but not murder, was sentenced to one year in prison, and another woman died before her trial. The accused, especially Alizon Device, confessed and incriminated each other with lavish tales of meeting the devil and having a familiar spirit in the shape of a black dog. The reasons for the confessions are still debated, explanations including schizophrenia and hallucinations because of mushrooms or ergot; some writers have noted the similarities to impossible confessions of child abuse, exposed in articles such as Lawrence Wright's "Remembering Satan," published in the *New Yorker* in 1993.

Harrison Ainsworth's 1849 novel *The Lancashire Witches* captures the historical setting, but does include supernatural elements. Alizon Device is innocent and good, but the other witches are evil and do much damage before they are executed—inaccurately, by being burned alive. Robert Neill's *Mist over Pendle* (1951) introduces a fictional character, and presents the witches as innocent dupes of a criminal mastermind, some of them likeable but others, such as Agnes Nutter, personally unpleasant; this novel has no supernatural elements. Incidentally, most modern readers are probably delighted by the idea of a witch named Nutter, and that Lancashire witch is likely the inspiration for the name in Neil Gaiman and Terry Pratchett's funny yet profound story of the relationship between an angel and a devil on the eve of the End Times depicted in St. John's Apocalypse, *Good Omens: The Nice and Accurate Prophecies of Agnes Nutter, Witch* (1990).

Because of the nature of the charges against the witches, many supernatural stories treat the witch as a negative figure who deserved to be executed, such as the movie *Black Sunday*. The 1993 Disney film *Hocus Pocus*, directed by Kenny Ortega and written by David Kirschner, Mark Garris, and Neil Cuthbert, is interestingly ambivalent. The three witches, executed in 1693, return from the grave, intending to live forever by stealing the souls of children; when they are foiled by teenagers, one turns to stone and two explode into dust. However, the witches are played with humor by Bette Midler, Sarah Jessica Parker, and Kathy Najimy, and many scenes evoke some audience sympathy. Another interestingly double-edged work is "Young Goodwife Doten" (1995), by Robert M. Price. The protagonist cannot conceive, and so she visits the local witch, Goody Watkins, who is in danger from the zealous witch hunter, Reverend Hoadley. The reader is fully set up to expect a standard post–Margaret Murray, pro-Wiccan story of the persecuted wise woman—and then Goody Watkins arranges to have Goodwife Doten impregnated by the devil. The child is born with wings and a tail, and Goody Watkins enjoys watching Goodwife Doten burned at the stake. That error—since witches in the English colonies in North America were hanged or pressed to death—is probably another play on the conventions of stories about witches.

Still, in general the author's sympathy, and the readers', is with the persecuted witch. Following the theory of Margaret Murray and others that medieval and early modern European witchcraft was a survival of pagan polytheism, works such as Marion Zimmer Bradley's *The Mists of Avalon* (1982) present early witches as oppressed, if not in personal terms, because their religion is threatened by Christianity. Just as Lucifer became a proud figure of rebellion for some Romantics and post-Romantics, the witch has become a symbol for those persecuted by the envious, the cruel, and those who take advantage of political or religious power over others. In Elise Matthesen's poem "Nettie's Garden" (1995), a witch's talisman gives a survivor of family violence, the toughness to survive. The persecuted witch, whether triumphing over circumstances or doomed by them, will likely become an even more common figure in future writing.

Familiars

One of the characteristics of the classic witch is her or his association with a helping spirit, often in the shape of an animal, called a familiar. The spirit is usually demonic and aids in magic; the witch may feed it blood or it may nurse from a supernumerary teat the witch possesses. Historically, familiars were reported more commonly in early modern English witch trials than on the continent. In fiction, familiars may be the witch's servant or master—or comic relief. Keeping a familiar spirit is prohibited in the Book of Leviticus (20:27) and is punishable by death.

Discovery of Witches (1647), by Matthew Hopkins of Essex, England, abounds in familiars he discovered as "witchfinder general." Elisabeth Clarke was said to be observed with familiars in the shape of a kitten, two dogs, a rabbit, a toad, and a polecat. A famous illustration shows familiars named by a witch who had been kept awake for four days: Holt, who looked like "a white kittling"; Jarmara, "a fat spaniel without any legs at all"; Vinegar Tom, "a long-legg'd Greyhound, with an head like an Ox"; Sack and Sugar, "a black Rabbit"; and Newes, "a Polecat." She also mentioned familiars named "Ilemauzer, Pyewacket, Pecke in the Crown, and Griezzel Greedigutt." Another historical witch, Jane Wallis of Huntingtonshire, England, confessed that the devil, appearing as the "Black Man," gave her three imps, one called Greedy Gut. Apparently feeding familiars could be a burden.

An illustration of Joan Prentis of the Chelmsford witches, executed in England in 1589, shows frog or toad familiars and two odd creatures, with doglike bodies and earless, toad-like heads, named Jacke and Gill.

Familiars abound in supernatural literature. Most recently, they figure extensively in the Harry Potter series written by J. K. Rowling: *Harry Potter and the Philosopher's Stone* (1997; U.S. ed. as *Harry Potter and the Sorcerer's Stone*, 1998), *Harry Potter and the Chamber of Secrets* (1998), *Harry Potter and the Prisoner of Azkaban* (1999), *Harry Potter and the Goblet of Fire* (2000), *Harry Potter and the Order of the Phoenix* (2003), and *Harry Potter and the Half-Blood Prince* (2005) as of this writing. Harry's familiar is an owl named Hedwig, Hermoine Granger has a cat named Crookshanks, and Ron Weasley had Scabbers, a rat; Professor Dumbledore's familiar is a phoenix, while the evil Voldemort's is a snake. Other familiars include other cats and owls and at least one toad. These familiars do not seem to talk, and most of them primarily help with errands such as sending and bringing mail.

Much of His Dark Materials series by Philip Pullman—*Northern Lights* (1995; retitled *The Golden Compass* in the United States), *The Subtle Knife* (1997), *The Amber Spyglass* (2000)—takes place in an alternate world in which all human beings (though not sentient animals) have familiars, called daemons. These creatures constantly accompany their companions, and it is taboo to touch someone else's. The familiars shape-shift until the companions reach adulthood, when they adopt one shape that reflects (and perhaps influences) their companions' natures. The familiar of the protagonist, Lyra, is named Pantalaimon. The daemons of witches have the ability to range further than other daemons; that of the witch Serafina Pekkala's is Kaisa, a large gray goose.

WITCHES, SEX, AND DEATH

Whether for good or ill, witches are traditionally deeply involved with that most basic of human functions, sex. Witches in every culture provide love spells; many also can cause or prevent erections, facilitate fertility, or give abortions. For instance, in fourteenth-century England, witches were said to create impotence by tying knots in a thread, and finding such a thread was legal ground for the husband to dissolve the marriage. The mandrake root, used for spells in Europe from the Roman empire to early modern times, was selected in part because it resembles either the male genitals or, if growing in two parts, female legs and hips. La Voisin foretold the future and performed other services, but it was saying the Black Mass as part of a love spell against King Louis XVI—and using his mistress as the naked altar—that caused her downfall.

In medieval and early modern Europe, especially, the witch herself, or himself, was a sexual creature. Sometimes this is seen as repellent: the witch may be ugly and old, copulating with the devil, who often appears as an animal and whose penis is often described as cold and painful. Sometimes it is viewed with a lurid fascination, especially stories of male and female witches in one big orgy after dancing at their sabbats. The range in art is quite striking, from the hags surrounding a black goat in Francisco Goya's painting "The Witches' Sabbath" (1821) to a quite attractive young witch (though overweight by today's standards) receiving the devil's tongue in her genitals, depicted in a striking pen-and-ink drawing by Hans Baldung in 1515. Many drawings and engravings show both old and young witches, with varying degrees of sexual allure.

Unsurprisingly, fiction and movies often depict the lustful witch. *Haxan*, a Flemish film from 1922, written and directed by Benjamin Christensen, is presented as a documentary on the history of witchcraft. Nikolas Schreck writes in *The Satanic Screen*, "Christensen didn't shy away from recreating the erotic fantasies that swirled around visions of the Devil's Sabbath. His writhing witches display more exposed flesh than was seen in the Satanic cinema for decades to come" (34). Less explicit but even more lurid, the classic Gothic novel by Matthew Gregory Lewis, *The Monk* (1796), features the temptation and degradation of the title character, Ambrosio, by his pupil Matilda, who embodies the morbid fascination of the sexual witch. Similarly, Valery Briussof's novel *The Fiery Angel* (translated into English in 1930) concerns a hero who is seduced by a witch and becomes involved in the sabbat. More recently, John Brunner's "All the Devils in Hell" (*Science-Fantasy*, 1960) is the story of a man tempted by a totally desirable and totally selfish witch and saved by his love for a plain but loving woman who sees through the witch. Such an idea sounds trite, but Brunner's story succeeds, thanks to excellent characterization, suspense as to whether the woman really has supernatural power or not, and the descriptions of sexual tension.

Stories of voodoo women and other exotic witches—that is, Hispanic or African American rather than European-American—often have an erotic charge. "Cerimarie," by Arthur J. Burks, is a fine example, first published as "Voodoo" under the pen name Estil Critche in *Weird Tales* (December 1924). For a contemporary reader of this tale about Haitian voodoo, it may be difficult to decide whether the lecherous descriptions or the racism is more unnerving. However, the lecherous appeal of the witch of color has by no means died out. Todd Grimson's novel *Brand-New Cherry Flavor* (1996), set in Hollywood, features the seduction of the heroine by Boro, a South American shaman complete with jaguar skin. The novel combines humor and horror, and manages to exploit the exoticism without the problems of Burks's piece. *Witch-Light* (1996), by Nancy Holder and Melanie Tem, is another erotic novel, this one featuring a WASP woman and a dark and handsome *brujo* (male witch); it takes place in New Mexico.

Small presses and collections of erotic fiction provide plentiful stories about the lustful witch, although they are still vastly outnumbered by erotica and pornography about vampires. In fact, the prevalence of the helpful witch as a cultural image may sometimes be turning writers about sexual compulsion and fascination into vampires instead of witches, male or female. Still, Satanic witches do appear in numerous hard-core pornographic novels, including *A Girl Possessed* (1973) by Richard E. Geis under the pen name Peggy Swenson.

This may be the most appropriate place to mention the almost universal associations of witches with animals. As seen in the character of Circe, the transformation of people into animals is deeply connected to the witch's power over, and association with, our own animal nature. Fiction includes many stories of witches changing people into animals, including John Collier's "The Lady on the Grey" (*New Yorker*, June 16, 1951). Similarly, the witch's ability to transform herself into an animal, and her association with familiar spirits in the shape of animals, may speak of her own animal nature. In medieval and early modern Europe, the witch sometimes turned into a cat, but it could also be a rabbit or dog. At least as far in the past as ancient Rome, and in countries around the world, witchcraft is also connected to the traditions of shape-shifters, from werewolves to leopard people. One excellent story concerning witches who turn into cats is "Ancient Sorceries" (1908) by Algernon Blackwood. Witches are also believed to be able to project their souls into natural animals, such as rats or birds, in order to travel or accomplish magic without revealing their human identities.

As universal a human concern as sex, death is also closely associated with the witch. In folk belief and legend, witches can both curse the living to death and raise the dead. In fact most cultures have some version of necromancy, in which witches gain information, and sometimes power, by the evocation of departed souls. This was the offense of the biblical Witch of Endor; in Renaissance and early modern Europe, necromancy was primarily practiced by sorcerers, men like John Dee (1527–1608/09).

Nickolai Gogol's story "The Viy" generally takes a satiric tone but achieves genuine scares with its presentation of a witch who returns from the dead as a scholar must stay and read prayers for her. In some traditions witches are said to live in graveyards; bones or graveyard dirt are used in many spells, from those of the ancient Thessalian witches to the mojo bag, discussed earlier, and the *gris-gris*, another African or African American charm. All this is apart from the idea that witches can be immortal, either in their own bodies or by possessing the bodies of others, which is quite common in fiction and often implied or explicit in folklore.

WITCHES AND THE TRIPLE GODDESS

Along with Margaret Murray, the poet, novelist, and scholar Robert Graves presented an idea that, while historically unjustifiable, shaped our contemporary concept of the witch and Wiccan and neo-pagan practice. In the case of *The White Goddess: A Historical Grammar of Poetic Myth* (1948, revised 1966), the idea was only part fabrication; the rest was overgeneralization. Also, he did not exactly present his concept as historical fact, as shown by the ambivalent subtitle. Graves proposed a European goddess whose worship dominated antiquity and survived in folklore and literature, a triple goddess identified with love, birth, and death, represented by the three forms of maiden, mother, and crone.

Certainly, there is a common association of witches with the number three, or three aspects. Hecate was often depicted in classical times as having three aspects, a characteristic that William Blake conveys in his 1795 painting of that goddess of sorcery. The three witches in *Macbeth* are called the weird sisters, linking them to the three fates, also female and often cruel. Yet one could also associate witches with the number four, for the four seasons and the associated celebrations of Beltane, Midsummer, Samhain, and Yule; or two, for the sun and the moon, night and day, or male and female. Indeed, some Wiccans and neo-pagans do base their craft more on those numbers than on the number three.

Still, Graves and his triple goddess have influenced both fiction and Wiccan or neo-pagan practice. She shows up in Susan M. Schwartz's introduction to the anthology *Hecate's Cauldron* (1982) and some of its stories (all original to the collection), such as C. J. Cherryh's "Willow" and Jayge Carr's "Reunion."

NEW TYPES OF WITCHES

The Domestic Witch

For eight years, ending in 1972, the most popular image of the witch in America was blonde, perky Samantha Stevens in the television show "Bewitched." Witches, on the show, were inherently different creatures, immortal or at least living for centuries, possessing vast powers, but looking like human beings and living among us. Instead of evoking the fear of a conspiracy, however, this is the setup for domestic comedy: Samantha is basically good, though mischievous and tempted to use magic on people who are unkind or pretentious. Most of all, the situation is played as domestic comedy. Samantha meets and falls in love with a mortal man, Darren, and agrees to subdue her magic to marry him. He is an up-and-coming man in advertising, a situation that creates constant worry that her magic might compromise his image at work.

This image of a domestic witch was not original to "Bewitched." Many critics have observed the similarity to the 1958 movie *Bell, Book and Candle*. Doubtless that was an influence on the TV series, including the link between witches and a counterculture lifestyle—in the movie, the setting in bohemian Greenwich Village, and in the television show, Samantha's cousin Serena, a Hollywoodish combination of early sixties mod, late-sixties hippie, and early seventies liberated partier.

However, the more important predecessor to *Bewitched* was a 1942 movie, *I Married a Witch*, directed by René Clair. One of the writers of the film was Thorne Smith, known for his humorous yet humanly touching supernatural stories. *I Married a Witch* provides a hard-to-beat "meet cute" (a term film critic Roger Ebert coined for first encounters in movies that lead to romance but are initially embarrassing or filled with tension). Jennifer is a seventeenth-century witch who returns to life to take revenge on her persecutor, a politician named Wallace Woodey. As the title indicates, they fall in love and marry.

The domestic witch provides an ironic twist to some older aspects of the witch while continuing others. After all, finding out that one's wife is a witch (albeit probably confessed under torture) was a historical actuality. More than that, as we have seen, this discovery is central to stories such as Hawthorne's "Young Goodman Brown" and the novel *Conjure Wife* by Fritz Leiber. The twist is that such discovery becomes, with the movies and television show, less a source of fear and more a source of confusion, chagrin, and unpleasant social consequences. In fact, in later seasons of "Bewitched," conflict came less from Darren's reaction to Samantha's magic and more from Samantha's mother—Endora, an archetypally unaccepting mother-in-law—and other troublesome relatives.

Furthermore, the traditional evil witch, though often associated with lust, seems incompatible with love. In fact, in "The Final Ingredient" by Jack Sharkey (*F&SF*, August 1960), a would-be witch discovers that no magic can be cast when the witch has any love in her heart—not even a love spell. The domestic witch contradicts this idea, but it also subtly continues it. The opposition between power and love is seen in *Bell, Book and Candle*, in which Gillian must give up her powers in order to marry; in "Bewitched," Samantha promises not to use her powers in order to please her husband.

The domestic witch is definitely the product of its time, hence an interesting comment on women's social place during those years. After World War II, women who had gone off to work had to be redomesticized, turning their

Familiars in Supernatural Literature

Greymalkin is the familiar of one of the witches in William Shakespeare's *Macbeth*; another witch refers to Paddock, a toad.

Brown Jenkin, a rat-like creature with a bearded human face and sharp canine teeth, is the familiar of Keziah Mason, an immortal witch who escaped the hanging in Salem; they appear in H. P. Lovecraft's short story "The Dreams in the Witch House" (*Weird Tales*, July 1933).

Enoch, in the short story of that name by Robert Bloch (*Weird Tales*, September 1946), is a murderous imp that sends its host, Seth, voluptuous dreams in exchange for brains to eat.

Pyewacket became a popular name in fiction and is the name of Gillian Holroyd's familiar, a Siamese cat, in the play (1950) and movie (1958) *Bell, Book and Candle*.

Carbonel, in Barbara Sleigh's *Carbonel: King of the Cats* (1955), is the King of the Cats but enchanted by an evil witch, Mrs. Cantrip; he gets a girl named Rosemary to learn some witchcraft in order to find Mrs. Cantrip and undo the spell.

Salem, a wisecracking black cat, is the familiar of Sabrina, the teenaged witch, both in Archie Comics beginning in 1962 and in the television show, 1996–2003.

Throgmorton is a huge tabby, somewhere between a familiar and a wizard in his own right, in the Chrestomanci series by Diana Wynne Jones, including *Charmed Life* (1977) and *The Lives of Christopher Chant* (1988).

Peach, short for Machu Picchu, is a scarlet, blue, and yellow macaw belonging to an advisor wizard, Tom, in Diane Duane's *So You Want to Be a Wizard?* (1983). There are hints that Peach was an ordinary bird before Tom became a wizard.

Loiosh, a small dragon-like creature called a jhereg, is the familiar of Steven Brust's Vlad Taltos in *Jhereg* (1983) and other books.

Jiji, a black cat, is Kiki's familiar in the 1989 movie *Kiki's Delivery Service* by Hayao Miyazaki.

Greebo, a tough, one-eyed tomcat, is the familiar of Nanny Ogg, the motherly witch in Terry Pratchett's Discworld books, including *Wyrd* Sisters (1988), *Lords and Ladies* (1992) and *Witches Abroad* (1991), in which he is transformed into a sexually attractive, bearded young man dressed in leather. Nanny Ogg insists he is gentle as a kitten.

Kit the Cat, a pale Siamese with blue eyes, appeared as the young witches' familiar in the first season (1998–1999) of the WB television show, "Charmed."

In the Earthsea books by Ursula Le Guin—*A Wizard of Earthsea* (1968), *The Tombs of Atuan* (1972), *The Farthest Shore* (1974), *Tehanu: The Last Book of Earthsea* (1990), and *The Other Wind* (2001)—the wizard Ged has a mouse familiar; other familiars include ravens and boars.

---

jobs over to the returning soldiers to instead keep their homes and raise their families. Yet, by the time of "Bewitched," the wheel was turning again, and women began to receive more education and enter a wider range of careers. Cultural critics have noted this ambivalence in the television series, but tend to polarize it. Some see the show as pro- or at least proto-feminist because Samantha has such power. As has been shown, witches can represent female power, and there are more female than male witches in the series, though characters include men such as Samantha's powerful father. Other commentators find "Bewitched" sexist because Samantha promises to stop using that power in order to please a man. Of course both insights are true—of "Bewitched," of the times, and perhaps of the whole idea of the domestic witch.

The Younger Witch

In fiction, young children who are witches are generally evil. Many such stories were written during a spate of horror fiction about evil children in the 1970s, although some of the more striking examples predate that fashion. Besides the eternal fear that one's children might turn out to be ungrateful or even harmful, increased by the generational tension of the late 1960s, there is the aesthetically pleasing irony when children, usually seen as more innocent than not, are depicted as witches.

A standout even among Arthur Machen's many powerful stories concerning magic and decadence or corruption, "The White People" (1899) is told in the form of a journal by a young girl undergoing a strange and terrifying supernatural initiation; it was the inspiration for T.E.D. Klein's novel *The Ceremonies* (1984). Another disturbing and potent short story of a young practitioner of magic is Jane Rice's "The Idol of the Flies" (*Unknown*, January 1942). The story convincingly depicts a child of pure malevolence and the temptations of an elusive state of consciousness in which he can practice magic. Ramsey Campbell, author of numerous short stories and novels concerning frightening magic, depicts the possession of a young girl by an old woman with supernatural powers in *The Influence* (1988). Other frightening stories of evil witches include August Derleth's "The Place in the Woods" (*Weird Tales*, May 1954) and "Timothy" (*SF Impulse*, September 1966) by Keith Roberts. One exception to the tendency of child witches to be evil, of course, is Wendy, "the good little witch," a long-running character from Harvey Comics.

Pre-teen and teenage witches, however, are more apt to be good than bad, and their stories are more apt to be funny or charming than horrific. These include Sabrina, the teenaged witch, and the three weird sisters in the television show "Charmed," discussed above. One subdivision is that of the students at a witches' school, which is referred to in *Bedknobs and Broomsticks* and other sources but has recently reached its height of popularity in the Harry Potter books, discussed above. While these witch schools primarily turn out benevolent alumnae, "The Cyclops Juju" by Shamus Frazer (1965) presents an account of evil magic (much like that of "Lukundoo," mentioned above) at a boys' school. Also, although it concerns sorcery more than witchcraft, Peter Straub's novel *Shadowland* (1980) should be mentioned for its chilling and evocative presentation of both a boys' school invaded by magic and a school set up by a magician to train and initiate one of the pupils of that school.

The Business Witch

A final recent face of the witch is that of a contemporary businessperson. In one way, this is nothing new: cunning folk were paid for their spells, although the ethics of many Wiccans and neo-pagans prevented them from taking money for magic. On the other hand, one charge against witches in many times and cultures, sometimes justified, is extortion of money by threats of supernatural harm. In addition, the image of the business witch is a natural outgrowth of the many deal-with-the-devil stories that take place in a modern setting. In fact, when the protagonist arrives to make a deal with the devil in "Blind Alley" by Malcolm Jameson (*Unknown Worlds*, June 1943), he first has an appointment with Madame Hecate, Consultant Witch, in suite 1313.

Most of all, the business witch had an entertaining irony: supernatural power juxtaposed to mundane payment and setting, ancient folklore and myth juxtaposed to modern values, and often sacred worship of the goddess juxtaposed with profane commercial practices. The anthology *100 Wicked Little Witch Stories* contains multiple stories of the business witch, including "Vend-a-Witch" by Adam-Troy Castro and "1-900-Witches" by Nancy Holder and Wayne Holder. In "Buyer Beware," by Tim Waggoner, a witch shopping at a used-car dealership uses magic to resist being conned into a sale, but the dealer is using magic too. "So Sweet as Magic . . .," a story by Bruce Elliott (*Fantasy Fiction*, August 1953), presents a traveler into an alternate world: in ours, stores sell supplies for stage magic, while in the other, stores sell the ingredients for effective spells and potions. Another story from *Unknown Worlds*, Robert A. Heinlein's novella "Magic, Inc." (September 1940, originally "The Devil Makes the Law"), is the ultimate business witch story. All businesses use magic, powered by demons and elementals (spirits of the four elements); the story concerns an attempt to create a monopoly and drive up the price of magic.

Stories concerning the business witch may also reflect a distrust of anyone who is motivated by money. "Sorcerer's Moon" (*Playboy*, July 1959) is one of Charles Beaumont's many brief, clever, and effective short stories. The magician involved, who is paid to raise a demon for harmful magic, directs the spell against his original customer when he is paid a higher price by the intended victim.

THIRTEEN WITCH MOVIES ADAPTED FROM LITERATURE

As noted previously, the witch has figured prominently in films from the very beginning of the movie industry. While it is in some cases difficult to distinguish movies about witches from movies involving related supernatural phenomena—notably demons or the Devil himself—some of the most successful films, adapted from novels, stories, or plays, are as follows:

1. *Bell, Book and Candle* (1958), directed by Richard Quine, screenplay by Daniel Taradash based on the 1950 play of the same name by John Van Druten. Though this was not the first movie about a mortal's romance with a witch (*I Married a Witch*, 1942), its genuine sweetness and the offbeat chemistry between the protagonists (James Stewart and Kim Novak) help make it the most famous. The Greenwich Village setting helped establish witches as bohemians—outsiders, but chic and charming rather than threatening. The play is more lighthearted, with less emotional depth.

2. *Black Sunday*, originally *La maschera del demonio* (1960), directed by Mario Bava, screenplay by Ennio De Concini after "The Viy" by Nikolai Gogol. This is the classic story of revenge by an executed witch, given style by Bava and allure by the witchy eyes and appealing figure of Barbara Steele. Gogol's short story, both amusing and frightening, has little in common with the movie, though both do feature a witch returning from the grave.

3. *Burn, Witch, Burn!*, also *Night of the Eagle* (1962), directed by Sidney Havers, screenplay by Charles Beaumont and others based on the 1953 novel *Conjure Wife* by Fritz Leiber. Both novel and movie depict a rational mathematics professor who discovers that his wife has been practicing witchcraft to protect him and advance his career—as do all wives of faculty. It has been called the best story of campus politics; it also is an early exemplar of the theme that witches exist in an unknown conspiracy.

4. *Witches' Brew* (1980) is another adaptation of *Conjure Wife*, more humorous and less frightening than the book or earlier movie; it is not nearly as good as *Burn, Witch, Burn!*, despite Terri Garr in the lead role. It was directed by Richard Shorr and Herbert L. Strock, with a screenplay by Syd Dutton based on Leiber's novel.

5. *The Witches* (1966), directed by Cyril Frankel, screenplay by Nigel Kneale from the 1963 book by Nora Lofts, *The Devil's Own* (also known as *The Little Wax Doll* and *Catch as Catch Can*). A woman is threatened by

witchcraft in Africa, then she comes home to England and teaches at a school which she finds is controlled by a coven of witches, who are about to sacrifice one of the students. Both the movie and the novel are better than a bare plot summary makes them sound.

6. *Rosemary's Baby* (1968), directed by Roman Polanski, screenplay by Roman Polanski from the 1967 novel of the same name by Ira Levin. Rosemary discovers that her New York apartment building is rife with witches, her husband has joined their coven, she has been drugged and raped by the devil, and her child will be its offspring. From religious doubt—"Is God Dead?" is a real *Time* magazine cover shown in the film—to fears of conspiracy and of what one's children might become, Levin and Polanski expressed many subtexts of the culture at the time. The movie is quite faithful to the novel, which combines supernatural horror with a tightly developed detective-story structure.

7. *The Devil Rides Out* (1968), directed by Terence Fisher, screenplay by Richard Matheson based on the 1934 novel of the same name by Dennis Wheatley. In production before *Rosemary's Baby*, this film helped start the supernatural boom of 1960s–1970s. However, with its sternly moral stance, it did not match the tone of the times as Polanski's film did, and it was never as popular. The coven members are mostly respectable older men, but one female is being tempted into the group. The head Satanist, based on Aleister Crowley, is more realistic and interesting in the movie than in the novel.

8. *Bedknobs and Broomsticks* (1971), directed by Robert Stevenson, screenplay by Bill Walsh and Don DaGradi based on Mary Norton's novels, *The Magic Bedknob; or, How to Become a Witch in Ten Easy Lessons* (1945) and *Bonfires and Broomsticks* (1957). This musical film by Walt Disney Productions shows the importance of children's literature in shaping a more benign image of the witch; it also features the idea of a school for witches, whose headmaster visits, aids, and falls in love with the adult protagonist. Events are set in motion when three children are sent from London to the countryside during World War II. The film is quite faithful to the books, although in the interests of social progress, magical animals replace cannibals as one threat.

9. *The Witches of Eastwick* (1987), directed by George Miller, screenplay by Michael Christofer from the 1984 novel of the same name by John Updike. The film and book differ surprisingly in tone, given that both follow the same basic story: three single women in small-town New England discover their witchy powers and summon a male devil, whom they must eventually reject. The book shows more realistic personal growth by the witches, yet also demonstrates their appetite for petty retribution. The movie focuses more on the devil (Jack Nicholson).

10. *Kiki's Delivery Service* (1989), directed by Hayoa Miyazaki, scripted by Hayoa Miyazaki based on the picture book *Majo no Takkyūbin* (1985) and its sequels by Eiko Kadono. This Japanese film was dubbed in English, changed very slightly, and released by Disney in 1998. A witch in training, Kiki takes her mother's broom and her talking black cat to a new town, in

which she opens a flying delivery company. As in other films by the director, the blend of the supernatural and real is seamless; the magic is charming but never trivial. Also common for the director, this is a coming of age film, as Kiki must learn about commerce, independence, and love.

11. *Practical Magic* (1998), directed by Griffin Dunne, screenplay by Robin Swicord based on the 1995 book of the same name by Alice Hoffman. Both book and film depict the lives of Gillian and Sally, members of a family thought to be witches for 200 years. Their aunts, raising the girls, sell love potions to a town that otherwise rejects them. Both book and film provide both horror and love, but the language and details of the book provide a deeper view of human nature, while in the movie the magic is more undeniable.

12. *The Witches* (1990), directed by Nicholas Roeg, screenplay by Allan Scott based on the 1983 book of the same name by Roald Dahl. A child and his grandmother are staying at the hotel at which the organized, worldwide conspiracy of witches is holding its annual convention, when he overhears their plan to exterminate all children, which smell bad to the witches. Despite being turned into a mouse, the child manages to use the witches' own potion against them. Both book and movie, though intended for children, are enjoyably creepy, as well as funny.

13. *The Chronicles of Narnia: The Lion, the Witch and the Wardrobe* (2005), directed by Andrew Adamson, screenplay by Ann Peacock and others based on the 1950 novel by C. S. Lewis. The image of the purely evil witch, not popular in cinema since the early 1960s, reappears here quite powerfully. The movie follows the book, including Lewis's Christian views that evil is deceptive, malefic, but not as powerful as a savior's self-sacrifice. The association of the witch with winter and the glacial malice with which she is played (Tilda Swinton) give an original yet mythic feel to the character.

Witches may be as old as mankind, according to many interpretations of cave paintings such as those at Lascaux, they are with us as we enter the twenty-first century, and they will almost certainly continue to inspire art and real belief in the foreseeable future. Perhaps a witch could prophesy what forms such fiction, drawings, folklore, ritual, music, poetry, drama, and events may take—and even what new technologies may be used to display them—but we ordinary human beings cannot.

BIBLIOGRAPHY

Primary

Ainsworth, W. Harrison. *The Lancashire Witches*. London: Henry Colburn, 1849.
Bacon, Peggy. *The Good American Witch*. New York: Franklin Watts, 1957.
Bassett, Ronald. *Witch-Finder General*. London: Jenkins, 1966.
Bradley, Marion Zimmer. *The Mists of Avalon*. New York: Knopf, 1982.
Brussof, Valery. *The Fiery Angel*. London: H. Toulmin, 1930.

Campbell, Ramsey. *The Influence.* New York: Macmillan, 1988.

Carr, Marina. *By the Bog of Cats.* Loughcrew, Ireland: Gallery Press, 1998.

Curran, Ronald T., ed. *Witches, Wraiths, and Warlocks: Supernatural Tales of the American Renaissance.* New York: Fawcett, 1990.

De Paola, Tomie. *Strega Nona.* Englewood Cliffs, NJ: Prentice-Hall, 1975.

Drake, David. *Cross the Stars.* New York: Tor, 1984.

———. *Old Nathan.* New York: Baen, 1991.

Dziemianowicz, Stefan, ed. *100 Wicked Little Witch Stories.* New York: Barnes & Noble, 1995.

Edghill, Rosemary. *The Book of Moons.* New York: Forge, 1995.

———. *The Bowl of Night.* New York: Forge, 1996.

———. *Speak Daggers to Her.* New York: Forge, 1994.

Frazer, Shamus. "The Cyclops Juju." In *The Tandem Book of Horror Stories,* ed. Charles Birkin. London: Tandem, 1965.

Gaiman, Neil. *American Gods.* New York: Morrow, 2001.

Gaiman, Neil, and Terry Pratchett. *Good Omens: The Nice and Accurate Prophecies of Agnes Nutter, Witch.* New York: Workman, 1990.

Garcia y Robertson, R. *Firebird.* New York: Tor, 2006.

Geis, Richard E. *A Girl Possessed.* As by "Peggy Swenson." Chatsworth, CA: Brandon, 1973.

George, Elizabeth. *The Witch of Blackbird Pond.* Boston: Houghton Mifflin, 1958.

Ghidalia, Vic, ed. *Wizards and Warlocks.* New York: Manor, 1972.

Gluckman, Janet Berliner, and George Guthridge. "Inyanga." In *100 Wicked Little Witch Stories.* New York: Barnes & Noble, 1995.

Gray, Muriel. *Furnace.* New York: Doubleday, 1997.

Grimson, Todd. *Brand-New Cherry Flavor.* New York: HarperPrism, 1996.

Haining, Peter, ed. *The Satanists.* New York: Pyramid, 1969.

———. *The Witchcraft Reader.* London: Pan, 1969.

Hand, Elizabeth. *Black Light.* New York: HarperCollins, 1999.

———. *Mortal Love.* New York: Morrow, 2004.

———. *Waking the Moon.* New York: HarperPrism, 1995.

Hawthorne, Nathaniel. *Tanglewood Tales for Boys and Girls.* Boston: Ticknor, Reed & Fields, 1853.

Hearn, Julie. *The Merrybegot.* Oxford: Oxford University Press, 2005.

Holder, Nancy. "The Only Way to Fly." In *100 Wicked Little Witch Stories,* ed. Stefan Dziemianowicz. New York: Barnes & Noble, 1995.

Holder, Nancy, and Melanie Tem. *Witch-Light.* New York: Dell, 1996.

Hopkinson, Nalo, ed. *Mojo: Conjure Stories.* New York: Warner, 2003.

———. *Skin Folk.* New York: Warner, 2001.

Huysmans, J.-K. *Là-Bas.* 1891. Trans. Keene Wallis as *Down There.* New York: A. & C. Boni, 1924.

Jeffers, Robinson. *Medea: Freely Adapted from the Medea of Euripides.* New York: Random House, 1946.

King, Stephen. *Thinner.* As by "Richard Bachman." New York: New American Library, 1984.

Klein, T.E.D. *The Ceremonies.* New York: Viking, 1984.

Koontz, Dean. *Darkfall.* New York: Berkley, 1984.

Lackey, Mercedes, Eric Flint, and Dave Freer. *This Rough Magic*. New York: Tor, 2003.

Leiber, Fritz. *Conjure Wife*. *Unknown Worlds* (June 1943). New York: Twayne, 1953.

Leland, Charles Godfrey. *Aradia; or, The Gospel of the Witches*. London: David Nutt, 1899.

Lewis, Matthew Gregory. *The Monk*. London: J. Bell, 1796.

Machen, Arthur. "The White People." In *The House of Souls*. 1899. London: Grant Richards, 1906.

Maguire, Gregory. *Wicked: The Life and Times of the Wicked Witch of the West*. New York: ReganBooks, 1995.

Meinhold, Wilhelm. *The Amber Witch*. Trans. Lady Duff Gordon. London: Oxford University Press, 1928.

Miller, Arthur. *The Crucible*. New York: Viking Press, 1953.

Mundt, Martin. "Hunger Gulag." In *100 Wicked Little Witch Stories*, ed. Stefan Dziemianowicz. New York: Barnes & Noble, 1995.

Neill, Robert. *Mist over Pendle*. London: Hutchinson, 1951.

Paxson, Diana. *The Paradise Tree*. New York: Ace, 1987.

Price, Robert M. "Young Goodwife Doten." In *100 Wicked Little Witch Stories*, ed. Stefan Dziemianowicz. New York: Barnes & Noble, 1995.

Prose, Francine. *Marie Laveau*. New York: Berkley, 1977.

Pullman, Philip. *The Amber Spyglass*. London: Scholastic, 2000.

———. *Northern Lights*. London: Scholastic, 1995. New York: Scholastic, 1995 (as *The Golden Compass*).

———. *The Subtle Knife*. London: Scholastic, 1997.

Reisert, Rebecca. *The Third Witch*. New York: Pocket, 2001.

Rhodes, Jewell Parker. *Voodoo Dreams*. New York: St. Martin's Press, 1993.

Rowling, J. K. *Harry Potter and the Chamber of Secrets*. London: Bloomsbury, 1998.

———. *Harry Potter and the Goblet of Fire*. London: Bloomsbury, 2000.

———. *Harry Potter and the Half-Blood Prince*. London: Bloomsbury, 2005.

———. *Harry Potter and the Order of the Phoenix*. London: Bloomsbury, 2003.

———. *Harry Potter and the Prisoner of Azkaban*. London: Bloomsbury, 1999.

———. *Harry Potter and the Philosopher's Stone*. London: Bloomsbury, 1997. New York: Scholastic, 1998 (as *Harry Potter and the Sorcerer's Stone*).

Saunders, Charles R. "Ishigbi." In *Hecate's Children*, ed. Susan M. Schwartz. New York: DAW, 1982.

Schwartz, Susan M., ed. *Hecate's Cauldron*. New York: DAW, 1982.

Serling, Rod, ed. *Rod Serling's Triple W: Witches, Warlocks, and Werewolves*. New York: Bantam Books, 1963.

Straub, Peter. *Shadowland*. New York: Coward, McCann & Geogheghan, 1980.

Updike, John. *The Witches of Eastwick*. New York: Knopf, 1984.

Ward, Don, ed. *Black Magic: Thirteen Chilling Tales*. New York: Dell Mayflower, 1967.

Wheatley, Dennis. "The Snake." In *A Century of Horror Stories*, ed. Dennis Wheatley. London: Hutchinson, 1935.

Wolfe, Gene. *Castleview*. New York: Tor, 1990.

Yolen, Jane. *The Flying Witch*. New York: HarperCollins, 2003.

Secondary

Ankarloo, Bengt, and Stuart Clark, eds. *Witchcraft and Magic in Europe: Ancient Greece and Rome.* Philadelphia: University of Pennsylvania Press, 1999.

————. *Witchcraft and Magic in Europe: Biblical and Pagan Societies.* Philadelphia: University of Pennsylvania Press, 2001.

————. *Witchcraft and Magic in Europe: The Middle Ages.* Philadelphia: University of Pennsylvania Press, 2002.

————. *Witchcraft and Magic in Europe: The Period of the Witch Trials.* Philadelphia: University of Pennsylvania Press, 2003.

————. *Witchcraft and Magic in Europe: The Twentieth Century.* Philadelphia: University of Pennsylvania Press, 1999.

Bessy, Maurice. *A Pictorial History of Magic and the Supernatural.* Feltham, UK: Spring, 1964.

Binder, Pearl. *Magic Symbols of the World.* London: Hamlyn, 1972.

Bond, George Clement, and Diane M. Ciekawy, eds. *Witchcraft Dialogues: Anthropological and Philosophical Exchanges.* Athens: Ohio University Press, 2002.

Cavendish, Richard. *The Black Arts: An Absorbing Account of Witchcraft, Demonology, Astrology, and Other Mystical Practices Throughout the Ages.* New York: Perigee Trade, 1968.

Drury, Nevill, and Gregory Tillett. *The Occult: A Sourcebook of Esoteric Wisdom.* London: Grange, 1997.

Elworthy, F. T. *The Evil Eye.* New York: Julian Press, 1958.

Ginzburg, Carlo. *Ecstasies: Deciphering the Witches' Sabbath.* Trans. Raymond Rosenthal. New York: Pantheon, 1991.

————. *The Night Battles: Witchcraft and Agrarian Cults in the Sixteenth and Seventeenth Centuries.* Trans. John and Anne Tedeschi. Baltimore: Johns Hopkins University Press, 1983.

Graves, Robert. *The White Goddess.* New York: Creative Age Press, 1948. Rev. ed. New York: Farrar, Straus & Giroux, 1966.

Green, Richard J. "How Many Witches." http://www.holocaust-history.org/~rjg/witches.shtml.

Grillot de Givry, Emile Angelo. *Witchcraft, Magic, and Alchemy.* Trans. J. Courtenay Locke. London: George G. Harrap, 1931.

Harris, Anthony. *Witchcraft and Magic in Seventeenth Century English Drama.* Manchester: Manchester University Press, 1980.

Hill, Douglas. *Magic and Superstition.* London: Hamlyn, 1972.

Hoyt, Charles Alva. *Witchcraft.* Carbondale: Southern Illinois University Press, 1981.

Hutton, Ronald. *The Triumph of the Moon: A History of Modern Pagan Witchcraft.* New York: Oxford University Press, 2001.

Johns, Andreas. Baba Yaga: *The Ambiguous Mother and Witch of the Russian Folktale.* New York: Peter Lang, 2004.

Jong, Erica, and Joseph A. Smith. *Witches.* New York: Harry N. Abrams, 2004.

King, Francis X. *Witchcraft and Demonology.* New York: Exeter, 1987.

Kors, Alan Charles, and Edward Peters, eds. *Witchcraft in Europe, 400–1700: A Documentary History.* 2nd ed. Philadelphia: University of Pennsylvania Press, 2000.

Lehman, Arthur, James Myers, and Pamela Moro. *Magic, Witchcraft, and Religion: An Anthropological Study of the Supernatural*. New York: McGraw-Hill, 2000.

Maple, Eric. *The Dark World of Witches*. London: Robert Hale, 1962; London: Pan, 1965.

———. *Witchcraft: The Story of Man's Quest for Supernatural Power*. London: Octopus, 1973.

Morrow, James. "James Morrow's Top 10 Books on Witch Persecutions." *Guardian Unlimited*, http://books.guardian.co.uk/top10s/top10/0,,1756750,00.html.

Murray, Margaret. *The Witch-Cult in Western Europe*. Oxford: Clarendon Press, 1921.

Russell, Jeffrey B. *A History of Witchcraft: Sorcerers, Heretics, and Pagans*. London: Thames & Hudson, 1982.

Schreck, Nikolas. *The Satanic Screen: An Illustrated History of the Devil in Cinema 1896–1999*. London: Creation, 2001.

Stein, Rebecca L., and Phillip Stein. *Anthropology of Religion, Magic, and Witchcraft*. Boston: Allyn & Bacon, 2004.

Thomas, Keith. *Religion and the Decline of Magic: Studies in Popular Beliefs in Sixteenth and Seventeenth Century England*. New York: Oxford University Press, 1997.

Trevor-Roper, Hugh. *The European Witch Craze in the Sixteenth and Seventeenth Centuries*. New York: Harper Torchbooks, 1967.

Wheatley, Dennis. *The Devil and All His Works*. New York: American Heritage Press, 1971.

© Variety/The Kobol Collection.

The Zombie

by June Pulliam

In the twenty-first century, the word "zombie" conjures up a familiar figure of a decaying corpse shuffling in a somnambulistic state, eyes glazed and arms held stiffly forward, in the mindless pursuit of human flesh. We owe this iconographic image to filmmaker George A. Romero's 1968 low-budget black-and-white movie *Night of the Living Dead*, which transformed the zombie in much the same way that James Whale's 1931 film *Frankenstein* altered Mary Shelley's creature or Tod Browning's 1931 film *Dracula* changed Bram Sto-ker's count. Today, writers and filmmakers who take zombie as their subject must acknowledge Romero's interpretation of the creature, if only to argue within the reality of their own fictional universes that his portrayal was inaccurate. The zombie itself is a malleable symbol—representing everything from the horrors of slavery, white xenophobia, Cold War angst, the fear of death, and even apprehensions about consumer culture—and has become an icon of horror perhaps because it is quite literally a *memento mori*, reminding us that our belief that we can completely control our destiny, and perhaps through the right medical technology, even cheat death, is mere hubris.

The zombie has two basic criteria. First, it must be the reanimated corpse or possessed living body of *one* person (or animal), so golems and creatures similar to what Dr. Frankenstein stitched together from the charnel house do not fall into this category. Golems are not zombies, but instead, corporeal beings created from other forms of matter. Similarly, Victor Frankenstein's creature is not a zombie because it is a crazy-quilt of the parts of *many* people rather than a single reanimated body. Yet a zombie is much more than the walking dead. Mummies and vampires, for example, are also reanimated corpses, yet most are not zombies because they do not have a second essential characteristic: a lack of free will. The zombie must be completely subordinate either to the will of someone else or to some monomaniacal drive, whether for living flesh, violence, revenge, or even resistance of the tyranny of entropy itself. The zombie's lack of volition often makes it a parody of slavery. Furthermore, this lack of free will generally makes zombies flat characters, unable to fully appreciate the wretchedness of their condition, unlike vampires, who frequently wax philosophical about being doomed to hunger for living blood. Thus, zombies are generally not the protagonists of stories about them.

Typical characteristics of the zombie narrative can include an emphasis on the creature's decaying form and extreme gore. The decaying body of the zombie is particularly evident when the creature is represented in visual media, and underscores the horrors of death itself. And in the past forty years, directors starting with Romero have added extreme gore to the list of attributes that are essential to zombie narrative.

The zombie itself is not new, but is a creature with deep roots in literature and cultural practices. Ethnobotanist Wade Davis's controversial monographs *The Serpent and the Rainbow* (1985) and *Passage of Darkness: The Ethnobiology of the Haitian Zombie* (1988) study the zombie phenomena in Haiti. Here an unscrupulous houngan, a type of voodoo priest, can be paid by someone bent on revenge to administer to an enemy a neurotoxin derived from the pufferfish. This neurotoxin very convincingly simulates death. The victim is then buried by the unsuspecting grieving family, only to be resurrected several hours later by the houngan and taken away to become uncompensated unskilled labor. The zombie is kept in "thrall" by the houngan through a combination of physical coercion and malnutrition (and in fact, many legends hold that feeding zombies salt or meat is sufficient to rouse them from their stupor and permit them to realize their abject condition, at which point they will either kill their master or run shrieking back to their graves). This zombie makes an ideal slave, as higher brain functions such as memory and intellect have been disabled by the toxin, while lower brain functions permitting the body to move and perform simple tasks still work.

Davis's studies were not limited to the biological phenomena of the zombie, but included sociological factors as well. He observed that the houngan would not be able to create zombies were it not for the cooperation of the surrounding community. Often those who become the "walking dead" are disliked by neighbors and even family, so nothing is done to prevent their fate, such as ensuring before burial that they are actually *dead*, either through cutting off the head or driving a dagger through the heart. Others are prevented from interfering with the houngan's plans out of the fear that they too could meet a similar fate should they run afoul of him or her. Finally, community members tacitly agree to see the victims of the houngan as irrevocably undead. On an island as small as Haiti, it is not unheard of for family members to actually *see* their dead, alive, and walking in a state of zombification. However, when these "dead" family members are sighted, relatives make no attempt to reclaim them. While it is possible through careful nursing to somewhat restore the faculties of someone in this state, the zombie is treated as an outcast by friends and family. Indeed, they deny that their family member lives at all, exhibiting an attitude similar to the ones held regarding rape victims in many parts of the world—both zombie and rape victim are seen as fundamentally and irredeemably unclean, and therefore, no longer fit to be a part of the family unit.

In Haiti, zombies are not figures of terror because of what they might do to the living. In fact, these zombies are not capable of harming anyone. Instead, the zombie—a creature between life and death, an outcast, something with no will of its own—is a fearful symbol of human bondage in this former colony where, in the late eighteenth century, the enslaved successfully threw off their oppressors in a bloody struggle with many times their number of British and French soldiers. A mere two decades after this revolution the word zombie first appeared in English, when the British poet Robert Southey in 1819 used it as a metaphor for imperialism in the Americas, indicating that the colonized had been robbed of free will (Fonseca 1240).

While there are mentions of zombies and walking corpses in fiction and journalistic accounts from the nineteenth century, the creature does not fully make its debut into popular culture until the early twentieth century with the publication of W. B. Seabrook's 1929 travelogue *The Magic Island*. Seabrook, an adventurer, traveled to Haiti and lived there with a family, collecting stories about zombies and voodoo practices, even claiming once to see a dead man resurrected. Though stories of zombies were not new to the United States or Europe, Seabrook's book is credited with igniting popular Western interest in the creature. And when the zombie makes its appearance in British and American culture, its most fearsome aspect is its lack of that Protestant human virtue, free will.

The earliest representations of zombies in American culture derive from Haitian folklore and voodoo practices. Victor Halperin's *White Zombie* (1932), starring Bela Lugosi, the first full-length feature film about this creature, was inspired by *The Magic Island*, and by the unsuccessful play *Zombie* (1932), itself based on Seabrook's book. *White Zombie* was mildly successful in the box office, and Lugosi went on to do four more obscure zombie films: *The Bowery at Midnight* (1942), *The Voodoo Man* (1944), *Zombies on Broadway* (1945), a comedy, and finally, the infamous *Plan 9 from Outer Space* (1958), in which he completed two scenes before he died.

White Zombie is set in Haiti, and the horror of the creature lies not in its being undead, but rather in its very lack of volition. All the zombies are manipulated by their master, Murder Legendre (Bela Lugosi), a houngan who, through a combination of drugs and black magic, puts the living into a deathlike state, then resurrects their "corpses" as slaves who perform grueling labor on the country's sugar plantations. But Legendre is more than someone whose superior occult knowledge makes it possible for him to enslave others; he is a man of superior *will*. Among his army of slaves are the island's executioner, who once nearly put Legendre to death; a magistrate; and even his own former master, another houngan who gave up his secrets only under torture. Legendre controls his zombies through more than just administering poison to them; he also exerts a sort of mesmerism on his victims. Midway through the film, Legendre makes out of sight of his zombies a gesture where one hand grapples with the other, performing a type of sympathetic magic that transmits his will to the nearest zombie. That Legendre can bewitch those with so much political and occult power bespeaks the superiority of his own mental abilities.

But the film's central horror is not so much that Legendre can enslave relatively powerful people but that his abilities can be used to enslave a *white* woman, Madeline. Legendre and many of his zombies are racially ambiguous, though those who labor in the cane factory are all unmistakably black. However, the wage slavery aspect of the plot, the only thread to involve dark skinned people, is unexplored. Madeline, the only one of Legendre's victims that the film is concerned with, is unambiguously white. Peter Dendle observes in *The Zombie Movie Encyclopedia* that "early zombie movies are most obviously concerned with the appropriation of female bodies, and the annihilation of female minds, by male captors" (3). Dendle's observation is accurate regarding gender, but he neglects the significance of race in these narratives.

White Zombie follows Madeline and Neil, a couple engaged to be married. But Monsieur Beaumont, a wealthy planter pretending to be the couple's benefactor, secretly pines for Madeline, and lures her and her fiancé to his estate with the promise that they can wed there in splendor. Moments before the ceremony, Beaumont begs Madeline to be *his* bride. When she refuses, he secretly administers to her the zombie powder acquired from Legendre. Madeline "dies" before consummating her marriage to Neil and is interred, resurrected, and brought to Beaumont, who now plans to enjoy her. We see Beaumont raptly watching his beloved play the piano for him, but her eyes are dead and her face is unresponsive. Dendle observes that in the zombie film "time and again the villains learn that to possess the woman's mindless body is unsatisfying" (3), and Beaumont is no exception. He soon realizes that not having Madeline at all is better than possessing an automaton, and so he entreats Legendre to administer an antidote to his beloved or just allow her to die. Legendre refuses to do either, and instead attempts to turn Beaumont into a zombie. Meanwhile, Neil refuses to believe that Madeline is dead and searches for her. Legendre tries to use his influence over Madeline to make her kill Neil, but her love for him is too strong and permits her to resist Legendre's manipulation, resulting in his demise. According to Haitian zombie lore, when the houngan dies, his slaves are free, so when Legendre is eventually killed, his undead slaves jump from a cliff to their deaths. Madeline, however, recognizes Neil, and is restored as his virginal bride.

While *White Zombie* is set in Haiti, the film's anxieties about the zombie are those of *white* Americans, especially men, rather than anything that black Haitians would find particularly fearful. However, voodoo and the power to control others are represented as deriving from a dangerous island of savages, in spite of the fact that this power has been appropriated by whites. The message is that Legendre, already corrupted by an insatiable desire for power, is enabled to make his worst dreams come true in this relatively unregulated environment. The result is a perceived threat to white male ability to control the chastity of white women. What is represented in *White Zombie* is not so different from what the Ku Klux Klan feared would occur if blacks were not terrorized into submission after the Civil War.

In the 1930s and 1940s, zombies appeared in the horror pulp magazines such as *Weird Tales* and *Strange Tales* as well as in comic books, a format I will discuss later in this chapter. Thorp McClusky's story "While Zombies Walked" (1939) owes a good deal to *White Zombie*. This story is similar to the film in that its central concern is the chastity of a Caucasian woman. Set in Haiti, here too zombies are made by a white man wishing both to create the ideal slave and to enjoy ultimate power over others. When Tony Kent's fiancée Eileen returns to Haiti to tend to her ailing uncle and uncharacteristically sends him a Dear John letter, he travels to the island to speak with her in person. Almost immediately upon his arrival, he discovers a land of horrors. Tony stops to ask directions of a man on the road, whose refusal to respond makes him appear insolent. Upon closer inspection, Tony discovers the seemingly impossible—the man has a cracked skull, yet labors in the fields. At the plantation, Tony tells Eileen's ill uncle and his large and menacing overseer, Reverend Barnes, about what he has witnessed, but Barnes insists that Tony is suffering from a heat stroke. Wishing to prove definitively to Tony that his eyes have deceived him, Barnes sends one of his workers to fetch the allegedly mortally wounded man, who only has clotted dirt in his hair where his injury should have been. But before Tony consents to leave, he demands to speak to Eileen in person. Eileen secretly attempts to warn Tony about the threat to her and her uncle, but her communication is detected by Barnes, who has no choice but to capture Tony as well lest he interfere with his plans for Eileen's family.

While imprisoned, Tony learns about the strange influence that Barnes has over Eileen and her uncle, a power derived from the effigies of each kept in a cloth bag around his neck. Soon after, Tony and Barnes have what is to be their final confrontation. In typical melodramatic villain fashion, Barnes confesses everything to Tony, describing how he had been denied success in the church by his superiors, who correctly perceived him as a man of questionable morality, and so dispatched him to the most forlorn of parishes in the hope that he would simply leave the profession. But this assignment only gives the ambitious reverend the opportunity to obtain dangerous occult knowledge that he uses for evil. Barnes intends to "influence" Tony into turning over to the reverend all his wealth, after which he plans to kill his rival and ravish Eileen. Naturally, before Barnes can make good his threats, he is thwarted by those he has harmed. Eileen and her uncle are free of Barnes's influence, and the dead return to their graves. The anxieties represented in "While Zombies Walked" are really not any different from those displayed in *White Zombie*. Here too whites, already morally corrupt to begin with, have greater power to wreak havoc when they come into contact with what is literally black magic.

Two other zombie stories from the pulps, August Derleth's "The House in the Magnolias" (1932) and Manly Wade Wellman's "Song of the Slaves" (1940), are both concerned with how slavery has transplanted to United States something malign that affects master more than slave. Derleth's "The House in the Magnolias" merely transfers the menace of voodoo to the contemporary United States. A female zombie master of mixed race comes to New Orleans after her reanimation and exploitation of the dead have worn out her welcome in her native Haiti. She emigrates with her niece Rosamunda, then a child, and no one else. The two inhabit a huge plantation outside the Crescent City. Amidst rumors of grave robbing, Rosamunda's aunt acquires several "slaves" who do the plantation's work by night. These dark family secrets are discovered by Jordan, an artist who comes to the house in the magnolias to paint, and must stay at the plantation for a few nights in order to complete his work. One night, he is knocked unconscious by the mistress who is not pleased that her niece has allowed a guest into their home. Rosamunda comes to his rescue and confesses all, and the two forge a plot to free the zombies so that she can escape her hellish life, since for some reason she is incapable of leaving on her own. In keeping with Haitian folklore about the zombie, Rosamunda feeds the undead salt. When they taste this substance, the zombies realize they are dead, shriek in terror at their condition, and run to their graves. The aunt dies in the fire that burns the house to the ground, while Rosamunda goes off to marry Jordan. So while anxieties of *White Zombie* and "While Zombies Walked" are located "over there" in Haiti, "The House in the Magnolias" is concerned with how, seventy years after the end of the Civil War, the curse of slavery still persists. But because these fears are transferred into the early twentieth century and the slave master is of mixed origins, white people are not directly responsible for the evils.

Wellman's story is also in the vein of zombie narratives derived from Afro-Caribbean folklore and has characteristics of Gothic literature as well. The story, set in the decade preceding the American Civil War, has a more contemporary feel in that the horrors of slavery are correctly attributed to the whites who kidnapped Africans and put them in bondage. In 1853, Gender, a greedy South Carolina planter, ventures to Africa to replenish his stock of slaves, in open defiance of recently enacted laws prohibiting the further importation of human chattel. While Gender ferries forty-nine unfortunate souls in the belly of his ship, much to his chagrin they persist in singing their "curse song" to get revenge on their captor. Meanwhile, the British are attempting to stamp out the slave trade, and their navy seizes cargos such as Gender's and takes their captains to justice. Gender's ship is about to be overtaken by such a ship when he gets rid of the evidence by throwing overboard his slaves, who are all chained together. The captain of the British ship, however, is not fooled by Gender's ruse, and vows to ruin his reputation in his community. The captain is as good as his word, sending letters to Gender's neighbors about his exploits at sea. Though Gender's neighbors are all slaveholders, they are nevertheless appalled by his actions and snub him completely. But social ostracism isn't the only torment that Gender suffers. In a denouement typical of the Gothic, Gender hears on the final night of his life the slaves' curse song once again just before seeing beneath his window their watery corpses that have come back to haunt him. It is the sight of these decaying bodies brought back to life finally that makes this a zombie narrative rather than a tale of haunting. These are not ghosts come to reproach Gender for his crimes, but the flesh and blood undead.

Jacques Tourneur's 1943 film *I Walked with a Zombie* is one of the two zombie films that owe much to nineteenth-century Gothic narrative. *I Walked* is very loosely based on Charlotte Brontë's *Jane Eyre*. As with other zombie films, it is set in the Caribbean. Also typical of zombie narratives of the time, the dark-skinned natives practice voodoo for good, mainly for improved health and psychological well being, while whites appropriate native practices for their own nefarious ends. Betsy, a Canadian nurse, comes to the island to care for the local sugar planter Paul Holland's catatonic wife, Jessica. In the process, she uncovers the root of her patient's malady. The beautiful Jessica cannot speak and has no will of her own, and so must be led childlike throughout her day. Similar to *Jane Eyre*'s Bertha Mason, Jessica spends her days locked in a tower, and Paul acknowledges her existence only a bit more than Edward Rochester acknowledges the presence of his own lunatic wife in the attic of Wildfield Hall. The Holland family physician is unable to diagnose Jessica's inexplicable state, which resembles an extreme form of neurasthenia. But the

"She's alive...yet dead! She's dead...yet alive!" Tagline from I Walked with a Zombie.

island natives know immediately that Jessica is neither alive nor dead, but a zombie.

Jessica's plight is similar to Madeline's in *White Zombie*: her sexual desirability has provoked the ire of powerful enemies who have the ability to transform her. But Jessica has not been made into a zombie by a houngan who wishes to keep her for himself. Instead, Dr. Rand, Jessica's physician mother-in-law, has arranged her fate as a way to keep her two sons on the island. Before Jessica fell ill, she planned on leaving the island with Paul's younger half-brother Wesley, with whom she had fallen in love. With Jessica ill, both of them remain on the island. However, the war between the two brothers has escalated as Wesley blames Paul for driving Jessica mad. The denouement reveals Dr. Rand's involvement through her tearful confession, but the ending is ambiguous: Dr. Holland openly questions Dr. Rand's sanity, claiming that she has been deceived by her own powerful imagination. The film concludes with Dr. Rand sadly agreeing with this assessment of herself, and an even more ambiguous representation of the power of Voodoo. The final scene juxtaposes a houngan using a doll to imitate Jessica coming to him before she is stabbed to death with a catatonic Jessica leaving the family estate in the middle of the night, only to be put out of her misery by Wesley, who runs her through the back with a spear. The viewer is lead to believe that perhaps Dr. Rand was correct after all.

Similar to previous narratives, the zombie in *I Walked* is a fearful creature because of its lack of will. One of the more horrifying moments in the film, for viewers in the 1940s at any rate, is when this lack of volition makes it impossible for two zombie characters to observe various racial and sexual taboos. In a scene suggesting the possibility of miscegenation, a black zombie comes into Jessica's bedroom in the middle of the night in order to initiate a spell being worked on her by the local houngan. Nothing happens beyond the black zombie sharing briefly the same intimate physical space with Jessica, but the *mise en scène* suggests possibilities that would have been unsettling to the minds of viewers at the time.

A second zombie film loosely based on a well-known Gothic novel is John Gilling's *The Plague of the Zombies* (1966). *Plague* is similar to *White Zombie* in that the undead are created by a white man through the use of voodoo. However, this Hammer studios film, whose story owes much to Bram Stoker's *Dracula*, relocates the zombie to nineteenth-century England. Another notable difference between *Plague* and *White* is the method of creation: zombies are not made with any mysterious power, but instead *wholly* through sympathetic magic. Both films have similar rationales for raising the dead. *White* hints that zombies have been made to serve as slaves, while this purpose is expressly articulated in *Plague*.

Before the film opens, Squire Hamilton, the young scion of a wealthy family, has returned from foreign lands to the paternal home in Cornwall to assume his deceased father's debts. The Hamilton family wealth is derived from a tin mine, which is no longer in operation because of an alarming number of industrial accidents. Since young Hamilton's return, each month a villager has died of a mysterious illness that the local doctor, Peter Thompson, cannot diagnose. Frustrated, Dr. Thompson writes to his mentor, Sir James Forbes.

Soon after Sir James comes to help his former student, Dr. Thompson's young wife, Alice, falls ill. Meanwhile, Sir James and his protégé embark on a scientific investigation to discover what is killing the villagers. They must conduct clandestine autopsies on the newly deceased, since the villagers would see this procedure as a gross violation of their loved ones. The need for secrecy leads Sir James and Dr. Thompson to the cemetery in the middle of the night to find only an empty coffin where the most recent victim should be resting. Meanwhile, Alice leaves home in a trance in the dead of night. This scene is similar to the one in *Dracula* where Lucy Westerna, in thrall to the Count, sleepwalks. But Alice does not make it home alive; instead, she is killed by a villager who died at the beginning of the film.

Alice is buried, and Sir James persuades her husband to assist in exhuming her for an autopsy. This disinterment scene owes a great deal to the passage in *Dracula* where the infected Lucy's eternal slumber is similarly interrupted, permitting her fiancé to give her peace by putting a stake through her heart and cutting off her head. The duo open Alice's grave, only to see her corpse transform before their eyes, from her pale, white almost virginal beauty to the dark, bluish countenance of the zombie. The newly awakened Alice does not recognize her husband or his old friend, and menaces the two before Sir James beheads her with a spade.

Sir James and Dr. Thompson's continued investigation resembles the work of Dr. Van Helsing and his band of vampire hunters. They use the most modern of Victorian technologies to rid England of this foreign-born plague, and they have Christianity on their side as well when the local vicar provides them with books on witchcraft from his own personal library. Eventually, Hamilton's secret is uncovered. His zombies, the male ones anyway, are working in his tin mine. And when the Voodoo dolls that Hamilton uses to control his army of the undead burn, true to Haitian zombie lore, the creatures turn on their master.

The racial politics of *Plague* are also similar to those of *White Zombie*. Whites, not blacks, have appropriated Haitian magic in order to make zombies, and their primary interest, or at least from what we see occurring on the screen, is the ability to possess the bodies of white women. When we do see black characters, they are tangential to the plot. In *Plague*, black characters exist mainly to beat the drums during Hamilton's zombification ceremonies and add an air of "savagery" to his decadence.

Plague represents a transition in the representation of the zombie in popular culture. While *Plague*'s zombies are created by voodoo, they are terrifying not

"In a world where the dead are returning to life, the word 'trouble' loses much of its meaning." Quipped by Kaufmann in Land of the Dead *upon discovering that someone blackmailing him for 5 million dollars has the power to break down the fortifications erected against zombie attack.*

simply because they do not have a will of their own, but because they are dead things, who will not stay nicely in their coffins. A good deal of screen time is given to showing the dead Alice transforming from the "beautiful memory picture" she was when placed in her coffin to a rotting hunk of flesh, albeit through very cheap special effects. The fixation on Alice's rotting countenance is similar to Romero's visual representation of zombies, whose terror resides in their being dead yet animated with a force that compels them to attack the living. Also, while *Plague*'s zombies have no drive of their own, they are similar to the more modern version in that their will is completely sublimated to the interests of capitalism. Hamilton's zombies toil in the mines, while Romero's zombies represent the working classes, particularly in the 2005 film *Land of the Dead*.

But before more modern zombie narratives can be discussed, it is first necessary to go back in time to consider a medium that was an outgrowth of the pulp horror and crime magazines, the comic books. In the 1930s, the zombie quickly became a staple of comic books, and by the 1950s, when superhero comics were in decline and horror and crime comics gained popularity, the creature appeared with great frequency. Zombie stories in the comics ascribed their existence to reasons more numerous than those found in either the pulps or film: they were created by black magic, by an irrepressible need for revenge that transcended the grave, or for no "rational" reason at all. And it was in this medium that the zombie was most dependably represented as a visibly rotting corpse. As a story-telling medium, comics had the advantages of both print and film. Of course, comic books had stories, but even more significant was the fact that readers could view an image over and over, something that fans couldn't do with films until the introduction of the VCR in the early 1980s. So, for the price of a dime, children were able to contemplate the lurid horrors of death through the figure of the zombie.

Unfortunately, horror comics in particular had been alarming child development experts, most notably Dr. Frederic Wertham, "a psychiatrist who tried to tie the gore and violence in the comic books of the day to juvenile delinquency in his 1953 book, *Seduction of the Innocent*" (Gatevackes). Congressional investigations led to the formation of the Comics Code Authority, a committee created by and composed of comic book publishers. For the next twenty years, this code put some horror comics out of business, since it prohibited "scenes dealing with, or instruments associated with walking dead, torture vampires and vampirism, ghouls, cannibalism, and werewolfism" (Gatevackes). Still, the zombie did not completely disappear from this medium, in part because compliance with the Code was voluntary, and some publishers, most notably EC Comics, refused to cave into pressure and abide by it.

In 1971, the Code became more lenient, especially toward horror comics. However, while vampires and werewolves would be permitted, zombies were still *verboten*. Marvel, already experiencing great success with its *Tomb of Dracula* and *Werewolf by Night* titles, circumvented the Code to offer zombie comics. This was effected by creating characters called "zuvembies," zombies by a different name, a subterfuge that incredibly satisfied the Comic Code Authority. Eventually the Code changed in 1989, permitting zombies to roam openly through the pages of comics, and Marvel retired the "zuvembie" name.

In the 1950s, zombies in comic books had been assuming that iconic form described in the beginning of this chapter, while during this same period the creature was still undergoing a radical transformation in the media of film and literature. During the 1950s, the zombie lost some of its connections with voodoo and the Caribbean and became a character whose lack of volition instead represented Cold War fears of about Communism's threatened lack of individuality. Richard Matheson plays with this idea in his 1954 novella *I Am Legend*. Set in a post-apocalyptic world of the near future (1975), the story suggests that recent bombings have created a strain of bacteria that kills humans, reanimating them as mindless shells driven solely by a hunger for human blood. Nightly, Robert Neville, the last man on earth, shelters in his suburban home, the final remnant of civilization, desperately trying to drown out the calls of the undead just outside who beckon him to join their ranks. The female zombies are represented as particularly horrifying, shamelessly flaunting their undead flesh in front of Neville, who has been deprived of female companionship for several years.

Matheson's undead are a cross between the vampire and the zombie. Certainly their need for blood and ability to be killed with a stake through the body make them the literary descendants of *nosferatu*. And to further confuse the issue, some of the undead believe themselves to *be* vampires, so that crosses repel those who in life were either familiar with the cultural icon of the vampire or were particularly religious. However, these undead are also slow and shuffling, underscoring their affiliation with the zombie. But it is the extreme mindlessness of these creatures that truly defines them as zombies. The undead who howl outside Neville's door are animated by a monomaniacal quest for blood, unable to appreciate any of the intellectual pursuits that he engages in, within his bomb shelter of a house. And like it or not, Neville will either be assimilated by this group or eliminated from the population. The story concludes with the revelation that there are two types of the undead: those created by the mutated strain of bacteria, and a group who predate this mutation and have learned to live with their affliction, and therefore thrive in this post-apocalyptic universe. Neville, the destroyer of the undead, sees himself as the last great hope for mankind, while this other group only sees him as a terrible legend, like the Bogey Man, something that must be eradicated.

Matheson's novella was made into two films, neither very good. The Italian film *The Last Man on Earth* (1964) by Ubaldo Ragona stars an ill-cast Vincent Price in the title role, and omits the crucial scene where he stakes a creature who crumbles to ashes and thus reveals the fact that there were some undead pre-dated the plague. The 1971 film *The Omega Man*, starring Charlton Heston as Neville, captures the eerie landscape of post-apocalyptic earth, but quickly becomes a silly action/adventure flick with poor production values. In a scene where Neville confronts a pack of undead, it is clear that only one is an actor and the others in the crowd are merely robed mannequins with hoods covering their faces. Another failing was the casting of Heston, who lacked the everyman quality of Matheson's Neville, and instead interpreted the character as more of an exceptional man fated to survive through force of his superior masculinity.

The 1964 film *The Earth Dies Screaming* is another science fiction zombie narrative in which the undead are not created through magical means. Some of *Earth*'s themes also anticipate Romero's *Night of the Living Dead* by four years. Aliens attack England and wipe out most of the population. A pilot lives through the initial invasion and makes his way across the blighted landscape looking for survivors. Searching for news on television and radio, he soon discovers that the airwaves have been affected by some sort of electronic interference. Soon after, alien robots invade Earth and begin bringing to life the dead, who are now perfectly docile and suitable for slavery. Similar to *I Am Legend*, *Earth* posits a post-apocalyptic world. But while *Legend*'s planet Earth is done in by a strange virus, *Earth*'s alien robots that cause electronic disturbances prefigure Romero's nebulous radiation cause that reanimates the newly dead.

The figure of the zombie had been evolving since its appearance in mass culture in the early twentieth century. However, George Romero's watershed 1968 film *Night of the Living Dead* crystallizes many of these elements into a form of the zombie that is arguably the most iconic representation of the creature to date. Romero's *Dead* series continues to alter the zombie, completely changing the focus of the creature's horror from its resonance with slavery and its lack of free will to its very existence as something the opposite of human—a dead thing that cannot be erased from the consciousness, since it will not completely die. The visibly decomposing bodies of Romero's undead in the relatively realistic medium of film add yet another dimension to the meaning of the zombie: the horrors of death itself.

Typical of the zombie in previous science fiction films, Romero's undead are created by a vague technology run amok, something about which the layperson knows so little that it too seems to have supernatural capabilities. In *Night*, it is not known with certainty what has animated the recently deceased, but the precipitating cause is thought to be radiation leaking to earth from a satellite. The dangers of radiation are an old familiar theme of science fiction films of the 1950s, causing men to shrink and women to grow into towering colossuses.

However, it is clear that the central horror of *Night* is the ubiquity of death itself. The film begins with Johnny and Barbara, a brother and sister quarreling during a visit to their father's remotely located grave: Johnny bitterly laments their mother's lack of consideration in burying their father in such an inconvenient location, thereby burdening her grown children with a lengthy annual trip to place flowers on his final resting place. Barbara chastises Johnny for his filial disrespect, which causes her brother to launch into an irreverent parody of all the dead interred within the cemetery, and of the events to come in the film. Johnny attempts to frighten his sister with his best Boris Karloff imitation, telling her in a deep voice that "they're coming to get you, Barbara." Perhaps it is his irreverence that raises the dead, who have now *indeed* come to get Johnny and Barbara, and anyone else with a pulse. His mock prophecy is fulfilled when one of the undead shambles up to the duo, killing Johnny. *Night* establishes the zombie as a fearsome creature *because* it is no longer living, with much visual attention paid to the decomposing bodies of the undead.

> *"They're dead. They're all messed up." Comment about the zombie infestation by a sheriff interviewed by a television news crew in* Night of the Living Dead.

After Johnny is killed brutally before Barbara's eyes, she escapes to a local farmhouse, where she tries to survive the night with a group of strangers. Soon all the occupants fight among themselves about the best place in the house for survival: the cellar or the attic. The discussion is reminiscent of the very real debate in the 1950s and early 1960s about how, and where, to hide for the few months thought necessary to survive a nuclear war, and it also introduces the theme of claustrophobic enclosure that runs through the *Dead* series. Of course, this infighting leads to the group's doom.

Romero's *Dead* series also establishes the zombie movie as a genre full of gore, something that will later particularly influence Italian filmmakers. *Night of the Living Dead* was released internationally under the title *Zombi*, which inspired Italian director Lucio Fulci's 1979 graphic film *Zombi II*. The film *Night* shows the zombie consuming living flesh in graphic detail that was fairly disturbing, even given that it was shot in black and white and its special effects were particularly low budget. Later installments in the series continue the tradition of extreme gore when zombies consume the living by tearing flesh and bone asunder amid jets of scarlet blood. A good deal of screen time is lavished on showing the red-mouthed leers of zombies with bad teeth, consuming bits of human flesh as if it were so much uncooked barbecue.

Romero's zombies also pose a critique of consumer culture in that the undead are animated by a single-minded drive for mindless consumption. The spectacle of the zombie feasting without cessation on human flesh is a central image in the whole of Romero's *Night* oeuvre. This idea of mindless consumption is particularly underscored in the second installment in the series. *Dawn of the Dead* (1978) is set in that cathedral of the modern world—the shopping mall—where the spiritual hunger can be temporarily assuaged by the purchase of just the right accessories.

Still another innovation of Romero's zombies is the establishment of "an indistinct boundary between monster and victim" (Gagne 26), causing the viewer to question the monster's essential difference from humans. This theme is further explored in subsequent entries in the series. *Dawn of the Dead* ponders on both human and zombie identity by juxtaposing flesh eaters outside of the mall with those within, whose habits of consumption of goods are so ingrained that they continue shopping in the face of annihilation.

The third film of the series, *Day of the Dead* (1985), expands this analysis of what it means to be human. An undisclosed amount of time has passed since the conclusion of *Dawn*. It is now clear that the reanimation of the newly dead is not a localized phenomenon, but a worldwide catastrophe. Because zombies now greatly outnumber the living, exterminating them is no longer a feasible solution for human survival. Thus, three research scientists are sheltering with military personnel in a nuclear silo, engaged in experiments to reprogram zombies into complete docility, in much the same way parents trick their children into comporting themselves as civilized adults. And indeed the zombies *do* seem capable of learning. Dr. Logan, the head researcher, manages to teach the zombie Bub to suppress his desire to make his human captors into dinner and instead take pleasure in reading (or at least flipping through the pages of a book) and listening to classical music.

But the military personnel responsible for safeguarding everyone fail to see the merit in the experiments, and when several of their number die procuring fresh zombies for science, Captain Rhodes, their sadistic commander, rebels. The soldiers themselves are mindless, valuing sex, alcohol, and marijuana over anything else, and are indeed difficult to tell apart from the actual zombies, particularly since they too have an insatiable blood lust. Dr. Logan attempts to convince the soldiers that they must be civil, since civility allows for communication, and if civility breaks down, then civilization itself deteriorates. But his pleas fall upon deaf ears. Rhodes is not impressed with Logan's teachable zombie Bub. Because the human Bub was in the military, he automatically salutes Rhodes, recognizing him as a superior officer. But when Rhodes flatly refuses to return the salute, Bub is enraged by his lack of civility. Meanwhile, Dr. Logan embarks on an impromptu experiment: he empties a gun and gives it to Bub to see what he would do. Bub points the gun at Rhodes, who responds by pointing his own sidearm, further illustrating that there really isn't that much difference between the two.

However, for all Logan's claims about how civility is what separates humans from other lower life forms, he himself is not a very good advertisement for civilization. Dr. Logan's gory experiments have earned him the nickname "Dr. Frankenstein": his lab is full of dissected zombies, and he frequently appears among his colleagues without bothering to change his soiled clothing or wash the blood from his hands. If Dr. Logan represents civilization, then it comes at a very terrible price to humans.

Also, *Day* begins exposing how power structures function to deny the inevitability of death. Rhodes and his unintellecutal subordinates are deeply racist and sexist, and these ideas nourish their fantasy that they themselves, all white men, are uniquely suited to survive. Of course, this is an illusion, and these men die horribly at the end of the film.

The fourth film in Romero's series, *Land of the Dead*, is set still later, and is the only film of the group to actually envision the new world order to emerge post-zombie. A band of survivors are re-establishing civilization on a peninsula in Philadelphia. The venture, funded by the wealthy Mr. Kaufmann, has kept intact old class structures. Wealthy whites live "in the grand old style" in Fiddler's Green, a condominium tower that boasts world-class shopping and dining, while within the barriers of the city but outside of the towers are the other people, a motley assortment of black, white, and brown, who make a living in the various service professions—protecting the city from zombie attack as members of the military; raiding neighboring zombie-infested towns for supplies; cleaning and cooking for the rich; or working in the flourishing prostitution, gambling, and drug trafficking trades that keep lower social orders too occupied to question the unequal distribution of resources.

Tension erupts almost immediately when one of Kaufmann's henchmen, Cholo, decides he has made enough money doing his employer's dirty work, disposing of the bodies of his enemies, and so he is now entitled to purchase his own condo in Fiddler's Green. But class mobility is an illusion in this society. Kaufmann rebuffs Cholo's attempt to move into his neighborhood, and sends one of his other henchmen to dispose of his bitter now-former employee. But Cholo escapes and steals Kaufmann's million-dollar armored truck used for supply raids and threatens to use it to shell the city if he isn't paid a ransom. Another of Kaufmann's henchmen, the more idealistic and revolutionary Reilly, is sent to kill Cholo before it is necessary that Kaufmann pay him. Reilly agrees, not out of any loyalty to Kaufmann, but because if Cholo bombs the city, more than just the wealthy of Fiddler's Green will suffer when the zombies are able to enter through the breached security fences.

Meanwhile, Dr. Logan's theories about zombies in *Day* are proved correct. The zombies *can* learn and work cooperatively. We see this earlier on in *Land* when one of the more intelligent of their number, Big Daddy, is able to communicate with the others through grunts. Eventually, the zombies work together to storm the island, destroying Kaufmann and his property. But even more importantly, this moment demonstrates that zombies are definitively not very much different from humans. As Reilly prepares to leave the city at the end of the film, he remarks on the zombies' similarity to humans in that they just

> *"You have no right!" Bellowed by Mr. Kaufmann in* Land of the Dead, *who is in a state of disbelief that anyone living or dead would defy his authority and violate personal property.*

"That's exactly why we're killing . . . to survive. We can't allow the dead to exist beside the living. Their brains are impaired, they exist for only one purpose. They have *to be destroyed."* Explained to Robert Neville in Richard Matheson's I Am Legend *by one of the infected who aren't brain damaged, and who will be re-establishing civilization in a post-apocalyptic world where much of the population has been turned in to bloodthirsty zombies by a mutant virus.*

want somewhere to be. And he is correct on all counts. We see that these zombies are justifiably angry that their own home in Uniontown is continually raided by humans who then harass their numbers. And the zombies in *Land* appear more similar to their human counterparts than they do in any of the other films in the series. When they first appear in *Land*, it isn't clear if we are viewing zombies or humans, as their faces are less distorted by decay than the zombies in previous films, and all wear clothing that marks them as individuals with a particular place in the old world.

Romero's films also definitively associate the zombie with the apocalypse, something done previously in *I Am Legend* and *The Earth Dies Screaming*. Many zombie films after *Night* similarly associate the undead with an apocalyptic world where the bottom rail is on top, so to speak, in that they hunt the living. J. R. Bookwalter's 1988 low budget 8mm film *The Dead Next Door* envisions the zombie as the result of human hubris. A scientist attempting to create a serum to keep people from expiring instead makes the first zombie, ushering in the end of the world as all know it. Now government zombie squads roam the country, attempting to eradicate the living-impaired and discover a cult who believes zombies were created by God as punishment for man's sins. Scooter McCrae's 1994 film *Shatter Dead* similarly posits a world where the existence of zombies spawns the creation of a cult. Here too zombies are sent to Earth by divine fiat, but cannot be killed by the usual means, or at all, since the source of their condition resides in the soul, not in the brain. To some, the presence of zombies is a wondrous thing, signifying that the Rapture cannot be far behind. For others, the presence of the undead is worse than the old way, since this condition has some disturbing drawbacks: these zombies do not crave human flesh, or anything for that matter, and also do not need to sleep, but are eternally imprisoned in bodies that have lost the power of regeneration. Thus, a zombie who is injured or maimed lives eternally as a sort of broken doll, and some of the undead rightfully fear that a caste system will soon develop where unmarred zombies are at the pinnacle, and the more shopworn among them on the lowest rungs of society.

The zombie became popular in Italy ever since the release of Romero's *Dawn* under the name *Zombi*. It is difficult to discuss the Italian zombie film without also describing its sister genre, the cannibal film. The Italian cannibal film is set in an exotic third-world locale and features dark-skinned people consuming in graphic detail the flesh of just about anything that moves. Both Italian zombie and cannibal films are similar to their earlier American and British counterparts in their representation of non-Europeans as violently savage Others.

Also, the Italian zombie and cannibal films are both characterized by graphic scenes of the consumption of bloody flesh. In Italian films, as visual attention is paid to the disturbing eating habits of the zombie as to the spectacle of the creature's own decaying flesh. And similar to the serial killer figure in the American slasher film, the Italian zombie frequently feasts upon scantily clad women, or preys on sexually active couples.

Lucio Fulci's 1979 film *Zombie* is a fairly typical example of the Italian zombie film. *Zombie* (not to be confused with *Zombi* or *Zombi 2*) is set on an unnamed Caribbean island where African drums beat a tattoo whenever anyone approaches the dwelling of the dark-skinned natives. A white doctor remains on the island, attempting to cure the natives of an unidentifiable disease that causes the dead to walk and crave human flesh. While the natives believe the origin of the phenomena is voodoo, the doctor thinks there is a scientific explanation, though he never finds one. The decaying bodies of the zombies get a good deal of screen time, and more often than not, their appearance is made after the camera shows a nude woman in a private setting. This juxtaposition of the zombie with the prerequisite topless young woman so often found in horror films manipulates the phenomenon described by Laura Mulvey in "Visual Pleasures in Narrative Cinema." The modern audience has become so comfortable with the objectification of female flesh on the screen that the significance of its appearance usually passes unnoticed and it is just another unconscious pleasure. In the Italian zombie film this phenomenon has yet another layer: naked female flesh, presented for visual consumption by the viewer, is juxtaposed with the zombie's very literal consumption of this very body. Not surprisingly, these women also receive the most abuse at the hands of both humans and zombies. The doctor's wife in *Zombie* exists to absorb violence. She goes from getting slapped by her husband to being the recipient of a splinter through the eyeball in one of the most graphic and disturbing scenes in all zombie cinema.

The 1983 Italian film *Zeder* is unusual as a zombie movie in that is more concerned with what happens when the dead are brought back to life than it is with what they eat. The basis of the plot is similar to Stephen King's 1983 novel *Pet Sematary*: special places possess magical powers to reanimate the dead. One such site is a fifth-century necropolis in Italy; in 1959, Paolo Zeder experimented with this ground by having his body secretly interred there. Zeder rose from the dead, but became a mindless fiend who preyed on the living. Twenty-seven years later, a former priest has himself interred in this ground, and a team of paranormal investigators monitors his progress with a television camera placed in his coffin. After a year in his grave, the priest has not decomposed and eventually awakens to wreak havoc on the living. The fearful spectacle of death presented in *Zeder* is not one of decay, but of the dead *living*. In one of the penultimate scenes, the video camera shows the priest's eyes flickering, then opening completely, a wicked smile playing across his lips as he laughs maniacally before rising from his own death. *Zeder* is also similar to *Pet*

Sematary in its assumption that the reanimated necessarily have homicidal intent toward the living.

Other Italian, and Spanish, zombie films are about the ancient, rather than the recently dead, rising from their graves. Perhaps this is to be expected in a continent where ancient history is a tangible presence amidst contemporary life. The Italian film *War of the Zombies* (1964) presents an undead army of Roman legionnaires who threaten the world with the rule of a black magician. The Spanish film *Tombs of the Blind Dead* (1971) takes as its subject medieval Knights Templar, who brought back from their last crusade eastern necromantic secrets of life and death. The order drank the blood of a virgin to make a pact with Satan that permitted them to live eternally, provided they drink more blood and consume human flesh. Soon the outside world learns of their crimes, and the knights are excommunicated and executed, but too late—they can continue their existence beyond death through the consumption of female flesh. The knights thrive well into the twentieth century, and at the end of the film they have escaped the confines of their monastery completely to consume more human flesh for three more sequels. The zombies of *Tombs* are the personification of death itself: their bloated faces filled with maggots, they feast upon the living who, moments before, were having sex or caring for their children.

In the past twenty years, the popularity of zombies has spread to the novel format as well. One of the most original and graphic of these novels is Simon Clark's *Blood Crazy* (1995), set in a post-apocalyptic world where overnight a virus has infected anyone over twenty-one with a drive to brutally annihilate the young by lavishing violence on them. Their juvenile victims, often their own children, are rent asunder, stomped into the earth, even crucified. The surviving youth now have to restructure society without adult guidance. While the adults in *Blood Crazy* are not the walking dead, since they are not deceased, they are zombies in that their higher reasoning has been obliterated, leaving them with nothing more than a drive to kill the young that is so powerful that it wipes out even the need for eating and sleeping. The infected adults are so single-minded in their purpose that they will do things such as make a living bridge of themselves over a river, those on the bottom willingly drowning to permit others to reach the young who must be wiped out at all costs. Other zombie novels include *Pet Sematary* (1983), which will be discussed in a later section of this chapter; Bentley Little's *The Walking* (2002), where the recently dead shamble miles to a lake in the middle of the Arizona desert, the site of a nineteenth-century town eventually flooded by the government to stop the evil located there; and Brian Smyth's *Deathbringer* (2006), where a sorcerer comes to a small Tennessee town and makes the newly dead into a zombie army to menace the living.

Literary zombies are generally flat characters, which is to be expected, since they are typified by the mindlessness of their drives. Notable exception can be seen in Tim Waggoner's hard-boiled dark fantasy *Necropolis* (2004) and Brian Keene's *The Rising* (2003) and *City of the Dead* (2005), novels that feature intelligent zombies. Waggoner's Necropolis is a newly created subterranean city of supernatural creatures, including werewolves, vampires, and zombies. While most of the zombies are devoid of free will, Waggoner's protagonist, Matthew Adroin, is a zombie *not* under the control of a master. Adroin, a hard-boiled private detective, knows what no one else does: Necropolis's fatal flaw that will destroy the city if not corrected. There is also a touch of humor in Adroin's zombie state. In Waggoner's universe, people are turned into zombies through a series of spells that not only bind them to their master, but ensure that their bodies do not deteriorate. But similar to many pharmaceuticals, these spells lose their efficacy after a while, and unfortunately for Adroin, the magic no longer prevents his own decay, so that he must resort to "restoring" himself with bits of his corpus that have fallen into his pockets.

"Every so often in history, there will come this colossal event that splits time in two. You know, like the birth of Jesus Christ. Everything before—B. C. Everything after—A. D. On my way to McDonald's, it happened again. After two thousand years of old Age, Anno Domini, had died a death. Naturally, like everyone else at the time I didn't know it. Any more than a passerby seeing that baby squawking in a manger somewhere in suburban Bethlehem would know that the world was going to change PDQ." Observed at the beginning of Simon Clark's Blood Crazy *by his hero Nick Aten about the world the day changed when everyone over 21 became infected with a virus compelling them to murder the young.*

Keene's novels posit an apocalyptic universe where a government experiment with a supercollider has loosed a demon that kills and inhabits humans, and later animals. Jim Thurmond, a construction worker, is one of the few remaining humans, having built a bomb shelter five years earlier to survive Y2K. But Keene's zombies are not the slow and mindless sort established by Romero. Of course, they hunger for flesh and reproduce prodigiously, but they are also fast and intelligent—they can think, drive cars, and even set traps for the living.

Zombies continue their popularity in contemporary graphic novels and comics. Eric Powell's humorous *The Goon* series (2003) pits the title character, a sort of mafia hit man with occult powers, against his arch nemesis, the Nameless Priest, and his army of undead soldiers. Robert Kirkman and Tony Moore's *The Walking Dead* series (2004) is more character driven and less concerned with gory representations of the living dead, and is very heavily influenced by Romero's *Dead* series as well as Danny Boyle's 2002 film *28 Days Later*. Rick, a small-town Kentucky police officer, is shot in the line of duty and put into a coma. He awakens a month later to discover that zombies have taken over the world and destroyed civilization. Rick heads toward Atlanta and is reunited with his wife and child, who have taken refuge outside of that city with a band of other survivors. *The Walking Dead* focuses on the usual struggles that ensue whenever a civilization is toppled by zombies, ranging from petty bickering about who does the laundry to more weighty

"The end is very fucking nigh." Message scrawled on a church wall in 28 Days Later.

matters concerning the best place to be in order to survive. Also, the series is rendered in black and white rather than color, which not only underemphasizes the gore but gives the work the feel of Romero's black and white film *Night of the Living Dead*. And most recently, *The Marvel Zombies* (2006) is Marvel Comics's most recent addition to its list of undead characters. *The Marvel Zombies* series is an arc of an *Ultimate Fantastic Four* story that occurs in a parallel universe where a virus from space turns superheroes into the flesh eating undead.

Zombies have also come into the world of video games, some of which have spawned their own comic books in turn. *Zombies Ate My Neighbors*, produced by LucasArts, is a shooter-style video game where teenaged protagonists must navigate their way through a suburban landscape besieged by a number of classic monsters including werewolves, vampires, and zombies. The game's sequel, *Ghoul Patrol*, however, was rather uninspired and effectively killed off the series. And in the 1996 game *Resident Evil*, a corporation clandestinely conducting biological warfare research has created a race of bloodthirsty mutants who are now out of control. *Resident Evil* has spawned a comic book series and several films.

As the zombie figure becomes more familiar in popular culture, many writers and filmmakers push to extremes the idea of the undead as representative of existential angst. The zombie not only represents a fear of (and denial of) death, but states of existence devoid of meaning and of questionable quality. David Sutton's short story "Clinically Dead" (1993) applies the zombie metaphor to the horrors of medical technology used to prolong life at any cost. When the nameless protagonist's elderly mother becomes critically ill, neither patient nor her only surviving family member is given any say in her medical care. Instead, her unconscious body is kept alive, and she is whisked away to a special hospital that cares for people whose bodies are failing. When her son visits her in this facility, he makes a horrifying discovery: not only do others also seem to have been transformed into the undead through science, but similar to zombies created by black magic, their animated flesh has been filled with a unified will to kill their "creators."

Edgar Wright's comic film *Shaun of the Dead* (2005) offers a similar, if parodic, commentary on modern life. The opening scene shows the film's hero, Shaun, pasty and slack-jawed at the conclusion of another monotonous night of drinking in his local pub. When the zombies appear in the film five minutes later, their presence is redundant among the workaday living, and at first they are barely noticed. If zombies are flat characters, then so are most of the living in this film. Hence, escaping doom involves not merely avoiding the bite of a zombie, but actively becoming a "round character," someone with a varied and meaningful existence.

R. Chetwynd Hayes's comic short story "The Ghouls" (1975) makes light of what is done more seriously with the undead in other works such as *White*

Zombie and *Zombie Plague*. In both of these films, it is hinted at that zombies make ideal workers. Not only is their condition similar to slavery but, better still, they do not attempt to shirk their duties, since they have no will of their own. In Hayes's story, a prime minister oversees a secret government program to convert the dead into productive civil servants who do not even need to be paid. The apparent mindlessness of lower-level civil service makes it completely unnecessary that these employees possess any critical thinking skills in order to do their jobs effectively.

Clive Barker's short story "Sex, Death and Starshine" (1984) likewise blurs the distinction between human and zombie and questions the quality of modern life. The Elysium Theatre, a grand palace of the arts about to be torn down to make way for an office building or big box store, is hosting its final show, a production of *Twelfth Night*. A truly incompetent actress has been cast in the role of Viola because her fame as a television star will guarantee that the public, who would otherwise avoid a production of Shakespeare, will spend money; this demonstrates that the truly crass world has succeeded the one that created the Elysium. One of the elderly trustees of the theater laments that the last show of the Elysium will not be a quality production, and wants to put someone else in the role—his dead wife Constantia, a gifted actress in her day. The zombie Constantia, embalmed soon after her death, has retained her beauty, and was so renowned in life for her thespian prowess that her presence on the stage inspires the deceased to rise from their own untended graveyard to see her perform. When Constantia is on stage with the human actors, it is as if the line between the living and the dead has been seamlessly crossed: the illusion of life created by great art is more compelling and beautiful than the genuine article. But the real irony is that only the dead can appreciate truly excellent theater as the living are all too obtuse.

Les Daniels's humorous story "They're Coming for You" features zombies who return from the dead and are curiously uninterested in taking revenge on their creator. The ironically named Mr. Bliss walks in on his young wife's dalliance with another man in their marital bed, prompting him to kill her and her partner in adultery and bury the two in the back yard. When Bliss finally has the courage to return to the scene of the crime, the two rise from their shallow grave and come to the upstairs bedroom where he waits. But they are not interested in nibbling on his flesh, but only intent on continuing their fairly athletic coitus. Bliss finds himself compelled to watch their performance, since the undead have a more meaningful and interesting existence than his own.

Don Coscarelli's witty film *Bubba Ho-tep* (2002), based on a Joe R. Lansdale story of the same name, likewise employs the zombie to explore existential angst. In an East Texas nursing home live an aging Elvis Presley and John Kennedy. The staff naturally believe that Elvis and the President are not who they say they are, but instead, like the other inmates of the home, grossly out of touch with reality. After all, Elvis's "real" identity is Sebastian Haff, an Elvis impersonator, whose career-ending fall from the stage broke his hip and forced

A Chronology of Important Zombie Films

1932   *White Zombie* (Victor Halperin)

1943   *I Walked with a Zombie* (Jacques Tourneur)

1958   *Plan Nine from Outer Space* (Ed Wood)

1964   *The Earth Dies Screaming* (Terence Fisher)

1964   *The Last Man on Earth* (Ubaldo Ragona)

1964   *War of the Zombies* (*Roma contra Roma*) (Guiseppe Vari)

1966   *The Plague of Zombies* (John Gilling)

1968   *Night of the Living Dead* (George A. Romero)

1971   *The Omega Man* (Boris Sagil)

1973   *Return of the Evil Dead* (Amando de Ossorio)

1973   *Tombs of the Blind Dead* (Amando de Ossorio)

1974   *A Virgin among the Living Dead* (Jesus Franco)

1979   *Dawn of the Dead* (George A. Romero)

1979   *The Fog* (John Carpenter)

1979   *Zombie* (Lucio Fulci)

1979   *Zombi 2* (Lucio Fulci)

1980   *The Gates of Hell* (Lucio Fulci)

1981   *The Evil Dead* (Sam Raimi)

1982   *Creepshow* (George A. Romero)

1983   *Zeder* (a.k.a. in the United States as *Revenge of the Dead*) (Pupi Avati)

1985   *Day of the Dead* (George A. Romero)

1985   *Re-Animator* (Stuart Gordon)

1985   *Return of the Living Dead* (Dan O'Bannon)

1987   *Evil Dead II* (Sam Raimi)

1987   *I Was a Teenage Zombie* (John Elias Michalakis)

1987   *The Serpent and the Rainbow* (Wes Craven)

1988   *Return of the Living Dead, Part II* (Ken Wiederhorn)

1988   *Zombi 3* (Lucio Fulci)

1989   *Pet Sematary* (Mary Lambert)

1990   *Night of the Living Bread* (Kevin S. O'Brien)

1990   *Night of the Living Dead* (Tom Savini)

1991   *Bride of Re-Animator* (Brian Yunza)

1991   *Night of the Day of the Dawn of the Son of the Bride of the Return of the Revenge of the Terror of the Attack of the Evil Mutant Hellbound*

Flesh-Eating Subhumanoid Living Dead, Part II (Lowel Mason and James Riffel)

1992 *Dead Alive* (Peter Jackson)

1993 *Army of Darkness* (Sam Raimi)

1993 *Return of the Living Dead, Part III* (Brian Yuzna)

1993 *Shatter Dead* (Scooter McCrae)

1994 *The Cemetery Man* (Michele Soavi)

2002 *Bubba Ho-Tep* (Don Coscarelli)

2005 *Land of the Dead* (George A. Romero)

2005 *Shaun of the Dead* (Edgar Wright)

him into a nursing home. And the man claiming to be President Kennedy is black. But each man has a perfectly "reasonable" explanation for his seemingly improbable situation. In the late seventies, Elvis, tired of fame and fortune, changed lives with an impersonator who could be his twin and liked drugs even more than he did. When the impersonator soon expired, the world believed the King was dead. And Jack Kennedy did not die after being shot in Dealey Plaza, but was whisked away to a secret hospital where his enemies dyed his skin brown, modified his memory, and placed him with some African Americans they said were his family so that he would forget he was ever the leader of the Free World.

Now each man suffers the daily indignities of living in a nursing home, an existence that is itself a sort of living death. But as improbable as Jack's and Elvis's situations seem, they are downright sensible compared to the explanation behind what is killing off residents in the home. An ancient mummy, Bubba Ho-tep, formerly part of a traveling road show attraction, has "escaped" when the bus carrying him ran off a bridge and into the creek below. Bubba Ho-tep's makers eternally cursed him by burying him without any of his names, depriving him of the identity he would need to move on to the next world. Now Bubba Ho-tep is doomed to roam the earth, sucking souls from people in order to continue to animate his hideously desiccated corpse. For Bubba Ho-tep, the nursing home is like the proverbial nest on the ground—the prey can't escape easily, and no one will believe an outlandish tale of a mummy running in the halls. Only when Jack and Elvis team up to rid the world of Bubba Ho-tep can they regain their sense of purpose and feel alive once more.

Bubba Ho-tep is not your typical zombie film, however. As stated previously, generally mummies *aren't* considered zombies, because they are usually not devoid of will or completely controlled by one basic drive. But this is not the case with Bubba Ho-tep, who is compelled to suck souls in much the same way Romero's zombies crave human flesh. Another important factor is Bubba Ho-tep's appearance, something that Lansdale is unable to convey fully through his story, since he is not working in a visual medium. While mummies share the shambling gait of the zombie, they are generally covered in bandages. But Bubba Ho-tep is very obviously and disturbingly a decaying corpse. And his decomposition is as terrible a spectacle as the visible aging of the nursing home residents. Also, Bubba Ho-tep's countenance and behavior are reminiscent of the figure of Death, sans black robe and scythe, come to harvest those who aren't really "living" much any more.

Some zombie narratives treat the inability to accept death. In Stephen King's novel *Pet Sematary,* residents of a rural main town use the Micmac Indian burying ground as a way to cheat death because this place's supernatural powers allow the bereaved to be reunited with their loved ones. But the Micmac burying ground, once a hallowed resting place for the tribe, has been corrupted by whites into a site of dangerous magic. Those buried in this space are physically regenerated, but lack a soul. Thus, while their bodies return to their loved ones, they no longer possess any memories of affection or attachment, but instead are animated only by an irrational desire to kill whoever was responsible for their resurrection.

William Sleator's young adult novel *The Boy Who Couldn't Die* (2004) explores the inability of adolescents to accept mortality. Sleator writes about a sort of zombie not seen often in Western popular culture, the astral zombie. Astral zombies, also derived from Haitian folklore, are individuals who still walk among the living, but have either sold their souls or had them stolen by a houngan who can then use them to carry out his or her wishes. This is the case for sixteen-year-old Ken Pritchard, who initially believes himself to be invulnerable. After all, he is a white male from a wealthy family that can give him things such as a private education and spring break vacations in exotic countries. His youth and privileged position have presented him with little opportunity to see misery, let alone death, first-hand. But all this changes when his best friend is killed in a plane crash, his body so mangled that an open casket funeral is out of the question. Ken, still at that age where he cannot imagine old people as ever having been young, naturally has difficulty accepting that a member of his cohort is mortal, and his friend's death precipitates an existential crisis.

Looking for something to placate his fears, Ken is attracted to an obscure ad in the back of a magazine that promises to make him safe from death. The ad leads Ken to Cheri Beaumont, whose appearance bespeaks the pedestrian nature of mortality more than it does exotic powers from another land. Cheri is a sagging and wrinkled middle-aged woman whose apartment reeks of cigarette smoke and is decorated with tacky ballerina ornaments. For the price of a concert ticket, she promises she can hide Ken's soul and make him immortal. But there is a catch. Nothing can be gained without sacrifice, so to live eternally, Ken must be willing to die a little first, and once his soul is hidden, it won't be easy, let alone cheap, to get it back.

Sleator's novel is remarkable in that his zombie is actually a round character capable of questioning the quality of his existence and ultimately changing things. This is in part due to the nature of the astral zombie, who is a good deal more similar to the living than more traditional types of zombies. Ken explores his newfound immortality by doing suicidal things such as provoking a fight with the school bully and swimming with sharks while on a family vacation. But Ken soon learns that immortality isn't all he thought it would be: food is no longer appetizing, and even kissing the most attractive girl in school after "winning" her from her bully boyfriend is uninteresting! Ken eventually comprehends the horror of his condition. After a vivid nightmare in which he knifes a stranger, he awakens to find himself in the family kitchen, clutching a butcher knife from which phantom blood disappears before his eyes. The next night, Ken discovers that a man was found stabbed to death in the vicinity where his dream was set and realizes that he is no longer in control of a vital part of his self; instead, his soul has been hijacked to accomplish someone else's will. Ken's ensuing struggle to regain control of his soul causes him to understand how truly special it is to be mortal and vulnerable.

The films *Ed and His Dead Mother* (1993) and *Braindead* (1992) also treat the inability to accept the death of loved ones. Both deal humorously with socially inept mama's boys unable to sever the parental relationship, even after the death of their mothers. *Braindead* is the more traditional of the two. In life, Lionel's mother is a demanding shrew who desperately tries to keep her son all to herself, even going so far as to spy on him while he takes an attractive young woman on a date to the zoo. It is here that Lionel's mother is bitten by a Sumerian rat monkey, turning her into a flesh-eating zombie who infects others with her bite. Worse still, Lionel's mother is ever more demanding dead than she was alive, and he must spend all his waking hours ensuring that she doesn't escape and harm anyone else, particularly the woman he loves. *Braindead*'s over-the-top gore further parodies the more recent incarnations of the genre.

Ed and His Dead Mother is less traditional in that Ed's inability to get over his mother's death derives from his almost unnatural affection for her. As with Lionel, Ed's relationship with his mother prevents him from having an adult relationship with a woman his own age, and his inability to get over her death further prevents him from maturing. Not surprisingly, Ed is easy prey for a slick-talking salesman who promises to return his deceased mother to him for a nominal fee. Of course, Ed's mother comes back as a zombie, but her reappearance among the living isn't as disturbing, at least at first, since her lust for flesh is more subtle, and if one didn't look too closely, it wouldn't be possible to detect any difference between Ed's undead mother and her formerly alive self. The zombies in both these films represent the idealized parent that we all create as children, the one who must be symbolically killed if we are to emerge as autonomous adults. Thus, both men must ultimately kill their zombie mothers if they are to become successfully heterosexualized and able to have adult relationships with women their age.

After the zombie narrative was firmly established as a subgenre with its own rules, parodies appeared. Parodic zombie narratives are particularly illuminating in that, to be effective, they must demonstrate a thorough knowledge of the genre. One of the earliest of these parodies is Sam Raimi's film *The Evil Dead* (1981). The plot is fairly simple. A group of college students drive to a remote mountain cabin for a weekend of partying. Instead, they discover the reason the cabin was so cheap. In the basement is a copy of the *Necronomicon*, a magical book that can raise the dead. And just in case the hapless finder of this tome is unable to read it, there is also a helpful version of the book on tape, which one of the group plays, thereby raising a demon who possesses each of the cabin's inhabitants and makes them into the walking dead who hunger for flesh.

The Evil Dead, with its cheesy special effects and gore so over-the-top that it can only be a parody of itself, questions the conventions of the genre. Ash, the film's hero, cannot seem to figure out if he is in a zombie film or a possession story. When his girlfriend's body is inhabited by the demon and her face is subsequently distorted into a bluish death mask with glassy eyes, he cannot quite bring himself to kill and dismember her (one of the few things that can stop a zombie), perhaps because he himself isn't quite sure if she is not just possessed. And the demon takes advantage of Ash's confusion about what rules apply. At one point, when Ash is prepared to dispatch the thing that was his girlfriend with a bullet to the head, the trickster-demon restores her pre-dead appearance and voice, causing him to vacillate long enough to be menaced further. But even when Ash finally realizes that he is in a zombie movie, ordinary human sentimentality prevents him from doing what is necessary. As Ash prepares to cut off his zombified girlfriend's head with a chainsaw, he is stopped cold at the sight of the necklace he gave her, dangling around her neck. This hesitation allows the demon to do still more damage. But in the end, it really doesn't matter how soon Ash realizes he is in a zombie movie, since the rules he has learned from this genre do not apply either, since they never really made logical sense. After all, how can you kill something that's already dead? You can't, which is why the film ends with the demon chasing Ash. *The Evil Dead* spawned two sequels: *Evil Dead II* (1987) and *Army of Darkness* (1993).

The Return of the Living Dead (1985) similarly plays with the conventions of the zombie narrative. *Return* is an explicit parody of Romero's *Dead* series. John A. Russo, who co-wrote the script for *Night* with Romero, was also one of the writers for *Return*, which poses the question asked by many fans: "How do you kill something that's already dead?" *Return*'s premise is this: the events depicted in *Night* really happened, but the directors had to change the story in order to avoid litigation. Inside a Louisville medical warehouse are stored the bodies of the reanimated dead, part of a vast government cover-up from events in 1968, after an experimental chemical developed by the military for killing. Marijuana came into contact with the newly dead, bringing them back to life with an insatiable desire for consuming brains. One of the zombies "safely" contained in an allegedly impervious container crafted by the Army Corps of Engineers escapes, contaminating a cadaver in the warehouse. Now two zombies are on the loose, and hapless people trapped in the warehouse rely on what they learned in *Night* to neutralize the undead menace. But alas, *Night* is not a source of factual information, and indeed, it is difficult to "kill" what is already dead. Burning the zombies in the incinerator of a mortuary next door at least gets rid of the individual undead, but causes a new problem when the ashes are borne aloft just before a rainstorm brings them down to earth, saturating the ground of the nearby cemetery and reanimating the dead interred within.

The zombies in *Return* are also capable of learning rapidly in order to adapt to their new environment. One zombie, a Confederate soldier, has no trouble operating the radio in an abandoned police car in order to convince the dispatcher that he is a police officer in need of reinforcements. The dispatcher obliges, and more officers are sent to the scene of the disturbance, only to be consumed by the waiting zombies as if they were nothing more than a pizza delivery. The zombies in *Return* are also articulate: they are able to tell their victims clearly that they are after brains—apparently their voice boxes didn't deteriorate.

There is also irony in where the besieged living has been forced to take shelter—the mortuary. The modern funeral industry has encouraged us to believe that death is not a part of life, transforming the corpse so that it appears that the deceased is only sleeping rather than beginning to decompose, and conveniently permitting us to forget this horrible reality. But death is with us always, no matter how hard we strain to deny this fact. Hence, the zombies' wish to eat brains (rather than the more general human flesh that other zombies consume) can be seen as attempting to reacquaint the conscious mind with the disturbing knowledge of death.

Another comic zombie film that is conversant in the conventions of the genre is *Re-Animator* (1985), which is loosely based on H. P. Lovecraft's 1922 short story "Herbert West—Reanimator." Lovecraft's tale of a mad scientist in the vein of Victor Frankenstein is arguably a zombie story. West, obsessed with the desire to isolate the mechanical processes that permit life, experiments with keeping alive humans who are soon to expire. This causes great suffering to his subjects, as the dead tissue is not anxious to return to life, and does so only with great pain. The story concludes with West's most recent and horrible experiment—keeping alive, separately, the head and body of a major killed during World War I. The "preserved" soldier makes a spectacular return with some of his fellow reanimated dead to take vengeance on their creator. *Re-Animator* emphasizes the humor in Lovecraft's story, taking what is told with tongue in cheek in the original to its most absurd extreme. Dr. Herbert West, a medical student at Miskatonic Medical School, has discovered a serum that can reanimate dead things, and one of the school's directors, Dr. Carl Hill, attempts to steal this secret from him. Instead, Hill becomes one of West's more horrifying experiments, suffering a fate similar to that of Lovecraft's Dr. West's major. Hill's torso shuffles around, his head tucked underneath his arm. While this scene in Lovecraft's story is merely horrifying, translated into a visual medium it becomes absurd. Hill's torso flails comically and finds it necessary to hold his severed head above his shoulders so that he can see. One of the film's more humorous, and graphic scenes, involves the headless Dr. Hill attempting to ravish the supine object of his affection, holding up his severed head in order to perform an obscene act upon the unwilling young woman.

The zombie also appears in more recent narratives incorporated with other more traditional folklore. Peter Tremayne's 1993 short story "Marbh Bheo" is an example of this type of story. "Marbh Bheo" tells of the Irish myth of the living dead. During the days of the Potato Famine, a greedy British landlord turns out his tenants to starve because they are unable to pay their rents. Wishing to change their minds, the parish priest gathers with the tenants to protest, only to be cruelly cut down by the lord's henchmen. The local cunning woman finds a corpse that is in relatively good condition in that it has lost no limbs and uses her ancient wisdom to reanimate it. Similar to the golem in Rabbi Lowe's tale, this creature is then controlled by the cunning woman to protect her people. But the marbh bheo goes further than Rabbi Lowe's golem: it actually seeks vengeance against not only the landlord, but his descendants many generations down, tearing them into pieces.

Other more recent works renew an interest in the zombie as genuine phenomena. Lisa Cantrell's novel *Boneman* (1992) returns the zombie to its Haitian roots through her story of a Haitian drug dealer who is also a houngan able to turn his rivals into zombies.

The zombie has also been subject matter for more mainstream directors. Danny Boyle's film *28 Days Later* is a modern version of Romero's dead. Boyle's zombies are neither bewitched nor the reanimated dead, but instead are irredeemably infected with a virus known as rage that causes perfectly docile humans to transform into red-eyed shells of their former selves, now animated by nothing more than the single-minded desire to tear asunder other humans. The virus has the same "magical" quality in Boyle's universe that radiation had in Romero's, in that it is capable of rapidly transforming everything in its path. And the nature of the virus itself, rage, is the *Zeitgeist* of the modern era, where everything is so impersonalized and moves so rapidly as to provoke constant and consuming impotent fury. The single-minded need to destroy other humans is the only thing that qualifies these creatures as zombies as they aren't dead. Also unlike Romero's undead, Boyle's zombies are fast, sweeping down upon their hapless victims with preternatural speed.

The zombie has become such a cultural icon that it has come full circle as a metaphor for someone who has no will, similar to the way poet Robert Southey used the term in the early nineteenth century. Joyce Carol Oates's novel *Zombie* (1995), a serial killer narrative loosely based on the life of Jeffery Dahmer, attests to this phenomenon. Dahmer experimented with making some of his victims into zombies by giving them a home lobotomy with a drill. Similarly, Oates's psychologically immature sex offender Quentin Q. is obsessed with making the perfect zombie, a beautiful young man who can be transformed into a willing sex slave that he can keep hidden indefinitely for his private enjoyment. Brad Gooch's novel *Zombie 2000* (2000) uses the zombie as a metaphor for his protagonist's lack of assertion and unnatural ability to be swayed by the desires of others much to his own detriment. And most recently, the term zombie is used by computer geeks to describe a terminal that has been maliciously taken over by a remote host.

BIBLIOGRAPHY

Novels and Short Stories

Barker, Clive. "Sex, Death and Starshine." In *Books of Blood, Volume 1*. London: Sphere, 1984.

Cantrell, Lisa W. *Boneman*. New York: Tor, 1992.

Cave, Hugh. B. "Mission to Margal." In *The Mammoth Book of Zombies*, ed. Stephen Jones. New York: Carroll & Graf, 1993.

Chetwynd-Hayes, R. "The Ghouls." In *The Night Ghouls*. London: Fontana, 1975.

Clark, Simon. *Blood Crazy*. London: Hodder & Stoughton, 1995.

Daniels, Les. "They're Coming for You." In *Cutting Edge*, ed. Dennis Etchison. New York: St. Martin's Press, 1986.

Derleth, August. "The House in the Magnolias." *Strange Tales of Mystery and Terror* (June 1932).

Etchison, Dennis. "The Late Shift." In *Dark Forces*, ed. Kirby McCauley. New York: Viking Press, 1980.

Gooch, Brad. *Zombie 2000*. Woodstock, NY: Overlook Press, 2000.

Grant, Charles L. "Quietly Now." In *The Arbor House Necropolis*, ed. Bill Pronzini. New York: Arbor House, 1981.

Haining, Peter, ed. *Stories of the Walking Dead*. London: Severn House, 1985.

Jones, Stephen, ed. *The Mammoth Book of Zombies*. New York: Carroll & Graf, 1993.

Keene, Brian. *City of the Dead*. New York: Leisure, 2005.

———. *The Rising*. North Webster, IN: Delirium, 2003.

King, Stephen. *Pet Sematary*. Garden City, NY: Doubleday, 1983.

Little, Bentley. *The Walking*. New York: Signet, 2000.

Lovecraft, H. P. "Herbert West—Reanimator." Originally published as "Grewsome Tales" in *Home Brew* (February–July 1922).

Matheson, Richard. *I Am Legend*. New York: Fawcett, 1954.

McClusky, Thorp. "While Zombies Walked." *Weird Tales* (September 1939).

Oates, Joyce Carol. *Zombie*. New York: Dutton, 1995.

Sleator, William. *The Boy Who Couldn't Die*. New York: Amulet, 2004.

Smith, Bryan. *Deathbringer*. New York: Leisure, 2006.

Sutton, David. "Clinically Dead." In *The Mammoth Book of Zombies*, ed. Stephen Jones. New York: Carroll & Graf, 1993.

Tremayne, Peter. "Marbh Bheo." In *The Mammoth Book of Zombies*, ed. Stephen Jones. New York: Carroll & Graf, 1993.

Waggoner, Tim. *Necropolis*. Waterville, ME: Five Star Press, 2004.

Wellman, Manly Wade. "The Song of the Slaves." *Weird Tales* (March 1940).

Comics

Kirkman, Robert, and Tony Moore. *The Walking Dead, Volume 1: Days Gone Bye*. Orange, CA: Image Comics, 2004.

Kirkman, Robert, and Sean Phillips. *Marvel Zombies*. New York: Marvel Comics, 2006.

Morrison, Grant. *Seven Soldiers of Victory, Volume 1*. New York: Marvel Comics, 2006.

Powell, Eric. *The Goon: Nothin' But Misery*. Milwaukie, OR: Dark Horse Comics, 2003.

Films

Army of Darkness. Directed by Sam Raimi. Dino de Laurentiis/Universal, 1993.

The Bowery at Midnight. Directed by Wallace. Banner/Monogram, 1942.

Braindead. Directed by Peter Jackson. Wingnut, 1992.

Bubba Ho-Tep. Directed by Don Coscarelli. Silver Sphere, 2002.

Burial Ground: The Nights of Terror [*Le notte di terrore*]. Directed by Andrea Bianchi. Esteban, 1981.

Dawn of the Dead. Directed by George A. Romero. Laurel, 1978.

Day of the Dead. Directed by George A. Romero. Dead Films, 1985.

The Dead Next Door. Directed by J. R. Bookwalter. Amsco Studios, 1988.

The Earth Dies Screaming. Directed by Terence Fischer. Lippert, 1965.

Ed and His Dead Mother. Directed by Jonathan Wacks. ITC, 1993.

The Evil Dead. Directed by Sam Raimi. Renaissance, 1981.

Evil Dead II. Directed by Sam Raimi. De Laurentiis, 1987.

I Walked with a Zombie. Directed by Jacques Tourneur. RKO, 1943.

Land of the Dead. Directed by George A. Romero. Universal, 2005.

The Last Man on Earth. Directed by Ubaldo Ragona. AIP, 1964.

Night of the Living Dead. Directed by George A. Romero. Image Ten, 1968.

Night of the Living Dead. Directed by Tom Savini. Columbia, 1990.

The Omega Man. Directed by Boris Sagil. Warner Bros., 1971.

Plan 9 from Outer Space. Directed by Edward D. Wood. Reynolds, 1959.

Re-Animator. Directed by Stewart Gordon. Empire Pictures, 1985.

The Return of the Living Dead. Directed by Dan O'Bannon. Orion, 1985.

Shatter Dead. Directed by Scooter McCrae. Tempe Video, 1994.

Shaun of the Dead. Directed by Edgar Wright. Big Talk, 2004.

Tombs of the Blind Dead [*La noche del terror ciego*]. Directed by Amando de Ossorio. Interfilme, 1971.

28 Days Later. Directed by Danny Boyle. British Film Council, 2002.

The Voodoo Man. Directed by William Beaudine. Banner/Monogram, 1944.

War of the Zombies [*Roma contro Roma*]. Directed by Guiseppe Vari. Galatea, 1964.

White Zombie. Directed by Victor Halperin. Edward Halperin/United Artists, 1932.
Zeder [a.k.a. in the United States as *Revenge of the Dead*]. Directed by Pupi Avati. A.M.A., 1983.
Zombie. Directed by Lucio Fulci. Variety, 1979.
Zombies on Broadway. Directed by Gordon Douglas. RKO, 1945.

Criticism

Davis, Wade. *Passage of Darkness: The Ethnobiology of the Haitian Zombie*. Chapel Hill: University of North Carolina Press, 1988.
———. *The Serpent and the Rainbow*. New York: Simon & Schuster, 1985.
Dendle, Peter. *The Zombie Movie Encyclopedia*. Jefferson, NC: McFarland, 2000.
Fonseca, Tony. "Zombies." In *Supernatural Literature of the World*, ed. S. T. Joshi and Stefan R. Dziemainowicz. Westport, CT: Greenwood Press, 2005.
Gagne, Paul R. *The Zombies That Ate Pittsburgh: The Films of George A. Romero*. New York: Dodd, Mead, 1987.
Gateveckes, William. "Marvel Zombies #1." *Popmatters*. January 19, 2006. *Popmatters*. January 21, 2006, http://www.popmatters.com/comics/marvel-zombies-1.shtml.
Mitchell, Charles P. *A Guide to Apocalyptic Cinema*. Westport, CT: Greenwood Press, 2001.
Rhodes, Gary D. *White Zombie: Anatomy of a Horror Film*. Jefferson, NC: McFarland, 2001.
Seabrook, W. B. *The Magic Island*. New York: Harcourt, Brace, 1929.

General Bibliography

BIBLIOGRAPHIES AND INDEXES

Ashley, Mike, and William G. Contento. *The Supernatural Index.* Westport, CT: Greenwood Press, 1995.

Bleiler, E. F. *The Guide to Supernatural Fiction.* Kent, OH: Kent State University Press, 1983.

Frank, Frederick S. *Guide to the Gothic: An Annotated Bibliography of Criticism.* Metuchen, NJ: Scarecrow Press, 1984.

Hall, H. W. *Science Fiction and Fantasy Reference Index, 1878–1985.* 2 vols. Detroit: Gale, 1987.

———. *Science Fiction and Fantasy Reference Index, 1985–1991.* Englewood, CO: Libraries Unlimited, 1993.

———. *Science Fiction and Fantasy Reference Index, 1992–1995.* Englewood, CO: Libraries Unlimited, 1997.

Lentz, Harris M., III. *Science Fiction, Fantasy and Horror Film and Television Credits.* 2 vols. Jefferson, NC: McFarland, 1983. (Supplement, 1994.)

Parnell, Frank H., and Mike Ashley. *Monthly Terrors: An Index to the Weird Fantasy Magazines Published in the United States and Great Britain.* Westport, CT: Greenwood Press, 1985.

Reginald, R. *Science Fiction and Fantasy Literature: A Checklist, 1700–1974.* 2 vols. Detroit: Gale, 1979.

———. *Science Fiction and Fantasy Literature, 1975–1991.* Detroit: Gale, 1992.

Senn, Bryan, and John Johnson. *Fantastic Cinema Subject Guide.* Jefferson, NC: McFarland, 1992.

Tuck, Donald H. *The Encyclopedia of Science Fiction and Fantasy through 1968.* 3 vols. Chicago: Advent, 1974–1982.

ENCYCLOPEDIAS

Barron, Neil, ed. *Horror Literature: A Reader's Guide.* New York: Garland, 1990.

Bleiler, E. F., ed. *Supernatural Fiction Writers.* 2 vols. New York: Scribner's, 1985.

Bleiler, Richard, ed. *Supernatural Fiction Writers: Contemporary Fantasy and Horror*. 2 vols. New York. Scribner's, 2002.

Burgess, Michael. *Reference Guide to Science Fiction, Fantasy, and Horror*. Boulder, CO: Libraries Unlimited, 1992.

Fonseca, Anthony J., and June Michele Pulliam. *Hooked on Horror: A Guide to Reading Interests in Horror Fiction*. Englewood, CO: Libraries Unlimited, 1999 (rev. ed. 2003).

Frank, Frederick S. *The First Gothics: A Critical Guide to the English Gothic Novel*. New York: Garland, 1987.

Fraser, Sherman A. *Cyborgs, Santa Claus and Satan: Science Fiction, Fantasy and Horror Films for Television*. Jefferson, NC: McFarland, 2000.

Hanke, Ken. *A Critical Guide to Horror Film Series*. New York: Garland, 1991.

Hardy, Phil, ed. *Horror*. London: Aurum Press, 1993.

Harris-Fain, Darren, ed. *British Fantasy and Science-Fiction Writers before World War I*. (Dictionary of Literary Biography, Vol. 178.) Detroit: Gale, 1997.

———. *British Fantasy and Science-Fiction Writers, 1918–1960*. (Dictionary of Literary Biography, Vol. 255.) Detroit: Gale, 2002.

———. *British Fantasy and Science-Fiction Writers Since 1960*. (Dictionary of Literary Biography, Vol. 261.) Detroit: Thomson/Gale, 2002.

Jones, Stephen. *The Essential Monster Movie Guide*. New York: Billboard, 2000.

Joshi, S. T., and Stefan Dziemianowicz, eds. *Supernatural Literature of the World: An Encyclopedia*. 3 vols. Westport, CT: Greenwood Press, 2005.

Kinnard, Ray. *Horror in Silent Films: A Filmography, 1896–1929*. Jefferson, NC: McFarland, 1995.

Maxford, Howard. *The A-Z of Horror Films*. London: Batsford, 1996.

Morton, Alan. *The Complete Directory of Science Fiction, Fantasy and Horror Television Series*. Peoria, IL: Other Worlds, 1997.

Newman, Kim. *The BFI Companion to Horror*. London: Cassell, 1996.

O'Neill, James. *Terror on Tape: A Complete Guide to Over 2,000 Horror Movies on Video*. New York: Billboard, 1994.

Pringle, David, ed. *St. James Guide to Horror, Ghost and Gothic Writers*. Detroit: St. James Press, 1998.

Sullivan, Jack, ed. *The Penguin Encyclopedia of Horror and the Supernatural*. New York: Viking, 1986.

Thomson, Douglass H., Jack G. Voller, and Frederick S. Frank, eds. *Gothic Writers: A Critical and Bibliographical Guide*. Westport, CT: Greenwood Press, 2002.

Tymn, Marshall B., ed. *Horror Literature: A Core Collection and Reference Guide*. New York: R. R. Bowker, 1981.

Tymn, Marshall B., and Mike Ashley, eds. *Science Fiction, Fantasy, and Weird Fiction Magazines*. Westport, CT: Greenwood Press, 1985.

Wolf, Leonard. *Horror: A Connoisseur's Guide to Literature and Film*. New York: Facts on File, 1989.

Wright, Gene. *Horrorshows: The A to Z of Horror Film, TV, Radio and Theater*. New York: Facts on File, 1986.

Young, R. G. *The Encyclopedia of Fantastic Film*. New York: Applause, 2000.

CRITICAL STUDIES (LITERATURE)

Birkhead, Edith. *The Tale of Terror: A Study of the Gothic Romance*. London: Constable, 1921.

Carroll, Noël. *The Philosophy of Horror; or, Paradoxes of the Heart*. New York: Routledge, 1990.

Cavaliero, Glen. *The Supernatural and English Fiction*. Oxford: Oxford University Press, 1995.

Heller, Terry. *The Delights of Terror: An Aesthetics of the Tale of Terror*. Urbana: University of Illinois Press, 1987.

Hogle, Jerrold E., ed. *The Cambridge Companion to Gothic Fiction*. Cambridge: Cambridge University Press, 2002.

Jackson, Rosemary. *Fantasy: The Literature of Subversion*. London: Methuen, 1981.

Jones, Stephen, and Kim Newman, eds. *Horror: 100 Best Books*. London: Xanadu, 1988.

———. *Horror: Another 100 Best Books*. New York: Carroll & Graf, 2005.

Joshi, S. T. *The Evolution of the Weird Tale*. New York: Hippocampus Press, 2004.

———. *The Modern Weird Tale*. Jefferson, NC: McFarland, 2001.

———. *The Weird Tale*. Austin: University of Texas Press, 1990.

Kerr, Howard, John W. Crowley, and Charles L. Crow, eds. *The Haunted Dusk: American Supernatural Fiction 1820–1920*. Athens: University of Georgia Press, 1983.

Kies, Cosette. *Presenting Young Adult Horror Fiction*. New York: Twayne, 1992.

Lovecraft, H. P. *The Annotated Supernatural Horror in Literature*. Ed. S. T. Joshi. New York: Hippocampus Press, 2000.

Messent, Peter B., ed. *Literature of the Occult: A Collection of Critical Essays*. Englewood Cliffs, NJ: Prentice-Hall, 1981.

Punter, David. *A Companion to the Gothic*. Oxford: Blackwell, 2000.

———. *The Literature of Terror: A History of Gothic Fictions from 1765 to the Present Day*. London: Longman, 1980 (rev. ed. 1996).

Railo, Eino. *The Haunted Castle: A Study of the Elements of English Romanticism*. London: Routledge, 1927.

Ringel, Faye. *New England's Gothic Literature: History and Folklore of the Supernatural from the Seventeenth through the Twentieth Centuries*. Lewiston, ME: Edwin Mellen Press, 1995.

Robillard, Douglas, ed. *American Supernatural Fiction: From Edith Wharton to the Weird Tales Writers*. New York: Garland, 1996.

Schweitzer, Darrell, ed. *Discovering Classic Horror Fiction*. Mercer Island, WA: Starmont House, 1992.

———. *Discovering Modern Horror Fiction*. Mercer Island, WA: Starmont House, 1985.

———. *Discovering Modern Horror Fiction II*. Mercer Island, WA: Starmont House, 1988.

Spacks, Patricia Meyer. *The Insistence of Horror. Aspects of the Supernatural in Eighteenth-Century Poetry*. Cambridge, MA: Harvard University Press, 1962.

Sullivan, Jack. *Elegant Nightmares: The English Ghost Story from Le Fanu to Blackwood*. Athens: Ohio University Press, 1978.

Todorov, Tzvetan. *The Fantastic: A Structural Approach to a Literary Genre.* Trans. Richard Howard. Cleveland: Press of Case Western Reserve University, 1973.

Voller, Jack G. *The Supernatural Sublime: The Metaphysics of Terror in Anglo-American Romanticism.* DeKalb: Northern Illinois University Press, 1994.

CRITICAL STUDIES (MEDIA)

Beck, Calvin Thomas. *Scream Queens: Heroines of the Horrors.* New York: Macmillan, 1978.

Becker, Susanne. *Gothic Forms of Feminine Fictions.* Manchester: Manchester University Press, 1999.

Benshoff, Harry M. *Monsters in the Closet: Homosexuality and the Horror Film.* Manchester: Manchester University Press, 1997.

Benton, Mike. *Horror Comics: The Illustrated History.* Dallas: Taylor Publishing Co., 1991.

Bradley, Doug. *Sacred Monsters: Behind the Mask of the Horror Actor.* London: Titan, 1996.

Brosnan, John. *The Horror People.* New York: St. Martin's Press, 1976.

Donald, James, ed. *Fantasy and the Cinema.* London: British Film Institute, 1989.

Dyson, Jeremy. *Bright Darkness: The Lost Art of the Supernatural Horror Film.* London: Cassell, 1997.

Freeland, Cynthia A. *The Naked and the Undead: Evil and the Appeal of Horror.* Boulder, CO: Westview Press, 2000.

Glut, Donald F. *Classic Movie Monsters.* Metuchen, NJ: Scarecrow Press, 1978.

Grant, Barry Keith, ed. *The Dread of Difference: Gender and the Horror Film.* Austin: University of Texas Press, 1996.

———. *Planks of Reason: Essays on the Horror Film.* Metuchen, NJ: Scarecrow Press, 1984.

Hogan, David. *Dark Romance: Sexuality in the Horror Film.* Jefferson, NC: McFarland, 1986.

Hopkins, Lisa. *Screening the Gothic.* Austin: University of Texas Press, 2005.

Huss, Roy, and T. J. Ross, eds. *Focus on the Horror Film.* Englewood Cliffs, NJ: Prentice-Hall, 1972.

Jensen, Paul M. *The Men Who Made the Monsters.* New York: Twayne, 1996.

Mank, Gregory William. *Women in Horror Films, 1930s.* Jefferson, NC: McFarland, 1999.

———. *Women in Horror Films, 1940s.* Jefferson, NC: McFarland, 1999.

McCarty, John. *The Modern Horror Film.* Secaucus, NJ: Carol Publishing Group, 1990.

Newman, Kim. *Nightmare Movies: A Critical History of the Horror Film, 1968–88.* London: Bloomsbury, 1988.

Paul, William. *Laughing, Screaming: Modern Hollywood Horror and Comedy.* New York: Columbia University Press, 1994.

Rasmussen, Randy Loren. *Children of the Night: The Six Archetypical Characters of Classic Horror Films.* Jefferson, NC: McFarland, 1998.

Schneider, Steven Jay, and Tony Williams, eds. *Horror International.* Detroit: Wayne State University Press, 2005.

Senn, Bryan. *Golden Horrors: A Critical Filmography of Terror Cinema, 1931–1939.* Jefferson, NC: McFarland, 1996.

Sennitt, Stephen. *Ghastly Terror!: The Horrible Story of the Horror Comics.* Manchester: Critical Vision, 1999.

Skal, David J. *Screams of Reason: Mad Science and Modern Culture.* New York: W. W. Norton & Co., 1998.

CRITICAL STUDIES (POPULAR CULTURE AND SOCIETY)

Daniels, Les. *Living in Fear: A History of Horror in the Mass Media.* New York: Scribner's, 1975.

Edmundson, Mark. *Nightmare on Main Street: Angels, Sadomasochism and the Culture of Gothic.* Cambridge, MA: Harvard University Press, 1997.

Hendershot, Cyndy. *The Animal Within: Masculinity and the Gothic.* Ann Arbor: University of Michigan Press, 1998.

Massumi, Brian, ed. *The Politics of Everyday Fear.* Minneapolis: University of Minnesota Press, 1993.

Meikle, Denis. *Jack the Ripper: The Murders and the Movies.* London: Reynolds & Hearn, 2002.

Nelson, Victoria. *The Secret Life of Puppets.* Cambridge, MA: Harvard University Press, 2001.

Skal, David H. *The Monster Show: A Cultural History of Horror.* New York: W. W. Norton & Co., 1993.

Twitchell, James B. *Dreadful Pleasures: An Anatomy of Modern Horror.* New York: Oxford University Press, 1985.

Notes on Contributors

EDITOR

S. T. JOSHI is the author of *The Weird Tale* (University of Texas Press, 1990), *The Modern Weird Tale* (McFarland, 2001), and other critical and biographical studies. With Stefan Dziemianowicz, he coedited *Supernatural Literature of the World: An Encyclopedia* (Greenwood Press, 2005; 3 vols.). His biography, *H. P. Lovecraft: A Life* (Necronomicon Press, 1996), won the Bram Stoker Award and the British Fantasy Award. He has prepared editions of works by H. P. Lovecraft, Ambrose Bierce, Lord Dunsany, Algernon Blackwood, H. L. Mencken, and other authors. He is founder and editor of *Lovecraft Studies* and *Studies in Weird Fiction*.

CONTRIBUTORS

MIKE ASHLEY is a retired Local Government Officer who is also a researcher and editor in the fields of science fiction, fantasy, and mystery fiction. He has published over 70 books, including *The History of the Science Fiction Magazine* (New English Library, 1974–1978 [4 vols.]; rev. ed. Liverpool University Press, 2000f.), *Starlight Man* [a biography of Algernon Blackwood] (Constable, 2001), and *The Mammoth Encyclopedia of Modern Crime Fiction* (Robinson, 2002), for which he won the Edgar Award. He also won the Stoker Award for *The Supernatural Index* (Greenwood Press, 1995) and is the recipient of the Pilgrim Award for his lifetime contribution to science fiction research. His wider interests in history has also resulted in his books on the British Monarchy and *The Mammoth Book of King Arthur* (Robinson, 2005).

RICHARD BLEILER is the Humanities Bibliographer for the Homer Babbidge Library at the University of Connecticut. He is the editor of *Science Fiction*

Writers (Scribner, rev. ed. 1999), *Supernatural Fiction Writers: Contemporary Fantasy and Horror* (Scribner, 2002; 2 vols.), and the compiler of *The Index to* Adventure *Magazine* (Starmont House, 1990), *The Annotated Index to* The Thrill Book (Borgo Press, 1992), *Reference and Research Guide to Mystery and Detective Fiction* (Libraries Unlimited, 2004), and, with E. F. Bleiler, *Science Fiction: The Early Years* (Kent State University Press, 1990) and *Science Fiction: The Gernsback Years* (Kent State University Press, 1998).

BERNADETTE LYNN BOSKY is a freelance writer and educator. She frequently contributes to encyclopedias and other reference works; her writing ranges from Renaissance alchemy to self-esteem, Sir Thomas Browne to John Wayne Gacy. However, she is most known for major articles about Charles Williams, Stephen King, and Peter Straub. She teaches nonfiction writing for Gotham Writers' Workshop and has many individual clients for writing instruction and editing; she tutors everything from graduate-level literature study to SAT prep. Happily middle-aged, she lives in Yonkers, New York, with her two husbands, Arthur Hlavaty and Kevin Maroney, and their sixteen pet fancy rats.

DONALD R. BURLESON is the director of a computer lab at Eastern New Mexico University in Roswell. He holds master's degrees in both mathematics and English and a Ph.D. in English literature, and has taught at several universities. He is the author of over a hundred short stories published in many magazines and anthologies. His critical works include *H. P. Lovecraft: A Critical Study* (Greenwood Press, 1983) and *Lovecraft: Disturbing the Universe* (University Press of Kentucky, 1990) and numerous journal articles. He is the author of several novels and of the nonfiction book *UFOs and the Murder of Marilyn Monroe* (Black Mesa Press, 2003).

MATT CARDIN is the author of the short story collection *Divinations of the Deep* (Ash-Tree Press, 2002) and the novella *The God of Foulness* (Delirium, 2004). His short stories, essays, and reviews have appeared in *Studies in Weird Fiction, The Thomas Ligotti Reader* (Wildside Press, 2003), *Dark Arts* (CD Publications, 2006), *Alone on the Darkside* (Penguin/Roc, 2006), *Strange Horizons*, and elsewhere. He has a master's degree in religious studies and a bachelor's degree in communication. He resides in southwest Missouri with his wife and stepson.

MARGARET L. CARTER, specializing in the supernatural in literature, especially vampires, received a Ph.D. in English from the University of California, Irvine, and had her dissertation published as *Specter or Delusion? The Supernatural in Gothic Fiction* (UMI Research Press, 1987). She has edited *Dracula: The Vampire and the Critics* (UMI Research Press, 1988), the first anthology of articles on Stoker's novel, compiled *The Vampire in Literature: A Critical Bibliography* (UMI Research Press, 1989), and written the monograph *Different Blood: The Vampire as Alien* (Xlibris, 2002). Her first mass-market vampire novel, *Embracing Darkness,* appeared in 2005 from Silhouette Intimate Moments.

SCOTT CONNORS discovered weird fiction through the Ballantine Adult Fantasy editions of Lovecraft and Clark Ashton Smith. He is currently writing a biography of Smith. His books include Smith's *Selected Letters* (with David E. Schultz; Arkham House, 2003) and *Red World of Polaris* (with Ronald S. Hilger; Night Shade, 2003), *A Century Less A Dream: Selected Criticism on H. P. Lovecraft* (Wildside Press, 2002), and Lovecraft's *Science Versus Charlatanry* (with S. T. Joshi; Strange Co., 1979). His essays and reviews have appeared in *Nyctalops*, *Fantasy Crossroads*, *Lovecraft Studies*, *Publishers Weekly*, the *Explicator*, the *New York Review of Science Fiction*, *Wormwood*, *Studies in Weird Fiction*, and *Faunus* as well as Don Herron's *The Barbaric Triumph: A Critical Anthology on the Writings of Robert E. Howard* (Wildside Press, 2004). He is the editor of *Lost Worlds: The Journal of Clark Ashton Smith Studies.* He is a graduate of Washington and Jefferson College.

STEFAN DZIEMIANOWICZ is the author of *An Annotated Guide to Unknown and* Unknown Worlds (Starmont House, 1990) and coeditor, with S. T. Joshi, of *Supernatural Literature of the World: An Encyclopedia* (Greenwood Press, 2005; 3 vols.). He is the editor of numerous anthologies of horror fiction, including *Weird Tales: 32 Unearthed Terrors* (Bonanza, 1988) and *The Rivals of Dracula* (Barnes & Noble, 1996). He is the founder and editor of *Necrofile: The review of Horror Fiction* (1991–1999) and the author of numerous articles and reviews for *Lovecraft Studies*, *Studies in Weird Fiction*, the *Washington Post Book World*, *Publishers Weekly*, and other journals. He has contributed to Neil Barron's *Fantasy and Horror* (Scarecrow Press, 1999) and other reference works.

TONY FONSECA is Electronic Resources/Reference Librarian at Nicholls State University in Thibodaux, Louisiana. He has coauthored two editions of the reference book *Hooked on Horror: A Guide to Reading Interests in the Genre* (Libraries Unlimited, 1999, 2003) and has written various reviews for *Necropsy: The Review of Horror Fiction* (www.lsu.edu/necrofile), a free e-zine which he also coedits. Currently, he is working on two articles for the *Dictionary of Literary Biography: Asian American Writers* (Gale Group).

PAULA GURAN is a recipient of the International Horror Guild Award and two-time winner of the Bram Stoker Award for Outstanding Achievement in Nonfiction in the field of horror and dark fantasy. She has written about dark fiction and those who create it for print publications including *Publishers' Weekly* and *Cemetery Dance* and online for Universal Studios, OMNI, and her own DarkEcho.com. She currently works with Writers.com as an instructor and heads its publishing arm, Writers.com Books and its imprints Caelum Press and Infrapress.

MELISSA MIA HALL is a frequent contributor to *Publishers Weekly* and has taught creative writing for University of Texas at Arlington's Continuing Education. Her fiction career began with "Wishing Will Make It So" (*Twilight Zone*, 1981). She contributed to Charles L. Grant's *Shadows* anthologies (Doubleday, 1983–1987) and many others: for example, *Women of Darkness* (Tor, 1988); *Post-Mortem* (St. Martin's Press, 1989); *Skin of the Soul* (Women's Press, 1990); *Whisper of Blood* (Morrow, 1991); *Marilyn: Shades of Blonde* (Tor, 1997); *Retro Pulp Tales* (Subterranean Press, 2004). Hall edited *Wild Women* (Carroll & Graf, 1997), and her contribution, "Psychofemmes," was reprinted in Ed Gorman and Martin Greenberg's *Year's 25 Finest Crime and Mystery Stories* (Carroll & Graf, 1998).

K. A. LAITY is the author of *Pelzmantel: A Medieval Tale* (Spilled Candy, 2003), which was nominated for the 2003 Aesop Prize and the International Reading Association Children's Book Award. She writes both fiction and nonfiction encompassing all varieties of the fantastique, medieval literature, popular culture, and contemporary religions. At present she is assistant professor of English at the University of Houston-Downtown, where she teaches medieval literature, creative writing, and film. Current work includes *Unikirja*, a collection of stories based on the Finnish epic; *The Kalevala*, a novel set in fourteenth-century Ireland and contemporary Boston; and a nonfiction book on Anglo-Saxon women as witches.

JOHN LANGAN is a Ph.D. candidate at the CUNY Graduate Center; he also adjuncts at SUNY New Paltz. He has written on Lovecraft, Leiber, and Ligotti; his fiction has appeared in the *Magazine of Fantasy & Science Fiction* and twice been nominated for the International Horror Guild Award. He lives in upstate New York with his wife and son.

ROB LATHAM is an associate professor of English and American Studies at the University of Iowa, where he directs the Sexuality Studies Program. A coeditor of the journal *Science-Fiction Studies* since 1997, he has is the author of *Consuming Youth: Vampires, Cyborgs and the Culture of Consumption* (University of Chicago Press, 2002). He is currently working on a book on New Wave science fiction.

STEVEN J. MARICONDA is a leading authority on H. P. Lovecraft and the author of *On the Emergence of "Cthulhu" and Other Observations* (Necronomicon Press, 1995), which collects his numerous papers on the Providence author. His articles and reviews have appeared in *Lovecraft Studies*, *Crypt of Cthulhu*, and other journals.

JUNE PULLIAM teaches horror literature and women's and gender studies at Louisiana State University Press and is managing editor of *Necropsy: The Review of Horror Fiction* (http://www.lsu.edu/necrofile). She is also coauthor of two editions of *Hooked on Horror: A Guide to Reading Interests in the Genre* (Libraries Unlimited, 1999, 2003) and of *The Horror Reader's Companion: A Guide to Horror Reading for Any Occasion, Mood and Taste* (Libraries Unlimited, 2005).

DARRELL SCHWEITZER is the author of the novels *The White Isle* (Owlswick Press, 1989), *The Shattered Goddess* (Donning, 1982), and *The Mask of the Sorcerer* (SFBC Fantasy, 1995), as well as about 275 short stories, numerous poems, essays, reviews, etc. He has written critical books on Lord Dunsany and H. P. Lovecraft, and edited critical symposia such as *The Thomas Ligotti Reader* (Wildside Press, 2003). He contributes to the *New York Review of Science Fiction*, *Lovecraft Studies*, and other journals. He has been coeditor of *Weird Tales* magazine since 1987. He has been nominated for the World Fantasy Award four times and won it once.

BRIAN STABLEFORD has published more than 50 novels and 200 short stories, as well as several nonfiction books, thousands of articles for periodicals and reference-books, several volumes of translations from the French, and a number of anthologies. He is a part-time Lecturer in Creative Writing at University College Winchester. His recent publications include a *Historical Dictionary of Science Fiction Literature* (Scarecrow Press, 2004) and a *Historical Dictionary of Fantasy Literature* (Scarecrow Press, 2005).

HANK WAGNER lives in northwestern New Jersey with his wife and four daughters. A respected journalist and critic, Wagner's reviews and interviews have appeared in *Cemetery Dance*, *Hellnotes*, *Dark Echo*, *Mystery Scene*, *Nova Express*, *Horror Garage*, and the *New York Review of Science Fiction*. With Stanley Wiater and Christopher Golden, he coauthored *The Stephen King Universe: A Guide to the Worlds of the King of Horror* (Renaissance, 2001). Wagner graduated from the University of Notre Dame in 1982, received a J.D. from Seton Hall University School of Law in 1985, and earned an LL.M. in Taxation from the New York University School of Law in 1991.

ALAN WARREN has written for such publications as *Take One*, *Film Comment*, *Isaac Asimov's Science Fiction Magazine*, *Publishers Weekly*, *Castle Rock*, and the *Armchair Detective*. His critical study of Roald Dahl was published in 1988 (Starmont House); a revised, enlarged edition appeared in 1994 (Borgo Press). His full-length study of television's "Thriller," entitled *This Is a Thriller*, was published in 1996 (McFarland). He is currently working on a critical study of Richard Matheson.

Index

Abe, Shana, 451
Abominable Dr. Phibes, The (film), 156
Ackroyd, Peter, 606
Adam and Eve, 36, 171, 511, 532, 629
Adams, Benjamin, 125, 697
Adomnan, 456
African curse, 133–37
Agrippa, Cornelius, 571–72, 575
Ahern, Jerry, 676
Ahern, Sharon, 676
Aickman, Robert, 200, 293–94, 450, 468
Aiken, Conrad, 467
Ainsworth, William Harrison, 169, 319, 320, 699, 706
Akenside, Mark, 68
Alchemy, 317–18, 320, 571–72, 581
Alcott, Louisa May, 385
Aldiss, Brian, 352, 633
Alexander (sorcerer), 567
"Alias" (TV show), 530
Alien (film), 24
Alien icon/motif, 1–3, 5, 29
Alienist, The (film), 492–93
Aliens, 29; chronology of films about, 14–15; in film, 6–29; in literature, 3–6; quality of "outsideness," 2
All About Eve (film), 527
"All My Children" (TV show), 531
Allen, Grant, 386
Allende, Isabel, 519
Allison, Jennifer, 431

"Ally McBeal" (TV show), 531
Alten, Steve, 463
Alter ego, 189, 191. *See also* Doppelgängers; *Strange Case of Dr. Jekyll and Mr. Hyde, The*
Altner, Patricia, 640
Amazing Randi, 410
American Beauty (film), 529
American Gothic (Bloch), 484–85, 606–7
"American Gothic" (painting), 282
American Werewolf in London, An (film), 683
"Amina" (White), 248, 359–60
Amityville, 273–74
Amityville II: The Possession (film), 51
"Ancient Sorceries" (Blackwood), 539–44, 546, 547, 557, 560, 694, 710
Andersen, Hans Christian, 199, 447, 454
Anderson, George K., 311, 316
Anderson, Poul, 454, 675
Anderson, Tracy, 428
Angel of Darkness, The (film), 493
Angel(s), 31–34, 60; chronology, 41; from first century to modern times, 40–43; origin of the term, 36; prehistory, 36–37; in supernatural literature and film, 54–60
Angels in America (Kushner), 58
"Ankardyne Pew, The" (Harvey), 290
Annie Hall (film), 527–28

Anstey, F., 450
Anthony, R., 705
Anthony, Susan B., 413
Antieau, Kim, 519
Appleton, Everard Jack, 458
Apuleius, Lucius, 566–67
Aquinas, Thomas, 40
Arabian Nightmare, The (Irwin), 150–51
Aradia; or, The Gospel of the Witches (Leland), 701–2
Arch Angels (Randisi), 497
Armin M., 481
Armstrong, Kelley, 681
Árnason, Jón, 446
Arnold, Matthew, 447
Arrival, The (film), 26
Arthur, King, 163, 511–12, 568, 569
Arthur, Robert, 177
Ash Wednesday (Williamson), 228
"Ash-Tree, The" (James), 142–43
Asimov, Isaac, 177
Askew, Alice, 432
Askew, Claude, 432
At the Mountains of Madness (Lovecraft), 84, 109–11, 125
Atherton, Gertrude, 323
Atkey, Bertram, 451, 458
Atkins, Frank, 460
Atwater-Rhodes, Amelia, 638
Atwood, Margaret, 220, 524
Auerbach, Nina, 624, 625, 640, 646
Austin, F. Britten, 467
Austin, William, 320
Automatic writing, 418
Autoscopic phenomena, 191
Aveni, Anthony, 581
Axton, William F., 131–32
Aymar, Jacques, 431

Baba Yaga, 699–700
Babbitt, Natalie, 333
Bacon, Francis, 575
Bacon, Peggy, 697
Bacon, Roger, 164, 165
Bad Seed, The (March), 483
Bailey, Dale, 557–58, 560

Baker, George A., 446
Balderston, John L., 395, 641
Ballard, J. G., 332, 611, 612
Bane, Diana, 430
Banister, Manly, 668
Banks, L. A., 636
Barber, Paul, 620
Barbour, David, 122
Baring-Gould, Sabine, 320
Barker, Clive, 280–81, 366, 433, 587, 608, 613, 680, 743
Barker, Nugent, 260
Barrie, J. M., 322
Barrow, Reginald, 35
Bartendale, Luna, 665
Barton Fink (film), 207–8
Barzak, Christopher, 451
Basic Instinct (film), 529
Bassett, Ronald, 706
Bates, Harry, 8, 9
Bathory, Elizabeth (Erzbet), 477, 702
"Batman" (TV show), 532
Baudelaire, Charles, 74–76, 78, 81, 83, 592, 595
Baum, L. Frank, 697
Baumgarten, Alexander, 67
"Baumoff Explosive, The" (Hodgson), 79
Bayley, Barrington J., 333
Beagle, Peter S., 680
Beale, Charles Willing, 294
Beauclerk, Helen, 328
Beauman, Sally, 522
Beaumont, Charles, 135, 179, 602–3, 716
Beckford, William, 70, 244
Bedelia (Caspary), 523
Bedknobs and Broomsticks (film), 717
Beerbohm, Max, 177, 200
Before I Wake (Bowman), 494
Begbie, Harold, 433
Beichler, James E., 411, 414
Bell, Book and Candle (film), 716
Bell, Michael E., 621
Beloved (Morrison), 228, 236
Belzoni, Giovanni, 382–83
Benchley, Peter, 463

Bender family, 478

Benét, Stephen Vincent, 173, 458, 692

Benjamin, Walter, 592, 595

Bennett, Charles, 152

Benson, A. C., 468

Benson, E. F., 150, 295, 399, 468, 625–26

Beowulf, 345–47

Béranger, Pierre de, 313

"Berenice" (Poe), 517

Berglund, Edward Paul, 122

Bergstrom, Elaine, 632

Bernal, J. D., 89

Besant, Walter, 322

Beware! The Blob (film), 19

Beyond Black (Mantel), 230

Bierce, Ambrose, 81, 114, 259

Bijns, Anna, 573

Bill, Alfred H., 662, 676, 680

Billson, Anne, 601

Birds, The (film), 558–60

Bishop, Michael, 331

Bishop, Zealia, 147

Biss, Gerald, 661, 662, 676, 680

Bitten (Armstrong), 681–82

Bixby, Jerome, 627

Black, Campbell, 429

Black House (King and Straub), 426, 495

Black magic, 422–23. *See also* Sorcerers

"Black Man with a Horn" (Klein), 123

Black Sunday (film), 154–55, 716

Blackburn, John, 132

Blackmore, Peter, 452

Blackwood, Algernon: "Ancient Sorceries," 539–44, 546, 547, 557, 560, 694, 710; *The Centaur*, 344; Derleth and, 114; "The Empty House," 289–90; ghost stories, 80, 224, 598; *Jimbo*, 295; John Silence stories, 433; Lovecraft compared with, 100; "The Nemesis of Fire," 388; "A Psychical Invasion," 433; Ramsey Campbell and, 280; "The Terror of the Twins," 200; "The Wendigo," 114; "The Willows," 80, 224

Blackwood, William, 197

Blair, Cherie, 421

Blair, Tony, 421

Blake, William, 329, 692, 711

Blatty, William Peter, 53, 60, 184; *The Exorcist*, 32, 33, 48, 60, 179, 180, 183, 607; *Exorcist III*, 183; *Legion*, 55, 183

Blayre, Christopher, 132

Bleiler, E. F., 132

Blish, James, 180, 674

Blixen, Karen, 326

Blob, The (film), 19

Bloch, Robert, 602; *American Gothic*, 484–85, 606–7; "Beetles," 399; "The Cloak," 600, 626; "The Dream-Makers," 600; Egyptian stories, 138–40; "Enoch," 713; "The Eyes of the Mummy," 398; "Fane of the Black Pharaoh," 117; "The Grinning Ghoul," 256–57; "The Laughter of a Ghoul," 256; "Left Feep Catches Hell," 179; Lovecraft and, 86, 101, 116–17, 122, 138, 256, 257, 599; *The Night of the Ripper*, 596; "The Opener of the Way," 139; "The Phantom from the Film," 600; *Psycho*, 260–61, 474, 475, 479, 481, 484, 600; "Return to the Sabbath, 600; *The Scarf*, 484; "The Secret of Sebek," 138, 139, 398–99; "Slave of the Flames," 324–25; stories about Devil, 178–79; *Strange Eons*, 122; "Sweet to the Sweet," 693; "The Faceless God," 117, 139; "The Shadow from the People," 116; "The Shambler from the Stars," 116; "The Traveling Salesman," 132; "A Toy for Juliette," 502; urban horror, 596, 599–600, 602, 603; "Wolf in the Fold" ("Star Trek" episode), 502; "Yours Truly, Jack the Ripper," 47, 325, 501–2, 596

Block, Lawrence, 519

Blood Crazy (Clark), 740

Blood Hunt (Killough), 630

Bloody Chamber and Other Stories, The (Carter), 523

Blum, Joanne, 189, 196
Bo, Ben, 430
Body Snatchers, The (film), 16–17
Body Snatchers, The (Finney), 16–17
Bond, Nelson, 344
Bone Collector, The (Deaver), 494
"Book, The" (Irwin), 147
Boothby, Guy, 321, 387
Boron, Robert de, 569
Boston, Lucy M., 450
Bottrell, William, 446
Boucher, Anthony, 177, 668, 669
Bowker, David, 433
Bowler, Tim, 430
Bowman, Eric, 494
Boy Who Couldn't Die, The (Sleator), 746
Boyce, Chris, 463
Bradbury, Ray, 11, 229, 292–93, 401, 452, 458, 599, 602, 626; *Something Wicked This Way Comes*, 547, 549, 552, 554, 557
Braddon, Mary Elizabeth, 624
Bradfield, Scott, 668
Bradley, Marion Zimmer, 345, 433, 512, 570, 701, 707
Brahen, Marilyn "Mattie," 172
"Brahman, the Thief, and the Ghost, The" (Sanskrit folk tale), 223
Brain from Planet Arous, The (film), 21
Braindead (film), 747
Braude, Ann, 413
Breaking down, horror tales about, 240
Brennan, Joseph Payne, 143, 461, 468, 671
Brentano, Clemens, 449
Bridges, Sallie, 569
Brite, Poppy Z., 427, 428, 634
Briussof, Valery, 709
Brodie-Innes, John, 449
Brontë, Anne, 227
Brontë, Charlotte, 227, 729
Brontë, Emily, 227
Brown, Crosland, 668
Brown, Fredric, 693
Brown, Robin, 463
Browning, Robert, 72

Brueghel, Pieter, 76
Brugger, Peter, 191, 193, 196
Brunner, John, 709
Bryant, Edward, 519
BTK killer, 481
Bubba Ho-tep (film), 743, 745–46
Buchanan, Robert, 315
"Buffy the Vampire Slayer" (TV show), 530–31, 644
Bugliosi, Vincent, 479
Bulgakov, Mikhail, 168
Bulwer-Lytton, Edward, 72, 74, 86; *The Coming Race*, 88; monstrous elements in the works of, 353–55; supernatural fiction, 354–55; *Zanoni*, 45, 73, 78, 321, 354–55
Bundy, Ted, 479–80
Bürger, Gottfried August, 621
Burke, Edmund, 68, 69
Burke, Rusty, 253
Burke, William, 478
Burkholz, Herbert, 429
Burks, Arthur J., 354, 709
Burleson, Donald R., 105
Burn, Witch, Burn! (film), 716
Burnett, Francis Hodgson, 227
Burnt Offerings (Marasco), 279
Butler, Octavia, 636
Byrne, Eugene, 333
Byron, George Gordon, Lord, 350, 621, 622, 633

Cabell, James Branch, 172–74
Cadnum, Michael, 668
Cady, Jack, 466, 556–57
Cain, James M., 526
Caine, Geoffrey, 668
"Call of Cthulhu, The" (Lovecraft), 102–4
"Call of Cthulhu, The" (role-playing game), 125
Calmet, Dom Augustin, 620
Cameron, Anne, 451
Camp, L. Sprague de, 179
Campbell, Eddie, 503, 597
Campbell, John W., Jr., 10, 88, 89, 428, 600

Campbell, Ramsey, 119–20, 123, 366, 400, 486, 609; haunted house stories, 294; *The House on Nazareth Hill*, 280; *The Hungry Moon*, 555–56; *The Influence*, 714; "Mackintosh Willy," 605, 606; overview, 605; urban horror, 601, 604, 605

"Canavan's Back Yard" (Brennan), 143

"Candidate, The" (Slesar), 147–48

Candles Burning (King and McDowell), 230

Cannon, Peter, 122, 124

Canticle for Leibowitz, A (Miller), 332

Cantrell, Lisa, 750

Cape Canaveral Monsters (film), 21–22

Čapek, Karel, 323, 324

Capes, Bernard, 132, 317

Capra, Frank, 32

Card, Orson Scott, 225, 367

Carey, Lisa, 451

Carmen (film), 527

Carnarvon, Lord, 138, 392–93

Carpenter, John, 125, 468

Carr, Caleb, 492–93

Carr, Jayge, 711

Carr, Marina, 701

Carrie (King), 231, 427, 551

Carrington, Hereward, 192

Carroll, Lewis, 270

Carter, Angela, 367, 523, 680–81

Carter, Howard, 138, 392, 393, 400

Carter, Lin, 124

Carter, Margaret L., 639–40

Case, David, 671–72

Case Against Satan, The (Russell), 179–80

Caspary, Vera, 523, 526

Cast a Deadly Spell (film), 125

"Casting the Rules" (James), 46, 141–42

Castle of Otranto, The (Walpole), 350

Castries, Thibaut de, 607

Castro, Adam-Troy, 715

Cave, Hugh B., 475

Cawein, Madison, 296

"Cell, The" (Case), 671–72

Chabon, Michael, 351

"Chadbourne Episode, The" (Whitehead), 249–50

Chambers, Julius, 460

Chambers, Robert W., 81, 114, 446

Chamisso, Adalbert von, 170

Chandler, A. Bertram, 676

Changeling, The (film), 302–3

Chappell, Fred, 121, 122

"Charlie's Angels" (TV show), 531–32

Charnas, Suzy McKee, 631–32, 634, 681

Charteris, Leslie, 464

Charwoman's Shadow, The (Dunsany), 170, 583–85

Chaucer, Geoffrey, 354, 585

"Cheese" (Coppard), 146

Cherryh, C. J., 711

Chetwynd-Hayes, Ronald, 258, 263, 742–43

Chicago (film), 529

Children of the Damned (film), 422

"Christ and Satan" (poem), 162

"Christabel" (Coleridge), 197–98

Christian, Selena, 430

Christianity, angels, demons, and, 33, 38–42, 60, 328. *See also* Devil, *specific topics*

Christmas Carol, A (Dickens), 226

Christopher, John, 464

Chronicles of Narnia, The (film), 718

Chronicles of the Mayfair Witches, The (Rice), 50

Church of Dead Girls, The (Dobyns), 494

Chute de la maison Usher, La (film), 298–99

Cipher, The (Koja), 609–10

Citro, Joseph, 464

City of Angels (film), 59, 235

City of the Dead (Keene), 50

Claiming Her (Brahen), 172

Clairvoyance, 419, 426–31

Claremont, Clare, 350

Clarens, Carlos, 153, 155

Clark, Dale, 178

Clark, Joan, 467

Clarke, Arthur C., 124

"Clay" (Thompson), 145

Cleanup, The (Skipp and Spector), 201–2

Cleopatra, 388, 389, 400, 511

Cleopatra (film), 525

Clifford, Hugh, 259

Cline, Leonard, 87

"Cloak, The" (Bloch), 600, 626

Close Encounters of the Third Kind (film), 23–24

Clute, John, 327

Coates, Paul, 194, 195

Cobb, Irvin S., 461–62

Cobban, J. Maclaren, 320

Colavito, Jason, 126

Colburn, Henry, 383

Coldheart Canyon (Barker), 280–81

Coleridge, Samuel Taylor, 70, 71, 130–31, 197, 465, 467, 521, 621–23

Coleridge, Sara, 446

Collette, 518

Collier, John, 176, 710

Collins, Max Allan, 483

Collins, Nancy A., 427, 632, 679

Collins, Wilkie, 224, 523

"Colour out of Space, The" (Lovecraft), 104

Columba, St., 456

Comic books, 50, 421, 586, 645, 732–33

Confessions of an English Opium-Eater (De Quincey), 70–71, 82

Conjure Wife (Leiber), 694, 698, 712, 716

Connell, Richard, 483

Connelly, Michael, 493–94

Conrad, Joseph, 466

Constantine (film), 50–51, 59–60

Conway, Daniel, 316

Cooper, Anthony, 349

Cooper, Susan, 450, 464

Copenhaver, Brian P., 410

Coppard, A. E., 146

Copper, Basil, 433, 640, 653

Coraline (Gaiman), 202–3

Corelli, Marie, 171–72, 177, 181, 323, 328, 392, 393

Cornwell, Patricia, 479

Cory, Patrick, 427

"Cosmic horror," 65–66, 71; cosmic pessimism and its antidotes, 72–76; cosmicism, 103; and the decadent world-view, 76–81; leading short stories of, 79; in science fiction, 88–92; and the sublime, 67–71

Costello, Matthew, 463, 468

Costello, Peter, 444

Counselman, Mary Elizabeth, 132

Course of the Heart, The (Harrison), 605

Cowper, Richard, 333

Cox, Greg, 640

Cox, Michael, 221, 223

Coye, Lee Brown, 121

Cram, Ralph Adams, 288–89

Crawford, F. Marion, 321, 625

Crawling Eye, The (film), 20–21

Crespigny, Rose Champion de, 432–33

Crichton, Michael, 261, 346, 463

Crisis apparitions, 237

Croker, T. Crofton, 445, 446

Cronenberg, David, 611, 612

Crookes, William, 409

Crouch, Blake, 496

Crowley, Aleister, 143, 583–84, 717

Csernica, Lillian, 697

"Cthulhu mythology," 115

Cthulhu Mythos, 97–98; chronology of, 124; Derleth Mythos, 112–18; later Lovecraft Mythos, 108–12; Lovecraft Mythos, 98–107, 461; in the media, 125–26; modern, 118–24

Cthulhu Mythos Bibliography and Concordance, A (Jarocha-Ernst), 98

Cunningham, Allan, 446

Curse, The (film), 125

"Curse Kiss, The" (Roscoe), 145–46

Curse of the Demon. See Night of the Demon

Curse of the Voodoo (film), 133, 154, 155

Curse of the Wise Woman, The (Dunsany), 133, 148–49

"Curse of Yig, The" (Bishop), 147

Curse(s), 129–33, 144–51, 157; African, 133–37; Egyptian, 137–44; family, 150; in film, 151–57; of King Tut, 391–93; short stories about, 142 (*see also specific short stories*)

"Daemon Lover, The" (Jackson), 519
Dahl, Roald, 718
Dahmer, Jeffrey, 480, 750–51
Daimons, 35–36. *See also* Demon
Danielewski, Mark Z., 281
Daniels, Jonathan, 329
Daniels, Les, 630, 743
Däniken, Erich von, 126
Danse Macabre (King), 222, 227, 228, 233, 554, 684
Dante Alighieri, 31, 38–40, 163, 179, 701
Danvers, Dennis, 681
"Dark Angel" (TV show), 532
Dark Half, The (King), 201, 204–5
Darker Than You Think (Williamson), 666–68
d'Arras, Jean, 448
Darwin, Charles, 99
Davenport, Basil, 177–78
Davids, Paul, 25
Davidson, Avram, 351, 451
Davidson, MaryJanice, 635
Davis, Andrew Jackson, 412
Davis, Frederic C., 363
Davis, Wade, 724–25
Dawn of the Dead (film), 735–36
Day, William Patrick, 640
Day Mars Invaded Earth, The (film), 22
Day of the Dead (film), 736–37
Day of the Triffids (film), 22
Day the Earth Stood Still, The (film), 8–9
de la Mare, Walter, 291–92, 297–98
De Paola, Tomie, 697
De Quincey, Thomas, 70–71, 74
Dead Ringers (film), 207
Dead Zone, The (film), 422
Dead Zone, The (King), 422, 485, 553
Dean, Joe E., 627
Deane, Hamilton, 641
Death. *See* Immortality

Deaver, Jeffrey, 494
Decadence and Decadent Movement, 78, 80, 81
Declare (Powers), 247–48
Dee, John, 112, 579–80, 587
DeFeo, Ronald, Jr., 273, 274
Delany, Samuel, 452
Demon, the, 31–34, 60–61, 161; aspects of, 44, 49; chronology of, 39; as djinn, 51–52; in film and other media, 46–54; from first century to modern times, 37–40; origin of the term, 34; prehistory, 34–36; in supernatural literature, 43–50. *See also Exorcist*; Possession
Demon, The (Lermontov), 45
"Demon Pope, The" (Garnett), 170–71
"Demons and Disenchantment" (Walter), 34
Demons by Daylight (Campbell), 120
Demons trilogy, 52
Dendle, Peter, 726–27
Denker, Henry, 511
Dennison, Walter Traill, 456
Derleth, August: "Bat's Belfry," 626; death, 121; "The Drifting Snow," 626; "The House in the Magnolias," 728–29; Lovecraft, Cthulhu Mythos, and, 86, 97–98, 101, 105, 108, 113–21, 125, 360, 361; "The Place in the Woods," 714
"Derleth Mythos," 112–18
Deshayes, Catherine, 702
Dessoir, Max, 416
Devereux, George, 193
Devil, 161–74, 176–84; autograph/ signature, 175–76; werewolves and the, 657. *See also* Devils
"Devil and Daniel Webster, The" (Benét), 173–74, 181
"Devil and Tom Walker, The" (Irving), 169–70
"Devil in the Belfry, The" (Poe), 170
Devil Is a Woman, The (film), 525
Devil Rides Out, The (film), 717
Devil Rides Out, The (Wheatley), 179

Devil upon Two Sticks, The (Le Sage), 167–68

"Devil Was Sick, The" (Elliott), 178

Devils, cinematic, 182 (*see also specific films*). *See also* Devil; Sorcerers

Devil's Elixir, The (Hoffmann), 169

Devil's Own Dear Son, The (Cabell), 173

di Filippo, Paul, 369, 452, 462

Diana, Princess of Wales, 421

Dibdin, Michael, 596

Dick, Philip K., 693

Dickens, Charles, 198, 226, 267–68, 353, 355, 383, 414

Dicks, Terrence, 431, 464

Diderot, Denis, 349–50

Dietrich, Marlene, 508

Digges, Jeremiah, 451

Dissociation, 191. *See also* Doppelgängers

"Disturb Not My Slumbering Fair" (Yarbro), 258

Dixon, Franklin W., 431

Dobyns, Stephen, 494

Doctor Strange (comic), 585

Doherty, Berlie, 450

Door of the Unreal, The (Biss), 661–62

Doppelgänger films, 204–10; chronology of, 206

Doppelgänger tales, 20th-century, 200–202

Doppelgängers, 187–89, 237; German Romanticism and, 189–91; golems as, 194–97; in popular culture, 210; psychology of, 191–97; young adult, 202–3

Dopperugengâ (film), 209

Dorsey, Tim, 497

Dostoevsky, Fyodor, 188, 191

Double Indemnity (film), 526

Doubles: Romantic and Victorian, 197–200. *See also* Doppelgängers

Douglas, Carole Nelson, 524

Douglas, Theo, 386

Doyle, Arthur Conan, 392–93, 410; "J. Habakuk Jephson's Statement," 467; *The Maracot Deep*, 462; mummy stories, 386; *The Parasite*, 624; "A Pastoral Horror," 669; Sherlock Holmes stories, 432, 433, 524–25, 626

Dr. Terror's House of Horrors (film), 155–56

Dracula (Stoker): critiques of, 638–40; films based on, 641–43. *See also under* Stoker

Drake, David, 260, 701, 703

Dreadstone, Carl, 400, 462

Dreamcatcher (King), 28–29

Dreamers, The (Manvell), 136, 137

Dream-Quest of Unknown Kadath, The (Lovecraft), 106–7, 111, 121, 251, 252

"Dreams in the Witch House, The" (Lovecraft), 111

Dresser, Norine, 646

Druids, 692

Dryden, Linda, 194, 195, 198

du Maurier, Daphne, 200–201, 231, 233, 522, 558

du Maurier, George, 513, 522

Duane, Diane, 713

Dudgeon, Robert Ellis, 462

Due, Tananarive, 230

Dumas, Alexandre, 314, 321, 657

Dunbar, Dayna, 434

Duncan, Lois, 228, 430, 431

Dunsany, Lord, 263, 585; "The Bride of the Man-Horse," 344; *The Charwoman's Shadow*, 170, 583, 584; *The Curse of the Wise Woman*, 133, 148–49; "The Curse of the Witch," 146; "A Deal with the Devil," 178; Jorkens stories, 146, 148–49, 178; Lovecraft and, 83, 100, 107; "Mrs. Jorkens," 451; "The Shield of Athene," 344; short stories, 107, 146; stories about Devil, 178; stories dealing with curses, 146

Dunwich Horror, The (film), 125

"Dunwich Horror, The" (Lovecraft), 100, 104–6, 110, 200, 553

Dwyer, James Francis, 467

Dyalhis, Nictzin, 450

"Dynasty" (TV show), 531

Dyson, Freeman, 90

Dziemianowicz, Stefan, 217, 511, 521

E. T.: The Extraterrestrial (film), 24–25

Eadie, Arlton, 680

Earth vs. the Flying Saucers (film), 13, 16

Earthbound (Matheson), 523

Eaters of the Dead (Crichton), 261, 346

Ebert, Roger, 219, 233, 237, 509, 526, 712

Eckert, Allan W., 430

Ed and His Dead Mother (film), 747

Eddington, Arthur, 89

Eddison, E. R., 259

Edghill, Rosemary, 696

Edward, John, 421

Eekhoud, Georges, 322

Egan, Greg, 333

Egbert, H. M., 518, 522. *See also* Rousseau, Victor

Egyptian curse, 137–44

Egyptian tombs and mummies, 376–77, 379, 381–82, 387, 403–4. *See also* Mummy(ies)

Eldridge, Paul, 132, 324, 326, 511

Eliade, Mircea, 268

Elizabeth I (Queen of England), 579–80

Elliott, Bruce, 178, 668, 715

Ellis, Bret Easton, 491–92

Ellis, Julie, 430

Ellison, Harlan, 49, 344, 502

Ellroy, James, 491

Elrod, P. N., 630

Emortality, 318, 331

"Empty House, The" (Blackwood), 289–90

Endless Honeymoon (Webb), 494–95

Endore, Guy, 259–60, 676–77

Engels, Friedrich, 592

England, George Allan, 323

Entartung (Nordau), 78

Entity, The (film), 51

Estes, Clarissa Pinkola, 681

Etchison, Dennis, 604, 609

Eulo, Ken, 611

Eureka (Poe), 73

Euripides, 701

Evans, Elizabeth, 477

Everett, Mrs. H. D. *See* Douglas, Theo

Eve's Bayou (film), 422–23

Evil Dead, The (film), 748

Evil Dead trilogy, 52–53

Exorcism of Emily Rose, The (film), 54

Exorcist, The (Blatty), 32–33, 48, 49, 60, 179, 180, 183, 607

Exorcist, The (film), 53, 54

Exorcist III, The (film), 55

"Extraterrestrial alien" motif, 5. *See also* Aliens

Eye Creatures, The (film), 18

Eyes of Laura Mars, The (film), 422

"Faceless God, The" (Bloch), 117, 139

"Facts in the Case of M. Valdemar, The" (Poe), 353, 423

"Fall of the House of Usher, The" (Poe), 283, 290, 622

Fallen, The (Bailey), 557

Fallen (film), 58–59

Familiars, 707–8; in supernatural literature, 713–14

Family curse, 150

"Far Below" (Johnson), 257

Farmer, Philip José, 344, 345

Farnese, Harold S., 115

Farrère, Claude, 320

Fatal Attraction (film), 528

Faulkner, William, 539, 544–46, 556

Faust, Johann Georg, 165

Faust (film), 181

Faust (Goethe), 44–45

Faust films, 574

Faust legend, 165–66, 168, 572–79, 657; Western writings inspired by, 576–77. *See also Tragical History of Doctor Faustus*

Faustus, 572; Prospero compared with, 577–79

Fear (Hubbard), 47, 51

Femme Fatale (Douglas), 524–25

Femme Fatale (film), 530

Femme Nikita, La (film), 528

Femmes fatales, 532–33; chronological
    listing of pivotal stories about,
    516–21; in film, 525–31; in TV shows,
    530–32. *See also* Sirens
Ferrera, Abel, 609
Féval, Paul, 315
Fevre Dream (Martin), 631, 632
Field, Eugene, 316, 449
Fight Club (film), 196
Fight Club (Palahniuk), 208, 209
Fincher, David, 196
Finney, Jack. *See Invasion of the Body
    Snatchers*
Firestarter (film), 422
Fischer, George Reuter, 122
Fish, Albert, 479
"Fisherman and His Soul, The"
    (Andersen), 447
Fitzball, Edward, 465
Fitzpatrick, Sonya, 421
Five Million Years to Earth (film), 23
Flamel, Nicolas, 571
Flammarion, Camille, 78
Flaubert, Gustave, 76, 77, 511
Floating Dragon (Straub), 555, 556
Florescu, Radu, 638
Flying Dutchman, The (opera), 465–67
Flying Saucers from Outer Space
    (Keyhoe), 16
Flynn, Michael, 676
Fodor, Nandor, 414
Fog, The (film), 559–60
Fonseca, Tony, 432
Forster, E. M., 345, 450
Fortune, Dion, 345
"Fortunes of Sir Robert Ardagh, The"
    (Le Fanu), 285–86
Foster, Alan Dean, 10–11, 24
Foster, George C., 323
Foster, Lori, 434
Fouqué, Friedrich de la Motte, 448
Fowler, Christopher, 202, 606, 613
Fox, [Ann] Leah, 412, 413, 415
Fox, John, 412
Frailty (film), 52, 59
France, Anatole, 174, 328
Frankenstein, 195

*Frankenstein; or, The Modern
    Prometheus* (Shelley), 70, 194, 196,
    342, 350–52, 382, 383, 581–82
Frankenstein (film), 363. *See also under*
    Shelley, Mary Wollstonecraft
Franklyn, Julian, 412
Franklyn, Roland, 120
Frayling, Christopher, 640
Frazer, James George, 99, 188
Frazer, Shamus, 714
Freeman, Mary E. Wilkins, 626
Freemantle, Brian, 467
Frenschkowski, Marco, 416
Freud, Sigmund, 190–92, 268, 274, 416
Frida (film), 529
Friesner, Esther, 451
Frighteners, The (film), 501
From Hell (film), 423
From the Dust Returned (Bradbury),
    229
Frost, Brian, 619, 640
Frost, Gregory, 496
Frost, Mark, 494
Frost, Robert, 296–97, 496
Fry, Rosalie K., 450

Gage, Matilda Joslyn, 413
Gaiman, Neil, 184, 202–3, 222, 346,
    433, 492, 586, 587, 700, 703
Gallon, Tom, 294–95
García Márquez, Gabriel, 545
Garcia y Robertson, R., 700
Garden, Nancy, 637
Garden of Eden, 36, 171, 511, 532, 629
Gardner, John, 342, 346, 463
Garmon, Larry Mike, 462
Garnett, Mayn Clew, 467
Garnett, Richard, 170, 328
Garrett, Randall, 399–400, 451
Garton, Ray, 608, 609
Gaunt, Mary, 397
Gautier, Théophile, 74, 384–85, 511,
    517, 521, 622–23
Gayton, Bertram, 323
Geasland, Jack, 207
Gein, Ed, 260–61, 479, 500
Geis, Richard E., 710

Gelder, Ken, 640

Geoffrey of Monmouth, 568–70

George, Elizabeth, 705

Gernsback, Hugo, 83

Ghost bones, 240

Ghost (film), 233

Ghost films, 230–32; chronological list, 232–37

Ghost manifestations: categories of, 237. *See also* Doppelgängers

Ghost ships and other hauntings, 464–68

Ghost stories, 234, 235; chronological list of novels, 226–30; classic short stories, 223–26; Dean Koontz on, 223; gnarled and twisted roots of, 218–20

"Ghost Stories of the Tiled House" (Le Fanu), 285

Ghost Story (Straub), 200, 216, 228, 555, 557

Ghost story writers, 220–23

"Ghost Village, The" (Straub), 539, 546–47

Ghostly sounds and lights, 237

Ghosts, 215–18; "singing bones" of, 240; on TV shows, 238–41

"Ghoul, The" (Smith), 245–46

Ghoul (Ronson), 247

Ghoul tales, top ten, 249

Ghoulish humor, 262

Ghouls: figurative, 258–64; influence of Edward Lucas White and Lovecraft, 248–58; origins of the term, 243–48; real-life, 260

"Ghouls" (Lee), 258

Ghouls (Lee), 258

Giant Ymir, The (film), 18

Gilden, Mel, 636, 637

Gilling, John, 730

Gilman, Charlotte Perkins, 196–97, 225, 226, 297

Ginzburg, Carlo, 695

"Girl with the Hungry Eyes, The" (Leiber), 601, 626

Glasgow, Ellen, 225

Gleason, Earl, 135

Gluckman, Janet Berliner, 696

Gods. *See* Cthulhu Mythos

Godwin, Mary Wollstonecraft, 382. *See also* Shelley, Mary Wollstonecraft

Godwin, William, 318, 319

Goethe, Johann Wolfgang von, 44–46, 166, 181, 190, 312, 352, 582, 621

Gogol, Nikolai, 198, 710, 716

Gold, H. L., 145, 150, 179

Golden, Christopher, 204

Goldenthal, Elliot, 347

Golding, William, 549

Golem as doppelgänger, 194–97

Gomez, Jewelle, 632

Gonce, John Wisdom III, 124

Gone with the Wind (Mitchell), 522

Gooch, Brad, 750–51

"Good Man Is Hard to Find, A" (O'Connor), 483–84

Gordon, George, 350

Gordon, Stuart, 125

Gothic horror, 69–70

Gothic Revival style and haunted houses, 272–73

Gourmont, Rémy de, 77, 511

Graham, Carter E., 116

Grant, Charles L., 228, 258, 400, 608

Graves, Robert, 345, 443, 711

"Graveyard Rats, The" (Kuttner), 256

Gray, John, 216

"Great God Pan, The" (Machen), 200, 253, 345, 358, 517–18

Greeley, Andrew M., 434

"Green Tea" (Le Fanu), 45–46

Greenberg, Martin H., 293

Gregory, Franklin, 666

Grey Shapes (Mann), 665–66

Grillparzer, Franz, 701

Grimassi, Raven, 701

Grimes, J. S., 412

Grimm, Jacob and Wilhelm, 367, 482

Grimson, Todd, 710

"Grinning Ghoul, The" (Bloch), 256–57

G-String Murders (Lee), 523

Guerard, Albert, 188

Guiley, Rosemary, 646

Guran, Paula, 230

Gurney, Edmund, 419
Guthridge, George, 696
Gutierrez, Cathy, 411–12, 414–15

H. G. Wells' The War of the Worlds,
6–7, 10, 16
Hadji, R. S., 608
Haeckel, Ernst, 99
Haggard, H. Rider, 345, 388, 521–22,
525
Haiti, 725–27
Haldane, J.B.S., 89
Haldeman, Joe, 452
Hales, E.E.Y., 331
Hall, Melissa Mia, 520
Hallam, Clifford, 187–88, 192
Halperin, Victor, 726
Hambly, Barbara, 630–31
Hamilton, Edith, 343
Hamilton, Laurell K., 258, 635
Hancock, Graham, 126
Hand, Elizabeth, 694, 695, 701
Hannibal (Harris), 487, 488
Hannibal the Cannibal. *See* Lecter,
Hannibal
Hardy, Phil, 153
Hare, William, 478
Harms, Daniel, 124
Harris, Charlaine, 635
Harris, Thomas, 260, 342, 366–67, 435,
487–88, 503
Harrison, Kathryn, 451
Harrison, M. John, 601, 604–6
Hart, Ellen, 434
Hartwell, David, 226
Harvest Home (Tryon), 550–51, 559
Harvey, Jayne, 637
Harvey, W. F., 290
*Hashish-Eater; or, The Apocalypse of
Evil, The* (Smith), 81–82, 87, 90
Hauff, Wilhelm, 190
"Haunted" (Oates), 226
Haunted Castle, The (Railo), 271
Haunted castles, 271–72
Haunted house films, 298–303
Haunted house novels, 276–81, 283
"Haunted House" (painting), 283

Haunted house poems, 296–98
"Haunted House" (Robinson), 298
Haunted house short stories, 283–96;
unjustly neglected, 294–95
Haunted houses, 267–69; in art,
282–83; in folklore, 269–71; iconic,
272–73; "real," 273–76
"Haunted Palace, The" (Poe), 284
"Haunter of the Dark, The" (Lovecraft),
111–12
Haunting of Hill House, The (Jackson),
227, 279, 424–25
Hauntings, sea, 464–68
Hawthorne, Julian, 623
Hawthorne, Nathaniel, 100, 167, 320,
548; *The House of the Seven Gables*,
167, 276–78; *Tanglewood Tales*, 701;
"A Virtuoso's Collection," 316;
"Young Goodman Brown," 167,
538–42, 544, 550–52, 554, 694, 712
He Loves Me ... He Loves Me Not
(film), 530
Headhunter (Slade), 488–89
Hearn, Julie, 706
Heautoscopy, 191, 196
Heine, Heinrich, 320, 449, 465–66
Heinlein, Robert A., 715
Hellblazer (Moore), 50
Henley, Samuel, 245
Henry, O., 317
Herdman, John, 187, 189, 190
Hering, Henry A., 466
Hermeticism, 570–72
Herschel, William, 68
Herskovits, Melville J., 193
Herter, Lori, 634
Hesiod, 343
Hewson, David, 497
Heym, Stefan, 326
Hichens, Robert, 322, 518
Hierens, William, 481
High-Rise (Ballard), 611–13
Highsmith, Patricia, 484
Hill, Susan, 522, 523
Hill House, 279
Hilton, James, 320
Hitchcock, Alfred, 484, 497, 499

Hix, J. Emile, 322

Hodgson, William Hope, 80, 82, 83, 86, 433; *The Ghost Pirates*, 79, 466; "The Hog," 79–80; *The House on the Borderland*, 78, 278–79; Lovecraft and, 83, 461; monsters in the works of, 358–59; *The Night Land*, 79, 598; sea monsters in the stories of, 459–61

Hoffman, Alice, 512, 527, 718

Hoffman, David, 316

Hoffmann, Ernst Theodore Amadeus, 46, 169, 190, 192, 411

"Hog, The" (Hodgson), 79–80

Hogg, James, 169, 197

Hohman, George, 692

Holden, Stephen, 232

Holder, Nancy, 699, 710, 715

Holder, Wayne, 715

Holmes, H. H., 478, 484–85, 607

Holt, Tom, 466

Holy Skirts (Steinke), 525

Home, Daniel Douglas, 413

Homer, 345, 443, 508, 532, 700

Homeward Bounders, The (Jones), 332

Hopkins, Linda, 382–84

Hopkins, Matthew, 706, 708

Hopkinson, Nalo, 699

"Horla, The" (Maupassant), 45, 46, 188, 194, 199, 224, 226, 594

Horler, Sydney, 626

Hôtel Transylvania (Yarbro), 629–30

Houdini, Harry, 358, 410, 415

"Hound, The" (Leiber), 601, 602, 670–71

House of Leaves (Danielewski), 281, 283

"House of Sounds, The" (Shiel), 290–91

House of the Seven Gables, The (Hawthorne), 167, 276–78

House on Nazareth Hill, The (Campbell), 280

House on the Borderland, The (Hodgson), 78–79, 278–79

Housman, Clemence, 659, 676, 680

Howard, Robert E., 261, 362–63, 518, 598; "The Black Stone," 113; ghouls and Little People in stories of, 253, 259; Lovecraft and, 113, 252, 361–63; "The Moon of Skulls," 509; myth-cycle, 98; "Pigeons from Hell," 156; in *Shadows Bend*, 122; "Wings in the Night," 508–9

Howe, Deborah, 636

Howe, James, 636

Howison, John, 465

Hoyle, Fred, 464

Hoyle, Geoffrey, 464

Hubbard, L. Ron, 47, 50, 149, 246–47

Hudson, T. K., 257

Huff, Tanya, 630

Hughes, Rhys, 366, 368

Hugo, Victor, 457

Huldra, 513

Humanoid races, 461–62

"Hunger" (Oates), 520–21

Hunger, The (Blaylock), 631

Hunter, Mollie, 450

Huxley, Aldous, 40, 176, 323

Huxley, Thomas Henry, 99

Huysmans, Joris-Karl, 75–76

Hyder, Alan, 363

Hyne, C. J. Cutcliffe, 323

I Am Legend (Matheson), 627–28

I Married a Monster from Outer Space (film), 19–20

I Walked with a Zombie (film), 729–30

I Was a Teenage Werewolf (film), 684

Immortality, 377; leading novels about, 327; leading short stories about, 330; progress in the flight from frustration, 332–34; rejuvenative, 320; science-fictional images of, 333–34. *See also* Mummy(ies); Witches

Immortals, 307–9; learning to love long life, 322–26; mythology (tedious punishments and accursed wanderers), 309–13; occult practitioners and Faustian, 317–22; twilight of the gods, 326–32. *See also* Wandering Jew

"In Kropfsberg Keep" (Cram), 288–89

In the Closed Room (Burnett), 227
In the Mouth of Madness (film), 125
Independence Day (film), 26–27
Inferno (Dante), 38–39, 163–64
Inhabitant of the Lake and Less Welcome Tenants, The (Campbell), 119–20
Interview with the Vampire (Rice), 624, 628–29
Invaders from Mars (film), 11–12
Invaders in the Dark (La Spina), 661–62
Invasion of the Body Snatchers (film), 16–17, 22
Invasion of the Body Snatchers (Finney), 547–49, 551, 557, 558
Invasion of the Saucer Men (film), 18
Irrefutable Truth about Demons (film), 51
Irving, Washington, 169, 224, 232, 352, 465
Irwin, H. J., 417
Irwin, Margaret, 147, 692
Irwin, Robert, 150–51
Island of the Burning Doomed (film), 22–23
It Came from Outer Space (film), 11
It Conquered the World (film), 17
It's a Wonderful Life (film), 32

Jaccoma, Richard, 668
Jack the Ripper, 478–79, 481, 501–3; compared with Dracula and Hyde, 594–96
Jack the Ripper stories, 596; chronology of, 597; *The Women of Whitechapel and Jack the Ripper* (West), 596–98; "Yours Truly, Jack the Ripper," 47, 325, 501–2, 596
Jackson, Melanie, 451
Jackson, Shirley, 216, 228, 232; "The Daemon Love," 519; *The Haunting of Hill House*, 227, 279, 424–25; "The Lottery," 539, 544–48, 551, 559
Jacobs, W. W., 441, 458
Jacob's Ladder (film), 51
Jacques, Brian, 466
Jaffe, Jody, 434

Jakes, John, 511
James, Henry, 200, 227, 228, 300
James, M. R., 45–47, 141–43, 152, 177, 217, 224, 280, 598, 625
James, William, 416
Jameson, Malcolm, 715
Janvier, Thomas, 460
Jarocha-Ernst, Chris, 98, 361
Jason, Daniel N., 464
Jeffers, Robinson, 701
Jesby, Edward, 452
Jesus Christ, 41, 79, 132, 314, 326, 334; Satan and, 162–63
Jewett, Sarah Orne, 100
Jews. *See* Judaism; Wandering Jew
Johns, Andreas, 700
Johnson, Robert Barbour, 257
Jones, Constance, 452
Jones, Diana Wynne, 325, 332, 713
Jones, Ernest, 619, 620, 638
Jones, Guy, 452
Jones, Stephen, 125, 217, 227, 433
Joplin's Ghost (Due), 230
Jordan, Michael, 444
"Jorkens in Witch Wood" (Dunsany), 146
Joshi, S. T., 142, 147, 148, 217, 219, 224, 511, 521
Joyce, James, 701
Judaism, 35–37. *See also* Wandering Jew
Jung, Carl Gustav, 199, 416
"Jungle, The" (Beaumont), 135
Jungle Book, The (Kipling), 141
Jungman, Ann, 637
Jurgen (Cabell), 172–73

Kadono, Eiko, 717
Kael, Pauline, 136
Kagan, Jeremy, 25
Kalogridis, Jeanne, 633
Kant, Immanuel, 68
Kaplan, Stephen, 274
Karloff, Boris, 342, 352, 363
Kast, Pierre, 332
Keats, John, 517, 621, 622, 633
Keene, Brian, 50, 740–41
Keller, David H., 174

Kelley, David E., 464. *See also* "Ally McBeal"

Kelly, Edward, 580

Kelvin, Lord, 78, 89

Kenyon, Sherrilyn, 636

Keppler, C. F., 188, 195–96

Kerruish, Jessie Douglas, 663–66, 680

Kesserling, Joseph, 497

Ketchum, Jack, 487

Keyhoe, Donald F., 16

Ki, 421

Kiki's Delivery Service (film), 717–18

Kill Bill Vol. 1 and *Kill Bill Vol. 2* (films), 530

Killer Inside Me, The (Thompson), 483

Killers, types of, 475. *See also* Serial killers

Killers from Space (film), 12–13

Killough, Lee, 630

King, Frank, 260

King, Stephen, 125, 240, 241, 365, 537–38, 560; *Black House*, 426, 495; "The Body," 553; on *Burnt Offerings*, 279; *Carrie*, 231, 427, 551; *Chronicle of a Death Foretold* and, 545; *Cujo*, 553; *Cycle of the Werewolf*, 673–74; *Danse Macabre*, 222, 227, 228, 233, 554, 684; *The Dark Half*, 201, 204; *The Dead Zone*, 422, 485, 553; *The Diaries of Ellen Rimbauer*, 238; on *The Doll Who Ate His Mother*, 280; *Dreamcatcher*, 28–29; *The Exorcist* and, 607; *Eyes of the Dragon*, 366; *Firestarter*, 422; "Jerusalem's Lot," 121; "The Man Who Would Not Shake Hands," 148; *Needful Things*, 184, 552–55, 561; on *The Nightwalker*, 486; *Pet Sematary*, 739–40, 746; "The Raft," 461; "The Reach," 427; *Rose Madder*, 344; *Rose Red*, 238, 276; *'Salem's Lot*, 538, 551, 552, 554, 555, 557, 561, 628–30; small-town horrors, 537–38, 550–56; *The Stand*, 366; *The Talisman*, 426; telepathy and telekinesis texts, 422; *Thinner*, 148, 694; *The Tommyknockers*, 552, 554;

works with psi themes, 426–27. *See also Shining, The*

King, Tabitha, 230

King in Yellow, The (Chambers), 81

King-Smith, Dick, 450, 463

Kipling, Rudyard, 140–41, 224, 248, 458, 658, 691

Kirkman, Robert, 741

Klause, Annette Curtis, 637–38

Klein, T.E.D., 123, 134, 599, 714

Kleist, Heinrich von, 190

Kline, Otis Adelbert, 354

Knight, Charlotte, 18

Knight, Damon, 116

Knight, H. R., 410

Koja, Kathe, 609

Konvitz, Jeffrey, 611

Koontz, Dean R., 223, 365, 366, 426, 693

Kopet, Arthur, 25

Kornbluth, C. M., 627

Kostova, Elizabeth, 633–34

Kotzwinkle, William, 25

Krutch, Joseph Wood, 108

Kubrick, Stanley, 345. *See also Shining, The* (film)

Kummer, Frederic Arnold, 176, 177

Kushner, Tony, 58

Kuttner, Henry, 256, 599

La Spina, Greye, 661, 662, 676, 680

Lackey, Mercedes, 630

Lady Eve, The (film), 526

Lady in the Water (film), 530

Lafferty, R. A., 345

Lagerkvist, Pär, 326

Lancashire Witches, 706

Lancashire Witches, The (Ainsworth), 169, 706

Land of the Dead (film), 737, 738

Landis, Theodor, 193, 196

Lane, Joel, 605–6

Lang, Andrew, 345

Lang, Fritz, 601

Lang, Peter, 136

Langford, David, 333

Lansdale, Joe R., 366, 402, 608

Larson, Erik, 484–85

Lassez, Sarah, 218

Last Wave, The (film), 125

Laura (Caspary), 523

Laura (film), 526

Laurie, Victoria, 434

Laveau, Marie, 703

Lawrence, C. E., 326

Laws, Stephen, 611

Laymon, Richard, 402, 503, 608

le Breton, Thomas, 323

Le Fanu, J. Sheridan, 199, 423, 424, 511, 521, 642; "Carmilla," 623; "Green Tea," 45–46, 199, 200; haunted house stories, 285–86; monstrous and horrific elements in stories of, 353; "Sir Dominick's Bargain," 170; vampire stories and, 625

Le Fay, Morgan, 701

Le Guin, Ursula, 714

Leave Her to Heaven (film), 526–27

Lecter, Hannibal, 474, 481, 482, 487, 503

Lee, Edward, 258

Lee, Gypsy Rose, 523

Lee, Stan, 148

Lee, Tanith, 631–32

Legend of Hell House, The (film), 301

"Legend of Sleepy Hollow, The" (Irving), 224

Legion (Blatty), 55, 183

Leiber, Fritz, 86, 117, 259, 602, 607; *Conjure Wife*, 512, 550, 694, 698, 712, 716; "The Girl with the Hungry Eyes," 511, 519, 601, 626; "The Hound," 601, 602, 670–71; Lovecraft and, 86, 122; *Our Lady of Darkness*, 86, 601; on Sirens, 511, 512; "Smoke Ghost," 225, 231, 600–601, 607; "The Terror from the Depths," 122; urban horror, 601–3; "The Warlock," 694

Leibniz, Gottfried Wilhelm, 67

Leight, Walter W., 399

Leinster, Murray, 461, 463

Leland, Charles, 701

Lem, Stanislaw, 205

Leman, Bob, 257

Lermontov, Mikhail Yurievich, 45, 47

Levin, Ira, 48, 180, 184, 206, 550, 551, 610, 613

Lewis, C. S., 43, 47, 179, 259, 331, 347, 467, 718

Lewis, Matthew Gregory, 32, 44, 168, 315, 581, 709

Lewton, Val, 152

Leyden, John, 465

Lichtenberg, Jacqueline, 632

Lie, Jonas, 445–46

"Ligeia" (Poe), 223, 516–17, 622

Ligotti, Thomas, 56, 86, 123, 294, 296

Lilith, 511

Linklater, Eric, 451

Lint, Charles de, 519

"Lips, The" (Whitehead), 134–35

Little, Bentley, 740

Loch Ness Monster, 463–64

Locke, John, 349

Lofts, Nora, 716

Lolita (film), 527

Long, Frank Belknap, 85–86, 108, 112, 113, 122, 123, 247, 459

Longfellow, Henry Wadsworth, 267

Longinus, 67

Lorrah, Jean, 634

Lorrain, Jean, 77

lost boy lost girl (Straub), 229, 235, 490

"Lottery, The" (Jackson), 539, 544–48, 551, 559

Loudon, Jane, 382

Lovecraft, H. P., 256, 263, 366; Bloch and, 16–17, 86, 101, 122, 138, 256, 257, 599; on cosmic/supernatural horror, 65–67, 91; death, 363; demons and, 47, 66; *The Dream-Quest of Unknown Kadath*, 251; "The Dreams in the Witch House," 713; *Fungi from Yuggoth*, 140; ghouls in stories of, 250–52, 257; "Herbert West–Reanimator," 749; "The Horror at Martin's Beach," 354; "The

Horror at Red Hook," 599;
indifferentism, 109–10, 112; "The
Invisible Monster," 354; later
Lovecraft Mythos, 108–12; life of,
99–100; literary techniques, 254–55;
Lovecraft Mythos, 98–107; Lovecraft
school, 81–88; on *Melmoth the
Wanderer*, 131; monsters in the stories
of, 354, 360, 459, 553; *At the
Mountains of Madness*, 84, 599;
mummy stories, 398; Old Ones, 102,
105, 109, 114–16, 120–23, 125, 202;
"Out of the Aeons," 398; Peter
Straub and, 201; "Pickman's Model,"
250–53, 257, 599; on religion, 66–67;
Rhys Hughes and, 368; Robert
Barbour Johnson and, 257; "The
Shadow out of Time," 5–6, 84–85,
111, 125; "The Shadow over
Innsmouth," 539, 542–44, 546, 547,
556, 557, 560; "The Shunned
House," 361, 626; "Supernatural
Horror in Literature," 1, 227; on
"The House of Sounds," 290; "Under
the Pyramids," 398; urban horror
and, 598–99; "The Whisperer in
Darkness," 5, 6, 83; on "The
Willows," 224; on witch-cults, 253;
writers influenced by, 361, 366 (*see
also specific writers*). See also Cthulhu
Mythos; "Dunwich Horror, The";
Necronomicon
Lovecraft Chronicles, The (Cannon),
122
Lovecraft's Book (Lupoff), 122
Lovely Bones, The (Sebold), 229, 234,
495
Lowe, Rabbi, 750
Lowndes, Marie Belloc, 501, 596
Lucan, 701
Lucas, Henry Lee, 500
Lucas, Henry Lee (film), 500
Lucian, 269
Lucifer, 172
"Lukundoo" (White), 133–35
Lumley, Brian, 86, 120, 427–28, 433,
633

Lupoff, Richard A., 122
Lycanthropy, 482–83, 486, 655, 657,
658, 660–63, 666, 669, 670,
673–76, 681, 683–84
Lymington, John, 22
Lyons, Arthur, 432

M., Armin, 481
Macbeth (Shakespeare), 698, 711,
713
MacDonald, George, 227, 316, 448,
511
Machen, Arthur, 359, 366; Celtic
mythology and, 252; "The Children
of the Pool," 468; "The Great God
Pan," 200, 253, 345, 358, 517–18;
"The Great Return," 80; Lovecraft
and, 80, 100, 252; "Novel of the
White Powder," 358; Rhys Hughes
and, 366, 368; *The Secret Glory*, 80;
tales of Little People, 100, 252, 253;
"The White People," 80, 714
Machinist, The (film), 209–10
Macleod, Fiona, 449
MacOrlan, Pierre, 466
Magic. *See* Sorcerers; Witches
Magic Island, The (Seabrook), 725
Magick, 583–84
Magnetism, 411
Maguire, Gregory, 698
Mahy, Margaret, 430
Majestic (Streiber), 27–28
Malory, Thomas, 569
Malvo, Lee, 480–81
Man from Planet X, The (film), 9–10
"Man of the Crowd, The" (Poe),
592–95
Mandeville, John, 347–48
Mann, Jack, 325, 663–65
Mansart, François, 272
Manson, Charles, 479
Mantel, Hilary, 230
Manvell, Roger, 136–37
Map, Walter, 448
March, William, 483
"Mark of the Beast, The" (Kipling),
140–41

Marlowe, Christopher, 165–66, 565, 574–76, 579

Marryat, Frederick, 132, 320, 456, 457, 465, 658–59, 680

Mars Attacks (film), 25–26

Marschner, Heinrich, 320, 350

Marsh, Jan, 515

Marsh, Richard, 357, 359

Marshall, Michael, 495–96

Martin, Ann M., 637

Martin, George R. R., 631, 668

Martyn, Wyndham, 325

Marx, Karl, 592

Masefield, John, 449, 459

Mass murderers, 475–76

Masterton, Graham, 217–18, 427

Mather, Cotton, 167, 168, 170

Matheson, Richard, 602, 603, 633; "Duel," 225; *Earthbound*, 523; "From Shadowed Places," 696; *Hell House*, 227; *Hill House*, 301; *I Am Legend*, 627, 733–34; Mesmerism and, 424; *Stir of Echoes*, 236

Matheson, Richard Christian, 600, 608

Matthews, Brander, 466

Matthewsen, Elise, 707

Maturin, Charles Robert, 45, 131–32, 169, 318, 319, 662, 669

Maugham, W. Somerset, 141, 584

Maupassant, Guy de, 199, 201, 224, 225, 424, 593, 623; "The Horla," 45, 46, 188, 194, 224, 226, 594; "La Nuit," 594; "Who Knows?", 286–87

Maxwell, Ann, 430

May, Rollo, 36, 49

McAlister, Kate, 635, 638

McCammon, Robert, 366, 630

McCarthy, Cormac, 490–91

McCarthy, Justin Huntly, 328

McCauley, Kirby, 240

McClusky, Thorp, 727

McDowell, Michael, 230

McGrail, Nuala Anne, 434

McGrath, Patrick, 367

McIlwraith, Dorothy, 87

McLaughlin, Mark, 124

McNally, Raymond, 638

McNaughton, Brian, 261–63

Medium, A., 415

Medium, The (film), 427

Mediums, 414, 417, 421, 426, 430–32

Meinhold, Wilhelm, 705

Melmoth the Wanderer (Maturin), 131–32, 169, 318–19

Melville, Herman, 457

Memnoch the Devil (Rice), 50

Mendlesohn, Farah, 329

Menzies, Sutherland, 656

Merlin, 568–70

Merlin, movies about, 570

Mermaid paintings, classic, 455

Mermaids (and mermen), 444–52, 512–13; in movies and TV shows, 453–54

Mesmer, Franz Anton, 411, 423–24

Mesmerism, 411–12, 414, 423

Metcalf, John, 295

"Metzengerstein" (Poe), 284

Meyrink, Gustav, 351

Michaels, Barbara, 426

Michel, Anneliese, 54

Middleton, Richard, 225

Midwich Cuckoos, The (Wyndham), 548–49

Miéville, China, 368–69, 606

Millard, Joseph, 23

Mille, Cecil B. de, 525

Miller, Arthur, 705

Miller, Elizabeth, 641

Miller, Karl, 188, 198

Miller, P. Schuyler, 452

Miller, Rex, 491

Miller, Walter M., Jr., 332

Millgate, Irvine H., 19

Milton, John, 31–32, 40, 166–67, 329, 352

Mind Parasites, The (Wilson), 119

Mitchell, Margaret, 522

Mocha Dick, 457

Molitor, Ulrich, 693

Monk (Lewis), 168

Monroe, Marilyn, 533

Monsarrat, Nicholas, 466

Monsters: curious facts about, 354; durable, 364–65; in film, 363–65; in literature, 341–63; from outer space, 364; on television, 365. *See also* Sea serpents and monsters

Monteleone, Thomas F., 613

Montesquieu, Charles le Secondat, Baron de, 78

Moon Dance (Somtow), 678–79

Mooney, Brian, 433

Moorcock, Michael, 333

Moore, Alan, 50, 503, 586, 597

Moore, C. L., 344, 626

Moore, James A., 202

Moore, Tony, 741

Mopsard, 261

Moreau, Joseph, 74

Morgan, Dexter, 496–97

Morgan, Hank, 570

Morrah, Dermot, 397

Morris, William, 510

Morrison, Toni, 217, 228, 236

Morrow, James, 184, 334

Mosig, Dirk W., 121

Moskowitz, Sam, 138

Mudgett, Herman. *See* Holmes, H. H.

Muhammad, John, 480–81

Mulholland Dr. (film), 207

Mulligan, Robert, 204

Mumford, Lewis, 591–92

Mumler, William H., 418

Mummy, The (film), 394–97, 400–402

Mummy!, The (Webb), 382–84

Mummy, or Ramses the Damned, The (film), 400

Mummy books for young readers, 391

Mummy(ies), 375–76; curse of King Tut, 391–93; in early films, 389–90; in Europe, 379–81; factual, 376–79; in fiction, 381–89; in later fiction, 397–401; in later films, 393–97; making, 380; origin of the term, 380–81; in recent literature and film, 401–4

Mundt, Martin, 693

Murnau, F. W., 181

Murphy, Pat, 681

Murray, Margaret Alice, 66, 101, 252, 261, 696, 702, 707, 711

Murrell, James, 702–3

My First Two Thousand Years (Viereck and Eldridge), 324, 329

Myers, Frederic William Henry, 419

Myers, John Myers, 345, 346

Mysteries of Udolpho, The (Radcliffe), 271–72

Mysterious Stranger, The (Twain), 171

Nabokov, Vladimir, 527

"Nameless Offspring, The" (Smith), 253–56, 263

Napoleon Bonaparte, 381, 390

Narrative of Arthur Gordon Pym of Nantucket, The (Poe), 352–53

Narrows, The (Connelly), 493

Nathan, Robert, 176

Navarro, Yvonne, 633

Navidson, Will, 281

Nazareth Hill, 280

Necromancy, 566, 574–75

Necronomicon, 101–2, 105, 112, 113, 126, 692

Needful Things (King), 184, 552–55, 561

Neele, Henry, 315

Neiderman, Andrew, 691

Neill, Robert, 706

Nelson, Victoria, 60

Neptune Rising (Yolen), 523

Nero, 477

Nesbit, E., 323, 450

Nevins, Francis M., Jr., 144

Newman, Kim, 333, 427, 428, 433, 635, 679

Newton, Isaac, 68, 349

Newton, Michael, 482

Nichols, Joel Martin, 461

Nickell, Joe, 431–32

Nietzsche, Friedrich Wilhelm, 257

Night Country, The (O'Nan), 556, 557

Night Land, The (Hodgson), 79

Night of the Demon (film), 47–48, 51, 151–54

Night of the Eagle (film), 716

Night of the Living Dead (film), 734–35, 748, 749
Nightmare Alley (film), 423
Nightwalker, The (Tessier), 486, 672–73
Niven, Larry, 259, 675
Nodier, Charles, 622
Nolan, William F., 608
Nollen, Scott A., 395–96
Nordau, Max, 78
Norris, Frank, 466
Norton, Caroline, 318
Norton, Mary, 717
Nostromo (film), 24
Noyes, Alfred, 467
Nutman, Philip, 608

O Brother Where Art Thou? (film), 529
Oates, Joyce Carol, 226, 295, 493, 520, 750–51
Obenski, Michael A., 421
O'Connelly, Neil, 200
O'Connor, Flannery, 483
O'Donnell, Elliott, 653
Odysseus, 443
Odyssey (Homer), 345, 700–701
Off Season (Cady), 556
Ogres, real-life, 260
Old Curiosity Shop, The (Dickens), 355
Old Dark House, The (Priestley), 299–300
Old English Baron, The (Reeve), 272
O'Leary, Patrick, 334
Oliver, Owen, 459
Omega Point hypothesis, 89–90
On Blue's Water (Wolfe), 524
O'Nan, Stewart, 550, 556, 557
Onions, Oliver, 238, 450, 518
"Opener of the Way, The" (Bloch), 139
"Operation Afreet" (Anderson), 675
Oppenheim, Sulamith, 450
"Orchard Pit, The" (Rossetti), 517
Ordo Templi Orientis (OTO), 584
Orpheus myth, 219
Oruene, T. O., 194
Ossenfelder, Heinrich, 621
Other, The (Tryon), 201, 204, 426

Otten, Charlotte F., 653
Oudemans, A. C., 457
Our Lady of Darkness (Leiber), 86
Our Town (Wilder), 551
Our Vampires, Ourselves (Auerbach), 624–25
Ovid, 692–93

Page, Carol, 646
Pain, Barry, 345
Paine, Michael, 400
Palahniuk, Chuck, 196, 197, 208
"Papa Benjamin" (Woolrich), 144–45
Paperhouse (film), 426
Paradise Lost (Milton), 32, 40, 59, 166–67, 329
Parapsychology, 415–20; defined, 417; prevalence, 420
Pargeter, Edith, 150
Parry, David M., 462
Patterson, James, 492
Paul, Jean, 187–90, 198
Paul VI, Pope, 33
Pausanias, 445
Paxson, Diana, 696
Pearce, Joseph H., 449
Pease, Howard, 467
Peattie, Elia W., 294–95
Pelan, John, 125
Pendle Witches, 706
Perez, Edwardo, 347
Peritti, Frank, 49, 55
Perrault, Charles, 482
Pessimism, 109, 118–19. *See also under* "Cosmic horror"
Pet, The (Grant), 228
Pet Sematary (King), 739, 740, 746
Peters, Elizabeth, 403–4
Petronius, 538
Pettee, Florence M., 397
Phantom from Space (film), 12
Phenomenon of Man, The (Telhard), 89–90
Phillips, Arthur, 404
Phillpotts, Eden, 328
Philosophical horror, 118
Phoenician Dragon, 444

Pickett, Lenny, 347

"Pickman's Model" (Lovecraft), 250–53, 257, 599

Picture of Dorian Gray, The (Wilde), 198

Pike, Christopher, 228

Pirie, David, 153, 156

Pizer, John, 188

Plague of the Zombies, The (film), 730–32

Planche, James Robinson, 622

Plato, 36, 130, 508

Plautus, 269

Pleasures of the Imagination, The (Akenside), 68

Pliny the Younger, 219–20, 269

Plutarch, 352

Podmore, Frank, 412, 419

Poe, Edgar Allan, 256–57, 296, 366, 493, 598; "Al Aaraaf," 73; Baudelaire and, 75; "Berenice," 517; "The Devil in the Belfry," 170; *Eureka*, 73–74; "The Facts in the Case of M. Valdemar," 353, 423; "The Fall of the House of Usher," 283, 290, 622; film adaptations of, 298–99; haunted house short stories, 283–84; "Ligeia," 223, 516–17, 622; Lovecraft and, 100; "The Man of the Crowd," 592–95; "The Masque of the Red Death," 353; Mesmer and, 411; "Metzengerstein," 284; "Morella," 622; "MS. Found in a Bottle," 465; *The Narrative of Arthur Gordon Pym of Nantucket*, 84, 352–53; prose fiction, 73; Rhys Hughes and, 368; "Some Words with a Mummy," 384; the supernatural and detectives in the stories of, 432; vampires and, 626; "William Wilson," 199, 201–4, 353

Poet, A (Connelly), 493

Polergeists, 237

Polidori, John, 319, 350, 621–22

"Pollock and the Porroh Man" (Wells), 133, 691

Polson, John, 205

Poltergeist (film), 234–35, 303

Pontopiddan, Erik, 456

Portal fantasy, 329–30

Possessed objects, 237. *See also* Demon

Possession, spirit, 426. *See also* Demon; *Exorcist*

Possessions (Moore), 202–3

Powell, Eric, 741

Powers, Tim, 247, 334, 466, 633

Powlik, James, 463

Powys, T. F., 308, 334

Practical Magic (film), 529, 718

Pratchett, Terry, 184, 713

Pratt, Fletcher, 325

Prayer for the Dying, A (O'Nan), 556, 557

Prest, Thomas Preskett, 622

Price, E. Hoffmann, 178, 360

Price, Robert M., 101–2, 110, 125, 707

Prichard, Hesketh Vernon, 387, 432

Prichard, Kate O'Brien Ryall, 387, 432

Priestley, J. B., 299

Prill, David, 493

Prince of Darkness (film), 51

Pritchard, Melissa, 229

Prometheus, 342–43

Pronzini, Bill, 135, 260, 400

Prophecy, The (film), 56–59

"Prophecy of Monsters, A" (Smith), 354, 675

Prose, Francine, 703

Prospero, 348–49, 577–79

Psychic detectives, 431–32; in fiction, 432–35

Psychic phenomena in popular culture, 420–23

Psychical research, 415–20

Psychics, 435; chronology of films about, 425; definition and origins, 409–11; Houdini and the skeptics, 410, 415; in science fiction and horror, 423–29; Spiritualism and, 411–15; in various literary genres, 429–30

Psycho (Bloch), 260–61, 474, 475, 479, 481, 484, 600

Psychokinesis (PK), 419–20, 422, 426–29

Pudd'nhead Wilson (Twain), 198
Pugmire, Wilum, 123
Pullman, Philip, 708
Pulver, Joseph, 123
Punk subculture, 607. *See also*
  Splatterpunk
Putnam, Nina Wilcox, 395

Quatermass and the Pit (film), 23
Queen of the Damned, The (Rice), 524
Quiller-Couch, Arthur, 316–17
Quinet, Edgar, 313–14
Quinn, Seabury, 399, 450, 668, 680

Rabid Growth (Moore), 202–3
Radcliffe, Ann, 271–72
Rader, Denis, 481
Railo, Eino, 271
Rais, Gilles de, 477, 702
Raleigh, Richard, 122
Ramses the Great, 400
Ramsland, Katherine, 646
Randisi, Robert, 497
Randle, Kevin D., 25
Rank, Otto, 190–91, 193, 194, 198
Rankin, Ian, 524
Rashômon (film), 423
Raven, Simon, 628
Reagan, Nancy, 421
Re-Animator (film), 749
Rebecca (du Maurier), 522
Rebecca (film), 526
"Recluse, A" (de la Mare), 291–92
Red Dragon (Harris), 487–88
Reeve, Clara, 272
Reilly, James E., 474
Reincarnation fantasy, 321
Reisert, Rebecca, 698
Repeated actions (ghosts), 237
Ressler, Robert K., 482
Return of Fursey, The (Wall), 174
Return of the Living Dead, The (film),
  748–49
Revolt of the Angels, The (France), 174
Reynolds, Alistair, 606
Reynolds, George W. M., 657
Reynolds, Jeremiah, 457

Reynolds, Mack, 429
Rhine, J. B., 428–29
Rhodes, Jewell P., 703
Rhys, John, 448
Riccardo, Martin V., 640
Rice, Anne, 332, 511, 512, 627,
  632, 646; *Interview with the Vampire*,
  604, 624, 628–29; *Memnoch the
  Devil*, 50; *The Mummy, or Ramses
  the Damned*, 400, 401; *The Queen
  of the Damned*, 524, 629; *Servant of
  the Bones*, 50
Rice, Jane, 680, 714
Richards, Justin, 431
Richardson, Viv A., 430
Richelieu, Cardinal, 190
Richepin, Jules, 77
Riddell, Mrs. J. H., 294
Rinehart, Mary Roberts, 298
Ring, The (film), 423
Riquelme, Paul, 641
Rising, The (Keene), 50
Robber Bride, The (Atwood), 524
Roberts, Jane, 698
Roberts, Keith, 714
Robertson, Morgan, 459, 467
Robinett, Stephen, 345
Robinson, Edwin Arlington, 298
Robinson, Lynda S., 404
Robinson, Phil, 624
Rogers, Richard, 188, 189, 191, 193
Rohmer, Sax, 140. *See also* Ward,
  Arthur Sarsfield
Rolt, L.T.C., 468
Romance of the Mummy, The (Gautier),
  384–85
Romanticism and the sublime, 69–70
Romero, George A., 204. *See also
  specific films*
Ronson, Mark, 247
Roscoe, Theodore, 145–46
Rose Red (King), 238, 276
Rosemary's Baby (film), 717
Rosemary's Baby (Levin), 181–83, 610
Rosenblum, Mary, 452
Rossetti, Dante Gabriel, 507, 517, 532
Roswell (film), 25

Rousseau, Victor, 449, 462, 518. *See also* Egbert, H. M.
Rowling, J. K., 708
Royle, Nicholas, 605, 606
Rudorff, Raymond, 628
Rule, Ann, 482
Rumbelow, Donald, 596
Russell, Jeffrey B., 410, 411, 433
Russell, Ray, 179–80, 243–44, 259, 263
Russell, W. Clark, 320, 466
Ryes, Stellan, 204
Rymer, James Malcolm, 622

Saberhagen, Fred, 628, 632
Sackett, Jeffrey, 676
Saint Leger, Francis, 449
Saintsbury, George, 131
Saki, 345
Salem witch trials, 704–5
’Salem’s Lot (King), 538, 551, 552, 554, 555, 557, 561, 628–30
Salmonson, Jessica Amanda, 221
Sampson, Ashley, 331
Sanders, Lawrence, 485
Sandman, The (Gaiman), 586–87
Sands, Lynsay, 635
Sanford, John, 491
Sardar, Gian, 218
"Sardonicus" (Russell), 243–44, 259
Sarrantonio, Al, 676
Sartre, Jean-Paul, 548
Satan. *See* Devil
Satanism, 329, 693, 696. *See also* Demon; Devil
Saul, John, 227
Saunders, Charles, 691
Scapegoat, The (Du Maurier), 200–201
Scarborough, Harold, 323
Schayer, Richard, 395
Schecter, Harold, 482
Schmidt, Eckhart, 190
Schmidt, Helmut, 419
Schmitt, Donald R., 25
Schow, David J., 600, 607–9, 611–12
Schreck, Nikolas, 709
Schubart, Christian, 313
Schultz, David E., 98, 114–15

Schwader, Ann K., 123
Schwartz, Susan M., 711
Schweitzer, Darrell, 348–49
Scot, Reginald, 703
Scotch, Cheri, 668
Scotland, Jay, 511
Scott, Walter, 45, 169, 464–65
Screwtape Letters, The (Lewis), 47, 179
Sea creatures, 441–42; early legends and folktales, 442–44; intermarriage with humans, 461; mermaids, mermen, selkies, and sirens, 444–55
Sea Demons, The (Egbert), 522
Sea hauntings, 464–68
Sea serpents and monsters, 455–64
Seabrook, William B., 693, 725, 726
Seabury, Charles, 457
"Seal Maiden, The" (Rousseau), 518
Séances. *See* Mediums
Searles, A. Langley, 245, 248
Sebold, Alice, 216, 229, 234, 495
Secret Life of Puppets, The (Nelson), 60
"Secret of Sebek, The" (Bloch), 138, 139, 398–99
Seduction. *See* Femmes fatales; Sirens
Selene of the Spirits (Pritchard), 229
Seligman, Kurt, 578
Selkies, 448–49, 451
Senf, Carol A., 640
Serenity (film), 423
Serial Killer Days (film), 493
Serial killer nicknames and aliases, 489
Serial killer profilers, 498
Serial killers, 473–75, 503, 671, 702; definitions, 475–76; fictional, 481–98 (*see also under* Harris, Thomas); in films and TV shows, 499–501; Jack the Ripper, 501–3; in plays, 498–99; prevalence, 476; remarks by, 481; songs about, 474; traits, 476
Serial killing, history of, 477–82
Serial Mom (film), 500–501
Serling, Robert J., 467
Serling, Rod, 603
Servant of the Bones (Rice), 50

"Seven Geases, The" (Smith), 82, 362
"Shadow out of Time, The" (Lovecraft), 5–6, 84–85, 111, 125
"Shadow over Innsmouth, The" (Lovecraft), 539, 542–44, 546, 547, 556, 557, 560
Shaft, The (Schow), 611–12
Shaftsbury, Anthony Ashley Cooper, Earl of, 349
Shakespeare, William, 165, 171, 515, 743; on ghosts, 220; *Macbeth*, 698, 711, 713; monsters in the works of, 348; *Othello*, 498; *The Tempest*, 348–49, 461, 577–79
Shapiro, Rochelle Jewel, 434
Sharkey, Jack, 712
Sharks, 463
Sharp, William, 449
Shaun of the Dead (film), 742
Shaw, George Bernard, 323, 324, 513
She (film), 525
She (Haggard), 521–22
Shea, Michael, 86, 428
Shelley, Mary Wollstonecraft, 343, 344, 351, 633; *Frankenstein; or, The Modern Prometheus*, 70, 194–96, 342, 350–51, 382, 383, 581–82; Greek mythology and, 342; immortality and, 319; *The Last Man*, 72; monsters of, 343. *See also* Godwin, Mary Wollstonecraft
Shelley, Percy Bysshe, 70, 197, 315, 329, 350, 351
Sherman, Delia, 449, 452
Sherrill, Stephen, 331
Sherwood, Thomas, 477
Shiel, M. P., 290–91, 326
Shining, The (film), 227, 228, 233, 275, 301–2
Shining, The (King), 228, 366, 427, 428
Shirley, John, 613
"Shunned House, The" (Lovecraft), 361, 626
Sickert, Walter, 597
Siddons, Anne River, 227
Sigmund of the Volsung, 665

Silence of the Lambs, The (Harris), 367, 487–88
Silver Bough, The (Tuttle), 525
Silverberg, Robert, 333, 399–400
Silverstein, Alvin, 318
Simak, Clifford D., 676
Simmel, Georg, 592
Simmons, Dan, 633
Sinclair, Iain, 606
Sinclair, Upton, 418
"Singing bones" of ghosts, 240
Siodmak, Robert, 601, 654
Siodmark, Curt, 13
Sirens, 507–13, 532–33; in art, 515; dangerous beauty, 514–16; men creating female, 513–14; in novels and novellas, 521–25; pivotal stories about, 516–21; in TV shows, 530–32. *See also* Femmes fatales; Sea creatures
Sirens (film), 529
Sisters (film), 527
Sixth Sense, The (film), 236, 422
Skal, David J., 640
Skipp, John, 201, 608, 609
Slade, Henry, 415
Slade, Michael, 259, 487, 503
"Slave of the Flames" (Bloch), 324–25
Slaves of Sleep (Hubbard), 149–50, 246–47
Sleator, William, 746–47
Sleigh, Barbara, 713
Slesar, Henry, 147–48
Slethaug, Gordon E., 196
Small-town horror, 537–58, 561; films, 558–61; leading stories of, 538
Smidt, Heinrich, 465
Smith, Clark Ashton, 81–83, 87, 101, 361, 363, 366, 598; "The Amazing Planet," 82; "A Bit of the Dark World," 86; "The Charnel God," 255–56; "The Colossus of Ylourgne," 361–62; death, 363; "The Dimension of Chance," 82–83; "The Empire of the Necromancers," 398; "The Eternal World," 82–83; "The Ghoul," 245–46; "The Gorgon," 343; *The Hashish-Eater; or, The Apocalypse of*

Evil, 81, 82, 87, 90; Lovecraft and, 361; "Marooned in Andromeda," 82; "The Monster of the Prophecy," 354; myth-cycle, 98, 113; "The Nameless Offspring," 253–56, 263; *Our Lady of Darkness* and, 86; "A Prophecy of Monsters," 354, 675; "The Seven Geases," 82, 362; "Symposium of the Gorgon," 343; "The Tale of Satampra Zeiros," 113; tales of Zothique, 85
Smith, Deborah, 451
Smith, Evelyn E., 627
Smith, Guy N., 463
Smith, Horace, 383
Smith, L. J., 637, 638
Smith, Thorne, 343–44
"Smoke Ghost" (Leiber), 225, 231, 600–601, 607
Smyth, Brian, 740
"Snout, The" (White), 359
Soal, S. G., 412, 413
Solaris (Lem), 205
Something Wicked This Way Comes (Bradbury), 547, 549, 552, 554, 557
Sommer-Bodenburg, Angela, 637
Somtow, S. P., 601, 630, 678–79
Son of Blob (film), 19
Sondheim, Stephen, 497
Sorcerer, The (Gilbert and Sullivan), 582–83
Sorcerers, 565–66; in classical world, 566–67; early modern, 572–80; medieval, 567–72; modern, 580–88. *See also* "Ancient Sorceries"; Black magic; Urban horror, since the 1960s; Witches
Sorrows of Satan, The (Corelli), 171–72
Southey, Robert, 130–31, 318, 621, 725
Spanky (Fowler), 202
Spector, Craig, 201, 608, 609
Spencer, William Browning, 123
Spengler, Oswald, 78
Spenser, Edmund, 701
Spirit possession. *See* Demon; *Exorcist*; Possession

Spiritualism, 411–15. *See also* Psychics
Splash! (film), 527
Splatterpunk, 607–9, 611, 614
Spoto, Donald, 526
Spree killers, 475
St. Leon (Godwin), 318
Stableford, Brian, 428, 511
Stagg, John, 621
Stanton, Elizabeth Cady, 413
Stapledon, Olaf, 89
Stapp, Henry, 419–20
Star Maker (Stapledon), 89
"Star Trek" (TV show), 502
Star Wars (film), 365
Steinke, René, 525
Stepfather, The (film), 500
Stepford Wives, The (Levin), 206, 550
Stephens, John Richard, 381
Sterling, George, 81
Sterling, Robert, 196
Stevens, Shane, 485
Stevenson, Burton, 390
Stevenson, Robert Louis, 188, 191, 201, 263; "The Body Snatcher," 259; *The Strange Case of Dr. Jekyll and Mr. Hyde*, 195, 199–200, 355–56, 593–96, 669–70
Stewart, Fred Mustard, 332
Stewart, Mary, 426, 570
Stine, R. L., 228, 403
Stockton, Frank R., 322, 458
Stoker, Bram, 357–59, 402, 483, 551; *Dracula*, 357, 521, 593–95, 598, 621, 623, 624, 628, 633, 635, 638–43, 654, 730, 731; influence of, 624–27; *The Jewel of Seven Stars*, 397; mummies, tombs, and, 388
Stonier, G. W., 331
Storm of the Century, The (made-for-TV movie), 560
"Story of the Inexperienced Ghost, The" (Wells), 224, 228
Strange Case of Dr. Jekyll and Mr. Hyde, The (Stevenson), 190, 195, 199, 355–56, 593–96, 669–70
Strange Story, A (Bulwer-Lytton), 45, 72

Straub, Peter: *Black House*, 495; *The Exorcist* and, 607; *Floating Dragon*, 555, 556; on ghost stories, 227–29; *Ghost Story*, 200, 216, 228, 555, 557; "The Ghost Village," 539, 546–47; on ghosts, 215; *Julia*, 234; *Koko*, 490; *lost boy lost girl*, 229, 235, 490; *Mr. X*, 201; serial killers in the stories of, 490; *Shadowland*, 715; on Stephen King, 555; *The Throat*, 490, 546; works with psi themes, 426–27
Straw Men, The (Marshall), 495–96
Strieber, Whitley, 27–28, 332, 601, 631, 642, 668, 678
Stroheim, Erich von, 178
Stuart, Don A. *See* Campbell, John W., Jr.
Sturgeon, Theodore, 429, 451, 628, 693, 700
Sublime, the, 67–71
Sue, Eugène, 132, 314
Suffer the Children (Saul), 227
Summers, Montague, 244, 619, 653
Sunglasses After Dark (Collins), 632
Supernatural (film), 426
Sutton, David, 742
Suzuki, Kôji, 235, 423
Swann, Thomas Burnett, 344, 345, 454
Swanwick, Michael, 166, 675
Swayne, Martin, 323
Swedenborg, Emanuel, 423
Sweeney, Joyce, 430
Swift, Jonathan, 308–9
Sylvester II, Pope, 165, 170–71

Talbot, Michael, 630
Tale of Two Cities, A (Dickens), 198
Talented Mr. Ripley, The (Highsmith), 484
Taralon, Jean, 218
Taylor, Lucy, 225
Teen Wolf (film), 684
Teilhard de Chardin, Pierre, 89, 90, 333
Telekinesis, 419–20, 422, 426–29
Telepathy, 418–19, 422, 426–29
Tem, Melanie, 634, 636, 681, 710

Tempest, The (Shakespeare), 461; Prospero from, 348–49, 577–79
Tenn, William, 344, 627
Tennyson, Alfred, Lord, 456, 569
Tentation de Saint-Antoine, La (Flaubert), 76–77
"Terrible Old Man, The" (Lovecraft), 100
"Terror from the Depths, The" (Leiber), 122
Tessier, Thomas, 427, 428, 486, 672
Texas Chainsaw Massacre, The (film), 500
Theogony (Hesiod), 342–43
"There Shall Be No Darkness" (Blish), 674
"There Will Come Soft Rains" (Bradbury), 292–93
Thessalian witches, 700
Theurgy, 567
They Came from Beyond Space (film), 23
Thing, The (film), 10, 125
Thing from Another World, The (film), 10
Thing in the Woods, The (Williams), 660
"Thing on the Doorstep, The" (Lovecraft), 111
Thinner (King), 148, 694
This Present Darkness (Peretti), 49
Thomas, Kevin, 233
Thompson, C. Hall, 118, 145
Thompson, Jim, 483
Thomson, William. *See* Kelvin, Lord
Thornburg, Mary K. Patterson, 194, 195
Thouless, R. H., 417
Thousand and One Nights, 244, 245
Throat, The (Straub), 490, 546
"Throne of Bones, The" (McNaughton), 261–63
Throne of Bones, The (McNaughton), 261–63
Thunstone, John, 626
Thurston, E. Temple, 317
Tiamat, 442
Tieck, Johann Ludwig, 190, 621

Tierney, Richard L., 121
Timberline Lodge, 274–75
Time Machine, The (Wells), 78, 248, 357
Tipler, Frank, 90, 333
Tishy, Cecilia, 433
Todd, Sweeney, 478
Tofina, La, 478
Tolan, Stephanie S., 430
Tolkien, J.R.R., 325, 363, 585
Tolstoy, Alexis, 623
"Tomb, The" (Lovecraft), 100
Tombs of the Blind Dead (film), 740
Tommyknockers, The (King), 552, 554
Toombs, Jane, 668
Topor, Roland, 610, 613
Tourneur, Jacques, 47, 152, 153, 177, 729
Towne, Mary, 430
Tragical History of Doctor Faustus (Marlowe), 165–66, 574–76, 579
Tremayne, Peter, 750
Trilby (du Maurier), 522
"Trouble with Water, The" (Gold), 145
Truzzi, Marcello, 432
Tryon, Thomas, 201, 204, 426, 550–51, 559
Turn of the Screw, The (James), 227, 300
Turner, James, 125
Turner, Lindsey, 347
Tut, King (Tutankhamen), 138; curse of, 391–93
Tuttle, Lisa, 224, 225, 227, 525
Twain, Mark, 171, 172, 174, 184, 198, 316, 554, 570
20 Million Miles to Earth (film), 18, 19
27th Day (film), 18–19
"Twilight Zone, The" (TV show), 603–4
"Twin Peaks" (TV show), 560
Twitchell, James, 638
Tylor, Edward Burnett, 99
Tymms, Ralph, 189, 190, 193, 194

Uhls, Jim, 196
Unbreakable (film), 422
Undercliffe, Errol, 120

Underhill, Tim, 490
Undying Monster, The (Kerruish), 663–64
Unfortunate Fursey, The (Wall), 174
Unknown (magazine), 246, 600–602, 666
Untermeyer, Louis, 136
Updike, John, 512, 699, 717
Upton, Smyth, 320
Urban horror, 592; iconic sites of, 609–14; since the 1960s, 604–9
Urban life, 591–92
Urban nightmares: 19th-century, 592–98; 20th-century, 598–603

"Vampire: The Masquerade" (roleplaying game), 645–46
Vampire criticism, 638–41
Vampire films, chronology of, 639
Vampire literature, young adult, 636–38
Vampire stories: early, 621–24; Stroker and his influence, 624–27
Vampire Tapestry, The (Charnas), 631
Vampires, 511, 619–21, 733; attitudes toward, 627; immortality and, 331–32; in the media, 530–31, 641–46; modern, 627–36; *vs.* the mortal/human, 634; parasitic, 633. *See also* 'Salem's Lot
Vampyre, The (Polidori), 319–20, 350, 621–22
Van Druten, John, 716
Van Praagh, James, 421
van Vogt, A. E., 429, 463
Vance, Jack, 86
Vanderdecker, Philip, 132
VanderMeer, Jeff, 368
Vansittart, Peter, 331
Vardoulakis, Dimitris, 187, 189
Varney the Vampyre (Rymer), 622, 623
Velde, Vivian Vande, 638
Verne, Jules, 457, 458, 460
Victor, Paul, 433, 434
Viereck, George Sylvester, 132, 324, 326, 511
Village of the Damned (film), 422, 558

Vinge, Vernor, 333
Virgil, 654–55
Visiak, E. H., 467
Voisin, La, 702
Voltaire (François Marie Arouet), 349
Voodoo, 709–10, 726
Voronoff, Serge, 322

Wade, James, 118
Waggner, George, 683
Waggoner, Tim, 740–41
Wagner, Hank, 538, 561
Wagner, Karl Edward, 121, 259
Wagner, Richard, 328, 466
Wakefield, H. Russell, 143–44, 468
Waldrop, Howard, 342, 344–45, 441
Walker, Adam, 69
Walker, John, 525
Walker, Stuart, 683
Walker, Tom, 169–70
Walking Wolf (Collins), 679
Walkowitz, Judith, 597
Wall, Mervyn, 174
Waller, Gregory A., 640
Wallop, Douglas, 176
Walpole, Horace, 44, 271, 284, 350
Walter, E. V., 34, 48
Walton, Bryce, 135
Wanderers, accursed, 309–13
Wandering Jew, 132, 311–12, 317, 318,
    320, 332–33; popularization of the,
    313–17
Wandering Jew, The (Sue), 132
Wandrei, Donald, 85, 87, 103, 116, 135
War of the Worlds, The (Wells), 3–4,
    6–8, 16, 21, 357
War of the Worlds (film), 6, 7, 9, 16.
    *See also H. G. Wells' The War of the
    Worlds*
Ward, Arthur Sarsfield, 389. *See also*
    Rohmer, Sax
"Warm, Dark Places" (Gold), 145
Watkin, L. E., 308
Watson, Ian, 468
Waugh, Charles G., 293
Webb, Catherine, 334
Webb, Don, 494–95

Webb, Jane, 382–83
Webber, Andrew, 188, 189
Weber, William, 274
Wedekind, Fritz, 596
Wegener, Paul, 204
Weinbaum, Stanley, 345
Weir, Peter, 125
Weird Tales, 47
Weisner, B. P., 417
Wellman, Manly Wade, 225, 433, 626,
    692, 728, 729
Wells, H. G., 179, 358, 359, 502;
    "The Flowering of the Strange
    Orchid, 623–24; "In the Abyss," 462;
    The Invisible Man, 357; *The Island of
    Dr. Moreau*, 357; Martians and, 3–4,
    6–8; monsters in the stories of,
    356–57; "Pollock and the Porroh
    Man," 133, 691; *The Sea Lady*, 451;
    "The Sea Raiders," 459; "The Story
    of the Inexperienced Ghost," 224,
    228; *The Time Machine*, 78, 248,
    357; *The War of the Worlds*, 3–4,
    6–8, 21, 357
Werewolf, The (film), 682–83
Were-Wolf, The (Housman), 659
Werewolf fiction, varieties of modern,
    668–69
Werewolf films, 682–85; essential, 682
Werewolf novels, essential, 664
Werewolf of London (film), 683
Werewolf of Paris, The (Endore),
    676–78
Werewolf short stories, groundbreaking,
    677
Werewolf(ves), 601, 602, 653–54; early
    modern, 659–68; feminist, 680–82;
    Gothic and Victorian period,
    656–59; origin of the term, 654–55;
    pre-Gothic, 654–56; psychological,
    669–74; science-fictional, 674–76; as
    symbol of racial and political identity,
    676–80
Wertham, Frederick, 479, 732
West, Paul, 596–98
Westlake, Donald E., 500
Wetzel, George T., 108, 250, 251

Weyland, Edward, 631

Whale, James, 352, 363

Wharton, Edith, 224, 225

What Lies Beneath (film), 422

Wheatley, Dennis, 179, 399, 461, 691, 695, 717

"Whimper of Whipped Dogs, The" (Ellison), 49

"Whisperer in Darkness, The" (Lovecraft), 5–6, 106, 107, 113

White, Edward Lucas, 133–35, 359–60, 364, 518, 691; "Amina," 248, 359–60; ghouls and, 248–51

White, T. H., 512, 570

"White People, The" (Machen), 80, 714

White Wolf, The (Gregory), 666

White Zombie (film), 725–31

Whitehead, Henry S., 134, 249–50

Whitten, Leslie, 628, 668

"Who Knows?" (Maupassant), 286–87

Wicca, 696–97, 701–2

Wicker Man, The (film), 559

Widen, Gregory, 56, 57

Wild Blood (Cade), 679

Wilde, Oscar, 80, 189, 198, 252, 322, 447, 511

Wilder, Laura Ingalls, 478

Wilder, Myles, 12

Wilder, Thornton, 551

Wilhelm, Kate, 520

Wilkins, Vaughan, 326

Willard, John, 298

"William Wilson" (Poe), 199, 201–4, 353

Williams, Alex, 218

Williams, Conrad, 606

Williams, Margery, 660

Williams, Raymond, 548

Williams, Tad, 349

Williamson, Chet, 228

Williamson, Jack, 324, 344, 666, 674, 675

Willingham, Bill, 700

Willis, Val, 450

"Willows, The" (Blackwood), 80, 224

Wilson, Charles, 463

Wilson, Clare, 414

Wilson, Colin, 118–19, 596, 628

Wilson, Edmund, 116

Wilson, F. Paul, 123, 636

Wilson, Gahan, 122, 693

Wilson, Lucy Sarah Atkins, 385

Winchester Mystery House, 275–76

Winter, Douglas E., 229

Wise Woman, 148–49

Wishmaster (film), 51–52

Witch (Rankin), 524

Witch-Cult in Western Europe, The (Murray), 66

"Witch doctors," African, 695–96

Witch hunts and persecution of witches, 167, 689–90, 703–8

Witch movies adapted from literature, 716–18

"Witch of Coös, The" (Frost), 296–97

Witch of Endor, 700

Witches, 325, 410–11, 689–90, 718; animals and, 710; aspects of, 690–94; business, 715–16; demons and, 39–40; domestic, 711–12, 714; familiars, 707–8, 713–14; fictional third-world malign, 691; as figures of power, 697–99; as healers and protectors, 694–97; lengendary/mythic, 699–703; new types of, 711–12, 714–16; sex, death, and, 708–11; Sirens and, 511–12; and the triple goddess, 711; younger, 714–15. *See also* "Young Goodman Brown"

Witches, The (film), 716–18

Witches' Brew (film), 716

Witches of Eastwick, The (film), 717

Witches of Eastwick, The (Updike), 699, 717

Wodehouse, P. G., 124

Wolf, Leonard, 638–39

Wolf in the Garden, The (Bill), 662–63

Wolf Leader, The (Dumas), 657–58

Wolf Man, The (film), 654, 666, 668, 682–84

Wolfe, Gene, 222, 226, 257, 524, 701

Wolfen, The (Strieber), 678

Wolff, Lycurgus, 662

Woman in Black, The (Hill), 523

Women of Whitechapel and Jack the Ripper, The (West), 596–98
Wonders of the Invisible World (Mather), 167, 168
Wood, Bari, 207
Woolf, Virginia, 295, 323
Woolrich, Cornell, 144–45, 156
Wordsworth, William, 131
Wright, Dudley, 620
Wright, Farnsworth, 103
Wright, S. Fowler, 308
Wuornos, Aileen, 480
Wuthering Heights (Brontë), 227
Wyndham, John, 22, 422, 459, 547–49
Wynne, Madeline Yale, 294
Wynne-Jones, Diana, 587

Yarbro, Chelsea Quinn, 258, 629–30, 633
Yolen, Jane, 451, 523, 700
Young, Edward, 69, 72

"Young Goodman Brown" (Hawthorne), 538–42, 544, 550–52, 554, 694, 712
"Yours Truly, Jack the Ripper" (Bloch), 47, 325, 501–2, 596

Zanoni (Bulwer-Lytton), 45, 72, 78, 321, 354–55
Zeder (film), 739–40
Zelazny, Roger, 333, 345
Zicree, Scott, 603
Zombie (film), 739, 750–51
Zombie films, 734–50; chronology of, 744–45; by Romero, 734–38
Zombies, 723–34, 745–51; characteristics, 724; in comics, 732–33; criteria for, 724; as metaphor for people with no will, 750–51; roots in literature and cultural practices, 724–25; stories from pulp magazines, 725–28
Zorro, legend of, 679–80